CW01646728

The Honourable The Irish Society and the Plantation of Ulster, 1608-2000

Arms of The Honourable The Irish Society combining the Arms (*Argent a Cross Gules in the first Quarter a Sword in pale point upwards Gules*) on the *Dexter* side of the Shield, Crest (*On a Wreath Argent and Gules a Dragon's expanded Sinister Wing Argent charged on the underside with a Cross throughout Gules*), Supporters (*On either side a Dragon Argent charged on the undersides of the expanded Wings with a Cross throughout Gules*), and Motto (*Domine Dirige Nos*) of the City of London impaling the Arms of Ulster (*Argent* a *Sinister Hand couped at the wrist Gules*). Unlike the Red Hand of The O'Neill, the Ulster (and Irish Society's) Hand is *Sinister* rather than *Dexter*. The Ulster hand is borne either in a Canton or in an Inescutcheon in the Arms of baronets.

It would seem that the Arms of the City of London were 'anciently recorded' but that the Crest (on a Peer's helmet) and Supporters long used were not officially granted by the Kings of Arms until 30 April 1957 (*College of Arms MS: Grants 119/154*), and a search of the official records of the College of Arms and of the former Ulster Office of Arms has proved unilluminating regarding the origins of The Society's Arms (*IS*).

The Honourable The Irish Society and the Plantation of Ulster, 1608-2000

The City of London and the Colonisation of County Londonderry in the Province of Ulster in Ireland

A History and Critique

JAMES STEVENS CURL

Phillimore

2000

Published by
PHILLIMORE & CO. LTD.
Shopwyke Manor Barn, Chichester, West Sussex

© James Stevens Curl, 2000

ISBN 1 86077 136 X

Printed and bound in Great Britain by
BUTLER & TANNER LTD.
London and Frome

In Memoriam

Robert Thomas Brown (1931-91)
former Education Officer of The Worshipful Company of Drapers of the City of London who revealed many of the archival riches on which this study is based

and

Theodore William Moody (1907-84)
a great pioneering scholar of the Plantation of Ulster

Forsan et haec olim meminisse iuvabit
(Perhaps one day it will be acceptable to recall even these things)

PUBLIUS VERGILIUS MARO (70-19 BC): *Aeneid*, **i**, l.203

And they the Successors of High Renouned Lud, will there reedifie a new Troy … They have O'Cane's Country, and whatever Ireland's Eden can afford, and therefore even in respect of their owne Reputation, they of themselves will performe this the most honourable action that they have ever attempted. Therefore let Coleraine reioyce, for the heart of England (London herselfe) will no doubt make her more beautifull …

THOMAS BLENERHASSET (*c.*1550-*c.*1625): Dedication to Prince Henry Frederick, Prince of Wales (1594-1612) in *A Direction for the Plantation in Ulster* (London: Ed. Allde for John Budge, 1610)

Contents

CHAPTER XII

County Londonderry, Ireland, The Irish Society, and Events from the 1880s to 1984 321

CHAPTER XIII

Conclusion
The Irish Society from the 1950s to the End of the Century 354

List of Illustrations

Sources for illustrations are given in abbreviated form *in italics* at the end of each caption, as follows:

A	The Author
AC	The Author's Collection
DB	Mr. David Bigger
GB	Mr. Geremy Butler, Photographer
CC	Crown Copyright. Reproduced with the Permission of the Controller of Her Majesty's Stationery Office
Colby(1837)	From Thomas Frederick Colby (1837): *Ordnance Survey of the County of Londonderry. Parish of Templemore* (Dublin: Published for Her Majesty's Government, Ordnance Survey Office, by Hodges and Smith)
WCC	By permission of the Worshipful Company of Clothworkers of the City of London
WCD	By permission of the Worshipful Company of Drapers of the City of London
GACL	Corporation of London, Guildhall Art Galleries
GLCL	Corporation of London, Guildhall Library
RIA	Royal Irish Academy
IRC	Irish Reference Library, County Hall, Coleraine, North Eastern Education and Library Board
IS	The Honourable The Irish Society
L	From Samuel Lewis (1837): *A Topographical Dictionary of Ireland, Comprising the Several Counties, Cities, Boroughs, Corporate, Market, and Post Towns, with Historical and Statistical Descriptions, etc.* (London: Lewis)
DMacL	Mr. Daniel MacLaughlin
WCMT	By permission of the Worshipful Company of Merchant Taylors of the City of London
CLRO	Corporation of London Records Office
GVS	George Vaughan Sampson (1814): *A Memoir, Explanatory of the Chart and Survey of the County of London-Derry, Ireland* (London: Printed by W. Bulmer for G. & W. Nicol)
PRONI	By permission of the Deputy Keeper of the Records, Public Record Office of Northern Ireland
StC	By permission of the Dean and Chapter, the Cathedral-Church of St Columb, Londonderry
AT	Miss Ann Taylor
TCD	By Permission of The Board of Trinity College Dublin
UFTM	Ulster Folk and Transport Museum Copyright
UM	Ulster Museum, Belfast

In some cases, sources will involve combinations of these: e.g. (*IS/CLRO*), which refers to The Irish Society's papers at the Corporation of London Records Office, and will be followed by some further identification; or (*A/CC*), which indicates a photograph by the Author, but that the negatives are now held by the Environment and Heritage Service, Built Heritage, Belfast, an Agency within the Department of the Environment for Northern Ireland.

Frontispiece: The Arms of The Honourable The Irish Society

Preface and Acknowledgements

> To administer with fidelity the accepted trusts; to hold with even hand the well-adjusted balance; to stimulate industry; to activate the spirit of peace and good-will; to promote the moral and religious welfare of the people, and to cherish everywhere that spirit of self-reliance which is the strength and glory of a community endowed by such civic immunities, and crowned with such historic fame: these must be the objects of a Society whose interests are so closely linked in with the interests of the Plantation in Ulster; and thus united they shall remain for ever and indissolubly one
>
> CHARLES REED (1819-81): Preface to *An Historical Narrative of the Origin and Constitution of 'The Society of the Governor and Assistants, London, of the New Plantation in Ulster, within the Realm of Ireland', commonly called The Honourable The Irish Society*; together with *Memoranda of Principal Occurrences* (London: The Irish Society, 1865)

Very few (least of all politicians or commentators in the media) seem to know anything about the connection between the City of London and the part of Ulster known as the county of Londonderry, a 'shire' specially created for colonisation by the City and its long-established Livery Companies.[1] It is an extraordinary story, involving coercion by the Crown, reluctant participation by nervous and unwilling members of the Companies, and a great deal of hardship, violence, and loss of life. The purpose of this book is to trace that story, drawing on historical archives (most of which survive in Guildhall, City of London, and in the collections of the Livery Companies), and focusing on the organisation constituted within the City to direct the affairs of the 'Plantation' or colonisation of Ulster after huge tracts of land became escheated to the Crown after the Flight of the Ulster Earls in 1607. That body was called 'The Society of the Governor and Assistants, London, of the New Plantation in Ulster, within the Realm of Ireland', later shortened as 'The Honourable The Irish Society', and has been in existence ever since its foundation in 1610 apart from a 20-year break from 1637 to 1657 following the celebrated trial of the City of London in the Star Chamber in 1635.

There can be no question that the Plantation of Ulster had momentous consequences, not only for Ireland, but for the political development of England. King Charles I's arbitrary rule and his never-ending search for funds led to the Star Chamber trial, the forfeiture of the City of London's property, mayhem in Ireland, and a political upheaval of huge import in the three Kingdoms of England, Scotland, and Ireland. The Crown's treatment of the City of London was a major contributory factor in the ending of personal royal rule, the establishment of the principle that the King reigned by the consent of Parliament, and the beginnings of modern political systems.

[1] For explanations concerning these Companies see Chapter II below.

In an earlier work, *The Londonderry Plantation 1609-1914: the History, Architecture, and Planning of the Estates of the City of London and its Livery Companies in Ulster,*[2] the present writer described the detailed sagas of the 'Proportions' or properties of the Twelve Great Livery Companies and their Associated Companies, copiously illustrated and annotated. Whilst The Irish Society and its holdings perforce were included in that book, space did not permit a detailed examination of The Society and its history. The present study attempts to make good that lacuna.

Why should a history of The Honourable The Irish Society be written towards the end of this millennium, nearly four centuries after that truly remarkable body was founded? First of all, widespread ignorance is never laudable, least of all when intelligent understanding has never been more imperative, and it is hoped this work will help to clarify certain matters. Mythologies are no substitute for dispassionate histories, though they well serve those among whose ends the shedding of light into murky corners is not on the agenda. Ignorance and myth are not confined to Ireland, or even to Ulster, where the amazing story of the Plantation did not loom large in schools curricula (and still does not do so): they are widespread in Great Britain and America to a frightening extent. The present writer recalls making an approach to a respected academic publishing house with a proposal concerning the Plantation of Ulster, only to be rebuffed with the mind-boggling statement that 'Forestry in Northern Ireland would not fit into the book-list'. Secondly, in a period of considerable change it is important to set down facts in an accessible and readable form as an antidote to wild stories and bad history, so the timing is right. There has been a huge upsurge of interest in Irish history (and especially in Ulster history) in recent years, to which any haunter of second-hand or antiquarian bookshops will attest: hardly any books on Irish history can be found these days, as they are sold often before they reach the shelves. Thirdly, The Honourable The Irish Society, once the reluctant agent for what might be described as Colonisation-on-the-Cheap on behalf of a parsimonious Crown, has changed through the centuries from an unwilling (and perhaps less than efficient) participant in the Plantation venture through several metamorphoses. In the 1630s, after it had created one of the last fortified cities in all Europe; built a Gothic Survival cathedral; laid out, built, and fortified a town (to designs by the brother of the founder of the Bodleian Library, Oxford); co-ordinated the efforts of the Twelve Great Livery Companies and their Associates in building villages, castles, and houses (and endeavoured to ensure they were inhabited by British settlers); re-edified and strengthened a fortress at Culmore on the west bank of the River Foyle to guard the approaches to the infant city of Londonderry; and expended an enormous amount of money, expertise, and effort, it and its parent, the City of London, were ignominiously tried and found guilty in a less than fair court, and The Irish Society was abolished. Late in the 1650s The Society was reconstituted and had to start to make good decades of damage and neglect, then it was caught up in international power-politics in the Franco-Jacobite wars after the Revolution of 1688, and its city of Londonderry withstood a siege of over 100 days that made the name 'Londonderry' resound throughout Europe. Painful reconstruction, yet again, and the disasters of the South Sea Bubble left The Irish Society in an unenviable position as an 18th-century ramshackle absentee landlord that had lost its grip on much of its holdings. From the beginning of the 19th century, partly as a result of change brought about by that curious phenomenon, the Evangelical Conscience, The Society became the instigator of good works, improvements, and a

[2] Curl (1986), *passim.*

transformation of the county of Londonderry into a prosperous part of the United Kingdom of Great Britain and Ireland. In particular, it was active in promoting town-planning, decent standards of design and building, model dwellings and farms, tree-planting, encouraging the creation of hedgerows, and land-reclamation: it was also an important agent of conservation of natural resources, including the fisheries, agricultural lands, woodlands, and turbaries,[3] all of which had been plundered and mis-used in the 18th century. As landholdings were lost from the late 19th century, The Society gradually became transmogrified into a charitable organisation, using revenues from the fisheries, shooting rights, turbaries, and residues of property to support all manner of good causes, including several schools.

As the 20th century draws to its close, The Society, with its headquarters in London and its local office by the Salmon Leap in Coleraine, has developed close relationships with local politicians, organisations, and authorities. Virtually all its income is disbursed in charitable grants, maintenance of properties, and, of course, administration, including the regular Deputations (or Visitations) when representatives of The Society visit the lands with which it has been associated for so long. The Society aims to promote the welfare of the county of Londonderry and its two main urban centres, the city of Londonderry and the town of Coleraine. It has a pastoral and financial rôle in the maintenance of its schools in the county, supports numerous other educational and religious organisations regardless of denomination, and takes pains to be even-handed in all its dealings. Established for State reasons to colonise part of Ulster and ensure the success of the Protestant (originally Anglican) Plantation, The Society has become a benevolent body concerned with the well-being of all in the territories for which it became responsible in the reign of King James I and VI. From 1974, The Society, which historically kept its affairs very close to its chest, became much more open and accessible, exchanging information and collaborating with all manner of local bodies.

In the volatile climate of contemporary Ulster, The Irish Society (which has a long history as a grant-making organisation) treads a conciliatory path. The historian, considering its remarkable story, can only conclude that, given the extreme reluctance of the City of London to get involved in Ulster at all, The Irish Society comes out of the whole saga very well indeed: sniped at from all quarters, cheated by its own agents, attacked by grasping adventurers, plotted against by some of the Livery Companies (the interests of which it protected), stealthily asset-stripped by bishops and ennobled *parvenus*, abused and denounced (like all landlords) by Irish Nationalists, robbed by the Crown which had forced the City of London to become embroiled in the first place, and libelled in countless pamphlets by strangers to truth or historical facts, The Society was, throughout its history, a reasonable and beneficent body. Its survival and its prestige are eloquent testaments to its many qualities.

The Honourable The Irish Society maintains close links with its two towns, Londonderry and Coleraine, and remains the custodian of a special relationship between north-west Ulster and the City of London, though that relationship has seen many metamorphoses throughout the terrible history of Ireland. The Society is a body that has existed for nigh on four hundred years, and takes its responsibilities and duties very seriously, seeing them as of great importance and significance. Mindful of the ever-changing circumstances of history, The Society has adapted its rôle to suit the times, while always being keenly aware of its historical *raison d'être* and the humane duties it has been obliged to shoulder. It still consists of 'six and twenty honest and

[3] See Select Glossary below.

discreet citizens of London'; its Governor (by tradition a past Lord Mayor of London) is still appointed by the Court of Aldermen of the City of London; and members of the Court of The Irish Society are obliged to retire after two years' service unless they become Deputy Governor. However, an inbuilt weakness of the past has been corrected by the re-appointment of retired members after a year's absence, thus ensuring a degree of continuity and a corrective to the collective amnesia that was such a problem (especially in the 18th century).

A few explanations may be necessary in order to clarify some matters. The dispassionate historian has a duty to endeavour to relate a truthful story, based, where possible, on documentary and other evidence (such as that found in buildings), avoiding bias, distortion, or humbug. The use of the word 'Londonderry' can cause offence in certain quarters, but no offence is intended: to call the county of Londonderry (a shire specially created for the City's Plantation from the county of Coleraine and parts of Counties Antrim, Donegal, and Tyrone) 'County Derry' is absurd, and has no historical justification whatsoever. There never was an Irish county called 'Derry'. The see of Derry, however, was thus historically, and it is historical nonsense to refer (as the B.B.C. has done on many occasions) to the 'Bishop of Londonderry' as no such person exists, or ever did exist. Since the Church Temporalities (Ireland) Act of 1833,[4] however, the Church of Ireland (Anglican) bishops of Derry have been the bishops of Derry and Raphoe. With regard to the city of Londonderry, the site should be referred to as 'Derry' before the early 17th-century charter, but it seems unfair on the Londoners to call it 'Derry' and ignore the fact that the post-1608 fabric was entirely the creation of The Irish Society. It is true that the Irish tend to shorten names of places: Carrickfergus (formerly Knockfergus) is colloquially known as 'Carrick', and similarly Londonderry is called 'Derry'. In 1984 the city council (where the Nationalists are now in the majority) voted to change its name to 'Derry City Council', for the 'London' prefix is anathematised by Republicans: nevertheless, 'Londonderry' is still the official name of the Londoners' city, which will be referred to by this nomenclature from the time of its charter and foundation, but as 'Derry' before then. This use of names is based entirely on reason and historical fact, and has absolutely no politico-religious significance in this study. The author has no axes to grind in any cause save that of truth, as far as he has been able to establish the facts.

Historical events, however, cannot be undone, much as many would desire to wish them out of existence. Haste to rebuild sites within the walls without first carrying out thorough archaeological investigations may be understandable where decisions are taken with political and economic agendas in mind, but time should always be found to examine every site as fully as possible before new buildings go up: the obliteration of archaeological evidence is inevitable when deep modern foundations are laid, and in some instances such destruction has taken place, which is regrettable given that we know very little about the details of the 17th-century built fabric of the Londonderry Plantation. It seems almost as though the changing of history is desired, but those who seek this should reflect that the convoluted history of Ireland is not one of pure Gaelic mythology, but involves peoples from Scandinavia, England, Scotland, Wales, France, Central Europe, and The Netherlands, among others. After all, even a few 20th-century leaders of the Republican movement have borne Lowland Scots names, so it ought to be recognised that in Irish history very few things are as straightforward as some might think. The legacy left by the Planters from the 17th century is now as

[4] 3 & 4 Will. IV, c. 37. See explanation below.

much a part of Irish heritage as are the great monuments of Gaelic Antiquity: that fact cannot be wished out of existence as though it never happened, and although built fabric can easily be destroyed, its annihilation impoverishes historical understanding and the imprints left upon time. Those who seek the elimination of traces of civilisations of which they themselves do not approve do their countries no service, and destructive agendas leave future generations groping in a windy limbo, like a people with no memory. Everything should be recorded, and time allowed to do the job properly: all historic sites in the county ought to be fully investigated prior to any redevelopment taking place.

Events such as those described in this book cannot be explained without some reference to the historical backgrounds that led to their occurrences and against which they happened. The book is therefore constructed on chronological lines as far as is possible (though some back-tracking and overlapping occur, for reasons that will become obvious), and draws together many threads. Those who wish to pursue certain lines of enquiry are referred to the Select Bibliography which, although full enough to satisfy the curiosity of readers, is by no means comprehensive. The References and Bibliography in the present writer's *Londonderry Plantation* of 1986 are much fuller, but the material given below has been carefully selected as germane to the subject this book attempts to outline.

The compiler of a study such as this owes many debts: it is many years since this one first began to study the Londonderry Plantation and fell under the spell of a landscape of enchanting loveliness (at the end of the century being wrecked by inappropriate and ugly developments that are wholly alien to any tradition in Ireland). The results of early studies were published in two monographs by the Ulster Architectural Heritage Society[5] and as a couple of short articles in *Country Life*.[6] Favourable critical reviews of the monographs expressed hopes that further investigations into aspects of the Plantation might be carried out, and encouragement was given to the major investigation of all the Company estates (supported by The British Academy, many Livery Companies, The Irish Society, the Society of Antiquaries of London, the Leicester School of Architecture, Derry City Council, Limavady District Council, Ballinascreen Historical Society, and many individuals), eventually published in 1986 as *The Londonderry Plantation 1609-1914* which was very well received by critics. Nearly a decade later, through the offices of Commander Peter Campbell, the Irish Representative of The Irish Society from 1974 to 1996, the present writer was invited to research and prepare this study, for which he is most grateful, as the work has been fascinating, enabling The Society to be investigated in far greater detail than was possible in the 1986 work on the general Plantation (that concentrated on the Companies and their lands).

Thus the author thanks Commander Campbell for instigating the enterprise; the Governor, Deputy Governor, and Court of The Honourable The Irish Society for listening to expositions of proposals and for giving encouragement to the work; Mr. Simon F. N. Waley (the Secretary to The Society); and Mr. Edward Montgomery (Commander Campbell's successor as The Society's Representative in Ireland) for

[5] Curl, James Stevens (1979): *Moneymore and Draperstown. The Architecture and Planning of the Ulster Estates of The Drapers' Company* (Belfast: Ulster Architectural Heritage Society) and Curl, James Stevens (1981): *The History, Architecture, and Planning of the Estates of The Fishmongers' Company in Ulster* (Belfast: Ulster Architectural Heritage Society).

[6] Curl, James Stevens (1980): 'Towns built against the odds. Estates of The Drapers' Company in Ulster' in *Country Life* (25 September), 1036-7; Curl, James Stevens (1981): 'An Unbiased Involvement. The Estate of the Fishmongers' Company in Ulster' in *Country Life* (26 November), 1897-8.

facilitating research and for other kindnesses. Acknowledgement is also made to the following for help of many kinds given in the course of the research for and the preparation of final drafts of the book: Mrs. Vivienne E. Aldous (of the Corporation of London Records Office, who generously shared her unrivalled knowledge of The Irish Society archive held there, and gave much time to thus help); Mrs. Margaret Alford (of The Irish Society's office in London); Mr. David Bigger; Mr. Nicholas Brannon; Mr. Geremy Butler; The Very Reverend Herbert Cassidy, Dean of Armagh; Professor Leslie A. Clarkson; Sir Howard Colvin; Miss Iona Cruickshank (of the Photography Department, De Montfort University, Leicester); Miss Rachel Cutts; Miss Caroline C. Dickson; Mr. and Mrs. Joseph Erwin; Mr. Mark Le Fanu (General Secretary, the Society of Authors); the Reverend Canon F. Fawcett; Mr. John Fisher (of Prints and Maps, Guildhall Library, City of London); Lady Freeman; Mr. Stephen Freeth (Keeper of Manuscripts, Corporation of London Guildhall Library, City of London) and his staff (especially Miss Charlie Turpie, Deputy Keeper of Manuscripts); Miss Penelope Fussell (Archivist, The Worshipful Company of Drapers of the City of London); Mr. R. G. G. Gallick and the staff of St Columb's cathedral, Londonderry; Mr. John A. Gamble; Miss Marjorie Geary and the staff of the Irish Reference Library, County Hall, Coleraine; The Hon. Janet Grant of the College of Arms, London; Mr Barrie Hartwell of The Queen's University of Belfast; Mr. and Mrs. James Hegarty; Mrs Sally Hofmann, Archivist, The Honourable Artillery Company; Miss Elizabeth Hoy and the staff of the North-Eastern Education and Library Board; Dr. Raymond Gillespie; Mr. Ralph Hyde (former Keeper of Prints and Maps, Guildhall Library, City of London, who gave generous encouragement to further investigations in reviews of the 1979 and 1981 monographs); Mr. Geoffrey Kelly; Professor Michael Kenneally; Professor Rhodri Windsor-Liscombe; Professor Charles H. A. MacCallum; Mr. and the late Mrs. Daniel MacLaughlin; Dr. William A. Maguire; Mr. Annesley Malley; Mr. Barratt E. Manning; Mr. Graham Mawhinney; Mr. Victor J. Miller; The Very Reverend Dr. W. W. Morton (Dean of Derry and rector of Templemore); Dr Timothy Mowl; Mr. Noel Osborne and Phillimore & Co. Ltd. (for permission to quote from *The Londonderry Plantation 1609-1914*); Mr. Trevor Parkhill; Mr. Patrick Perratt (National Art Library, Victoria and Albert Museum); Mrs. Ann Perry (Senior Assistant Librarian, Division of Learning Development, Kimberlin Library, De Montfort University, Leicester); Madame Michèle Picard; Mr. N. M. Plumley (Curator and Archivist, Christ's Hospital, Horsham, West Sussex); Dr. Vivienne Pollock; Mr. Rodney C. Roach; Dr. Philip S. Robinson; Madame Françoise Roux (of the Centre Canadien d' Architecture, Montreal); Mr. Stuart Ó Seanóir (Assistant Librarian, Manuscripts Department, Trinity College Library, Dublin); Mr. James R. Sewell (City Archivist, Corporation of London Records Office); Mr. Michael Smallman (of The Queen's University of Belfast); Mr. Jeremy Smith (of Prints and Maps, Guildhall Library, City of London); Miss Ann Taylor; Mr. Trevor Todd (Royal Institute of British Architects); Dr. David Watkin (of Peterhouse, University of Cambridge), and Mr. Thomas Woodcock (Norroy and Ulster King of Arms of the College of Arms, London). All gave of their time and expertise with great patience, generosity, and kindness: they are most warmly thanked.

As former Senior Research Fellow of the School of Architecture, De Montfort University, Leicester, the author was supported by that University, especially by Professors George Henderson, Alan Short, and Brian Swanick. He also acknowledges the quiet encouragement given by Professor Dorota Iwaniec, his wife, who helped in very many ways, not least by generous gifts of books and unwavering moral support.

Mrs. Margaret Reed prepared the text and disks from less than tidy manuscripts and is warmly thanked. Research for the book was supported in part by the Arts and Humanities Research Board of the British Academy and by the Authors' Foundation to which bodies the author extends his gratitude. Mr. Noel Osborne and the staff of Phillimore & Co. Ltd., especially Mrs. Carolyn Oliver and Miss Nicola Willmot, did an enormous amount of work to bring this study to press, and the author records his sincere thanks for all their efforts in this respect.

Lastly, the book is dedicated to the memory of the late Mr. Robert T. Brown (formerly Education Officer of the Drapers' Company, who many years ago steered the present writer through labyrinthine archives with deftness, humour, and infinite courtesy, and, indeed, helped to lay the foundations for this and other studies) and the late Professor Theodore W. Moody (whose magisterial pioneering studies of the Plantation were carried out before the 1939-45 war, and so include references to some archival material that has not survived). Mr. Brown became a close friend, and it is a source of some sadness that he died at a relatively early age. Professor Moody's work remains monumental, and one can only salute a great scholar with deference and respect.

James Stevens Curl

Leicester, Holywood, and London, 1997-2000

List of Subscribers

Peter N. Acheson
Dr. Ian Adamson, OBE, MLA, FRSPHH
The Lord Alderdice
J.P. Alexander
Very Rev. Dr. D.H. Allen
David St.C. Baird
Dr. Jonathan Bardon
Bellaghy Bawn
P.A. Beddows Esq.
Philip William Beddows
Mr. and Mrs. D.A. Bigger
John L. Bird, OBE, CC
Beth Black
Councillor Toye Black
William A. Bolton
Kenneth Bond, AWA Architects
Nick Brannon and Audrey Horning
John Brazil
Mr. David R. Brewster and Mrs. Judith E. Brewster
The Rt. Hon. The Viscount Brookeborough, DL
Michael Fotheringham Broughton
Mr. Tony Byrne
Commander Peter Campbell, LVO, OBE, DL
Brian Joseph Carty
Causeway Institute of Further and Higher Education
The Reverend David L. Cawley, FSA
Colonel W.R.H. Charley, OBE, JP, DL
D.M. Christie
Gordon Clark
Wallace Clark
David Clarke
Board of Governors, Coleraine Academical Institution
Coleraine Borough Council
Coleraine High School
Timothy J.M. Conway
Robert L.D. Cooper
Russell Craig
Tony Crowe
Will Dalzell
Mr. Brian Dane
Albert Frederick Danton
Mr. and Mrs. A.M.L. Davidson
Andrew J.L. Davidson
William Davies
Denis F. Desmond
Rev. T.P. Donnelly
Tom and Patricia Douglas
Billy Dove, MBE, JP, CC
Mrs. Patricia Drummond
Dr. Eull and Mrs. Dorothy Dunlop
K.F. Dunn
W.A. Eakins
Dr. Harold Elwood
Brigadier J.G.G. de P. Ferguson, OBE, DL
J.H.Y. Fergusson
Dorothy I. Fleming
M.J. Foster
Foyle and Londonderry College
Mr. J.A. Gamble, FRGS
Garvagh Historical Society
George and Linda Gilmore
Peter Good
Robin Gray, BA, MRTPI
Greenhill House
Augusto J. Gregori
Mr. James Grew, CBE, JP, DL
Keith Haines
Emil W. Hamilton
S. McK. Hammond
Professor Robert Harris
S. Michael Henry
Hewitt & Gilpin
The Hon. Mr. Justice M.J. Higgins
Adrian J. Hill
Desmond and Barbara Hill
Mrs. Terence Hill
Dr. W.J.C. Hill
Mr. and Mrs. Desmond Hodges
Air Marshal Sir Reginald and Lady Harland
R. Blakiston Houston
David H.S. Howard
Jim Hunter
R.J. Hunter
W.F. Graham Hunter
Mary Cecil Hurley
Professor Dorota Iwaniec
Dr. Astrid James
Marlene Jefferson, MBE
Dr. E.G. Jenner, MBE
Harry Johnston
Neil C. Johnston
Andrew Kane
Dr. D.A.J. Keegan
R.D. Kells

Georg F. Kempter
J.A. Kilner, BA, MSc, FCIOB
Nigel Kinnaird
D.W. Laing
Noel Lamb Esq.
J. Cecil Leitch, BSc
Limavady Borough Council
Maurice Lindsay
Linen Hall Library, Belfast
Julian W.S. Litten, FSA

The Livery Companies of the City of London:
The Worshipful Company of Barbers
The Worshipful Company of Brewers
The Clothworkers' Company
The Worshipful Company of Cordwainers
The Worshipful Company of Curriers
The Worshipful Company of Cutlers
The Worshipful Company of Dyers
The Fishmongers' Company
The Worshipful Company of Ironmongers
The Leathersellers' Company
The Worshipful Company of Pewterers
The Clerk, The Saddlers' Company
The Worshipful Company of Skinners
The Tallow Chandlers' Company
The Vintners' Company

Professor Adrian Long
Dan MacLaughlin
Annesley J. Malley
Bill Mathews
Graham Mawhinney
Nigel May
Robert McCartney, QC, MP
Proinsias and Margaret McCaughey
Councillor David McClarty, MLA
Dr. Alan D. McClure, OBE, DL
David John McConaghy
Wm.J. McCourt
Denis F. McCoy, FRIAI
John McDowell
Sir John McFarland, Bt
Shaun McGibbon
George A. McIlrath, OBE, JP
Hugh McIlveen
Russell McKay
Robin McKinney
Isambard W.J. McMinn
Robert Fraser McMinn
Mr. J.E. McPeak, BA, PGCE
Ian B. McQuiston
A.J. Miller
Dr. Mervyn Miller
Douglas Mobsby
Professor Fabian Monds, CBE
Edward Montgomery
Herbert Montgomery
Mildred M. Moore
Museum, Apprentice Boys' Memorial Hall, Londonderry
Alderman Sir Richard Nichols
Sir Michael Nicholson
Rev. Thomas Nicholson
O'Connor Kennedy Turtle
Sean O'Dwyer
Alderman Michael Oliver
Dr. Andrew Parmley, Phd, MusM, CC
Christopher Peacocke
John W.D. Pinkerton
The Rt. Hon. Sir Robert Porter, QC
Gerald A.G. Pulman, Past Deputy Governor
Queen's University Belfast
Mrs. Margaret Reed
Isobel Reilly
W.N.B. Richardson, DL
Andrew Alwyn Riddell
River Faughan Anglers Ltd.
Wm. Ross, MP and Mrs. Christine Ross
St Columb's College, Derry
Keith A. Sargant
Charles and Susan Scott
Ella Scott-Simpson
J.D. Shaw
Robert Shillingford, MBE, AE, Deputy Governor 1968-69
David H. Smith
Brian Smyth
Daniel Smyth
John Spanner, TD, CC
Jim Spence
W. Bristow Stevenson
Nial Stewart
Mr. and Mrs. Paul Teesdale
Dr. R.W. Temple
Timothy P. Traill Esq.
David Trimble
Professor R.G. Ussher
John Vaughan
Verbal Arts Centre (N.I.) Ltd
Mr. Simon Waley
Alderman Sir Christopher Walford, Governor 1997-2000
J.C. Warnock Consulting Engineers
Dr. David Watkin
John White, OBE, FPS
D.E. Wickham, MA, ARHistS
Dr. and Mrs. Peter Willis
Philip J. Willoughby, JP, Deputy Governor 1995-96
R.T.D. Wilmot
Mr. and Mrs. Hal Wilson
T. Woodcock Esq., Norroy and Ulster King of Arms
Michael C. Wylie

Note on Currency Equivalents

> Blessings on him who invented … the common currency that buys all things, the balance and weight that equalises the shepherd and the king, the simpleton and the sage
>
> MIGUEL DE CERVANTES SAAVEDRA (1547-1616): *Don Quixote* (1605), pt. 2, ch. 68

Throughout this study figures are given relating to expenditure, etc., incurred by the City of London in relation to the Plantation of Ulster. However, any discussion of cash value during the 17th century is fraught with difficulties for the simple reason that a monetary figure then bears no resemblance to the sums computed at the end of the 20th century. A few attempted definitions are therefore necessary, though it is almost impossible to arrive at hard-and-fast accuracy.

Historically, the Pound Sterling was based on a pound weight of silver, of the value of 20 Shillings or 240 Pence. *Sterling* may derive from the Old English *Steorling*, meaning a coin decorated with a star, some of the early Anglo-Norman Pennies having on them a small star-shaped decoration; another explanation is that the word comes from *Stær* (a starling), alluding to the four birds (called *martlets*) on coins of the time of King Edward the Confessor (reigned 1042-66); and yet another is that *Sterling* was a corruption of *Easterling*, meaning a merchant of the Hanseatic cities or Baltic coasts and coinage minted by those settlements, but this interpretation may be spurious, for *Moneta esterlingorum* probably meant not 'the coin of the Easterlings', but 'coinage of Sterling pennies'. The first English silver 'Sterlings' date from *c.*775.[1]

Currency was sometimes calculated in *Marks*, a denomination of weight employed for gold or silver throughout western Europe that can be seen as an early form of 'Common European Currency'. A *Mark* was usually two-thirds or half of a Pound. In England, after the Norman Conquest in 1066, the ratio of 20 Sterling Pennies to an Ounce was the basis of monetary calculation, so the value of a *Mark* was fixed at 160 Pence (13s. 4d. or two-thirds of a Pound Sterling). Many of the 17th-century papers relating to the Plantation refer to monetary transactions in *Marks*, and the term remained in general use until around 1770. The *Mark* continued in use by Hamburg merchants and others who kept their accounts in *Marks* and *Schillings* (16 *Schillings* = 1 *Mark*), throughout the 18th century, and in 1871 the *Mark* (worth 100 *Pfennigs*) became the currency of the new German Empire. By 1875 the silver *Mark* of the German Reich was worth slightly less than an English silver Shilling, and generally replaced the old *Thaler* (corrupted to *Dollar*) as the main unit of German currency.

A *Carat* is a proportional measure of one twenty-fourth used in stating the fineness of gold. If gold consists of 22 parts of pure gold and 2 parts of another metal it is said to be 22 carats fine, or 22-carat gold. *Carat* was sometimes confused with weight, and

[1] *O.E.D.* (1933), **x**, 927-8.

some historical sources state a *Carat* was one twenty-fourth part of an Ounce, or even one twenty-fourth part of a Pound Troy. The term *Troy* refers to a standard system of weights used for precious metals, hence *Troy Ounce* and *Troy Pound*. The *Pound Troy* or *Troy Pound* was divided into 12 Ounces of 20 Pennyweight, unlike the *Pound Avoirdupois*, which was once the standard system of weights used in Great Britain for all goods *except* precious metals, precious stones, and medicines, and was subdivided into 16 Ounces. A *Pennyweight* was the actual weight of a silver Penny, and there were 20 Pennyweights per Troy Ounce, so 240 Pennyweights per Troy Pound. Each Pennyweight equalled 24 Grains, and each Grain was the smallest unit of weight, equivalent to one five thousand seven hundred and sixtieth part of a Pound Troy. It is obvious that coinage could be debased by adding other metals to produce alloys, and this certainly worsened e.g. Scotland's economic position at certain times.

When we consider that, for the Plantation of Ulster, £60,000 was levied on the 55 Livery Companies in 1610-16 to buy out interests, build and fortify a city and a town, erect a fortress, and do much else besides, it is apparent that the historical figures are meaningless in today's terms. £4,000 would not build much of a cathedral in Londonderry today, and indeed would hardly be sufficient to renew the stone dressings of one buttress. It is also pointless to consult official Government figures, for claims about strength of currency, inflation, standards, etc., are not trustworthy. In 1717 an Ounce Troy of 22-Carat gold was reckoned to be £3 17s. 10½d. Sterling.[2] Allowing for fluctuations in the market, an Ounce of gold in the late 20th-century would fetch around £187 to £205, but the figure cannot be compared with £187-£205 in 1717 or in 1617 which would, in either case, have been a small fortune, being based on gold and silver. In 1999 a Pound gold coin could be purchased for about £50, and represented 0.25 Troy Ounces, so an Ounce Troy would cost around £200 in 1999, although figures have fluctuated: at the end of September 1999 an Ounce Troy was quoted at £171.

But it is not a question of an easy conversion using one standard. Any calculation should take into account what it cost to rent land, rent housing,[3] provide accommodation, pay wages, and so on. In 1999 it was estimated that George Augustus Frederick (1762-1830), Prince of Wales (later King George IV [1820-30]), had debts of £269,878 in 1786, which could be computed as £15,000,000 in late 20th-century terms,[4] but that figure is undoubtedly too low. Even multiplying £269,878 by £50 (the average price of a gold Pound in 1999) gives £13,493,900 as a bare minimum: taking into account wages, rents, and other checks, the figure probably exceeds £20,000,000 by far more than a margin. If that sum is imagined in 1616 it would be astronomical, but attempts to relate prices of gold now and then by means of simple formulae are clearly not sufficient, and figures come out far too low for what was achieved.

Various rather crude comparisons have been attempted, including the price of a cow then and now, but cows have not enjoyed anything like a stable price in the market, and at the end of the 20th century to use a cow as a sensible basis for currency calculations would not be wise, given the crises concerning bovine diseases, demand, legislation, and other matters. Possibly land rental as a percentage price over several years might offer some scope, but even that has problems, and it is dangerous to try any fixed formula or to be dogmatic.

[2] *Encyclopaedia Britannica* (1959), **xviii**, 382.

[3] Information from the financial pages of *The Sunday Telegraph* (25 April 1999) and Spink & Son Ltd. (April and September 1999).

[4] Smith, F. A. (1999): *George IV* (New Haven and London: Yale University Press), *passim*.

i Railway-bridge over the River Bann, (built 1921-4), from the north, with the tower of St Patrick's parish-church, Coleraine, in the background. (*A*)

In the 1970s, when working on nineteenth-century working-class housing, the present writer estimated that if the average weekly wage of a skilled London tradesman was something like the equivalent of four or five times the weekly rent for a self-contained flat or small dwelling that left just about enough to rear a family and leave something over for entertainment and clothing. This was confirmed by a study of the literature (printed and MSS.) of the time. When it is remembered that *four* self-contained architect-designed model dwellings could be erected in 1851 for £458 14s. 7d. (e.g. the Prince Albert Model Houses erected at the Great Exhibition and designed by Henry Roberts [1803-76]), some idea of the phenomenal inflation since then may be gained.[5] Those unfortunates today who pay for crippling mortgages (a system to which Roberts was vehemently opposed because of its inflationary influences on house *prices*) might well look at 20 or 25 per cent of income devoted to housing with envious eyes. When it is remembered that £1,000 per annum in 1933 was a reasonable income, enabling a man to marry, keep a servant, have children, live in a house, and run a car, a very considerable multiple of that figure would be required today for anything approaching the same standard of living.

A further illustration can be given concerning the railway-bridge over the River Bann near Coleraine in County Londonderry. The first viaduct had been erected in 1860, but by 1900 its condition was giving cause for concern. It was decided to replace it by a new structure about a quarter-of-a-mile downstream from the old bridge, and in 1914 authority was granted to realise the scheme. Land was obtained after negotiation with various bodies, including The Honourable The Irish Society, by May 1919, and work began in 1921. The contractors were Armstrong, Whitworth, & Co. Ltd., the bridge was designed by Bowman Malcolm, and work was completed under the supervision of W. K. Wallace: the new viaduct had 11 spans, and one of the spans was a bascule arrangement to enable ships to pass through **[i, ii]**. This re-aligned bridge enabled the sharp curves of the track on either side of the 1860 structure to be replaced by gentler bends. In 1924 the Bann bridge opened: with the re-alignment of tracks, embankments, and other works, it cost around £100,000.[6] Had it been built before the 1914-18 war it would have cost about £10,000. So a factor of a multiplier

[5] Curl (1983), *passim*.
[6] Currie (1974), 77-81, and *passim*.

ii Railway-bridge over the River Bann from the south. The structure in the centre controls the section that can be moved to allow ships to pass. (*A*)

of 10 has to be applied to construction works of such a type between 1914 and 1924, only a decade. Today, such a structure would cost many times what it did in 1924, and even a million pounds would fall far short.

So how can we come to any viable conclusions regarding expenditure on the Plantation? It is clear that the City of London poured an enormous treasure into the Londonderry venture, causing very considerable distress to many Liverymen and their dependants. It is little wonder the Liverymen of the City of London were anxious to avoid being embroiled in the 'Busynesse' at all, and feared for the calls made on their dwindling purses. An accurate estimate of what that treasure might be in modern terms is almost impossible, but it is obvious it ran to the equivalent of many millions of pounds. On paper the Livery Companies put up £62,000 by 1635, and The Irish Society's total disbursements by then totalled £110,000 not counting £30,000 expended on the Company Proportions.[7] When it is remembered that The Society had built and fortified the city of Londonderry and the town of Coleraine, improved and strengthened Culmore Fort (built earlier before the involvement of the Londoners), erected a large Gothic Survival cathedral-church, and paid for ships, arms, ordnance, labour, administration, and much else, such a sum in today's money would be as a drop in the ocean. Londonderry's walls alone cost something like £10,357, and the cathedral-church was completed in 1633 for an outlay of about £4,000. Using calculations based on modern prices of gold it is doubtful if Londonderry's walls could be built for anything like £2,071,400 or, ludicrously, £517,850, while the cathedral most certainly could not be erected for £240,000 or £800,000 in the year 2000.

Exercises involving modern techniques of quantity surveying would not be helpful, however, for labour, material, banking, administrative, and other costs would be wholly out of kilter with those of the early 17th century, so to compare like with like is not really possible. If the crude multiples used (4 × 15) to calculate the Prince of Wales's debts in 1786 are inadequate, then so are any that might help to shed a light on figures for the pound 1610-35. A factor of 100 (at least) would be needed to translate the income of £1,000 in 1933 to 1999 terms, and even then it is doubtful if £100,000 would be enough to keep a non-working wife, children, a car, and servants in anything like the affluent style of the 1933 man on £1,000 per annum.

[7] Moody (1939), 365; Smith (1966), 26.

It is submitted that the £110,000 laid out by The Irish Society in the first phase of its existence would have to be a lot more than £11,000,000 today (assuming a multiplier of 100, as with the 1933-99 example), and that a multiple of 1,000, giving £110,000,000 would hardly cover the extent of the construction work, wages, and provision of armaments, among much else, but, given the defects pointed out by Bodley, Phillips, Pynnar and others (described below), is probably a lot nearer the mark. If this figure approximates to real expense, it goes a long way to explaining why the City of London not only broke with the arbitrary rule of King Charles I, but tended to side with those who eventually constituted the Whig oligarchy.

Similarly, one could not build the four Henry Roberts flats for just under £30,000 today (and here we can make a precise comparison because detailed specifications survive), so a factor much higher than 60 or even 100 has to be applied to construction costs in 1851. Thus the factor of 1,000 applied to the 1610-35 figures is not so far-fetched, although £4,000,000 for St Columb's would hardly be sufficient to build it, and it is doubtful if £10,357,000 for Londonderry's walls and gates would be anywhere near enough.

Although Government figures should be treated with caution (as contemporary economic figures are usually made out to be better than they are, for political reasons), it is interesting to look at the Central Statistical Office's notes on the Internal Purchasing Power of the Pound. As the C.S.O. stated in 1980, 'no single indicator will be ideal for all purposes'. If we assume that the purchasing-power of a pound in 1914 is 100p, its comparable purchasing power (according to the C.S.O.) in 1980 would be

$$100 \times \frac{11.1}{260.8} = 4.26\text{p}$$

Now inflation since 1980 has been considerable, so if *official* recognition accepts that there has been such a huge decline in purchasing power between 1914 and 1980, the difference between 1609 and 1999 must be enormous, and suggests that a factor considerably in excess of 1,000 might not be all that far out.

Such estimates are necessarily only reasonable deductions based on many observations, figures, comparisons, and other criteria, and are not offered as incontrovertible facts. However, they do begin to give some indication of the enormous burden the Crown placed on the City when it pushed the Londoners into being involved in the Plantation of Ulster. They also point to the huge responsibilities of The Honourable The Irish Society, and, though they take no account of human suffering and other aspects that are difficult to measure, suggest something of the magnitude of the undertaking and its calls upon the pockets of the Liverymen of 55 Companies. It is little wonder those Liverymen were less than keen to become involved in something that must have seemed singularly unattractive at the time.

CHAPTER I

Historical Outline of Events before the Involvement of the City of London in Ulster

> [English rule acted] like a running sore, constantly irritating the Gaelic regions beyond the Pale, and deepening the confusion …
>
> SIR HENRY JAMES SUMNER MAINE (1822-88):
> *Early History of Institutions* (London: Murray, 1875)

The Historical Background I: The Medieval Period

A detailed history of Ireland, or even of Ulster, before the intervention of the City of London from the 17th century, is not possible here. Only the briefest of outlines will be attempted in order to set the scene.[1]

It is now more or less accepted that the Anglo-Norman invasion of Ireland began in 1167 when Diarmait Mac Murchada (Dermot Mac Murrough – d. 1171), King of Leinster from *c.*1132 until he was deposed in 1166, received permission in Aquitaine from King Henry II of England (reigned 1154-89) to recruit troops to help him to regain his Kingdom. Mac Murchada had got into difficulties first by abducting Derbforgaill, wife of Tigernán Ua Ruairc (O'Rourke), King of Bréifne, in 1152, thereby setting 'all the countrie in uprore' (as Meredith Hanmer [1543-1604] put it in his *Chronicle of Ireland* [1633]). Then, after a failed bid to become High-King of Ireland, Mac Murchada was banished by Ruaidrí Ua Conchob(h)air (Roderick O'Connor – High-King from 1166 to 1183 – d. 1198), and fled to Bristol. Having offered his fealty to the English King, he sailed from Wales with his forces, and soon regained his territories.

His most important ally (from 1170) was Richard fitz Gilbert (or de Clare), known as 'Strongbow' (d. 1176), who had been deprived of the earldom of Pembroke by Henry II in 1154. Strongbow married Aífe (*c.*1152-*c.*1189), daughter of Mac Murchada, in 1170, and, on the last's death (1171), succeeded to the kingship of Leinster, where he energetically settled tenants from his English and Welsh estates, and waged war to make his holdings secure. King Henry, however, threatened to confiscate Strongbow's lands unless he received recognition of the English King's overlordship of Strongbow's Irish acquisitions, and in 1171 landed in Ireland where he received the submissions of the Kings of North Leinster, Bréifne (approximately equivalent to Counties Leitrim and Cavan), Airgialla (the modern counties of Londonderry, Monaghan, and Tyrone, Armagh west of the Bann, parts of Fermanagh and Louth, and [probably] part of

[1] For further information see Connolly (ed.) (1998); Foster (1988); Foster (ed.) (1989); Moody, Martin, and Byrne (eds.) (1982).

Meath), and Ulster (approximating to the modern counties of Antrim and Down east of the Bann), as well as those of other Irish lords. He also recognised Strongbow as Lord of Leinster and Earl of Strigoil (the last a title taken from Strongbow's castle at Chepstow in Monmouthshire, Wales).

The Anglo-Norman (or Cambro-Norman) invasion was given further apparent legality by the papal letter (or Privilege Bull), *Laudabiliter* (probably prompted by the Archbishop of Canterbury, Theobald [or Tedbaldus (d. 1161) – Primate from 1138] through his intermediary, John of Salisbury [d. 1180]) of 1155 issued by Pope Hadrian IV (1154-9 – himself a native of Hertfordshire, in England) to King Henry II as an instrument, it has been claimed, by which the Irish Church would be reformed and brought more into line with European norms, and led to colonisation and settlement between *c.*1170 and *c.*1270 by significant numbers of tenants or town-dwellers, notably in Leinster and Munster. The influence of the English Church in this business should not be underestimated, for Canterbury, primatial see of England, unquestionably played a pivotal rôle in Irish ecclesiastical affairs during the 11th and 12th centuries. The first recorded bishop of Dublin, for example, Dúnán (or Donatus), was probably consecrated at Canterbury by Archbishop (from 1020) Æthelnoth (Egelnodus – d. 1038) around 1028 in the reign of King Canute (or Cnut) the Great (*c.*994-1035). The Irish Church seems to have accepted Roman primacy after the Synod of Whitby (664), but it is difficult to establish how real this was in practice. From 841 Scandinavians had established permanent bases in Ireland, and developed important settlements at Dublin, Waterford, Wexford, Cork, and Limerick, gradually becoming Christianised. The Scandinavian-Irish clergy had close links with their kinsmen in England, and it was to Canterbury they looked for leadership and indeed for legitimacy. Those links were strengthened under Lanfranc (*c.*1005-89), Archbishop of Canterbury from 1070 to 1089, who consecrated Gilla Pátraic (or Patricius) [1074]) and Donngus (or Donatus [1085]) as bishops of Dublin. Under Anselm (1033-1109), Archbishop of Canterbury (1089-1109) and later Saint, a wide recognition of the primacy of Canterbury was secured from the Churches in Wales, Ireland, and (to a lesser extent) Scotland, and it was Archbishop Anselm who consecrated Samuel as Bishop of Dublin and Máel Ísu Ua hAinmere (or Malchus) as first recorded bishop of Waterford (both 1096).

Archbishop Anselm attempted to bind the Irish Church more closely to that of England, but Bishop Samuel of Dublin had ambitions of his own: from *c.*1097 until 1102 he claimed metropolitan jurisdiction in defiance of Canterbury. Thus an ominous rift developed. The first formal establishment of a single authority for the Irish Church seems to have been attempted at the Synod of Ráith Bressail (1111), which divided the country into two provinces to be administered by the archbishops of Armagh and Cashel, and each province was subdivided into 12 dioceses. This arrangement reflected ecclesiastical structures in England.

However, when an episcopal election in Dublin was disputed (1121) by Cellach of Armagh after the death of Samuel, Bishop of Dublin, Gréne (Gregorius) was consecrated by Ralph d'Escures, or Ralph de Turbine (d. 1122 – Archbishop of Canterbury from 1114). Under Archbishop Theobald of Canterbury the English Church took an ever-stronger position in attempting to bring Ireland into line: in 1140 Patricius, Bishop-elect of Limerick, sought consecration from Theobald to gain legitimacy for his office, but there was another powerful personality at work who advocated radical reform of the Irish Church. Máel Máedóc Ua Morgair (or Malachy – 1094-1148) had experienced great difficulty (1129) in overcoming the opposition of the *hereditary* secularised ecclesiastical dynasty of clann Sínaich (which had enjoyed a virtual monopoly of clerical offices at Armagh for two centuries) when he was appointed Archbishop of Armagh. In fact, Malachy did not succeed in taking possession of the insignia of office or the temporalities of the Church until 1134. Accordingly, Malachy visited Rome in 1139 to obtain papal recognition for the archbishoprics of Armagh and Cashel, and was instructed by Pope Innocent II (1130-43) to call a general council in Ireland to formalise a request for papal endorsement of ecclesiastical reorganisation. Once back home Malachy introduced the Cistercians to Ireland at Mellifont and the Augustinians at St Mary's Abbey, Louth, both in 1142, so 12th-century reform of the Irish Church was well under way, supported by the Papacy, *before* the Anglo-Norman invasion. It should be remembered that Irish political structures were largely dependent upon the possession of land, and with those systems monasteries and churches, controlled by Irish magnates and family groups, were closely connected. Malachy's difficulties at Armagh stemmed from the fact that Church properties and offices had long been under the control of an hereditary dynasty of laymen, but it is doubtful if he could have succeeded in weakening, let alone breaking, that control unless powerful centralising forces from Canterbury and Rome had been at work. Once heads of monastic houses recognised the authority of a primate, archbishops, and bishops in ecclesiastical matters (rather than that of local lords and chiefs or the hereditary powers of family groups), and the senior clergy recognised the full authority of Rome through an appropriate hierarchy, Ireland could be more easily controlled, under threat of excommunication, if need be. Thus an Anglo-Norman invasion can be seen as a means by which the authority of laymen and local factions could be undermined and replaced by more centralised control deriving from legitimate powers delegated by Rome.

A crisis seems to have developed from 1152 following the Synod of Kells (which transferred to the Cistercian house at Mellifont), when Ireland was officially divided into four ecclesiastical provinces (Dublin, Tuam, Armagh, and Cashel), and this was given Roman *Imprimatur* when Cardinal Paparo, papal legate, arrived with the *Pallia* for the four archbishops. Canterbury would have viewed these developments with disfavour and as a gross diminution of its rights, for not only did Canterbury claim primacy over York, but looked to the precedents of consecrating Irish bishops (of Scandinavian origins or not) as evidence for its primacy over Ireland as well.

It is not unreasonable, therefore, to see the Anglo-Norman intervention as prompted by a Canterbury that felt slighted, and by a Papacy anxious to achieve greater conformity throughout Europe. There may also have been one factor in the whole momentous affair that most historians have glossed over: in December 1170 the Archbishop of Canterbury (from 1162), Thomas Becket (1118-70), was martyred in his own cathedral, and King Henry II was obliged later to do public penance for his death. Less than 11 months later, the King, then pursuing the conquest of Ireland, issued the summons for the important Synod of Cashel, and a few days later received the submissions of the four Irish Kings. Henry also obtained promises of clerical obedience from the Irish bishops and clergy: armed with these new strengths, the English King was in a much better position to bargain with Rome, and in May 1172 he received Absolution from papal legates for any part he might have had in the death of Becket (canonised in 1173). In the following September Pope Alexander III (1159-81) wrote to the Irish lords advocating fealty to King Henry. It is difficult to avoid concluding that these events were connected, and that the see of Canterbury, backed by the Papacy, encouraged King Henry to intervene in Ireland, partly, perhaps, as some sort of recompense for the death of Becket. Papal authorisation (or approval) of Anglo-Norman intervention seems to have been endorsed by the Irish prelates at the Synod of Cashel (1172), the last of the great reforming assemblies held by the Church in Ireland during the 12th century. Those prelates seem to have recognised that further reform and centralisation were necessary, for dynastic control of Church offices and lands had continued in places, and indeed would continue in the more isolated parts of the country (like Ulster) where the Gaelic chieftains held sway. Thus the death of Becket, the see of Canterbury, the Papacy, and King Henry's imperative need to find himself once more in good odour with the Church appear to have been at least partly responsible for the consolidation of English overlordship in Ireland.

By the Treaty of Windsor (1175) between King Henry II and the Archbishop of Tuam (Cadla Ua Dubhthaig [Catholicus O'Duffy (d. 1201)] on behalf of Ruaidrí Ua Conchob(h)air), witnessed by the Archbishop of Dublin (from 1162), Lorcán Ua Tuathail (Laurence O'Toole [d. 1180]), the High-King made submission to the English monarch, and was confirmed as King of Connacht. Thus Ireland appeared to accept English overlordship.

During the pontificate of Pope Honorius III (1216-27)[2] support was given to the young King Henry III (1207-72 – reigned from 1216 on the death of his father, King John [*c.*1167-1216 – declared King of Ireland in 1177, reigned as King of England from 1199]), and papal recognition was given to the rights of the English Crown in Irish episcopal elections in 1219. Further approval seems to have been given to English hegemony by the Canonisation of Laurence O'Toole by Pope Honorius in 1225 and by the Letters of Excommunication issued against those who might attack royal castles in Ireland (1223). Furthermore, the Pope put pressure on France to abandon her projected invasion of England, so it would seem that the Papacy viewed England and the English Crown with at least a certain benevolence.

Certain events relating to the papal intervention in the British Isles are commemorated in frescoes in the Vatican Library in Rome (entrance to the so-called Secret Cabinets): the themes of these paintings concern various acts by which the Papacy legitimised temporal power, and include the Coronation (800) of Charlemagne by Pope Leo III (795-816), the Coronation (1155) of the German King Frederick I Barbarossa (1152-90) as Roman Emperor, the grant of the papal Bull of Privilege in relation to King Henry II's overlordship of Ireland **[1]** (the last two acts by Pope Hadrian IV), and the bestowing of the Kingdom of Mona (the Isle of Man), 'in the Irish Sea', by King Reginald of Mona (1187-1226), upon the apostolic see during the pontificate of Honorius III **[2]**. The Manx episode is very interesting in the Irish context, for Reginald wished to hold his Kingdom of the Papacy and King Henry III, avoiding having to do homage to the Irish Church or to be subject to Irish episcopal domination. Again, it should be remembered that the Manx aristocracy was of Scandinavian blood, and therefore would feel easier under Canterbury and Rome than under a Gaelic bishop.[3]

Now the fact that no fewer than two of the handful of frescoes in a small room in the *Biblioteca Apostolica*[4] depict episodes in the transfer of power (both spiritual and temporal) in Ireland and the Irish Sea (and the legitimising of that power), and that those two paintings have equal status in the decorative scheme to that accorded to the

[2] For details of the Pontificate of Honorius III see Sayers (1984), *passim*.
[3] Sayers (1984), 64, 93, 164, 185.
[4] Studied by the present writer in September 1999.

1 Fresco-painting in the *Gabinetto Segreto*, *Biblioteca Vaticana* (or *Apostolica*), showing Pope Hadrian IV granting his assent to King Henry II of England's overlordship of Ireland. (*A*)

papal *Imprimatur* of Roman emperors, no less, cannot be insignificant. The Henry II and Manx frescoes point to two Popes accepting the claims of English Kings to overlordship in Irish temporal and ecclesiastical affairs, and must lend credence to the Papacy's backing of English intervention in Ireland. It is curious that this appears to have escaped (or has been ignored by) most commentators.[5]

Whatever the reasons, arguments, and machinations that led to *Laudabiliter* (the authenticity of which is still questioned in certain quarters, despite the independent evidence[6] that the papal approval for English intervention in Ireland was given) and military invasion, the demographic, economic, and social consequences were immense: Ireland's Gaelic identity was irrevocably changed. Furthermore, the colonisation of Ireland was part of enormous movements of peoples from north-western Europe leading to the establishment of villages and towns in north-eastern and central Europe as well as in Ireland. Such a massive demographic shift, or series of shifts, was rather like an explosion, as settlers spread out from north-western Europe, and it would be historically inaccurate to view the English or Anglo-Norman colonisation of parts of Ireland as an isolated incident, divorced from the European experience as a whole.[7]

[5] Sayers (1984) gives a very full account of the relations between the Papacy and England between 1216 and 1227.

[6] Including commemorative frescoes in the Vatican itself.

[7] Connolly (ed.) (1998), 17-18, 24, 68-9, 554-5, and *passim*; Foster (ed.) (1989).

2 Fresco-painting in the *Gabinetto Segreto, Biblioteca Vaticana* (or *Apostolica*), depicting Reginald (1187-1226), King of Mona (Isle of Man) 'in the Irish Sea', in the presence of the papal legate, bestowing his kingdom upon the apostolic see during the pontificate of Honorius III. (*A*)

Nevertheless, in spite of the English King's ambitions, the affronted archbishops of Canterbury, and the desire of the Papacy to bring Christendom under strict control from Rome, the Anglo-Norman 'conquest' was 'but slight and superficial, so the Pope's donation, and the Irish submissions, were but weak and fickle assurances',[8] as Sir John Davies, or Davys (1569-1626 – poet, from 1603 Solicitor-General, and from 1606 Attorney-General for Ireland), noted in his *A Discoverie of the Trve Cavses why Ireland was never entirely Subdued, nor brought vnder Obedience of the Crowne of England, vntill the Beginning of his Maiesties happie Raigne*, which he published in London in 1613, with a dedication to the King.[9] It all seems to have run out of steam, probably because European affairs diverted attention and resources, but many Anglo-Normans established themselves in strategic parts of Ireland, and put down healthy social and cultural roots.

It should be made clear, however, that the feudal Anglo-Norman lords did not carry out, or attempt to implement, a considered colonisation as part of State policy. Davies noted that the 'conquest of Ireland was made piece and piece, by slow steps and degrees, and by several attempts, in several ages. There were sundry revolutions, as well as of the English fortunes, as of the Irish; sometimes one prevailing, sometimes the other; and it was never brought to a full period …'.[10] The Anglo-Normans were concerned to exploit their feudal prerogatives, and so their strongholds were created

[8] Davies (1787), 8.

[9] *Ibid.*, 1-213. See also Curl (1986); Moody (1939); Moody, Martin, and Byrne (eds.) (1982); Robinson (1984, 1994).

[10] Davies (1787), 9-10.

purely for military reasons, although where these were sited in favourable positions for the advancement of commerce and trade they might also be associated with urban settlements. In some cases lordships became highly organised, successful, and prosperous, attracting skilled craftsmen and traders, but in many others they were failures. Anglo-Norman or English settlements were largely the creations of individuals, working for self-aggrandisement rather than for anything like the State, and colonisation was spasmodic and incomplete, leaving large parts of virtually untouched Gaelic civilisation almost intact.[11]

In the north of Ireland, John de Courcy (d. *c.*1219), who had arrived in Ireland in 1176, invaded Ulster in 1177 and commenced a zealous policy of colonisation. A great patron of the Church, he encouraged devotion to Irish Saints (especially fostering the cult of St Patrick), and was responsible for bringing the Cistercians over to found abbeys such as Grey and Inch in Co. Down. The title of Earl of Ulster was granted to Hugh de Lacy (d. 1242) in 1205 by King John, and this earldom was an important instrument of English power. Strong castles were built at Carrickfergus (Co. Antrim), Dundrum (Co. Down), and in other places, but although some English influences permeated the Gaelic fastnesses of Ulster (essentially the lands west of the River Bann, but also the Glens of Antrim and a few other areas), the earldom waned and the overlordship was destroyed by the invasion (1315-18) of Edward Bruce (d. 1318) and his Scots. The assassination of William de Burgh (1312-33), Earl of Ulster, led to further disintegration of English power in Ulster, leaving isolated pockets surviving in the vicinity of Coleraine, in some coastal enclaves in Down, and around Carrickfergus (as it is called today).

The Historical Background II: The Tudor Period

By the time of the establishment of the Tudor dynasty (1485) English lordship in Ireland was really effective only in the Pale (the area around Dublin comprising the county of Dublin and parts of Counties Kildare, Louth, and Meath), in which conditions approximated to those in English lowland counties. From this period the monarch's representative, or chief governor of Ireland, became known as the Lord Deputy (really the Viceroy), nominally the deputy to a Lord Lieutenant, who ruled through an executive from Dublin Castle. At first the Lords Deputy were local magnates (notably the Earls of Kildare), but this was to change, as will be explained below.

An immense upheaval occurred with the reign of King Henry VIII (1509-47) whose break with Rome (1533-4) left England diplomatically isolated and potentially vulnerable to attack by foreign powers. The reaction in Ireland led to the Kildare rebellion (1534-5) led by 'Silken Thomas' (Lord Offaly, then 10th Earl of Kildare [from 1534 to 1537]), who not only repudiated his allegiance to Henry VIII, but appealed to Charles V (Holy Roman Emperor from 1519 to 1556) for help and support in a Roman Catholic crusade against English sovereignty, but the Emperor, preoccupied with problems in Europe, not least the growth of Protestantism, failed to provide aid, so the rebellion collapsed and Kildare and five of his uncles were executed in 1537.

The immediate result was that, from the Kildare rebellion until around a century later, only Englishmen were trusted with the Lord Deputyship position. The job had enormous prestige and offered those who held it opportunities for enrichment and a means of rising to greatness in England. It could also ruin careers, the most spectacular

[11] Connolly (ed.) (1998).

example of which was that of Thomas Wentworth, 1st Earl of Strafford (1593-1641), Lord Deputy from 1632 and Lord Lieutenant from 1640, who was impeached and beheaded, so the Lord Deputyship could be a poisoned chalice. When Lord Leonard Grey, Viscount Grane (d. 1541), became Lord Deputy in 1536, he pursued a vigorous policy of attacking the castles of grandees and seeking formal submission to English overlordship as well as demanding hefty tributes and homage. This resulted in the formation of the Geraldine League led by the Ulster Gaelic chiefs Manus O'Donnell (Maghnus Ó Dom(h)naill), Lord of Tirconnell (d. 1563), and Conn Bacach ('The Lame') O'Neill (Ó Néill – *c.*1484-1559), expressly to counter Grey's aggression and to oppose royal ecclesiastical supremacy in Ireland, made law in 1536.[12] Grey presided over the Parliament in Ireland which enacted the important statutes of 1537 abolishing papal authority,[13] establishing English order, dress, and language (including the compulsory teaching of English in parish schools),[14] and the suppression of several monasteries[15] (in which the Irish, it has to be said, to a large extent, joined the scramble for pickings). The League was defeated at the battle of Bellahoe (or Ballyhoe) in 1539, but had actually offered the sovereignty of Ireland to James V, King of Scots (reigned 1513-42), who permitted some of his subjects from the Western Islands to support the Irish, and who had been encouraged by Pope Paul III (1534-49) to take up arms against the heretic King Henry (excommunicated in 1533 by Pope Clement VII [1523-34]), but James otherwise failed to act. The dissolution of the Irish monasteries and friaries proceeded apace from 1539, but the measure was not really effective in Gaelic or Gaelicised Ireland (notably Ulster) for many decades thereafter as English writ was ineffective there.

Grey also had had to contend with other uprisings led by the 14th Earl of Desmond (d. 1558) and The O'Brien (Ó Briain) of Thomond, but he dealt with those in 1536 and again in 1539. In 1540, however, the Geraldines (supporters of the Earls of Kildare) attacked settlers within the Pale, and Grey found himself in grave difficulties as his sister, Lady Elizabeth Grey, had married (1520) Gerald Fitzgerald, 9th Earl of Kildare (1487-1534), so he was suspected as the relative of a rebel (although Kildare had been Lord Deputy himself in 1513-20, 1524-8, and 1532-4). Kildare died in the Tower of London just as the Kildare rebellion (led by his son, 'Silken Thomas') started, and Grey was beheaded nearly seven years later on Tower Hill in 1541, another victim of the tainted cup that the Lord Deputyship so often became.

From 1534 there began a concerted effort to extend English power beyond the Pale to full sovereignty throughout Ireland. The Tudor Conquest (it was nothing less) was resisted in a series of conflicts culminating in the Nine Years' War. In 1541 the Kingdom of Ireland was officially created,[16] and a constitutional framework was set up to integrate the Gaelic lordships within the Tudor State. This was largely accomplished by means of Surrender and Regrant: the Gaelic lords were to recognise the King as Sovereign, renounce their Irish chieftainships, and surrender all their ancestral lands (or 'countries') in exchange for regrants of land and peerages; promises were to be given to aid the promotion of English laws and customs (together with assurances of rendering military service and paying rents to the Crown) in return for

[12] Under 28 Hen. VIII, c.5.
[13] 28 Hen. VIII, c. 13.
[14] 28 Hen. VIII, c. 15.
[15] 28 Hen. VIII, c. 16.
[16] 33 Hen. VIII, c. 1.

which charters for land and noble titles would be bestowed; and the lords were to establish the duties and rights of their kinsmen and vassals by means of arbitration. For example, Conn O'Neill was created 1st Earl of Tyrone in 1542 under Sir Anthony St Leger (*c.*1496-1559 – Lord Deputy 1540-8, 1550-1, and 1553-6), and abandoned the prestigious O'Neillship title. Contrary to the belief that the Gaelic lords were bribed with freeholds of commonly held clan lands, the Crown desired to create stability by feudalising *existing* tenures, and wished to establish the principle of primogeniture as in England, but in the short-term accepted the succession of the *Tánaiste* (designated successor of a chieftain, not necessarily a relative or even a legitimate offspring). In the case of the 1st Earl of Tyrone, succession was to pass to his (supposedly) illegitimate son, Matthew (Feardorcha) Kelly (d. 1558), created 1st Baron of Dungannon (1542), which led to civil war when Tyrone's eldest legitimate son, Shane (Seán '*an Diomais*' [The Proud]) O'Neill (*c.*1530-67), slew his half-brother, Dungannon, in 1558, claimed the O'Neillship as electee of the clan (he was called 'The Great O'Neill'), and, on the death of Tyrone in 1559, demanded the earldom. Thomas Radcliffe, Lord Fitzwalter, Earl of Sussex (1523-83), Lord Deputy from 1556 to 1564 in succession to St Leger, mounted a series of military campaigns culminating in Shane O'Neill's submission in 1563. Shane appears to have been promised the earldom in that year, but this was never implemented. In 1565 Sir Henry Sidney (1529-86) became Lord Deputy and determined to proceed with colonisation and centralising of power. In 1566 O'Neill approached Charles IX, King of France (1550-74), for aid, and offered his allegiance. Proclaimed a traitor, O'Neill attacked the English garrison at Derry, but was defeated in battle by Hugh O'Donnell at Farsetmore, near Letterkenny, while trying to re-establish his authority over Tirconnell. In 1567 O'Neill was murdered by the MacDonnells in Co. Antrim, possibly at the instigation of Sidney.

Sixteenth-century Ireland must have been a very uneasy and dangerous place as two cultures fought, one for supremacy, and the other to survive. Matters were exacerbated by England's isolation from much of Europe, and by the religious differences. Under King Edward VI (1547-53) attempts were made to make Ireland conform to the reformed religion[17] by prescribing the use of the Book of Common Prayer, but the accession of Queen Mary I (1553-8) encouraged hope of a revival of Roman Catholicism, given further impetus when the Queen married Philip of Spain (1527-98), son of Emperor Charles V, in Winchester cathedral in 1554. Legitimacy was conferred on claims that Ireland was a kingdom under the Bull *Rex Hiberniae* of Pope Paul IV (1555-9) in 1555, which affirmed papal authority in the matter of the governance of Ireland. In 1556 Philip became King Philip II of Spain, but, in spite of the creation of King's and Queen's counties (Offaly and Leix [Laois] respectively, with their main settlements re-named Philipstown and Maryborough [1557]),[18] the repeal of the statutes made against the see of Rome,[19] and an enactment declaring the regal power over Ireland to be vested in the Queen,[20] military campaigns were waged by Sussex against the Scots in Ulster, the O'Connors in Offaly, and Shane O'Neill in Ulster, and schemes were prepared for the colonisation and settlement of Leix and Offaly. Clearly, Ireland was to be 'planted' or colonised with English settlers whether England had a Protestant or a Roman Catholic on the throne.

[17] 2 & 3 Edw. VI, c. 1, and 5 & 6 Edw. VI, c. 1.
[18] 3 & 4 Philip & Mary, c. 2.
[19] 3 & 4 Philip & Mary, c. 8.
[20] 3 & 4 Philip & Mary, c. 14.

The Historical Background III: The Elizabethan Period and the Rise of O'Neill

The accession of Queen Elizabeth I (1558-1603) led to yet more difficulties, for her international standing was very shaky. Regarded as the illegitimate child of an adulterous liaison, her claims to be Queen of England, let alone of Ireland, were not universally recognised. Indeed, Philip II of Spain was seen in some quarters as the rightful King of Ireland, but that monarch, mindful of the delicate system of checks and balances in European politics, broke off his negotiations with Irish Roman Catholics in 1564 and delegated any claims to the thrones of England and Ireland to Mary, Queen of Scots (1542-87).

When Turlough (Toirdhealbhach or Terence) Luineach O'Neill (*c.*1531-95) succeeded Shane as the O'Neill chieftain in 1567, the English decided to back Hugh (Aodh) O'Neill (*c.*1550-1616), son of Matthew, 1st Baron of Dungannon, as their man, and established him in 1568 as 3rd Baron of Dungannon in succession to the murdered Brian O'Neill, 2nd Baron, slain by his cousin and rival, Turlough Luineach, in 1562. Sir Henry Sidney (Lord Deputy 1565-7, 1568-71, and 1575-8) wrote to Sir Francis Walsingham (*c.*1530-90) that he had with him the 'young Baron of Dunganan, Shane's eldest brother's son, whom I had bred in my house from a little boy, then very poor of goods and full feebly friended'. This appears to be one of the sources for claims that O'Neill was brought up and educated in England, but although he certainly visited England and stayed in London on several occasions, the notion is mistaken, yet often has been reiterated. In truth, O'Neill appears to have been brought up in the Pale by a New Englishman, Giles Hovenden (who farmed property granted to O'Neill's grandfather, Conn, near Dublin), and in 1567 sued out of his Livery (though failed to pay his full 'fine').[21] The Hovendens were not Protestant zealots, but nevertheless for a time O'Neill maintained some semblance of Conformity with the Established Church. Had O'Neill been brought up at Sidney's home in Kent (Penshurst), we may be sure he would have been thoroughly indoctrinated in Protestantism.

During Elizabeth's reign the policies of Queen Mary's reign were reversed, and in 1560 Parliament restored the supremacy of the Crown in matters ecclesiastical, ordering attendance at parish-churches on pain of fines.[22] In 1569 the O'Neill lordship was officially abolished,[23] and a *post-mortem* attainder was passed against Shane O'Neill. In 1570, the Crown made peace with Turlough Luineach, who had greatly increased his power and prestige by marrying (1569) Agnes Campbell, the Lady of Kintyre, widow of James MacDonnell, and half-sister of the Earl of Argyll. This union facilitated the supply of Scots mercenaries to fight for the illegal O'Neill lordship. Then, in 1570, Queen Elizabeth's position in Ireland was further threatened by Pope Pius V (1566-72) who issued the Bull *Regnans in Excelsis* (1570), excommunicating her and, in effect, calling for her deposition. However, this made matters worse for the Queen's Roman Catholic subjects and antagonised Spain, France, and the Empire, because papal power was being increasingly challenged, in Europe too, and there were other more pressing problems to be dealt with on the Continent.

In 1571-5 an attempt, called 'The Enterprise of Ulster', was made to colonise the southern part of eastern Ulster by allocating responsibility to private 'Undertakers',

[21] Brewer and Bullen (eds.) (1868): *Cal. Carew MSS 1575-88*, 339; Connolly (ed.) (1998), 412; Morgan (1999), 93.
[22] 2 Eliz., c. 1, c. 2 .
[23] 11 Eliz., c. 1.

notably Sir Thomas Smith (1513-77) and his illegitimate son, also Thomas (1546/7-73), who were granted lands in north Down and in the Ards peninsula.[24] The Smiths raised funds through a joint-stock company which they promoted by means of printed literature, but their armed forces were undisciplined and unreliable. The local lord of Clanaboy, Sir Brian Phelim O'Neill (murdered in 1574 in captivity), took exception, burning and destroying, and the younger Smith was killed in Comber. A much greater undertaking in the Enterprise was attempted by Walter Devereux, 1st Earl of Essex (*c.*1541-76), who raised money by mortgaging his estates in England to colonise a large part of County Antrim, but by 1573 his men, disappointed by the lack of booty, wanted to go home, and he was lured by Sir Brian Phelim O'Neill into a false sense of security. No real results were achieved (apart from the construction of a fort by the River Blackwater to subdue and contain the Tyrone O'Neills), however, and Essex is today remembered as the instigator of massacres of O'Neills in Belfast and of MacDonnells in Rathlin. Essex boasted that the Belfast killings 'hath broken the faction and made them all afeard'. Considering he was entertaining his victims at a feast it is difficult not to regard Essex's behaviour as less than civil. The story of the Enterprise is salutary, however, and is a typical incident in the unedifying history of Ulster: the State attempted to get private individuals to carry out State policies at minimum cost, and indeed chronic under-funding (or lack of means altogether) was a familiar problem throughout. Private Undertakers (accompanied by armed men in search of plunder), minimum State support, and brutality on both sides only served to destabilise the country without putting anything in place that would improve matters.

Sir John Perrot (*c.*1527-92), provincial President of Munster, was more successful in his territories. Having ruthlessly suppressed the Desmond rebellion of 1569-73, he then prepared the ground for the Plantation of Munster. During his period as Lord Deputy (1584-8) he also determined to bring English law and systems of land tenure to Ulster. As part of this policy he proposed 'shiring' the province, i.e. creating six new counties, but this was theoretical rather than real, and very little was achieved in a land becoming more unstable by the year. Unrest was endemic.

The threat to Queen Elizabeth posed by the Queen of Scots's claims was removed by Mary Stuart's execution in 1587, and Philip II of Spain in 1588 despatched the 'Invincible Armada' partly to back his claim to the thrones of England, Scotland, and Ireland to which he had been nominated by Mary, and partly to punish Elizabeth for her support given to Protestant rebels in the Spanish Netherlands from 1585. Having Plantagenet blood in his veins as well, Philip's claims to the thrones had considerable substance, a fact not unnoticed by the Irish lords. The story of the Armada is very well known, but its grisly aftermath less so. Many ships of the Spanish fleet were wrecked, stranded, or burned off the coasts of Ireland in September and October 1588, including *La Trinidad Valencera*, *Nuestra Señora de la Rosa*, *San Marcos*, *La Sancta Maria Rata Encoronada*, *El Grangrin*, *San Juan*, *La Lavia*, another *San Juan*, an unnamed ship, *La Duquesa Santa Ana*, *Falcon Blanco*, *La Juliana*, and *La Gerona* or *Girona*. The last was a Neapolitan galleass (a warship propelled by oars and sail, with a ram before the prow to hole enemy ships): she was estimated to have many hundreds on board when she was wrecked on the north Antrim coast near the MacDonnell stronghold of Dunluce, and some of her treasures have been recovered in recent years. Only nine lives were reported as saved after she foundered.

[24] Robinson (1994), 48-52, and *passim*.

Very few Spaniards survived the disaster, and many of those who struggled ashore were stripped naked, robbed of all their belongings, and killed. Some, however, were succoured by their Irish co-religionists, but it is clear that the Spaniards suffered what is now called a 'culture-shock' when they encountered the Irish natives. The account left by Captain Francisco de Cuellar, who was on the run for a year in Ireland before he managed to flee to Scotland and from there escaped to Antwerp, is of considerable historical interest, for it describes conditions in Ireland at the time, as he moved among the 'savages', some of whom helped him. He had no high opinion of the Irish as 'Christians', thinking them 'no more … Christian than Mahomet'. On occasion de Cuellar was able to converse with a few Irishmen in Latin, and eventually found refuge among the O'Rourkes. The greatest danger he and other survivors faced, however, was that posed by English patrols which hanged Spaniards without compunction.

Subsequently de Cuellar travelled to O'Cahan's country (the present County Londonderry), where he had some narrow escapes from marauding Englishmen, and eventually was given help by a 'truly Christian … bishop … disguised as a savage' (to avoid being recognised by English patrols) and living in a castle. De Cuellar calls the Bishop 'Don Reimundo': this was Raymond (corrupted as 'Redmond') O'Gallagher (Réomonn Ó Gallachair – [1518-1601]),[25] Roman Catholic Bishop of Derry (1569-1601), and the 'castle' may have been at Anagh or in Derry itself. In 1588 O'Gallagher was called 'a most seditious papist, and a man very like to procure great aid for the Spaniards' by the English. After several days with the Bishop, Mass was said and 18 persons in all embarked for Scotland in a 'wretched boat'. De Cuellar found the King of Scots unfriendly, and he and his companions lived in Scotland for more than 'six months as naked as we had arrived from Ireland' before some of them landed in the Spanish Netherlands.[26]

The Bishop of Derry had a reputation for assisting survivors of the Armada to escape. He aroused the enmity of the dangerous and unprincipled Meiler (or Myler) MacGrath (or Magrath) (*c.*1523-1622), who had been nominated by the Pope as Bishop of Down and Connor, but claimed to become a Protestant and got himself appointed Archbishop of Cashel and Bishop of Emly (1571), later collecting the bishoprics of Waterford and Lismore and over 70 benefices for good measure. This multiple pluralist, in whose dioceses no provision was made for divine service (so that the inhabitants knew little of religion), was infamous for 'his simony, rapacity, and evil example' which 'did incalculable harm' to Irish Protestantism. Wentworth referred to the 'ugly oppressions of that wicked bishop Melerus'.[27] This appalling apostate (who wavered between Roman Catholicism and Protestantism to the end of his long life) drew up a list of 'Popish bishops, doctors, and seminary priests', including Raymond O'Gallagher, who was accused (falsely, as he had to keep a low profile) of riding 'from place to place with pomp and company, as was the custom in Queen Mary's days'. O'Gallagher was also denounced because his clergy 'even changed the time according to the Pope's new invention' (i.e. the Gregorian calendar).[28] De Cuellar's pious prayer that the Bishop of Derry, 'an honourable and just man', should be watched over by God and delivered 'from his enemies' fell on stony ground:

[25] Daly and Devlin (1997), 9-10.

[26] Hardy (1966), 37-138, and *passim*. This is an excellent account of the sufferings and adventures of the unfortunate Spaniards.

[27] *D.N.B.* (1917), **xii**, 769-71.

[28] Hardy (1966), 128.

O'Gallagher was killed by English troops in 1601,[29] doubtless to the satisfaction of the Archbishop of Cashel. He was buried in Old Glendermott graveyard.

With Sir William Fitzwilliam (1526-99), Lord Deputy from 1571 to 1575 and again from 1588 to 1594, one of the most greedy and corrupt of administrators, matters in Ireland grew more fraught, as his policies were marked by cupidity, first treating with the lords, then attacking them.[30] The partition of Monaghan (1590-1), following the death of Rossa MacMahon (Mac Mathghamhna), Lord of Monaghan, was achieved when Hugh Roe MacMahon, who had bribed Fitzwilliam so that he could succeed to the lordship, was executed instead in 1590. This alarmed the lords of Ulster, and none more so than Hugh O'Neill, 3rd Baron of Dungannon, who was created *Tánaiste* of Turlough Luineach O'Neill in 1584, yet also received his patent as 2nd Earl of Tyrone, granting him all his grandfather's lands, in 1587. From that time, the State attempted to curb Tyrone's growing power, playing him off against other lords, and alternately appearing to support him, then withdrawing that support. Tyrone himself was a curious mixture of impetuousness and extreme caution, even timidity, and his career is marked by a devotion to duplicity which ultimately failed in its objectives, but earned him a reputation for astuteness and ability that he probably never possessed, though some commentators have regarded him in the best possible light, even proposing that he was one of the most brilliant politicians in Irish history. His behaviour was inconsistent, often illogical, and veered between braggadocio and grovelling attempts to ingratiate himself and be restored to a status he himself had undermined. He often had difficulty in controlling his temper, and was given to undignified outbursts which terrified some observers and disgusted others. His apologists have seen him as an 'adept politician and a gifted soldier who made the most of limited resources',[31] but the fact is that by 1603 he left much of his country in ruins, its people starving, and his own position greatly weakened. There is no doubt that aspects of his behaviour were guaranteed to cause difficulties, as when he eloped with (or perhaps abducted) Mabel, sister of Sir Henry Bagenal (*c.*1556-98), marrying her in 1591. Bagenal, Marshal of the Army, became chief commissioner for the government of Ulster, and was opposed to his sister's union with Tyrone (perceiving it as an affront to his family). He thus became a powerful enemy of the Ulster Earl, and his refusal to pay Tyrone his sister's dowry became one of O'Neill's main 'griefs' or grievances. Mabel Bagenal soon wearied of Tyrone's behaviour, left him, and laid sundry complaints about him before her brother. She died shortly afterwards, and so did not live to know of her brother's death in battle with her husband.

The Historical Background IV: The Last Decade of Elizabeth's Reign and the Nine Years' War

The Nine Years' War began in 1593, sparked by Fitzwilliam's breaking of the MacMahon lordship. The Ulster lords saw this incident as a precedent, for, after all, traditional Gaelic organisation and customs, contrary to popular belief, were alive and well, and indeed thriving in some territories, especially Ulster (by then a much larger territory than that existing at the time of the Anglo-Norman invasion). It should be emphasised also that at that time Ulster was the most Gaelic part of Ireland, and had

[29] Colby (1837), 34.
[30] Healy (1913), *passim*.
[31] Connolly (ed.) (1998), 412; Morgan (1999), 214-21.

remained so partly for geographical reasons. In secret the Ulster lords formed a confederacy bound by oath which set aside traditional rivalries, leadership being given by Tyrone and his son-in-law, Red Hugh O'Donnell (Aodh Ruadh Ó Domhnaill [1572-1602]), Lord of Tirconnell from 1592, by which date Tyrone and O'Donnell had achieved supremacy in Ulster. At the start of the war Tyrone proceeded with extreme cunning, putting on a show of loyalty to the Crown by assisting Bagenal in actions against the Maguires of Fermanagh, while at the same time egging on his kinsmen to prepare to rise against the State. This appears to have been part of Tyrone's plan of playing for time, for as early as 1592 the Ulster lords had sent emissaries to the King of Spain who was recognised by them as Sovereign of Ireland after the death and testament of Mary, Queen of Scots. Surviving documents reveal and prove approaches made to King Philip by Tyrone and O'Donnell,[32] and in 1593, James O'Hely, Roman Catholic Archbishop of Tuam, went to Spain to solicit the aid of Irish noblemen in the service of King Philip in preparing for a great rebellion in which Tyrone, O'Donnell, and Maguire were to play leading rôles. However, the ship sent to Ireland by the King of Spain on what today would be called 'a fact-finding mission' foundered in the Bay of Biscay, carrying with it the Archbishop and several noblemen to the bottom of the sea.

Further attempts were made to 'shire' and partition Tyrone's country, and the spectre of the fate of MacMahon strengthened the resolve of the Ulster lords to resist. In 1594 an English force sent to relieve Enniskillen was routed by Maguire at the 'Ford of the Biscuits' on the Arny River in Fermanagh. Early in 1595 Tyrone revealed his true colours when he ordered the destruction of the fort, garrison, and bridge on the River Blackwater. Shortly afterwards Maguire and O'Donnell recaptured Enniskillen, and in June Tyrone attacked Bagenal's forces at Clontibret, Co. Monaghan. At this point the Government proclaimed Tyrone a traitor. English reinforcements were rushed to Ireland as Tyrone now had over 6,000 men in arms, including 4,000 musketeers and 1,000 cavalrymen, although he was short of artillery, which made the taking of well-fortified castles and towns difficult without ruses or betrayal. Tyrone's major successes were really ambushes carried out using guerrilla tactics, culminating in the destruction of Bagenal's army at the Yellow Ford between Armagh and the Blackwater in 1598 during which action Bagenal was killed. A curious feature of the war up to then was that English offensives were little more than expeditions to establish or relieve garrisons, with the result that Irish victories became more numerous, and Sligo and Cavan fell to the Ulster lords. Indeed, the war spread to Connacht and Leinster in 1595, and to Munster in 1598.

In 1595 Tyrone and O'Donnell had invited King Philip to create the Archduke Albert (d. 1621 – Habsburg Governor of the Spanish Netherlands) Sovereign Prince of Ireland, and in September again approached the King asking for help, promising him allegiance, and expressing a desire to secure him the Kingdom. Letters from Tyrone and O'Donnell implored aid in the cause of 'Catholic liberty' to destroy the 'ministers of satanic fury and the impious disturbers of the Christian state'.[33] Furthermore, Turlough Luineach O'Neill died in September, and the O'Neill lordship (illegal under the enactments of 1569) passed to Tyrone, who was inaugurated at Tulla(g)hogue, Co. Tyrone, and soon styled, according to Gaelic custom, as 'The

[32] Archivo General de Simancas, Estado, lejagos 838; Falls (1950), *passim*; Morgan (1999), *passim*.
[33] Archivo General de Simancas, Estado, lejagos 839, *passim*.

Great O'Neill'. Yet during the latter part of 1595 Tyrone was seeking pardon, and in October O'Donnell and he submitted, but this was again only playing for time, as Spanish envoys arrived in the Spring of 1596, and the Ulster lords called on the 'gentlemen of Munster' to join them in making war on the English, even though Tyrone had received his pardon in May. In September Spanish ships landed arms and munitions at Killybegs, Co. Donegal **[3]**, and in the following month a Spanish fleet intended for the invasion of Ireland and England was dispersed by a storm off Cape Finisterre (another fleet was also driven back by a storm in 1597). The Irish victory at the Yellow Ford in August 1598 encouraged further rebellions in Munster (where the English Plantation was destroyed), and various southern lords joined Tyrone's rebellion.

1598, then, was an eventful year in the whole messy affair. Apart from Tyrone's victory over Bagenal in August, King Philip II of Spain died in September, and the Government in London received intelligence of an intrigue between Tyrone and the King of Scots (James, son of Mary, Queen of Scots, and Henry Stuart, Lord Darnley, born 1566, King James VI from 1567 on his mother's enforced abdication). It appears from some sources that James offered Tyrone men and arms if the latter would prevent the English from establishing a presence in Lough Foyle. But in 1599 it seems that Charles Blount (1563-1606), 8th Lord Mountjoy (from 1594 – who was to be sworn in as Lord Deputy in 1600), entered into secret negotiations with King James on behalf of Robert Devereux (1566-1601 – 2nd Earl of Essex, Lord Lieutenant from 1599), assuring the King of Scots of Essex's support for James's claims to the English throne using Irish troops if necessary, and the King made the establishment of a strong garrison at Derry a condition of any such moves. Thus the fundamental strategic importance of Derry and Lough Foyle in national and international affairs was underlined.[34]

If these tales are true, they contrast with events in 1591 when Sir Brian na Múrtha O'Rourke (Ó Ruairc), Lord of Leitrim (or west Bréifne), went to Scotland, apparently seeking the protection of King James after his lordship had been invaded and occupied by English troops in 1590, but in reality attempting to recruit Scots mercenaries to fight for him in Ireland. In April 1591, following a demand from Queen Elizabeth, James VI had O'Rourke arrested and handed over to English custody: in November that year he was hanged at Tyburn Tree on the charges contained in his indictment, having proudly refused to stand trial. Those charges included helping Spaniards who had survived the Armada disaster, making war on his neighbours, denying the sovereignty of the Queen, and other matters, including dragging the Queen's 'picture att a horse-taile, and disgracefully' cutting it 'in pieces'. Clearly, King James, with one eye on the English throne and another on the difficulties of holding his own realm together in the face of various factions, was not willing to incur the animosity of his more powerful neighbour to the south.[35]

One of Tyrone's problems was that the Old English (descendants of the Anglo-Norman conquerors and settlers), also called the Anglo-Irish, thought of themselves as Englishmen born in Ireland, yet were predominantly committed to the spiritual leadership of the Pope while remaining loyal to the English Crown. When the State began its demands for conformity to Protestantism and the New English (fairly recent

[34] Atkinson (ed.) (1895); *Cal. S.P.I., 1598-99*, 120; Bagwell (1888-90), **iii**, 366-8.

[35] *D.N.B.* (1917), **ii**, 702-5, and **xiv**, 1158-60; Archivo General de Simancas, Estado lejagos 839, f. 97; Moody (1939), 55.

3 The Phillips/Raven 'A Plat of the Harbor of Calbeg' [Killybegs] 'in the Countie of Dunagal'. This perfect natural harbour on the west coast of County Donegal was used by the Londoners and by the English garrisons in Counties Donegal, Fermanagh, and Tyrone. It had also been used by Spanish ships, e.g. in 1596. (*WCD/GB*)

arrivals in Ireland, and increasingly Protestant in religious persuasion), attracted by the possibilities of obtaining land, positions, and wealth, began to settle in greater numbers, the Old English started to be displaced, and were painted in dark colours as servants of Rome, as disloyal to the Crown, as corrupters of the law, and as having lost their Englishness by marrying into the Irish nobility and speaking Irish. Although Old English merchants had been among those who supplied Tyrone with firearms, Tyrone's appeal in 1599 to the Old English to join him in the fight for the Faith and the Fatherland,[36] leading to the establishment of an autonomous Roman Catholic Ireland run by the Irish lords and the Old English, did not bear fruit. The Old English were not to ally themselves with the Gaelic Irish in any significant numbers until the great rebellion of 1641.

A feature of the Nine Years' War was the curious inertia, even lack of purpose, that characterised Government military campaigns against Tyrone, whose every submission was received, followed by a pardon. Clearly Tyrone, with his vast 'country' and enormous prestige, was thought of as essential to fill a vacuum, which explains the spasmodic aggression followed by appeasement that was the essence of official reaction to Tyrone. It has long been true that English intervention in Ireland has been marked by fitful bursts of activity and apparent determination, followed by half-baked policies and sloth, then appeasement and turning of blind eyes, and back again to resolute action. The point is that most English activities were prompted by events, and were reactions, rather than following any coherent plan of State policies. Exceptions were the Anglo-Norman invasion and settlement, the Tudor Conquest, and the

[36] *Patria* was the Roman concept of the Fatherland, and entered Irish political thinking under the influence of Renaissance ideas. Tyrone invoked it when appealing to the Old English, but this frightened the Government more than attracting possible allies.

Plantation of the 17th century, but even these were chronically under-funded, marked by vacillation, and incomplete.

In 1599 Lord Lieutenant Essex began a vigorous series of campaigns against the Irish lords. More troops were raised in England, and seasoned soldiers from The Netherlands were ordered to Ireland. Such activities were prompted by worries that the new King of Spain, Philip III (reigned 1598-1621), would move to give Tyrone (whom he held in great respect) help, and indeed that monarch stayed any Irish ship that did not carry Tyrone's pass. Spanish ships sailed into Lough Foyle with arms and ammunition, and, following a rout of English forces near Wicklow by Phelim MacFeagh O'Byrne (Feidhlim mac Fiachaidh Ó Broin) in May 1599 and the death of Sir Conyers Clifford (*fl.* 1580-99),[37] President of Connacht, in a skirmish with Irish insurgents under the O'Rourkes in the Curlew mountains, Co. Roscommon, in August, Essex met Tyrone which led to a truce, immediately after which Tyrone wrote to Pope Clement VIII (1592-1605) for financial aid. The truce infuriated Queen Elizabeth and her advisers, for by then it was clear, even in London, that Tyrone used his pardons and truces simply to gain time, enabling him to re-arm and acquire strategic advantages, while lulling the English into an agreeable, if ill-advised, state of inactivity. When Tyrone wrote to Essex saying he could not persuade O'Donnell and other allies to agree to the articles of peace (which the English State declared to be a 'dishonourable and dangerous treaty' with the arch-enemy Tyrone, and the Queen herself described as 'full of scandal to our realm and future peril to the state'), Essex was in trouble. What he seems to have aimed at was a formal recognition of the rights of Tyrone and other lords to their lands, but his enemies also insinuated that he had promised to secure a full recognition of papal supremacy in Ireland. This, with other problems, led to Essex's execution in London in 1601. It was another instance of a glittering career foundering in Ireland.

Determination rather than vacillation followed under Mountjoy from 1600. Tyrone suffered the first of many setbacks in Munster, where Hugh (Aodh) Maguire was killed in March. Plenary Indulgences were granted by Pope Clement VIII to supporters of Tyrone, but he refused to excommunicate those who were loyal to the Queen, which should have served as an ominous warning to the Irish lords. More arms and money (with Indulgences from the Pope for all those who should rise in defence of the Faith) arrived in Tirconnell with Mateo de Oviedo, appointed titular Roman Catholic Archbishop of Dublin, but in May an English expeditionary force under Sir Henry Docwra (*c.*1560-1631) landed at Culmore, near Derry, and immediately raised earthworks to guard the narrows of the Foyle. Docwra's campaigns prevailed over the Irish, and he began the restoration and new buildings at Derry itself. With such strategic advantages, Docwra lost no time in persuading the O'Dohertys in Inishowen and the O'Cahans in the nominal county of Coleraine to abandon the overlordships of O'Neill and O'Donnell for concessions, and serious rifts became apparent in the doomed confederacy. Mountjoy and Docwra swiftly established small but well-armed garrisons within easy reach of each other, with the express intention of destroying the supply-lines to the Irish guerrillas, and fomenting dissent. Niall Garbh O'Donnell (1569-1626), cousin of Hugh, joined forces with Docwra in October 1600, although more Spanish gold and arms were to arrive in Teelin, Co. Donegal, later in the year. Docwra was also joined by Sir Art O'Neill (son of Turlough Luineach), who had ambitions to step into Tyrone's shoes.

[37] Clifford was the author of 'A Brief Declaration relating to the Province of Connaught, how it stood in 1597', held in manuscript in the archiepiscopal library at Lambeth Palace (MS.642. f.22).

Then, in 1601, a Spanish fleet landed troops at Kinsale, Co. Cork, under the command of Don Juan del Águila, which was singularly inconvenient for the Ulster lords. Mountjoy at once hastened to attack the Spaniards before Tyrone and O'Donnell could join up with their allies, which they attempted to do in October by forced marches to the south. Mountjoy had invested Kinsale, and del Águila became greatly concerned by the failure of the Irish to support him. More Spanish ships landed supplies and forces at Castlehaven, Co. Cork, and Tyrone and O'Donnell joined forces at Bandon before proceeding to Kinsale. Used to surprise attacks and guerrilla warfare, Tyrone was unwilling to risk a conventional, pitched battle against well-trained English troops, but del Águila, having been cooped up for such a long time, prevailed upon his allies to engage the enemy. On 24 December 1601 Mountjoy's forces routed those of Tyrone and O'Donnell. The last fled to Spain, and the long march home to Ulster by Tyrone was made more difficult by attacks on the remnants of his army by a populace brutalised by war.

In 1602 del Águila surrendered to Mountjoy and returned to Spain with the survivors of the campaign. Interestingly, del Águila formed a high opinion of Mountjoy and Sir George Carew (1555-1629), the English commander and President of Munster (to whom he sent gifts of citrus-fruits and wine when he got home), but he brought back very unfavourable reports concerning the Irish, whom he found to be untrustworthy, weak, disorganised, tardy, and absurdly over-confident of their own invincibility. Meanwhile, Donnell Ballagh O'Cahan (d. *c.*1617), principal vassal of Tyrone, and lord of most of the lands between the Foyle and the Bann (known as O'Cahan's 'country' or the county of Coleraine), threw in his lot with Docwra on condition that he would hold his lands (somewhat reduced in area) direct from the Crown, and would no longer be under the O'Neill overlordship. Events moved quickly thereafter, for Hugh O'Donnell died[38] in Spain, Mountjoy destroyed the O'Neill inaugural chair at Tulla(g)hogue, and, early in 1603, Mountjoy was authorised to offer Tyrone a pardon (yet again) in return for his surrender. In March, however, the Queen died, the 'unthrifty and inauspicious war' having clouded the last years of her life. Just as Elizabeth had 'supported the revolted states of Holland', so the 'King of Spaine' turned 'the tricke upon herselfe towards her going out, by cherishing the Irish rebellion', as Sir Robert Naunton (1563-1635) put it. Naunton also saw the 'Irish action' as 'a mallady, a consumption of her times, for it accompanied her to the end; and it was of so profuse and vast expence that it drew neare unto a distemperature of State, and of passion in herself; for towards her last, she grew somewhat hard to please with her armies ...'.[39] Sir John Davies estimated that it had cost two million pounds (an astronomical sum then) and the largest army in Europe to defeat Tyrone.[40]

The war was a huge drain on State resources, and on the Irish side brought famine and disease in its wake as, one by one, Tyrone's allies sued for peace. The Crown found the maintenance of garrisons in remote parts far too expensive to sustain, and there must have been considerable relief in Dublin and London when, after much negotiation at Tulla(g)hogue and Mellifont, Tyrone, with the Treaty of Mellifont (1603), gained his pardon and a new patent for his lands. He also kept his earldom. Perhaps even more significant, he retained control of the O'Cahan lordship,

[38] Allegations that he was poisoned by English agents are most likely wholly unfounded.

[39] *On the death of Queen Elizabeth.* See also Falls (1950) for one of the best accounts of the period.

[40] Russell and Prendergast (eds.) (1874a): *Cal. S.P.I. 1606-8*, 273.

which was in contravention of the arrangement made with Docwra, who was overruled by Mountjoy.[41] Clearly, the Irish lords who had sided with the Crown were to be abandoned to the tender mercies of Tyrone and others. This suggests, or even proves, that Gaelic organisation in Ulster was far too firmly entrenched to be changed overnight without vast expense and a great deal of trouble. At that point, therefore, it is clear that the Government intended to leave well alone, hoping that time and a steady following of example would gradually change matters. Hands were later forced by Tyrone's attempts to get involved yet again in international politics, and he probably overestimated his own powers while underestimating the new monarch who came to the throne in 1603.

The Historical Background V: The Accession of King James I and VI and the Flight of the Earls

In March 1603, the Queen died and was succeeded by James VI, King of Scots, as James I of England and Ireland. Mountjoy was re-appointed Lord Deputy, and, accompanied by Tyrone and Rory (Ruaidhrí) O'Donnell (1575-1608), brother of the Lord of Tirconnell (who, as has been noted above, had died at Simancas in 1602), went to London to kiss the new King's hands. In July Mountjoy was created Earl of Devonshire, and in September O'Donnell became 1st Earl of Tyrconnell, being granted the greater part of County Donegal, except Inishowen (granted in 1601 to Sir Cahir O'Doherty [1587-1608], who had grown to manhood under the aegis of Docwra) and certain fisheries and forts which were retained by the Crown.

The implications of Tyrone's warrant of pardon (September 1603) and the raising of O'Donnell to an earldom were enormous. First of all, they were astonishing acts of clemency, and did not find favour in all quarters (Davies noted that the war 'was ended almost in the instant' when the Crown 'descended' on King James's head, 'and so there remained no occasion to amend the former errors committed in the prosecution of the war', and Sir John Harington (1561-1612) lamented that he had 'lived to see that damnable rebel Tyrone brought to England, honoured, and well liked'[42]). Secondly, they demonstrated that the Crown was concerned about a vacuum of power in Ulster and considered that the only way of controlling things was through the Irish lords, now given earldoms and other titles, all of which suggests that Gaelic social order was thriving, was far too robust to be ignored, and was anything but moribund, as often has been claimed. Yet there were formidable problems that had not been resolved, not least of them connected with the rivalries and murderous feuds endemic in the old Gaelic culture. The new King gave instructions that the collection of rents in Ireland should be more zealously pursued, and emphasised the necessity to carry out surveys to establish the bases for all revenues due to the Crown. Certain allies of Docwra, such as Donnell Ballagh O'Cahan (to be knighted in 1607), were offended by once again being subservient to Tyrone. Sir Niall Garbh O'Donnell (who had been promised Tirconnell by Docwra) was upset by the grant of Inishowen to O'Doherty as well as by the elevation of his cousin as Earl of Tyrconnell. In 1604

[41] The O'Cahan case is dealt with in Russell and Prendergast (eds.) (1872, 1874a): *Cal. S.P.I. 1603-6* and *1606-8, passim.*

[42] Davies (1787), 194; *D.N.B.* (1917), **xiv**, 1089.

Docwra's infant settlement of Derry was incorporated by charter as a city,[43] but Docwra, allegedly disgusted by the Crown's treatment of himself and his Irish allies, sold up in 1606, and in 1614 published *A Narration of the Services done by the Army employed to Lough Foyle under the leading of me, Sir Henry Docwra, knight.* This document suggests that Docwra felt his own honour had been impugned, and that guarantees given to O'Cahan, O'Doherty, and O'Donnell had been dishonourably broken.[44]

In 1605 another personality rose to eminence when Sir Arthur Chichester (1563-1625) was sworn in as Lord Deputy, a position he held until 1615. A soldier, he had seen service on the Continent, and was sent to Ireland during the Nine Years' War. He became governor of Knockfergus (Carrickfergus) from which base he carried out devastating raids deep into Tyrone's country, and in 1603 was granted Belfast Castle and its surrounding lands, including the Lagan fisheries and the Admiralty of Lough Neagh on which he directed naval operations against Tyrone. He was no friend of the Irish, and his antagonism was probably exacerbated by the fact that his brother, Sir John Chichester, was killed by MacDonnells in 1597 (commemorated in the elaborate funerary monument [the finest of its type and period (*c.*1619) in Ireland] to Chichester, his wife Lettice [d. 1620], daughter of Sir John Perrot, and son in the church of St Nicholas, Carrickfergus).[45] Chichester must be credited with the founding of Belfast (from which he took his title as Baron Chichester of Belfast in 1612),[46] a settlement that steadily grew in importance, notably in the 19th century when its expansion as 'Linenopolis' was phenomenal. One of Chichester's first proclamations was that all persons in the realm of Ireland were to be free, natural, and immediate subjects of the King, and not subjects of any lords or chiefs. He also promoted the Common Law with regular Assize Courts, and created freeholdings. Protestant bishops were established in their sees, including George Montgomery (1566-1620), appointed Bishop of Derry, Raphoe, and Clogher in 1605,[47] who vigorously pressed the Anglican episcopal claims on lands originally presented to the founders of churches by Gaelic lords, and who, throughout his tenure of the see, advocated a sound financial basis for the diocese and the importation of English and Scots clergy. Seminary priests and Jesuits were commanded to leave Ireland, and the laity was directed to attend Divine Service in accordance with the law, those who did not being fined or imprisoned. The Book of Common Prayer was translated into Irish, but proselytism was made difficult by the shortage of zealous Irish-speaking Anglican clergymen, and a showdown with Roman Catholics failed to develop. It should also be remembered that on 5 November 1605 the Gunpowder Plot (by which certain Roman Catholics in England sought to destroy King and Parliament) was discovered. This only served to turn the authorities further against Roman Catholics. Thereafter, attempts to enforce conformity with the Established Church tended to enfeeble the Roman Catholic Church in Ireland without entirely replacing it with Protestantism except in a nominal way, with resulting bitterness and dissatisfaction on all sides. Furthermore, Rome sent numbers of travelling friars

[43] At which point it was granted Arms, the escutcheon of which depicts a skeleton of human bones sitting on a stone, leaning, the *Dexter* elbow on the knee, and resting the head on the hand, the *Sinister* hand resting on the hip proper in *Dexter* chief a castle or tower. This may be a reference to the death by starvation of Walter MacWilliam de Burgh (Burke) when imprisoned by William de Burgh, Earl of Ulster, in Greencastle, Co. Donegal, in 1332.

[44] It was published in *Miscellany of the Celtic Society* (Dublin: The Celtic Society, 1849).

[45] Potterton (1975), 8, 17, 88-9.

[46] For Chichester's career see *D.N.B.* (1917), **iv**, 232-5, and for his family's rise as Earls and later Marquesses of Donegall, see *Burke's Peerage* (Townend [ed.] [1963], 743-4).

[47] Orr (1997), 17-20.

to Ireland who not only provided spiritual succour, but acted as advisers and scribes for the uneducated, associated Irish identity with Roman Catholicism as a bulwark against English aspirations in Ireland, and ensured Protestantism never took root with the mass of the populace. The failure to establish Protestantism throughout Ireland as the religion of the majority should not be underestimated in importance: it was the single most significant factor in the history of Irish Nationalism. Under the protection of the Gaelic lords ceremonies of ordination to the priesthood took place with full and solemn liturgies in Derry in the 1590s, and the Ulster chiefs had previously demonstrated their support for Rome and their identification with the great Roman Catholic powers of Europe by adopting the 'Gregorian' calendar in 1584 when celebrating Easter (Britain did not follow suit until 1751-2[48]). Similar conformity with Continental practice may be seen in the Republic of Ireland in the latter part of the millennium, as the country converts to kilometres and other standards far ahead of Britain.

In his determination to bring Ulster under the rule of English law, Chichester ordered the implementation of Perrot's plan to 'shire' Ulster (delayed by the war), and detached Cavan from Connacht, adding it to Ulster which thus consisted of nine counties (Antrim, Armagh, Cavan, Coleraine, Donegal, Down, Fermanagh, Monaghan, and Tyrone – each of which was divided into baronies). By 1607 Ulster had also been organised into military districts, each centred on a fortress, and each under the command of a governor. It should be noted at this point that neither before Perrot's or Chichester's shiring, nor after, was there ever a county called 'Derry', although the diocese was *always* called 'Derry'. Docwra's settlement was named 'Derry', a corruption of the Irish *Doire*, meaning an 'oak-grove', or 'place of the oaks', and sometimes had an Irish suffix which designated it as an eminence crowned with oak trees.

As a result of Chichester's zeal, the authority of the Gaelic chiefs was undermined, and powers of jurisdiction were made to conform to English practice. Furthermore, the Irish system of *gavelkind* (by which land, on the decease of the occupant, became part of the common stock, and the whole area was subdivided among male members of the sept[49] [both legitimate and illegitimate]) was abolished, and all land was to descend thereafter according to the common law. Tyrone, Tyrconnell, and Cúchonnacht Óg Maguire, or Mág Uidhir (d. 1608), Lord of Fermanagh, began to assert their rights as landlords. Donnell Ballagh O'Cahan became the butt of Tyrone's vindictiveness, not least because O'Cahan had married, then repudiated, one of Tyrone's daughters. Perceiving O'Cahan as a traitor to the Irish cause, Tyrone demanded O'Cahan's submission and the payment of an annual rent: to show he meant business, Tyrone seized a large chunk of O'Cahan's 'country', and drove off all the cattle he could find belonging to O'Cahan. The latter, claiming he had as much interest in his lands as an English freeholder had in his, and supported by the bishop of Derry (who may have had his eye on the land himself, so his motives may not have been entirely altruistic), sought the services of the Attorney-General, Sir John Davies, and in 1607 put his case before Chichester and the Privy Council, reminding them that he had been given certain assurances when he threw in his lot with the Crown. It was decided that O'Cahan should retain two-thirds of his lands, the remaining third to be held by

48 24 Geo. II, c. 23. It is called 'Gregorian' from the Bull of Pope Gregory XIII (1572-85) of 24 February 1582.

49 Territorial group of pre-Plantation Irish under the local control of a minor chieftain, also perceived as a division of a clan.

Tyrone (who behaved outrageously during the hearing, snatching papers from O'Cahan's hands, and demonstrating a bellicosity that was clearly out of control) pending the final decision by the King. As noted above, O'Cahan was knighted (June 1607), and it seemed he was in good odour with Chichester and the State. But Tyrconnell was also disgruntled with his position, and Maguire with his as well. Sir Niall Garbh O'Donnell had caused himself to be inaugurated to the illegal O'Donnell chieftainship, with the customary ceremonies, at Kilmacrenan, in 1603, so on Mountjoy's orders was arrested by Docwra, pleaded his cause in Dublin, and was pardoned by the King. The Privy Council determined that he should only hold lands on either side of the River Finn that were his own patrimonial inheritance, so he again felt badly treated following Docwra's assurance. It was not a happy state of affairs.

In order to resolve the disputes Tyrone and O'Cahan were summoned to London. It appears that Tyrone, Tyrconnell, and Maguire, by 1607, were yet again in contact with Spain and the Papacy, with the intention of starting another rebellion against the Crown. However, the Government had got wind of the plot, and Tyrone and Tyrconnell, unattracted by the prospects of arrest and imprisonment (and with good reason, as the histories of O'Cahan and Niall Garbh O'Donnell were to show), with their families and followers, sailed from Rathmullen (also spelled Rathmullan), Co. Donegal, in September, in a ship brought by Maguire's influence from France to Ireland, an event known as the Flight of the Earls. The fugitives were landed in France (rather than the intended destination, Spain), the vessel having sailed up the Seine and landed its passengers, but remonstrances from the English ambassador compelled the party to retire to the Spanish Netherlands, and it was from Louvain (Leuven) that Tyrone sent his extraordinary list of 'griefs' or grievances in which the reader may seek in vain for an explanation of the flight. In 1608, debarred from Spain for diplomatic reasons (Spain and France were anxious not to become embroiled in hostilities against Great Britain), the by then embarrassing party travelled to Rome, where Pope Paul V (1605-21) granted them accommodation and a small pension: Tyrconnell, however, died in Rome in July, and Maguire in Genoa in August. Tyrone was attainted for high treason and stripped of his titles by 5 August 1608, yet continued to use them. In 1613, by which time probably aware at last of his follies, he made overtures through Robert Carr, Earl of Somerset (d.1645), for his restoration and pardon, but by then the Plantation of Ulster was well under way, and the Crown was not prepared to risk any more temporary submissions and bogus protestations of loyalty from the discredited Irish Earl. Tyrone seems to have hoped for a rupture between England and Spain, but Spain was in decline, and had no resources to squander on yet another probably doomed attempt to eject an ascendant power from Ireland. Reports reached London of Tyrone, *vino plenus et ira* (full of wine and rage), and in 1616 the body of Prince O'Neill (as he was known in Rome) was buried beside that of Tyrconnell in the church of San Pietro in Montorio, where St Peter is said to have been martyred on the slopes of the Janiculum. This is itself significant, for the church was erected in *c.*1472 at the expense of the 'Catholic Kings' of Spain, Ferdinand V of Castile and II of Aragon (d. 1516) and Isabella (d. 1504), and indeed the royal House of Spain maintains a close connection with San Pietro in Montorio to this day (part of the monastic buildings are [in 1999] a Spanish college).[50] Thus the exiled Ulster lords were cared for, even after death, by the Spanish Crown, an eloquent testimony to an alliance that had culminated in failure at Kinsale, an English victory that also led to Dutch survival and, eventually,

[50] Baedeker (1930), 467-8; Hare (1897), **ii**, 312.

4 Inscribed slabs over the tombs of Hugh O'Neill, 4th Baron of Dungannon, and Rory (Roderick) O'Donnell, Earl of Tyrconnell, in the church of San Pietro in Montorio, Rome, based on a drawing by James Molyneux, 3rd Earl of Charlemont (1820-92), and a photograph by Frederic Charles Bigger first published in *Ulster Journal of Archaeology* (May 1899) **v**/3, 118. It contains some minor inaccuracies of transcription, but this is understandable as the original is not clear in parts. The O'Neill slab (*left*) is embellished with his Arms (*Two Lions rampant combatant Gules standing on Water therein naiant a Salmon Proper and between them a Dexter Hand couped at the wrist in Chief two* [there ought to be three, but one appears to be missing] *Estoiles*) surmounted by a variant of the earl's coronet, and the O'Donnell slab (*right*) is decorated with Tyrconnell's Arms (*Issuing from the Dexter side of the Shield a Sinister Arm vested and cuffed the Hand Proper grasping a Passion Cross erect with Supporters of Dexter a Lion Sinister a Bull*) also surmounted by a variant on the earl's coronet. It appears, however, that the Supporters ought to be *guardant*, or with their faces turned to be full-faced, and both Mottoes have been omitted. (*IRC by permission of the Ulster Archaeological Society*)

independence for The Netherlands. It seems, therefore, that the Ulster lords were maintained in Rome not only by the Papacy, but by the Spanish monarch, Philip III. The first to be buried on the liturgical north side of the nave before the altar of San Pietro in Montorio was Tyrconnell (1608), followed by Hugh (Aodh), 4th Baron of Dungannon (1585-1609), and then Tyrone (1616). Two handsome inscribed ledger stones **[4]** over the graves of Tyrconnell and Dungannon record the struggles against 'heretics', and include Arms featuring an arm sleeved issuing from the *Dexter* side a Passion Cross *Gules* (O'Donnell) and the Red Hand of Ulster (O'Neill). These stones appear to have been restored in 1843, partly at the expense of Francis William Caulfeild (1775-1863), 5th Viscount and 2nd Earl of Charlemont, a generous gesture given that Toby Caulfeild, 3rd Lord Caulfeild, Baron of Charlemont, had been murdered by followers of Sir Phelim (Feidhlimidh) O'Neill in 1642, as will be described below. Tyrone himself is baldly commemorated by a simple slab inscribed with the legend that his bones lie below, which might indicate that he had run out of good will among his hosts and patrons by the time he died. Francis Joseph Bigger, writing in 1899,[51] stated that this slab could no longer be seen, which might indicate that the present slab is later than 1899, or that it was covered up then. In any case the 'Ossa' (bones) of 'Ugonis Principis Onelli' are merely recorded as being there.[52]

The two main slabs were further repaired in 1848, having been injured during the upheavals of the period. Dungannon's tomb is inscribed thus:

D. O. M.[53]	To God, Best and Greatest
HVGONI BARONI DE DONGANAN	To Hugh, Baron of Dungannon —
HVGONIS MAGNI ONELLI PRINCIPIS	eldest son of the Great O'Neill,
ET COMITIS TIRCONIÆ PRIMO GENITO	Prince and Earl of Tyrone —
PATREM ET RODERICVM COMITEM	who, for singular piety towards God
TIRCONNALLIÆ AVVNCVLVM PRO	and his parents, followed his father
FIDE CATHOLICA QVAM MVLTOS ANNOS	and his uncle, Roderick, Earl of Tyrconnell
CONTRA HÆRETICOS IN HYBERNIA	for the Catholic Faith which,
FORTITER DEFENDERANT RELICTIS	for many years, they bravely defended
STATIBVS SVIS SPONTE EXVLANTES AD	against the heretics in Ireland,
COMVNEM CATHOLICOR(?) AXILVM VRBEM	to the City of Rome,
ROMAM PRO SVA SINGVLARI IN DEVM ET	common asylum of Catholics.
PARENTES PIETATE SEQVVNTO CVIVS	His early death destroyed utterly
IMMATVRA MORS SPEM DE EO	the hope, held by all for him,
RESTAVRANDÆ ALIQVANDO IN ILLIS	on account of his remarkable
PARTIBVS CATHOLICÆ RELIGIONIS OB	qualities of mind and body,
EIVS INSIGNES ANIMI ET CORPORIS DOTES	of at some time restoring
AB OMNIBVS CONCEPTAM ABSTVLIT AC	the Catholic Religion in those parts,
DICTO RODERICO AVVNCVLO FATO SIMILI	and joined him to the said Roderick,
ABSVMPTO CONIVNXIT	his uncle, struck down
OCCIDIT TAM SVIS QVAM TOTI CVRIÆ	by the same lamentable fate
FLÆBILIS NONO•KAL•OCT•MDCIX	on the ninth of the Kalends of October 1609
ÆTATIS SVAE XXIIII	in his 24th year.[54]

The 'same lamentable fate' points to a Roman fever, which claimed many lives of northerners who settled there. Other members of the Ulster lords' party, for example, died soon after arriving in Rome.

[51] Young and Bigger (eds.): *Ulster Journal of Archaeology* (May 1899) **v**/3, 115-38.

[52] D. O. M. Hic Quiescunt UGONIS PRINCIPIS ONELLI OSSA (Here repose the bones of Hugh, Prince O'Neill).

[53] Abbreviation of *Deo Optimo Maximo*.

[54] i.e. 23 September 1609. The Romans reckoned days before the beginning of a month, so the ninth day of the Kalends of October was 23 September. The inscription was transcribed from the slab by the present writer in September 1999. Tyrconnell is also spelled 'Tyrconnel', 'Tirconnel', and 'Tirconnell'.

Tyrconnell's tomb has a longer and grander inscription:

D. O. M.
RODERICO PRINCIPI ODONALLIO
COMITI TIRCONALLIÆ IN HYBERNIA
QVI PRO RELIGIONE CATHOLICA
GRAVISSIMIS DEFVNCTVS PERICVLIS
IN SAGO PARITER ET IN TOGA
CONSTANTISSIMVS CVLTOR ET DEFENSOR
APOSTOLICÆ ROMANÆ FIDEI
PRO QVA TVENDA ET CONSERVANDA E PATRIA PROFVGVS
LVSTRATIS IN ITALIA GALLIA BELGIO
PRÆCIPVIS SANCTORVM MONVMENTIS
ATQ•IBIDEM PRINCIPVM CRISTIANORVM
SINGVLARI AMORE ET HONORE
SANTISS•ETIAM•P•AC•D•PAVLI PP•V
PATERNO AFFECTV SVSCEPTVS
IN MAXIMIS CATHOLICORVM VOTIS DE FELICI EIVS REDITV
SVMMVM DOLOREM ATTVLIT SVIS
ET MOERCOREM OMNIBVS IN HAC VRBE ORDINIBVS
IMMATVRA MORTE QVAM OBIIT III KALENDAS SEXTILES
ANNO SALVTIS MDCVIII ÆTATIS SVAE XXXIII
QVAM MOX SECVRVS [?SECVTVS] EODEM TRAMITE
VT EADEM CVM BEATITATE FRVERETVR
CALFVRNIVS FRATER
PERICVLORVM ET EXILII SOCIVS
IN SVMMA SPE ET EXPECTATIONE BONORVM
DE EIVS NOBILITATE ANIMI
QVAM VIRTVS ET OPTIMA INDOLES EXORNAVIT
SVI RELIQVIT DESIDERIVM ET MÆSTITIAM COEXVLIBVS
XVIII KAL•OCT•PROXIME SEQVENTI(?S) ANNO ÆTATIS XXV
VTRVNQVE ANTECESSIT ÆTATE ET FATI ORDINE
FRATER PRIMOGENITVS
HVGO PRINCEPS
QVEM PIE ET CATHOLICE PRO FIDE ET PATRIA COGITANTẼ
PHILIPPUS III HISPANIARVM REX
ET VIVVM BENEVOLE AMPLEXVS ET IN VIRIDE ÆTATE
MORTVVM HONORIFICE FVNERANDVM CVRAVIT
VALLISOLETI IN HISPANIA IIII IDOS SEPTEMB•A•S•MDCII

To God, Best and Greatest
To Roderick, Prince O'Donnell,
Earl of Tyrconnell in Ireland,
who, for the Catholic Religion,
endured the gravest dangers
both in the soldier's cloak and in the toga,
a most constant supporter and defender
of the Apostolic Roman Faith,
for protecting and preserving of which, became a fugitive from his own country.
Having seen the principal monuments of the Saints
in Italy, France, and Belgium,
and there been received with the singular love and honour
of Christian Princes and the paternal affection
of the Most Holy Father and Lord, Pope Paul V,
amid the greatest prayers of Catholics,
for his happy return, he brought supreme sorrow
and grief to his and all orders in this city,
by his untimely death which he suffered
on the Third of the Kalends of August[55]

[55] i.e. 30 July 1608.

in the Year of Salvation 1608 in his 33rd year.
Whom there soon followed along the same path
that with him he might enjoy the same happiness,
his brother Calfurnius,[56]
companion of his dangers and exile,
in highest hope and expectation of good things.
From the nobility of his mind,
which virtue and the greatest natural disposition adorned
he left his longing and sadness to his fellow-exiles,
on the 18th of the Kalends of October next following[57] in his 25th year.
There went before both, in age and order of fate,
their elder brother,
Prince Hugh,
whom, as one intending piously and Catholically for Faith and Fatherland,
Philip III, King of Spain,
affectionately embraced while living,
and took great care to bury honourable when dead, in his green age,
at Valladolid in Spain, the 4th of the Ides of September, in the Year of Salvation 1602.[58]

Tyrone had, apart from the 4th Baron of Dungannon, other children: Henry or Énrí (*c.*1586-*c.*1617 – self-styled 4th Earl of Tyrone despite his attainder of 1608), Margaret (d. 1655 – Viscountess Mountgarret), Alice (a celebrated beauty [d. 1663], who married Randal MacSorley MacDonnell, 1st Earl of Antrim),[59] Seán (1599-1640 – self-styled 5th Earl of Tyrone, whose death meant that, even if the attainder had been lifted, the earldom of Tyrone and barony of Dungannon would have expired, as he was the last male of the line, apart from his illegitimate son, Hugh, or Hugo [1631-60]), Conn na Creaga (1601-22 – who was left behind during the Flight of the Earls and died in the Tower of London), and Brian (1604-17 – murdered, supposedly by an English agent, in Brussels).[60]

The facts that both Dungannon and Tyrconnell have elaborate, even magnificent, incised slabs marking their places of entombment, and that Tyrone does not may be significant. Tyrone is said to have been buried with great pomp and his body laid to rest between those of his son (Dungannon) and Tyrconnell,[61] but the absence of a memorial suggests that he had lost favour among those who counted. What is clear, though, is that the Ulster exiles were supported financially until the end of their lives by the King of Spain and the Papacy.

Nearly four centuries have passed, so it is difficult to assess Tyrone's personality with any certainty. He does not seem to have been much loved by those lords (like O'Cahan) who, traditionally, were his *uirríthe*, and to whom he behaved punitively and tyrannically. Early in his career he aroused distrust in many, while his violence and temper (he may, like Turlough Luineach O'Neill, have been a heavy drinker) made some afraid of him and others despise him. There must also be doubt concerning his prowess as a military strategist, for what success he did have in skirmishes with English forces seems to have been due to good fortune and to the incompetence of his

[56] i.e. Cathbarr.
[57] 14 September 1608.
[58] i.e. Hugh Roe (*Aodh Ruadh*) O'Donnell on 10 September 1602. The Ides were the 15th of March, May, July, and October, and the 13th of the remaining months. Days were reckoned forward, so the 4th of the Ides of September was the 10th of the month. This inscription was transcribed by the present writer in the church of San Pietro in Montorio, Rome, in September 1999.
[59] All by Joan (d. 1591), daughter of Aodh O'Donnell and half-sister of Tyrconnell.
[60] All by Catherine (d. 1618), sister of Arthur, 1st Viscount Magennis of Iveagh. See Mosley (ed.) (1999) *Burke's Peerage & Baronetage*, 2153.
[61] *D.N.B.* (1917) **xiv**, 1090.

opponents. He did not follow up his victories: at one stage (October 1597) he could easily have over-run the Pale, but instead made one of his 'submissions' to the State; and in 1598, after his success at the Yellow Ford against Bagenal, he not only failed to profit from his victory, but did not even prevent the remnants of Bagenal's force from retiring to Newry. Tyrone does not seem to have possessed much foresight, and was probably incapable of thinking on a broad scale, contenting himself with brief fights, but unable to push home his advantage. He was also prodigal with time, and wasted many precious months during which he could probably have become master of all Ireland had he possessed any vision.

One has the distinct impression that his reputation in Roman Catholic Europe was greatly inflated, but that when he actually arrived on the Continent many people who counted turned away from him. The parallels with the 'Young Pretender', 'Bonnie Prince Charlie', in the following century, are interesting. As a force, Tyrone no longer mattered much after his flight, and the realities of his character and behaviour began to dim his mythological prowess as a leader. While he lived, though, he remained a threat to the English and Scots presence in Ulster, and rumours of his impending return did not facilitate the suppression of unrest. That is why English agents in Rome watched him with care, and doubtless noted his dissipations and decline with considerable satisfaction. In the final analysis, though, Tyrone's decision to court alliances with Spain was fatal to his cause, for it committed the future of Ulster to international politics over which Tyrone himself had no control,[62] and Great Britain would never have tolerated any threat from a major Continental power operating in Ireland (or anywhere else in the British Isles), for the State had to put survival first in any reckoning. Tyrone attempted to draw Spain into the affairs of the three kingdoms, which was at least fraught with danger, and bound to rouse the Government in London to promote effective counter-measures.

Tyrone's apologists have stressed his Roman Catholicism, patriotism, nobility, powers of leadership, astuteness, piety, and much else. Yet the Government obviously never considered Tyrone's religious persuasion as a problem when giving him support before 1587, and it is possible that, given different circumstances, Tyrone might have raised the O'Neills to a similar position of influence as the Campbells enjoyed in Argyll in keeping the Gaelic Western Islands and Highlands subdued for the Crown of Scotland (and later of England), for the Campbells became earls and then dukes while remaining Gaelic chieftains. Be that as it may, it is clear that Tyrone's chief concern was the pursuit of power and influence: to abjure Roman Catholicism would not have secured his power-base, for a most significant element of any Irish Gaelic lord's standing was his control over local Church affairs (often dynastically controlled, as has been indicated above), so it would not have been sensible to encourage Protestant clergymen from Oxford and Cambridge to accept livings in Ulster. Such a move would have undermined an important part of his and his family's authority. Tyrone was motivated by ambition, which became over-weening, and eventually reached into areas over which he had no control: that was his undoing.[63]

[62] *Irish Historical Studies* **26**/101 (May 1988), 8-32.

[63] This chapter draws heavily on numerous sources cited in the Select Bibliography, but especially on *Analecta Hibernica* (from 1930); Atkinson (ed.) (1893-5); Bagwell (1885-90, 1909); Brewer and Bullen (eds.) (1867-73): Butler (1918); Byrne (1903); Curl (1986); Hamilton (ed.) (1860-90); Hardy (1966); Harris (1770); Hill (1877, 1878, 1889); Maxwell (1923, 1954); Moody (1939); Moody, Martin, and Byrne (eds.) (1978 and 1982); Morgan (1999); Morley (ed.) (1890); Mosley (ed.) (1999); O'Donovan (ed.) (1856); Robinson (1984, 1994); Russell and Prendergast (eds.) (1872-80) and Townend (ed.) (1963).

CHAPTER II

The Beginnings of the Plantation of Ulster and the First Involvement of the City of London in the Venture

> That wise and gracious King taking it into his care and Princely Consideration the restoring and future settlement of that defaced Kingdom lately torn in pieces with a long and miserable War to the effusion of much English Blood and wasting of an unspeakable Mass of Treasure, and taking timely Occasion to perform the Work of that Care by the Advantage given him in the Fugacy of the Rebels Tyrone and Tyrconnell, he resolved upon the present Plantation of Ulster with British. That Country having heretofore been the Nursery of all Rebellion in that Kingdom, and considering that the Ability of particular and private Undertakings would not be sufficient to answer and fortify so great a Work, he was pleased to invite the City of London to undertake a principal Part thereof

SIR THOMAS PHILLIPS (*c.*1558-1636): Preface (1629) in Form of a Petition from Sir Thomas Phillips to King Charles I, quoted in DAVID ALFRED CHART (1878-1960) (ed.), *Londonderry and the London Companies 1609-1629* (Belfast: His Majesty's Stationery Office, 1928), 1

Aftermath of the Flight of the Earls

There seems little doubt now that the Flight of the Earls was at least a gamble which led to disaster for Tyrone, his allies, and the survival of Gaelic culture. Chichester seems to have been (or appeared to be) surprised, even shocked, by the event, which may indicate he knew nothing of any treasonable plot, but he was also stunned by the implications, for huge tracts of Ulster became escheated to the Crown. Bills of Indictment were brought in by the Grand Juries of Donegal and Tyrone (December 1607), charging the earls and their associates with high treason and declaring their lands forfeit to the Crown. It is interesting to note that the foreman of the Donegal Jury was none other than Sir Cahir O'Doherty, Lord of Inishowen, who no doubt sought to enrich himself at the expense of Tyrconnell. The Flight, however, precipitated the Government into full-scale intervention in Ulster. Tyrone's pardon and restoration in 1603 can only be explained by the unwillingness of the Crown to disturb things to excess: it was probably hoped that the 'unstable equilibrium'[1] that existed from the end of the Nine Years' War to the final break with Tyrone might continue and even settle down into something like very gradual piecemeal Anglicisation by osmosis, but the premeditated Flight of the Earls forced the Government's hand. It seems clear that the astonishing pardons and restorations were prompted as much by lack of funds as unwillingness to tackle a thorny problem. The war had been extremely exhausting and expensive, so a draconian settlement could hardly be contemplated. It was Tyrone and O'Donnell's unrealistic and foolish action in attempting to involve Spain once more, followed by the Flight, that really left the Government with no

[1] Moody (1939), 24.

options, for containment, accommodations, and appeasement had been tried again and again and again, and had not worked. There is no doubt that the Government had hoped the problem would simply go away, but once its hand was forced it acted with unusual speed and resolution. Those who have perceived the Plantation as a rapacious attack on the Irish have not really seen things clearly, for, given the politico-religious state of affairs in western Europe at the time, a major grasping of nettles was essential, and the Crown would have been grossly irresponsible if it had not acted to fill the vacuum left by Tyrone, O'Donnell, and others, who had been given every chance, more than once.

At first, O'Cahan's position might seem to have improved once Tyrone had disappeared from the scene, but Sir Donnell began to adopt a fearful and hostile stance towards the Government, as well as having territorial disputes with the bishop of Derry. More trouble simmered in the vicinity of Derry, where Sir George Paulet (d. 1608) had been appointed Governor in 1606 through Mountjoy's influence, but Chichester was concerned about Paulet's fitness for the position. Very soon there were major quarrels between the bishop and Paulet (who claimed all see lands in Derry, the site of the ancient cathedral, and even the episcopal palace and parish-church which Docwra had built), and, even worse, between Paulet and Sir Cahir O'Doherty (whom Paulet accused of treason). Chichester warned Paulet to post sentries and keep a good watch, but the Governor ignored the advice. Incompetent, stupid, and ill-tempered, Paulet seems to have annoyed everyone, including his own men, who despised him. In April 1608 O'Doherty, who had premeditated a rising, seized Culmore Fort by treachery, and attacked Derry just before daybreak. The infant city was sacked and burned (including Bishop Montgomery's fine library), and many of its inhabitants (including Paulet) killed. When news of the disaster reached Chichester, he at once sent a strong force north to Ulster under Marshal Sir Richard Wingfield (d. 1634), and O'Doherty was killed at Kilmacrenan where his head was struck off and set up on the Newgate in Dublin. What is said to be his great sword, a fine example of Italian Renaissance workmanship, survives in the Tower Museum, Londonderry.[2]

From that time on, Chichester and the Government abandoned policies of appeasement and leniency towards the native Irish in Ulster. After the Flight of the Earls, Sir Donnell Ballagh O'Cahan and Sir Niall Garbh O'Donnell had hoped to enhance their positions and have Docwra's assurances implemented, but their pleas were ignored, for it had become a widespread belief (again not without reason) that Irish chiefs simply could not be trusted, that their word was anything but their bond, and that the security of the State would be under permanent threat if the Ulster chiefs were not removed. Furthermore, although O'Cahan had taken no part in O'Doherty's revolt as he was confined in Dublin Castle at the time, having been arrested by Sir Thomas Phillips (of whom more anon) the previous February, he was charged by the Lord Deputy with presumption of treason. One of his brothers, however, was implicated, and made a statement that incriminated Sir Donnell (probably with an eye to grabbing O'Cahan's 'country'). O'Donnell was also impugned, but in spite of his protests of loyalty to the Crown, was committed to stand trial in Dublin: however, after three days of deliberation in June 1609, the jurors would rather have starved than find him guilty, so the Attorney-General had to dismiss them, and O'Donnell and his son were sent to the Tower of London, where both of them died, Sir Niall

[2] Bonner (1975), *passim*.

as late as 1626. O'Cahan fared no better. He was confined without trial until 1609, when he, too, was sent to the Tower, where he appears to have died in 1617. Thus vast tracts of Ulster were seized for the Crown.

Surveys, the Genesis of the Plantation, and the First Frameworks of the Scheme

In July 1608 surveys of Counties Armagh, Cavan, Coleraine, Donegal, Fermanagh, and Tyrone were authorised, and by September it was clear that almost all those territories had become escheated to the Crown. However, the events of 1607-9 had left enormous problems, for the native Irish, bereft of their lords and their lands, were in a sullen and dangerous temper. There was a permanent sense of instability, and nowhere was this more palpable than in O'Cahan's former 'country' (County Coleraine) and in and around Derry. Law and order had broken down, robbery and violence were commonplace, and local jurymen refused to convict, even if the evidence were absolutely beyond question. The wrecked city of Derry was a testament to the dangers that faced settlers, who knew they would never enjoy any security until the escheated lands were 'planted' with large numbers of British colonists, well-armed and loyal to the Crown. Ulster was a hostile and terrifying place.

It is clear, however, that on the very day of O'Doherty's death, Sir Geoffrey Fenton (*c.*1539-1608), His Majesty's Secretary in Ireland, was able to write to Robert Cecil (*c.*1563-1612), 1st Earl of Salisbury (from 1605 – in whose powerful hands lay virtually the entire administration of the State), that conditions were now suitable for a universal settlement of Ulster,[3] so it looks as though from at least 1607 (the year of the Flight) there were those who saw a major intervention in Ulster as something inevitable, and that the sooner a resolution could be found, the better for everyone. It should be remembered that another 'Plantation' was under way at the time, for in May 1607 the first emigrants from England arrived in Virginia, and very soon the colonisation of the escheated lands in Ulster had the keen attention of the Government. Quite apart from transforming them into a peaceful, law-abiding country, the entire Kingdom would be better secured against native rebellion, foreign invasion, and attempts to restore Roman Catholicism. The Tudor State, from around 1534, as mentioned above, had been isolated and unstable, and certainly under Elizabeth isolation and instability had increased. The realm had been endangered on several occasions, not least during the Nine Years' War, and the various attempts by Spain to invade England and Ireland had been beaten as much by appalling weather as by the skills of English forces and the incompetence of the Spaniards and their allies. Under James I and VI, King of Great Britain and Ireland, there was still instability, even though the power of Spain was in decline, but from 1618 to 1648 much of Europe was to be decimated by the Thirty Years' War (which diverted Continental attention from Great Britain and Ireland), at the end of which Protestantism was secured in Scandinavia, Northern Germany, and The Netherlands.

As the implications of having control of the escheated counties sank in, enthusiasm grew. Farming methods would be greatly improved; lands could be settled on 'Servitors', or soldiers, who needed to be treated generously by the Crown; and towns and villages would be built, thus aiding the economy and bringing civilisation to a 'rude and

[3] Russell and Prendergast (eds.) (1874a): *Cal. S.P.I. 1606-8*, 609. Cecil seems to have been one of the prime movers in the entire Plantation venture.

unreformed part of Ireland', as Davies noted in his *Discoverie*.[4] Francis Bacon (1561-1626), the English Solicitor-General (from 1607), embraced the idea of an Ulster Plantation, and wrote A *Discourse on the Plantation of Ireland*, which he presented to the King in 1609. In this work he argued that the majority of those granted lands in Ulster should be men of substance and not the needy, as it was essential to ensure the colonisation was thorough and backed by suitable investment. He also insisted that the settlers should build their houses in fortified towns to avoid destruction (as had happened to the dispersed and isolated houses of the Munster Plantation in 1598), and that the State should provide the means of building towns, churches, bridges, causeways, roads, and other public buildings. Bacon emphasised the strategic and political reasons for colonising Ulster, pointing out its geographical proximity to Great Britain and its capabilities of receiving large numbers of settlers. The escheated lands had large areas of excellent farmland; the rivers teemed with fish; there was plenty of livestock, including game; there was stone, clay, and limestone; and there were substantial areas covered with forests to provide building materials.

Near the end of 1608 Chichester sent Davies and Sir James Ley (1550-1629), the Chief Justice, to London with instructions (Remembrances touching the Plantation and Settlement of the Escheated Lands in Ulster[5]) to prepare a scheme for the Plantation in consultation with the Privy Council. He was anxious that Davies, Ley, and others should become acquainted with the county of Coleraine, and that evidence should be collected concerning the O'Cahans and others, their holdings, and any implications of involvement in plots; furthermore, the importance of the fisheries was emphasised, and all facts concerning these should be ascertained. From the very start false claims to land by Irish natives should be looked upon with great care, and the need to colonise the lands with new blood was stressed. No person should acquire land to make him more powerful than his neighbour (this was a clear reference to endemic Irish problems with chiefs and vassals), and there was an urgent need to build strong castles and houses to secure the country.

By January 1609 two important documents had been produced by a special committee established in London: *A Collection of such Orders and Conditions as are to be observed by the Undertakers upon the Distribution and Plantation of the Escheated lands in Ulster* and *A Project for the Division and Plantation of the Escheated lands in Ulster*.[6] The forfeited lands were to be divided into 'Proportions', described as 'Great' (2,000 English acres), 'Middle' (1,500 English acres), and 'Small' (1,000 English acres), with bogs and woods to be exempt from rents in all Proportions. There were to be three distinct classes of grantees:

(i) British, who would settle their Proportions with English and Scots tenants;
(ii) Servitors, who had seen military or civil service in Ireland, who would settle their Proportions (positioned in places that were most dangerous, for the defence of other colonists) with British and Irish tenants;
(iii) Irish, who could take Irish (and presumably any other sort of) tenants.

Each Undertaker with a Great Proportion was to build a strong castle with a court about it protected by a bawn (a fortified wall, often with towers, or 'flankers', at the corners); each with a Middle Proportion was to erect a stone or brick house and bawn; and each with a Small Proportion was to build at least a bawn. Undertakers

[4] Davies (1787), 208.
[5] Russell and Prendergast (eds.) (1874b): *Cal. S.P.I. 1608-10*, 54.
[6] *Analecta Hibernica* (1938), 8; Hill (1877), 90-116; Irish Society (*c.*1898), 19-25; Moody (1939), 33; Schultes (1822), 1-3.

were to settle British tenants on their lands, and require them to build houses near the castles and bawns for reasons of security. In addition, Undertakers were to have stores of arms placed conveniently so that weapons could be supplied to able-bodied men, and reviews and musters were to take place every six months. All British Undertakers were required to take the Oath of Supremacy before their letters patent could be sealed, and they had to conform to the liturgy and articles of the Established Church. No Undertakers were to alienate (transfer to the ownership of another) or demise (grant or transfer an estate by will or lease) their Proportions to the Irish or to any persons who failed to take the Oath, and all Undertakers were to reside on their Proportions for five years after getting the letters patent, or to ensure some other suitable person was in charge. Rents for British Undertakers were to be £5 6s. 8d. per annum per 1,000 acres, and the first two years' rent was to be remitted. In addition most British Undertakers were to hold their lands in fee-farm (tenure by fee simple [unconditional inheritance] at a fixed rent without services), and were required to set up manors over which they had authority, to hold courts baron twice a year, and to provide leases for their tenants. New Undertakers were allowed to sell or export all produce from the state for seven years, and for five years were permitted to import livestock, tools, provisions, and building materials without having to pay Customs duties. Timber would be provided for building purposes from the Crown forests of Ulster.

Rents were higher and remissions were for shorter periods where Irish tenants were involved, on the grounds that the Irish did not have to travel so far or subject themselves to as much expense or upheaval. Servitors should have estates in fee-farm at an annual rent of £8 per 1,000 acres if the land were inhabited by Irish, but only £5 6s. 8d. if there were British tenants. Irish landowners would again hold their estates in fee-farm, but would be liable to pay £10 13s. 4d. per annum per 1,000 acres, and were required to build 'English' houses and run their estates on the same lines as could be found in the English Pale. Any whiff of rebellion would not be tolerated, on pain of forfeiture. Allocation of Proportions would be by lot.

The *Project for the Plantation* set out rules for dividing each county: half the land would be subdivided into Small Proportions; a quarter into Middle Proportions, and a quarter into Great Proportions. Each Proportion was to have a parish-church, and 60 acres of glebe land were to be assigned to each incumbent of a parish of 1,000 acres, adjusted for larger areas. Land was also set aside to maintain free schools, as well as to support the college of the Holy and Undivided Trinity in Dublin (founded 1592). Therefore each county had its total area calculated, with total areas for Church lands, areas allocated to the Proportions, and the methods by which lands were to be distributed among Undertakers or grantees were described. Ordinary Irish natives were to be settled on the lands of Servitors and Irish grantees, as well as on the glebe and Church lands (i.e. lands allocated for the benefit of incumbents or land granted to the bishops of the Established Church). Armed followers of Gaelic chieftains were to be banished or forced into military service.

Chichester saw dangers in these proposals. Allocation of land by the luck of the draw could lumber an Undertaker with an impossible task, should his Proportion be in wild and dangerous country; time allowed for building-works was too short; holders of Great Proportions were required to hold their estates by knight-service *in capite* (i.e. direct from the Crown with an obligation to perform military service for the Crown as a condition of holding lands), and therefore had considerable extra burdens which put them at a great disadvantage; too little land was assigned to the native Irish, who were in a restless mood, expecting Tyrone and the Irish lords to return at any time; Servitors would be reluctant to take on estates unless conditions were made less onerous; building requirements were too expensive; and rigid application of areas and subdivisions was inflexible and unimaginative. When it is remembered that many Irish swordsmen, followers of their chiefs, had taken to the woods, whence they waged unremitting guerrilla warfare, attempts to create settlements by British colonists were bound to be hedged with dangers, and the prospects were unattractive.

Nevertheless, matters of State, the instability of Ireland, and international affairs dictated that nettles should be grasped and that the long-standing problem of Ulster had to be solved. In those difficult days the Crown moved with resolve and unwonted alacrity. The Plantation of Ulster began, with momentous consequences that resound through the centuries.[7]

Tentative Approaches to the City of London

The Government gradually realised that the rushed surveys of 1608 were inadequate – but it is hardly surprising they were so inaccurate – for inspection and measurement of lands could be very dangerous, especially if the natives were unfriendly. There are records of several instances of surveyors being threatened or killed: Richard Bartlett (*fl.*1595-1608), for example, was beheaded in Tirconnell in 1608, and was probably tortured first. Davies, recalling this episode in a letter of 28 August 1609 to Lord Salisbury, noted that the surveyors (he called them 'geographers') had difficulty in forgetting 'what entertainment the Irish … gave to a map-maker [Davies called him 'Barkeley'] about the end of the late great Rebellion …': when he came into Tirconnell the 'inhabitants took off his head, because they would not have their country discovered'.[8] Some of the maps are excessively (and understandably) vague in certain areas, and one can imagine prudent English surveyors indicating territories drawn more from hearsay and conversations heard in a tavern rather than from first-hand observation. Another difficulty for the surveyors was that they had to note the names of places, townlands, and so on, from spoken Irish, and therefore had to try to use phonetic methods of recording information gleaned. The surprising thing is that they were so accurate, for although some of their attempts produced names that were almost unintelligible in written form, as having derived from the Irish, they often correspond with spoken versions in local dialects, even today. Given the appalling difficulties faced by the 17th-century surveyors (including very real danger of being attacked and murdered), they did a remarkable job.

On 21 July 1609, therefore, Chichester and the Irish Government were authorised to establish a commission to carry out a thorough investigation of the escheated lands, including a new, corrected survey; to distinguish temporal and Church lands; to subdivide the counties into Proportions (with maps showing where these were); to determine all controversies and disputes concerning lands; and to take all necessary measures to further the Plantation according to the *Project*. Work on the survey began on 31 July 1609, and was completed on 30 September, an astonishing achievement. One of the commissioners was Sir John Davies, whose letter recalling the Bartlett episode was written while the survey was under way, and while a Deputation from the

[7] Curl (1986); Hill (1877); Moody (1939).
[8] Ford (1915), 26; Irish Society (*c.*1898), 83.

City of London was inspecting 'O'Cahan's Country', an important visitation which will be outlined below.

Very soon it had become clear that the Crown lacked the wherewithal and the will to carry out the ambitious Plantation scheme in the face of native resistance, poor-quality grantees with limited resources, and much else. In fact, the Plantation project was far too ambitious for the means available, and was bedevilled by shortage of funds throughout its history. The economic interests of Undertakers meant that they actually conspired with the natives to put the entire Plantation of Ulster in jeopardy. For their part, the Irish stubbornly stayed put (at whatever costs) with the enticing possibility of being able to butcher their landlords should the occasion arise. However, the British Crown was not alone in its paucity of treasure. Attempts by France and Britain to establish colonies in North America suffered from chronic under-funding, and this fact is well documented. The Virginia Plantation and French settlements in what is now Canada were very seriously under-resourced, as their historians have demonstrated.[9]

These were hesitant and inauspicious beginnings for the Plantation of Ulster, but already moves were afoot to resolve some of the problems by turning to a source that was more likely than individuals to be able to finance the venture, and which was already, slowly but surely, becoming enmeshed in the hoary problem of what was to be done about Ulster: the City of London was to become intimately involved in the colonisation of O'Cahan's country, but the Londoners at that time had little inkling what the extent of their intervention would be. Precedents, however, had been established long before, in that the resources of the City of London have often been tapped to further State policies. After Tyrone's rebellion, City money was used to prosecute the Nine Years' War, so there seemed to be nothing untoward about approaching the Londoners yet again for help in getting the Ulster Plantation started. In 1598-9 the Londoners had provided loans totalling the then gigantic sum of £80,000 to aid the Crown in dangerous times.[10]

A key figure in the venture was Sir Thomas Phillips (*c.*1558-1636), a 'pushing soldier-of-fortune',[11] who had seen service in France and seems first to have arrived in Ireland in 1599 where he was involved in the Nine Years' War. Through the influence of Robert Cecil (with whom he seems to have remained on good terms), Phillips served as an officer under Chichester, who soon came to respect Phillips's competence and qualities. In 1602 Phillips led troops in a successful assault on Tyrone's fortress at Toome, and was rewarded with the command of the castle and fort there, with a Company of 150 Foot. After Tyrone's submission Phillips was put in charge of the priory in Coleraine in 1604 which until that time still functioned as such.[12] Chichester knew the strategic importance of Coleraine, and sought to settle British colonists there, partly as a check on the Scots from the Western Isles. For a short time (1605) the priory site, its buildings and lands, together with certain fishing rights in the Bann, were held by James Hamilton (1559-1643), created Viscount Claneboye in 1622. Hamilton sold his interests (under pressure from Chichester) in Coleraine to Phillips in September 1605, who also obtained a 21-year grant of the Customs and Subsidies of all merchandise, wares, or goods carried by boat in or out of Coleraine, Portrush, and Portballintrae; ferry-rights over the Bann at Coleraine and Toome; a

[9] See, for example, Reps (1965, *c.*1972, 1980), *passim.*
[10] Moody (1939), 62.
[11] *Ibid.*, 60.
[12] Russell and Prendergast (eds.) (1872): *Cal. S.P.I. 1603-6*, 178.

licence to hold Wednesday markets and a three-day annual fair at Coleraine; and the castle and fort at Toome with 30 acres adjoining.[13] In 1607 Phillips was knighted, and by 1608 was military superintendent of the county of Coleraine and Glenconkeyne. He also obtained a licence to distil *Aqua Vitae* within the county and in the Route, Co. Antrim (the beginnings of Bushmills and Coleraine whiskeys). During O'Doherty's rebellion Phillips gave succour to refugees from Derry and district, and expended much of his limited capital as well as a lot of energy on attempts to establish Coleraine as a fortified colony with a market. After his arrest of O'Cahan, Phillips petitioned Cecil for a grant of some of O'Cahan's lands adjoining Coleraine to help him to improve the little town and restore his ruined finances.[14] Phillips had also repaired the parish-church at Coleraine, where there was a 'good congregation every day to hear Divine Service, to the discomfort of the ill-disposed'.[15]

By 1609 it was clear that the Plantation of Ulster was in sore need of a larger injection of money, colonists, and organisation. The Government was concerned that Derry, 'the fairest-begun city that ever was made in such a short time, and so well-seated upon a goodly river', … was all 'wasted, save only the rampiers of the forts …'. It was a place of 'little strength', and lay at the 'mercy of any' that would attempt 'to seize upon it', [16] as Cecil was informed by letter. The county of Coleraine, O'Cahan's 'Country', was particularly tricky, because its former lord, Sir Donnell, was languishing in captivity, there was some doubt about the legality of the seizure of his lands, and the inhabitants of the territory were restive. Sir Toby Caulfeild (1565-1627), later 1st Baron Charlemont, noted that there was 'not a more discontented people in Europe'[17] so something drastic had to be done, and at some time early in 1609 Cecil, presumably acting with the full approval, if not prompting, of the King, began to put out feelers to the City of London.[18] Phillips went to London to plead his claim for a share of O'Cahan's lands near Coleraine, and it seems that Cecil at once took his protégé into his confidence, perceiving that Phillips would be a useful ally who knew the country well and was fully acquainted with the problems and with what had to take place to resolve them. Phillips particularised to 'his Lordship in writing the commodities of that Country which might raise the Profits, to make the Londoners the more sensible of their Service'.[19] This probably refers to the 'Project of Sir Thomas Phillips for the Londoners' Plantation in the county of Coleraine and the Derry, sent to Robert, Earl of Salisbury',[20] a prolix document setting out probable costs to be borne and profits likely to accrue, which seems to have been the basis of the paper *Motives and Reasons to induce the City of London to undertake the Plantation in the North of Ireland*, dated 25 May 1609.[21] It proposed the best places for the City of London to 'plant' were Derry and Coleraine, both of which could be fortified to provide security 'to those that shall be sent thither to inhabit'. The King would create corporations in both settlements and would grant the City of London the land bounded by the River Foyle, the sea, and the River Bann, with no reference to any boundary to the south. In addition, the two

[13] Erck (ed.) (1846, 1852), 191, 194-6, 231, 257, 477-8 .

[14] Russell and Prendergast (eds.) (1874a): *Cal. S.P.I. 1606-8*, 281, 520.

[15] Russell and Prendergast (eds.) (1874b): *Cal. S.P.I. 1608-10*, 248; Boyd (1933), 27.

[16] Russell and Prendergast (eds.) (1874b): *Cal. S.P.I. 1608-10*, 194; Moody (1939), 60.

[17] Connolly (ed.) (1998), 561.

[18] Chart (ed.) (1928), 11-12.

[19] *Ibid.*

[20] Brewer and Bullen (eds.) (1867-73): *Cal. Carew MSS* for 1609, 148-53.

[21] Irish Society (*c.*1898), 42-45; Russell and Prendergast (eds.) (1874b): *Cal. S.P.I. 1608-10,* 207-10; Schultes (1822), 17-21.

5 Sir Clement Edmondes (*c.*1564-1622), the learned City Remembrancer. From a portrait in oils on canvas by the Dutch portrait-painter, Daniel Mytens (1590-*c.*1648). (*GACL/1423/Record 11493*).

towns would each have a thousand acres or more for their commons, rent-free, the rest of the territory to be 'planted with such Undertakers as the City of London' thought fit. Coleraine and Derry would be granted the proceeds of the Customs on all imports and exports for 21 years, Admiralty rights on the coasts of Donegal and Coleraine for the same period, and the salmon fisheries of the Bann and Foyle. The Londoners would be licensed to export the produce of their lands, would have access to the timber in the forests of Glenconkeyne and Killetra, and 'sea and river commodities'.[22] The possibilities of trade were rosily outlined, and the region would provide employment for a great population which could be moved out of overcrowded, insanitary London. Furthermore, the Londoners would develop a huge new trade area including western Scotland. Cecil wrote at once to the Remembrancer of the City, Sir Clement Edmondes (*c.*1564-1622 **[5]** – whose position made him the official mouthpiece of the City of London), requesting that he should acquaint the 'Lord Mayor' (Sir Humphrey Weld) 'with the Busyness'. Very soon Phillips met Weld, who began to be attracted to the idea, and called in two prominent London Aldermen, Sir John Jolles, Draper, and William Cokayne, Skinner (*c.*1550- 1626), both of whom were acquainted with recent Irish history, and with whom he discussed the Privy Council's offer to the

[22] Moody (1939), 66-7.

City. A meeting was then arranged at Sir John Holles's house with Phillips, who used all his powers of persuasion to get the Londoners interested in the Plantation.[23] This 'Holles' may be an error for 'Jolles', but it could also refer to the well-connected Sir John Holles (*c.*1564-1637), who had fought in Ireland under Lord Deputy Fitzwilliam, and who was to be created 1st Earl of Clare in 1624. However, Jolles seems to have been the man mainly involved in the Plantation venture, rather than Holles. This encounter seems to have been a great success, and very soon afterwards, in July, a special Court of Aldermen was held, with 'divers selected commoners', at which the *Motives and Reasons* document was read, and at once a Precept (the means by which the Lord Mayor, acting in this instance as the mouthpiece of the Crown, communicated commands to the Companies) and copies of the *Motives and Reasons* and *Orders and Conditions* were issued to all the Livery Companies of the City, requiring each of them to summon a 'competent number of the most grave and substanciall Men' to consider the Plantation project with due thought and to nominate four senior men 'of the most Judgment' to meet similar nominated Deputations from other Companies in order that their view on the matter might be communicated to the Crown in writing.[24] The Court of Aldermen received the report on 14 July, by which time the City had had more meetings with Phillips, who was quizzed on factual matters, availability of resources, and an estimate as to what profits might accrue by the venture. Phillips reported back to Cecil, reminding him that the project would involve surrendering his own properties at Coleraine on which he had expended much energy and capital. He proposed that his estate be purchased by the Crown for £2,500.[25]

The Court of Aldermen, having obtained the report from the Livery Companies, appointed a Deputation of 15 Aldermen and Liverymen to thrash out various points concerning the 'Busyness' with the Council of Ireland, and it was decided to send a Deputation to view the lands to be settled (and also to verify the official glowing account provided by the Crown and Phillips). A further Precept was sent to the Companies requiring them to prepare lists of all their members who would contribute money to the scheme together with the amounts subscribed and, more ominously, to take the names of members who refused to disgorge funds.

Almost at once there were difficulties. Many Liverymen summoned by the Companies did not attend, and were duly fined, while others, clearly worried, felt it 'were best never to entermeddle' in the 'Busyness' at all, fearing (not without reason, as it turned out) that Ulster would become a bottomless pit into which their gold would pour. As a Fishmonger plaintively observed, the 'Busyness' was likely to be 'exceading chargeable'.[26] The impecunious and nervous Ironmongers produced 46 names, of which 22 found it prudent to be out of Town. The Court of Assistants of the Skinners' Company went as far as to inform the Lord Mayor they would not 'undergo' the Plantation, but under pressure 25 members promised donations, but 12 refused outright. The Barber-Surgeons had many objections, and, of those who reluctantly agreed to pay, the largest amount was one pound.[27]

[23] Chart (ed.) (1928), 12. Sir John Jolles was Master of the Drapers' Company in 1605-6 and 1610-11, and Lord Mayor of London 1615-16. He was one of the first members of the Court of Assistants of The Irish Society .

[24] Moody (1939), 69. See also City Records, Misc. MSS 237.8.

[25] Russell and Prendergast (eds.) (1874b): *Cal. S.P.I. 1608-10*, 248-50.

[26] Moody (1939), 70.

[27] *Ibid.*, 72.

As Moody put it, 'at the outset' the Companies 'on the whole showed no enthusiasm for, and some positive hostility to, investing money in Ulster'. This is hardly surprising, given the history of the previous six decades or so. Ulster was far away, inconvenient, and dangerous to get to, with a hostile, embittered, poor, and 'Papist' population of 'Irishry' associated with wildness and treachery in the minds of the Londoners. To many Liverymen the Plantation did not seem like a good idea.

The Livery Companies and the City of London

During the 19th and 20th centuries large numbers of articles and tracts were published in Ireland attacking the Livery Companies. These polemics are so plentiful and windy it would be pointless (and infinitely tedious) to list them all, though the diligent historian must needs wade through their turgid prose. What is truly amazing is that the vast majority of these diatribes display a woeful ignorance of what a London Livery Company is and was. The general consensus seems to have been that a London Company was a sort of department-store selling haberdashery or groceries. Looking up historical facts seems to have been beyond most of the authors of these worthless effusions, for it is clear that they basked in their self-important ignorance rather than risk having their illusions shattered by anything resembling truth.[28]

At this point, therefore, it might be useful to clarify what is meant by the 'London Companies', which have a central place in the history of the City of London, and are of considerable antiquity. Many Companies have or had their own premises, or 'Halls', for meetings, regular feasts, and other purposes. The Livery Companies get their name from the mode of dress, the wearing of a *Livery*, often of peculiar magnificence, which was a badge of membership of a particular Company. These organisations were similar to the guilds that flourished in medieval Europe: they were concerned with trade, with the giving of alms and support for charities, and took part in religious observances, yet were secular in character. When craftsmen, dealers, and merchants obtained charters for managing their callings, they formed fraternities, the membership of which contributed money to a common stock, and could make laws by licence of the Crown. A hall, or guild-hall, therefore, was a place where a fraternity or commonalty could gather together into one combination, supporting a common charge by contributions. Each Company was headed by an elected Master and two or three Wardens who, acting alone or in association with a Court of Assistants, carried on the administration of the Company. Trades or crafts were overseen by inspection of work or products and by the carefully controlled training of apprentices; money was raised by letting the corporate estates and by 'fining' or raising levies on members; and charity was dispensed from the legacies of deceased members or from cash raised by rental or investment income. Under the Court of Assistants in rank were the Liverymen who were eligible to join the Court if vacancies occurred, and next came the Freemen or Yeomanry from whose ranks came the Liverymen on payment of a 'fine'. The hierarchy was completed by the large number of Journeymen (called the Commonalty) who were subject to strict rules laid down by the Company for the regulation of work, trade, etc.[29]

[28] Some of these publications are listed in the Select Bibliography, but no attempt has been made to record them all, for they would fill many pages. For a typical taste of the sort of material they contain see L.L.D. (1883), *passim*.

[29] Herbert (1834-7), iii-iv, 1, 36-7. See also Doolittle (1982), 3-5, Johnson (1914-22), and Leigh and Taylor (eds.) (1997), *passim*.

During the Middle Ages the Thirteen Great Companies (known variously as 'the substantial Companies', 'the principal Crafts', the 'Chief Misteries', the 'wealthier and superior Companies', the 'Most Worshipfull Fellowships', and other fulsome epithets) emerged as the wealthiest and most influential, paying the highest annual sums (called *fermes*) to the Crown or to other bodies, and sent the most members to the Court of Common Council for the governance of the City of London. From these Companies the Lord Mayors were chosen, and they alone could enrol the Sovereign among their members. With the redundancy of armour and the development of firearms, the Armourers' Company declined, leaving the Twelve Great Companies which bore the brunt of all levies on the City by the Government. These are, in order of precedence, the Mercers', Grocers', Drapers', Fishmongers', Goldsmiths', Skinners', Merchant Taylors', Haberdashers', Salters', Ironmongers', Vintners', and Clothworkers' Companies. By Elizabethan times these Companies comprised the 'chief commercial staple and manufacturing interests' of the Kingdom, 'besides including the most eminent of the citizens amongst their members'.[30] As they had their origins in the pre-Reformation world, the Companies retained their ancient titles that reflected this. For example, the Company of the Mystery of Grocers of the City of London was under the Patronage of St Antony the Great (*c.*251-356), often called St Antony of Coma, or St Antony of Egypt; the Guild or Fraternity of the Blessed Virgin Mary of the Mystery of Drapers of the City of London acknowledged its Patroness in its title; and the Mystery of Fishmongers of the City of London, unsurprisingly, was under the protection of St Peter (d. *c.*64), the Fisher of Men. The Art or Mystery of Ironmongers, predictably, had as its Patron St Laurence (d. 258), being associated with the gridiron on which the saint was roasted, thus achieving his martyrdom, but the Mystery for a time was devoted to St Eligius, or Eloi (*c.*588-660), whose principal emblem was an iron horseshoe. The Mystery of Vintners was under the protection of St Martin of Tours (c.316-97), who was particularly associated with charity, the healing of lepers, and, of course, with wine-growing areas of France (which country has some 500 villages and over 4,000 parish-churches named after him). Both the Guild or Fraternity of Skinners and the Art or Mystery of Salters were especially devoted to Corpus Christi.

Some fantasists have seen the word 'Mystery' as indicative of dark goings-on, secret societies, and quasi-Freemasonic junketings. Such notions are absurd, and should be discarded, for the word (also spelled *Mistery*) derives from the medieval Latin *misterius*, an altered form of *ministerium*, meaning occupation, service, craft, trade, profession, calling, or skill, although there may also be some confusion with *Maistre*, an old form of *Master* or *Mastery*, indicating well-developed professional skills. A very important aspect of a Company was the welfare of members, both material and spiritual. Sick members were cared for and given financial support, and in many instances the Mysteries or Guilds established almshouses. Furthermore, the Companies attended regular guild church-services, and often maintained a priest to say Masses for the repose of the souls of departed brethren and sisters (women were admitted as associates in the fraternities). One of the most important aspects of medieval life was the welfare of the soul after death. Thus chantries (endowments for the maintenance of one or more priests to say or sing daily Masses for the souls of those providing the money) were established, but these were very expensive for individuals, so the setting up of chantries was often only possible if numbers of people formed an association for the purpose. Several medieval guilds built special chantry-chapels attached to a church,

[30] Herbert (1834-7), 38.

and maintained an altar and a priest for the care of the souls of the departed and for the peace of mind of the living, who knew that after death their Company would continue to succour their souls. Funerals were therefore important and magnificent occasions, attended by all the members, and the coffin would be covered by richly-embroidered palls such as those which survive in the possession of the Fishmongers', Saddlers', and other Companies to this day.

By the time the City began its involvement in the convoluted history of Ulster, the organisation of London's Government was similar to that of the pyramidal structure of the Companies: at the top of the pyramid were the Aldermen, each representing a Ward. One of their number was chosen each year as the Lord Mayor, and they were responsible for managing the affairs of the Corporation; for regulating public services, laws, and order; for the control of trade in the Port of London; for the overseeing of public markets; and for providing water-supplies and street-lighting. For these tasks the Aldermen were assisted by the Common Council, with representatives from the Wards. The Liverymen (those who had assumed the clothing of certain Companies) had their place in Common Hall, the third of the City's Courts. Members of Common Hall could elect or nominate officers of the City, and could express critical opinions. Under the Common Hall layer were members of the Corporation who held the Freedom, which was an essential handle for anyone wishing to trade within the Square Mile, and the Freemen could elect Aldermen and members of Common Council. Thus, by the time of the beginnings of the Plantation, the Companies were fully assimilated into the City's government, and the City and the Companies were interdependent. The City needed the Companies and the riches of their members in order to satisfy the regular (and rapacious) demands made by the Crown, while the Companies needed Guildhall (the seat of power of the Corporation) to enforce the rules and obligations of the Freedom. As a means of raising money the Stuart dynasty called in the charters of Livery Companies and provided new ones for large financial considerations; thus many Companies operate under charters dating from the 17th century. Regular extortion, pressures to produce money to prosecute the Irish wars and the Plantation of Ulster, and many other instances tended to impoverish the Companies, with the result that eventually, as we shall see, the City turned against the Crown and supported Parliament during the Civil Wars (1642-6 and 1648-52). It was a momentous change of allegiance.[31]

The Inspection of the Lands and the Agreement with the Crown

The Privy Council held an important meeting with a delegation from the City in July 1609, and on 1 August it was resolved by the Common Council of the City that 'Fower wise, grave, and discrete Citizens' should 'be choosen' and 'presentlye sente' to Ulster 'to viewe the place for the intended plantacon in Ireland'. John Broad (Goldsmith), Hugh Hamersley (Haberdasher), John Rowley (Draper), and Robert Treswell (Painter-Stainer) were selected to form the Deputation.[32] Only a couple of days later the Common Council decided to excuse Hamersley and substitute John Munns (Mercer). The Deputation was instructed to 'survey and view the place and groundes intended

[31] The subject of the Companies of the City cannot be covered fully here. Doolittle (1982), Hazlitt (1892), and Herbert (1834-7), are among many sources which may be consulted with benefit.

[32] Moody (1939), 72, drawing on the Journal of the Court of Common Council of the City of London, 27, f. 398-9, LB DD, f. 64v, 65. See Corporation of London Records Office Misc. MSS 237.8, and Irish Society (*c.*1898), 79.

for the new plantaçon' and identified in the *Motives and Reasons*, in order to establish their potential for settlement; to survey the land, rivers, and coast; to study the produce of the country; and to make maps of the area visited. For all this, expenses of £300 were allowed (a very large sum then),[33] and Phillips, with his unrivalled knowledge, was identified to act as cicerone. Chichester was instructed to give the Deputation every help. Furthermore, in a private communication to Chichester the Privy Council emphasised the importance of getting the City involved and warning that only the most favourable impressions were to be received by the Deputation; the guides were to select the most attractive routes; were to lodge the Londoners comfortably (and preferably in English houses); were to emphasise the potential profits to be gained by the City; and were to shield the Deputation from anything disagreeable that might put them off.[34] Murdered surveyors, for example, were not, apparently, discussed.

On 22 August the members of the Deputation landed at Carrickfergus and travelled up to Coleraine, where they stayed for a couple of days before proceeding to Limavady where they met the Lord Deputy and his party (which was engaged in preparing the new commissions of inquiry and surveys alluded to above). More persuasion was used on the Londoners, who were shown the valleys of the Rivers Roe and Faughan, before being taken to Lifford, and, after four days, travelled to Derry from where Phillips returned with them to Coleraine. The party was then taken through the forests of Loughinsholin (to see the wealth of timber available) and on to Toome, where a smith demonstrated how good steel could be made from local ore. The Deputation travelled with Phillips back to Coleraine by boat down the River Bann, and the party started back for London near the end of September.[35]

One has a distinct impression of wool-pulling by the Government commissioners, for the Deputation had seen all the most attractive parts of the country (including the great Rivers Bann and Foyle, both of which had plentiful fish), but had been spared the wild landscapes of the Sperrin mountains and the foothills, not least because that country was too dangerous. A glimpse of English surveyors carrying out their duties under the watchful eyes of armed guards, clearly, would not have encouraged confidence, so doubtless the Londoners were shielded from seeing them. Chichester wrote to Cecil that Phillips, 'to his great charge and trouble', daily accompanied the Deputation 'from one place to another', which was a 'great comfort to them'.[36] Treswell, also writing to Cecil, noted the Deputation had not viewed all parts of the country, but what he and his colleagues had seen far exceeded their expectations. He assured Cecil that a favourable report would be presented to the Common Council.[37] Phillips at once began felling thousands of trees to be seasoned for use in the following spring,[38] and Chichester arranged to have typical products of the country sent to London: these included beef, eels, herrings, hides, iron-ore, pipe-staves made of timber, salmon, tallow, and yarn.[39]

The Londoners were no fools, however, and they made several demands which were answered in writing by Chichester, including a request that no grants of land should be made to other Undertakers on either side of the Foyle towards Lifford or

33 Russell and Prendergast (eds.) (1874b): *Cal. S.P.I. 1608-10*, 316.
34 *Ibid.*, 266-7.
35 *Ibid.*, 267-8.
36 *Ibid.*, 286, 297.
37 *Ibid.*, 290-1.
38 *Ibid.*, 290.
39 *Ibid.*, 286.

west of the Bann towards the River Ballinderry. It will be recalled that early notions of colonising O'Cahan's 'Country' were extremely vague about the southern boundary, but the Deputation at once saw the advantages, even necessity, of obtaining the barony of Loughinsholin, with its dense woods, which nominally lay in County Tyrone. Chichester urged Cecil to make an early decision and to facilitate the Londoners, as the least trouble would inhibit them.[40]

In November the Deputation presented to the Court of Aldermen a map of the country together with much information, including the requests made to Chichester. In December they reported to the Common Council which set up a special committee (made up of leading Aldermen, Sheriffs, and representatives of the Companies) to prepare the conditions on which the City would undertake the Plantation. By mid-December it was decided: that a sum of £15,000 be raised from the Companies; that the city of Derry (with 4,000 acres 'laid' [i.e. assigned] to it) and the town of Coleraine (with 3,000 acres laid to it), the county of Coleraine (estimated to be 15,000 acres of temporal land), and the districts of Glenconkeyne and Killetra in the south, should comprise the Londoners' property; that all established private interests of other landlords should be extinguished; that fishing-rights on the Rivers Bann and Foyle, the Customs on all exports and imports, the control of Culmore Fort, the right to export all products of the territory without controls, Admiralty rights on the coasts of Donegal and Coleraine, the patronage of all ecclesiastical livings (advowsons), and a monopoly of control over the export of flax, hemp, hides, and unwoven yarn produced in the north of Ireland should be demanded by the City; that the City would build 200 houses in Derry and provide sites for a further 300; that 100 houses would be erected in Coleraine, with sites for 200 more; that fortifications should be erected for the protection of Derry and Coleraine; that some sort of organisation to manage the Plantation should be set up in London, with the powers to appoint agents who would live in Ulster; that Corporations should be established in Derry and Coleraine; that forces paid for by the Crown should be maintained in Ulster for the defence of the Plantation; and that a Bill be prepared to go through Parliament so that demands should be settled and confirmed.[41]

The City's proposals were put before the Privy Council, but that body could not accept that the sum proposed was adequate, so the City raised its estimate to £20,000.[42] By this time the City was well aware of the anxieties of the Crown to get on with the Plantation, and in 1610 a new City committee was established (to include the four deputies who had visited Ulster) with powers to deal directly with representatives of the Crown. At first the Crown resisted the Londoners' demands for Glenconkeyne and Killetra, arguing that the woodlands should be preserved, possibly as royal forests. Agreement could not be reached, so matters were referred to the Privy Council.

A Precept for obtaining the first £5,000 of the estimated costs was issued to the Companies, and on 28 January 1610 Articles of Agreement between the City and the Crown for the Plantation of the city of Derry, the county of Coleraine, and the barony of Loughinsholin were signed. The Privy Council had caved in, and the Crown had acceded to nearly all the City's demands. As Moody noted, the 'City had made the most of its unsought compact with the Crown'.[43] This Agreement has 27 clauses which can be summarised below:

40 Russell and Prendergast (eds.) (1874b): *Cal. S.P.I. 1608-10*, 297.
41 Curl (1986), 32-3; Moody (1939), 75-6.
42 *Ibid.* See also Brewer and Bullen (eds.) (1867-73): *Cal. Carew MSS, 1603-24, passim.*
43 Moody (1939), 78.

1. £5,000 to be expended to buy out the interests of existing parties, leaving £15,000 to be spent on the Plantation;
2. 200 houses to be built at Derry, with sites provided for 300 more. 4,000 acres on the west (Donegal) bank of the River Foyle, excluding bogs and barren mountains, to be laid to the city of Derry;
3. the bishop and dean of Derry to have convenient plots provided for their dwellings;
4. Coleraine to be built on the 'Abby' (i.e. Antrim) side of the River Bann, and 100 houses erected, with room for 200 more. 1,000 acres on the Antrim side to be laid to the town, and, if the King were to erect and maintain a bridge over the Bann in perpetuity at his own charge, 2,000 acres more on the other side, otherwise the 2,000 extra acres were to be provided on the Antrim side (this was obviously partly for reasons of defence and partly for those of economics);
5. the measure and account of lands to be according to the last official survey, and estimated in balliboes (a balliboe was theoretically about 60 acres, but actually meant any economic unit of land. The Irish had no concept of measurement, and land was therefore assessed, not by area, but by how many livestock could be fed on it. Clearly a barren mountain could only feed so many animals, but rich lowland pasture of much smaller area could feed the same number of creatures, yet the balliboe figure might be identical for each portion of land. So almost at once there was a great deal of confusion. An English acre is 4,840 square yards, but an Irish acre was 7,840 square yards, and very soon a 'Plantation acre' based on 60 balliboes per acre distorted things even more, so that 2,000 acres could mean, in fact, a much greater area);
6. all the county of Coleraine and the rest of the territory to be colonised by the Londoners to be cleared from all interests, except the inheritances of the bishop and dean of Derry, and certain portions of land to be assigned to three or four Irish gentlemen (at the most) then living and settled in the county. Those Irish gentlemen to become freeholders of the City of London, and were to pay a small rent;
7. woods, grounds, and soil of Glenconkeyne and Killetra, extending from the border of County Coleraine to the River Ballinderry, to be granted to the City of London in perpetuity, the timber from the woods to be used for the purposes of the Plantation, and, expressly, not to be made merchandise;
8. the soil of the woods to be undertaken in a similar manner to that of the county of Coleraine;
9. the City of London to have the patronage (advowsons) of all churches (i.e. ecclesiastical livings) in Derry, Coleraine, and all the lands to be planted;
10. the 7,000 acres laid to the city of Derry and town of Coleraine to be held in fee-farm at a yearly rent of 53s. 4d.;
11. the city of Derry and town of Coleraine to be held of the King in free burgage;
12. the residue of all the county lands and woods and all land to be undertaken to be held of the King in common socage;
13. Customs on all imported and exported goods to be enjoyed by the city for ninety-nine years within the city of Derry, in the town and county of Coleraine,

and in all ports or creeks, with a yearly payment of 6s. 8d. to the King. The Londoners to have similar rights over Portrush;

14. the City of London to hold in perpetuity the salmon and eel fishing in the River Bann from Lough Neagh to its mouth, and in Lough Foyle, and all other kinds of fishing in the 'River of Lough Foyle, so far as the river floweth';
15. the City of London to have the right to transport, export, and dispose of all prohibited wares growing upon its lands;
16. the City of London to hold the office of Admiralty (effectively Vice-Admiralty) of the coasts of Donegal and Coleraine, with all royalties, including the right to all its ships and cargoes lost at sea or shipwrecked between Ballyshannon and Olderfleet, and on all coasts, in ports, and creeks;
17. the City of London to have the rights of fishing and fowling upon all the coasts (including Derry and Coleraine), and the rights to draw nets and pack fish on any part of the coast, and in all the lands to be undertaken (including the River of Lough Foyle and the Bann all the way to Lough Neagh);
18. no flax, hemp, hides or raw yarn to be exported without licences from the City's officers;
19. all the City of London's lands to be freed from all patents of privilege granted to individuals, and from all compositions and taxes which might have been imposed by the governors of those lands;
20. the City to hold the fort at Culmore and its contiguous lands in fee-farm, and maintain troops there;
21. Derry and Coleraine town to have Liberties extending three miles in every direction;
22. municipal privileges (modelled on those of Dublin, London, the Cinque Ports, and Newcastle upon Tyne) to be granted to Derry and Coleraine;
23. all individual interests to be extinguished (except those identified in Article 6) in Derry, Coleraine, and the county, and to become free to the City of London;
24. sufficient forces, maintained at the King's charges, to be maintained for the safety of the settlements;
25. Acts of the English and Irish Parliaments to be passed and given the royal assent to 'settle and secure' the Plantation;
26. the City to have scope to make any reasonable demands of the Crown that could not have been foreseen for a period of seven years;
27. the City of London to commence work on the great undertaking at once, so that 60 houses would be built in Derry and 40 in Coleraine by 1 November 1610, 'with convenient fortifications', the rest of the houses to be built by 1 November 1611.[44]

These Articles of Agreement seem specific in only a few instances, the rest of the document being couched in vague terms. Words such as 'convenient', 'sufficient', and even the mention of land area in balliboes are all very miasmic. According to the 1608 survey, for example, the area of good farming land in the county of Coleraine was 516 balliboes, or 30,990 English acres; in the 1609 'Project of Plantation' the total area of all the land in the county was 547 balliboes, or 34,187 English acres,[45] giving an average of between sixty and sixty-two balliboes per acre. By the time the City obtained

[44] Moody (1939), 78-80; Brewer and Bullen (eds.) (1867-73): *Cal. Carew MSS. 1603-24*, 36-8.
[45] Brewer and Bullen (eds.) (1867-73): *Cal. Carew MSS. 1603-24*, 16.

its charter (of which more later) a balliboe was reckoned to be about fifty-seven acres. According to the early 17th-century papers, the area of the county of Coleraine was 34,187 English acres, but when the Ordnance Survey published its findings regarding the county of Londonderry in 1830-2 the real area was 307,278 acres, which means the earlier settlers must have had a bit of a shock when they found out the scale of the project and the size of their lands. All these anomalies must be explained by the fact that the surveyors made no strenuous efforts to risk their lives in hostile territory by attempting to measure acres. On the contrary, they enquired of local Irish inhabitants how many balliboes there were in any given district, and then multiplied the result by 60.[46] As the balliboe was not a unit of uniform area, as explained above, it could vary enormously in size according to its quality. Furthermore, the Irish, not keen to give anything away to the strangers who were to be agents for the confiscation of their lands, would tell tall stories, lie in their teeth, and give grossly distorted figures, mostly on the small side.

The new survey maps prepared under the aegis of the committee appointed in 1609 arrived in London early in 1610, and *Conditions to be observed by the British Undertakers of the escheated lands in Ulster*, otherwise known as *The Printed Book* or as the *Articles of Plantation* was published.[47] This document was similar to the *Orders and Conditions*, but there were changes, the most important of which were:

- tenure was to be by free and common socage (ordinary tenure without knight-service) of the Castle of Dublin;
- no rents would be payable until September 1614;
- the building of houses, castles, bawns, and forts, and the installation of tenants, were to be completed by Easter 1613;
- land was to be distributed on a more rational basis, allowing for groupings or associations of neighbouring Planters;
- large parcels of land in which there would be several adjoining Proportions were to be allocated to British Undertakers to facilitate their defence;
- the numbers of tenants and types of tenancies on each Proportion were specified.

Successful Undertakers were to take out their letters patent and to receive their grants of Proportions by 24 June 1610, and during April and May lands to be assigned were selected by the Privy Councils of England and Scotland. Servitors and Irish grantees were allocated lands, and Irish natives on the Proportions assigned to British Undertakers were to remove themselves by May 1611. By the autumn of 1610 British Undertakers were arriving in Ulster to start work. All was not well, however, for resentment was rife among the Irish, who were not sufficiently provided for, and, in any case, were expected to leave their ancestral lands, abandoning them to foreigners. Worse was to come, for although Chichester had sent three ships out of Derry with swordsmen bound for Sweden, most of them returned to become the terrible 'wood-kernes', scourges of the settlers, and a constant danger to the Plantation. Furthermore, the Servitors, who were intended to keep the native Irish in order and be a first line of defence in times of trouble, were few on the ground, and often in the wrong place. Even more serious, many British Undertakers, contrary to Bacon's urgings, were not men of substance in any sense, and did not have resources of capital or intellect to carry out their obligations. Some Undertakers disposed of their Proportions, having

[46] Russell and Prendergast (eds.) (1874b): *Cal. S.P.I., 1608-10*, 393.
[47] Printed by Robert Barker (1610). See also *Bulletin of Institute of Historical Research* (1935), **xii**, 178-83.

taken one look at their lands and quailed at the prospect, while others, unable or unwilling to find British tenants, did not evict the Irish, but retained them on their Proportions, often charging them high rents, contrary to the terms of their grants. On their side, the Irish were determined to remain on their lands, often by ingratiating themselves with their landlords and paying exorbitant rents if requested to do so, thus tempting the Undertakers into the paths of greed. There was another problem: the settlers from Britain did not arrive in the required numbers. Reasons are not hard to find. Although Great Britain[48] and Ireland are geographically close, the journeys (especially from England) were long, arduous, and often dangerous. Apart from the problems of a sea that can become very unpleasant very quickly, there were pirates lurking around the coasts, and Ulster itself had not really been pacified. One can imagine the chirpy Londoner or the farmer in Herefordshire not wishing to swap familiar, comforting, cheerful places (such as his local inn) for gloomy, violent, unknown, foreign Ulster, a place with hardly any infrastructure worth the candle.

Origins of The Irish Society

It seems that the Articles of Agreement between the City of London and the Crown were not tablets of stone, but were an outline in general terms. Only a couple of days after the Articles had been concluded they were read before the City's Court of Common Council and duly ratified. The City then determined that, to direct and manage the Plantation, a new body of 26 citizens of London should be set up to consist of a Governor, a Deputy Governor, and 24 Assistants, the Governor and five of the Assistants to be Aldermen, while the Deputy Governor and the remaining Assistants were to be Commoners (i.e. of the Commonalty), and the Recorder of the City was to be one of the Assistants. Each year the Deputy and half of the Assistants were to retire, their places being taken by election at the first Common Council meeting held after the Feast of the Purification of the Blessed Virgin Mary (2 February). Thus each Deputy held office for one year, and each Assistant for two years. This was a very curious arrangement, for it made continuity almost impossible, and half the new body's members had to learn everything from scratch each year. Alderman William Cokayne, who was to be knighted in 1616, was the first Governor **[6]**; another Skinner, William Towerson, was the Deputy Governor; and the Assistants were Sir Henry Montagu (*c.*1563-1642 – Recorder of London from 1603, later [1620] created Baron Montagu of Kimbolton, Viscount Mandeville, and later still [1625] 1st Earl of Manchester), Sir Henry Howe, Sir John Jolles, Sir Thomas Myddelton, Grocer (1550-1631 – later [1613] Lord Mayor **[7]**), Sir William Romney, Haberdasher (d. 1611), Sir John Swynnarton (all Aldermen), William Dyos (the City Remembrancer), two Mercers (one of whom was John Munns), one Grocer, one Draper (John Rowley), one Fishmonger, two Goldsmiths (one was John Broad), two Merchant Taylors, one Haberdasher, one Salter, two Ironmongers, one Vintner, one Clothworker, one Leatherseller, and one Painter-Stainer (Treswell). So the Aldermen and Commoners were all Liverymen.

This new body was authorised to hold courts, to direct operations in Ireland, to administer funds raised for the purposes of the Plantation, to determine all matters

[48] Contrary to fatuous comments in the tabloid 'newspapers' and in the utterances of politicians, 'Great Britain' does not mean an overweening nomenclature for the Nation-State: it is simply the official name of the political unity of England, Scotland, and Wales, used in 1604 after the Union of the Two Crowns, and formally adopted in 1707 with the Union of the Parliaments of England and Scotland. Ireland was never part of Great Britain, nor was Northern Ireland: the inscription on passports makes this clear.

6 Tomb of Sir William Cokayne (*c.*1550-1626), Skinner, first Governor of The Honourable The Irish Society, who was knighted in 1616, and was Lord Mayor of London 1619-20. This splendid monument was destroyed in the Great Fire of 1666, although Cokayne's damaged effigy partly survives, and can be seen in the crypt of Wren's cathedral today. Engraving by Wenceslaus (or Wenzel) Hollar (1607-77) and published in William Dugdale (1658): *The History of St Paul's Cathedral in London* (London: Thomas Warren). (*GLCL/Pr. 460/PAU [1] Record 5926*)

relating to the 'Busyness', and to control the undertaking on behalf of the City. Any decisions by its courts were to have the authority of the Common Council itself, and the courts could make appointments of officers. Meetings were to be held in the Wardrobe in Guildhall at times decided by the Governor or his Deputy, and Cornelius Fish, City Chamberlain, was nominated to receive and disburse the money collected subject to warrants signed by the Governor (or his Deputy) and three Assistants.[49]

In essence this body, in its organisation and functions, was not unlike the governing bodies of early 17th-century joint-stock companies (e.g. the Virginia Company or the East India Company), and its relationship to the Common Council was similar to those of the councils, governing committees, or committees of management to the joint-stock companies, but it must be emphasised that at first the City's Plantation management committee was really a standing committee of the Common Council. It had powers to execute, through its agents in Ireland, policies determined by the Common Council of the City of London (in accordance with Government policy); to administer funds raised by the Common Council; and to collect rents and perform the duties of estate management, but it was, in the beginning, subject to the authority of the Court of Aldermen and the Common Council. Later it developed its own momentum, and although closely connected with the City (there never was any clash of interest as its members were intimately connected with the government of London), became virtually autonomous.

Thus came into being the Society of the Governor and Assistants, London, of the new Plantation in Ulster, within the Realm of Ireland, also referred to as the Governor and Assistants, Governor and Committee, London Company, or London Society.

[49] Moody (1939), 82.

Later, after the Restoration of the Monarchy in 1660, it became known as The Honourable The Irish Society, usually shortened to The Irish Society, and it is by this more convenient nomenclature that it will be referred to hereafter.

7 Sir Thomas Myddelton (1550-1631), Grocer, one of the first members of the Court of Assistants of The Irish Society, who became Lord Mayor of London in 1613. Portrait in oils. (*GACL/1345/Record 11414*)

The Dignity of Baronets

On the King's side there were certain financial obligations to keep troops in Ulster, as well as other matters requiring funds. In order to raise money the King determined to establish a new titled degree, the lowest that is hereditary, ranking below a baron but having precedence over all ranks of knighthood except that of the Garter. The dignity of baronet was instituted in 1611 to raise capital for the settlement and securing of Ulster by means of fees or fines paid for the dignity. Only armigerous families with suitable lands to their name could apply, and the numbers of baronets were to be restricted. It appears that the King perceived the new degree as a chance for the knightly classes to better themselves, for, in return for a large payment, an hereditary baronetcy could be acquired, and the smaller fee payable each time an heir to the fortunes of a family was knighted could be avoided. A baronet is still a commoner, however, because one of the principles of the dignity was to confer rank, precedence, and an hereditary title, but not a peerage. Each new baronet was obliged to maintain 30 soldiers in Ireland for three years, which was quite a demand, and could only be expected of those with adequate resources. The close connection between the dignity and Ulster is made overt by the badge of the baronetage, the Red Hand of Ulster, the bloody hand (or baronet's hand), or hand *Gules* in a field *Argent* (the Arms of Ulster). It was granted by the King to English baronets to be borne on a canton or in an escutcheon on their shields, and is an allusion to the purpose for which the degree was instituted. It is curious that even here English interpretation of things Irish resulted in an heraldic oddity: the O'Neill hand is *Dexter* couped at the wrist, *Affrontée Gules* (full-faced red), while the Red Hand on every baronet's escutcheon is *Sinister* (i.e. the left hand). The Red Hand of Ulster also features in The Irish Society's Arms **[Frontispiece]**.

Raising of Capital

Before much more could be done, money had to be gathered in. Early in 1610 a Precept was issued to 50 Companies requiring payment of the appropriate contributions towards the first £5,000, and the remaining five Companies received their Precepts for two instalments in May. Procedure in each Company was straightforward: the Court of Assistants appointed a committee to decide the amount to be paid by each member according to his circumstances towards the total sum required of each Company by the Common Council. Funds trickled in very slowly, and a second Precept demanding settlement of the first £5,000 was issued in February. This still did not work, and in March the Aldermen ordered that all arrears in respect of the first instalment should be paid at once, and that a second sum of £5,000 should be collected and paid before Lady Day (25 March), at that time the start of a new year under the old Julian calendar. Some coercion was necessary by that time, for the Precept demanding the second £5,000 also gave powers to the Masters and Wardens of individual Companies to have members who failed to pay their dues committed to prison.[50] Although the required payments arrived in time from the Fishmongers', Merchant Taylors', and Vintners' Companies, a large part of the first instalment failed to materialise. In the case of the Clothworkers' Company, the Wardens were summoned to appear before the Lord Mayor and Aldermen in June to answer for the Company's arrears, but even that did not bring results, and two Wardens of the Company languished in gaol for some months before the money materialised.

Thus, at the very start of the venture, it was abundantly clear that, to put it mildly, commitment to the Plantation project was by no means universal in the City of London. Even most of the wealthier Companies showed no great alacrity in paying up, while some of the smaller Companies were in serious difficulties at a very early stage of the project. The Mercers claimed to be in decline, and objected to being assessed for a full twelfth part of the total levy, but after several protests and meetings with the Lord Mayor, no relief was obtained. They then appealed to the Privy Council, which body refused to meddle in the government of the City, apart from recommending that the petition be noted. Repeated attempts to get off the hook were to no avail, and two Wardens of the Company were committed to prison in May, as five days after Lady Day the premier Company had paid neither instalment required of it. Three reluctant Drapers were behind bars in June, while other members were threatened with gaol unless they produced money; all defaulting Grocers were ordered to pay their contributions into the Hall immediately or face imprisonment; the Skinners were so reluctant to contribute that the Renter-Warden was obliged to pay a sixth of the total sum levied and to claim this back from the common stock; the Vintners requested of the Common Council that their contribution should be reduced; and the Ironmongers petitioned the Lord Mayor and Aldermen that the new demands were insupportable, but there was to be no release. The Ironmongers were forced to borrow heavily to make up their share, and the Company was obliged to quadruple the quarterage (the payments made by members of the Company to the common stock of the Guild). It was noted that even this would be insufficient to 'serve to undergo so great a plantation', so Liverymen, widows of Liverymen, and the Yeomanry had to expect further demands. The Goldsmiths' Court of Assistants, mindful of the difficulties of collecting money from individual members, resolved to meet the whole of their share by borrowing money and letting property,[51] and the Barber-Surgeons had to dip into their common stock for part of their levy, and raised the rest by 'fining' members. By July the Court of Aldermen had committed the Wardens of the Salters',

[50] Moody (1939), 84 and *passim.*

[51] Curl (1986), 35; Moody (1939), 87.

Brewers', and Cooks' Companies to be locked up for failure to deliver to the Chamberlain the sums rated.[52]

It soon became apparent that the prisons would be overflowing with Wardens and other respectable Liverymen, while the howls of protest from the Companies had become too loud to be ignored. The City's Common Council accordingly adjusted the levies to reflect the changed or changing fortunes of the Companies. For the next two instalments, totalling £10,000, levies on the Mercers', Goldsmiths', Skinners', Salters', and Ironmongers' Companies were reduced; those on the Grocers', Merchant Taylors', and Haberdashers' Companies were increased; while those on the Drapers', Fishmongers', Vintners', and Clothworkers' Companies remained as they were.

The Londoners, it was now clear, had little faith and less enthusiasm for committing precious resources to a distant, alien, hostile, unstable, unknown, tiresome, Gaelic land. Just as mention of Northern Ireland or 'Ulster' brings a glazed look onto the eyes of the bored and uncomprehending Englishman, so, in the 17th century, the Londoners had a distinct and uneasy feeling that the 'Busyness' would prove more than 'chargeable', but rather a never-ending drain on resources, and would be extremely difficult to manage. They were not to know that the official Government estimate of 34,187 English acres (based on suspect 'surveys') of the county of Coleraine to be planted was actually 307,278 acres,[53] but they were very aware of the small matter that a large part of the country probably belonged to someone else, for Sir Donnell Ballagh O'Cahan had never been brought to trial, and had been incarcerated, first in Dublin, and then in the Tower of London, from which he petitioned and complained of the illegality of the proceedings, and issued reminders that he had served on the English side during the last phase of the Nine Years' War. This did not increase the City of London's confidence in the whole murky affair.

Changes in the Articles

In the summer of 1610 the first major changes were made to the Articles of Agreement drawn up earlier. These alterations were the result of discussions between the Governor of The Irish Society and the Privy Council, for problems had arisen requiring resolution: these concerned Sir Thomas Phillips, Church lands, advowsons, and the fisheries. In due course it was agreed that:

1. the City would surrender to Phillips 2,000 acres of land in Killetra contiguous to the castle of Toome;
2. the advowsons in the area to be planted should be shared between the City and the bishops in a ratio of nine to six respectively; and
3. the termon lands (from the Irish *termonn*, or *tearmann* [meaning Church-territory or liberties, privilege, sanctuary, or protection], applied to land belonging to, or forming the precinct or liberties of a religious house, which was free and exempt from all secular charges or imposts) should be handed over entirely to the Anglican bishops of the sees in which the Londoners' estates lay.

(In fact, these termon lands had already been assigned to the bishops before the City's contract with the Crown, which was an ominous foretaste of endless disputes and problems that were to bedevil the Londoners' Plantation. It is clear that communications were very poor, and often one lot of people had no idea what other groups had agreed or were doing).

52 Curl (1986), 35; Moody (1939), 87.
53 Moody (1939), 451.

Another demand that the bishop of Derry should have a share of the fishing of Lough Foyle as well as of the tithe-corn and hay of the parish of Derry was successfully resisted by the City's Common Council, but the Londoners were rattled, and began to worry about what other surprises were in store or what had already been determined about which they had been kept in the dark. So, with several advowsons lost to them, a hefty chunk of Loughinsholin appropriated for Phillips's use, and the termon lands already assigned, a certain amount of disquiet began to be apparent.

When the original Articles had been signed, the question of compensating Phillips for his estates at Coleraine had not been resolved. Very soon the *modified* Articles had to be altered. It was decided in 1611 to grant Phillips O'Cahan's former castle at Limavady together with 3,000 contiguous acres, and the grant of lands to him at Toome was reduced to 500 acres adjoining the fortress. In return Phillips surrendered his lands east of the River Bann, his market rights at Coleraine, his ferries, his estate at Derry, and his patent to distil whiskey in the county of Coleraine and in the Route. However, his new properties were not conveyed to him until 1612, a delay which seems to have soured his relations with the Londoners.

Thus two parcels of land were removed from the City's estates to accommodate Phillips, and there were many other parts that had to be detached from the areas to be owned and settled by the Londoners: these were, for example, the very considerable Church lands that were scattered throughout the county of Coleraine and the barony of Loughinsholin, and there were the lands of the 'native freeholders' dispersed through the three baronies of County Coleraine, which accounted for a fair acreage. Native Irish would also be settled or permitted to remain on Church and glebe lands, and on Phillips's estate, so about a third of the total area was available for settlement by the Irish who would be scattered in pockets throughout the region. In theory, this was to ensure they would be surrounded by colonists, kept in order, and discouraged from rebellion, but, as we shall see, the theory did not work out in fact.

The Londoners had further worries. The letters patent embodying the City's grant had not yet been procured, and it was to be some time before anything like a legal basis was drawn up, which was no way to encourage reluctant Planters. In spite of shaky title, The Irish Society began to let the fisheries in the early part of 1611. Shortly afterwards there was a further momentous shift when the Common Council approached the Livery Companies to see if they would be prepared to take on parts of the territory and colonise these at their own expense, the lands to be allocated according to the funds paid. The Companies would still share in any profits from fisheries, rents, and other sources. When it was clarified that the Companies would be required to pay into the joint stock of the Plantation whether or not they accepted land, eight great and 10 inferior Companies agreed to become landowners.

By this time many individual members, terrified by the apparently endless calls on their purses, surrendered their interests to their Companies on condition that no further contributions towards the Ulster Plantation would be required of them. As for the Companies, it became more and more obvious that the £20,000 common stock was wholly insufficient, and that more Precepts, levies, final demands, threats, and incarceration were inevitable and likely to go on for a long time. Some Companies attempted to extricate themselves. The desperate Haberdashers were willing to surrender their £1,124 already paid together with all their interest in the Plantation to anyone willing to pay the fourth instalment of the first £20,000 and to be responsible for all future charges which the Company might normally have to pay. Two Haberdashers,

William Freeman and Adrian Moore, took over the Company's interests. The Court of Aldermen assessed the much decayed Bowyers and Fletchers, who were exempted from all future payments, doubtless to their great relief.

By the summer of 1611 the original £20,000-worth of capital had almost been expended, so the Common Council determined to call for £10,000 more in two Precepts of July 1611 and July 1612. As this was an increase of half as much again of sums in the original Articles of Agreement, the Companies were given the option of ceasing payments but forfeiting their investments. Surprisingly, only two Companies (the Brownbakers and Coopers) backed out, thus losing their contributions. Collection of the new levies proved as difficult as ever, so gradually Company members were permitted to withdraw from being compulsorily levied provided they surrendered their Plantation interests to the Company as a body. Participation by Companies was by dipping into the common stock, and in some cases members' interests were bought out by the Companies. By 1613 the Mercers, Grocers, Fishmongers, Goldsmiths, and Ironmongers (of the Twelve Great Companies) were contributing as Companies, while the Drapers, Merchant Taylors, and Vintners were gradually obtaining the shares of members who no longer wished to subscribe. In some inferior Companies the process of individual levies on members seems to have failed quite early in the history of the Plantation.

Some of the reluctance to part with money at all, let alone more and more money, must have been because the Crown had not formalised the titles to the lands. The reasons for this are probably not ascertainable now, but may have been something to do with uncertainties about entitlement or about the abilities of the City of London to sustain the impetus. They may also have been affected by the attitudes of Chichester and Phillips (whose initial enthusiasm for the Londoners' intervention had evaporated). The main problems centred on the acquisition of private interests from 1610, but the lack of proper title, shortage of money, and reluctance of individuals to part with their lands at all made progress slow and uncertain. Sir Toby Caulfeild, for example, who held estates at Kilrea and Agivey before 1607, and whose lands had never been forfeited to the Crown, resisted all attempts to hand his properties over, and with good reason. Nevertheless, Caulfeild and other interested parties eventually were persuaded to dispose of their lands, and by 1613 the whole of the county of Coleraine with other lands was in the hands of the City of London (apart from Church lands, Phillips's properties, glebe lands, and the estates of the native freeholders [but even those lands were held of the City in fee-farm]). Relations between the City and the Crown were under strain by 1612. The Irish Society listed the main problems:

- the refusal of landowners to surrender their interests;
- doubts about rights of title in Loughinsholin and elsewhere;
- difficulties of collecting rents;
- the retention of certain fishing rights by individuals;
- the rights to brew beer and distil whiskey still being exercised by individuals even though the Articles of Agreement had extinguished those rights; and
- the inclusion (contrary to undertakings given) of high, infertile, and boggy ground in the lands 'laid' to the main settlements.

Furthermore, The Irish Society was reluctant to evict Irish tenants until the Plantation was further advanced in order to avoid a complete collapse of the rural economy. However, it seems that The Society was very slow in settling British colonists, and that the agents of The Society were encouraging Irishmen to come into Loughinsholin as labourers. Chichester was anxious that the Irish should not entertain any false hopes of remaining, and demanded that better progress should be made. For its part, The Irish Society complained that £25,000 had been expended as well as any rents that had been collected – sums far in excess of those agreed with the Crown – and yet had no title to the lands.[54]

Meetings were then held between the Privy Council and the City, and various problems were discussed. The City obtained agreement to most of its demands, including that the natives could stay on the land until the spring of 1615, but Chichester was worried, mostly about security, for the Londoners' Plantation, far from being a strong and well-defended area, was very weak, especially in the southern, mountainous and well-wooded areas. Accordingly, a fort was built on Church lands at Desertmartin, defended by Government troops.

The Charter of Londonderry

Then, at last, a charter was prepared which passed the Great Seal of England in March 1613, and contained four main sections:

1. a new county to be called County Londonderry was to be formed, and was to consist of County Coleraine to which parts of Counties Antrim, Donegal, and Tyrone would be added, and would include the lands granted to the City of London as well as Church lands, Phillips's lands, and the estates of Irish freeholders.

   That part of County Antrim (some 17,997 acres) that was detached and incorporated within County Londonderry lies north-eastwards across the River Bann, and extended round the coast to include Portstewart: it was to provide the hinterland of Coleraine, which was to be developed on the eastern bank of the river, and was obtained from Sir Randal MacDonnell (d. 1636), who had made a timely submission to Mountjoy in 1602 during the Nine Years' War, and had been rewarded with extensive lands in County Antrim. His compliance with the Plantation scheme led to his being created Viscount Dunluce (1618) and Earl of Antrim (1620).

   That part of County Donegal (some 12,615 acres) that was to be included within the new county lay north-westwards across the Foyle and included the city of Derry with a large piece of territory stretching from Muff in the north to about two miles north of St Johnstown on the Foyle, and at its widest point extended about three miles north-west of Derry.

   From County Tyrone the barony of Loughinsholin (about 170,852 acres) was detached and added to County Coleraine, so that the new County Londonderry extended southwards as far as the River Ballinderry, and, excluding the Rivers Bann and Foyle, and Loughs Beg and Neagh, contained 508,742 acres, a huge increase on the 34,187 English acres originally envisaged in the *Project*;[55]
2. Derry became Londonderry, to emphasise the connection with London, and was constituted a corporation to be called the 'Mayor and Commonalty and Citizens of the City of Londonderry', with a Mayor, two Sheriffs, a Chamberlain, 12 Aldermen, and 24 Chief Burgesses forming collectively the Common Council,

[54] Chart (ed.) (1928), 39-40.
[55] Moody (1939), *passim.*

although The Irish Society had to approve, and had powers of veto or amendment over, any laws or regulations made that could affect the infant city. In general, the government of Londonderry was to be modelled on that of London, and a Recorder (who had to be English-born), well-versed in the laws of England and Ireland, was to be appointed during the pleasure of The Irish Society. All civic officers and officials were to take the Oath of Allegiance before the Mayor, and any failure to administer oaths would be punishable by The Irish Society. No art, 'Mistery', or manual occupation was to be practised in the city by those who were not Freemen, and citizens practising any art or mistery were to be organised into Guilds or Fraternities for the encouragement and regulation of the trades. The city was declared a seaport and the only place for unloading ships from Loughs Foyle and Swilly, and there were many other matters relating to Customs, laws, wharfages, tolls, etc.[56] Two Burgesses were to represent the city in the Dublin Parliament. Under the Plantation these Burgesses, exclusively British and Protestant, were to represent the towns, thus helping to secure Ulster. There were several curious features about the government of the city of Londonderry, though: its Common Council was subordinate to The Irish Society; it had considerable powers over the county, especially in law-enforcement; and the city and county were more closely interconnected than was the case with London and Middlesex.[57] Thus The Irish Society had enormous powers over a vast area, and none of its land was conveyed to the new corporation as it was part of the grant to The Society. The first persons to hold office in Londonderry were selected by The Irish Society: John Rowley, Draper, one of the City of London's four-man Deputation to view the lands, and The Society's Agent in Ulster, was first Mayor of Londonderry and also an Alderman; Robert Goodwin, Draper, was the Town-Clerk and Chamberlain; George Carey was the Recorder; William Gage, Rowley's brother-in-law, who had supervised the first parties of tradesmen to arrive from England, was an Alderman; while others were usually members of London Livery Companies, had close connections with London, or were pre-Plantation British inhabitants of Derry whose interests had been bought out;[58]

3. The Irish Society was legally incorporated and given authority to regulate every aspect of government in the city of Londonderry.[59] It had thus graduated from being really a standing committee of the Court of Common Council, and, as a result of the 1613 charter, became a corporate body, with an independent existence, endowed with all powers and functions once assigned to it by the Common Council. Furthermore, it was now the legal owner of all the property mentioned in the Articles of Agreement with powers to convey property, and had control over the city of Londonderry, the town of Coleraine, and the county lands. Thus The Irish Society's financial and political powers were similar to those held by the governing bodies of other contemporary joint-stock companies such as the Virginia Company;[60]
4. the Crown granted to The Irish Society the city of Londonderry with 4,000 acres adjoining it on the west bank of the Foyle (excluding bogs and barren

[56] Reed (1865), *passim.*
[57] Moody (1939), 130.
[58] *Ibid.*, 131-2.
[59] Reed (1865), *passim.*
[60] Russell and Prendergast (eds.) (1874b): *Cal. S.P.I., 1608-10*, 378-9, 487-8.

> mountain); the former 'Abby' of Coleraine, its lands, and the town of Coleraine with 3,000 acres on the east bank of the River Bann; the fortress of Culmore and 300 acres; all the lands in the baronies of Anagh, Keenaught, Coleraine, and Loughinsholin, excluding the lands of the bishop and dean of Derry, those of the archbishop of Armagh, and those of Sir Thomas Phillips; the rents, fealties, and duties reserved to the Crown in Phillips's grant of 1612; rights to erect manors, provided each included at least 1,000 acres, with rights to hold courts in the manors; all the River Bann from the sea to Lough Neagh; all the lough and river of the Foyle from the sea to Lifford, together with all the fishings, except those belonging to the bishop and dean of Derry; all rights to establish and charge for ferries; the advowsons of all churches, vicarages, and chapels in Derry and Coleraine, and of thirteen churches and rectories in the county; all Customs, subsidies, tonnage, poundage, etc., arising within the city and county, the town of Coleraine, the port of Portrush, and in Lough Swilly, the Foyle, and the Bann, for ninety-nine years;[61] the office of Admiral and what pertained to it in Donegal, and round the coast to Olderfleet (Larne); all wrecks at sea between Ballyshannon and Olderfleet, of all ships belonging to The Society and to the inhabitants of the city of Londonderry; the right to export all goods produced in County Londonderry even if such exports were normally prohibited by Irish law; and exemption from all royal exactions in respect of the lands granted, except for rents and services reserved by the charter.[62]

In addition, the Crown promised not to make any other grants within The Society's territories, undertook to provide troops for an indefinite period to protect the Plantation, and agreed to consent to any enactment of the Parliaments of England and Ireland to confirm the grant.[63] On its side, The Society was required to pay annual rents to the King: £2 13s. 4d. for the city, the town, and the 7,000 acres 'laid' to them; £201 6s. od. for the county lands; and 13s. 4d. for the Customs. So only just over £200 was to be paid into the Exchequer of Ireland each year, which looked like a bargain.

However, The Society was required to convey to the bishop and dean of Derry, within one year, four acres within the city of Londonderry contiguous to the ruined tower of St Columcille; to keep an armed garrison at Culmore Fort; to convey 60 in every 1,000 acres to the incumbents of all the churches in the county as rent-free glebes; to cut and use the timber in Loughinsholin for building purposes only; and to commission an accurate survey of the barony of Loughinsholin.[64]

It is curious that in the grant those sections of the Articles of Agreement dealing with the Irish freeholders, the fortifications, and the buildings were left out, so The Irish Society was not legally bound by the charter to abide by important and essential stipulations of the original Plantation documents, although grants to Undertakers in the other escheated lands specifically stated that land alienated to the Irish would be subject to forfeiture. Thus the City of London, required to colonise one of the most important (from the strategic view) parts of the Plantation, was left with many loopholes, grey areas, and fuzzy edges in what should have been a much tighter and unambiguous set of agreements. There were no real incentives *not* to lease land to

[61] Reed (1865), 88-90, and *passim*. *Admiralty rights* meant The Society could appoint a Deputy Vice-Admiral to the office.

[62] *Ibid.*, 92-7 and *passim*.

[63] *Ibid.*, 95-7.

[64] *Ibid.*, 83-6, 134-5.

Irish natives, and the Londoners do not appear to have been obliged legally to carry out aspects of Plantation policy that were enforced elsewhere.

In the case of Coleraine, it was incorporated in 1613, and was to have jurisdiction extending within a radius of three Irish miles from the town-centre. It had a constitution similar to that of Londonderry, but there were no Sheriffs, no Chief Burgesses (only Burgesses), and the government of the town was quite distinct from that of the county. The Town-Clerk was Clerk of the Court and Clerk of the Peace,[65] a market was to be held three days per week, and the town was constituted a port and the sole place for the unloading of ships entering the Bann. As was the case with Londonderry, byelaws were subject to the approval of The Irish Society, as was the election of civic dignitaries. The Corporation could send two Burgesses to Parliament, and could facilitate the creation of Guilds, Fraternities, or Misteries. The first dignitaries of Coleraine were closely connected with the City of London and its institutions: Tristram Beresford (b. 1574), Alderman, was Mayor, and Rowley's second-in-command as Agent to The Irish Society; Thomas Raven (*c.*1572 -1640), Alderman, was the City's surveyor in Ireland; and Elias Jermyn (or Jarman), who supervised building-works at Coleraine, was a master-carpenter of the City of London.[66] The governing bodies of Londonderry and Coleraine each included men closely involved in the City of London, but, in the case of Coleraine especially, prominent Servitors and other holders of land in the vicinity were involved in local government. Sir Randal MacDonnell, for example, was an Alderman, as were Sir Edward Dod(d)ington, who had fortified Dungiven, and Sir Francis Cooke, constable of the fort at Desertmartin.

The County of Londonderry and The Irish Society in 1613

So, in 1613, the new county of Londonderry had been created, and The Irish Society had not only been given legal incorporation, but enormous powers and considerable landholdings as well. But there were snags, primarily connected with title. This problem appears to have had its origins when O'Cahan petitioned the Government in Ireland against the operation of Tyrone's patent of 1603. As was discussed earlier, O'Cahan had been promised (by Docwra, and, apparently, by Chichester) the removal of Tyrone's overlordship of his (O'Cahan's) lands, and in the articles drawn up (1602) between Docwra and O'Cahan the Bann fisheries were expressly reserved for the Crown, together with other fisheries. However, all this was over-ridden by Mountjoy's refusal to amend the Treaty of Mellifont (1603) which restored Tyrone to his power, titles, and lands. O'Cahan therefore found himself once more under Tyrone. Docwra had tried (1604) to get rights granted to Tyrone's tenants, but to no avail. By 1606, therefore, O'Cahan felt betrayed and embittered. Tyrone claimed the Bann fisheries as his rightful property, which was a contributory factor in the *débâcle* that led to the dispute which prompted the incarceration of O'Cahan and the Flight of the Earls.[67] It would appear that Tyrone, in 1604, had granted Phillips, among other lands, woods, and rights, certain control over the Bann fisheries, but also that James Hamilton had obtained a patent from the King (i.e. Chichester) granting him rights over the fisheries of the Bann from Lough Neagh to the Salmon Leap and from the Salmon Leap to the sea. Hamilton granted some of these rights to Phillips in 1606, and Phillips, in an indenture

65 Reed (1865), 174-5.
66 Moody (1939), 140.
67 Russell and Prendergast (eds.) (1874a): *Cal. S.P.I., 1606-8*, 65.

between him and the King (1610), surrendered his rights. Hamilton surrendered his interests in the Bann from the Salmon Leap to the sea together with the 'ground and soil covered with water between the banks of the said river'.[68]

The Bann fisheries were the 'pearl of the adventure',[69] and the main enticement to induce the City of London to get involved in the Plantation. The King, through his Council and ministers, undertook to buy out interests and bestow rights on the Londoners, but, as with many undertakings given by the foxy James I and VI, this did not actually happen. While the Londoners were promised, in the various articles and contracts, fishing rights to the salmon and eel in the Bann from Lough Neagh to the sea, and the fisheries of the Foyle (as described above), the City ended up having to pay to buy out other interests,[70] including those of Hamilton 'in full satisfaction and discharge of all his rights and interests in and to the fishings in the rivers of Band [*sic*] and Laighfoyle'.[71] In other words, the King only paid part of the purchase price, the Londoners having to pick up the tab for the rest. However, the tangle was by no means sorted out, for other parties also had interests, and these proved to be a thorn in the corporate flesh of The Irish Society for many years to come.

Thus began the long sagas of deceit, chicanery, and betrayal of trust, to be exacerbated later by contradictory grants being dished out by the Crown in complete disregard of the obligations and signed agreements with the City of London, that were to haunt The Irish Society for centuries thereafter, and occasioned enormous expenses for litigation in endless disputes. It seemed, in 1613, that the legal bases had been fully established, but the City of London was to be the butt of animosities from all quarters thereafter. In the firing-line was The Irish Society, and it would not only have to struggle to maintain its rights granted by the Crown, but would also have to fight the Livery Companies themselves.

At least half the problems were caused by the vague terms upon which the City of London was induced to take part in the Plantation of Ulster, but the rest of the difficulties can be ascribed to greed, falsehoods, and the behaviour of the Crown and its agents. Given that the entire undertaking was of State importance, the Crown was to behave in an irresponsible and incredibly devious manner, while individuals, interested only in the main chance of personal aggrandisement, put considerations of State low on their lists of priorities. Furthermore, The Irish Society, with its built-in weakness of lack of continuity of membership, often lost sight of what had been agreed, and was treated as a kicking-boy by all and sundry.

So The Irish Society, given the task of securing its lands for the successful Plantation of Ulster, had an almost impossible task. The Irish, vengeful, resentful, embittered, and hostile, awaited their chance to undo the Plantation, but were only part of the problem. Nevertheless, the City, The Irish Society, and the Livery Companies were set on a course from which there would be no return journey.[72]

[68] Moody and Simms (eds.) (1968) 43, and *passim*.

[69] Healy (1913), 2.

[70] Moody and Simms (eds.) (1968), 52-3.

[71] *Ibid.*

[72] This chapter derives from a great wealth of material. Bagwell (1909), Beckett (1966), Butler (1918), Davies (1787), Erck (ed.) (1846, 1852), MacNevin (1846), Moody (1939), and Moody and Simms (eds.) (1968 and 1983) provided many insights, while Brewer and Bullen (eds.) (1867-73) and Russell and Prendergast (eds.) (1872-80), give useful background information. See also Chart (ed.) (1928), Curl (1986), Hill (1877, 1889), Irish Society (*c.*1898), Maxwell (1923, 1954), Reed (1865), and Schultes (1822). *Analecta Hibernica*, 3 (1931) and 8 (1938), are also essential reading. For the Livery Companies see especially Doolittle (1982), Hazlitt (1892), Heath (1869), Herbert (1834-7), Johnson (1914-22), and Leigh and Taylor (eds.) (1997).

CHAPTER III

The New County of Londonderry and the Beginnings of the Plantation of The City of London

> At this Court the Precept ... for the Irish Plantation was read. This Court thereupon have referred themselves unto the Committees by them formerly appointed for this Business authorising them to make answer for this Company ... as followeth. That in all humility they return thanks to His Majesty in gracious remembrance of them in the offer of the same Precept. But forasmuch as they are ... men that live by merchandise and therefore are inexperienced in managing a Business of this nature and withal want means and ability for the accomplishment thereof this Company are not willing to have a hand or intermeddle in the same
>
> Minute of The Court of Assistants of The Mercers' Company giving an answer to the Lord Mayor's Precept of 1 July 1609 on 11 July, quoted in IRISH SOCIETY (*c.*1898), 60

General Description of County Londonderry

The new county created specifically for colonisation by the City of London consisted of the recently shired county of Coleraine (formerly O'Cahan's 'Country' – the territory to the north of the Sperrin Mountains bounded by the sea and the Rivers Foyle and Bann); the heavily wooded barony of Loughinsholin (formerly one of the five baronies[1] of County Tyrone, detached and added to County Londonderry) that lay south-east of O'Cahan's 'Country'; the settlement of Derry and its hinterlands lying to the north-west of the River Foyle in County Donegal; and Phillips's town of Coleraine together with its immediate surrounding lands situated on the north-eastern side of the River Bann in County Antrim. Thus Derry (Londonderry) acquired several townlands[2] in County Donegal, and Coleraine had various townlands in County Antrim 'laid' to it. County Londonderry therefore consisted of four baronies (those of Anagh, Keenaught [later Limavady], Coleraine, and Loughinsholin [the last formerly in County Tyrone]) plus various townlands in Counties Donegal and Antrim to provide the Liberties[3] of Londonderry and Coleraine.

The southern boundary of the new county coincides with the River Ballinderry for some five miles from Lough Neagh, then meanders north-west along the highest

[1] Territorial division of a county, composed of several townlands. Historically, there were 273 baronies in Ireland that served as bases for administrative and taxation purposes until the early 20th century. An Irish barony was an approximate equivalent of an Anglo-Saxon hundred (a subdivision of a county or shire, having its own court, and historically supposed to be capable of supplying 100 warriors).

[2] A townland is a division of land of varying extent (from one to over 7,000 acres), and was the smallest administrative division, not necessarily associated with or containing an urban settlement. Historically there were over 60,000 townlands in Ireland.

[3] A Liberty is a district, extending beyond the bounds of a city or town, subject to the control of the municipal authority.

points of the Sperrins (including the peaks of Oughtmore, Meenard, Sawel, and Learmount), before continuing through lower rolling landscapes towards the Foyle Valley south-west of Londonderry. West of the Foyle, the boundary follows a gently curving form starting some four miles upstream from Londonderry, and ends by the bank of Lough Foyle about a mile north of Culmore. To the north the county is bounded by the shores of Lough Foyle and the open sea almost as far east as Portrush in County Antrim, then sweeps south in a curve to the River Bann about four miles upstream from Coleraine. The eastern extremities of the county south of this coincide with the River Bann and the western shores of Lough Neagh.

The rocky, bleak heights of the Sperrins thus dominate part of the south of the county, and the lower slopes contain peat-bogs. Further down, towards the gentler landscapes between the mountains and Lough Foyle, the country is lush and rolling, with several fertile valleys and one peak (Loughermore). The Sperrins are drained to the north by the River Faughan, its tributaries (including the Burntollet that flows from the high lands of Loughermore), and the River Roe with its tributaries (the Owenbeg, Owenreagh, and Gelvin, among others). Thus the Rivers Foyle, Faughan, and Roe all flow into Lough Foyle which is sheltered from the Atlantic by the long, hilly peninsula of Inishowen in County Donegal. Where the Foyle joins its lough a triangular spur of land (Culmore Point) projects from the western bank, commanding the narrows and therefore providing an ideal spot from which to protect the new settlement of Londonderry some four miles upstream. The 'Hill of Derry' on which Londonderry was to be built is partly encircled by a bend of the river, and commands vistas in several directions: south-west upstream towards Lifford; north-west to the Inishowen peninsula; north-east towards the lough; south-east into the Faughan Valley; and eastwards to the lowlands stretching towards Limavady. Between the Rivers Faughan and Roe, on the southern shores of Lough Foyle, is a very wide and fertile band of lowlands, and in the Roe Valley itself is a particularly rich belt of farmland (with its northernmost extremity at Magilligan Point) bounded to the east by a range of basalt hills stretching from the Sperrins in the south to the north coast and including the peaks of Carntogher, Benbradagh, Craiggore, Keady, and the majestic Binevenagh above Magilligan. This range is drained to the east by the Rivers Macosquin, Aghadowey, Agivey, and Articlave into the Lower Bann Valley, and the main massif of the Sperrins is drained into Lough Neagh by the Rivers Moyola and Ballinderry. Between the Rivers Agivey and Moyola the lowlands of Loughinsholin are drained by the River Cla(u)dy into the Bann, and the impressive peak of Slieve Gallion rises above the lowlands between the Moyola and Ballinderry rivers.

Coleraine, like Londonderry, is sited on a river-bank, and in its vicinity is rich, fertile land. Unlike the Foyle, the Bann is relatively narrow and shallow below Coleraine, and has a bar at its estuary that has long posed a hazard to shipping, especially in the days of sail. The currents and eddies at the river-mouth can be extremely powerful. Some two miles upstream from the town is a massive rock-formation the full width of the river (the Salmon Leap) where the river-level drops about two metres (over six feet).

The river-valley of the Lower Bann contains remnants of woodlands, and around Castle Roe and Camus it is possible to obtain a flavour of what the landscape must once have been like. The northern boundary of the barony of Loughinsholin stretched from the Bann south of Movanagher as far as Meenard, and a very large part of the lowlands bounded by the Sperrins, the Bann, and the Ballinderry was covered with extensive woodlands (as large as the New Forest in Hampshire) in the 17th century. Indeed, Loughinsholin contained some of the best timber in Ireland, especially in Glenconkeyne and Killetra, but at the foot of Slieve Gallion was also iron ore, which required vast amounts of timber for smelting. These huge woodlands were the fastnesses into which the Irish wood-kernes melted away, only to re-emerge and endanger the Plantation. Thus the natural resources of the forests were systematically plundered, not just for building purposes (a legitimate use), but for making iron, for shipbuilding, for pipe-staves,[4] for profit, and for security. Removal of the protective forests that were home to Irish guerrillas had a safety dimension as well as offering handsome profits to despoilers.[5] **[8-10]**

Tentative Beginnings of the Londoners' Plantation

The first Englishmen who inspected the lands to be settled by the City of London were impressed by the possibilities of a 'rich and fruitful' area[6] capable of sustaining the numerous garrons (small Irish horses), sheep, goats, pigs, and cattle found there as well as crops of barley, flax, oats, and rye. Land near Coleraine, especially in the Route, was excellent for growing corn, so brewing and distilling were carried on in the vicinity. Game, such as deer and rabbits, was plentiful, while edible birds abounded. Fish were found in most of the rivers, and the salmon-fisheries of the Foyle and Bann were celebrated. In 1635, for example, the waters of the Bann gave up 62 tons of salmon in one day alone,[7] while their eel-fisheries were among the richest in Europe. William Laud (1573-1645), Archbishop of Canterbury (from 1633), no less, considered the eels from Ulster to be the 'fattest and fairest' known to him.[8] Around the coasts the sea teemed with fish, drawing fishermen from as far afield as Brittany and Flanders, especially as the native Irish had little interest in sea-fishing.

For the Londoners, faced with a considerable amount of building-works of all kinds, the territories offered timber in plenty (especially ash, elm, and oak), but there were also supplies of limestone and sea-shells (for preparing lime), sand (for mortar and plaster), clay (for making tiles and bricks), and hard stone (for rubble walls). Freestone occurred in the Dungiven area, although it did not compare in quality with good English stone. Not only were the hardwoods suitable for timber-framed buildings, but could provide shingles for roofing. Slate (of poor quality) occurred in the west of the new county, while wood and peat provided fuel.[9] Examination of 17th-century records shows that (unsurprisingly) the Londoners built timber-framed houses roofed with shingles in areas where the woods were plentiful (e.g. Bannside and Loughinsholin), but in the west they built mostly of stone, although small numbers of timber-framed buildings occurred in places such as Ballykelly (Fishmongers' estate) and Eglinton (Grocers' estate), where they stood in contrast to the rubble-built and rendered houses that formed the majority of buildings. It appears that in some instances timber-framed buildings were made in Coleraine from timbers floated down the Bann from Loughinsholin, and then shipped to the west of the county.[10]

4 Boards or staves used to make pipes or casks.

5 Sampson (1802), Ch. I; Sampson (1814), 17, 242; Schultes (1822), clxxviii and *passim*.

6 Russell and Prendergast (eds.) (1874a and b): *Cal. S.P.I., 1606-8*, 19, 216, and *1608-10*, 280.

7 Moody (1939), 44.

8 In a letter to Wentworth, 28 August 1637.

9 Russell and Prendergast (eds.) (1874b): *Cal. S.P.I., 1608-10*, 207-10; Brewer and Bullen (eds.) (1867-73): *Cal. Carew MSS., passim.*

10 Robinson and Brannon (1981-2), *passim*; Robinson (1984, 1994), *passim*.

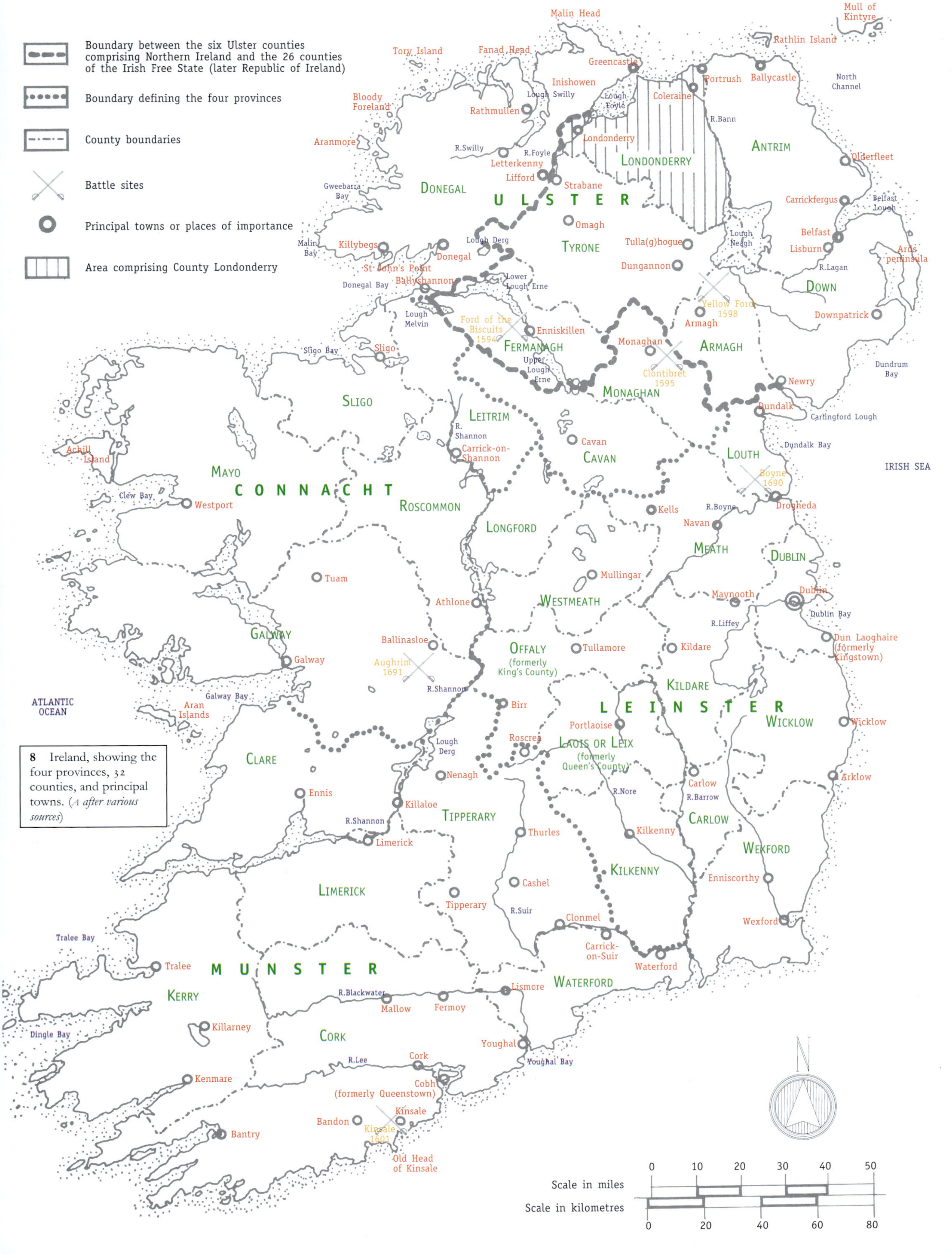

8 Ireland, showing the four provinces, 32 counties, and principal towns. (*A after various sources*)

9 The Jacobean Plantation of Ulster *c.*1610.
(*A after various sources*)

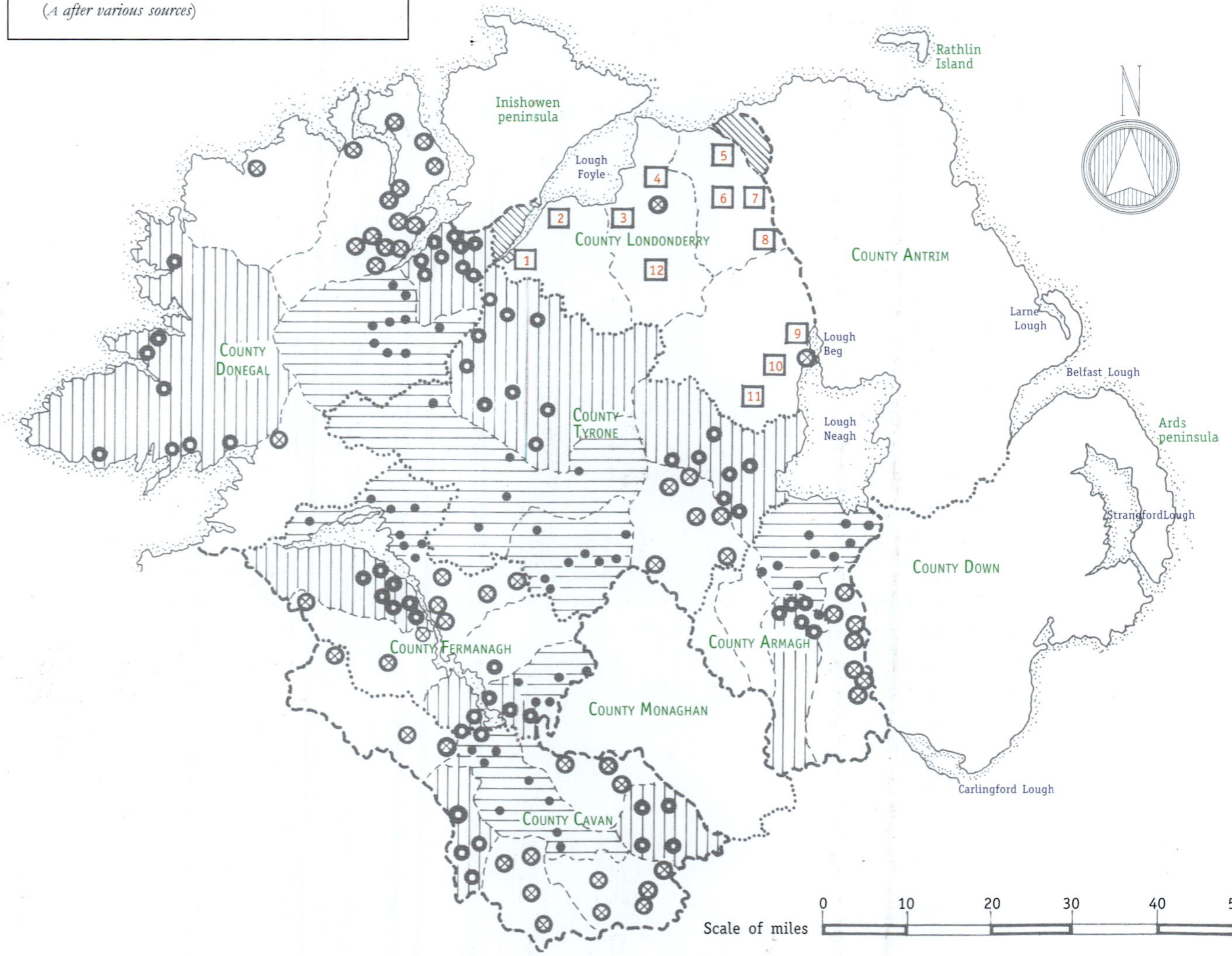

- Main settlements of the London Livery Companies
- Estates of The Honourable The Irish Society
- Boundary of the official scheme for the Plantation of Ulster in *c.*1610
- County boundaries
- Boundaries of baronies
- Expanses of water
- Baronies granted to Scots Undertakers
- Baronies granted to English Undertakers
- Estates of English Servitors
- Main centres of Scots Undertakers' estates
- Main centres of English Undertakers' estates

Note: the number within each square denoting a London Livery Company Proportion refers to the Lot number and approximate position of each main settlement

1 Goldsmiths' Company (New Buildings)
2 Grocers' Company (Muff, later Eglinton)
3 Fishmongers' Company (Ballykelly or Walworth)
4 Haberdashers' Company (Ballycastle and Artikelly)
5 Clothworkers' Company (Killowen and Articlave)
6 Merchant Taylors' Company (Macosquin)
7 Ironmongers' Company (Agivey)
8 Mercers' Company (Movanagher — later abandoned for the hilltop settlement of Kilrea)
9 Vintners' Company (Bellaghy or Vintnerstown)
10 Salters' Company (Magherafelt and Salterstown)
11 Drapers' Company (Moneymore)
12 Skinners' Company (Dungiven)

The two English Servitors' estates in County Londonderry are those of Sir Thomas Phillips at Limavady and Moyola, opposite Toome

While County Londonderry certainly had attractions and possibilities for settlers, there were many disadvantages. Travel to that part of Ireland was not easy or without dangers, for the sea was by no means safe: apart from storms and piracy (mentioned above), making landfall at Coleraine could be very difficult as navigation into the Bann from the sea was notoriously tricky (which explains why the Londoners were anxious to use Portrush as a harbour). Travel within the new county could also be dangerous, for although the route between east and west was protected by fortified centres to some extent, other parts (notably the woodlands and the high lands to the south) were inhabited by disaffected Irish (notably the wood-kernes), and lawlessness was rife. The region was not easy to reach from Dublin either, for the former O'Neill fastnesses of Tyrone lay in the way. As far as appearances are concerned, much of the new county would have presented an uninviting impression to the Londoners, for the Irish had no tradition of urban living, and any settlements there were consisted of an untidy number of single-storey windowless 'cabins' on a roughly elliptical plan roofed with turf. Even ecclesiastical buildings were very small and undistinguished compared with the architectural riches of England, while castles were little more than fortified tower-houses of small aesthetic importance. Irish agriculture was extremely primitive, so even the countryside looked wild and unkempt. Land was not enclosed, and ploughing was done by the inefficient (and cruel) method of attaching the plough to the tails of animals.[11] Straw was burned from corn, and threshing was not done. Food was unappetising, consisting mostly of milk, butter, oatmeal, and wild plants (e.g. sorrel and cress), while flesh, if eaten at all, was mostly pork. However, the chieftains and upper classes had a more sophisticated cuisine, encouraged, no doubt, by the export of hides, horses, linen yarn, and salmon in exchange for wines and other items. Even at the beginning of the 17th century linen yarn from Ulster was considered the finest in the Kingdom, and was the most important commodity for export. Englishmen also noted that linen yarn, flax, beef, mutton, and barley were plentiful and cheap, and could be bought in the markets at Derry and Coleraine.[12] Nevertheless, the first settlers, used to the bustling uproar of London or the long-established customs of an English market-town in the shadow of some great cathedral, must have experienced a severe culture-shock, and one can only imagine the tears, panic, onset of depression, and all the other likely unpleasantnesses occasioned by the hostile, alien environment of County Londonderry. There was hardly any infrastructure, and settlers were prey for unscrupulous suppliers. To obtain even a few necessities for making artefacts, finishing houses, or the bare essentials for daily life cannot have been easy.

Construction Work at Coleraine

For various reasons (not least their limited resources) the Londoners decided to concentrate on making one centre secure, and first efforts were focused on Coleraine. John Rowley was appointed its Chief Agent by The Irish Society, and Tristram Beresford (b. 1574) was appointed Rowley's assistant in 1610. Soon, various tradesmen, including masons, bricklayers, smiths, and carpenters, arrived in Ulster to carry out works under the general direction of William Gage (d. 1632), who was from Northamptonshire, and was Rowley's brother-in-law (Gage's sister, Mary, was Rowley's wife). They brought with them tools and certain building materials, and appear to have been

[11] Moody (1939), 45, quoting various sources.

[12] Brewer and Bullen (eds.) (1867-73): *Cal. Carew MSS., passim.*

supervised on a day-to-day basis by Elias Jarman (or Jermyn) and Peter Cobb, both master-carpenters (and both *fl.* 1600-28), who were paid 18s. per week for their pains. Chichester received instructions from the Privy Council to ensure that the tradesmen were provided with victuals at uninflated prices and labourers to help with quarrying stone, felling and transporting trees, burning lime, and so on. While houses in Londonderry and Coleraine were to be demolished so that the City's plans could be implemented, all materials were to be stored for re-use, and sufficient buildings were to be left standing for the time being to house tradesmen and labourers. The fort at Culmore was also to be used for storage.[13]

To augment the limited numbers of tradesmen it was necessary to encourage English settlers to move to Ulster without delay, and notices were posted in London offering land at 4d. per acre to all who would do so. Barnabe Rich (*c.*1540-1617), a former soldier who had served in Ireland, produced a rosy account (1610) entitled *A New Description of Ireland ... no lesse admirable to be perused than credible to be beleeved: neither unprofitable nor unpleasant to bee read and understood, by those worthy Cittizens of London that be now Undertakers in Ireland* that was intended to attract Londoners to move to Ulster, but expressly warned against the potential dangers of allowing 'Papists' of any origin to settle there. Even Rich's glowing tract did not succeed in enticing immigrants who were (not unnaturally) unenthusiastic about uprooting themselves, making an arduous (and probably one-way journey), and facing a hard life in an underpopulated, under-resourced, dangerous, and foreign land. However, the main difficulties facing the first attempts to build in Ulster were not posed by 'Papists' or Irish guerrillas, but those caused by the poor calibre of a motley crew of demoralised, drunken, badly paid, isolated, and overstretched English workers who at first do not appear to have been employed to great advantage, and indeed do not seem to have been adequately or sensibly directed until Rowley and Beresford were firmly established in Ulster. A land that was said to be overflowing with everything that could be desired was in fact hard and inhospitable: obtaining decent food, ale, tools, and materials in London was one thing, for established markets, shops, and supplies existed there, but in Ulster it was very different. Conditions were dreadful, and the agents (not helped by a lack of ready cash and the non-existence of banking facilities) were unable (and possibly unwilling) to pay wages because sufficient funds were not at first available. Relations with artisans were very poor in the beginning, and it seems that the pioneering workmen, uprooted from their natural habitats, were treated very badly: if tools, for example, were supplied, the costs of these were deducted from wages (although this was probably intended to discourage the theft or pawning of tools), and the agents appear to have missed no opportunity of holding back pay, overcharging for basic necessities, or making life even more difficult for men who must have rued the day they ever agreed to go to Ulster. Things were so bad that Jarman/Jermyn and Cobb were even accused of over-pricing when their building estimates were undercut by Antonie Lipsett (*fl.* 1600-28), another Londoner who produced drawings for buildings on the Drapers' Company's lands. Matters were resolved by permitting Jarman/Jermyn and Cobb to carry out works provided they did not draw their salaries (by then reduced in any case to 15s. per week).[14]

[13] For a detailed story of developments in Coleraine see the late Hugh Alexander Boyd's unpublished paper (1933), 'A History of Coleraine from the Londoners' Plantation to the Restoration 1609-1660' in the possession of The Honourable The Irish Society. See also King, R.G.S. (ed.) (1936), *passim*; Loeber (1981), 40, 62; Moody (1939), 275; Moody and Simms (eds.) (1968), 85, 89.

[14] Loeber (1981), 40; Moody and Simms (eds.) (1968), 85, 89; Moody (1939), *passim*; Curl (1986), *passim* and especially 183-4.

10 County Londonderry showing the baronies of Tyrkeeran (Tirkeeran) or Anagh, Kenaught (Keenaught) or Limavady, and Half Coleraine or Coleraine (formerly constituting O'Cahan's 'Country' or the county of Coleraine), to which the barony of Loughinsholin (containing the great unexploited woods of Glenconkeyne and Killetra) had been detached from County Tyrone and added to the new county, together with the Liberties of Londonderry (detached from County Donegal) and the Liberties of Coleraine (detached from County Antrim) (*A after L*)

An infusion of £4,000-worth of capital oiled the wheels somewhat, and works began in earnest in Coleraine once Rowley and Beresford were resident on site. In order to secure that settlement Sir Josias Bodley (*c.*1550-1617), Director-General of the Fortifications and Buildings in Ireland, the brother of Sir Thomas Bodley (1545-1613 – founder of the Bodleian Library, University of Oxford), approved (and probably helped to prepare) plans for fortifying Coleraine by constructing a thick earthen rampart some four metres wide, with a ditch, around the fledgling settlement. In 1609 Bodley, with Sir William Parsons (*c.*1570-1650 – Commissioner of Plantations and Surveyor-General in the Plantation of Ulster), had carried out a survey of the escheated lands, and having spent some time on the Continent, was in a good position to apply modern designs to military architecture. In his various works he was assisted by two Netherlanders, Levan de Rose and Joyes Everard (who was later to be involved in the Salters' Estates in County Londonderry), but it is not known how much the plans of Coleraine owed to these individuals. What is certain, though, is that there was a scarcity of expertise in County Londonderry, and it is more than likely that Bodley and his colleagues were responsible for designing some buildings as well as for approving and advising on plans for the fortifications at Coleraine.[15]

When Lord Carew (as Sir George had become in 1605) visited Ulster in 1611 to report on conditions, he found Coleraine to be laid out on a regular plan within earthen dykes and ditches forming five sides of the fortifications, with the River Bann forming the sixth side of a very irregular, roughly hexagonal shape, although the 'rampier' was only about half its intended height, and only two of the intended seven bastions were anywhere near finished **[11]**. The ramparts extended from where the Methodist church stands today past the north side of St Patrick's churchyard (where traces may be detected), along the east end of the parish-church, across Kingsgate

[15] Russell and Prendergast (eds.) (1880): *Cal. S.P.I., 1615-21*, 501.

---

11 Plan of Coleraine, *c.*1611, probably made by Thomas Raven at the instigation of Carew. At the bottom is the River Bann into which two timber 'Pallesados' project for defence. On the extreme right are a lime-kiln and a shipwright's house. The town is very underdeveloped, and the 'owld Church' stands with its 'new Rofe and wales Repayred', isolated at the top left of the main street leading to the central market place (the Diamond). On the opposite bank of the river is 'the owld Castle of Colerane', which presumably was that used by the Clothworkers' Company as its headquarters. The large complex of buildings between the 'Pallesados' is the old 'Abby' or priory, a former Dominican foundation established by the Anglo-Normans in *c.*1244. Sir Thomas Phillips used the priory as his residence until Coleraine was handed over to the Londoners. The key to the reference-letters reads as follows:

A The New Row Conteinenge 30 Tenements
B The Rowe on ye west side of the former streete Conteinenge ['26' cancelled] tenements — 23
C A Rowe of 10 tenements neare finished
D A Rowe of 5 tenements 3 finished the other 2 neare finished
E fowdacions layd for 13 houses and the frame almost redey to rayse
F fowdacions and frame making for 12 tenements. Redey to rayse
G A Rowe of Tenements of stonewales Conteineng 12 houses whose wales are building
H A Howse for 2 Smithes to Dwell and to worke in
I A Howse aJoynenge to ye owld Abby of 72 foote long 27 foote wide 2 storeye high
K A Maultinge house of 92 foot longe 21 foot wide
L A Brewhouse of 70 foot longe 20 foot wide
M A Bridge or key into ye Bann of 60 foot longe 12 foot Broad: with one ster by key
N A wharfe *and steyers* to goe downe to ye Bann
O 3 Tenements for a Butcher and Smyth: & Glazyer
P A fayre mill dam with a mill howse for 3 milles
Q The owld Church with a new Rofe and wales Repayred
R Pallesados intended to be bult into ye ryver
S the owld Castle of Colrane

On the extreme left of the drawing between the 'Pallesado' and the bastion is a 'Postarne gate' which was probably not realised: near it is a 'Beast Markett'.

(*From an original coloured drawing [582 x 435mm paper size]* [TCD/*MS.1209/ 24*])

THE PLAT OF COLE RANE
A The New Rowe Conteinenge 30 Tenements
C A Rowe of 10 tenements neare finished:
H A Howse for 2 Smithes to Dwell and to worke in
K A Maulthinge howse of 92 foot longe 21 foot wide:
L A Brewhouse of 70 foot longe 20 foot wide
O 3 Tenements for a Butcher and Smyth: & Glazyer.
P A Tyre mill dam with a mill howse for 3 milles
A Scale of yardes
THE MARKET PLACE
Gardens
Gardens and Backsides
The Beast Markett
The Abby Gardens
Porte
The Lime Kill
The New Brewhouse
Barm: flu:

Street, and along Society Street, at the end of which they ran west towards the river. Gates, fully fortified, were to be constructed, and on the river bank, between two 'Pallesados' extending into the water, was a jetty for the ferry to Killowen on the opposite bank (although a bridge had existed during the Middle Ages), and a quay for unloading cargoes. The area enclosed by the ramparts was laid out with three parallel north-south streets intersected by two parallel streets running east-west, but these two sets were not at right angles to each other. Where the northern east-west street joined the two westernmost north-south streets was a large rectangular market-place, and, in the approximately triangular area between the market-place, east gate, and south gate, rows of 'tenements', some 43 in number, had been built of birch and oak frames with brick chimney-stacks. These dwellings consisted of one storey with rooms in the roof-space over, and the timber frames were prefabricated on the ground before being hoisted into position on foundations of stone or brick. Carew described three of these units linked to form a dwelling for the parson of St Patrick's church, and it has to be admitted that, at 18 feet by 12 feet (approximately 5.49 by 3.66 metres), each 'tenement' of one-and-a-half storeys was extremely small. Some 50 more 'tenements' were being erected, but those were bigger, having larger ground-floor dimensions, and being two-and-a-half storeys high. 30 'tenements' stood on the east side of New Row and 23 on the west side; 10 were situated on the south side of Church Street between the market-place and New Row; five stood opposite the church; and foundations were laid for 13 houses in the rest of Church Street and on the south side of the market-place. Twelve stone-built houses were sited near the south gate. Other buildings included a large maltings near the quay, a brewery, a wharf with steps, 'tenements' near the wharf for a butcher, a smith, and a glazier, a 'beast-market', and an 'owld Church with a new Rofe and Wales Repayred'. Other structures included lime-kilns, a shipwright's house, a mill-dam, mill-race, and mill-house for three mills, a pound, accommodation for labourers, and workshops. Not least were the stores for arms, gunpowder, lead, and other items for defence. Some 250 workmen lived in Coleraine, and there were other artisans living at the Salmon Leap, near the lime-kilns at Portrush, and in the woods near Movanagher. In the last instance nearly 100 lumberjacks, sawyers, and carpenters were employed to prepare timber for the Plantation, and they were housed in around 20 'cabbons' that had either been commandeered or built for the purpose. Not all the workmen engaged in Loughinsholin were Londoners, though: some were Irishmen, and relations between the two races seem to have been reasonably peaceful, in the early stages at least.[16] Timber was felled and taken downstream to the Salmon Leap where it was transferred to another barge belonging to The Irish Society for the last stretch of the journey to Coleraine. Horses and oxen were also available for heavy work, and carts were built to transport materials.[17]

Much of the lime for the building of Coleraine was obtained from County Antrim limestone provided by Sir Randal MacDonnell, but lime was also obtained from the screw-shells of the gastropod *Turritella Communis* that can be found in large quantities along the shores. Thus The Irish Society was obliged to keep several boats: apart from the heavy craft needed to transport timber down the Bann for building purposes, lighter ferry-boats plied to and fro across the Bann, up to the Salmon Leap, from the

[16] Moody (1939), *passim*; Curl 1986), *passim*; Brewer and Bullen (eds.) (1867-73), *Cal. Carew MSS. 1611*, 68-9, 70-2, 218-21.

[17] *Ibid.*

Leap to Loughinsholin (especially Movanagher), and served the City of London's caravel, a sailing-ship which communicated with Carrickfergus and England. In short, Coleraine was a hive of activity and construction work, and settlers began to arrive in reassuring numbers.

When Carew visited the woods of Loughinsholin he found great stocks of squared timbers, poles for scaffolding, small timbers for laths, prefabricated sections for shipbuilding, partly completed frames for houses, and much else that indicates things were being properly organised at last, planning was advanced, and structural methods were reasonably sophisticated. Seasoned wood, prepared squared timber, and numbered parts for timber-framed buildings were barged down the Bann to the Salmon Leap, and transferred to another boat (or carted the last distance) for Coleraine. Some 50 men and many horses and oxen were needed to move the timber from the woodland clearings in Loughinsholin to Bannside, and from there downstream. Much manhandling was needed at the Salmon Leap whether the timber was moved to a second barge or carried by cart on the rest of its journey. Not all the timbers ended their journey at Coleraine: much was loaded into larger ships at the little town and transported by river and sea to Londonderry and other destinations in the west of the county (at least one consignment *en route* from Coleraine to the River Foyle for construction works on the Goldsmiths' and Grocers' estates was lost in a shipwreck). By early 1611 it would appear that more than 500 men were on the payroll of The Irish Society in Ulster, and very soon the obligations of the Londoners at Coleraine had been honoured.[18]

At this point it is important to lay to rest a canard that has risen again and again, and is even enshrined in stained-glass windows in Londonderry and Coleraine. George Vaughan Sampson (d. 1827), in his *Statistical Survey of the County of Londonderry* (1802), states that the Diamond [market-square] in Coleraine was 'laid out with regularity … some of … [the houses around which] … are yet in preservation. It is said that these houses were *framed in London*[19] in the reign of Elizabeth and James the First. The frame is of hard black oak, framed in what is called cage-work; the interstices were filled up with wicker-work and clay; some of which I have very lately seen in perfect preservation. According to the fashion of the day, these houses had pent ways, or piazzas; these have been built in front, but the roofs remain on one side of the market-place'. The *Ordnance Survey Memoirs of Ireland*, collected by the surveyors during the great mapping exercise under Colonel Thomas Frederick Colby (1784-1852) in the 1820s and 1830s, state that 'wooden frameworks' for houses were 'brought from London'[20] and that 'oak frames' were 'built in London at the expense of the London societies'.[21]

Like much in the *Memoirs* and a great deal of supposed 'history', the stories of houses 'framed in London' and shipped to Ulster are pure mythology, and there is absolutely no evidence it ever happened, let alone during the reign of Elizabeth. There would have been no point whatsoever, as the new county of Londonderry was endowed with plenty of good, mature timber, which is why Loughinsholin, specifically, was detached from Tyrone to provide the Londoners with that commodity. In any

[18] Moody (1939), *passim*; Robinson (1984), *passim;* Curl (1986), *passim. The Calendar of the Carew MSS* is incomplete regarding the Carew Survey. The complete original is in the archiepiscopal library, Lambeth Palace, MS 630, ff. 42-8.

[19] My italics. See Sampson (1802), 286.

[20] Day, McWilliams, and English (eds.) (1995), 59.

[21] *Ibid.* 129. The error was repeated in Betts (1913), 42, Camblin (1951), 32, and King, R.G.S. (ed.) (1936), 3.

case, by 1610 there was a growing shortage of timber in England, the woods having been stripped for shipbuilding, building construction, and the smelting of iron ore. Bringing frames to Ireland would have been rather like exporting coal (not an abundant naturally occurring substance in London) to Newcastle. It is perhaps significant that Sampson, in his *A Memoir, Explanatory of the Chart and Survey of the County of London-Derry, Ireland* (1814), refers (erroneously) to the 'pentways' as having been mostly removed by then, but omits any reference to the spurious London-made 'frames'.[22] While it would have made sense to send London-made nails, ironwork, tools, locks, lead bars, and so on to Ulster, it would have been absurd to ship bulky, scarce, prefabricated timber-framed houses to a site where, only a few miles upstream, were more than enough trees for every purpose, and an army of men working to make up the frames. It appears that Rowley arranged for the first cut to be made in the rock at the Salmon Leap (hence The Cutts) in order to facilitate the transportation of timber for building purposes from Glenconkeyne to Coleraine.[23] To go to all that trouble, employ hundreds of men to cut, prepare, and transport the timbers to Coleraine and elsewhere in the county, *and then* import frames from London (where the timber would have to have been brought in from outside anyway), is simply beyond all reason. All the hard evidence shows that the tales of frames imported from London are pure fantasy, and demonstrates the dangers of repeating tall stories in print, which are then cited as 'facts'. Besides, there is hard evidence from the history of developments on the Drapers' Company estates that at least some of the timber-framed houses had close-studded or half-timbered walls (i.e. with spaces between the upright square timbers equal to the width of the studs). Such prodigal use of timber would have been very difficult in a contemporary England denuded of woodlands, but possible in Ireland where there was plenty of it. Close-studding was also strong, so better from the point of view of defence than box-framing, with its large panels (framed by timber) requiring infill of wattle-and-daub, brick nogging etc.[24]

From written and archaeological evidence, most of the houses in Coleraine were constructed of timber with brick chimney-stacks and slate roofs. Slate found in excavations at New Row is of a schistose rock formation, probably quarried at New Buildings on the Goldsmiths' estate near Londonderry and shipped to Coleraine.[25] In Carew's reports there also appear to have been composite structures with panel-like timber façades set between stone party-walls.[26] It is complete nonsense to assume that the construction works were carried out by artisans without any plans. Among the papers of the Drapers' Company are two drawings of plans for 'howses' with precise dimensions, central chimney-stacks with a fireplace on each side facing the two main rooms, and an arrangement of what is known as the 'lobby-' or 'baffle-entry' in which the main door opened into a lobby to the side of the chimney-stack so that protection against draughts could be achieved. Stairs on the other side of the stack led to the upper floor (which was illuminated by dormer-windows), and a bread-oven was provided within the stack.[27] Although they do not appear to have survived, equally detailed drawings for the works at Coleraine and Londonderry must have been prepared by the employees of The Irish Society.

22 Sampson (1814), 206-9.

23 Boyd (1933), 33.

24 Alcock, Barley, Dixon, and Meeson (1996), *passim*; Curl (1986), 182-6; Curl (1999), 89, 646; Robinson (1984, 1994), 140-1.

25 Robinson and Brannon (1981-2), 173-8.

26 *Ibid.*, and Brewer and Bullen (eds.) (1867-73): *Cal. Carew MSS.*, *passim*, but see original in Lambeth Palace.

27 Curl (1986), 183, Brunskill (1978), 106-7; Alcock, Barley, Dixon, and Meeson (1996), *passim*.

Sampson's references to 'pent ways' or 'piazzas'[28] need some explanation. Pent-ways or pentices were essentially roofed corridors to protect pedestrians during inclement weather, and were not uncommon in England. Sometimes they were created by setting the front wall back at the ground-first-floor level so that the upper floors protected the walkway (e.g. at the Rows, Chester, the Pantiles, Tunbridge Wells, Kent, and the Pentice, Winchester, Hampshire), and in other instances they consisted of a row of posts carrying a lean-to roof. Coleraine had the last arrangement, and some traces are clearly visible in the drawings of the Book of Coleraine, a survey apparently produced under the direction of John Claudius Beresford (1766-1846) which shows plans of street-fronts to scale and elevations of whole frontages (not to scale).[29] This Book was formerly thought to date from around 1816, but Sampson's contention that the 'pent ways' had largely disappeared by 1814 might suggest the document is earlier. However, as will be seen below, the book was compiled over several years, and work on it was continuing in 1827, which means that the 'piazzas' survived in part even then, so Sampson is inaccurate, or perhaps did not realise they had been incorporated within many of the properties. The term 'piazzas' is derived from the Italian *piazza*, meaning a place or urban square surrounded by buildings. In Italy, piazzas were often surrounded by colonnaded or arcaded walkways set under the first floors of the buildings: a good north-European example is the Place des Vosges, Paris (from 1605), and Inigo Jones (1573-1652) designed the celebrated unified square at Covent Garden, called the Piazza (1631-7 – demolished), with arcaded ways at ground-floor level, for Francis, 4th Earl of Bedford (1593-1641). These walks became known as 'piazzas', and the term was later applied to any pentice or covered way, so it was in this sense that Sampson used the word in his work. It is intriguing that Sir Francis Bacon (1561-1626) seems to have been introduced (1608) by Inigo Jones to Sir Josias Bodley, who probably gave Bacon first-hand advice and material for his book on the Plantation.[30] Although the 'piazzas' at Covent Garden were very grand and Classical, and are much later, it is not beyond all possibility that Bodley was involved (even in an advisory capacity) in the creation of the 'piazzas' in Coleraine, and that Jones might have suggested the idea of providing such an amenity in the brisk northern climate of Ulster **[12-19]**.

The Book of Coleraine also shows an elevation of St Patrick's church as it was partly rebuilt and repaired by The Irish Society from 1610 **[20-21]**. Instead of battlements there was a series of shaped gablets surmounted by finials at the tops of the walls, and the south transept was also capped by a large shaped gable. It appears to have been a building of little architectural distinction, was subsequently altered on several occasions, and was replaced by the present church in 1884. Nevertheless, in spite of the fact that there was not much in the new settlement that would have passed muster as fine building, Sir John Davies (or Davys) waxed enthusiastic about progress on the Londoners' estates in a letter to Cecil.[31] He declared that the agents 'of London have made far better preparation for the erection of their new Town at Colrane than [the Commissioners for the Plantation] expected', for 'they found there such store of timber and other materials brought in place, so many workmen so busy in several places about their several tasks, as methought I saw Didoe's colony building

[28] Curl (1999), *passim*; Sampson (1802), 286.

[29] The book was in the possession of Mr. Daniel MacLaughlin of Coleraine, in 1998, to whom the author is indebted for permission to consult it and reproduce some of the images.

[30] Spedding (ed.) (1868-90), **iv**, 66, 110.

[31] 24 September 1610.

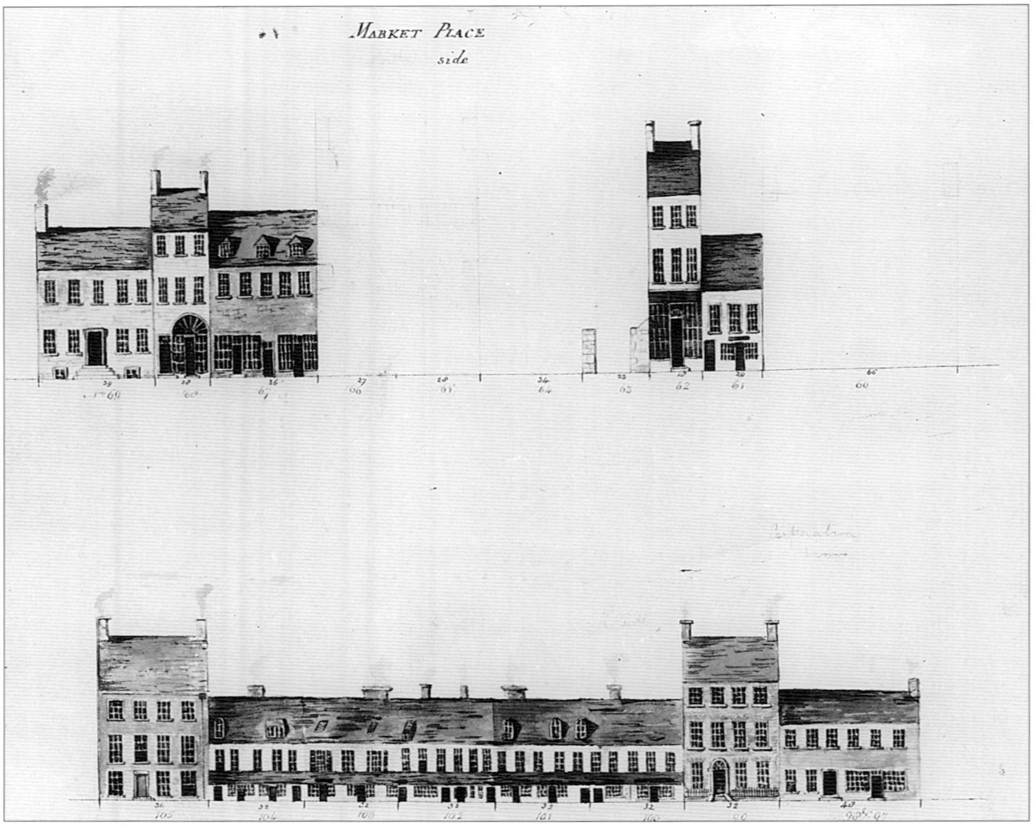

12 Elevation of houses facing the market-place in Coleraine from the 'Book of Coleraine' of *c.*1816-27. The covered way, pentice, or 'piazzas' are clearly visible in the lower elevation, though by that time had been filled in to increase the volumes of the ground floors of the houses. (*DMacL./ UFTM/AF89/ L1759/16*)

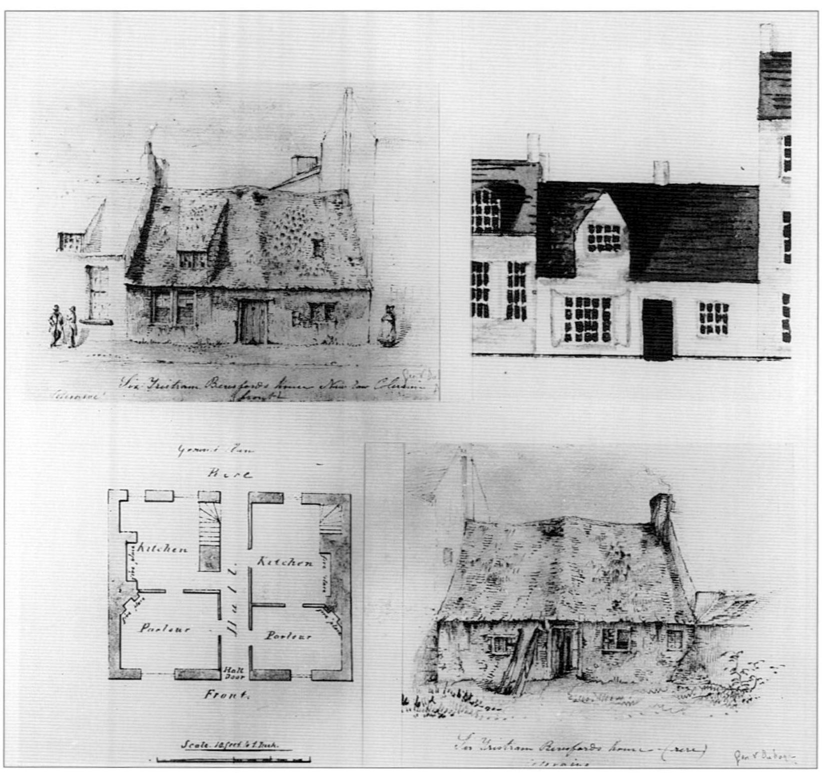

13 Plan and two elevations of 'Sir Tristram Beresford's House', New Row, Coleraine, from the Ordnance Survey Memoirs of 1828-33, showing the cat-slide dormer. There is no evidence that Beresford lived in such a poor dwelling, but the drawing does indicate a typical Irish Society house, 1½ storeys high. The drawing on the top right is from the 'Book of Coleraine' and has been claimed to show the same house. The dormer and fenestration have been changed, however, and so has the position of a chimney. Given the dates, the house (if it is the same) must have been virtually rebuilt in *c.*1827-30, and the O.S. Memoir sketch prepared very shortly before the alterations. (*RIA/DMacL./UFTM/AF89/L1882/5*)

14 East side of New Row, Coleraine, from the 'Book of Coleraine', showing buildings still standing in the decade or so after the Napoleonic wars. According to the drawings nearly all the windows are of the sliding-sash type. *(DMacL/UFTM/AF89/L1759/13)*

15 West side of New Row, Coleraine, from the 'Book of Coleraine', showing the range of buildings from Lawrence's Mill to Gaol Lane. The so-called 'Beresford House' is in the range at the bottom. *(DMacL/UFTM/AF89/L1759/9)*

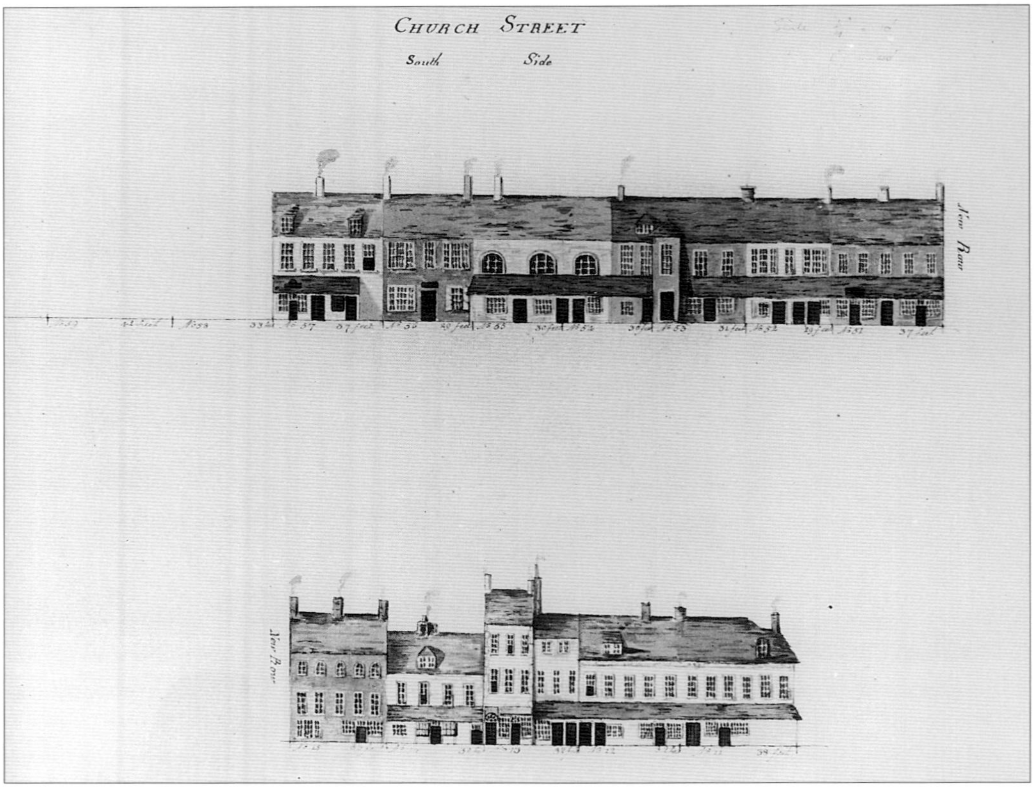

16 South side of Church Street, from the 'Book of Coleraine'. Surviving covered ways, pentices, or 'piazzas' are clearly visible in front of many houses, though filled in and incorporated into the dwellings. (*DMacL/UFTM/AF89/L1759/5*)

17 North side of Church Street, from 'The Book of Coleraine'. The trees behind the wall stand in the churchyard of St Patrick's parish-church, and the position of the surviving ramparts is noted on the right. (*DMacL/UFTM/AF89/L1759/1*)

18 North side of Bridge Street, from the 'Book of Coleraine', showing the Customs-house and other buildings, some of which are very handsome. The house third from the right seems to have a portion of the 'piazzas' partially intact. (*DMacL/UFTM/AF89/L1759/19*)

19 Hanover Place, from the 'Book of Coleraine', showing houses and a warehouse, encroachments on the citadel, and a row of thatched cottages (typical of the sort of thing The Irish Society was anxious to replace). (*DMacL/UFTM/AF9/L1759/20*)

20 South elevation of St Patrick's parish-church, from 'The Book of Coleraine'. In the south transept is a Gothic Survival window under a straight hood-mould. The curved gablets should be noted. (*DMacL/UFTM/AF9/L1759/4*)

21 St Patrick's church, Coleraine, from the south-eastern corner of the churchyard, from the tercentenary window in the town-hall, Coleraine. (*A*)

Carthage in Virgil'. He quoted the passage that referred to the Tyrians in their eagerness pressing forward with the work, some tracing and building walls to rear the citadel, while others cleared ground for the erection of houses and enclosed it with a furrow.[32] One further point needs to be made about developments at Coleraine. In modern terminology the 'density' of development was very low, and long gardens were attached to the rear of the houses. In the opinions of some, the ramparts enclosed an embarrassingly large area, sparsely built upon, but by 1611 The Irish Society, it seemed, had met its obligations in its contract with the Crown, and Carew's survey gave a precise account. It is clear that the work at Coleraine involved creating defences to make the infant settlement reasonably secure should the Irish attack, so one safe base would be established before the ruinous property at Derry could be re-edified.

[32] Virgil: *Aeneid*, **i**, 423-5, 436. See Mackail (tr.) (1908), 14.

Rowley's Instructions from The Irish Society, 1612

The Londoners experienced considerable difficulties in obtaining the surrender of lands at Derry, and Chichester himself noted that they could do 'Little ... until the differences betwixt them and the now inhabitants' could be resolved.[33] In fact the terms of the Articles of Agreement were largely ignored at Derry. In the Spring of 1612, however, Rowley travelled to London, and in November of that year was issued with 'Instructions given to Mr John Rowley, agent, receavour, and treasurer for the affairs of the City of Londons plantation in Ireland'.[34] In this document Rowley was reminded, in no uncertain terms, of his duties, and, in particular, was to keep 'Mr Berrisford' fully informed of all matters, especially those connected with payments, the 'taking up of moneys', and 'directions or anything of moment'. Clearly The Irish Society was anxious to keep a tighter rein on its agents, and there is a note of concern in the tone of the 'Instructions'. Some of the communication to Rowley deals with the renting of houses: tenancies were to be granted for 21 years, and rents varied from £2 per annum with an initial 'fine' of £5 to £5 per annum and a fine of £8 for the larger houses. Interestingly, similar rates were to be applied to houses in Londonderry, except that in the new city houses (conforming to designs 'already conceived') were all to be built of stone, with door- and window-frames of timber. This confirms that houses were planned and drawn up in London (as was the case with the Drapers' Company developments), and a 'master workman', one Riggs, is named in Instruction 29 as suitable to supervise their erection.

The Irish Society saw Londonderry as having far greater potential, where the 'building would yield more profit than at Coleraine',[35] but there was clearly a shortage of cash, for private individuals were encouraged to build houses at their own expense in both Coleraine and Londonderry, the land to be leased for 60 years at a quit-rent of 6s. 8d. However, the best parts of undeveloped lands in Londonderry were to be reserved for The Irish Society's own houses. Incomplete gates and drawbridges at Coleraine were to be finished, and one of the gate-houses, it was suggested, might house the lock-up. Customs-houses (no more than small rooms in 'convenient' houses) were to be provided at Londonderry and Coleraine by the river sides.[36] Private individuals were also to be encouraged to build corn-mills on lands leased for 60 years provided such structures did not prejudice the salmon-fishings.[37] Private enterprise was again called upon to build a pier or jetty at Portrush as Coleraine was a 'hard haven', dangerous at all times, and hardly passable in winter'.[38] The cutting of stone at the 'Leap at Castlerow' was to proceed with 'no hurt to the salmon fishings' in order to facilitate the carrying of goods up and down the Bann, and Rowley was reminded that stone excavated should be used for building-works at Coleraine.[39] Economies were obviously well to the fore when the 'Instructions' were drawn up, and Rowley was asked to 'inquire what money hath been made of pipe-staves or others in our woods by Mr Berrissford or others': he was to collect these monies and to use them for building-work.[40] Item 44 in the 'Instructions' makes it

[33] Russell and Prendergast (eds.) (1877): *Cal. S.P.I., 1610-1614*, 7, 65, 228.
[34] Given in Moody and Simms (eds.) (1968); 84-93.
[35] Instruction 4.
[36] Instruction 15.
[37] Instruction 19.
[38] Instruction 20.
[39] Instruction 21.
[40] Instruction 23.

clear that The Irish Society was aware its woods were being plundered and timber exported 'contrary to our order and contrary to the articles' between the Crown and the City: Rowley was told bluntly that the 'great disorder' in the woods had to stop, and that Rowley's tenants should be brought to heel. Furthermore, if Rowley pleaded ignorance of any misdemeanours that would be no excuse and he would be held responsible.

The clerks of works were to keep their books in such a fashion that the names of all workmen should be entered with information concerning the days worked and those not, and weekly accounts rendered.[41] Much 'disorder' was committed by drunken workmen, who spent their 'time and substance' in the 'great number of taverns and ale houses'. The Irish Society gave instructions to reduce the number of taverns to two or three in Coleraine and four in Londonderry, while 'not above ten ale-houses' should be provided at Coleraine and 'not above' twenty in Londonderry.[42] One wonders, therefore, what half-built Coleraine can have been like, for almost every other house must have purveyed drink, streets were muddy and unpaved, and the infant town cannot have been very appealing. Draconian measures were to be taken: 'idle and disordered' workmen were to be shipped back to England;[43] the *Dove* (The Irish Society's ship) and other boats were to be let out 'for freight for London or any other place' as it was considered there would be 'small employment for them' during the winter;[44] the smiths were 'not to be trusted with iron and steel worth above £10 at a time';[45] all ship-carpenters were to be dismissed except one to 'take general charge of all ... shipping boats, barges, etc.';[46] all 'needless' officers or workmen were to be sacked, and the surveyor, Thomas Raven (*c.*1572-1640), 'who hath a great stipend', was to have his salary cut to 20 marks per annum (about £13 6s. 8d.), which cannot have improved his relations with The Society. Raven, incidentally, must be regarded as another who had sufficient skills to design buildings, and he may have been responsible for some of the built fabric on the Londoners' lands. As will be seen, the disgruntled Raven was to assist Sir Thomas Phillips and Richard Hadsor in their devastating report on the City of London's Plantation in 1622.[47] Other instructions are concerned with attracting craftsmen to settle in the two towns, promoting trade, encouraging markets, and so on. Gold and bills of exchange were provided to the tune of £2,017 10s. (a gigantic sum) to pay 'arrearages' of workmen's wages, together with exhortations to be 'frugal'. Beresford had constantly complained about shortages of funds, and wrote 'continually' to The Society of 'great want of money to pay workmen and for other occasions'. This caused The Irish Society to 'much marvel considering the sums' already disbursed, and to instruct Rowley, on his arrival in Ulster, 'to examine the reason for such wants, what moneys' Beresford had 'received by rents, in bills of exchange, and in specie from hence', what the arrears of wages came to, and how they were paid. Throughout, there is more than a whiff of a suggestion that fingers were in the till, and that cash was flowing into pockets unintended by The Society. Keeping tabs on its agents cannot have been easy, for communications were bad and slow and The Society itself changed half its membership

[41] Instruction 7.
[42] Instruction 31.
[43] Instruction 32.
[44] Instruction 33.
[45] Instruction 34.
[46] Instruction 40.
[47] Chart (ed.) (1928), *passim*.

each year, which would have done nothing for continuity. Tristram Beresford, it should be noted, did not miss his opportunities, and laid the foundations of his family's fortunes. His son (also Tristram [d. 1673]) married Rowley's eldest daughter, Anne, became a baronet in 1665, and sat as Member of Parliament 1656-8 and 1661-6. His great-grandson, Sir Marcus (1694-1763), was created 1st Earl of Tyrone in 1746, and *his* son (George de la Poer Beresford [1735-1800]) became 1st Marquess of Waterford in 1789.[48]

Other instructions concerned the preservation of game, the necessity of controlling the importation of anything that could be produced locally in Ulster, free travel on ferries for craftsmen and labourers, free travel on ferries on market-days to encourage trade, and details of the establishment of the two Corporations with lists of the men selected by The Society as Town-Clerks, Aldermen, Recorders, Sheriffs, and Members of Parliament. Rowley was also commanded[49] to 'settle a course for the division of the City's lands' and to send all details of lands in the four baronies divided first into four parts then every fourth part divided into three 'for the better satisfying of the Companies in London to assign every one their proportion, for thereby they will be willing to disburse the several payments and to perform their buildings, etc., which we are enjoined by the articles to perform, having a respect to the goodness or barrenness of the soil, to the nearness of the town and the largeness of the balliboes'. Thus moves were afoot to unload the burden of colonising the county lands on to the shoulders of the Companies.

As far as buildings were concerned, the instructions relating to houses have been noted above. The Irish Society also instructed Rowley to build 'a town house at the Derry and under the same to make a place for the court de guard and a prison' to be 'set in the market-place so as it may scour as many streets as may be' and supplied with a bell hung 'in the top'.[50] Mindful of defence, The Society raised the question of the 'building of the walls of the Derry and making the ditch', reminding Rowley 'to beware of error committed at Coleraine in making the circuit of the town too great'.[51] In particular, Rowley was to consult Captain John Vaughan, Captain Hart, and other military men about the design of the defences at Londonderry.

Captain John Vaughan appears to have been a person of some substance in a land not over-endowed with such. He became Mayor of Londonderry in or around 1617, the year he was knighted, was appointed to the Irish Privy Council in 1620, was again Mayor of Londonderry (1627-9), and remained the military commander of Londonderry until his death in 1643. From various sources Captain Sir John Vaughan was probably the leading personality in Londonderry from *c.*1608 to the 1640s, and played a considerable part in the building of the city. Captain Henry Hart became an Alderman of Londonderry, and held an estate, as a Servitor, in County Donegal: he later became Governor of Londonderry and Culmore Fort, and the Vaughans and Harts intermarried (General George Vaughan Hart [1752-1832] was a direct descendant of both families, and retained his connections with Londonderry and Culmore).[52]

[48] *Burke's Peerage* (1963), 2512. See Townend (ed.) (1963).
[49] Instruction 16.
[50] Instruction 36.
[51] Instruction 41.
[52] Brewer and Bullen (eds.) (1873): *Cal. Carew MSS.*, 385; Moody (1939), 281; Russell and Prendergast (eds.) (1880): *Cal. S.P.I. 1615-25*, 296, 406, 517.

The Londonderry Plantation immediately before and after the issue of Rowley's Instructions

As has been mentioned above, relations between The Irish Society and Phillips began to deteriorate in 1611. It seems that Phillips had attempted to stop Beresford's men from spoiling the woods, and very soon Phillips was told to desist from meddling in The Society's affairs.[53] Phillips also experienced delays in obtaining legal title to his new estates. He eventually obtained grants in common socage of the Limavady and Moyola properties at the end of 1612, but had been without rents or lands for almost 18 months, and had to petition the Privy Council to obtain his entitlements. By that time Phillips had changed from being a champion of the Londoners' involvement to their most hostile critic. Other individuals had interests that conflicted with the City of London's grants, but in spite of the money allocated by The Irish Society to buy such interests out, the Irish executive was dilatory and the inhabitants of 'The Derry' were reluctant to surrender their rights until they received ready cash. Not until Chichester was instructed to pay out the compensation money at once (March 1612) were the Londoners able to do much at Londonderry. Other interests bought out were the rectory of Coleraine (from the diocese of Connor); the lands adjacent to Coleraine (from Sir Randal MacDonnell); fisheries of the Foyle and Bann (from Chichester himself and Sir James Hamilton, who seem to have acquired such rights by circuitous means); the castle at Culmore (from Chichester); the castle at Dungiven (from Captain Edward Dod(d)ington); grange lands in Loughinsholin and Agivey (from Sir Toby Caulfeild); and other parcels of property. But by 1613 all the new county of Londonderry was carved up between The Irish Society, the Church, Sir Thomas Phillips, and the native freeholders.

Rowley's Instructions, in which The Irish Society hammered home its obligations, suggest that trouble was brewing, and indeed the first signs of a serious breach between the Crown and the City occurred during 1612. The main problem was that the Londoners had not obtained title to everything agreed in the compact with the King, but the Government began to be concerned that native Irish tenants were being retained by The Irish Society on the grounds that artisans could not be fed without the co-operation of the Irish. No Undertakers, it was claimed, were as dilatory in sending British settlers to Ulster as the Londoners, and indeed it appeared that Irish from Tyrone were being encouraged to move to Loughinsholin, and were more numerous there than ever before. Chichester and Phillips were now overtly anxious about the security of the Plantation.

In December 1612 the King himself intervened and demanded to be fully acquainted with the state of the Plantation of Ulster.[54] A survey was necessary 'because the Londoners here pretend the expense of great sums of money ... and yet ... the outward appearance of it in their works are very small ...'.[55] Sir Thomas Phillips and other magnates were required to prepare certificates of the state of the Plantation, and a royal official was ordered to carry out a valuation of all work done by the Londoners. This official was Bodley, and his first survey took place between 2 February and 25 April 1613.[56] Chichester began to sense that the City of London had bitten off more than it could chew. The Londoners had little incentive to remove the natives (who took care to pay their rents and be as obliging as possible to their landlords)

[53] Moody (1939), 114.
[54] Chart (ed.) (1928), 31-2, 33-8.
[55] *Ibid.*, 39-40.
[56] Moody (1939), 159; Moody, Martin, and Byrne (eds.) (1982), 225.

because they could not find many British colonists, and it is quite clear that their estates would have got into serious trouble without their Irish tenants.

Carew, in 1611, had found little evidence of progress in the scheme of Plantation in the countryside, and noted that the natives paid their rents to the agents of the City who were not trying to replace them with British settlers: it seemed that the Londoners were getting away with behaviour that would not be tolerated among the private Undertakers.[57] On their side, the Londoners did not obtain full title to their lands until 1613, as has been made clear earlier. Thus a vast amount of effort and cash had been expended, largely on trust, until matters were formalised.

The Smithes-Springham Investigations

Once the Londoners had received their title two commissioners were sent to Ulster to establish the current state of the Plantation. The City of London had expended large sums of money over three years and was anxious to know exactly what had been achieved. Furthermore, alarm-bells were ringing concerning the conduct of John Rowley, who had acquired 81 townlands annexed to the bishopric of Derry from Brutus Babington (d. 1611), Bishop of Derry (1610-11). In 1612 Dr Christopher Hampton (1552-1625 – Bishop of Derry from 1611 to 1613, and Archbishop of Armagh from 1613 until his death) wrote to the Privy Council to acquaint them with this, and also to draw attention to Rowley's spoliation of the woodlands in order to export timber to Spain (of all places!). The King's letter of 21 December 1612 also hinted that both Rowley and Beresford might have misused the funds placed at their disposal,[58] and it was clear that matters required some investigation. As the City was about to begin major building operations in Londonderry itself, it was necessary that the site should be viewed and a programme of development decided upon. There was also the question of the distribution of the City of London's lands to the Livery Companies which had to be resolved. Finally, the new civic constitutions of Londonderry and Coleraine required formal inauguration from a Deputation sent from London.

In June 1613 the Common Council appointed Alderman George Smithes (or Smythes – d. 1615) and Mat(t)hias Springham, Merchant Taylor (both Assistants of The Irish Society), to travel to Ulster, accompanied by Clement Moss, the City Solicitor. The Smithes-Springham mission remained more than two months in County Londonderry, where several cans of worms were uncovered, although the City's Plantation seems to have been favourably regarded in Ireland. Rowley and Beresford were found to have pursued their own fortunes and personal trading deals to the detriment of The Irish Society's interests. For example, The Society's own brewery in Coleraine was not in use, but Rowley had set up his own establishment at Castle Roe; the agent was erecting a mill only a mile away from The Society's water-mill outside Coleraine; the Saturday market was held under Rowley's aegis on Church lands at Killowen (leased from the bishop) where he had set up a market-cross decorated with his own initials; and he and Beresford had systematically spoiled the woods of Loughinsholin for personal gain. Thus these two servants of The Irish Society had indulged in wholesale theft of City property, had misused the woods, and had abused their positions to acquire property and capital contrary to the interests of the City of

[57] Brewer and Bullen (eds.) (1867-73): *Cal Carew MSS. 1603-24*, 210-25.

[58] Moody (1939), 144.

London they were supposed to uphold.[59] The stench of corruption was all-pervasive, and some 400 workmen had not been paid for long periods with the result that they were in debt, demoralised, and completely at the mercy of The Society's agents who supplied the workers with provisions 'on tick' at double their actual value; these inflated charges were deducted from the overdue wages and commission was charged by the clerk on the whole disgraceful transaction, Smithes and Springham at once paid all arrears to the workmen, dismissed the unscrupulous clerk, and set up a fund from which artisans were to be regularly paid, at intervals no longer than four weeks.

Rowley, Beresford, and others had cornered the market in transportation, so the commissioners made a compact with one carter to do all the carrying in and around Coleraine at a fixed fee of four pence per load. Rowley and his accomplices had also defrauded The Irish Society by overcharging for timber transportation in and from the woods: therefore the commissioners contracted with two carters to transport all squared and unsquared timber at rates much lower than those fraudulently claimed by the agents. Further waste in shipping was drastically reduced, and every effort was made to regularise matters.

Only 63 houses stood in Coleraine (there were supposed to be 116, and some lay open to the weather). Some old thatched houses and many pre-Plantation Irish cabins survived. Several new houses were jerry-built, and had already cost much in repairs, while much was still unlet. In fact, for an outlay of over £10,000 only £302 had been received in rent, so the commissioners ordered that vacant houses should be let on 21-year leases, the tenants to be responsible for keeping them in good order. By this and other means the commissioners ensured an annual income of £518 from rents. The commissioners regretted that the ramparts at Coleraine had not been built of stone, that they enclosed too great an area, and that they could not be defended by so small a population. They had cost a great deal, were unfinished, and were already in poor repair, so needed a large injection of capital to secure them. Streets were unpaved and extremely muddy: accordingly, Smithes and Springham ordered paving to begin at once, and saw the works finished. The commissioners also instructed that the interior of St Patrick's church (which they considered very foul) should be rendered (plastered) and limewashed, and that more pews should be provided. An extortionate sum had been expended on making the unfinished cut in the Salmon Leap: this work was to be completed and orders were given that the two other Leaps should be cut to facilitate the passage of boats and timber down river.

Smithes and Springham then turned their attention to Londonderry, where 32 houses were used as 15 habitations, for the houses (like many in Coleraine) were far too small. They viewed and 'trod out' the ground with the assistance of 'Captain Paynton' (or Panton) and other experienced men. Evidently Smithes had brought plans of the walls from London, and the final designs appear to have been adapted from those by Sir Edward Dod(d)ington (*fl.* 1602-1618) or by Paynton (or both). In the event, it was decided that no work on the walls should start until sufficient stone and lime were available, and construction began in 1614, the contractor being the London tiler and bricklayer, Peter Benson (*fl.* 1614-42), who completed the work (under the superintendence of Captain Sir John Vaughan) in 1618 at a cost of £10,755. Benson ultimately had to petition the King for payment of arrears of £1,157 2s. 10d. as late as 1624, a huge sum to be owed.[60]

59 Moody (1939), 146; Curl (1986), 60.

60 Moody (1939), 150; Loeber (1981), 20.

Of the lands 'laid' to Londonderry, much was of poor quality, and would only produce about £100 per annum. It was found that some good land on the east bank of the Foyle at Rossnagalliagh once belonged to a former nunnery in the new city, so it was annexed to augment income. Culmore Fort was under inept command, and had to be strengthened. Accordingly, Smithes and Springham issued instructions that walls should be built around it and Captain John Baker put in charge of this important strategic spot.

Existing charters of the two urban settlements were surrendered and replaced by new ones. As matters had been fixed before Smithes and Springham left London, the commissioners who were to unmask Rowley's and Beresford's corruption were obliged to instal them as mayors, and Rowley lost no time in requesting new Arms for the infant city. In 1613 Daniel Molyneux or Molineux (1568-1632), Ulster King of Arms, combined the earlier Arms granted to Docwra's settlement (a skeleton of human bones [or Death] seated on a stone, or rock, leaning the *Dexter* elbow on the knee and resting the head on the hand, the *Sinister* hand resting on the hip proper in the *Dexter* chief a castle or tower) with in chief the Arms of London (*Argent* the Cross of St George *Gules* in *Dexter* chief a sword erect *Gules* and with the legend or motto *Vita Veritas Victoria* [Life, Truth, Victory]). Although the skeleton is popularly believed to be that of Sir Cahir O'Doherty, it cannot be, as it appeared on Arms granted four years *earlier* than his death, and the allusion to Walter de Burgh's death by starvation in 1332 holds more water. Molyneux, in the grant of 1613, refers to the skeleton as an allusion to 'Derrie' being 'raysed from the dead by the worthy undertakinge of the noble Cittie of London, in memorie of which it is henceforth called and knowen by the name of London-Derrie', which makes a great deal more sense, if the resurrected skeleton on a rock is seen as the new city on its rocky eminence.[61]

Communion plate was presented on behalf of The Irish Society to the churches in Coleraine and Londonderry. Fishing rights on the two main rivers were let for three years, to bring in £866 13s. 4d. per annum. Other tasks, such as a census of the native tenants, an accurate survey of Loughinsholin, definition of lands for native freeholders, mapping of glebe lands, and the building of a fort at Desertmartin, were set in hand. One of the largest jobs was to survey the county lands, and the commissioners found that virtually nothing had been done about this. To rectify matters, Thomas Raven, Dod(d)ington, and others worked with the commissioners to inspect, value, and divide these areas into 12 'Proportions', the areas of which varied according to the value and usefulness of the land. The commissioners were aware that the 'planting' of British colonists in remote mountainous regions was fraught with dangers, and so more land was added to Proportions that had a lack of advantages. Proportions were determined taking into account resources, access, nearness to towns, defensive possibilities, and quality of land rather than crude measurements of area. Any shortages of building materials (e.g. timber) on any Proportion were to be made good by arrangement with The Irish Society's agents. Londonderry itself and Coleraine, of course, were not to be subdivided, but were to remain in the ownership of The Society, any revenues to be shared out among the Companies that had contributed to the joint stock. By the summer of 1613 the Londoners seem to have laid out about £30,000 on the Plantation, a considerable part of which seems to have disappeared.

[61] Burke (1884), 619-20 (that states that the Arms were granted in 1623, which cannot be correct as Rowley died in 1617); Colby (1837), 35, 86-7; Lacy (1998), 49, 9. Information also supplied by Norroy and Ulster King of Arms.

Smithes returned to London in November and reported to the Common Council. Rowley was dismissed from the City's service, Springham (who had stayed on in Ireland) was to take charge of all money and other resources in Rowley's hands, and the latter was summoned to London for questioning. Auditors were appointed to look into the accounts. Springham appeared before the Court of Common Council in August 1614 to report on his reforms: these included a drastic reduction of the prices in several contracts; the introduction of piecework contracts for the building of the stone houses in Londonderry (which speeded up construction); an agreement with Lipsett to carry out all carpentry work at a fixed price per house; the sacking of superfluous labourers; the sale of all unnecessary boats and barges; the provision of materials for Benson's use in building the walls at Londonderry; and the collection of many debts owing to The Irish Society. In the same year Smithes succeeded Cokayne as Governor of The Society.

Distribution of the Proportions to the Livery Companies

Not until the end of 1613 were the 12 'Proportions' allocated to the Livery Companies. 55 Companies that had been levied by means of Precepts for contributions to the joint stock were organised into 12 associations, each headed by one of the 12 Great Companies. The 'Associated Companies' were grouped with a Great Company so that each group's total levy was a twelfth part of the £40,000-worth of capital raised so far. Some Great Companies had no Associates at all: the Merchant Taylors had oversubscribed by £1,186 and the Grocers by £874, so each held a Proportion and was given shares in other Proportions (the Merchant Taylors thus became an Associated Company of the Clothworkers, and the Grocers became an Associated Company in the Vintners' Proportion). The Drapers had the Tallow-Chandlers as Associates for a brief period before buying out their interests in 1618; the Goldsmiths acquired the Cordwainers, Painter-Stainers, and Armourers as Associates; and the Vintners had nine Associated Companies.

Inventories of each Proportion were drawn up, townlands were allocated, and each estate was granted to a Company group by lot, the City Swordbearer performing the office of drawer with considerable *élan*. Thus it was quite literally the luck of the draw that determined the ownership of good or bad lands, of landlocked bare mountains, or of lush valleys. Some Companies, such as the Goldsmiths, Grocers, and Fishmongers, were more fortunate than the Drapers and Skinners (both of whom were granted fragmented lands in the dangerous south, where the wood-kernes romped). Conveyances of the Proportions were made to the Companies with the cooperation of The Irish Society, the Recorder acting as adviser. From that time, therefore, each Company or group of Companies became the owner of a Proportion of county lands, and each estate was managed by one of the Great Companies which allocated shares to its Associates. In all cases, however, the Companies were obliged to be bound by the Articles of Agreement, had to conform to the general compact between the City and the Crown, and were under the general direction of The Irish Society to ensure the proper running of the estates for the general good of the Plantation as a whole **[22-23]**.

Once the Proportions had been allocated the City revealed that all the capital raised had gone, and the Companies were liable for more levies to pay for the fortifications and other buildings in the towns. £5,000 was levied at once. Thus although

22 'A Generall Plat of the lands Belonginge to the Cittie of London as they are devided and let out to the 12 Companies & as they doe Butt and Bound ech upon other the perticuler platts where of doe followe more at large described' by Thomas Raven (1622). This shows the new county of Londonderry divided into the Proportions of the Livery Companies. Londonderry, Coleraine, and other settlements and places are marked, including Lifford (Liffer), Toome, Ould Fort of Towne (Toome), Salterstown, Moneymore, Magherafelt, Movanagher, Vintnerstown (Bellaghy), Agivey, Mahereboy, Ballykelly, Dunluce, Castle Roe, Lough Beg, Magilligan, Ballycastle (County Londonderry, *not* County Antrim), Limavady (Sir Thomas Phillips's lands), Dungiven, Muff, Crosalt, Nutown (New Buildings on the Goldsmiths' Proportion), Strabane, Greencastle, Redcastle, Whitecastle, and Muff Culmor (Muff, County Donegal, and Culmore Fort). (*WCD/GB*)

the Companies had been allotted estates which they were obliged to develop and settle, they were also required to fund the 'undivided lands' of The Irish Society, the proprietor of all lands in County Londonderry not owned by the Companies, the Church, or the freeholders. However, in return for their contributions it was intended that The Irish Society would pay dividends to the Companies. All parties (the City of London, The Irish Society, and the Companies) had to adhere to the Articles of Agreement and the charter, and were responsible for the completion and management of the Plantation.[62] The Companies, furthermore, were disadvantaged because their manors were not properly conveyed to them for a few more years.

[62] Moody (1939), Ch. VI; Curl (1986), 60-62.

However, the state of play can be best shown in the following table. The Great Companies are given in **bold type**, in Order of Precedence, and the Associated Companies are given in *their* Order of Precedence within each group:

Lot number of each Proportion and name of major settlement	*Livery Companies*	*Order of Precedence now and in (1616)*	*Levy on each Livery Company in Pounds Sterling (Total levy on each group)*	*Approximate area of each Proportion in acres and (square miles)*	*Name of Manor, date of conveyance, name of first farmers, and (date of agreement to farm)*
8 Movanagher (destroyed in the 17th century and replaced by Kilrea)	**Mercers** Masons Innholders Cooks Broderers	1 30 32 35 48 (50)	3,920 150 300 300 233 (4,903)	21,600 (33.5)	Manor of Mercers, 17 October 1618. No farmer as Company retained direct control.
2 Muff (renamed Eglinton in the 19th century because it was confused with Muff just over the county boundary in Donegal)	**Grocers** No Associates as more than the full levy was raised	2	5,000 (5,000 plus 874 subscribed to Vintners Proportion)	15,900 (24.9)	Manor of Grocers, 17 October 1618. Edward Rone (2 May 1615, for 61 years @ £116 13s. 4d. per annum) However, Rone died and the property was leased to Robert Harrington on 29 October 1619 for 57 years from 1 May 1620 @ the same rental proposed in the Rone agreement.
11 Moneymore (second settlement of Draperstown developed in the 19th century)	**Drapers** Tallow-Chandlers (bought out soon after)	3 21 (20)	4,608 380 (4,988)	38,800 (60.6)	Manor of Drapers, 20 July 1619. Sir Thomas Roper (7 May 1619, for 55 years for 'fine' of £450 and £230 per annum for 21 years, £260 p.a. thereafter). However, an agent was placed in charge 1622-28, and the Proportion was leased to Peter Barker for 60 years from 1 November 1627 for a 'fine' of £500 and £200 p.a. Barker died in 1631 and the property was then leased to Sir John Clotworthy (d.1665—created 1st Viscount Massereene in 1660) on 23 October 1633 for 61 years from 1 November 1632 @ £200 p.a.
3 Ballykelly	**Fishmongers** Leathersellers Plaisterers Musicians Basket Makers Glaziers	4 15 46 (47) 50 (52) 52 (54) 53 (55)	3,390 1,450 60 30 48 48 (5,026)	24,100 (37.7)	Manor of Walworth, 24 October 1618. James Higgins (10 February 1617, for 60 years for 'fine' of £400 and £167 p.a.). This arrangement was changed when two thirds of the Proportion were leased to Christopher Freeman on 24 January 1631 for 31 years from 1 November 1630 @ £160 p.a., while Higgins took a lease of one third of the Proportion for 40 years from 1 May 1632 @ £55 13s. 4d. p.a.
1 New Buildings	**Goldsmiths** Armourers Cordwainers Painter-Stainers	5 22 (21) 27 (26) 28	4,459 60 370 66 (4,955)	11,050 (17.25)	Manor of Goldsmiths' Hall, 10 September 1617. John Freeman (26 January 1615, for 20 years @ £106 p.a.)
12 Dungiven (with second bawn at Brackfield [also known as Crosalt])	**Skinners** Whitebakers Girdlers Stationers	6 and 7 in alternate years 19 (18) 23 (22) 47 (49)	2,903 720 570 800 (4,993)	49,000 (76.5)	Manor of Pellipar, 22 March 1618. Sir Edward Dod(d)ington (July 1616, 58 years 6 months @ £112 p.a.). Dod(d)ington died(*c.*1618) and his interests passed to his widow and her second husband, Sir Francis Cooke. The property was leased to Tristram Beresford and George Carey (in trust for Lady Cooke) on 26 June 1627 for 47 years 4 months from 1 May 1627 @ £125 p.a.
6 Macosquin	**Merchant Taylors** No associates as more than full levy was raised	7 and 6 in alternate years	5,000 (5,000 plus 1,186 subscribed to Clothworkers' Proportion)	18,700 29.25)	Manor of St John the Baptist, October 1618. Valentine Hartopp (18 July 1617, 51 years from 1 November 1617, for 'fine' of £500 and £150 p.a.). However, Hartopp, in Moody's words a 'needy and grasping adventurer', assigned his lease to Ralph Wall in 1621, who obtained a new lease dated 30 July 1622 for 46 years from 1 November 1621 @ £150 p.a.

4 Ballecaslan (Bally Castle [not to be confused with the town in County Antrim]—with another settlement at Artikelly)	**Haberdashers** Wax-Chandlers Founders Turners	8 20 (19) 33 51 (53)	4,724 120 90 102 (5,036)	23,100 (36.1)	Manor of Freemore, 15 April 1617. Sir Robert McClelland (6 August 1616, 51 years for £1,000 [representing the first 3 years' rent payable by 25 December 1616] and £350 10s. od. p.a. payable from 1620). By 1633 the rent was £200 p.a.
10 Magherafelt (with another settlement, castle, and bawn at Salterstown)	**Salters** Dyers Cutlers Saddlers Joiners Woolmen	9 13 18 (17) 25 (24) 41 43	2,914 900 345 590 246 30 (5,025)	23,250 (36.4)	Manor of Sal, 12 February 1619. William Finch *et al.* (May 1616 @ £160 p.a., but subsequently leased to Ralph Whistler, 20 June 1627, 51 years, for a 'fine' of £400 and £100 p.a. rent).
7 Agivey	**Ironmongers** Brewers Pewterers Barber-Surgeons Carpenters Coopers Scriveners	10 14 16 17 (27) 26 (25) 36 44 (45)	2,230 700 360 350 300 420 570 (4,930)	19,450 (30.4)	Manor of Lizard, 7 November 1618. George Canning (14 August 1617, 41 years @ £150 p.a. from 1 November 1619).
9 Bellaghy (called for a brief period Vintnerstown)	**Vintners** Grocers Curriers Plumbers Poulters Tylers and Bricklayers Blacksmiths Weavers Woodmongers Fruiterers	11 2 29 31 34 37 40 42 — (44) 45	3,120 874 66 120 120 120 96 150 320 96 (5,082)	32,600 (50.9)	Manor of Vintners, *c.* October 1618. John Rowley and Baptist Jones (9 May 1616, 57 years from 1619 @ £120 p.a.). Rowley died *c.* July 1617, so the lease passed to Jones, 20 April 1619. Jones died in *c.* January 1624, and the property was leased to Henry Conway on 20 July 1625 for 51 years from 1 May 1625 @ £120 p.a.
5 Killowen (with a second settlement at Articlave). In the 19th century Castlerock was also developed as a holiday resort	**Clothworkers** Merchant Taylors Butchers Bowyers Fletchers Brownbakers Upholders	12 6 and 7 in alternate years 24 38 39 — (48) 49 (51)	3,390 1,186 230 30 30 130 66 (5,062)	13,450 (21.0)	Manor of Clothworkers, June 1618. Sir Robert McClelland (probably 1618, 51 years @ £250 p.a., but £600 8s. 4d. to be paid in advance for first 3 years of rent). The rent was reduced to £150 per annum, payable in advance, in October 1626.
Undivided lands	The Honourable The Irish Society	N/A	Monies collected from the Companies	29,900 (46.8)	N/A. The properties were essentially Coleraine and Londonderry, with their Liberties and Culmore Fort.

Thus the levy on each group was £5,000, making a total of £60,000, but some groups had to pay more to make up the £5,000 quota, while other groups that had overpaid were reimbursed.[63] In addition to the City of London's lands the table under shows the remaining picture:

Proprietor	*Lands*	*Area in acres and (square miles)*
Sir Thomas Phillips	Limavady and contiguous areas. Moyola and district (i.e. opposite Toome)	13,100 (20.5) 6,300 (9.8)
Anglican Church (Church of Ireland)	bishops' lands incumbents' lands	102,100 (159.6) 14,300 (22.3)
native Irish freeholds	parcels of land allocated to Irish gentlemen	52,050 (81.4)

[63] These figures are derived from Chart (ed.) (1928), *passim*; Curl (1986), 69-71; and Moody (1939), 183, 442-461. For Orders of Precedence see Leigh and Taylor (eds.) (1997), 36-7.

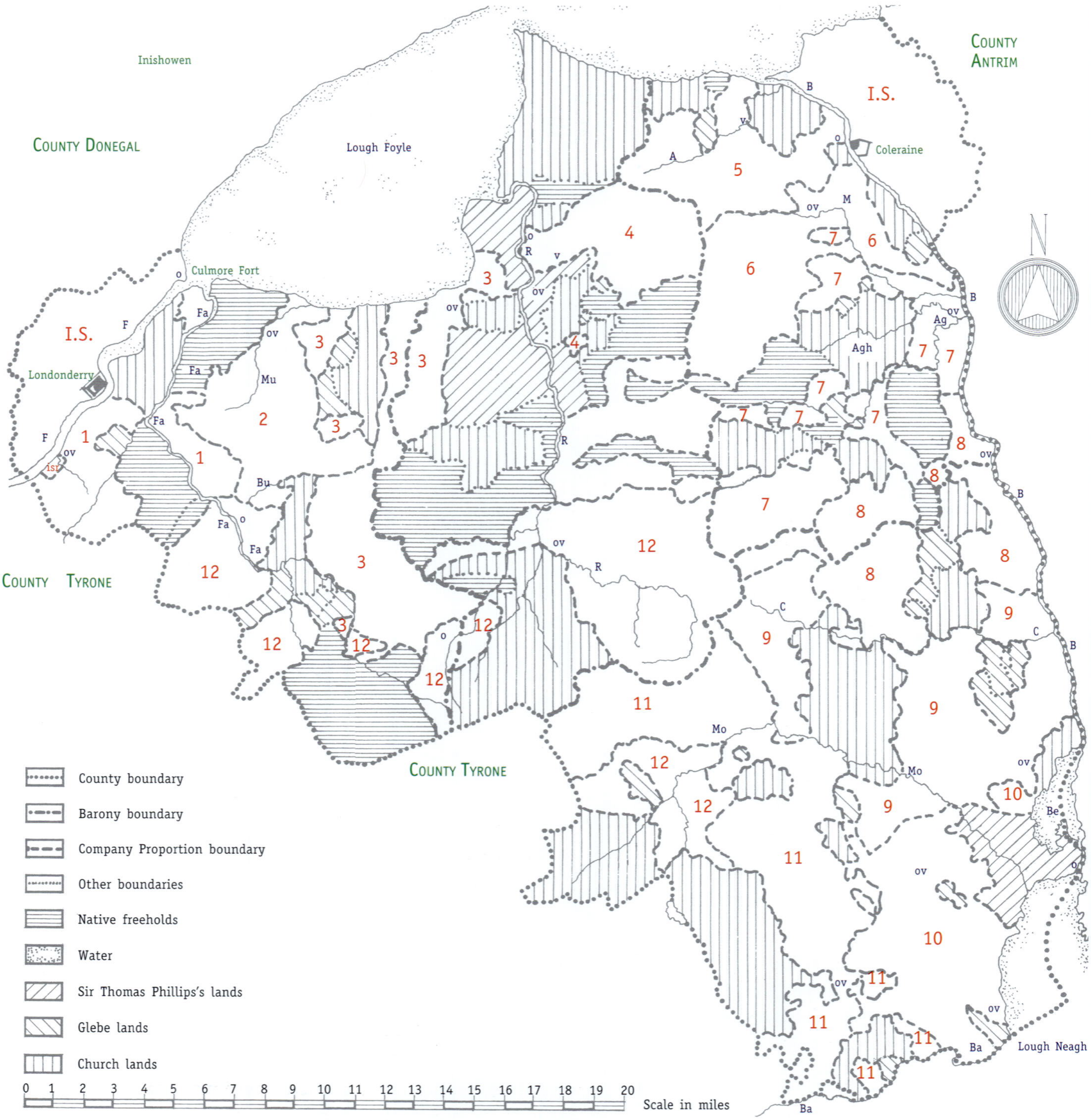

Proportion 1 (Goldsmiths)
Proportion 2 (Grocers)
Proportion 3 (Fishmongers)
Proportion 4 (Haberdashers)

Proportion 5 (Clothworkers)

Proportion 6 (Merchant Taylors)
Proportion 7 (Ironmongers)
Proportion 8 (Mercers)
Proportion 9 (Vintners)
Proportion 10 (Salters)

Proportion 11 (Drapers)
Proportion 12 (Skinners)

Sir Thomas Phillips's Lands

ov: New Buildings
ov: Muff (later Eglinton)
ov: Ballykelly (Walworth)
o: Ballycastle
v: Artikelly
o: Killowen (old Irish castle opposite Coleraine)
v: Articlave
ov: Macosquin
ov: Agivey
ov: Movanagher
ov: Bellaghy (Vintnerstown)
ov: Magherafelt (to the north)
ov: Salterstown (near Lough Neagh)
ov: Moneymore
ov: Dungiven
o: Cros(s)alt (Brackfield)
ov: Limavady
o: Toome

The Irish Society's lands (Liberties of Londonderry and Coleraine) : I.S.
The Irish Society's lands at Rossnagalliagh : isr

A : River Articlave
Agh : River Aghadowey
Ag : River Agivey
B : River Bann
Ba : River Ballinderry
Be : Lough Beg
Bu : River Burntollet
C : River Clady (or Claudy)
F : River Foyle
Fa : River Faughan
M : River Macosquin
Mo : River Moyola
Mu : River Muff
O : River Owenbeg
R : River Roe
v : village
o : castle or fort
ov : castle and village

23 The county of Londonderry with the distribution of property following the parcelling of the lots to the City Companies. The extremely fragmented nature of Proportions 7 (Ironmongers) and 12 (Skinners) should be noted. *(A after various sources, including Company Proportions maps, Curl [1986], Moody [1939], Sampson [1814], and Simington [ed.] [1937]).*

The total area of the lands throughout the county of Londonderry, therefore, was 508,700 acres (794.9 square miles), of which The Irish Society held 5.9 per cent, the Livery Companies 57.3 per cent, Phillips 3.8 per cent, the Church 22.8 per cent, and the native freeholders 10.2 per cent. Fragmented, land-locked Proportions (e.g. those of the Drapers' and Skinners' Companies, situated partly in the dangerous and partly mountainous areas to the south) were larger than the more fertile, lowland Proportions that were nearer Londonderry and Coleraine (and therefore more secure). The proportion of land owned by the Anglican Church (over a fifth of the total) should be noted. Although the proportion of native freeholds estated by The Irish Society (some 16 or 17 in all, comprising just over 10 per cent of the total area of the county), seems quite small, these were also situated in hilly and relatively unproductive country, a point not lost on the various Deputations and surveys of later years. Two native freeholds were forfeited after the 1615 Irish conspiracy, and many Irish sold their lands to the Planters. By 1639 there were as many British as Irish in possession of the 'native freeholds'. However, this does not mean the Irish were driven off the land. According to the intentions of the scheme of Plantation, the native Irish were to remove themselves from the City of London's lands, but deadlines passed again and again, and the Irish largely stayed put. The fact of the matter was that, for whatever reasons, the Londoners could not (or would not) attract settlers in sufficient numbers, and so the Irish remained, otherwise the entire agricultural economy would have failed. Furthermore, the Irish paid their rents in order to stay on, and it was better from the Londoners' point of view to have rents coming in rather than none. This failure to comply with one of the most important aspects of the Plantation scheme was to sour relations with the Crown, and had momentous consequences.

A few more words will suffice on the Company estates as these have been dealt with in some detail in the present writer's earlier works.[64] The term 'farmer' has little to do with agriculture, and really means a *firmator* or *fermier*, meaning one who undertakes the collection of taxes, rents, etc., paying a fixed sum from the proceeds. Farmers therefore paid the sums outlined above to the Companies and had obligations to build 'English' houses, fortified manor-houses, and bawns, to enclose land, and so on. However, The Irish Society reserved rights to fell and carry away timber growing on the Proportions, to hunt, fish, and ride there, and to seek for, dig, and carry off stone, slate, loam, gravel, sand, and other materials for building purposes. Farmers had the liberty to cut down timber for the construction of houses, repairs, making carts, ploughs, gates, etc., and for fuel, but for this they had to pay an annual rent of £1 5s. od. and to render to The Society as lord of the manor homage and fealty, suit of court, the obligation to grind all corn and grain grown on the Proportion at The Society's mills, and heriots (fines) for every alienation of land and the death of each tenant. The duties to enclose and subdivide the lands by means of strong hedges, mounds, fences, ditches, etc., and to build a substantial fortified house were onerous, as were the requirements to keep arms on the premises and not to demise or let premises to anyone who would not take the Oath of Allegiance and Supremacy before a Justice of the Peace.

In some cases the individuals concerned were able to lay the foundations of their fortunes, though others were highly conscientious agents of the Companies. George Canning (d. 1646), for example, served the Ironmongers very well, and carried out

[64] Curl (1986), *passim*.

works on the Proportion with its 'capital' at Agivey. His son, William, was killed during the Irish rebellion of 1641, and his direct descendant, George Canning (1770-1827), became Prime Minister in 1827, but a promising career was cut short by George's death soon afterwards.[65] The Cannings, who obtained a grant of the Manor of Garvagh, County Londonderry, were raised to the peerage as Barons Garvagh in 1818. Ralph Whistler, farmer (1627-35) of the Salters' Proportion, was an indefatigable despoiler of the woods to make pipe-staves, in spite of which misdemeanour his descendants were long associated with the estate. Gabriel Whistler repaired Magherafelt church in 1699, and was the ancestor of the celebrated American painter, James Abbott McNeill Whistler (1834-1903). Mention has already been made of the remarkable rise of the Beresfords, and Sir Robert McClelland (or MacLennan) (d. 1641), who was involved in the Proportions of the Haberdashers and Clothworkers, became a peer of Scotland as Baron Kirkcudbright (in which town the McClelland castle stands to this day).

Some of the Livery Companies, however, were only nominal participants in the Plantation. The Haberdashers, for example, gave up their interest to two of their number (William Freeman and Adrian Moore), and the Coopers and Brownbakers (the last no longer exist) forfeited their disbursements, withdrawing from the scheme altogether. The Bowyers and Fletchers, who had fallen on hard times, were bought out by the Ironmongers, and other 'inferior' Companies backed off. The Fishmongers acquired the Musicians' shares as well as those of the Leathersellers (who themselves had bought out the Plaisterers' interests). So keen were the Leathersellers to unload that they let the Fishmongers have their shares at two-thirds of their disbursements. Thus the Fishmongers were left with only the Basketmakers and the Glaziers as their associates. The Drapers bought out their single associate, the Tallow-Chandlers, in 1618 for £374 11s. 0d., which was slightly less than had been disbursed. Other 'inferior' Companies seem to have got rid of their alarming obligations to the Plantation in similar ways.[66] The fact that the Companies had to provide The Irish Society with the funds to build Londonderry and Coleraine as well as the fortress of Culmore must have scared the Liverymen, especially as a fairly large chunk of the (then) huge sum of £60,000 seems to have vanished into thin air.[67]

[65] *D.N.B.* (1917), **iii**, 872-83; Townend (ed.) (1963), 987-8.

[66] Moody (1939), 154-5.

[67] Material in this chapter is drawn from a variety of sources indicated in the footnotes, from the extensive matter listed in Curl (1986), *passim*, and also from the definitive texts of Moody (1939) and Moody and Simms (eds.). (1968 and 1983). Considerable use was also made of the material listed in Aldous (ed.) (1993) in the Corporation of London Records Office. See also *Analecta Hibernica* 3 (1931) and 8 (1938), Bagwell (1909), Betts (1913), Boyd (1933), Brewer and Bullen (eds.) (1867-73), Camblin (1951), Chart (ed.) (1928), Colby (1837), Hill (1877, 1889), Irish Society (*c.* 1898), Portlock (1843), Robinson (1984, 1994), Russell and Prendergast (eds.) (1872-80), and Schultes (1822).

CHAPTER IV

Surveys, Progress and Setbacks, Settlers, Planning and Buildings, and Commissions

> The plan of the new town of Derry was … most interesting … The layout consisted of two main streets which crossed one another at right angles, the crossing being emphasised by the formation of a large square, in the centre of which was a building containing a market house, town hall, and prison. The steep slope of the ground did not prevent a rectangular plan from being adopted and consequently a steep gradient resulted in some of the streets. The town had four gates, one being placed at each end of the two main streets and these, with the market house at the crossing, must have added considerably to the character of the streets
>
> GILBERT CAMBLIN (1913-87): *The Town in Ulster. An account of the origin and building of the towns of the Province and the development of their rural setting with 62 Plates and Maps from contemporary sources* (Belfast: William Mullan & Son [Publishers] Ltd., 1951), 33

Bodley's Survey of 1614-15 and the King's Letter to Chichester

As has been mentioned above, the first official survey of the Ulster Plantation for the Crown was that of Carew (1611). In 1613 Sir Josias Bodley conducted his first survey. In June 1614 the Lord Deputy received orders to have a new survey carried out so that progress could be assessed, and once more Bodley was asked to perform the task, which he did in September. His report (the second Bodley survey) was highly critical of the Londoners' Plantation. Anxiety in high places had been growing concerning the efficiency and the will of the City to carry out its obligations. Bodley's investigations are a devastating indictment. He opined[1] that the 'Cittie of London' had never intended 'his Maties satisfaccion' but viewed the Plantation as an unwelcome drain on resources. Furthermore, evidence of the claimed expenditure was scant; the City had not established any of the colonists claimed (the only British people on the Londoners' Plantation were tradesmen, labourers, a few settlers who had been there before the Londoners, and a handful of brave adventurers who had gone to Ulster of their own accord); the defences of Coleraine were wholly inadequate and, in order to save money, had not been carried out to his approved plans; the state of the new houses in Coleraine was appalling, and several buildings were not even capable of keeping the weather out; the fortifications of Londonderry were not ready (although stone and lime had been prepared), while one of the two old fortresses that had survived O'Doherty's sack of Derry had been demolished[2] and the other was ruinous and beyond repair, so Londonderry, intended to give protection and succour to settlers

[1] Moody (1939), 160 ff. Bodley's report was copied by the then Clerk to the Goldsmith's Company, Henry Carter, in 1615-16, and abstracts of this were used by Moody in his pioneering and indispensable study.

[2] *Ibid.*, 161.

in the Inishowen peninsula and county lands, was hopelessly undefended; some levelling and paving of streets had been carried out in Londonderry, but the 100 or so houses only consisted of a single room and a roof-space; high rents, short tenancies, and the fact that very few of the intended acres had been assigned to the towns for the support of civic government tended to depress confidence and fail to lift the local economy out of its less than buoyant condition; and the few inhabitants (not surprisingly) were demoralised, uncooperative, and could not be expected to remain long. Bodley stated categorically that some £20,000 had 'gone some other waies than directlie' towards the 'buildinges and plantinges', that about £35,000 had been spent (although reduced by the rents taken in), and that it seemed clear that private interests had been financed by funds rightfully belonging to the City of London.[3]

In the countryside things were very bad. The Companies had sent agents to Ulster, but only a few cheap houses had been put up in order to increase the value of the land; instead of the 800 or so armed British settlers intended by the Crown, there were very few, and the armaments in Londonderry and Coleraine were wholly inadequate; furthermore, the Irish were present in great numbers, clearly intending to stay put, while The Irish Society saw no need to remove them. In short, Bodley found that The Irish Society had not built the houses required (either in numbers or up to standard in terms of accommodation or quality of construction), nor fortified the settlements, nor 'planted' the country, and that the Londoners had not given 'anie testimonie by their course of proceedinge' that they had 'any purpose' other that to make money out of the 'busynesse'.[4] The Londonderry Plantation lay open to attack, money was missing, and accomplishments failed to relate to alleged expenditure. From the Londoners' point of view, they had originally been required to sink £20,000 into the venture, had actually spent £45,000 (with no end to the expenditure in sight), had no prospect of immediate profit, and had not achieved the political and colonial objective required of them. It was a devastating state of affairs.

By early 1615 all the cash raised by the City had gone, £10,000 had been borrowed, and further levies were raised from the ever-reluctant Companies. More obligations were placed upon the Londoners as a result of Bodley's survey. The Companies were required to prepare detailed descriptions of their Proportions for The Irish Society which, in turn, was to draw up a detailed report on the Plantation. It is clear that Bodley's survey alarmed the King, who wrote to the Lord Deputy in very strong terms on 25 March 1615.[5] Using the Royal 'We', the King said he had 'receaved latelie ... a relat'on of the p̱sent estate of the plantac̄on in Ulster, sett downe with some clearnes and order by the pen of Sr Josias Bodley, according to the exactnes of the survey thereof taken lately by himself by or commandment'. The King was impressed by Bodley's 'care and industrye in p̱formance of that service', and had 'examined, viewed, and reviewed with or own eyes everie pte thereof'. His Majesty found, 'greatlie to' his 'dis-contentment, the slow p̱gression of that plantac̄on; some fewe of the Brittishe undertakers, s'vitors, and natives having as yett proceeded effectuallie to the accomplishing of such things in all points' as was 'required of them by the articles of the plantac̄on; the rest, and by much more the greater p̱te, having either done nothing at all, or so little, or by reason of the [slightness] thereof to so little purpose, that the work seems rather to us to be forgotten by them, and to p̱ishe under their hands, than any whitt to be advanced by them; some having begun to build and not to plant,

[3] Moody (1939), 161.
[4] *Ibid.*, 162.
[5] Johnson (1914-22): **iv**, 505-7.

others began to plant and not to build, and all of them in geñall reteyning the Irish still upon their lands, the avoiding of wch was the fundamental reason of that plantac̃on'. Ominously, the King noted he had 'made collection of their names ... and ... their endeav^{rs} or neglicences ... in this s'vice', which he would 'reteyne as a memoriall': all defaulters would be 'sure to feele accordingly the effectes' of the King's 'ffavour as there shalbe occasion'. King James reminded the Lord Deputy that if he (the King) 'had intended onlie' his 'p̱sent profitt', as it seemed most Undertakers 'over greedelie' had done, he 'might have conv'ted those large territories of' the 'escheated lands to the greate imp̱vem^{t} of the revenewe' of the Crown: however, he 'chose rather, for the safetie of that countrye, and the civillizing of that people, to dep̱te with the inheritance of them [the lands] at extreame under values, and to make a plantac̃on of them'.

As the Crown had been 'induced' to commence the Plantation 'out of reason of state', the King felt justified to 'make bould with' the rights of anyone who had neglected his 'duties in a s'vice of so much ymportance'. He threatened to 'resume into' his hands the estates of any Planter who had 'failed to p̱forme, according to [the] originall intention', the articles of the plantation, and 'to bestow them upon some other men more active and worthie of them than themselves'. Nevertheless , although the King had a 'just p̱vocation to proceed ... with rigor against' defaulters, he was prepared 'to assigne ... a further tyme' to the end of August 1616 'w^{ch} ... shalbe finall and peremptorie', after which he would 'seize into ... [his] ... hands the lands of any men whatsoev^{r}, without respecte of persons, whether he be a Brittishe undertaker servitor or native', found 'defective in p̱forming any of the articles' of the plantation 'to wch he was enioyned'. As soon as the 'lymitted tyme of favo^{r}' expired, Sir Josias Bodley would carry out a 'p̱ticular survey' of the plantation, and anyone found 'to be defycient in anie point to wch he' was bound would have his Proportion or Proportions seized. The King would have no truck with feigned lack of knowledge of what was required (or, as he put it, 'p̱tend ignorance'), Bodley was required to 'take a reviewe of the relation of his last survey', after which, 'with as much convenient speed' to 'signifye to the Londoners, and to every undertaker, servitor, and native, and to their servants or assignees that dwell upon their land, their seva'll defectes and omissions, either in matter or in forme, that all thinges accordinglie may be reformed and p̱formed'. In other words Bodley was to prepare check-lists of action to be taken to make good all poor and sub-standard works and to ensure that anything required to be done, which had not, was implemented. By the time Bodley was to make his next survey in 1616 the Undertakers (including the Londoners) were expected to have remedied all matters required. The King's instructions applied not only to the current Lord Deputy, but to 'anie other Deputie that hereafter for that tyme shalbe', and gave powers to 'seize' any estates or Proportions belonging to any Undertaker found wanting.[6]

King James's celebrated letter, therefore, was at pains to emphasise the ideals behind the Plantation, the 'reason of State' that had prompted the venture, and much else. In a postscript in the King's own hand, Chichester was exhorted in terms that resound down the centuries: 'My Lo. In this s'rvice I expect that zeale and uprightnes from you, that ye will spare no fleshe, Englishe nor Scottishe fo no private man's worth is able to countervaile the safetie of a kingdom, wch this Plantac̃on being well accomplished, will p̱cure'.[7]

[6] Johnson (1914-22): **iv**, 505-7. See also Chart (ed.) (1928), 47-9, where the letter is given in full, though Johnson's transcript appears to be more accurate. See also Russell and Prendergast (eds.) (1880): *Cal S.P.I. 1615-1625*, 15; Irish Society (*c.*1898), 393-5.

[7] Chart (ed.) (1928), 49; Johnson (1914-22), **iv**, 507.

This letter undoubtedly put the fear of God into the Undertakers. Rowley (by then Agent of The Drapers' Company), wrote[8] that it 'hath not onlie stirred upp the most that are for the oth^{r} companies to be planting & buildinge, but also all the Servito^{rs} & undertakers, soe as manie of those workmen whom I intended to have imploied and that weare long sut^{rs} to me to be settled under you are now unwillinglie settled wth others'. He warned the Drapers that 'there is now noe expectation of favour to any and the least to London, much being looked for at yor hands'.[9] The writing was clearly visible on the wall.

The most optimistic of the adventurers must have been left in no doubt that the King meant business, and hopes of making a fast buck and of neglecting obligations evaporated. That is not to say that The Irish Society or the City of London had intended any sharp practice, for there is no evidence that this was so, in spite of a plethora of intemperate 19th-century Irish polemics to the contrary. Certain individuals (and Rowley seems to have been one of them[10]), sent to Ulster, probably abused their positions, but everything appears to have been done that could be done to bring them to heel. It was not just the justified anger of the King that concentrated minds however, for other threats soon spread alarm, and their effects were far-reaching.[11]

The Native Conspiracy or The Great Northern Plot

On 18 April 1615[12] Chichester, who made sure he was kept very well informed about events in Ulster, intimated to the English Privy Council that there was a plot by Irish natives to massacre the settlers in Ulster and undo the Plantation. Emboldened by the 'paucity and poor estate of the soldiers', the 'weakness' of the Undertakers, and encouraged by 'news beyond the seas' that made them 'bold', some Ulster Irish hatched a plot to resist the huge changes promised by the Plantation scheme. The inaction and inefficiency about which Bodley, Chichester, Phillips, the King, and others were concerned doubtless raised hopes in Irish breasts. Implicated in the plot was Rory O'Cahan, one of the native freeholders, and his associates included another O'Cahan, kinsmen of the exiled Tyrone, including a freeholder in County Tyrone, Brian Crossagh O'Neill; two brothers of Sir Niall Garbh O'Donnell; one Edmund O'Mullarky, a friar; Alexander MacDonnell (a nephew of Sir Randal, therefore making the MacDonnells of Antrim and the Isles suspected as part of the conspiracy); and a priest, Laughlin O'Laverty. The Great Northern Plot involved plans to rescue Tyrone's son, held in Fort Charlemont; to attack and destroy Coleraine, Londonderry, Lifford, Dungannon, Carrickfergus, and other settlements (with everyone in them); to massacre all settlers and tradesmen, only sparing Beresford, Sir Richard Hansard (d. 1619), and Rowley (who were to be held hostage pending the release from the Tower of London of Sir Donnell O'Cahan, Sir Niall Garbh O'Donnell, the latter's son, and Sir Cormac McBaron O'Neill); and to kill Sir Thomas Phillips (Rory O'Cahan boasted he would cut off Sir Thomas's head) and recover the O'Cahan properties at Limavady.

However, as Moody noted, the conspirators were indiscreet to the point of foolhardy noisiness (part of the plot included O'Cahan and others drinking all day in

[8] May 1615.

[9] 20 May 1615, see Moody (1939), 164-5.

[10] Johnson (1914-22), **iii**, 23, calls Rowley a 'grasping man' whose 'administration of the Plantation' was not satisfactory. See also Hill (1877), 419-25.

[11] Chichester's letter to the English Privy Council, 18 April 1615. Moody, Martin, and Byrne (eds.) (1982), 226. See also Moody (1939), 166-7.

[12] Russell and Prendergast (eds.) (1880): *Cal. S.P.I. 1615-1625*, 38-9.

Coleraine and then, through various agents, to get the guard to betray the town and open the way for Irish to enter through the fortifications), and were, on the whole, a 'fatuous set, in whose hands the plot had not the remotest chance of success'.[13] The whistle seems to have been blown by Alexander MacDonnell's servant, who, about to be hanged as an 'idle person', saved his life by giving valuable information about the plot to Phillips and others. When it was revealed that the conspirators hoped to gain the assistance of men from MacDonnell's territory, the Highlands and Islands of Scotland, and Spain, a frisson ran through the authorities. The plotters were certainly no match for Phillips, whose agents kept him well-informed, and soon the ringleaders were under arrest. Seventeen were tried at the Assizes in the half-built city of Londonderry, 11 were released, and six were found guilty and condemned on 31 July 1615. Two O'Cahans, two O'Neills, O'Laverty, and one O'Kennan were hanged, drawn, and quartered, the heads afterwards being set up on the city gates.[14] The presence, among the conspirators, of a friar and a priest suggests that resistance to the imposition of Anglicanism and the suppression of Roman Catholicism was at least a significant factor in the matter. As a result of the conspiracy two native freeholds were forfeited to The Irish Society, one of which was let for life to George Carey, Recorder of Londonderry, for £5 6s. 8d. per annum.[15]

In a strange dredging up of this case early in the 20th century it appears there were moves to elevate the executed six as martyrs, but a discreet veil was drawn, and the campaign was quietly dropped when wiser counsels prevailed.[16] Nevertheless, it must be emphasised that the implications of the conspiracy were enormous, for it had been hatched in County Londonderry among the very natives The Irish Society and the Companies were so keen to retain on their lands and in the area the City of London was supposed to secure, and indeed was the first effort (however ineffective) at a rising since Tyrone's submission.

Chichester's Concerns, The Irish Society's Reactions, and Settlers

Chichester warned the Privy Council that unless the new county could be better protected it would fall sooner or later, while Coleraine could not withstand an attack by the MacDonnells (who had been regarded as loyal to the Crown, but now, in view of Alexander MacDonnell's apparent involvement in the Conspiracy, had to be seen at best as unwilling allies and at worst as implacable enemies of Protestant colonists).[17] The Irish Society was told in no uncertain terms that improvements had to be made: it was even suggested that Coleraine should be strengthened by building a keep or fortress there. At once Precepts were sent out to the Livery Companies to provide the wherewithal for defence, and arms were despatched to Londonderry and Coleraine. At a Court of the Ironmongers' Company, for example, as early as 19 April 1615, it was ordered that 'two muskets and four Calivers be sent over for defence of the parts of Ireland',[18] and other Companies also reacted. The Londoners put the question of the Coleraine keep on ice, however, clearly resenting any more demands over and above existing commitments to what was rapidly becoming an expensive nightmare.

[13] Curl (1986), 62-4; Moody (1939), 159-165.
[14] Gillespie (1987), *passim*, Lacy (1998), 96-7.
[15] Russell and Prendergast (eds.) (1880): *Cal. S.P.I., 1615-25*, 29-82; and *passim*; Chart (ed.) (1928), 9, 46-7; Moody (1939), 165-6.
[16] Gillespie (1987), *passim*; Lacy (1998), 97.
[17] Russell and Prendergast (eds.) (1880): *Cal. S.P.I. 1615-25*, 38-9, and *passim*; Moody (1939), 166-7.
[18] Irish Society (*c.*1898), 396.

In September 1615 another Precept to the Companies was issued requiring immediate payment of sums due '*upon pain of imprisonment* and such further punishment as the qualities of … contempt … deserve', and in November The Irish Society demanded certificates from the Companies concerning buildings erected and the progress of 'planting' or settling tenants. Clearly information had to be gathered in preparation for the expected inquiries from the Government. Early in 1616 more information about the Proportions was demanded by The Irish Society from the Companies, which bodies were also instructed (2 March 1615/16) to arrange for skilled English workmen and their families, with all tools and baggage, to be settled in County Londonderry by the spring 'for the increase of our nation … and the strenthening of … towns and places'. Urgently needed were weavers of linen, cloth, fustian (coarse, twilled cotton fabric including velveteen and corduroy), and 'new stuffs', feltmakers, 'trimmers of hats' and hat-band makers; locksmiths; farriers; tanners and fellmongers (men who prepared hides for the tanners); shoemakers; girdlers (makers of waist-belts, often capable of carrying light articles, e.g. a weapon or a purse, and frequently decorated); iron-makers and blacksmiths; glass-makers and cutters; pewterers; 'coast fishermen'; turners (men who worked with woods and metals turning them on a lathe to fashion them; the term is also applied, historically, to potters); basket-makers; tallow-chandlers (makers of candles from animal fats, especially from sheep and cattle); dyers; and curriers (those who dress tanned leather). Interestingly, these new tradesmen were to be respectable and God-fearing, unlike the rootless boozers (defined by The Irish Society as 'common drunkards or persons of defamed or ill life') who appear to have comprised the early consignments sent to the City's lands. Clearly, the tone of the settlements was to be improved. Twelve poor boys from 'hospital and other poor children' from London were to be sent to County Londonderry to serve as apprentices and servants, thus discouraging the taking on of Irish children in these rôles.[19] It seems that in a few instances apprentices were 'enticed' away from their London masters so that they could be sent to Ulster.[20] Ten Christ's Hospital boys were settled in Londonderry and two in Coleraine: they must have been bewildered and very frightened. Finally, those Companies that had advowsons in their Proportions were to 'with speed re-edify the Churches and furnish their several Ministries with a bible and a book of common prayer and with a Communion cup to administer the Sacrament of the Lord's Supper'.[21] The Society acknowledged that the Companies had 'already

[19] Moody (1939), 168.

[20] Curl (1986), 64-5; Hardy (ed.) (1937), 175-6.

[21] Irish Society (*c.*1898), 421-2. The author is also indebted to the late Mr. Hugh Alexander Boyd of Ballycastle for information on ecclesiastical matters in County Londonderry. On the matter of the Christ's Hospital boys, the Court Minute Book for the period *c.*1615-18 (Guildhall Library MS. 12806/3) and a search of the Children's Registers for the period *c.*1600-18 (MS. 12818/1) produced source material relating to the children, for some of the names match the list of householders in Londonderry of 1628 (see King, R.G.S. [ed][1936] – e.g. Hugh Joanes [admitted to Christ's Hospital 20 May 1601 and discharged as apprentice to William Cooke, 27 July 1615], Peter Morgan [admitted to C.H. 7 July 1601], John Smith [admitted to C. H. 19 March 1605 and discharged as apprentice to David Alline, 5 May 1615], and Thomas Brooke [admitted to C. H. 13 January 1606/7]. Other Christ's Hospital boys discharged in 1616 include a Thomas Edmondson (October): could this be the ancestor of the Edmistons who were long established in business in County Londonderry? It would appear, therefore, that the Christ's Hospital records account for at least four of the boys. The others were probably from other London hospitals, especially the Bridewell. What seems to have happened is that the 'Xts Hospitall' boys was a term applied to *all* the apprentices, whether from Christ's Hospital or other establishments. Without wading through the entire unindexed lists of children placed in the hospitals from about 1600, the identities of most of the children remain obscure. However, four out of twelve is a third, and that is something. There does not appear to be any surviving reference to the indentures among the Christ's Hospital records. Mr. Stephen Freeth, Keeper of Manuscripts, and Miss Charlie Turpie, Deputy Keeper of Manuscripts, Guildhall Library, gave valuable assistance here, as did Mr. N. M. Plumley, Curator and Archivist, Christ's Hospital, Horsham, Sussex.

disbursed great sums of money for fortifying and building Londonderry and Coleraine 'besides their several' Proportions in the 'Country which things being brought now to good pass they are desirous that comfort and benefit might redound unto them in time to come and be for the honour of the City of London'. The Society stressed that there was 'nothing so needful as forthwith' to populate County Londonderry with loyal English settlers.[22]

The hoped-for 'honour of the City of London', to a very large extent, was wishful thinking, as the subsequent history would show. Apart from the constant barrage of criticisms leading to various sequestrations of rents, the trial in the Court of the Star Chamber, the break with the Crown, and the interminable litigation with bishops and other individuals, all of which will be outlined hereafter, the hostility to the Londoners on the part of the native Irish would continue unabated, reaching a crescendo of vitriolic hatred in the countless pamphlets churned out during the 19th century. Politics, nationalism, disestablishment of the Church of Ireland, religion, and the Irish land controversies all contributed to the hostility, but the seeker after facts need not waste too much time wading through that mass of polemic, mythology, and untruths. On the whole, the City of London comes out of the story very well, certainly compared with some grasping Undertakers, and it is very clear from the *documentary* evidence that the City and The Irish Society did everything possible to answer criticisms and do what was required by the Crown. It was when the King's demands became impossible that the system broke down.

Strangely, it seems that the references to the 12 apprentices and to the various tradesmen are the only surviving proofs of any early 17th-century attempts by The Irish Society to promote emigration from England to Ulster, and even those exist because the Precepts and mention of them can be found in some Company records, The Irish Society's own records for the period having become unusable or lost (following a disastrous 18th-century fire at Guildhall, London). Moody felicitously refers to some of this material as 'burnt fragments', 'remains', and other papers, 'now in irretrievable confusion'.[23] However, an MS. volume contains 'An abridgement of the principal matters contained in the records belonging to ... The Irish Society', compiled in 1821-2 by Henry Schultes, author of the useful *Concise View* of 1822.[24] The present writer, having been privileged to have a glance at the 'irretrievable confusion', can vouch for the accuracy of Moody's description, so much of the material has to be garnered from Company and other sources. It is clear from these that efforts *were* made to encourage settlers with skills to move to the Londonderry Plantation, though the evidence that comes down to our own times is not overwhelming.

However, as Philip Robinson[25] has shown, sources such as the muster rolls (registers of men capable of bearing arms) of 1618 and *c.*1630 give lists of adult British men, those with predominantly English names being (by 1630) numerous in the areas around Londonderry, Limavady, Coleraine, and in the areas immediately west of the River Bann (i.e. the Proportions of the Merchant Taylors', Ironmongers', Mercers', Vintners', Salters', and Drapers' Companies). A glance at the list entitled *A Particular of the Howses and Famylyes in London Derry*,[26] signed by Tristram Beresford, Agent for

[22] Irish Society (*c.*1898), 419-20 (record of a Precept from The Irish Society sent to The Ironmongers' Company making certain requisitions).
[23] Moody (1939), 422.
[24] Aldous (ed.) (1993), IS/B/4; Schultes (1822), *passim*.
[25] Robinson (1984, 1994), 92-108, 112-14, 119, 122-3, 186, 212-24.
[26] King, R. G. S. (ed.) (1936), *passim*.

The Society, dated 15 May 1628, is sufficient to show that there were indeed many English names on that register (they were in the majority), although 'Evan Jenkin' has a Cambrian ring, while 'Donnell McKenney' and 'Owen O'Galloher' could only have been Irish. There are very few Scots surnames recorded in Londonderry in 1628. Because Sir Robert McClelland, from Galloway, 'farmed' the contiguous Clothworkers' and Haberdashers' Proportions, there were numerous Scots colonists on his lands, but the main influx of Lowland Scots Presbyterian settlers did not begin to arrive until later.

In 1616, however, The Irish Society was prodding the Companies to get on with their requirements under the various agreements. 'The Governor and Committees ... authorized by act of Common Council for the governing and managing of that weighty business' on behalf of the City of London ... had, by 'best endeavours care pain and diligence advanced the said' Plantation as much as possible 'thereby to satisfy His Majesty and the Lords of the Council who from time to time' took a 'strict account' of 'how the same' proceeded or prospered 'according to expectation'. The Companies were reminded in a Precept of 27 July 1616 to 'hasten ... to perform what is enjoined' by 'sending out tenants tradesmen and artizans the sooner to people and profit' each Proportion. The Ironmongers, for example, were told that 'forasmuch as amongst other wants occasioned by delay or negligence' there were not 'yet' any freeholders 'instated' ... 'whereby the Company' could not be 'supplied or served at Assizes or Sessions as' was fitting, to the considerable annoyance of the King, the Lords, and the Lord Deputy. The Society informed the Ironmongers that a 'great prejudice' could 'ensue thereby for want of Government to the great encouragement of malefactors and other lewd persons that for want of punishment do daily increase to the great disturbance' of the Plantation. The Ironmongers (and other Companies) were 'required' to 'forthwith advise and consult together' of such freeholders as they meant to settle on their lands and either by themselves in London or through their agents in Ulster to ensure freeholders were 'instated and established according to such conditions as by the Charter granted by His Majesty' so that 'the Country' would be 'served upon all occasions'. This Precept warned the Companies that action was required immediately, and ended with the peremptory order 'Whereof fail you not'.[27]

Londonderry and its Early Development

The earliest known map of Derry is dated 27 December 1600, and is a rather crude sketch of Docwra's camp based on the medieval Augustinian abbey protected by substantial earthern ramparts. Entitled 'The Iland and forte of the derry', it also shows a fort around the ruins of a church at the highest point of the hill, another fort around the O'Donnell tower-house by the river, and an isolated round tower.[28] It appears to have been drawn by Richard Barth(e)let (or Bartlett), who flourished 1595-1608, and, as has been mentioned earlier, was murdered in Tirconnell in 1608.

Dowcra's settlement is shown in greater detail in a drawing, supposedly of *c.*1600 or *c.*1603, in the library of Trinity College, Dublin, copied in an engraving **[24]** published in Colby's *Memoir of the City and North Western Liberties of Londonderry*.[29] It depicts the O'Donnell 'castle', the fortified town (or 'great fort'),[30] and a proposed planned

27 Irish Society (*c.*1898), 421-2.
28 P.R.O. SP 63/207 Pt. VI, No 84 (i), P.R.O.N.I. T.1493/36, or T/1965/2C/IS .
29 Colby (1837), plate opposite 98.
30 Schultes (1822), clxvii.

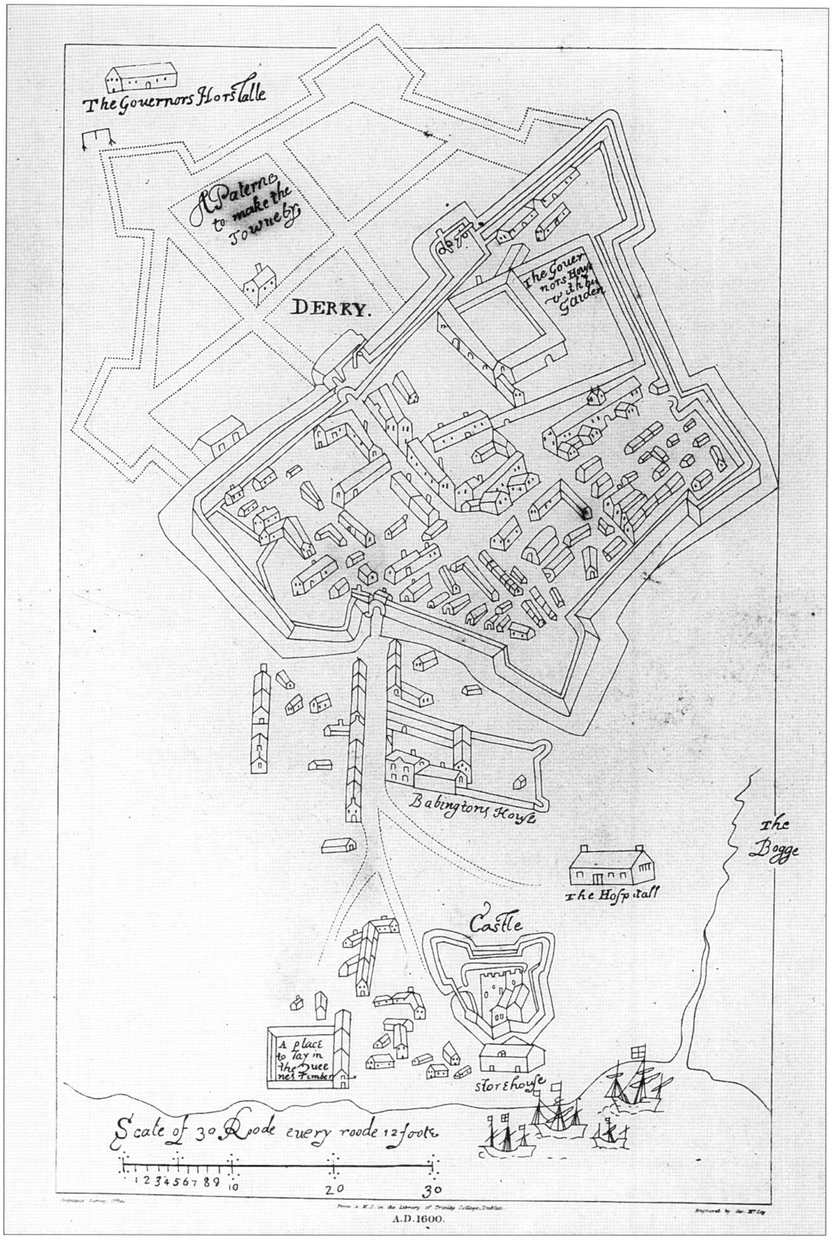

24 Derry in *c.*1600 or *c.*1603. At the bottom is the River Foyle, on the banks of which are stores and 'a place to lay in the "Queenes Timber"', so the image dates from before the Queen's death in March 1603. Near the river is the O'Donnell castle, and a 'Hospitall' stands in a relatively isolated position near the 'Bogg'. The large building labelled 'Babington's House' with bawn and flankers probably was occupied by Edward or Edwin Babington, Contractor Commissary of Stores in the English army, or possibly by Ury or Uriah Babington, merchant, of London. The massive fortifications are shown, and a proposed extension ('A Paterne to make the Towne by') is indicated. Colby based this drawing on an original in Trinity College, Dublin, probably by Richard Griffin or Griffen. (*Colby[1837]/AC*)

extension to the south called 'A Paterne to make the Towne by'. From a defensive point of view this plan makes a great deal of sense, for the regular planned extension was intended for high ground. The later plan that was adopted, and that extended the town to the river-bank, left Londonderry seriously exposed to fire from the river. Colby credits the plan with the 'Paterne' to one 'Griffen', presumably Richard Griffin (or Griffen), who lived in Derry and was an inhabitant of the settlement before the advent of the Londoners. In 1613 he was named as one of the Sheriffs of the new city of Londonderry.[31] There are puzzling aspects of this early plan, however: a large

[31] Moody (1939), 448.

house labelled 'Babingtons House' with bawn and flankers is shown on a site to the east outside the main fortress roughly where Shipquay Street runs today. Who this Babington was is unclear, but Brutus, Brute, or Bruce Babington (d. 1611), Bishop of Derry (1610-11), did not arrive on the scene until 1610, and though other members of his family appear to have settled in Ulster from that time[32] 'Babington' cannot have been the bishop. Most likely he was Edward (or Edwin) Babington (1543-1601), Contractor Commissary of Stores in the English army, who was Brutus Babington's brother.[33] Another candidate seems to be Ury (or Uriah) Babington (d.1605), merchant, of London, who was 'contractor for supplies for the army of Queen Elizabeth'.[34] Edward (Edwin) and Ury (Uriah) may have been the same person, and indeed William Babington, another brother of the bishop, had a son called Ury or Uriah,[35] but this cannot be the Derry 'Babington' as he would have been too young. This branch of the Babington family hailed from Nantwich, Cheshire, and the 'Babington' of the picture-map was probably the son of Richard Babington (or Bebington) of Nantwich, who married in *c.*1555. Further confirmation that the Babington of 'Babingtons House' cannot have been the bishop is found in the legend 'A place to lay in the Queenes timber' at the bottom of the drawing which makes the plan 1603 or earlier (i.e. dating from the reign of Queen Elizabeth I). The drawing shows the old church, the fortifications, and a proposed development, all of which pre-date the advent of the Londoners and the 1611 plan that evolved into the realised town plan. Dowcra's town, however, occupied only a very small part of the area enclosed within the Londoner's walls today, so it cannot have been very impressive. There was little sense of order in the arrangement of streets and buildings, and, if the picture-map had any degree of accuracy, the houses and other structures, huddled within the fortifications, had little or no architectural pretensions.

When George Montgomery (1566-1620), Dean of Norwich from 1603, was appointed to the dioceses of Derry, Raphoe, and Clogher[36] by King James I and VI in 1605, the prospect of moving to north-west Ulster cannot have been enticing, even though Sir John Davies saw the bishop as a 'new St Patrick'. Mrs Montgomery could not remember the names of the dioceses except 'Derye' and prayed to God that He might make 'all merry',[37] a pious hope that did not have much prospect of fulfilment. It must have been a wrench to move from Norwich to Derry, but accommodation was found in an English house, and there were enough English people in the settlement to provide some sort of social structure. During the O'Doherty rebellion Mrs Montgomery and her sister were held prisoner by the Irish for some time, and when the bishop was translated to Meath in 1610 it must have been something of a relief. Virtually everything, it should be recalled, except the church, was 'spoiled, ransacked, and fired' by O'Doherty and his men, and Davies lamented in 1609 that 'the fairest-begun city that was ever made in so short a time, and so well seated upon a goodly river' was all 'wasted saving only the rampiers of the forts', and a 'place of little strength', lying 'at the mercy of any that will attempt to seize upon it'.[38]

Montgomery, therefore, could be said to have had something of an uphill task to function as bishop of Derry. At the very beginning of his episcopate in Ulster he

32 Moody and Simms (eds.) (1968 and 1993), *passim*.
33 Burke's *Landed Gentry of Ireland* (1958), 42. I am indebted to Mr Annesley Malley for this reference.
34 Burke, A. P. (1897), 18. I owe this item also to Mr Malley.
35 Recorded in both Burke's *Landed Gentry of Ireland* (1958), 42 and Burke, A. P. (1897), 18.
36 Moody and Simms (eds.) (1968 and 1993), *passim*.
37 Lacy (1998), 77.
38 *Ibid.*, 80.

arranged for the compilation of a major ecclesiastical survey of his three dioceses, meticulously recording the old Gaelic organisation of the Church, including its financial bases. Determined to ensure that the Church would become well endowed, thus attracting British parsons to serve it, he petitioned the King to restore monastic lands to the bishoprics, to increase glebe lands drawn from the bishops' temporal lands to support parish-churches, and to ensure each parish would be adequately supported. In particular, he advocated that both settlers and natives should pay tithes. He also promoted the establishment of grammar schools to encourage 'civilitie, learning, true religion, and loyaltye' and a rejection of 'barbarous and disloyall courses'. The bishop believed that unrest could be 'contayned within the bounds of alleageance and good order', and that youth, adequately educated in schools and by example, would eschew the 'barbarous, disloyall, and superstitious' ways of old thus sparing the King 'infinit treasure and much blood of his civill subjects'.[39]

Although Montgomery remained in good odour with the King, his apparently excessive concern with the financial structures of his dioceses drew criticism from Chichester and others. Nevertheless, he managed to lay the foundations for a flourishing diocese of Derry that thereby became attractive to aspiring prelates. However, the wealth, land ownership, and income established under Montgomery did not always work to the advantage of the Plantation, and a tendency to acquire lands, advowsons, and fishings led to frequent clashes with The Irish Society over many years to come. 'Uncertainties of distinction between the temporal' and Church 'property led to prolonged disputes between the' bishops of Derry and The Irish Society. The first Protestant bishop of Derry was, in fact, Montgomery, 'whose importunity was largely responsible for' the Crown's 'decision to assign termon[40] and erenagh[41] land' to the Ulster bishops as episcopal demesne.[42]

Once the Government had been forced by events into a more positive policy in regard to Ulster, leading to the Plantation, and the City of London was pressured into participation, plans were drawn up for the two main settlements of Londonderry and Coleraine. The earliest 'Platt of the Derrie', dated 1611, survives in the library of Trinity College, Dublin, and shows the outline of Dowcra's fortifications within which stood the old abbey-church and 'The house wherein ye Ld. Bpp: Dwells': the proposed new settlement was to cover a much greater area, was designed on a grid pattern of streets laid out around an off-centre market-place, and the whole was surrounded (except on the river side) by a wall with bastions and a ditch. Presumably this plan was related in some way to the Carew survey, but it does not tally with that eventually fixed upon as the basis for the new town **[25]**.

The site of Derry is a hill on the west bank of the River Foyle (which flows around its eastern side in a gentle curve), and commands fine views. It is perhaps the most splendid situation of any Irish city, and at one time the hill was an island, the river surrounding it in two branches. Although the water-level gradually dropped and the land rose, the low ground on the western side of the hill (once the course of the western branch of the Foyle) remained damp, so that even in 1600 the English troops found that the hill of Derry was still virtually an island, and it was referred to as such

[39] Colby (1837), 49-55.

[40] Church land enjoying special privileges of protection and sanctuary in pre-Plantation times belonging to, or forming the precinct or liberties of a religious house, free and exempt from all impositions or secular charges, but subject to annual payments to the bishop of the diocese. *See also* Select Glossary below.

[41] An *erenagh* was an hereditary tenant of ecclesiastical land in pre-Plantation Ulster.

[42] Moody and Simms (eds.) (1968), 6.

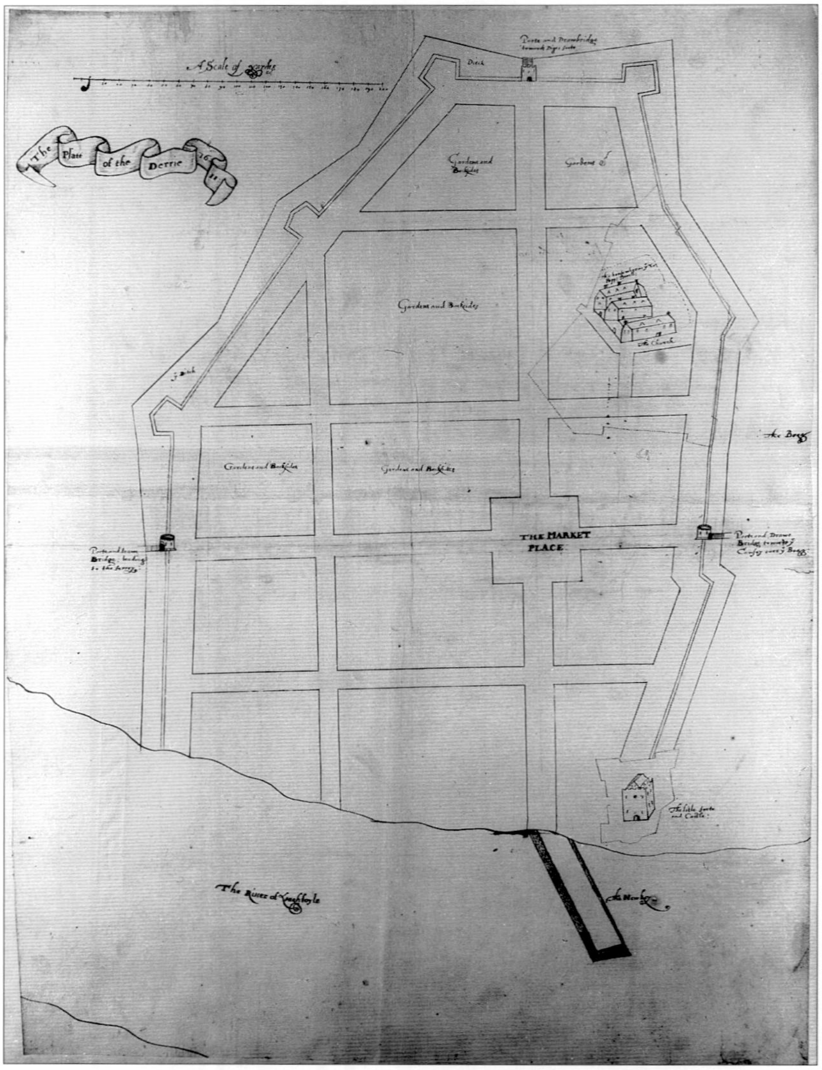

25 'The Platt of the Derrie', *c.*1611. A 'Scale of Yardes' of the original is 211 mm. representing 200 yards. The captions include 'The River of Loughfoyle', 'The litle forte and Castle', 'The New key', 'The Market Place', 'Gardens and Backsides', 'Gardens &c', 'Porte and drawe Bridge: leading to the ferrey', 'Porte and Drawbridge towards Diges forte', 'Porte and Drawe Bridge towards ye Cawsey over ye Bogg', 'The Bogg', 'Ditch', 'The Church', and 'The house wherin ye Lo. Bpp: Dwells'. (*From an original drawing [790 × 574 mm paper size][TCD/MS.1209/24*])*

all through the 17th century. The sodden valley separating the hill of Derry from higher ground to the west is commemorated by the suburb known as the Bogside (a name that resounded in the media from the late 1960s), but even before the Plantation began, causeways had been constructed over the 'Bogges'. The hill of Derry could only be approached from the eastern bank by boat until the first bridge was erected in the fast-flowing waters in 1790.[43] It was also isolated to a certain extent by the boggy Pennyburn depression between it and the Inishowen peninsula to the north, while the marshy valley to the south between Newtowncunningham and the Foyle east of Carrigans also helped to protect it.

Doire (or Daire) of old was well wooded, the oaks that gave it its name being plentiful. Derry was also called *Daire Calgagh*, the oak-wood of Calgagh (meaning fierce warrior), translated into Latin by Adomnan, Abbot of Iona (*c.*700), as *Roboretum Calgaghi*. Around the end of the 10th century Derry became known as Derry-

[43] For a detailed description of the geology and geography see Colby (1837), *passim*, Lacy (1998), 1-5, and Portlock (1843), *passim*.

Columbkille (or Columbcille), after the saint. Colby suggested that the post-Plantation appellation of Londonderry could be interpreted as a compound of the Celtic *Lonn-Dún* (strong fortress) added to Derry, so that *Lonndún-Doire* would mean something like 'ship-town of Derry' or 'strong fortress of the oak-grove', perhaps with further connotations relating to ships, which is exactly what post-Plantation Londonderry actually was.[44]

By 1611, however, as has been mentioned earlier, much of the construction effort had been at Coleraine. Very little had been done at Derry except for repairs to the old Augustinian abbey-church, a few new houses built, and various workshops, lime-kilns, saw-pits, wharves, and other structures erected. It is not clear when the plan of the new settlement was finalised, or who was responsible for it, but it is beyond dispute that Londonderry was to be virtually a brand-new walled city on a site cleared of earlier fabric.[45]

An ordered town-plan based on a grid, with a central market-square, the whole protected by a fortification, of course, was nothing new. In antiquity there were Hellenistic and Roman precedents, and medieval new towns had been created in large numbers, including those in Wales (e.g. Caernarfon, Conwy, and Flint), the *bastides* in France (e.g. Montpazier, Aigues Mortes, Villeneuve-sur-Lot), and the colonial settlements in eastern Europe (e.g. the many 'Neustadts'), several of which had regular grid-patterns of streets. With the Renaissance period countless proposals for new model towns on regular lines were made, and some were realised, including Vitry-le-François, designed by Hieronimo Marino in 1545 for King François Ier (1515-47) to replace Vitry-le-Brûlé, destroyed in the wars with Emperor Charles V in 1544. Vitry is situated on the banks of the River Marne, some 100 miles east of Paris, and its layout has similarities to the plan of Londonderry: it was fortified, had a central market-square, and a simple grid-pattern for the streets. Completed around 1560 in the reign of François II (1559-60), Vitry was only slightly bigger than Londonderry.[46] There is a further intriguing (though slight) connection. François II was married (1558) to Mary, Queen of Scots (1542-87 – Queen from 1542), mother of King James I and VI by her second husband, Henry Stewart (or Stuart), Lord Darnley (1545-67), and King James, of course, was one of the chief protagonists in the saga of the Plantation of Ulster.[47] In addition the plan of Charleville-sur-Meuse (1608) is related to that of Londonderry, and its almost contemporary date is interesting. Based on principles devised by Leon Battista Alberti (1404-72) in his *De re aedificatoria* (1485) and Andrea Palladio (1508-80) in his *Quattro libri dell' architettura* (1570), Charleville as well as Vitry-le-François may have influenced the design of Londonderry which in turn seems to have provided a model for various towns in Virginia.

The key to this inter-relationship goes back to the earlier Plantation of Munster in which Sir Walter Ralegh (or Raleigh – *c.*1552-1618) was involved, having obtained huge tracts of land in Counties Cork, Waterford, and Tipperary in 1586. Raleigh and his cousin, Sir Richard Grenville (*c.*1542-91), were involved in the tentative beginnings of a Plantation at Roanoke Colony, North Carolina (1585-6), and the plan of Fort Raleigh resembles that of Culmore Fort, County Londonderry. The triangular Fort Carolina, Florida (1564), built by Huguenot settlers, also may have influenced Forts Raleigh and Culmore, and these exemplars may have prompted the plan of Jamestown

44 See Colby (1837), 17.
45 Moody (1939), 104.
46 Lacy (1998), 90-91; Reps (1965, 1972, 1980), *passim*.
47 Lacy (1998), 90, also notes this possibility.

in the Plantation of Virginia (1607) which was partly funded by 56 Livery Companies of the City of London. Raleigh is also credited with the introduction of the potato to Ireland, and raised a crop of this American plant in his garden at Youghal, Co. Cork, in the late 1580s or early 1590s.

Further connections between Ireland and British North America are suggested by later events. The plan of Londonderry may have influenced William Penn (1644-1718) and his surveyor-general, Thomas Holme, in the design of Philadelphia, Pennsylvania, laid out at the narrowest point of the peninsula bounded by the Rivers Delaware and Schuylkill from 1682. Indeed, there are very many parallels between the 17th-century English urban developments in America and Ulster.[48]

At the time of Carew's 1611 survey, the projected new City of Londonderry remained a plan on paper, but the bishops' house on the south side of the repaired church was built, and there was evidence of a great deal of activity, though efforts were concentrated at Coleraine. It was not until the Smithes-Springham investigations of 1613 that the layout of Londonderry appears to have been finalised when the Londoners 'trod out' the ground, and the new city began to resemble the plans prepared by Thomas Raven in the 1620s **[26]**.

As a plan on paper the proposed city looks impressive, but it was built on a hill rising steeply from the river, so from the east, as indicated earlier, the entire settlement was exposed to possible artillery-fire from the river and the opposite bank. Furthermore, there was high ground on hills near by, so cannon could easily lob balls and shells *over* the thick walls (an outer wall of stone backed by a thick earthern rampart now hidden behind an inner stone facing). The huge amounts of earth were excavated from a ditch, some ten metres wide, that lay around the south and eastern perimeter.

These fortifications erected by the Londoners are of great European importance, and at Londonderry the survival of virtually the whole circuit of walls is remarkable. Of course, there have been changes made to them, most significantly the new gates (the finest architecturally of which is the Bishop's gate), but the layout of the 17th-century street plan, the walls, and the Anglican cathedral constitute one of the grandest, biggest, and most impressive historic monuments in all Ireland, and ought to be recognised as such.[49]

The Proby-Springham Commission

In order to ensure that further official criticisms should be deflected, the Governor of The Irish Society, Alderman (later Sir) Peter Proby (d. 1624), announced to the Common Council that a further commission of inquiry on the lines of the Smithes-Springham investigation would be set up, and in May 1616 Proby, with Springham and the ever-reluctant Clement Moss, set off for Ulster, armed with a set of instructions to examine progress, to find out how the City's money had been expended, and to establish to what extent the works carried out actually met the requirements of the Crown as set out in the various agreements.

The instructions included orders that the commissioners should receive copies of former instructions issued to Smithes (dead by 1616) and Springham together with the results of the earlier inquiry; that they should 'demonstrate the care' taken to 'remove

[48] See Reps (1965), 6-15, and Reps (1972, 1980), *passim*. See also *D.N.B.* (1917), **xvi**, 629-49.

[49] Milligan (1948); Mullin (1986).

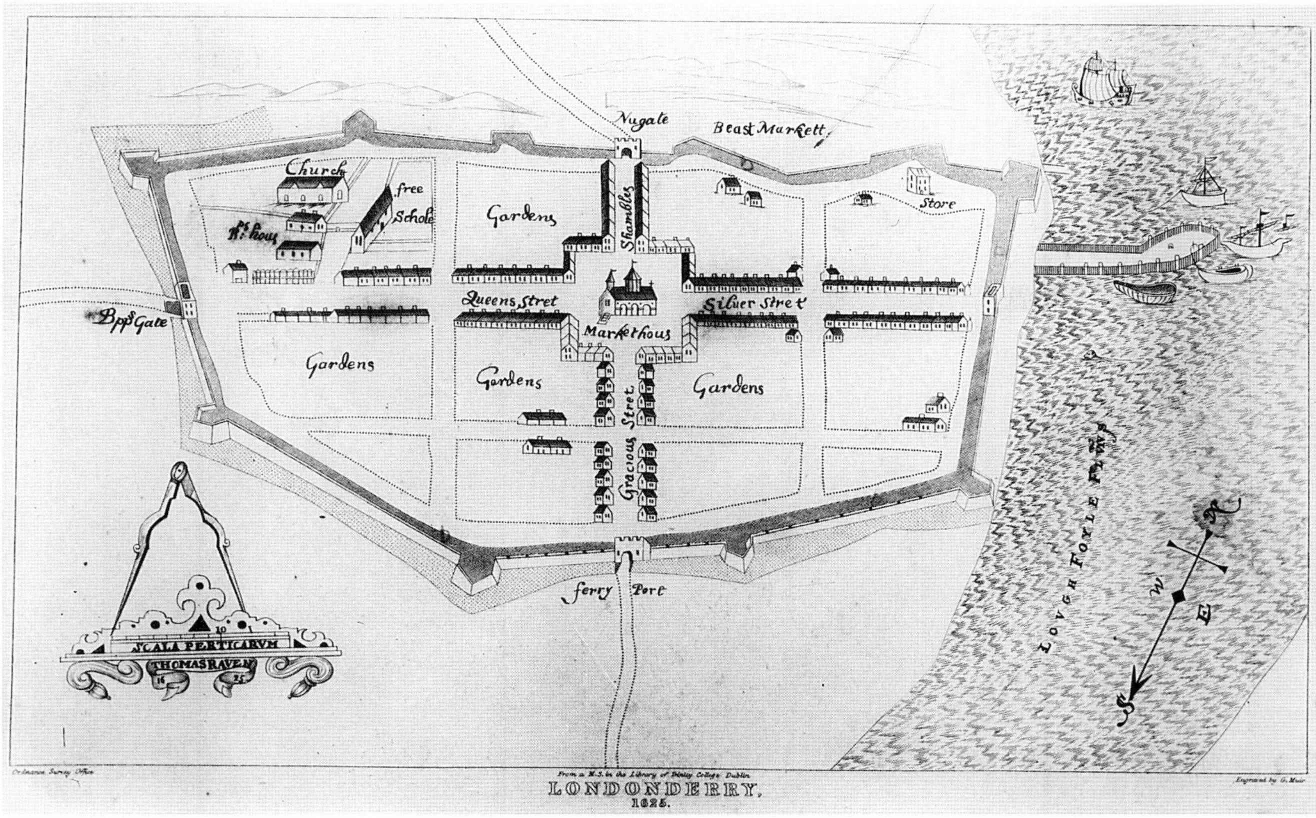

26 Londonderry in 1625, from an original in Trinity College, Dublin, by Thomas Raven, showing the fortifications, the central market-square (Diamond) with its market-house, the old church used as the cathedral (with adjoining Bishop's house), and general layout. The low density of development is striking. *(Colby[1837]/AC)*

the Natives', the 'sevall Companies having already planted and placed divers nombers of Brittish on their proporčens and are every day sending over more families to inhabite there so it will be now noe great time ere the Cittie pforme what is ... expected'; that Tristram Beresford, Mayor of Coleraine and The Irish Society's Agent and Treasurer, should be interviewed and statements obtained from him 'concerning his yployment' and all accounts, debts, etc.; that the fortifications at Coleraine be inspected and to order the making good of any defects forthwith; that all buildings and houses should be seen and notes made concerning condition, numbers, leases, and rents; that the number of artisans in Coleraine be established, and every encouragement given to more to be 'drawn over ... towards the peopling of that place'; that the 'imperfect' development of Coleraine whereby houses were built only on one side of the High Street be considered, and a course directed 'how the said Towne' could be made more uniform and 'brought to a better form' by encouraging the erection of more houses by allowing £20 towards every house of four or five rooms and granting leases of 60 years; that 'Cabbens in the town' be systematically demolished as houses went up to avoid 'noysomeness, danger of fire, and other inconvenience'; that the state of the store and all accounts be determined to establish where all the 'armes, nails, and other things for the service of the touns' had gone, for it was important to find out if the 'Cittie of London hath not been abused by embesseling or unord issuing out of the said provisions'; that 'by reason of the ill passage for shipping' the possibilities of building a 'peere or jetty' at Portrush be investigated, together with how it might be financed; that the project for 'cutting the leapes in the river of the Bann' which had proved 'of unneccessarie charge', the 'passage that way being so dangerous' and its use fraught with 'uncertaintie' be examined; that Culmore Fort be inspected to establish how it was 'kept and maynteyned' in view of the charge to the City of £60 per annum; that 'speciall care' be given to report on the welfare of 'those children sent lately over for servants and apprentices out of the hospittals in London';[50] that pressure to have 'new workes of charge as tonhouses [town-houses], gaoles, &^{c} 'built both in 'the Derrie and Coleraine' should be resisted unless absolutely necessary to prevent London from bearing 'the burthen of extraordinarie disbursem^{ts}'; that the commissioners should inform themselves 'concerning the farme of the fishings, being one of the many healps towards the returne for' London's expenses, should investigate complaints that the lessees were 'so covetous of gaine and profitt' they had transported 'the fishe wholly out of the plantac̃on' leaving the 'townes unserved of that commoditie', and should establish who might be more suitable lessees when the present leases for the fishings expired; that the accounts relating to the Customs be inspected, and the possibilities of leasing the Customs to 'farmers' be investigated, provided leases did not exceed six or seven years; to establish how and where markets were organised and served, with a view to reforming abuses and destroying monopolies that were creating discontentment; that the new parson appointed by the City of London to the living at Coleraine (one William Vincent) be heard to find out what his sermons were like, that he should be advised 'to instruct o^{r} people in the rules of religion' and effect the 'reformac̃on of such Irish and others' by 'faire meanes and ꝑsuasions to come to church thereby to make the plantac̃on more blest and happy, and that 'the said Vincent ... be allowed a convenient house in the toune to be built or repaired at the Citties charge and to have fortie acres' Irish of land 'in some fitt place' that would avoid 'disaccomodating any of the inhabitants' given to him;[51] that the whole question of the advowsons be investigated; that the 'fishings in Clonleigh to which the Bishop of Derry' laid 'clayme' be looked into and sorted out, and that the rent due for the 'Bishopp's house' be collected; that the houses and land leased by Rowley at Coleraine be repossessed and relet to him or to any other person 'for the most benefitt of the Cittie'; that two townlands allowed to Rowley be 'retorned back to London'; that enquiries should be made as to how 'Surveyor Rowen [*sic*]' had 'discharged his trust', and, if he had failed, he was to be called to account and consideration given to whether it be fit to continue him any longer in service; enquiries should be made as to how the 'lands wanting and due from' Sir Randal MacDonnell and Sir Thomas Phillips should be procured; that 'Rowen' (actually Raven) should investigate the Company Proportions to ensure that all lands properly due to the Londoners were duly mapped and allotted; that all alleged infringements of the Liberties or charter of Coleraine by Sir Randal MacDonnell were to be put right, and all privileges of Coleraine 'mainteyned according' to the charter in order to avoid 'discontentmen^{t} and confusion in orderlie Govermen^{t}'; that all money paid to the Crown by The Society's Agent be accounted for 'to see that no wrong be done to the Cittie nor any ꝑticular Companie'; that levies on the country towards the charge of Knights and Burgesses of the Parliament be clarified; that according to the charter the two towns should have laws and ordinances for their better government, so these were to be discussed and reported back to London; that

[50] It should be noted there is no mention here of Christ's Hospital, but only of 'hospittals' (i.e. charitable institutions for the reception and education of needy young). If the apprentices were, in fact, drawn from several institutions, this could well explain why only four names of the 'Christ's Hospital' boys match those in County Londonderry in 1628.

[51] Vincent enjoyed a long tenure of the rectory of Coleraine from 1615 (he died *c.*1639), and was granted the prebend of Aghadowey from 1628.

the lands of the native freeholders 'lately … attained by reason of notorious offences' should be taken over by the City and policies evolved 'to prevent wrong' thereafter; that the Mayor and Aldermen of London be assured of the care the 'Cittie of London … [was taking] … to give them all contentm^{t} & encouragm$^{t'}$, and that the commissioners were 'to remove all misunderstanding'; that the fortifications, walls, and gates of Londonderry be viewed and reports prepared on progress, the payment of workers, and the standard of workmanship; that proposals to build a quay and wharf at Londonderry be evaluated 'for the good of the townes and profitt' of The Society; that the best means of providing and maintaining buoys and beacons as navigation aids be established; that houses in Londonderry should be let so that they would be 'tenanted as soune as may be', allotting some portions of land to each house, but that in the leases it was to be made clear tenants 'should have no power to lett, sell or alienate' their properties without first consulting The Irish Society; that any parcels of land on the Proportions 'diminished' or 'deteyned by any pson' should be restored to their rightful owners; that the best means of repairing and enlarging the church in Londonderry be found as congregations were 'so straightened for want of roome' they were 'forced to stand wthout doors', which was not appreciated by the inhabitants; that all the Companies should ensure the churches on their Proportions were in good repair and sufficiently large; that complaints of John Wilkinson, late Recorder of Coleraine, against agents and officers of The Irish Society be carefully examined to establish the 'true grounds of the proceedings and who set him on worke so to disturbe the plantac̃on as th^{by} the Comons' were 'discouraged and the Committees disgraced'; that the 'several merits' of all officers employed on the Plantation be examined in order to give them the 'best contentment or encouragement … provided' this did not involve any 'new charge to the Cittie'; that lands of 'Widow Gothane' be dealt with as the commissioners 'found fitting'; that two swords of office be presented to the Mayors of both towns as a 'guifte from London' in the hopes that their carriage would ensure 'just government' thereafter; and that wide discretionary powers were to be used concerning any other problems that arose, everything left to the 'care, judgem^{t}, and integritie' of the commissioners to ensure London's contentment and the 'worthy discharge of the great trust' placed on Proby and Springham.[52]

The commissioners duly arrived in Ireland and obtained various documents from the Lords Justice and the Government in Dublin. Proby and Springham were called to a special 'conference' at which they were reminded of the City of London's obligations to remove the native Irish from the Londonderry Plantation. They then proceeded north armed with warrants to obtain 'convoyes', as the 'Countrie about the Citties Plantac̃on' was exceedingly dangerous for 'travaile', so some idea of conditions may be gained. The commissioners spent some time interviewing Beresford, inspecting his accounts, and establishing the background information necessary prior to the site-visits. Beresford lived in Coleraine and did not visit Londonderry very often as he had appointed a deputy, John Wray, who resided in the infant city. Beresford's position of 'Mair at Coleraine' the commissioners thought was 'very troublesome and a hindrance to the Citties business at Derrie'.[53]

It was found that the Coleraine fortifications, as had been reported earlier, were 'over spacious', had cost too much, and, being made of earth, needed constant repair. However, the ditch surrounding the ramparts had acquired dams and sluices so that

[52] Irish Society (*c.*1898), 424-32.
[53] *Ibid.*, 433.

it could be filled with water 'and made more defensible', and 'pallisadoes' had been built out into the Bann 'beyonde the lowe water marke' to afford some degree of protection. Two 'substanciall drawe bridges' had just been constructed. Although 116 houses had been erected, they were inhabited by 63 families because the houses were so small that inhabitants had made 'two or three' single houses into one. 35 families had taken leases, but 'paid their rents very badly', most failing to pay their dues on a regular basis, if at all. Jerry-built timber frames were deteriorating due to inroads made by the rain: it appears that dormer-windows and even roofs were only clad in timber boards, so the commissioners gave instructions that repairs should be carried out at once, and that slates should be used on roofs and dormers. So rapid was the decay of the timber frames that it was decided all future houses should be constructed of stone. It is interesting that Proby and Springham also found that 'some of the houses that were built wth bricke' had begun to 'decay and by reason of the bleakness of the weather the walls of the other houses are much decayed'. This must mean that the bricks were insufficiently burnt, or that mortar was of very poor quality, or that the rain, penetrating wholly inadequate roof-coverings, was damaging the walls by soaking them and then freezing, causing spalling and collapse. Walls 'were but of loame and lime and readie to fall down', complained the commissioners.[54] In terms of appearance, Coleraine was unattractive and its development was lop-sided, as construction in Church Street (the High Street) and New Row left the north side of Church Street unbuilt. The commissioners prevailed upon the Mayor to call a public meeting at which they offered advantageous terms (e.g. £20 subsidies, low rents [6s. 8d. per annum], and 80-year leases) to entrepreneurs willing to build houses with a minimum of three rooms on the north side of Church Street. Edmund Hayward (or Haward, who was to become active as a developer on the Merchant Taylors' Proportion at Macosquin) undertook to erect nine such houses of stone on the new terms.[55] Thus attempts were made to sort out the Main Street, which was 'not built in any uniformity'.[56] The matter of pulling the 'Cabbens' down and replacing them with proper houses seems to have been left for the time being, but some rudimentary principles of town planning and order were to be applied in relation to new buildings.

With regard to the arms supplied by the Londoners, most were 'disposed to the sev'all inhabitants' in Londonderry and Coleraine, the rest being 'kept safe' in Londonderry under the direction of the Mayor. As for the 'nailles and other materials' held in stores in the two towns, Proby and Springham had inventories made, and established the stores were badly run: accordingly, the commissioners sold their contents, sacked the men in charge, and let the houses used as stores so that 'rents to the Cittie' were 'much the more'.[57] Other matters considered at Coleraine included the problems caused for shipping by the bar at the mouth of the Bann (where the construction of a wharf or jetty was 'not fesible'), the site of a proposed safe harbour at Portrush (reckoned to be 'so rockie and open to the North seas that it is very dangerous', but that, if the town and surrounding county were to build a harbour at Portrush, the City of London would contribute £200 'towards that charg when it shod be performed'), and certain difficulties relating to the complaints made by John Wilkinson, the late Recorder of Coleraine, to the King and the Privy Council against the agents and officers of The Irish Society. Some degree of 'public participation' was

[54] Irish Society (*c.*1898), 434.
[55] Moody (1939), 169-176.
[56] Irish Society (*c.*1898), 434.
[57] *Ibid.*, 435.

again encouraged concerning the last matter, for the commissioners called a meeting of the 'whole towne of Coleraine' to investigate Wilkinson's actions. The Irish Society suspected somebody had egged Wilkinson on to stir up the King's wrath, and probably thought Phillips might have been working behind the scenes. Wilkinson's criticisms were read out, and included denunciations of the Londoners for negligence in the management of the Plantation and failure to introduce British colonists. Unfortunately we cannot determine what the rest of Wilkinson's complaints were, as records appear not to have survived (they are presumably lurking amid the 'irretrievable confusion' of burnt fragments in Guildhall, London), but at the meeting a unanimous show of hands rejected Wilkinson's charges as untrue, frivolous, and malicious, and cleared Beresford of all accusations of wrongdoing and negligence. The Irish Society appears to have been given what amounted to a vote of confidence by the townspeople.[58] It is clear, even after so many years have passed, that Wilkinson's actions were resented as casting aspersions on The Society, its agents, and the City of London.[59] It should be remembered that he had been summoned before the Court of Aldermen with the Governor and Assistants of The Society, Captain Dod(d)ington, and various representatives from Coleraine. The Court found Wilkinson's accusations to be false, which is why he lost his Recordership. Wilkinson's house and 40 acres of land accordingly were assigned to the rector, Vincent, whose preaching and teaching won due approval.[60]

Sir Randal MacDonnell had failed to surrender all his promised lands in County Antrim intended as the areas 'laid' to Coleraine. The commissioners extracted from him a written undertaking to deliver these lands to The Irish Society's Agent, Beresford.[61] One of the bones of contention between The Society and MacDonnell appears to have been the exact amount of land to be 'laid' to Coleraine, for the Ulsterman wanted to hand over as little as possible, preferably 'bogge mosse and mountains' rather than good agricultural land. It seems that Raven's surveys and MacDonnell's estimates did not tally, so the ubiquitous Sir Josias Bodley was called in 'to determine that difference'.[62]

Proby and Springham found that the 'farmers' of the fishings had kept to their agreements with the 'Cittie and duly paid their rent' and had 'well served' the markets with salmon at very reasonable rates, but, as the leases were nearly up, the existing 'farmers' offered an increase of £200 per annum rent, undertaking also to supply the markets of Londonderry and Coleraine with salmon, and to ensure London was also provided for. This matter was referred back to London for a decision by The Society, as was an examination of the books relating to the profits from the Customs, for an idea was floated to lease the Customs to the two towns.

Livings for which the City possessed the advowsons were presented to various English clergymen with the agreement of the bishop of Derry and The Irish Society's Agent. It is interesting that the earliest incumbents in Plantation Coleraine were Cambridge graduates, which itself is significant: The Irish Society, representing the City of London, inclined more towards Parliament than the Crown as the century progressed, and Oxford leant more towards high church and traditional monarchy than did Cambridge, which tended to be sympathetic to Calvinism, though not in all

58 Irish Society (*c.*1898), 441.
59 Moody (1939), 170.
60 Irish Society (*c.*1898), 437.
61 *Ibid.*, 438.
62 *Ibid.*, 438.

colleges. However, in 1616 many derelict churches were still roofless and instructions were issued 'for the covering of them' and their repair, as the Plantation would prosper 'the better when we beginn with the house of God'. Some ecclesiastical fabric was medieval, as may be detected in several places to this day, notably at Dungiven and Macosquin. Unfortunately the bishop was in England during the commissioners' visit, so no progress could be made on the Clonleigh fishings problem, and the rent owed by the previous bishop had to be regarded as written off as 'his estate proved poore'.[63] It was impossible to let the repossessed house occupied by Rowley without sufficient land (which The Society appears to have granted him), so the commissioners had little option other than to re-lease the house and land to Rowley for 21 years at £20 per annum, hoping he would be 'a good tenant to the Cittie'.

As the Crown maintained a garrison at Desertmartin, Sir Francis Cooke, the commander, held the lands there for that use. Markets in Londonderry and Coleraine were poor affairs and very small, but there was evidence that hides, tallow, and yarn were being transported in considerable quantities by individuals who had acquired unhelpful monopolies. Native freeholds of those attainted for taking part in the Conspiracy were resumed into the ownership of The Irish Society: one freehold was let for life to George Carey, Recorder of Londonderry.

At the infant city the commissioners found the fortifications were proceeding, but gave instructions that the walls should be raised some three feet (approximately one metre) and escarpments created where deemed necessary for defence 'on the Hille towards the Bogge' and in other places. The drawbridges had been erected and one of the gates was under construction. With regard to these fortifications, as mentioned above, Captain Sir Edward Dod(d)ington, Captain Baker, of Culmore Fort, Captain Panton, and Captain Sir John Vaughan all seem to have been involved in various advisory and supervisory rôles, but Baker and Vaughan were the key figures, and Benson[64] was the main contractor. Work, by 1616, was proceeding well, and under the Beresford-Wray régime 'the Workmen' were 'well paide', Proby and Springham hearing 'no Complainte' concerning 'want of paie', so those difficulties seem to have been overcome.[65]

The fortifications of Londonderry, however, were to be set out and measured by Raven, who did the same at Culmore Fort. Having examined 'his businesses and taken an accompt thereof', the commissioners extended Raven's employment as surveyor for two more years to enable him to carry out his duties at Culmore and Londonderry, and also to measure any Company lands if the agents required this to be done **[27a & b]**. Although 'no complaynt of any land deteyned' was made by any of the Twelve Companies, the surveyor would be on hand to examine the same and to put to rights any problems that arose in this respect: in effect The Society put the City's surveyor at the disposal of the Companies to watch over their interests. In his various tasks Raven may have been assisted by Simon Kingsland (who had prepared maps of various Proportions in 1613, and who had acted as book-keeper of all stores in Coleraine), for the county surveys were carried out with remarkable speed, although mountainous, boggy, remote, or heavily wooded terrain was mapped with understandable vagueness. With regard to the fortifications, Raven presumably determined their exact lines and plans, so their final form is partly due to him, though

63 Irish Society (*c*.1898), 437.
64 Loeber (1981), 20-21.
65 Irish Society (*c*.1898), 440.

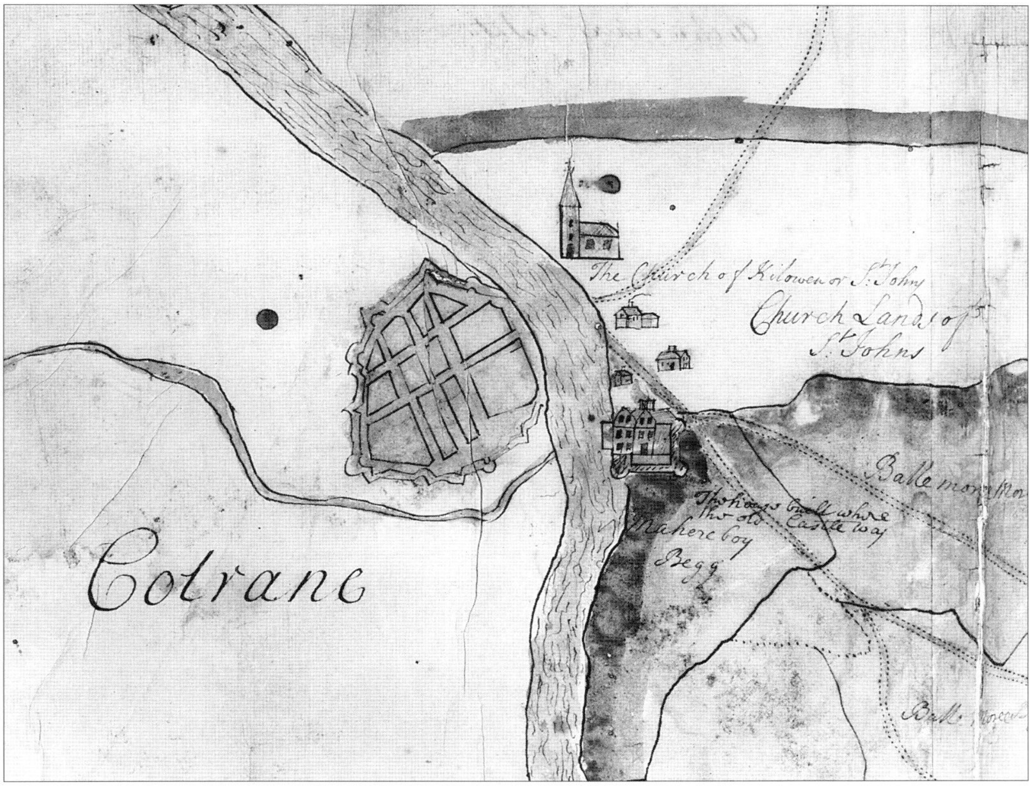

27a Detail from 'A Platt of the Lands belonging to the Right Worshipfull Company of Clothworkers in Ulster in the Realm of Ireland, 1616': a map (or a copy of a map) by Thomas Raven on paper on canvas. It shows 'Colrane' and the Clothworkers' settlement at Killowen. Note that the Clothworkers' 'Castle' or 'Hall' has moved downstream from its position on other plans: it seems to have stood roughly where County Hall is sited today. (*WCMT/208.Q.5/GB*)

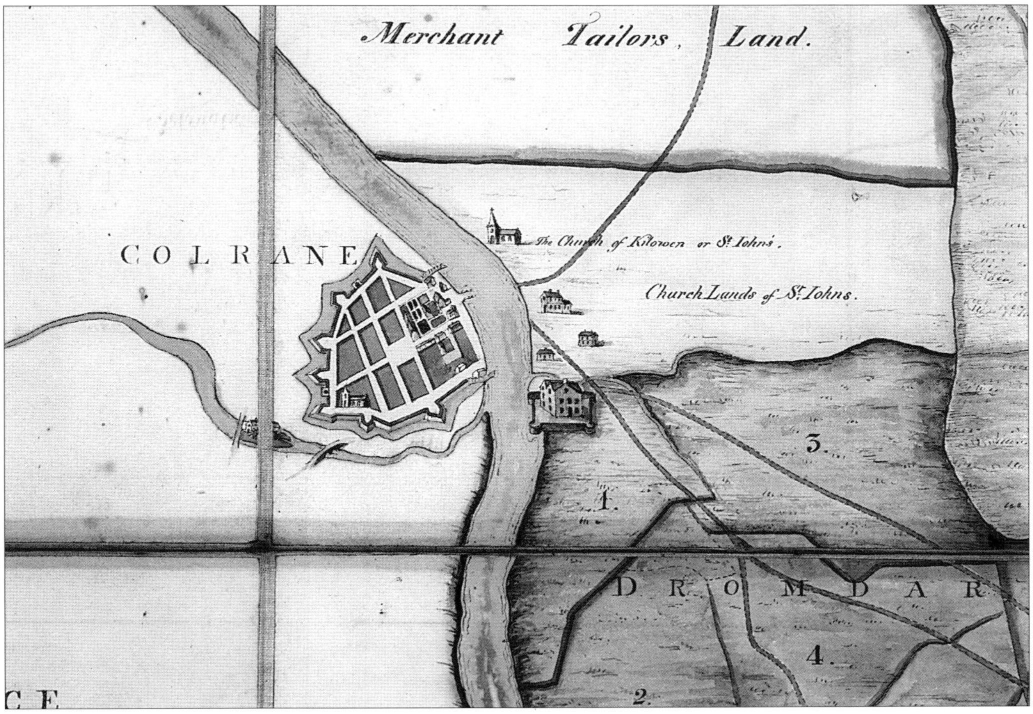

27b Detail from a version of the Raven 1616 map dating from *c.*1829 showing Coleraine, St John's parish-church and the settlement at Killowen, and Clothworkers' Hall. (*WCC/GB*)

the structures as finished were under the direction of the military experts, and subject to changes demanded by The Irish Society's commissioners.

Proby and Springham professed themselves pleased with the 'Castle of Culmore', for it was in a state of 'good forwardnesse being very stronge and well wrought', but would require a total of eight 'pieces of ordinance' (i.e. guns) to make it effective. It seems that Captain Baker himself supervised the building of Culmore Fort to Raven's plans and layout, and was in charge of the garrison there for which he was paid an annual salary of £52. At Londonderry they found 214 houses, a considerable increase on the numbers recorded in 1613, so the City's contract with the Crown was fulfilled in that respect, albeit some five years late. Benson seems to have been a very important figure in the edifying of Londonderry, where he became chief mason and erected several stone houses within the walls as well as overseeing the building of many others. Unlike the satisfied workmen, who were paid on time, Benson did not obtain the final instalments due to him for the construction of the fortifications until the 1620s, but nevertheless managed to acquire lands near Lifford in County Donegal, and built a house, a bawn, and a village there. He was also involved in the creation of the Ironmongers' castle at Agivey and the Mercers' castle at Movanagher, and appears at the time of his death (24 August 1642) to have enjoyed some 20 years as a person of substance. He seems to have contributed to the creation of many houses built under the aegis of The Irish Society in Londonderry.[66] Thus it would appear that the most significant people involved in building at Londonderry in the second decade of the seventeenth century were Baker, Benson (probably of considerable importance), Dod(d)ington, Lipsett, Panton, and Raven.

Mindful of instructions, the 1616 commissioners avoided any commitment to a market-house, town-house, or prison, although 'much ymportuned for the same': plans to erect civic buildings were therefore shelved for the time being. Nevertheless, they thought a market-house and town-house should be erected in Londonderry to 'serve to divers good uses and be a strength to the towne' while also freeing the three houses then being used by the city council to be let for 'gaine'. Leases of most of the houses at Londonderry were granted for 30 years to 'as many … thought fitt to take them', with a 'porc̃on of land … allotted to evy house'. The 'Island of Derry' was in fact divided and distributed for gardens and orchards, and 'the Bogge' leased 'out to sundry persons at small rents in hope that the same may be made firme and goode meadowe in time to come'.

Public worship was found to be neglected in Londonderry because the existing church was too small for the needs of the parish (there was 'hardly room for halfe' of the inhabitants). The enlargement of the church was 'needful and necessarie' but the commissioners brought 'a plott with an estimate of the charge for making' another building. Clearly, this 'plott' (or plan) was prepared in Londonderry, and had windows and a 'steple' which gave the inhabitants 'great contentment'. In other words the drawings of a proposed new church had been seen by individuals in Londonderry. Tantalisingly, little is known of these proposals, unless the building with western tower, spire, tall nave, and lower chancel shown in Raven's 'Plan of the Cittie of London: Derrie as it stand built and fortifyed' **[28]** on a site to the east of the main square represents the intentions.[67] Perhaps Raven, Baker, or Benson had made the designs, which were shown to various committees in London, and the commissioners

[66] Loeber (1981), 20-21.
[67] Chart (ed.) (1928), pl 3 facing 12, 149, 167.

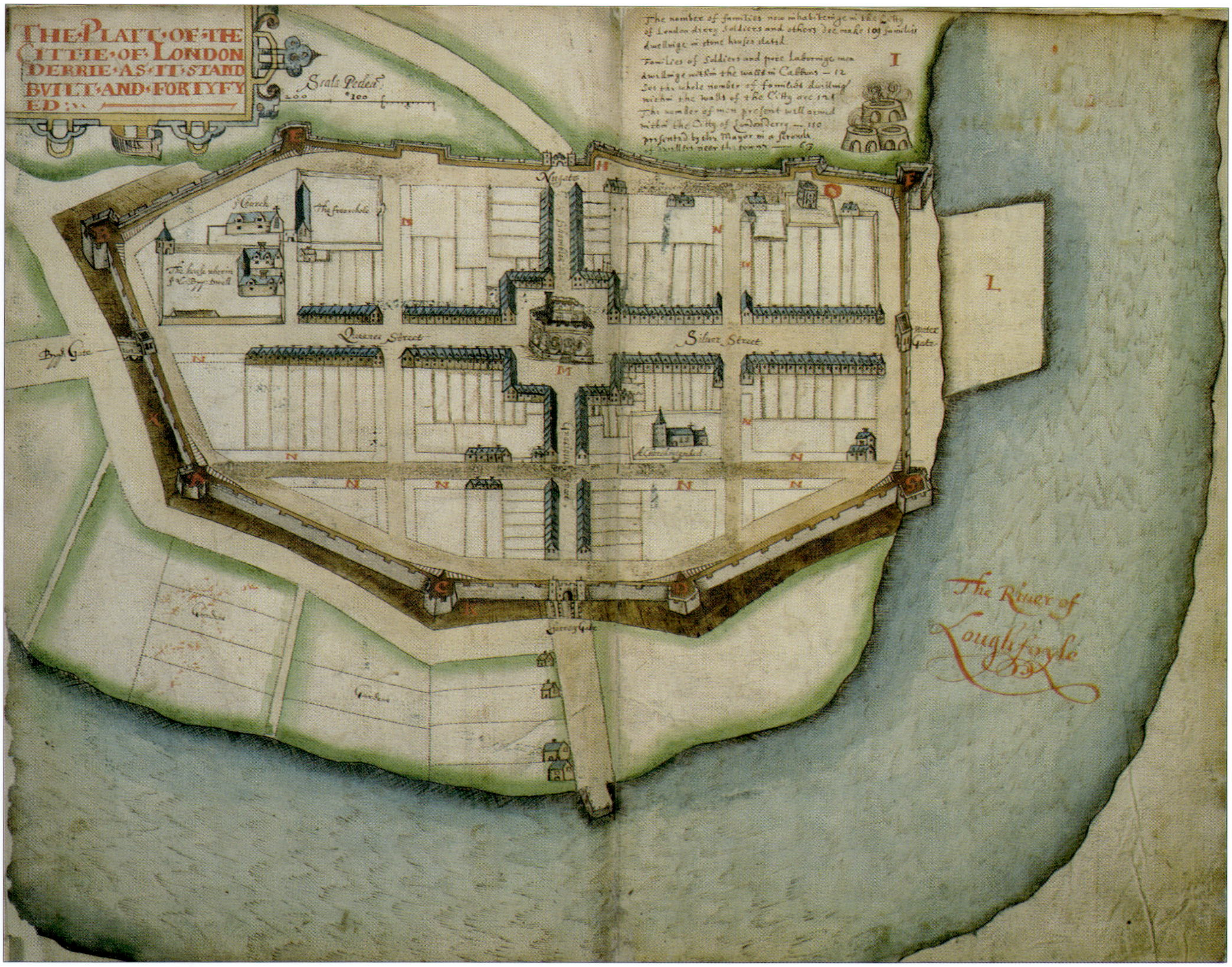

28 'The Platt of the Cittie of London: Derrie as it Stand built and Fortyfyed.' Raven's picture-map of 1622, drawn for Sir Thomas Phillips, showing the completed walls of Londonderry, the old church, the Bishop's Palace and bawn, the street-pattern, and the rows of houses, mostly of 1½ storeys, set in their own plots. Note the long back gardens. It should also be noted that the site of the present cathedral is vacant, and that Phillips/Raven proposed a cathedral-church on a different site south-east from the market-square. At the top right-hand corner of the walled city is an Irish tower-house (the 'Castle' shown on the *c.*1600 map), and outside the walls are 'Lyme-Kilns'. There were 109 families living in the houses (which had slate roofs), and 12 families of poor labourers and soldiers lived in 'Cabbons' within the walls. Only 110 armed men were available to defend the city. In the centre of the market-place Phillips and Raven proposed a rather exotic citadel for a 'great strengthe to the Cittie'. (*WCD/GB*)

urged The Irish Society to order materials for the realisation of the proposals, which, however, were not carried out.

Springham determined to provide a free school in Londonderry at his own expense, and it was agreed to make an annual grant for its maintenance. 300 acres of land were provisionally allocated for the support of this establishment. The commissioners noted a gratifying improvement of security, and there were now sufficient arms for defence in both Londonderry and Coleraine, while Culmore promised to be a strong fortress. By far the most satisfactory aspect of the Plantation, however, was the income from the fisheries, although there were ominous (and unresolved) disputes with George

Downham (d. 1634 – the new bishop of Derry from 1616 to 1634, who had succeeded John Tanner [d. 1615], bishop from 1613 to 1615) concerning the fishings at Clonleigh, and, even at that early period, a few rumblings of confusion over the advowsons. The bishop soon became an enemy of The Irish Society and of the Londoners generally because he came to believe his lack of success in the enforcement of conformity could be attributed to the continuing presence of 'unconformable natives' on Plantation lands. Indeed, the failure to replace these 'Papists' with 'British or conformable Irish' (i.e. Irish converts to Protestantism[68]) on the allotted lands was a major concern of the King, the Privy Council, the Lord Deputy, the Anglican Church, and several conscientious Undertakers. Specifically, the bishop noted that, as the Irish did not spend much on food, English clothes (preferring Irish apparel), building, or agriculture, they were often in a position to outbid the English settlers (who spent money on food, drink, clothes, buildings, and agriculture), with the result that the English settlers gave up and went home. He also perceived that the Companies and their 'farmers' were anxious to ensure that income from rent kept coming in to help recoup the enormous outgoings, so it was not in the interests of the Londoners to pursue enforcement of conformity in matters of dress, speech, education, religion, housing, or anything else, even though such a stance was contrary to the King's policies to secure the State.[69] It was not only the Londoners who were failing to implement one of the key objectives. Richard Boyle (1566-1643), 1st Earl of Cork (from 1620), one of the Lords Justices of Ireland, noted that it was 'clear … King James's policy of planting civilization and Protestantism … has not had the good effect which was expected of it' because far too many Undertakers 'countenanced' and encouraged 'Papists'[70] on their lands. Boyle himself had been enormously successful in establishing order and prosperity in Munster, having bought out all the interests there of Sir Walter Raleigh (*c.*1552-1618) in Counties Cork, Tipperary, and Waterford in 1604. There, he built bridges, harbours, towns, and fortresses, set up industries, planted settlers from England, and made sure the natives were kept in order. Cromwell was later to declare that if every province in Ireland had had a Boyle it would have been impossible for the Irish to raise the Great Rebellion.[71] Boyle's strictures, though aimed primarily at the Hamiltons (created Earls of Abercorn in 1606) of Co. Tyrone, who had 'drawn thither Papists',[72] could have been applied to many others. Later, in 1625, Downham was to become one of the sequestrators of the rents in County Londonderry, which he, the archdeacon, and Sir John Vaughan were to deliver to Sir Thomas Phillips.

It will be recalled that Phillips had obtained new estates in and around Limavady to compensate him for the loss of Coleraine. By the time King James wrote his famous letter to the Lord Deputy Phillips was becoming extremely apprehensive. His lands included the ancient O'Cahan castle, so he was at the epicentre of the imprisoned chieftain's 'Country', and certainly a target for assassins. Wedged between the Fishmongers' Proportion to the north and west, Church lands to the north, south, and east, a patch of glebe lands to the north, the Haberdashers' Proportion to the

[68] As Simington (ed.) (1937) makes clear, some Irish natives did conform, certainly when the Civil Survey was made during the Cromwellian Protectorate.

[69] Reynell (ed.) (1896) **iii**/1, 55. See also Mahaffy (ed.) (1900): *Cal. S. P. I. 1625-1632*, 509-12.

[70] Mahaffy (ed.) (1900) *Cal. S. P. I. 1625-1632*, 511.

[71] *D.N.B.* (1917), **ii**, 1022. Boyle's tomb in the collegiate church of St Mary, Youghal, Co. Cork, is a spectacular example of showy Jacobean funerary architecture, designed and made by Alexander Hills of Holborn, London, in 1620 (see Potterton [1975]).

[72] Mahaffy (ed.) (1900) *Cal. S. P. I. 1625-1632*, 511.

north-east and south-east, and lands of native freeholders in the north-east, to the east, and to the south, his estates were extremely vulnerable, given that any security offered from the Fishmongers' and Haberdashers' Proportions would not be worth much, while Irish natives teemed all around. It was little wonder that Phillips and the bishop became allies in their concern for the future of the Londonderry Plantation.

Throughout the county the question of encouraging the Established Church remained a problem in spite of the bishop's vociferous appeals. English parsons may have been reassuringly familiar figures for the few British settlers, but they were ineffective as proselytisers among the Irish, not knowing the language. There is also abundant evidence (including the events surrounding the 1615 Conspiracy) that Roman Catholic priests and friars were numerous and active among the native population, implacably opposed to the Plantation with its corollaries relating to implementation of uniformity with Anglican worship, English habits, English agricultural methods, English speech, English education, and English law.

Proby and Springham duly delivered the swords of office to the mayors. A new water-bailiff was appointed for Lough Foyle (i.e. to protect the fishings), and the supply and maintenance of sufficient beacons and buoys for navigation were entrusted to Captain Baker of Culmore. The existing wharf at Londonderry was judged to be adequate for its purpose for the time being. However, there were signs of discord between The Irish Society and the civic officials of both Londonderry and Coleraine, for when the commissioners invited the local dignitaries to make proposals for bye-laws and ordinances, the invitations were refused and all discussion about these matters curtailed. Furthermore, there was something very odd about the Wilkinson affair at Coleraine. In the instructions given to Proby and Springham[73] mention is made of settlers who had 'quitted their houses and left' the town, which indicates all was not well. The commissioners were asked to ensure that care was taken 'for the said towne'. This seems to confirm Bodley's indications that there was discontentment with treatment by The Irish Society, or rather by the Agent and officials of The Society on the spot (i.e. Rowley and then Beresford). The systems of municipal government that had been established 'had not fostered in the local officials any sense of attachment' to The Society.[74] Furthermore, a careful reading of any shadowy evidence that survives suggests that there was more in the Wilkinson business than at first meets the eye. First of all, Wilkinson's actions in sticking his neck out by complaining to the King and the Privy Council early in 1616 were not entirely prompted by personal pique, for some of the townsmen of Coleraine indicated at the public meeting that they had collected money to enable Wilkinson to travel to London to press for 'favor to obteine certain thinges for the good of the said town and inhabitants'. This might indicate that the normal channels through the Agent were not working, and that some decided to 'go to the top'. Anybody who has worked in any large organisation will be familiar with the problems of obstructive personalities in positions of power, more interested in keeping the lid firmly on problems than admitting there are any which might involve action and decision-making of an uncongenial nature. The commissioners do not appear to have interviewed disgruntled persons individually (which might have been more informative), relying on shows of hands at a public meeting, where those with complaints could well have kept them to themselves to avoid opprobrium and possible unpleasantness (even discrimination?) from Beresford and others. At the

[73] Irish Society (*c.*1898), instruction 31, 431.

[74] Moody (1934), 175.

public meeting Proby and Springham recorded that Wilkinson had 'promissed to effect' the requests made by townspeople who had paid for his mission, but 'abused them in his trust and exhibited the said complaints' in the name of the inhabitants of Coleraine 'without their direccon'. The commissioners examined the 'peticon preferred' in the names of 'the inhab^ts of Coleraine' and the various letters 'to the Committee against Wilkinson': the townspeople were then asked if the petition and the letters were their 'free and voluntary act which by holding up their hands they acknowledged and affirmed'. This might indicate that Proby and Springham suspected that witnesses had been 'leant on' by somebody or more than one person, but the public meeting 'cleared Mr. Beresford of the imputations inserted in Wilkinson's complaints', and that seems to have been that. Nearly four centuries later the affair still reeks of coercion, manipulation, and even intimidation, and one suspects the unfortunate settlers were very likely at the mercy of an unscrupulous and bullying Agent. It is probably of great significance that the commissioners made Beresford sign an 'oath to behave himself truly and faithfully in his place and ymployment of Agent and Treasurer there for the Citties use'. A copy of this document was presented to The Society in London.[75] However, The Irish Society seems to have done what it could to sort things out, and, of course, would have had considerable difficulties finding anybody else to be sent over from London to take over as Agent, for ropes would have had to be learned all over again. The surviving evidence suggests that the commissioners felt it was a case of putting up with the 'Devil they knew'.

Other matters dealt with by Proby and Springham included payments to the Burgesses who sat for Londonderry and Coleraine in the Irish Parliament and other incidental sums disbursed to individuals such as Baker, Carey, and Rowley. 'The 12 Children sent over from X^t Hospitall' had 'arrived all safe and well': the commissioners 'placed tenn of them' at 'London Derry ... and two ... at Coleraine'. Their indentures were to be delivered by Proby and Springham to the 'Thier of Christs Hospitall to be there kept for there use'.[76] This time, it should be noted, the reference to Christ's Hospital is clear and precise. It should be remembered that Christ's was in Newgate Street, City of London, at that time, only moving to Horsham in the 19th century, so it was perfectly feasible for the commissioners to promise to deliver the indentures in person. Unfortunately these papers have eluded rediscovery.[77]

These efforts by the City of London did not deflect the attention of the Crown, however, and it was not long before further investigations were set in hand. In the meantime The Irish Society was doing what it could to keep its agents in order and to prod the Companies to show greater zeal in implementing the King's wishes. All these efforts were not enough. Alarm-bells were sounding, and the City of London was under the spotlight.[78]

75 Irish Society (*c.*1898), 442.

76 *Ibid.*, 435, para 11.

77 The Keeper of Manuscripts, Libraries and Guildhall Art Gallery, Corporation of London, and the Curator and Archivist, Christ's Hospital, Horsham, West Sussex, kindly tried to find these, without success.

78 See also Aldous (ed.) (1993), Bagwell (1909), Betts (1913), Bodley (1910), Boyd (1933), Brewer and Bullen (eds.) (1867-73), Carson (1968), Chart (ed.) (1928), Colby (1837), Curl (1986), Erck (ed.) (1846, 1852), Freshfield and Freshfield (1898), Harris (1770), Hill (1877, 1889), Irish Society (*c.*1898), Johnson (1914-22), Lacy (1998), Moody (1939), Orr (1997), Perceval-Maxwell (1990), Portlock (1843), Robinson (1984, 1994), Russell and Prendergast (eds.) (1872-80), Schultes (1822), Smith (1966), and Townshend (1904).

CHAPTER V

Bodley's Third Survey, the Pynnar and Phillips Surveys, the Quarrel with the Crown, and Building Endeavours to 1641

> My continued zeal to your Majesty's Service solicits me not to be idle at any time in the work committed to my charge and, being no orator, I have made bold ... to discover ... the truth in writing, wherefore in this book I have collected the whole proceeding of the London Plantation in the North of Ireland with every particular since the first undertaking therein, and have made bold to present the same to your Majesty's most judicious view, to the end, their abuses appearing unanswerable ...
>
> Preface in form of a Petition from Sir Thomas Phillips to King Charles I, quoted in CHART, DAVID ALFRED (1878-1960) (ed.): *Londonderry and the London Companies 1609-1629. Being a Survey and Other Documents submitted to King Charles I* (Belfast: His Majesty's Stationery Office, 1928), 1

Introduction

Proby and Springham left Londonderry on 12 August and submitted their report and accounts to auditors before presenting them, with estimates for 'all future workes of fortificaсons and reparaсons and addition to the Church of Derrie and Steeples for the churches of both townes', on 1 October 1616.[1] The Irish Society approved their report, but, while gratifying progress had been made, and Londonderry itself was a hive of building activity, it was obvious that Bodley's criticisms were well founded, so improvements had to be implemented to deflect the ire of His Britannic Majesty. The City noted many of the most flagrant abuses had been nipped in the bud, but there was still much to be done, although in some respects the covenant with the Crown had been resolved, albeit rather later than intended.

However, all was not well on the Company Proportions. On the Ironmongers' estate workmen were 'fearful to work in the woodes except there be 10 or 12 in a companie',[2] there were almost daily instances of violent robbery, and several very nasty murders of settlers (e.g. on the Mercers' Proportion at Lislea). Canning complained of 'mischeifes and miseries' inflicted on the settlers, causing those in and around Agivey to 'stand continually upon' their guard, and, when travelling, to 'take good strength' with them. He asked the Ironmongers' Company for more arms and bullets, and it is obvious from his comments and other evidence that life was no picnic for the Londoners or their agents.[3] Proby reported on the Ironmongers' estates in some detail, demonstrating that nearly all tenants, both British and Irish, had Irish sub-tenants on their lands, although the occasional British name appears. Of 127

[1] Irish Society (*c.*1898), 423-43.

[2] Quoted from Richard Hunter's documents, f. 135, by Moody (1939), 329.

[3] Curl (1986), *passim*, Hill (1877), *passim*, Moody (1939), *passim*, and Robinson (1984, 1994), *passim*. See also M.S. 17276, Guildhall Library, City of London.

under-tenants, all but nine were Irish (as the O'Cahan, McReddy, McGrath, and O'Quig names testify), despite the indisputable fact that the tenants of the Ironmongers' Company were expressly bound by covenant not to sublet to the Irish natives at all.[4] On the other Proportions the same conditions prevailed, and it is absolutely clear that the Companies found it easier to ignore the presence of Irish under-tenants than to persuade reluctant Englishmen to risk all by settling in Ulster. However, all this was contrary to the intentions of the King, the Lord Deputy, and the Privy Council, a fact that did not escape the watchful eyes of Sir Thomas Phillips, Sir Josias Bodley, and others. On 12 December 1616 The Irish Society reacted by sending a Precept to the Ironmongers' Company demanding that it named its freeholders, for it was clear 'no care had been taken ... to satisfy' The Society or the Lords of the Council in 'so great a business'. If the Ironmongers failed in the objects of the Plantation, they were reminded that 'the blame must be upon' them and not The Society. As a result of the reports of the commissioners it became obvious that the Companies would be leant upon for further funds in the immediate future.[5]

Bodley's 1616 Survey and its Immediate Effects

In July 1616 Tyrone died in exile in Rome, doubtless to the great relief of the Government, but the climate was changed further when Chichester was replaced as Lord Deputy by Sir Oliver St John, an experienced Planter himself, who, in the aftermath of Tyrone's death, determined that all natives were to remove themselves from the City's lands by May 1618. As usual, this notice had little effect, and once again excuses were found to avoid implementing the evictions.[6] What is more, if the Irish remained on the lands of British Undertakers after 1 May 1619, they were to be fined 10 shillings each, and afterwards to pay further fines at the command of the Lord Deputy. This was a clear signal that the Government had no intention of implementing the Crown's objectives, and that the segregation of Irish natives would not be enforced: so long as they paid the fines, they could stay. There was one little problem: who was to collect those fines?

In November 1616 Bodley carried out his third survey on behalf of the Crown, and predictably found the castles and bawns on the Company Proportions woefully incomplete and inadequate, while there were very few British tenants but many Irish natives residing on the county lands, confirming Proby's observations earlier. Lawlessness was obviously on the increase too, and Bodley was in no doubt that the retention of the native population on Company Proportions posed great dangers, because that population not only covertly supported the wood-kernes with food and shelter, but provided the ranks from which the guerrillas were recruited. Clearly, County Londonderry in 1616-17 was not a safe place, and was becoming more disordered: The Irish Society, intended as the agency by which the new county would be organised and brought to calm waters and prosperity, had failed in the objectives required of it, through no fault of its own. The main problems were its agents and employees, the Companies' 'farmers' (and *their* under-tenants) who proved difficult to control from London, tardy and unreliable communications, human frailty, dishonesty, and greed, and the hostility of other Undertakers, settlers, and, of course, the Irish themselves.

4 See Moody (1939), 333, and *passim*.
5 *Ibid.*, 167-176; Irish Society (*c.*1898), *passim*.
6 Moody (1939), *passim*.

Even John Rowley, the dismissed Agent of The Irish Society (who might have been expected to be a severe critic of his former employers), who was by then Agent of the Drapers' Company,[7] opined that Bodley was not 'well affected' towards the City, and thought that various individuals were casting beady eyes on the Londoners' holdings: 'manie are in the hope to cure from the Kinge such of the Citties lands as are not Planted accordinge to the Kings booke of Plantac̃on', he wrote to the Company on 26 October 1616.[8] Bodley was well tuned to potential dangers, however, and intelligence of the frequent outrages committed by the wood-kernes in 1616 could not be suppressed. Indeed he and the Justices of the Peace had been active in anti-insurgent work in the autumn of 1616, obliging parishes to arm men (placed under commanders approved by the Lord Deputy, no less[9]), and regular forays from the fort at Desertmartin were made, leading to the killing of some 40 dangerous Irish guerrillas[10] who appear (ominously) to have been followers of the Antrim MacDonnells.

As a result of Bodley's unflattering findings, the Privy Council called The Irish Society before it: the City of London stood accused of breach of contract with the Crown and with failure to implement the Articles of Plantation. Lists of faults were prepared by the Crown and sent to The Irish Society for responses. Although both the list of defaults and the answers were sent to the Attorney-and-Solicitor-General for consideration, no further immediate action was taken. Again and again, the Londoners were to manage to persuade the Crown that retention of Irish natives was necessary to avoid complete collapse of the rural economy, to obtain some income to ease the pain of so much outlay, and to ensure the land did not revert to a wilderness, to the ruin of the City of London. At the end of 1616 it seemed once more that matters were going to be allowed to drift. However, Bodley's third survey and its repercussions were indicative of the first formal moves accusing The Irish Society (and therefore the City of London) with a breach of its obligations under the various agreements negotiated with the Crown.

Pynnar's Survey

The new Lord Deputy (from August 1616), Sir Oliver St John (1559-1630 – Viscount Grandison from 1623 and Baron Tregoz from 1626), who had been one of Chichester's most trusted advisers and one of the original commissioners for the Plantation of Ulster from 1608,[11] began to enquire about the removal of the natives almost as soon as he was sworn in, and he and the Government appointed commissioners to ensure that Irish natives on the Londoners' lands were transferred to Church lands, the estates of Servitors, and the native freeholders.[12] Phillips, Beresford, the Mayor of Londonderry, and other agents and Undertakers were instructed to ensure the message went home. As has been mentioned above, further threats, rumblings about fines, and other noises failed to accomplish anything. The Government then decided to order yet another survey, and on 28 November 1618 the Director-General and Overseer of the Fortifications and Buildings in Ireland, Captain Nicholas Pynnar (*fl.* 1600-44), a distinguished soldier (who had seen service as a Captain of Foot in Docwra's army,

[7] Johnson (1914-22), **iii**, 20, 23, 31, 34, 126, 128, 376.
[8] Drapers' Company archives, Ma. Dr. B45.
[9] *Ibid.* See also Moody (1939), 178.
[10] Russell and Prendergast (eds.) (1880): *Cal. S.P.I. 1615-1625*, 146-7, 195.
[11] *D.N.B.* (1917), **xvii**, 637-9.
[12] Chart (ed.) (1928), 49-50.

having gone to Ireland from The Netherlands in 1600), was appointed to carry it out. Pynnar had worked in Italy in 1606-7, so may have known something of Italian Renaissance architecture and other sophisticated subjects conspicuous by their absence in County Londonderry.[13] His remit included all the six escheated counties of Ulster, and he worked on his survey from 1 December 1618 until 28 March 1619: his findings were later published by Walter Harris (1686-1761) in *Hibernica* (1757).[14] The *Dictionary of National Biography*[15] is dismissive of the survey, stating that 'its importance has been probably overestimated', but that is not really borne out by the facts.

The survey owed its origins to an intimation given by the Privy Council to the Lord Deputy in March 1618 that the Government was becoming deeply concerned about the Plantation of Ulster because of the general slackness of the Undertakers which had provoked the King. His Majesty was resolved to brook no further connivance, but would punish 'those that have soe grossly failed, as eyther in lawe, or pollicy of state', as 'hee may justly doe'.[16]

The Irish Society, seeking to anticipate more trouble, wrote to the Companies reminding them of the current state of their Proportions, any deficiencies in terms of buildings, numbers of British tenants, supplies of arms for the tenants, and other relevant matters.[17] Pynnar's comprehensive report estimated that in the six escheated Ulster counties there were 6,215 adult British males capable of bearing arms, distributed as follows:

Armagh	642
Cavan	711
Donegal	1,106
Fermanagh	645
Londonderry	642
Tyrone	2,469 [18]

Thus Counties Armagh and Londonderry were severely undermanned, but his figures (based on the findings of the Government-appointed commissioners) were augmented by his own observations, and he came to the conclusion that there were around 8,000 men of British birth or descent capable of acting in the King's name. However, no more than 25 per cent of the area of the six escheated counties was fully inhabited or developed to anything like the extent necessary for the safety of the Plantation or its settlers: there were 107 'castles' (i.e. fortified houses) with bawns, 19 'castles' without bawns, 42 bawns unattached to any 'castle' or house, and 1,897 dwelling-houses of stone or timber frames, in villages, in the 'English' manner, plus many other isolated houses he had not inspected.[19]

Chart's romantic notion that the Plantation settlements 'could have been compared with Chester or Warwick'[20] is fanciful in the extreme: in 1616 Canning wrote to the Ironmongers' Company that on its Proportion 'there wilbe a towne of sixe houses, wch is a great towne in this Countrey',[21] so there cannot have been much in the way

13 Loeber (1981), 85-6.

14 Harris (1770), 139-241. See also Hill (1877), 451-590, and the Carew MS. 613 in the archiepiscopal library at Lambeth Palace (see Brewer and Bullen [eds.] [1873]: *Cal. Carew MSS 1603-1624*, 392-423).

15 *D.N.B.* (1917), **xvi**, 530.

16 Moody (1939), 184.

17 *Ibid.*, 185.

18 Hill (1877), 451-590; Irish Society (*c.*1898), 467-8; Moody (1939), 184-191.

19 Moody (1939), 185.

20 Chart (ed.) (1928), viii.

21 Moody (1939), 317, quoting sources from the Ironmongers' Company records. See Curl (1986), 349-366.

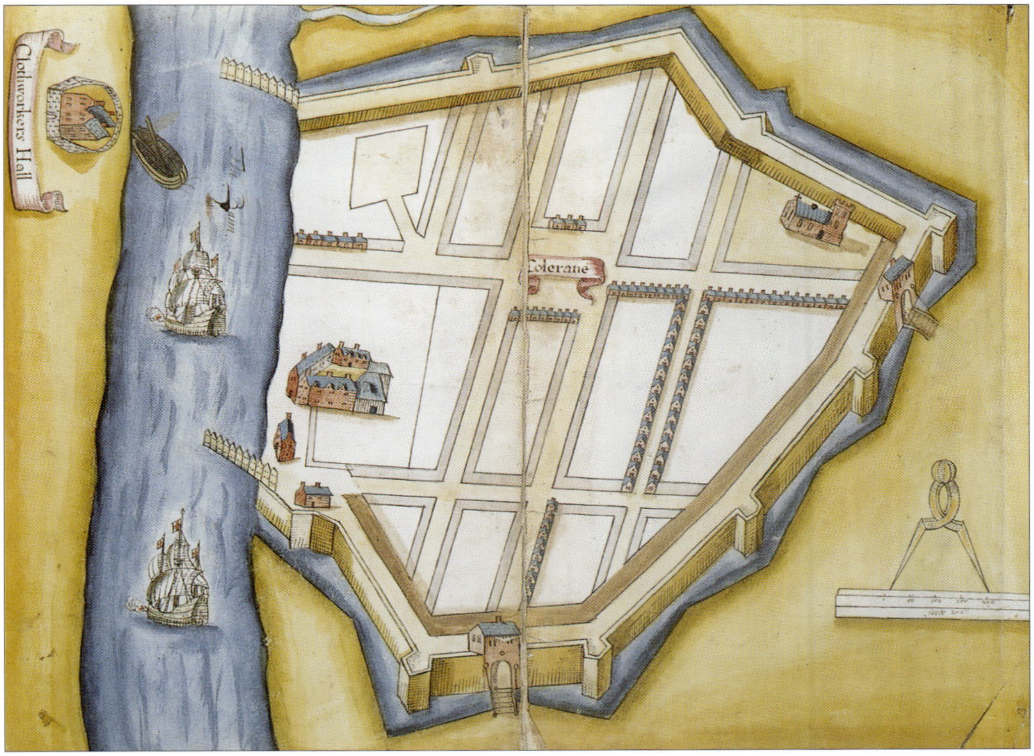

29 Plan of Coleraine, from Nicholas Pynnar's Survey of the counties of Cavan, Fermanagh, Donegal, Tyrone, Armagh, and Londonderry, with a map of the city there (fol.46r), Culmore Fort, and the town of Coleraine (fol. 49r), taken by virtue of the King's commission in 1618-19. Folios 56-57 contain the names of several British Undertakers, Servitors, and Irish natives. On the left, on the west bank of the Bann, is Clothworkers' Hall. The two 'portes' or town-gates are shown, together with the parish-church, the rows of small houses (note how much undeveloped land is enclosed within the 'rampiers'), and the complex of buildings of the former Dominican priory. The ramparts are surrounded by a water-filled moat, and there are drawbridges. The river-bank is unprotected save for the two pallisades projecting into the Bann. (*From an original coloured drawing [406.4 mm x 311.1 mm] on paper [TCD/MS. 864. fol 49r]*)

of a reassuring town or village anywhere, and certainly nothing to compare with the city of Chester or the town of Warwick. Pynnar concluded that there was a 'great want' of building on the escheated lands, with the result that the survival of the British settlements was by no means secured. Very few English colonists ploughed their lands or used 'husbandrie', as they were 'fearful to stock themselves with cattle or servants for those labours'.[22] Clearly there was a widespread lack of confidence. The settlers sublet their lands at high rents to Irish natives who did not grow crops, but only raised stock, because they themselves had no security of tenure as they could be removed at any time. Interestingly, it appears that determined Scots colonists practised arable farming, and that if it had not been for them there would have been a serious famine. Reading between the lines, it would appear that the colonists (especially English settlers) had developed a dependency on the Irish tenants who, if removed, would leave a vacuum and reduce the Planters to starvation, but who, if allowed to remain, posed a perpetual threat to the safety of the Undertakers, their dependants, and their tenants. It was a very thorny dilemma. Pynnar noted wryly that 'the abode

[22] Irish Society (*c.*1898), 467.

and continuance of those inhabitants upon the land is not yet made certain',[23] an understatement if ever there was one.

At Londonderry, Pynnar found the infant city 'encompassed about with a very strong wall, excellently made and neatly wrought; being all of good lime and stone'. There were four gates, all battlemented, but 'to two of them there is no going up, so that they serve no great use; neither have they made any leaves for their gates; but make two drawbridges serve for two of them, and two portcullises for the other two. The bulwarks are all very large and good, being in number nine; besides two half bulwarks; and for four of them there may be four cannons, or other great pieces; the rest are not all cut so large, but wanteth very little. The rampart within the city is 12 feet thick of earth; all things are very well and substantially done, saving there wanteth a house for the soldiers to watch in, and a sentinel house for the soldiers to stand in, in the night, to defend them from the weather, which is most extreme in these parts'.[24] He noted that since the last survey Springham's free school was in operation (it had been completed in 1617), and was supported by The Irish Society by means of an annual grant in lieu of the 300 acres allotted to the school for its maintenance by Proby and Springham.[25]

All this sounded reasonable, but Pynnar counted only 92 houses in Londonderry with 102 families inhabiting them, although Proby and Springham had claimed 215. There was not enough land, Pynnar noted, for the projected 100 houses. The discrepancy is accounted for, Pynnar suggested, because The Irish Society reckoned one room as a 'house'. To Pynnar it was absolutely clear that both Londonderry and Coleraine had far too few inhabitants, and would be impossible to defend as there were not enough able-bodied men to do so.[26] He thought Culmore Fort was complete, with platforms for artillery on the walls, and that it was adequately garrisoned.[27] Thus, although The Irish Society could claim that the fortifications of Culmore and Londonderry completed the Londoners' obligations, the paucity of housing and acute shortage of manpower might enable the Crown to challenge any such assumption.[28] Developments at Coleraine, for example, included only three more houses since Bodley's survey, and those had been erected by private individuals who had been allowed £20 each by The Irish Society.[29] Furthermore, the 'rampiers' at Coleraine were disintegrating (they were being washed away by the rain), and were hopeless for defensive purposes (being too extensive, as was indicated above, for the numbers of men available, and of insufficient size or strength to support heavy artillery). Pynnar reckoned only about a sixth of the length of the defences could be guarded with the manpower available. There were only two small timber 'ports' (gates) doubling as guard-houses for the soldiers. Undeveloped parts of Coleraine were dismal and filthy, and the shapeless market-place was squalid and filled with piles of refuse so that the inhabitants could hardly walk across it.[30] Clearly competent civic government and basic management were wholly lacking, in spite of The Irish Society's efforts, through the commissioners, to effect improvements. It sounds as though Beresford could do as little (or as much) as he liked **[29]**.

23 Irish Society (*c.*1898), 467.
24 Hill (1877), 451-590.
25 Chart (ed.) (1928), 54-5, 68, 108; Moody (1939), 186.
26 Hill (1877), 573-590.
27 *Ibid.*, 575.
28 Moody (1939), 186-9.
29 *Ibid.*, 186.
30 Hill (1877), 575-6.

On the 12 Company Proportions Pynnar found 118 timber-framed or stone houses had been built, mostly in settlements protected to some extent by castles and bawns in various stages of completion. However, some buildings would be too difficult to defend, and, as Phillips showed later, many were left uncompleted and roofless.[31] There were also houses scattered in isolated positions on the Proportions, and these would fall easily to determined attack. Several churches were being built, some were being repaired, and others were completed. On some Proportions (e.g. those of the Clothworkers, Grocers, Ironmongers, and Mercers) nearly all of the population consisted of Irish natives (who paid high rents), and Pynnar identified the City of London's lands as having the greatest numbers of natives of all in the six counties.[32] In the other nine Proportions the few British settlers (many of whom had erected houses at their own charge) were still waiting for titles to their lands and showed every sign of throwing in the towel and returning to England, so unsatisfactory and dangerous were their circumstances. The Companies argued that they could not evict the Irish natives because without them they would have no income and the rural economy would collapse, while the Government warned that retention of the Irish endangered everything the Plantation was intended to achieve.[33] It appears that some Companies began to believe that they were not bound by the City's charter to plant with British settlers. It is not clear how this 'specious view', as Moody[34] called it, gained currency, but even the Companies' lessees began to believe it, the implication being that the City's lands were not subject to the general conditions of the Plantation of Ulster, but only to the various stipulations of the charter of King James I and VI to The Irish Society (20 March 1613).[35] By the 'Printed Book' for all Plantations (1608), however, which preceded the Londoners' Articles, *all* Undertakers were obliged to plant with British and not to alienate or demise to the 'mere Irish' upon pain of forfeiture.[36] Eventually, in 1626, the Crown was to see that 'the Charter passed to the Londoners' was 'greatly prejudicial to the Crown in many material things', and that the 'Plantation as it now stands unsettled doth evidently endanger the whole Kingdom',[37] simply because the Articles of the General Plantations were not repeated verbatim in the charter, but assumed to be as read. Nevertheless, that the 'Londoners held themselves within these general rules' is clear from the repeated requests for permission to retain the Irish on the lands for a time until British settlers could be found.

The expression 'mere Irish' has been interpreted by hostile and ignorant commentators to imply some sort of gratuitous slur on the native Irish, but 'mere' simply means pure-bred, undiluted, or unmixed. *The Oxford English Dictionary*[38] goes so far as to say the word is 'now often misunderstood as a term of disparagement, the adjective being apprehended' as 'having no greater extent, range, value, power, or importance than the designation implies'. The fact that 'mere' or 'meer' is also applied to the 'Englishe', the Saxons, the English language, Tuscan song, and other nouns should be sufficient to dispel any misapprehensions.

31 Chart (ed.) (1928), *passim*.
32 Irish Society (*c*.1898), 468.
33 Hill (1877), 589-90; Moody (1939), 184-91.
34 Moody (1939), 190.
35 Given in full in Irish Society (*c*.1898), 155-362.
36 Chart (ed.) (1928), 79; Moody (1939), 137.
37 *Ibid.*
38 1933.

Pynnar's survey confirmed that virtually no progress had been made towards the segregation of the Irish, and although some of his figures were called into question by the returns of the Companies to The Irish Society, there can be no doubt that the Irish were in the majority on the Londoners' Plantation and that they paid the bulk of the rent collected by the Companies, while the rents paid by the British were forced ever upwards, obliging English and Scots settlers to 'take their lands at great rates' to their considerable 'distress'.[39]

The Aftermath of Pynnar's Survey

Pynnar's findings were sent to London in May 1619.[40] In July, The Irish Society reminded the reluctant Companies of the conditions under which they had received the estates, drawing especial attention to the fact that some freeholders had sold their lands in contravention of the covenants, and that many churches on Company Proportions were 'backward and unready',[41] which fact did nothing to promote adherence to the Anglican Church.

When the King learned the gist of what was going on, he informed the Lord Deputy[42] that the Londoners might have their estates seized by the Crown, but that, being ever merciful, he proposed to grant new patents provided he received double the rents and 'fines' for failing to honour contracts. He made it clear that he was not releasing the Undertakers from any of the requirements of the original agreements, but was simply remitting the forfeiture and resettling the estates to tighten things up.[43]

In 1620 the Privy Council called the Governor and some of the Assistants of The Society, informing them that the King believed the City of London stood in breach of its agreements with the Crown,[44] and a list of faults was prepared that formed the basis of the Crown's case. This followed the precedent of action taken after Bodley's survey of 1616. The Irish Society then demanded of the Companies lists of castles, bawns, houses, and other structures they had built or were erecting; details of what churches stood on their Proportions and of their condition; numbers of British tenants and inhabitants and information about freeholders; inventories of arms supplied and distributed; details of all monies expended and all income received; and full particulars of any letting of the Proportions or any parts thereof. Company returns to The Society were in some instances very vague, and it appears that some Livery Companies had not the slightest idea of what was going on in their Proportions at all.[45] Returns from the Drapers', Goldsmiths', and Merchant Taylors' Companies tend to confirm Pynnar's findings, but the Merchant Taylors 'understood' their lands to be tenanted entirely with British Planters, but had no knowledge of the numbers involved. The Mercers' Company claimed six freeholders and the rest of their Proportion let to British tenants, but Pynnar established that most of the Mercers' lands were let to Irish, and that 46 townlands were in the hands of the Clandonnells, 'the wickedest Men in all the Country'.[46] The Mercers' Proportion was the only one remaining in any Company's

[39] Irish Society (*c.*1898), 468.
[40] Russell and Prendergast (eds.) (1880): *Cal. S.P.I. 1615-1625*, 247-8.
[41] Moody (1939), 190.
[42] 8 September 1619.
[43] Moody (1939), 192.
[44] *Ibid.*
[45] *Ibid.*, 191.
[46] Hill (1877), 582; Irish Society (*c.*1898), 467.

immediate hands after the Ironmongers let their estates in August 1619, but in all cases the Companies had expended more on their Proportions than they had received from rents and other sources.

Once more The Irish Society and the Companies protested that difficulties would arise if the Irish were evicted, and, in an accommodating move, the Privy Council recommended that Irish natives who conformed in matters of religion and took the Oath of Allegiance could be accepted as tenants on a quarter of the lands of the City, and so could have access to over 80,000 acres in addition to those lands available for settlement under the original arrangements. Although (as is clear from the Civil Survey of 1654-6) some Irish became Protestants, probably for financial reasons as much as anything else, many remained true to the Church of Rome.[47]

The Undertakers were given until 1 May 1622 to eject Irish natives from the remaining 75 per cent of the lands, and were further prohibited from retaining Irish servants in their houses. However, even though Undertakers were prepared to pay double the existing rents for these terms, the Privy Council advised the King not to proceed any further until yet another survey should be carried out as part of a major official inquiry into the state of Ireland, both secular and ecclesiastical.[48] This marked the overture to the Lord Deputyship of Sir Henry Cary (d. 1633), 1st Viscount Falkland (from 1620), who was not sworn in until 18 September 1622.[49] Falkland succeeded St John in February 1622, and the inquiry was instituted on 20 March of that year.[50] Among its sections is a heading labelled 'The Plantation' that contains surveys of the colonies in King's and Queen's counties, Leitrim, Longford, Munster, Ulster, and Wexford. Each section was signed by the commissioners responsible for it.[51]

The seven commissioners for Ulster came to the conclusion that much had been accomplished, but that there were major problems. Many Undertakers were absentees; Irish natives were taken on as tenants instead of British; rents were extortionate; legal titles were withheld from tenants; freeholders were few on the ground; structures were unimpressive and jerry-built; houses were scattered too widely and not grouped together for defence so that their occupants were in danger from the wood-kernes; and copies of the Articles of Plantation were not provided for the poorer settlers who were therefore potential victims of the chief Undertakers, their agents, and rapacious lawyers. The commissioners confirmed earlier recommendations permitting Undertakers to lease 25 per cent of their lands to Irish natives for 20 years or for lives[52] on condition the Irish lived in villages, went to the Established Church, wore English clothes, ploughed in the English fashion (i.e. using halters rather than tying the plough to animals' tails), made their offspring learn a trade, and enclosed a minimum of a quarter of their lands.[53]

Ulster was divided into three groups of two counties each. Donegal and Londonderry were considered as one group, the Crown commissioners assigned to them being Richard Hadsor (one of the 'Kings Council for Ireland'[54]) and the looming figure of Sir Thomas Phillips. The ground-work of the survey appears to have taken

[47] See Simington (ed.) (1937), *passim*.

[48] Moody (1939), 192.

[49] *D.N.B.*, **iii**, 1149-51; Moody (1939), 193.

[50] Russell and Prendergast (eds.) (1880): *Cal. S.P.I. 1615-1625*, 346-7.

[51] British Museum Add. MS. 4756, ff.2-4, 6-133, 79v-133.

[52] A system by which a life was nominated (often a grand personage, e.g. royalty) on whose death the lease would terminate. By the 18th century it was usual to nominate three lives.

[53] British Museum Add. MS. 4756, ff.97v-133.

[54] Russell and Prendergast (eds.) (1880): *Cal. S.P.I. 1615-25*, 249, 356.

place from August until October 1622, and generally followed the pattern set by Pynnar, although the final report is far more detailed and is illustrated by the extraordinary use of coloured picture-maps by Thomas Raven.[55]

It was an ominous end of the beginning for the Londonderry Plantation, for by 1622 Phillips was wholly disenchanted with the Londoners. Far worse was to come, however, and the events of the rest of the century tore the nation apart, while one disaster followed another in Ulster. The 17th-century Plantation was to put a very considerable burden on the City of London and its Livery Companies, and played no small part in the momentous and historic rift between the City and the Stuart monarchy, in the Civil War and its outcome, and indeed in the ensuing saga of the curious relationship between Ulster and the Government in London.

The Phillips/Hadsor Survey

The Phillips/Hadsor documents are among the most fascinating dealing with the early Plantation.[56] As has been described above, Phillips had fallen out with the Londoners very early in the whole adventure, especially in relation to their spoiling of the woods, failure to remove the Irish natives, and tardiness in granting proper titles to lands. Phillips, not unnaturally, was concerned about the security of his own lands if the Londoners continued to default on their obligations, and by 1621 was negotiating with Raven to make surveys of the City of London's Plantation. It appears that Raven had been discharged from The Irish Society's service (there had been question-marks over his future employment at the time of the Proby/Springham investigations), and the commission of 1622 gave him a chance for revenge. The Phillips/Hadsor survey contained detailed observations about the built fabric, condition, and population of Londonderry, Culmore, Coleraine, the 12 Proportions of the Companies, and Phillips's own lands, setting out defects and omissions as well as suggestions for improvements.[57] The survey tabulated problems, and was augmented by a series of picture-maps entitled 'A true survey of the Present Estate of the Plantation of the County of London derry Taken by us, Sir Thomas Phillips, K^{t} and Richard Hadsor Esq. by Vertue of his Ma,^{ts} Commission …' which is almost identical to the official return. Two copies of these Raven maps survive: one is in the archiepiscopal library at Lambeth Palace[58] and the other in the archives of the Drapers' Company. The two versions differ slightly in matters of detail, and the annotations are not by the same hand. For example, some chimneys are shown in different positions, the timber-framed houses are sometimes not the same, and positions and designs of doors and windows are often changed.[59] It would appear that the Drapers' copy is the more accurate of the two, for it tallies with other material, and may be a corrected version. Other copies may have been taken, and a copy of the Lambeth version was made in 1836 for the celebrated Ordnance Survey of Ireland (deposited in the Public Record Office Northern Ireland) which was used by Chart in the *Phillips MS* volume published by HMSO in 1928. The attractive coloured picture-maps and accompanying annotations are very informative about the condition of the Londoners' Plantation in 1622, and in the absence of other

[55] Chart (ed.) (1928), *passim*; Curl (1986), *passim*.
[56] Chart (ed.) (1928), *passim*.
[57] British Museum Add. MS. 4756, ff. 119-23.
[58] Carew MS. 634.
[59] These variations are described in detail in Curl (1986), *passim*.

evidence should be treated with respect, though not necessarily as entirely accurate **[3, 22, 28, 30-35]**.

In Londonderry stout gates had been added to the gateways (or portes), and a town-hall was under construction in the 'Diamond' (central square). Streets were paved and all the houses (Phillips reckoned 102 as against The Irish Society's 219) were of stone. In addition were 26 other houses built by private individuals and around a dozen 'cabbons'. The 'Platt of the Cittie of London Derrie' **[28]** showed that the settlement had several defects:

1. it needed around 300 more houses and many more 'brittish sent over to guard the Towne', for as it was it stood 'a meere baite for an Enemy';
2. a food store to provide victuals for six months was essential as there was no possibility of the settlement's withstanding a siege without it;
3. there was a distinct lack of heavy artillery, platforms for the guns, and ammunition;
4. guard-houses and shelter for sentries were non-existent;
5. a stone quay to replace the timber structure was necessary not least to 'yeald good proffit by cranage and wharfage';
6. in the bog adjoining the city a cut was desirable, which, filled with water, would improve defence and provide power for water-mills;
7. 40 freeholders created by The Irish Society were essential in the 4,000 acres 'laid' to the city;
8. a new church was needed large enough to serve the city;
9. instead of the town-hall a fortified citadel containing municipal rooms was required **[30]**.

Phillips did not find much fault with Londonderry's walls, and approved Culmore Fort **[31]** with its strongly built bastions, ramparts, and walls. However, there was no possibility of the Fort's being able to withstand a prolonged siege as The Irish Society had not made provision for sufficient ordnance, ammunition, gun-powder, or victuals.[60]

At Coleraine, however, matters were anything but satisfactory. The earthen fortifications were full of holes through which men and beasts could pass easily, and the timber-framed guard-houses were a 'disgrace' to the town. 52 houses were of timber-framed construction and 18 were of stone, but that total of 70 houses erected by The Irish Society was counted as 125 by the Londoners. 21 other stone houses had been erected by individuals with the help of grants of £20 each from The Irish Society, but these only consisted of one room and a garret. In addition were five unsubsidised houses and 57 thatched cottages and 'cabbons' (which The Irish Society had tried to get rid of some time before). Coleraine had 145 families and could call upon 100 armed men for defence in addition to 24 men living outside the town. Quite clearly, with such a small number of men available, Coleraine could not be defended.

The commissioners recommended that new gateways of stone should be built and the riverside frontage of the town (which was wide open) fortified **[32]**. The 'rampiers' should be faced with stone, a citadel-cum-town-hall erected in the market-place, a bridge built over the Bann, and a new quay created. The problem of the bar at the mouth of the river was raised yet again, and the commissioners recommended a heavy expenditure to make the river navigable and safe. The 3,000 acres 'laid' to the town should be partially divided into freeholds. It appears that the 'whole number of Britisshe men inhabyteinge and now found resident in the City of London Derry, the Towne

[60] Chart (ed.) (1928), *passim*; Moody (1939), 191-210; Curl (1986), 72-80.

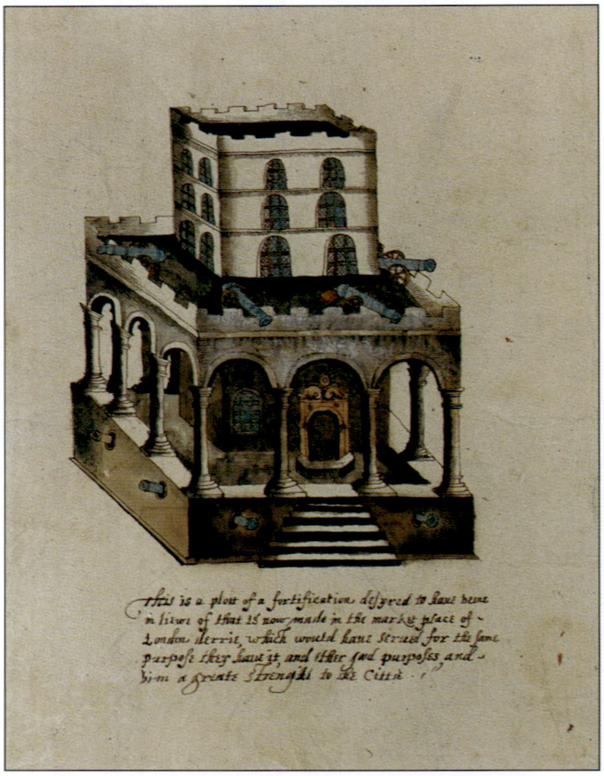

30 Detail of a copy of the Phillips/Raven 'Plott of a fortification desyred to have beene in liewe of that is now made in the market place of London Derrie, which would have served for the same purpose they have it, and their good purposes and bin a great strengthe to the Cittie' made at the time of the Ordnance Survey in 1836 by J. Butler Williams, acting under instructions from Colonel Colby. (*PRONI/CC*)

31 'The Fort of Coolemore 3 miles from London derry Seaward' in the series of Phillips/Raven picture-maps. Phillips emphasised the importance of this fort to protect the narrows of the River Foyle downstream from Londonderry from any attack by sea, and stated it was 'very needful there were a magazine of victuals for one year, and more store of munitions'. (*WCD/GB*)

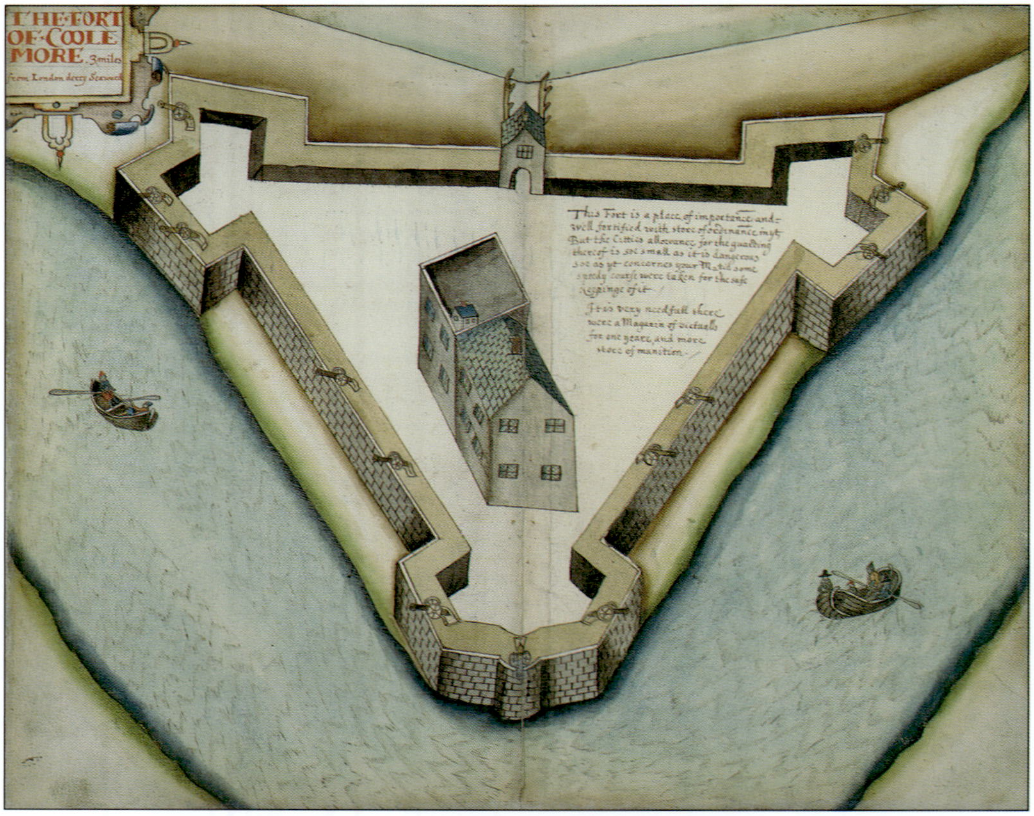

32 The Phillips/Raven 'A Plat of the Towne of Colerane as it now Stands Built and Fortified': a picture-map of Coleraine (1622) showing Phillips's suggestions for improvements. The paucity of dwellings should be noted: there were 145 families living within the walls, including 18 soldiers and 100 well-armed men to defend the town. In addition 50 men 'were about theire necessary affaires in the Cuntry' and there were about 24 others 'dwellinge neere the Towne'. As the ramparts did not extend along the river-bank between A and D, Phillips suggested that the part 'that doth lie dangerously open' should be 'fortified with a strong stone wall with convenient flankers, as in the plat described'. A bridge (C) should also be built across the Bann, as its 'want ... doth impoverish the town, and is a great hindrance of those parts of the country that lie beyond the water'. Phillips also noted that the 'wall or rampier' being of earth, should be faced with stone; that the gates should be rebuilt of stone; that 200 more houses should be built; that a store for victuals should be provided; that ordnance and munitions should be available; and that adequate guard-houses should be erected. This drawing also shows the former Dominican priory complex; the Clothworkers' castle and settlement across the river at Killowen; and a moat filled with water around Bodley's ramparts. (*WCD/GB*)

of Colrane, Fort of Culmore and upon the whole 12 Proporc̃ons planted by the Londoners doth contain 979, whereof armed 749. A third part of the 979 ... are not serviceable men.' For such a large area the British, in short, were thin on the ground. Phillips reckoned that, taking into account the inhabitants of Church lands and Irish freeholders, the native Irish outnumbered the British by about four to one. This is not surprising, for although the Londoners offered land at a few pence per acre to attract settlers, the Irish paid high annual rents to remain, and the Londoners, anxious to recoup their massive outlay, saw little reason to upset matters by evicting the natives. Procrastination over the agreed policy to plant British settlers and remove the Irish inhabitants was more and more apparent. Failure to assign freeholds of sufficient size, quality, and numbers also worked against the spirit of the Plantation, creating social imbalance, a shortage of jurors, and a curiously impoverished order. Lawlessness, lack of confidence, and absenteeism were rife.[61]

[61] Chart (ed.) (1928), *passim*; Moody (1939), 191-210; Curl (1986), 72-80.

As far as the built fabric of the Company lands was concerned, the commissioners and Raven revealed a shocking story. Many manor-houses lay unfinished and rotting, often used as pounds for cattle: obviously these structures could not withstand any determined attack, and thus provided no security, especially as they were not built on sites that would have secured the safety of the country. Phillips estimated that 131 stone and timber-framed houses had been built on the Proportions in addition to 109 small 'cabbons', but many stood in isolated positions (rather than grouped in villages), and so there was not much chance of the settlers giving each other mutual protection. The detailed notes on Raven's picture-maps make dismal reading.[62]

Phillips and Hadsor urged that many more British settlers should be sent to Ulster at once; that freeholds of sufficient size (according to the Articles) be granted to those capable of pursuing the aims of the Plantation; that extra villages ought to be created in every Proportion for the protection of the settlers; that bridges be built, passes cut, and communications improved; that more armed men should be stationed in each Proportion capable of tracking down any who attacked the settlers or their property; that castles, bawns, and manor-houses be completed, strengthened, and garrisoned; that what remained of the woods be properly conserved and

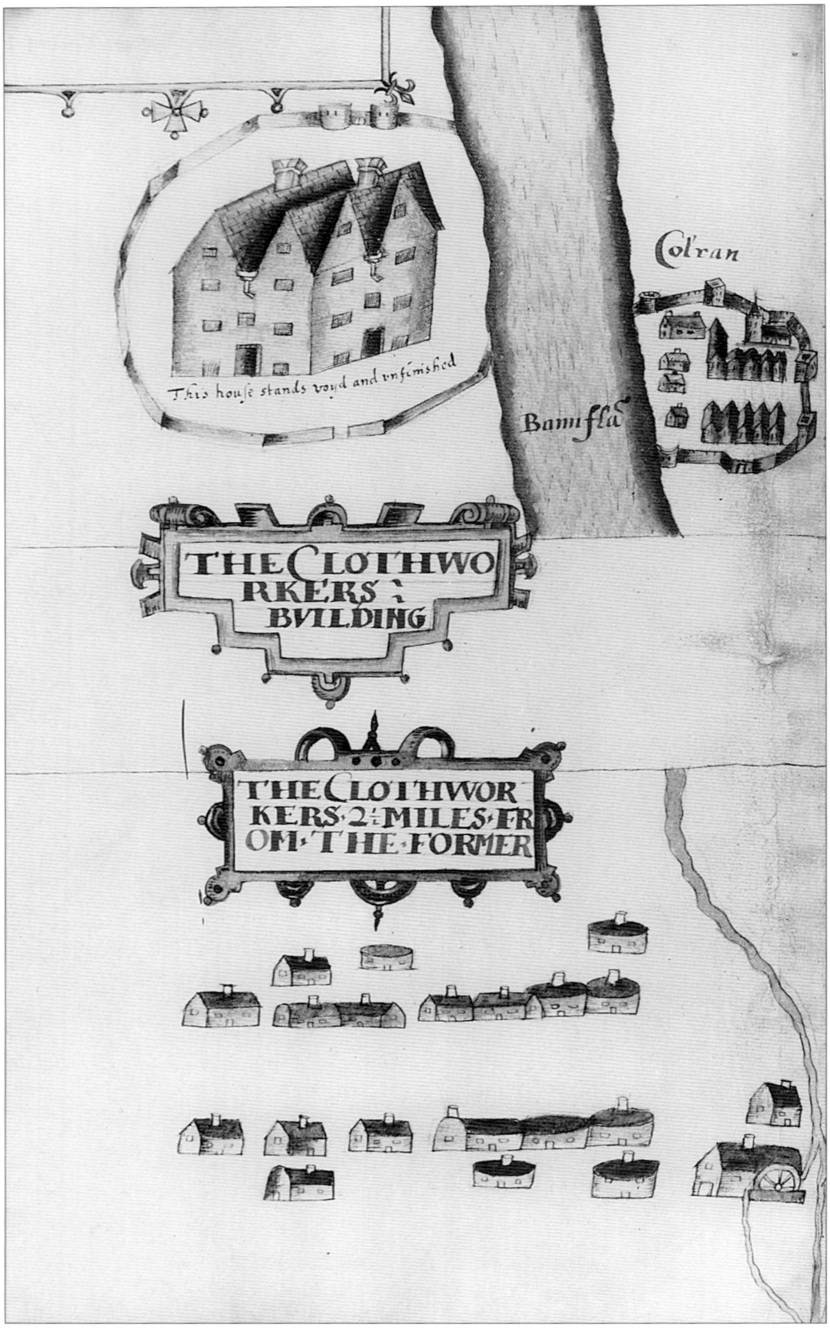

33 The Phillips/Raven 'The Clothworkers Building' at Killowen, and 'The Clothworkers 2½ Miles from the Former' at Articlave, 1622. The castle stood 'voyd and unfinished', had a central valley between roofs, and gables on at least three of the four elevations. Articlave had no architectural pretensions, and consisted of a series of thatched 'cabbons' and a mill. There do not appear to have been any houses of the 'English' type. The scale is hopelessly inaccurate, as the Clothworkers' Hall is surrounded by a wall containing a greater area than that comprising Coleraine. (*WCD/GB*)

62 Chart (ed.) (1928), *passim*, Curl (1986), *passim*.

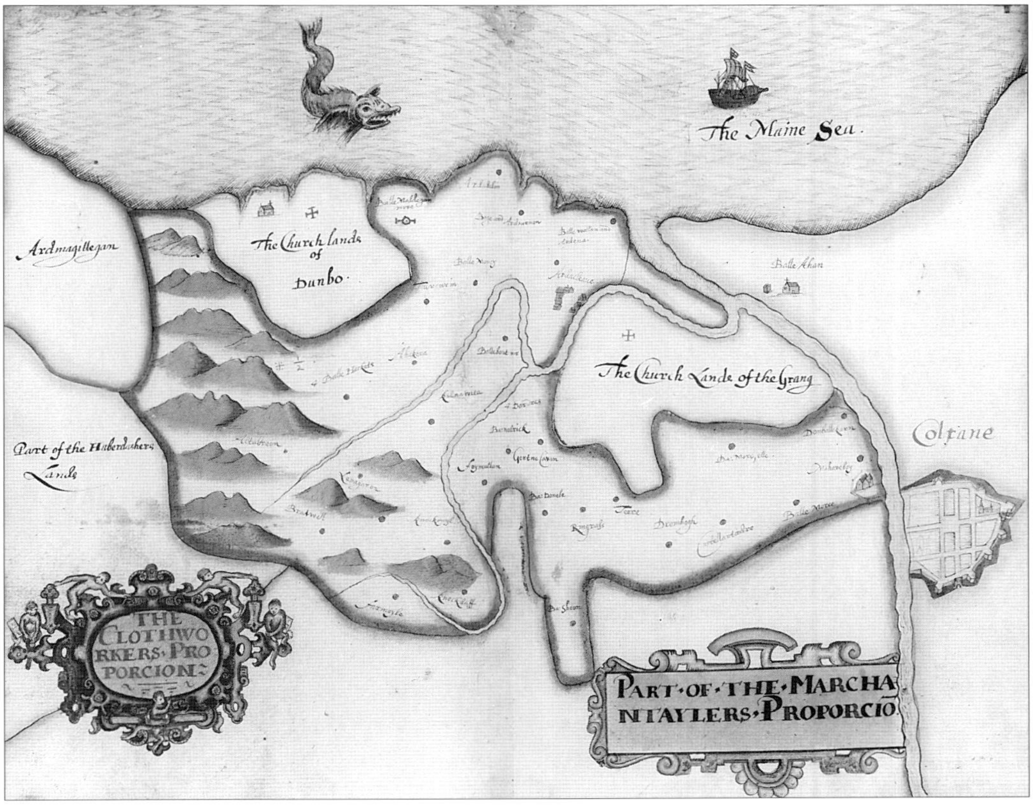

34 The Phillips/Raven 1622 picture-map of 'The Clothworkers' Proporcion' and 'Part of the Marchan-Taylers Proporciõ', showing 'Colrane', Clothworkers' Hall, the River Bann, the Clothworkers' village of Articlave and parcels of Church lands. (*WCD/GB*)

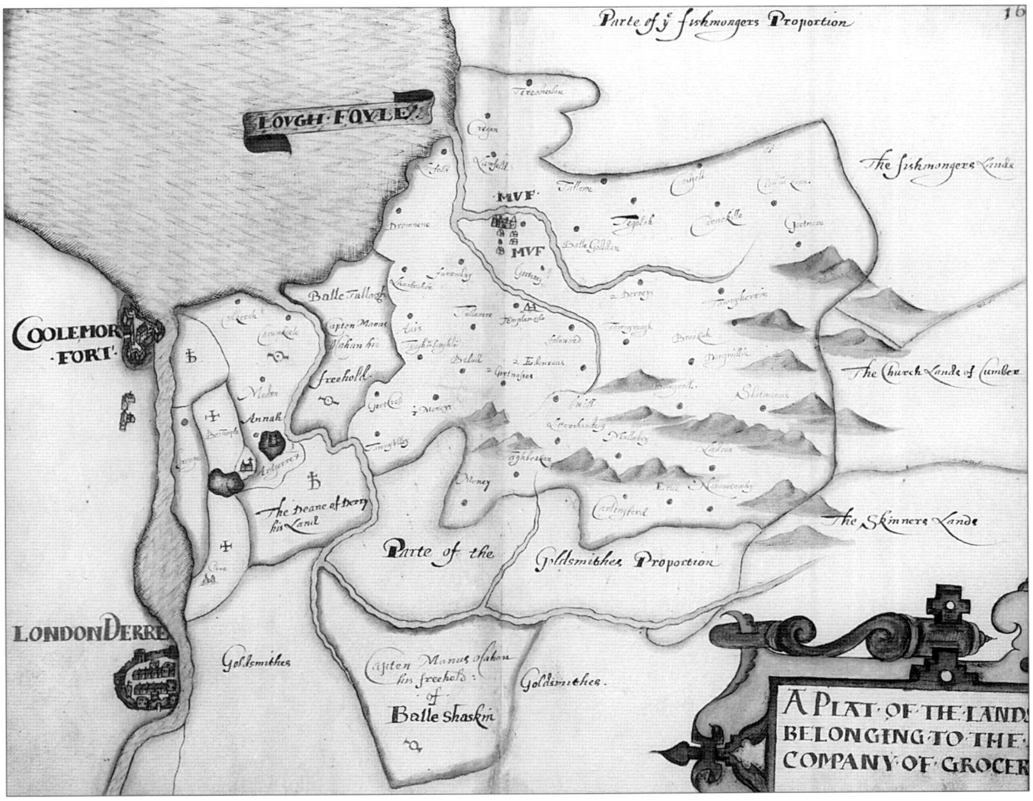

35 The Phillips/Raven 'A Plat of the Lands Belonging to the Company of Grocers', showing the Proportion in relation to the River Foyle and its Lough, 'London Derre', and 'Coolemore Fort'. The Grocers' 'capital' at Muff (now Eglinton) is clearly marked. (*WCD/GB*)

managed; and that arrangements to improve the workings of the law be made, with Assize-Courts and Sessions established in a more central location than Londonderry. The commissioners claimed that if reforms were not implemented immediately then the Plantation would be destroyed, for British tenants were few and in a sorry state, while the Irish, paying high rates for yearly tenancies, could hardly be expected to contribute to forward planning. There were also problems with the lands 'laid' to the urban settlements which remained for the most part in the hands of The Irish Society, so that there was insufficient income to support institutions such as Springham's school. The Calvinistically-inclined George Downham, Bishop of Derry, during the Visitation of his diocese (1622), also found it puzzling why educational endowments (such as those enjoyed in Donegal and Dungannon) did not exist in Londonderry, although he noted that the trend towards the displacement of native clergy by British parsons was well advanced.[63]

Many of the findings of Phillips and Hadsor were confirmed in a petition by the Mayor, Commonalty, and Citizens of Londonderry presented to the commissioners for Irish Causes in *c.*1623, the year in which The Irish Society's powers of control over Londonderry Corporation were due to expire under the Charter of 1613. In 1619 John Wray, by then the Mayor, and other leading citizens had written to The Irish Society pointing out that the poverty of the place was such that it could not survive without continuing help from London, and that the subordinate status of Londonderry should be continued for the mutual advantages of both London and Londonderry. The *c.*1623 petition raised the question of the sole place of worship, created from the ruins of the old monastery, which was far from having the 'dignity of a Cathedral Church'. The acres intended to provide support for Springham's school had, by some curious means, been withheld, so the school was under-endowed and therefore not free. Thus poor children grew up in idleness and ignorance, 'the bane of this Kingdome'. Furthermore, only 1,500 acres had been assigned by The Irish Society for civil purposes, which proved wholly insufficient. High rents, short leases, and other problems stirred up grievances, caused confidence to evaporate, and prevented the evolution of free Burgesses. Although theoretically the settlers were allowed to export products of the City's lands, in practice they were forced to buy licences to trade in certain goods, e.g. linen yarn. Restrictions on the export of wool, sheepskins, and other products had been introduced, and there were more problems relating to the manufacture and purchase of whiskey. Shortage of banking facilities inhibited trade and prosperity. The Irish Society leased the fisheries to individuals who failed to serve local markets with salmon because it was more profitable to export the lot. Furthermore, as is clear from another petition of 1623 from the inhabitants of Loughinsholin, heavy fines were imposed on all those who failed to serve as jurymen, yet the poor British tenants could afford neither the time nor the expense of arduous (and dangerous) travel to attend juries and were, in any case, reluctant to leave their families to the tender mercies of the Irish natives, as disorder was rife. County Londonderry was becoming more volatile by the year. Any Aldermen or persons of substance tended to abandon the infant city, leaving its government to impoverished tradesmen. Abatement of rents, enjoyment of the lands 'laid' to Londonderry, the 'farm' of the Customs and fishings, and other benefits were requested to ameliorate conditions. So bad were conditions that the charter of incorporation was offered to be laid 'at His Majesty's Royal feet'.[64]

[63] Orr (1977), 26.

[64] Moody (1939), 191-210; Curl (1986), 72-80 and *passim*.

Events from 1623

From 1623 the Government, in both Dublin and London, began to take Phillips's criticisms to heart, not least because in that year there were serious incidents of robbery, terrorism, and concerted attacks on settlers, notably in isolated places. Phillips organised counter-terrorist measures; strict regulations regarding under-tenants (including attempts to register their names) were brought in; and a close eye was kept on travellers and movements of livestock and goods.

In 1622 Viscount Falkland, the new Lord Deputy, before he departed for Dublin, interviewed the Governor and some of the Assistants of The Irish Society in London, as he had got wind of 'great defects of munition and arms' leaving the settlers in danger of 'Sodain Massacre'. The Irish Society was instructed to provide sufficient supplies to remedy the problem. Once more the Companies were to prepare reports on the state of their Proportions. In July 1623 Phillips was summoned to Dublin to give his views on the state of affairs in County Londonderry, and Falkland determined that Phillips should be sent to London to report directly to the Government (which was in no hurry to hear him, for he had to cool his heels for 10 months before he was permitted to have his say). Meanwhile, the Privy Council gave instructions that the entire defensive system in Ireland should be surveyed.

In January 1624 Falkland issued a proclamation ordering all Roman Catholic priests to be banished from the country and to depart within 40 days. This was a curiously-timed action, for delicate negotiations were under way to arrange a marriage between the Prince of Wales (later King Charles I) and Princess Henrietta Maria (1609-69), youngest daughter of King Henri IV of France (1589-1610). It appears that Falkland had been prompted to issue his proclamation after hearing an inflammatory sermon by James Ussher (1581-1656), Bishop of Meath (1621-5), who was a tireless protester against any toleration of 'Popery', and was not renowned for his conciliatory views. During 1623 other plans had been laid to bring about a union of Prince Charles with the Infanta Maria, daughter of King Philip III of Spain (1598-1621), but by early 1624 the Spanish match was abandoned and attention turned to an alliance with a French princess. The Privy Council ordered Falkland to desist from his attempts to ban Roman Catholic priests at such a sensitive stage of the devious negotiations (which appear to have included some assurances that the lot of Roman Catholics in Great Britain and Ireland would be improved). The international situation looked decidedly grim at the time, with the Thirty Years' War (1618-48) waged between the Protestants of the 'Union' and the Roman Catholic 'League'. This shattering war (or rather series of wars) began in Bohemia when the Protestant magnates refused to elect Ferdinand of Austria to the throne, and instead offered it to Frederick V (1596-1632), Elector Palatine of the Rhine (1610-20), who had married Princess Elizabeth (1596-1662), daughter of King James I and VI of Great Britain. However, this aggrandisement of an Elector was unacceptable to most other Protestant princes, as well as to the imperial House of Habsburg, so Frederick, crowned King of Bohemia in Prague in 1619, found himself cast in the role of isolated rebel. Frederick and Elizabeth, the 'Winter King and Queen', subsequently lost both their Kingdom and their Palatinate after their defeat by the imperial army under Marshal Johann Tzerclaes (1559-1632), Graf von Tilly (from 1622), in 1620. Great Britain, therefore, once more found itself dangerously isolated, and an alliance with France became imperative, political expediency over-ruling religious zeal.

Under Pope Gregory XV (1621-3), however, the Sacred Congregation for the Propagation of the Faith was instituted by the Bull *Inscrutabili Divinae* (1622) in order to co-ordinate missionary activities *in Partibus Infidelium*, not only in heathen countries but in places which had become Protestant, and this encouraged Counter-Reformation activities. The Pope provided massive financial assistance for the Catholic League and the Emperor Ferdinand II (1619-37): through his influence the dignity of Elector Palatine, vacated by King James I and VI's son-in-law, was transferred (February 1623) to Duke Maximilian I of Bavaria (1573-1651), thus securing a majority of Roman Catholic Electors. The Papacy was prepared to sanction the marriage between Prince Charles and the Infanta Maria of Spain (in return for substantial concessions relating to the penal laws against James's Roman Catholic subjects), so hopes were raised among the Irish natives, and those hopes were not shattered by the marriage of Prince Charles and Princess Henrietta Maria in 1625, by which time King James was dead and the very pro-French Urban VIII (1623-44) had been elected Pope.[65]

In April 1624 a report on the condition of all forts and castles in Ulster was submitted to the Privy Council. This confirmed Phillips's contention that Londonderry and Coleraine were ill-prepared to withstand a possible attack by which north-west Ulster could easily pass to the control of disaffected Irish. The Privy Council ordered the immediate strengthening of defences at Coleraine, Culmore, and Londonderry, and Sir John Vaughan, who commanded the garrison at Londonderry, was instructed to use as much of the City's rents as was necessary to pay for the work. Vaughan pointed out that the tenants were nearly all in arrears, were too poor, and that rents in the Company Proportions were remitted directly to London. He had no chance of raising the necessary wherewithal by trying to squeeze money out of demoralised, poverty-stricken settlers.

Such anxiety to improve the defence of Ireland was no doubt inflamed by the breakdown of the Spanish-British marriage negotiations. In 1624 it was feared that a Spanish invasion, led by exiled Irishmen, was imminent, while the wood-kernes, by then well-armed, were active and dangerously effective.[66] Official interest in the Londoners' Plantation was deeply resented by The Irish Society and its agents, for it was claimed that the City of London was not bound, like other Undertakers, by the Articles of Plantation, but by the special Articles of Agreement and charter under which it held its lands. Beresford, in particular, was to argue that The Irish Society and the Companies had not only carried out what was required of them, but had exceeded their obligations: in any case, they were not, he argued, Planters, but had purchased their lands. As Moody has shown,[67] the figures given by Phillips do not tally with those of the various investigations from 1624, and it appears that Phillips was painting a blacker picture than that which existed in reality. Nevertheless, it is clear that the Plantation was in a parlous state.

In May 1624 the Privy Council commanded the City to carry out a series of reforms, to which the Londoners replied that they had never wanted to get involved in the Plantation, but had reluctantly done so in order to obey the King's wishes at great loss to prosperity and well-being. Not surprisingly, the City complained that its various rights were being eroded by other interests: these involved the fisheries, trade, patents for the selling of wines and whiskey, and other matters that appeared not to

65 Kelly (1986), *passim.*
66 Moody (1939), 216-7.
67 *Ibid.*, 218.

have been resolved by the Crown before the City became enmeshed in the Plantation project. It seemed to the Londoners that more and more was being asked of them, and it appears, as Moody has pointed out, that the 'City's contentions were sound in law and in fact'.[68]

By July[69] Phillips, obviously alarmed, petitioned the King, and explained he had been involved in many costly (and time-consuming) journeys to acquaint the Government with the state of the Plantation. The King ordered that Phillips should be seen at once, and, following consultations involving The Irish Society, a new set of Articles was drawn up. Matters relating to the fortifications, the provision of arms, the building of a new church in Londonderry, and the construction of a stone quay were again addressed. In September 1624 a programme was approved by the King, known as the '23 Articles'.[70] Phillips was appointed overseer at a salary of £200 per annum, and The Irish Society was required to implement reforms that were based on the Phillips/Hadsor Survey of 1622.

Briefly, The Irish Society was to erect a new church in Londonderry to be beautified and adorned with adequate seating; to provide platforms, sheds, and ordnance for the fortifications; to build guard-houses and sentry-boxes; to construct a stone quay to replace the timber structure at Londonderry; to ensure that 200 houses that would really serve as such would be provided in Londonderry, and that these should be occupied by skilled craftsmen and tradesmen (and that if occupants could not be found the Crown would ensure by means of compulsion that such persons would be found, impressed, and transported to ensure the proper numbers would be established); existing houses that were below standard for family occupation or conversion for shops were not to be counted in any reckoning of houses; once the 200 houses were built, fitted and occupied, then 300 more were to be erected at a rate of 50 per annum; every 'tenement' was to have convenient land left to it for 'curtilage and garden'; rents were to be calculated at 5 per cent of the cost of building; lands 'laid' to the City of Londonderry were to be 'set to men able to labour, stock, and manure it for the good and profit of the tenants ..., and for the supply of the markets where the tradesmen and artificers' could purchase goods (though lands were not to be granted to tradesmen who would 'thereby be diverted' from their 'proper calling', and they were to be possessed in 'freehold' (effectively long leases so that land would not be alienated); 'portes' (i.e. town gates) were to be built of stone at Coleraine, with guard-houses big enough to house enough men capable of defending the ramparts (which were to be kept in good repair); as facing of the 'rampiers' with stone would be costly, a new garrisoned citadel was to be built in Coleraine's market-square, supplied with suitable arms; 200 more houses were to be built in Coleraine under similar conditions to those laid down for Londonderry; the lands 'laid' to Coleraine were to be treated in the same way as those 'laid' to Londonderry; all trees and undergrowth were to be grubbed up and removed from the banks of the Bann to a distance of 200 yards on both banks of the river as a precaution against surprise attack; four or five ferries were to be established to cross the Bann, and no other ferries were to be recognised; Culmore Fort was to be strengthened, maintained, and garrisoned, with provisions and ordnance supplied; all Company castles and bawns were to be secured, guarded day and night, and well-stocked with arms; two new forts should be built and

[68] Moody (1939), 221. See Irish Society (*c.*1898), 491-6.
[69] 1624. Irish Society (*c.*1898), 497-8.
[70] Irish Society (*c.*1898), 501-6.

garrisoned by The Irish Society (one at the foot of Slieve Gallion and the other 'under the mountain' between Londonderry and Dungiven); six British freeholders were to be settled on each Proportion, each with a minimum of one balliboe, and 10 British tenants granted life interests on the estates at a shilling an acre for life; provision was to be made for Irish tenants who 'conformed'; deeds allocating lands in fee simple to the native freeholders were to be drawn up immediately; Culmore Fort, Londonderry, and Coleraine were to be provided with supplies sufficient to withstand four-month sieges (20 men at Culmore, 200 at Londonderry, and 100 at Coleraine); if The Irish Society or the Crown were incapable of bridging the River Bann at Coleraine, private entrepreneurs should be encouraged to build a bridge and given rights to charge tolls in perpetuity; another bridge should be erected over the River Roe near Limavady; and a new ironworks should be provided near Slieve Gallion, fuelled by timber provided from the woods of Loughinsholin. In relation to the permits given to allow 'conforming' Irish (i.e. those who learned English, wore English clothes, attended Established Protestant churches, and took the Oaths of Allegiance and Supremacy) to have life tenancies, there was a sting in the tail: the City of London was to pay double the rent due to the Crown for the concession. The Irish Society was required to put these Articles into immediate effect.

The Society responded by preparing lists of grievances, claiming that the Londonderry Plantation was a special case, and not bound by the general Articles of Plantation. It insisted it had done everything required of it, and objected to what it perceived as onerous new demands. It agreed to build a new church at Londonderry, to attempt to encourage tradesmen to settle in Ulster, and carry out other requirements, but baulked at the construction of a citadel at Coleraine, two new forts in Loughinsholin, and much else. It was felt that the Crown's demands were becoming excessive, especially as the Londoners had expended far more than they had ever been required to provide.[71]

The Accession of King Charles I and its Immediate Consequences

King James died in March 1625, and attention was diverted from Ireland by the accession of the new monarch, Charles I (1625-49), and his marriage to a French princess. In the autumn of 1625 the Privy Council, feeling that The Irish Society was dragging its feet, ordered immediate compliance with those Articles concerned with defence, and took steps to sequestrate all the Londoners' revenues in Ulster and divert these towards the implementation of the Articles. However, The Irish Society ensured that the rents were collected and sent to London, and the Companies also managed to avoid having their revenues seized by Phillips and his agents. This act of defiance was an ominous start to the new reign, already marred by the outbreak of war with Spain in September and an abortive naval expedition to attack Cadiz in October/November.

In 1626 Beresford was instructed by the Lord Deputy to provide copies of the rent-rolls for the Londonderry Plantation, and ordered not to interfere with the next sequestration scheduled for May. The Irish Society was informed that costs of defence should properly be borne by those benefiting from the lands, and that the Crown had, for 16 years, maintained troops in Ulster, whereas if the Londoners had 'planted with British, as they were bound by their contract', there would have been no need

[71] Moody (1939), *passim*.

for the Crown to station garrisons in County Londonderry at all. The City responded by pointing out that the Crown troops stationed in County Londonderry, far from benefiting the Plantation, created intolerable burdens, for the soldiers had to be fed and housed, and the Londoners had received no payment for these services. Indeed, so onerous were the demands of the military that several settlers had simply given up, abandoned their holdings, and returned to Great Britain.

Phillips, deprived of his salary, and stopped from collecting the sequestrated rents by the 'insatiable covetousness' of The Irish Society, once again approached the King, and there was much to-ing and fro-ing, the City insisting it had a special contract, and the Crown claiming the Londoners were endangering the whole of Ulster. Matters were further complicated by King Charles's offer of the '26 Graces', or concessions, to his Irish subjects in return for money to support the forces (1626), a gesture that aroused concern among Protestants in Ireland and led to a condemnation by Protestant bishops of any signs of toleration of Roman Catholicism (November 1626). This stance was not unconnected with Ussher, who had become Archbishop of Armagh (and Primate of All Ireland) in March 1625. The careful policies of canny King James were rapidly discarded, and in 1627 war broke out with France during which a British expedition to support the Huguenots at La Rochelle came to grief in June/November.

To a certain extent these wars diverted attention from Ireland, but there was a growing feeling that the new King would do anything to raise money. Within a very short time he had got involved in wars with Spain and France, broken faith with the Papacy, demonstrated military incompetence to the Huguenots, aroused the suspicions of Protestants on both sides of the Irish Sea, raised expectations among the Roman Catholic Irish, and started on a disastrous course that would alienate the City of London. Early in 1628 the King received a delegation from Ireland and in May issued 51 'Graces' in return for a promise of a subsidy of £40,000 per annum for three years, but approval of this arrangement was blocked in the Irish Parliament. It was not a happy state of affairs.

The Royal Commission of Inquiry

In 1627 commissioners, to include the Lord Deputy, the Lord Primate, the Bishop of Derry, the Attorney-General of Ireland, the Solicitor-General, Sir John Vaughan, and others, assisted by Phillips, were appointed to inquire into the City of London's Plantation, and reported adversely. In May 1628 a sequestration of rents was ordered by the King. Phillips claimed that Beresford and his men had done everything they could to obstruct the inquiry, while British settlers complained of their hard lives in the 'remote and unpleasant northern parts of Ireland', and denounced Phillips for undermining confidence and fomenting discontent. Another petition (signed by a significant cross-section of British and Irish inhabitants) supported Phillips and claimed the anti-Phillips faction was being whipped up by The Irish Society and its agents.

That summer, British Undertakers, in return for 'fines' and double rents, were permitted to have Irish tenants on 25 per cent of their lands, subject to certain conditions relating to dress, speech, and methods used in agriculture, but the requirements to conform in matters of religion appear to have been quietly dropped. The Londoners appealed against the sequestration of revenues, and insisted that County Londonderry, once the most barbarous part of Ireland, was the 'best civilised' as a result of their efforts (which included a vast expenditure far exceeding that originally required by the Crown). Once more The Irish Society claimed its privileges had been eroded or withdrawn, that its fishing-rights had been intruded upon, and that excessive burdens were being placed upon the settlers. In July the sequestration order was withdrawn on condition that The Irish Society carried out its various obligations.

Much statistical material was gathered in by the spring of 1629, including intelligence that there were 1,412 able British men and 2,293 Irish on the City's Plantation (this figure did not include the Irish on lands other than the Londoners' holdings). Beresford's assessment of the houses built in Londonderry[72] was that there were 265 of them, but Moody[73] has shown that many of these were not built by The Irish Society at all. Once again, deficiencies in fortifications, shortages of able-bodied men and arms, and other long-standing problems were identified. The commissioners reiterated the urgent need for more houses, many more British settlers, and improvements in trade. In particular, a supply of money for lending on reasonable security was urgently necessary.

Sir Thomas Phillips's 'Collection' of 1629

In addition to the evidence produced and recommendations made by the commissioners, Phillips presented a detailed history of the Plantation to King Charles in 1629. This covered the period 1609-29, and included copies of letters, Articles, and other material. Phillips's 'Collection' is a prime source for all historians of the Plantation.[74] Phillips tabulated all the sums raised by the Livery Companies; the rents paid by The Irish Society to the Crown; and estimates of the Londoners' income from and expenditure on the Plantation (1610-29).

Income (including rents from properties, rents from the fisheries, income from the 12 Proportions, rents from the lands 'laid' and not 'laid' to the towns, the Customs, rents from the native Irish, and monies from royalties, the spoiled woods, and the 'country lands') was estimated by Phillips to have been £98,665, but expenses (building construction, fortifications, paving, quays, arms and buildings related to defence, repairs, lime-kilns, victuals, entertainment, various charges paid to the Companies, salaries, payment to agents, travel, tools, losses through shipwrecks, rents to the King, buying-out of private interests, civic swords, maces, communion plate, bibles, etc, and the building of the cathedral) he reckoned as £68,730.

Phillips was a severe critic of the Londoners, and his estimates of expenditure are clearly too low, as the evidence of payments from the Companies makes clear. Phillips reckoned that over £10,000 had been made from the spoliation of the woods, but no evidence has emerged to show that either The Irish Society or the Livery Companies saw any income from that source, and indeed it would seem that the illegal profiteering was carried out by individuals who abused their positions. As Moody has shown,[75] Phillips made out that the £60,000 levied by Precept on the Companies was 'profit', and introduced other distortions, such as omitting the huge costs involved in the cutting of the Salmon Leap. In fact, the *total* sum received by the Companies up to 1641 never amounted to more than £2,000 per annum.[76] But then Phillips's consuming passion was to discredit The Irish Society, the Companies, and the City of London.

[72] King (ed.) (1936).
[73] Moody (1939), 243-5.
[74] Chart (ed.) (1928), *passim*.
[75] Moody (1939), 252-8.
[76] *Ibid.*, 251.

In this aim he succeeded beyond his wildest imaginings. Claiming the purest of motives for himself, he denounced the Londoners for deception, neglect of obligations, greed, cynicism, exploitation, and much else. He implored King Charles to 'cast ... his princely eye upon the important and material things contained' in his documentation of the Plantation; to 'revoke the Londoners' Patent'; and to 'reassume' the Plantation 'into his Royal hands'.

The Aftermath of the Inquiry and Phillips's 'Collection'

On 1 April 1629 a proclamation was issued that forbade the exercise of ecclesiastical jurisdictions derived from Rome and that ordered the dissolution of all Roman Catholic religious houses. In December of the same year, the Franciscan chapel in Cook Street, Dublin, was raided and 16 religious houses were suppressed. Severe riots followed, and decrees were issued ordering the suppression of every Roman Catholic religious house in Ireland. This did not contribute to calm.

In 1630 the Attorney-General and various lawyers began to study the report of the commissioners, and the Privy Council was consulted throughout. It was decided to prepare a case for trial, and The Irish Society was subjected to inquisitions. Phillips provided a large amount of material, and formal proceedings began against the City of London in the high court of the Star Chamber.[77] The City was accused of having procured a grant of exorbitant rights and privileges; of having deliberately violated the Articles of Agreement; and of having betrayed the trust of King James I and VI to the peril of the Kingdom of Ireland, the decay of 'True Religion', and the 'utter ruin' of the Plantation. Frantic activity ensued, the City calling on the Companies for full details concerning income, expenditure, population, buildings, letting arrangements, and so on, and the Crown setting up yet another commission to examine the state of the Plantation.

All this involved the City in further monetary outlay and The Irish Society was obliged to issue further Precepts to raise capital for the expenses of the inquiry and for the costs of building the cathedral-church in Londonderry, then under construction. In 1633 The Irish Society was added to the list of defendants, the Londoners petitioned the King and Privy Council for relief in the suits begun against them, and an offer of £20,000 plus Culmore and Admiralty rights in Ulster was made to the Privy Council, but to no avail.

From the very beginnings of his reign, King Charles had called upon the City of London for enforced loans to prosecute the wars with France and Spain. The usual lever of incarceration was employed, and by 1627 the new King owed the City the huge sum of £200,000. This was insufficient, however, and so to facilitate further borrowing, the existing debt was to be written off in return for grants of Crown lands to the City, which actions were to raise an additional sum of £120,000. Needless to say, the Livery Companies were extremely reluctant to provide yet more funds. In 1634 the City was required to provide seven warships, and the Lord Mayor, Sir Robert Parkhurst (d. 1636), who was also Governor of The Irish Society, was intimidated by the Privy Council into complying with the demands of the Crown.

[77] So called after the chamber in the Palace of Westminster in which the court (which inherited its jurisdiction from the medieval King's Council) sat. By the 17th century membership of the court was almost entirely confined to Privy Councillors, and there was no jury. Under King Charles I it began to be identified as an arbitrary and oppressive tribunal, and tended to be employed to enforce unpopular policies, notably in ecclesiastical matters, thereby incurring the enmity of the Parliamentary and Puritan opponents of the King and Archbishop Laud. It was abolished in 1641.

Things looked very bad for the City from 1632 when Thomas Wentworth (1593-1641) was appointed Lord Deputy: he quickly allied himself with the City's adversaries, advocating that the Plantation be taken away from the Londoners. The eyes of all men, wrote a contemporary observer, were 'fixed upon' the trial in the Star Chamber in 1635, which ended with the City of London and The Irish Society being found guilty of all charges, condemned to pay a colossal fine of £70,000 to the King, and to surrender their patent. This all represented a tremendous loss for the City, and created a smouldering resentment against the King. Several attempts were made to buy the Crown off, but it was not until 1637 that it was agreed the City should pay a fine of £12,000 and surrender all its properties and rights in Ulster in return for a pardon and new charters. Clearly the Crown saw the whole business as a means of raising much-needed cash. The Londonderry Charter was duly cancelled in the Court of Chancery (1638), and in 1639 deeds and all records pertaining to the Londonderry Plantation were passed to the Attorney-General. Thus, by the Chancery judgement, The Irish Society ceased to exist.

For some four years after the Star Chamber trial, the fate of the forfeited lands remained in limbo, and there was much official dithering about what was to be done. In 1638 the King was petitioned by the settlers who found themselves with void titles. John Bramhall (1594-1663), Bishop of Derry (1634-61), a friend of Wentworth, was appointed sequestrator of The Irish Society's rents, but he also claimed certain lands for the bishopric and rights to the fisheries that had never been intended in the earliest grants. All this was to give rise to much litigation later.

As a result of the commission appointed in 1639 receivers of rents were operating in 1640, and the rents from the two towns were double the amount The Irish Society had ever levied, while the rents from the 12 Proportions were three times those received by the Companies. Thus the new régime imposed punitive rack-renting far above fair or normal levels, and the settlers found to their alarm that they were far worse off under the Crown than they had been under the relatively benign rule of the Londoners. To his credit, Wentworth (created 1st Earl of Strafford in 1640) was concerned that the rack-renting would cause 'clamour', and indeed it quickly ruined confidence, businesses, trade, and many tenants who could not pay their rents. However, the Irish House of Commons prepared a remonstrance indicting Wentworth's policies and drawing especial attention to the 'extreme and cruel usage of certain … Commissioners …' towards the 'inhabitants of the City and County of Londonderry, by means whereof the worthy Plantation of that County is almost destroyed, and the said inhabitants are reduced to great poverty, and many of them forced to forsake the County … to the great weakening of the Kingdome in this time of danger' which was presented to the King in January 1641. The Londonderry Plantation was only an element (but it was a key one) in the impeachment of Wentworth. The King demonstrated his indecisiveness and lack of backbone by abandoning his protégé, who was beheaded in May 1641.

Meanwhile, opposition to the King was growing. The rapacious demands for money, the arbitrary misuse of power, and the ecclesiastical policies of William Laud (1573-1645), Archbishop of Canterbury from 1633, stiffened opposition. In 1639 the King attempted to extort money from the City for the wars against the Scots occasioned by the abortive imposition of a new liturgy on the Church of Scotland without first asking the consent of the Scottish Parliament or the General Assembly. The latter body abolished episcopacy and defied royal authority, thus initiating the movement against the King's arbitrary rule in England. In 1640 the Scots Covenanters' army defeated that of the King, and Charles was forced to summon the Long Parliament. By doing so he gave his enemies an organisation that was able to mobilise forces of resentment and resistance to active opposition.

Several attempts by the King to raise money for the Bishops' Wars against the Scots Covenanters were resisted and ended in failure, or only partial success. The recall of Parliament eased matters slightly, but the City was smarting from the loss of the Londonderry Plantation, and it is not surprising that the Ulster lands became an important topic for consideration. The City told Parliament that a loan would be granted to the King provided the Irish estates were restored to its ownership. In 1641 a petition was presented to the English House of Commons containing a history of the Plantation and Parliament accepted the following:

- the City had been forced by the Crown to undertake the Plantation;
- The Irish Society was properly constituted and was not an irregular body;
- there was no proof that the City was bound by the general Articles of Plantation, but only by the charter and the Articles of Agreement;
- as The Irish Society did not receive its patent until more than 3 years after the Articles of Agreement had been signed, the failure to complete buildings at Coleraine and Londonderry within the period stipulated was no fault;
- there was no proof that The Irish Society or Companies had leased any land to 'Papists', or that religion was in decay in County Londonderry, or that freeholds had not been created, or that the Londoners had spoiled or gained profit from the woods;
- as parsons had enjoyed possession of glebe-lands no hardships had occurred if the lands had not been legally conveyed;
- forfeiture of lands was not warranted even if a breach of covenant had occurred;
- the Court of the Star Chamber (by then abolished) had no rights of jurisdiction in cases of freehold or of breach of contract or trust;
- the draconian sentences passed were illegal as no *individual* was guilty;
- insufficient evidence of crime had been provided;
- the Star Chamber sentence was unjust and unlawful;
- the settlement forced on the City by the Crown was not binding as it had been made under duress;
- the King should refund the fine and any rents received;
- the patent of pardon should be cancelled;
- all those found guilty in the Court of Chancery should be discharged;
- the Londoners and all undertenants, including everyone dispossessed by the Crown, should be restored to the positions they had enjoyed before the trial.[78]

Thus Parliament supported and exonerated the City, and the position was to be that of 1635. So in 1641 a Bill was prepared for the restoration of the Londoners to their Irish estates as the King reversed the Star Chamber sentence, but by then (true to form) he was in no position to implement this. Furthermore, the City of London knew full well who had deprived it of its lands and to what body it owed the reversal of an arbitrary action concerned more with raising revenue than with matters of justice.

[78] Moody (1939), 412-3. Most of the above from Mahaffy (ed.) (1900, 1901): *Cal. S. P. I. 1625-1632* and *1633-1642, passim.*

Many of the proprietors who had lost money and lands as a result of the Star Chamber débâcle were shrewd and pushing adventurers who had considerable influence in the Irish Parliament, and Beresford and others played no small part in the spectacular fall of Wentworth. Of enormous importance, however, was the alienation of the City of London, which began to back Parliament with its wealth and prestige against the erratic King whose policies had proved disastrous nationally and internationally. The credibility of the King had been fatally weakened.

Building Endeavours up to 1641

Apart from the very considerable expense and labour involved in the building of the walls of Londonderry and the town and ramparts of Coleraine, the erection of the Anglican cathedral in the infant city was the major work of construction undertaken by The Irish Society, and resulted in the most architecturally distinguished of its 17th-century creations. The foundation-stone was laid on 21 August 1628, and the building was completed in 1633. For some time the inhabitants of Londonderry had complained about the lack of suitable accommodation for public worship, and the various surveys and reports confirmed that a new building was necessary. Proby and Springham had noted the need in 1616, and the City of London had been ordered by the Privy Council to build a new church in 1624. It is clear that the settlers had been using for worship part of the old Augustinian abbey-church that had been hastily repaired and stood approximately where St Augustine's church stands today. Presumably it was the necessity to retain this place of worship whilst the cathedral was being erected that led to the decision to build the new edifice on a site at the south-western corner of the city on the highest land within the walls previously intended for houses and gardens. The 'Plat of the Cittie of London: Derrie as it stand Built and Fortyfyed' by Raven (1622) shows a church with tower, nave, and chancel **[28]** on a site at the junction of what was to become Richmond and Linenhall Streets: this church was never built and it is not known what prompted Raven to show it in the sector to the east of the Diamond.[79]

The designs for St Columb's cathedral appear to have originated in London, although the author of the plans has eluded discovery. The structure is exactly contemporary with the church of St Katharine Cree in the City of London (1628-31), but the latter building is stylistically very different, mixing Classical nave-arcades with late-Gothic (Perpendicular) features in the windows and the plaster ceilings (that were modelled on stone vaulting). Edmund Kinsman, Master of the Masons' Company in 1635, may have been involved in the building of St Katharine's church, and he was certainly active in other City churches during the same period, so it is not impossible that he could have been involved in the genesis of the new cathedral in Londonderry. About two decades earlier he probably built the north aisle of the chapel at the Charterhouse in London, and in 1618 he was engaged in building the mortuary-chapel for the Cecil family (the Salisbury chapel) at the church of St Etheldreda, Hatfield, Hertfordshire, both contracts under the general direction of Francis Carter (d. 1630). The mortuary-chapel has Gothic fenestration, and it is known that Kinsman was involved in several building-works where Gothic was used. When St Columb's was begun he was a senior figure in the Masons' Company and the City of London. In 1636 he rebuilt the Gothic 'lanthorn' on the tower of the church of St Mary-le-Bow,

[79] Chart (ed.) (1928), Plate 3.

London; in 1633-4 he prepared plans for the rebuilding of St Alban's church, Wood Street, also in London (with Matthew Banckes, Master of the Carpenters' Company in 1637); and in 1638, with two other London masons, rebuilt the tower at Goudhurst church, Kent.[80] St Katharine Cree was consecrated by Laud on 16 January 1631 using a form that caused Puritan eyebrows to rise. Not only did he (at the time Bishop of London) wear full canonicals, but bowed towards the altar. Laud's brand of churchmanship (which today would be termed vaguely 'high-church') was wholly unacceptable to the Scots Covenanters and to the low-church Calvinism of the Church of Ireland as represented by the then Bishop of Derry, George Downham.

St Columb's cathedral in Londonderry was built by William Parrott (or Parrat or Parratt), who contracted with The Irish Society to erect the structure for £3,400 (its final cost was £4,000). Parrott was closely connected with the Merchant Taylors' Company, and contributed to the development of their settlement at Macosquin. In 1638 he carried out works at Dunluce Castle, Co. Antrim, and was Mayor of Coleraine in 1642.[81] However, Parrott appears to have worked under the general supervision of Sir John Vaughan, who is commemorated in an inscription in the western vestibule under the tower. It reads:

AN DO 1633	IN TEMPLO VERVS DEVS EST VEREQ(UE) COLENDUS	CAR REGIS 9

IF STONES COVLD SPEAKE
THEN LONDONS PRAYSE
SHOVLD SOVNDE WHO
BVILT THIS CHVRCH AND
CITTIE FROM THE GROVNDE
VAUGHAN AED

The Latin framed is a copy of an older inscription (that may have been brought from the pre-Plantation buildings at Tempull Mór or the abbey-church to give a sense of continuity) set above it. However, Colby records the smaller framed inscription as:

IN TEMPLO
VERVS DEVS
EST VEREQUE
CORDE MEVS

or as

IN TEMPLO
VERVS DEVS
EST VEREQUE
CLEMENS

[80] Bradley and Pevsner (1997), 228-9; Colvin (1995), 587-8; Hatfield House, Hertfordshire, Cecil papers, **143**, f.142 *et.seq.*; Guildhall Library, MS.7673/1.

[81] Loeber (1981), 83-4.

The first being 'in monkish rhyme' and the second 'of purer Latinity'.[82] So the True God inhabited both the Temple (i.e. the building) and truly the heart, or the True God is in the Temple and is truly merciful (the older inscription looks more like 'CLEMENS'). Clearly the newer version suggests second thoughts, and reads 'The True God is in the Temple and is truly worshipped' (or 'honoured'). The rest of the abbreviated Latin inscription refers to the Year of our Lord 1633 and the ninth year of the reign of King Charles **[36]**.

The new building, not much larger than an English parish-church, was decidedly backward-looking in style, and probably owes much to the conservative tradition encouraged by the Worshipful Company of Masons of the City of London which was not to succumb to the imported Classical styles to any great extent until the Restoration period and the ascendancy of Sir Christopher Wren (1632-1723) and his colleagues. While no evidence for such a supposition has been discovered, it is not impossible that Cecil may have been involved in obtaining designs through the Hatfield masons Kinsman and Carter, and it is possible that Kinsman or some of his senior contemporaries active in the Masons' Company of the City of London were involved in the creation of Londonderry's Anglican cathedral. There was little sign of the Classical innovations at St Katharine Cree: instead, the form and style were firmly late-Gothic, and it would be fair to describe the church as an example of the Gothic Survival. This stylistic conservatism may have had its origins in a desire to build a reassuringly familiar type of building that would remind settlers of home, but the avoidance of Classical references may also have been due to a deliberate rejection of the architecture favoured by the Stuart Court (e.g. the Queen's House, Greenwich [1616-35], the Queen's Chapel, St James's [1623-5], and the Banqueting House, Whitehall [1619-22], all by Inigo Jones, and all associated with the King and his French Roman Catholic Queen) and, through extension, by the high-church party (e.g. the fine Classical choir-screen[83] erected in Winchester cathedral [1637-8] under the aegis of Walter Curl [1575-1647], Bishop of Winchester [from 1632], a zealous supporter of Laudian high churchmanship).

As erected, the cathedral-church of St Columb (the dedication suggests a desire to establish a continuity with the pre-Plantation custom) consisted of a six-bay clerestoreyed nave with lean-to aisles (the lead-covered roofs of which were of a very low pitch, and concealed behind crenellated parapets), a short four-stage western tower, and a south porch (over the door of which was the original inscription relating to the building of the church that is now inside the vestibule under the tower). The short chancel was included within the body of the nave, and there were rather curious circular towers set at the south-east and north-east corners of both tower and aisles. Windows appear to have been of three lights in the clerestorey at east ends of the aisles, of three lights in the north aisle wall, and of four lights in the south aisle wall. All these lights were defined with stone mullions and had cusped heads, the groups of lights being set in segmental-headed openings over which were hood-moulds. So the fenestration was of a late-Elizabethan Gothic type. Construction was of rubble (some of which may have been recycled from earlier Irish buildings) with sandstone dressings **[37]**. Some mouldings (e.g. at the top of the plinth) are occasionally Classicising, which makes the building unmedieval in detail (but surviving mouldings are probably those inserted as part of draconian 18th-century repairs, and not part of

[82] Colby (1837), 103.

[83] Part of which survives in the Museum of Archaeology, Cambridge. For Gothic Survival see Colvin (1999), 217-44.

36 Inscription on the date-stone in the entrance-vestibule of St Columb's cathedral, Londonderry, with the earlier 17th-century stone set above. (*A/CC/UM*)

37 St Columb's cathedral, Londonderry, in *c.*1689, from the south. The original date-stone and inscription can be seen over the south porch. The rather curious circular towers should be noted, together with the Perpendicular Gothic fenestration of the aisle and clerestorey. This image, derived from Nevill's engraving of the siege, may not truly reflect the appearance of the building as completed in 1633, but it is as near as we are likely to get as further details are unlikely to be found after so long. (*Colby[1837]/AC*)

38 Interior of St Columb's cathedral, Londonderry, looking west towards the organ, *c.*1875. The ceiling, in the form of a Gothic vault, the crenellated corbels, and the nave arcades are shown before the major alterations of the 1880s, 1920s, and after. On the left is the cathedra, or bishop's canopied throne. (*DB*)

Parrott's building). However, the nave arcades, with their elegant moulded pointed arches springing from octagonal piers were once, in the words of Arthur C. Champneys, 'rather good work' **[38]**. Champneys regarded the cathedral – 'for the time when it was built' – as 'an interesting specimen of the Gothic of the time, though there appears to be nothing about it that is distinctively Irish. It was of far greater interest before the original short chancel, with a barrel-vault in the form of a four-centred arch, and a stilted chancel arch of the same kind springing from large corbels, was, five-and-twenty years ago, rebuilt, with very unnecessary alterations, though the east window appears to reproduce, nearly or precisely, the old tracery'.[84] The 'rather good work' of the arcades was drastically repaired and reworked in the late 19th and 20th centuries, as is clear from old photographs. However, the original *design* of the arcades

[84] Champneys (1910), 202-3.

is certainly very fine, and Champneys formed a judgement from which it would be hard to dissent. The piers resemble those in the church of the Holy Trinity, Staunton Harold, Leicestershire (1653-65), though the arches in the latter building are lower, less elegant, and plainer, with double chamfers, unlike those of St Columb's which are finely moulded. The Leicestershire church is a unique example of a traditional, backward-looking, Gothic Survival building created by a devout Anglican (Sir Robert Shirley, Bt. [1629-56]) as a deliberate act of defiance against the Presbyterianism and Republicanism rampant during the Commonwealth or Protectorate. Shirley, a Royalist, died in the Tower of London, and was buried under the chancel of his new church. His architect was Richard Shepherd, Shepperd, or Shepheard (d. 1673), of a family of master-masons from near Repton, Derbyshire.

It is interesting that an old-fashioned Gothic style associated primarily with pre-Reformation England should have been chosen for both Londonderry cathedral and Staunton Harold church. In both cases the architecture had connotations with politics and religion: in the former it was to be a symbol of the Established Church in a foreign land, to impress with its grandeur and to suggest the homeland of the settlers; in the latter it was an act of defiance by a Royalist and an Anglican 'When All Things Sacred Were Throughout Ye Nation Either Demollisht or Profaned'. Shirley claimed the new building was evidence of his having 'done the best things in ye worst times and hoped them in the most callamitous'. Unfortunately there is no documentary evidence available as yet which establishes any connection between Shepherd and Londonderry, although he or someone with the same name was active in Derbyshire in 1629-32. Parrott's connections (if any) with Derbyshire or Shepherd have not been discovered, although there is one tantalising thread: Parrott worked for Randal MacSorley MacDonnell (1609-82), 2nd Earl of Antrim (succeeded 1636), who married (1635) Catherine (*c.*1603-49), daughter and heir of Francis, 6th Earl of Rutland (1578-1632), and widow of George Villiers (1592-1628), 1st Duke of Buckingham (from 1623). Catherine (or Katherine) Manners (Baroness De Ros of Helmsley in her own right from 1632), Roman Catholic daughter of the (probably) Roman Catholic earl, nominally converted to Anglicanism to marry Villiers (1620), and reverted to Roman Catholicism when she married Antrim. The Manners family, of course, had properties in Derbyshire and Leicestershire. Parrott's contribution was probably the restoration of the chapel at Dunluce Castle, Co. Antrim, which was undertaken for Catherine (1637-40), and for which he was paid the huge sum of £1,800 at a bond of £3,500,[85] so it must have been a very considerable work.

Of the 17th-century cathedral in Londonderry, however, only six westernmost arches of each of the two nave arcades (much reworked and refaced), the north and south walls, and the general patterns of the aisle and clerestorey windows, are in any way original. Everything else (apart from some of the monuments) is of 19th- or 20th-century date, including much of the stonework of the windows. Presumably, like St Katharine Cree, the ceiling was of plaster to resemble late-Gothic stone vaulting, and 18th-century views of the interior show such a ceiling, but this was probably a replacement of the earlier version.

In 1634 The Irish Society received a royal licence to grant the cathedral-church in mortmain (i.e. inalienably) to the bishop of Derry. The building was to be consecrated and dedicated not only as the cathedral-church of St Columba of Derry, but as the parish-church for the use of the inhabitants of Londonderry and the parishioners of

[85] Loeber (1981), 83-4.

39 Rowley monument in the north transept of St Patrick's parish-church, Coleraine, of *c*.1620, probably London work, but re-assembled (?in the late 19th century) with no understanding. The Corinthian capitals should carry an entablature (part of which is missing, though what appears to be the original cornice is placed upside-down at the bottom, just above the skulls with Ionic head-dresses). The curved element beneath the panel with inscription is also upside-down. (*A/CC/UM*)

Templemore. Thus, from its completion, the building was both a cathedral and a parish-church. This coincided with the arrival of Bramhall as bishop, who was an ally of Wentworth and Laud. Bramhall was convinced that the appalling state of the Church of Ireland was partly due to poverty, and in his diocese he effected a doubling of rents from rectories and tithes. He was also opposed to slackness in liturgical matters, and introduced learned sermons and a dignity of ceremony to services. Unfortunately his politics alienated Puritans, Calvinists, Roman Catholics, and Presbyterians, and he was charged with treason by the Irish Parliament in 1641. Through the intervention of the King he was released, but by then the reforms he had tried to introduce in the Church lay in ruins. Furthermore, his position as sequestrator of rents identified him as an opponent of The Irish Society which, with the City of London, was becoming associated with Parliamentary anti-Royalist, anti-high-church opinion. His anti-London stance is borne out in a letter of 20 May 1635 to Phillips in which he congratulated Phillips for his part in the Star Chamber matter. 'To surprise that great and rich city after so long a siege was a work worthy' of 'an old experienced captain', and the bishop went on to praise Phillips's 'faithful services and noble achievements in these then miserable parts'.[86]

St Columb's was provided with bells by the Crown in 1638 at a cost of £500. Wentworth wrote to Laud (7 August 1638) that these were 'merrily ringing forth as well his Majesty's piety and bounty'.[87] King Charles's 'bounty' had not been extended to The Irish Society and the Londoners, however, who not only had expended great sums on the unsought Plantation, but had been obliged to finance the King's wars and other projects. Furthermore, there is ample evidence that the Crown failed to keep to the terms of the various agreements it had forced on the Londoners by granting monopolies, rights, and patents contrary to the interests of the Plantation, and especially to the wellbeing of the Londoners and their tenants.[88]

Another building with some architectural pretensions was the town- or market-house in the Diamond, Londonderry, a simpler structure with an arcaded ground floor above which seem to have been rooms for meetings, legal proceedings, and so on. It is shown on a picture-map by Thomas Raven of 1625 reproduced by Colby[89] **[26]**.

[86] Moody and Simms (eds.) (1968) 199. See also Mant (1840-1); Phillips (1933).
[87] Colby (1837), 104.
[88] Russell and Prendergast (1880): *Cal. S.P.I. 1615-1625*, 502.
[89] Colby (1837), between 98 and 99.

40 Funerary monument of Ann Munro (d. 1647) in the south transept of St Patrick's parish-church, Coleraine. (*A/CC/UM*)

Generally, however, the domestic architecture (if the term can be applied to such undistinguished buildings) appears to have been unremarkable, and virtually nothing of it survives except for fabric revealed in excavations, yet even at the end of the 20th century many opportunities to carry out archaeological investigations were being missed, and evidence destroyed by modern building foundations. Culmore Fort has not fared well either, and its extensive defences shown by Raven and others cannot be seen today, although there are traces of earthworks here and there. The stone structure that stands on the site is probably partly the 17th-century guard-house, but has been extensively rebuilt.

From the early period of the Plantation is the Rowley monument in the north transept of St Patrick's church, Coleraine. The carving is of excellent quality, probably dates from *c.*1620, and is very likely London work.[90] Unfortunately, it has been re-assembled with ludicrous lack of understanding **[39]**. The Corinthian capitals do not carry an entablature, and indeed part of the entablature has been reset upside-down *below* the tablet, while the element above the fragment of the entablature is also upside-down. Part of this fine memorial appears to be missing. Its inscription includes a reference to 'Londons honor' and 'Derries weale pursude' with 'Temperance, Zeale, and Religion'. Also worthy of note is the monument to Ann Munro or Monro (d. 1647) in the south transept, crowned with three *putti*, also probably of London workmanship **[40]**.

The fate of the built fabric erected under the aegis of the Londoners throughout County Londonderry demonstrates how unstable conditions actually were, and is indicative of later attitudes where historical continuity seems to have meant very little. Even major structures such as the cathedral have undergone such draconian alterations that very little of any historic interest still exists (these changes will be outlined below). At Coleraine, virtually nothing of the early work survives at all, and what does exist (e.g. the monuments in the church) has been treated with no understanding whatsoever. As for the 'piazzas', the last vestige of those vanished in the 1930s with hardly a ripple of interest being shown. If no value is placed on history, an understanding of history, or conservation of historic fabric, that says more about attitudes than requires any further comment.[91]

[90] Information from the late Mr. Edmund Esdaile.

[91] Some events described in this chapter are dealt with in greater detail in Curl (1986), 74-95. See also Beckett (1966), Bramhall (1842), Carte (1736, 1739), Chart (ed.) (1928), Mahaffy (ed.) (1900, 1901, 1903), Mant (1840), Moody (1939), Moody, Martin, and Byrne (eds.) (1982), Orr (1997), Perceval-Maxwell (1990), Phillips (1933), Reid (1867), Robinson (1984, 1994), Russell and Prendergast (eds.) (1880), Schultes (1822), Simington (ed.) (1937), Smith (1966), and Townshend (1904).

CHAPTER VI

The Great Rebellion, the Londonderry Plantation from the Restoration of the Monarchy, and Events to the End of the Seventeenth Century

> Upon the restoration of King Charles the Second, the City of London petitioned the Crown for a reversal of the judgement given against their first letters patent; but as the proceedings necessary to be adopted in this respect, it was considered, would be tedious, the King proposed to grant a new charter, to embrace all the possessions and rights the City originally possessed
>
> HENRY SCHULTES (d. 1843): *A Concise View of the Origin, Constitution and Proceedings of The Honorable Society of the Governor and Assistants of London, of the New Plantation in Ulster, within the Realm of Ireland, commonly called The Irish Society. Compiled, Principally, from their Records* (London: printed by order of the Court of The Irish Society by Gye and Balne, 1822), 62

The Great Rebellion

It is rather odd that the Charter of Coleraine did not figure in the draconian confiscations, and thus Coleraine's status was actually not much affected by the Star Chamber or Chancery judgements. This anomaly, of course, was probably another error. However, the Roman Catholic Irish viewed matters in County Londonderry with more than a passing interest, and the frictions between Wentworth's policies, the Presbyterians, and the low-church Anglicans did not escape them. Clearly English rule was in disarray, and in October 1641 ominous news reached London. A great rebellion had broken out in Ireland, and nowhere was it more ferocious than in Ulster. Sir Phelim O'Neill (Sir Feidhlimidh Ruadh ['The Red'] Ó Néill, Prince of Ulster – *c.*1605-53) seized Fort Charlemont by a ruse, and Sir Toby Caulfeild, 3rd Baron Charlemont, was murdered (1642). The insurgents were joined in 1642 by Owen Roe O'Neill (Eóghan Ruadh Ó Néill – *c.*1582-1649), a nephew of the 2nd Earl of Tyrone, who had seen service as an officer in the Spanish Netherlands. As soon as he heard of the rebellion he hastened to Ulster intending to destroy the Plantation, and superseded Sir Phelim O'Neill as commander of what became the Confederate forces. This time, inevitably, the Old English of the Pale and the Ulster Irish became allies, signalling a general rising of Roman Catholics throughout Ireland that became the Eleven Years' War, or War of the Confederation (1641-53). Part of the so-called 'general crisis' of the mid-17th century, it was linked to the Civil Wars in Great Britain (1642-52) and to some extent to the Continental Thirty Years' War (1618-48), but the Continental powers were far too preoccupied to intervene in Ireland, although some individual Irishmen serving in European armies returned to Ireland to take part in the great rebellion. Unlike events in the Nine Years' War, the fact that the Old English joined their Irish co-religionists demonstrates the seriousness of the rebellion, or the 'Wars of the Three Kingdoms'.

It is worth noting why the Old English took the stance they did. For two decades before the 1641 rebellion the Old English had been aggrieved by the activities of the Court of Wards and Livery established in 1622. In a nutshell, all those who held land by knight-service *in capite* became liable for all sorts of financial payments in lieu of the medieval requirements to provide military service as a condition of holding lands, and the Court set about 'discovering' land which had been alienated without Crown permission and levying 'fines' accordingly which fell heavily upon the Old English in the vicinity of Dublin. The Court, then, was really an instrument for taxation and, by 1622 when English control extended throughout Ireland, it began to be used to further religious and financial policies, and therefore caused consternation among the Old English, who claimed there were 'manie wilfully erroneous decrees and judgements of that Court by which the heires of Catholic noblemen and other Catholiques were most cruelly and tyrannically dealt withall, destroyed in their estates and bredd in dissolučion and ignorance ... and the whole land filled up with the frequent swarmes of escheators[1], feodaries[2], Pursuivants[3] and others ...'. In short, a Roman Catholic heir who failed to sue out of Livery (i.e. institute legal action as heir to obtain possession of lands passed to the Court) became in fact a mere lessee of his own lands until he 'sued' and paid his 'fine'. Costs were high, so many heirs settled to pay the Court for leases rather than lay out money for the 'fine'. The financial demands of the Court fell most heavily upon the Gaelic Irish and Old English landed proprietors, against whom the Court also discriminated on religious grounds. Under King Charles I it is true (as has been mentioned above) that there were attempts made (largely through need) to offer 'Graces' or concessions to the King's Irish subjects in return for hard cash (e.g. in 1626, 1628, and 1634), but under the 1634 Statute of Uses[4] those who had the use of land became liable for feudal incidents just as much as if they had full seisin (possession as of freehold), so the burden of livery and feudal incidents could not be avoided even by renting the land. From 1620 a large number of Roman Catholic proprietors sued out of their Livery, and in 1633 and 1636 over 100 licences and pardons of alienation[5] were granted in each year, the largest numbers between 1622 and 1641. The 'Planted' counties of Ulster were hardly affected by the activities of the Court because common socage[6] tenure was more usual, but in Leinster and Munster considerable antagonism was aroused by the impositions made on landowners and their heirs.[7]

A detailed history of the wars cannot be attempted here. Briefly, in 1642 Royalists in Ireland had secured the Pale, east Ulster, and Munster, but the outbreak of the Civil War in England in August left the Royalists in Ireland very much on the defensive, short of supplies, money, and support. Thereafter, matters were confused by shifting alliances. Religious divisions were exacerbated as sectarian massacres took place. Wholesale butchery of Protestant settlers and widespread destruction of property quickly reduced much of Ulster to ruin, although, surprisingly, both Coleraine and Londonderry were to survive, and became refuges for those fleeing the wrath of the Irish in the country. However, settlements such as Moneymore (Drapers' Company),

1 Official who watched over property that fell to the Crown: a confiscator.
2 Officer of the Court of Wards appointed to receive all the rents of the Wards lands within his circuit.
3 Official with power to execute warrants.
4 10 Chas. I, sess. 2., c. 1.
5 Remission of, or overlooking of, an offence caused by the action of transferring ownership.
6 Tenure of land by services other than knight-service.
7 Kearney (1955), *passim.*

Magherafelt (Salters' Company), and the fort at Desertmartin quickly fell to the insurgents. Coleraine, which had been supplied with arms and ammunition some time before, withstood a siege of around 100 days until it was relieved by forces from Londonderry,[8] the strong walls of which, protected by 19 'pieces of ordnance', ensured its survival and that of the many refugees who sought their protection. Contrary to some accounts, no attack was made on Londonderry by the Irish during the 1640s (probably because the fortifications were too strong for the poorly-armed insurgents to attempt to breach them), and Coleraine also survived because of massive efforts to improve the defences, though British forces in the countryside in the vicinity of the Bann suffered heavy losses.

Almost as soon as news of the rebellion reached London, Parliament approached the City for a loan of £50,000, and shortly afterwards the King promised to restore the Ulster estates to the Londoners. As The Irish Society had ceased to exist the Common Council had the problem of deciding in what name or names the estates should be vested. Early in 1642 attempts were made to coax £100,000 out of the City, but the Common Council decided it should relieve the distressed settlers, as no troops had been sent to Ulster after the first loan had been made. In the event, the Companies provided guns, other arms, ammunition, and victuals, and an Adventurers' Act was passed for the 'speedy and effectual reducing of the rebels in His Majesty's Kingdom of Ireland' offering 2½ million acres of land in Ireland for all who contributed.[9] Parliament called upon the City for a loan of £100,000 for the 'relief and preservation of Ireland', and this time the Companies subscribed. The King wrote petulantly that the loan should have been made to him and not to Parliament, and threatened to proceed against the Companies as well as to question the City's Charter. However, the King's credibility was no more, and various levies on the Companies were expressly raised for the support and assistance of the settlers.

It is clear from *A Particular of the Howses and Famylyes in London Derry* of 1628 that several Irish natives resided within the walls at that time.[10] Once the 1641 rebellion began and floods of refugees descended on Londonderry and Coleraine, however, plans were implemented swiftly to defend the infant city and the partly developed town. It was decided to 'expell' the native Irish from the city 'as … needful for … safety' and to issue a proclamation that 'no man or woman so expelled … shall, on pain of death, return … or make their abode within two miles of the same …' Suburban houses were destroyed and gardens and orchards cut down.[11] Various officers were appointed to guard sections of Londonderry's walls and to ensure they were kept in good repair.

In April 1642 the Scots general, Robert Monro (d. *c.*1680), landed with 2,500 men at Carrickfergus to assist his fellow-countrymen in the suppression of the rebellion. Up to then virtually nothing was sent to Londonderry from Dublin, Scotland, or England to help the defenders, thus the refugees who had sought shelter were in a very bad way, suffering starvation and other privations. Irish forces under Sir Phelim O'Neill were threatening Londonderry, but the authorities in the tiny city did not relish the possibility that Scots troops might become the garrison, and the English Parliament specifically refused the Scots access to Londonderry while allowing

[8] Curl (1986), 91-5.
[9] 16 Chas I, c. 33.
[10] King, R. G. S. (ed.) (1936), *passim.*
[11] Lacy (1998), 102.

Carrickfergus and Coleraine to be handed to them. This was probably to avoid antagonising the City of London, for the Scots were as foreign to the Londoners as were the Irish.

The large number of Scots soldiers sent to counter the Irish insurgents in Ulster had a profound effect on the religious flavour of the province. Most Ulster settlers tended to side with the English Parliament against the arbitrary and erratic rule of the King, but the Mayor of Londonderry stood by the King, probably more out of dislike of the Scots than for love of King Charles, but there was also the religious aspect: the Scots tended to be Presbyterians, while the City of London's sympathies still lay with the Anglican Church. In 1643 an army under the command of Sir Robert Stewart (d. *c.*1670), Governor of Londonderry following the death of Sir John Vaughan, defeated an Irish army under O'Neill at Clones, County Monaghan, and from around that time the Irish insurgents gradually inclined to support the cause of the King, again probably more out of hatred of Puritanism, Parliamentarianism, and Scots Presbyterianism than of devotion to the monarchy. It was a convoluted business.

In 1644 the Solemn League and Covenant for the elimination of 'Popery, Prelacy, and Profaneness' was signed in St Columb's cathedral, pledging all to abolish episcopacy and the hierarchy of the Anglican Church (deans, chapters, etc.). Use of the Prayer-Book was forbidden under pain of fines and imprisonment, and the peal of bells was silenced. Bishop Bramhall had fled to England in 1641, where he published a polemic defending the principles of monarchy and episcopal authority, but his stance did not gain him the favour of the Parliamentarians. He was exiled in Europe after the Royalist defeat at Marston Moor (2 July 1644): while abroad he attacked Presbyterianism in a tract of 1649, and defended Anglicanism against its Roman Catholic critics. In 1661, after the Restoration of the Monarchy, he was to become Archbishop of Armagh and Primate of All Ireland.[12]

By 1643 the Presbyterians of Londonderry, then vociferous as well as numerous, made representations to the General Assembly of the Church of Scotland to be sent a minister. Two ministers duly arrived, but were refused permission to preach in the cathedral. After public demonstrations in support of Presbyterianism the ministers were allowed into St Columb's, the altar was removed, and a Lord's table replaced it. It would appear that mob rule won the day, for the Mayor and others were forced to bow to the Presbyterianism of the large numbers of Scots who had sought succour within the walls of Londonderry. Religious and political upheavals were both complex and confusing, however, and nothing demonstrates this with more clarity than the events leading to the first siege of Londonderry.

King Charles I was beheaded in January 1649, an event that fragmented opinion among those who earlier had opposed the monarch and his policies. The Presbyterians of the north of Ireland, for example, revolted by the regicide and extreme Republicanism of Parliament, rose in arms against their former allies, those loyal to that Parliament. In Londonderry the garrison was commanded by Sir Charles Coote (d. 1661), Lord President of the province of Connacht, and later (1661) 1st Earl of Mountrath. After the death of the King, Londonderry was attacked by Royalist forces (largely Presbyterian) under the command of Hugh Montgomery, 3rd Viscount Montgomery of the Ards (*c.*1623-63), created 1st Earl of Mount Alexander (20 June 1661), and Sir Robert Stewart, who had obstructed the approaches to the city from his stronghold at Culmore Fort. In May the besiegers were reinforced by more Royalists,

[12] Orr (1997), 30-36.

but this time they were of the Anglican persuasion, and a short time later Roman Catholic Scots Highlanders and some Confederate Roman Catholic Irish also joined in the fray. Soon the Presbyterians began to feel uncomfortable among their uncongenial allies, and at the end of July began to abandon their positions. Astonishingly, Owen Roe O'Neill, who had been hindered by a chronic shortage of cash and supplies, began to make approaches to factions loyal to Parliament in Ireland, and Coote, grasping his opportunity, persuaded O'Neill to come to his rescue. On 8 August O'Neill's forces drove the besiegers off, and the Irish leader (who is said to have used a secret passage through the walls [now blocked] to enter the city) was entertained by Coote in Londonderry, thanked for his efforts, and given badly needed supplies and ammunition. Thus O'Neill, forced by circumstances to treat with the Parliamentarians, actually weakened the Royalist cause, but he probably hoped to come to a beneficial arrangement with the victorious side. Subsequent events showed that any such illusions were misplaced, for Oliver Cromwell (1600-58) turned his attention to Ireland, having defeated the Royalists in Great Britain, and landed at Dublin only a week after the lifting of the first siege of Londonderry. By 1653 Ireland was brought to heel by the Parliamentary Republicans. Cromwell was Ireland's first commoner Lord Lieutenant, and ruled through Henry Ireton (1611-51 – Deputy 1650-1), Charles Fleetwood (d. 1692 – Lord Deputy 1654-7), and his younger son, Henry Cromwell (1628-74 – Lord Deputy 1657-8, then Lord Lieutenant 1658-9).

Detailed surveys were made, providing information concerning land ownership in the middle of the century. Many Irish who had risen in the wars were dispossessed and transplanted to the west of Ireland, their lands being allotted to adventurers and settlers. Furthermore, many Ulster Presbyterians were transplanted to Kilkenny, Tipperary, and Waterford. Once the survey by inquisition, known as the Civil Survey,[13] had been completed (Cromwellian organisation was efficient and speedy), the Privy Council ordered that all rights in the Londonderry Plantation should be restored to the reconstituted Irish Society, and on 24 March 1657 Cromwell granted a new charter restoring all rights under the charter of King James.[14] Clearly it was of the utmost importance for the security of Ulster that the county of Londonderry should be speedily repopulated with English settlers,[15] and very soon The Society and the Companies resumed control of their former estates. In 1658 new conveyances were made to the Twelve Great Companies, but there was much reconstruction to be done in the aftermath of a long and bloody war that left the native Irish who had joined in the great rebellion far worse off than before. However, it was going to be more difficult than ever to attract Protestant settlers to Ulster after all the atrocities and massacres. This time, though, there was a difference, for the Irish, and the Roman Catholic Irish in particular, were now hated and mistrusted. Things would not be allowed to go on as they had.

The Restoration and the 1662 Charter

During the Protectorate, as has been mentioned, The Irish Society obtained a re-grant of its charter with additional privileges, but with the Restoration of the Monarchy in 1660 the Cromwellian settlements had to be confirmed under the new régime. King

[13] Simington (ed.) (1937), *passim*.
[14] Given in Moody and Simms (eds.) (1968), 246-320.
[15] Smith (1966), 38-9.

Charles II (1660-85) was petitioned by Alderman Sir Thomas Adams, Bt. (1586-1668 – Governor of The Irish Society 1662-8) and others, and the King responded by agreeing to grant a new charter. On 10 April 1662 letters patent were prepared that incorporated most of the contents of the original charter, but there were some important changes. Certainly the 1662 charter granted and confirmed all the lands, rights, and privileges granted by King James I and VI, but the entire preamble was new, much longer, and specifically referred to the restoration to The Irish Society of everything 'as fully and beneficially' as would have been the case 'if no repeal of the said letters patent had ever been made'.[16] Furthermore it made clear that the original charter was granted without any obligations or qualifications under other agreements. This arrangement satisfied the desire of the City in its petition of 1660 to have a grant made absolutely, and, in effect, returned to the position of 1613. The charter of 1662 confirmed the grant to The Irish Society of the 'city, fort, and town of Derry, and the whole island of Derry, town of Coleraine, and divers other towns, villages, hamlets, baronies, lordships, manors, territories, castles, messuages, lands, tenements, and hereditaments, royalties, franchises, privileges, and immunities'. It also made absolutely clear that The Irish Society had been licensed to grant to the 12 'Chief Companies of our City of London (which had taken upon themselves the greater part of the burthen of the said plantation) divers great quantities, parcels, and proportions of the said lands, tenements, and hereditaments, according to their several disbursements', retaining anything 'not properly devisable'. The word 'devisable' needs some explanation. It does not always mean 'dividable' or 'divisible', but sometimes something apportioned, assigned, or disposed (as with real property). Under the law, any grant of freehold land, or of rights arising out of or connected with land classed as real property is known as a *devise*, especially if assigned by means of a testament or will. The charter therefore refers to anything that could not be divided, separated, parted from, distributed, or conveniently disposed, granted, apportioned, or assigned, to be retained by The Irish Society 'for defraying of the charge of the general operation' of the Plantation.[17]

Under the Charles II charter the county was confirmed as County Londonderry and the name of the new city also Londonderry. For the 'better ordering, directing, and governing all and all manner of things, for and concerning the city and citizens of Londonderry … and the Plantation to be made within the same city and county of Londonderry, and all other businesses belonging to the same …' there should henceforth '*for ever … six and twenty honest and discreet Citizens of the City of London*,[18] … who should be called The Society of the Governor and Assistants, London, of the New Plantation in Ulster, within the Realm of Ireland'. The charter confirmed the composition of The Society (a Governor, a Deputy Governor, and 24 Assistants, the Governor and five Assistants to be Aldermen of the City of London, the Recorder to be one of the Assistants, and the rest to be drawn from the Commonalty of the City). It is odd that The Irish Society was not reconstituted in a way to ensure greater continuity, for the drastic change of personnel each year was left unaltered, resulting in a state of affairs that cannot have been healthy or efficient. Other matters covered in the charter relate to the government of the settlements, the Liberties of Coleraine and Londonderry, and Culmore. The Society was granted the water, ground, and soil

[16] Irish Society (*c.*1898), 159.
[17] *Ibid.*, 157.
[18] My italics.

of the River Bann from Lough Neagh to the open sea (including the rocks and Salmon Leap), and the fishing for salmon and eels therein; the water and soil and fishing of Lough Foyle and the river from the sea upstream to Lifford (except for the 'piscaries', belonging to the bishop and dean of Derry in the Bann and 'bay and river' of Foyle); timber from the woods to be used for Plantation purposes only; rights of hawking, fowling, hunting, and the protection of game; building stone, sand, and materials of construction; powers to create manors; rights to profits, etc., arising from the courts; powers over markets, trade, export, customs, and other rights; grants of admiralty rights and rights of all wrecks, flotsam, and jetsam, around the coasts, shores, ports, and creeks; ferry rights and profits; advowsons and right of patronage of various rectories and churches; various rights relating to the castle and town of Limavady 'late in the tenure or occupation or possession of Sir Thomas Phillips'; and much else besides.[19]

The charter gave protection to all Church lands and everything specifically excluded from the Londoners' grants. In the light of subsequent events it is salutary to consider the charter's very clear grant to The Irish Society of the Bann and Foyle, with the 'whole ground and soil thereof', and the 'whole piscary, fishing, and taking of fishes, as well salmon and eels as all other kinds of fishes whatsoever'.[20]

Thus The Irish Society, although re-established as a body and in ownership from 1657, owed its legal status to the 1662 charter which contained much that was in the original charter of 1613. By Act of Parliament all Excise and Customs, including duties on imported spirits, passed to the Crown in perpetuity,[21] so the charter was slightly altered in 1665. The Society surrendered to the Crown all its rights to the Customs, great and small, in the county and city of Londonderry and town of Coleraine, for which it eventually (by 1685) received £6,000 as compensation.[22] Furthermore, the Crown released The Irish Society from its obligations to maintain a garrison at Culmore on condition that it paid £200 per annum to the Governor together with profits from the 300 acres attached to the fort for its upkeep, but The Society was still obliged to keep the Fort in good repair.[23]

Once again the 12 Proportions were transferred to the Great Companies and their Associates (if any), by authority of a royal licence to hold in mortmain of 7 April 1663. Thus the Crown had granted permission to the Society to alienate property to the Companies ('mortmain' [literally 'dead hand'] is the condition of property held inalienably by an ecclesiastical or other corporation), and the licence was very similar to the earlier document of 1615 with some significant differences. In 1615 reference had been made to work done and to be done, and to the 'great somes of money' expended, but the 1663 documents went further, referring to the 'severall Companies of London whoe had laid out and disbursed vast sums of money in building and planting', and expressing willingness that the 'said severall Companies, guilds, or fraternities' should 'receive the full benefit of our said gratious intention, and be severally and speedyly reinvested and reestated in all and singular the castles, mannors, terretories, lands, tenementes, royaltyes, and all and singular other the premises with the appurtenances whereof they were disposed as aforesaid, and thereby receive some gaine and benefitt of their great travell and expence taken and bestowed therein'. This

19 Irish Society (*c.*1989), *passim*; Schultes (1822), 66-7.
20 Irish Society (*c.*1898), 242-3.
21 14 & 15 Chas. II, cc. 8, 9.
22 Schultes (1822), 69; Smith (1966), 42.
23 Freshfield and Freshfield (1898), 232-4.

later document does not specify work to be done on the Plantation, and the 1662 charter simply refers to 'the further and better settling and planting of the said county, towns, and places, with trade and inhabitants', just about the sole reference to what the Crown expected The Irish Society to do.[24]

The Court of Wards and Livery and the onerous tenures *in capite* and by knights-service were abolished in 1662,[25] in which year an enactment was passed to encourage 'Protestant strangers' to 'inhabit and plant in the Kingdom of Ireland'.[26] From this period The Irish Society, restored, became virtually autonomous, with extensive land holdings and many rights relating to timber, hawking and hunting, the fisheries, building materials, and the estates of the Companies. Although The Society was primarily concerned with Londonderry, Coleraine, and the lands 'laid' to the two settlements (i.e. the Liberties), it also had public responsibilities connected with the furtherance of the Londonderry Plantation.

It is interesting that the third Secretary of The Irish Society, John Sprackling (who succeeded the cautious Clement Moss in 1662), was called the Clerk, a title that recurred from that time, although the nomenclature of Secretary seems to have been favoured.

The Plantation from the 1660s

Although much of the built fabric of County Londonderry had been badly damaged or destroyed during the upheavals from 1641, the Beresfords and others had stayed put, so there was a degree of continuity. Episcopacy was restored, and George Wild (1610-65) was appointed Bishop of Derry, one of the 10 bishops and two archbishops consecrated in St Patrick's cathedral, Dublin, in 1661. Under Wild's aegis attempts were made to enforce conformity with the Established Church, and several dilapidated places of worship were restored. In 1665, however, plague created havoc in London and elsewhere, and the City was destroyed by fire in 1666. Losses included City churches and Company halls, and the impact of these cataclysmic events cannot be overstated. Among the losses in the conflagration appears to have been The Irish Society's charter. The existing charter is an exemplification of letters patent and was made in 1667 at the request of The Society.[27] Still reeling, the City sustained a further major disaster when the greater part of Londonderry was burned in 1668. It is all the more remarkable, therefore, that The Irish Society was able to rebuild Londonderry, supply the timber for a new bridge to connect Coleraine and Killowen, and even pay a dividend to the Companies in 1676. However, there was increasing friction between the English and the Scots settlers (the latter were arriving in increasing numbers), and there was a general decay in trade, not unconnected with a chronic shortage of finance and with enactments that restricted commerce.[28] The very small number of settlers cannot have helped. Sir William Petty (1623-87), Physician-General to the Cromwellian army in Ireland from 1652, had carried out a major survey of Ireland in order to facilitate the confiscation and regrant of all the properties of those who could not prove 'constant good affection' to the English Government during the recent wars. He quarrelled bitterly with Benjamin Worsley (*c.*1617-77), Surveyor-General of forfeited estates in Ireland from 1653 to 1658, whom he impugned for inaccuracy, with the result that

24 Irish Society (*c.*1898), 155-9, 399-418.
25 14 & 15 Chas. II, c.19.
26 14 & 15 Chas. II, c.13.
27 Smith (1966), 39 n.
28 Moody, Martin, and Byrne (1982), *passim.*

Worsley's 'Grosse Survey' was rejected. Petty was entrusted with the mapping of estates to be apportioned among Cromwellian adventurers, and his became known as the 'Down Survey' because it was measured 'down' on maps, and augmented the work of the Civil Survey which established the exact position and extent of the forfeited estates. Petty, in 1659, found that the city of Londonderry only had a population of 586 inside the walls, 369 of which were English or Scots, and the rest Irish natives. Outside the walls were 110 English and Scots settlers and 78 Irish natives. Thus Londonderry, just before the Restoration of the Monarchy, was neither prosperous nor thriving.[29]

Spoiling of the woods seems to have become an even greater problem from the 1660s, exacerbated by the demands of the ironworks on the Salters' and Vintners' Proportions. So serious had this become that The Irish Society was obliged to ask the Companies to introduce new clauses into leases in 1685 to prevent further damage. Relations between The Irish Society and the bishops of Derry deteriorated after the Restoration, the bishops laying claim to the Quarterlands (divisions of land in the Liberties described below) in the vicinity of Londonderry and also claiming certain fishing-rights. The Irish Society resisted these claims, and after much litigation and controversy won the contest for the Quarterlands, but the question of the fishing-rights recurred with tedious regularity. Other bones of contention included the stealthy acquisition of advowsons by the bishops. What appears to have happened is that the bishops made appointments and then claimed precedents for the next gifts of livings. Some of these difficulties seem to have stemmed from the lack of continuity in membership of The Society, resulting in a kind of collective amnesia,[30] and will be elaborated upon below.

After the death of Bishop Wild, Robert Mossom (d.1679) was promoted to the vacant see in 1665, and consecrated in 1666. Like Wild, his main preoccupations were grappling with Nonconformity and ensuring that churches were kept in good repair. In 1667, he noted that the churches, 'especially those within the 12 London proportions', were 'generally ruinous and not one, except that within the city, is in repair and accommodated fit for God's worship; neither are the inhabitants, such is their extreme poverty, any ways able to build or repair them, so that the holy offices of God's public worship are, for the most part, administered either in a dirty cabin, or in a common ale-house'. That was not all, for the parsons were 'generally and necessarily non-resident, not having any houses upon their cures nor being able, through meanness of their estate and numerousness of their families, to build themselves houses, nor could they find habitations to be hired upon the place'.[31] The bishop noted the country was so impoverished through want of trade that the tenants could not pay their rents,[32] and 'much land' had been 'laid waste', threatening the 'undoing of the country'. He approached The Irish Society and the Companies with proposals that each Company, the inhabitants of each parish, and the bishop should contribute to the repairs of churches. He also proposed the establishment of a grammar-school, with maintenance for the 'master and usher' paid by The Society, regular visitations to ensure everything was being run properly and that the 'right principles of piety, loyalty, and literature' were instilled. Furthermore, he proposed that each Company should

[29] *D.N.B.* (1917), **xv**, 999-1005; *D.N.B. Missing Persons* (1993), 732-3; Lacy (1998), 109.

[30] The long-running battles between The Irish Society and the bishops are fully chronicled in Moody and Simms (eds.) (1968, 1983), *passim*.

[31] Moody and Simms (eds.) (1968), 407-10. See also Kilroy (1994), *passim*.

[32] Moody and Simms (eds.) (1968), 408.

'send over one or 2 of their poor children to this school in Ireland with exhibitions for their maintenance', and that some of these youths, 'in due time', should be elected to scholarships in the University of Dublin and eventually 'preferred to livings within the' diocese of Derry. Other less mentally endowed boys were to be 'put out apprentices in London Derry or in Coleraine' and afterwards would support The Society's and Companies' Plantation. Mossom also suggested making 'an humble address' to his Majesty the King for a royal bounty to help provide for parsons' 'residence upon their cures'. Other proposals by the bishop included the establishment of a much-needed bank in Londonderry, capital to be provided by The Irish Society and the Companies out of rents, and by 'persons of quality and state in the city and county of London Derry'. The proposed bank would be run by 'such officers and agents as' the Society or Companies might appoint. Other proposals include ideas for improving trade, 'preserving amity among the British' (this seems to be a reference to quarrels between English and Scots settlers, and between those of differing religious persuasions), and the rôle of The Society as a resolver of 'all matters of difference or contention'.

The Irish Society responded very favourably to the bishop's proposals. In a letter signed by John Lawrence (Governor of The Society from 1667 to 1676, and again in 1690-1) to the King, it is clear that the bishop's ideas had been embraced, and by 1671 £540 had been provided for repairs to churches. The King also provided £350 from arrears of subsidies due to him from the diocese, and this was used for the relief of impoverished clergy. Yet in 1668 the bishop was failing to pay rent on property to The Society, and there were ominous indications of differences concerning fishing rights.[33] Meanwhile the bishop carried out a visitation of his diocese from April to the end of June 1668, establishing the condition of buildings and the state of each parish, but in the following year The Society had to write firmly to the bishop about the fishing-rights, quoting its charter to prove its case.

Mossom's episcopacy was also marked by his attempt to deter Presbyterianism and to frustrate 'factious preachers which run out of Scotland ...' throwing their 'foam of seditious doctrine among the people'. However, Presbyterians were very numerous, and the Government in Dublin favoured a line of least resistance, notably under John, Lord Robartes (1606-85), Lord Deputy from 1660 and Lord Lieutenant from 1669 to 1670, and John, Lord Berkeley (d. 1678), Lord Lieutenant from 1670 to 1672. Zealous attempts to enforce conformity with the Anglican Church were further undermined by the first payments of the *Regium Donum*, a royal contribution towards the salaries of Presbyterian ministers, in the autumn of 1672.

Mossom was succeeded by Michael Ward (1643-81), Bishop of Derry 1680-1. Through the influence of Robartes, Ezekiel Hopkins (1643-90) rapidly rose in favour, and became Bishop of Derry in 1681. Disputes concerning fishing-rights in the Foyle and Bann, and in relation to lands within the Liberties of Londonderry, known as the Quarterlands, became more convoluted, time-consuming, and expensive. In fact, The Irish Society had to expend a huge amount of energy and effort on retaining what was clearly its own property under the original agreements with the Crown.

From the granting of the new charter, then, The Society and the Companies were restored to their lands, and The Society was confirmed in its powers for the furtherance of the Plantation. The Companies became owners of their estates, but The Society retained certain rights set out in the conveyances (especially those relating to the woods and the fisheries). Specifically, the Companies *and The Society*, having 'expended

[33] Moody and Simms (eds.) (1968), 413-4.

very great sums of money in building and planting', were granted rights and The Society 'should for ever hereafter quietly and peaceably have, hold, possess, and enjoy the countyes, countreys, barronies, cittyes, towns, villages, lands, tenements, rents, rivers, fishings, hereditaments, and all other things',[34] which goes beyond the notion of The Society as some kind of body established for the common good. In fact, The Society had considerable freedom regarding its revenues and disbursements.

Although County Londonderry was relatively poor in the post-Restoration period, a new quay was built at Coleraine in 1679 to facilitate trade, especially the export of timber (contrary to the original Plantation agreements), and several ships were built at Bannside. Some 25 years after the Restoration, however, a nascent prosperity pervaded the county, and there was a thriving export trade in beef, pork, Irish linen, hides, and leather (as well as timber), while ships carrying wine, vinegar, sugar, indigo, cotton, and salt landed their cargoes in Londonderry and Coleraine.

The death of the King in 1685 and the accession of his brother, the Duke of York, as King James II and VII (reigned 1685-8) raised the hopes of the Roman Catholics but plunged Protestant Ireland into gloom. The Edict of Nantes, guaranteeing religious freedom for French Protestants, was revoked in the same year, and many Huguenots fled from France. In 1686 a royal warrant was issued for payments to the Roman Catholic archbishops and bishops, the existing land settlements were openly questioned, and very soon Roman Catholics were elevated to positions of power in Ireland. Richard Talbot (1630-91) was created Earl of Tyrconnell in 1685 and was sworn in as Lord Deputy in 1687. Almost immediately he began to discriminate against Protestants, and Roman Catholics were appointed to influential posts throughout the country. New charters were issued to cities and corporate towns, and almost everywhere (including the Irish House of Commons) Roman Catholics were in the ascendant. Despairing Protestants, facing ruin, left Ireland, many selling their lands for what they could get. It was said that in 18 months Tyrconnell had reduced Ireland from a 'place of briskest trade ... to ruin and desolation'.[35] It would also appear that Tyrconnell and the King had come to an arrangement whereby Ireland would be made a French Protectorate should the English Crown be placed on a Protestant head. Irish troops were sent to England, but attempts to fill the ranks of English regiments with Irishmen were resisted by the officers.

Matters came to a head in 1688 when the Queen, Mary of Modena (1658-1718), gave birth to a son, James Francis Edward (1688-1766 – later to be known by the Jacobites as King James III and VIII, and by others as the 'Old Pretender'), and less than three weeks later leading English Whigs *and* Tories invited William of Orange (1650-1702) to invade England. The tiny city of Londonderry, with a population of about 2,000, was about to experience its greatest trial, and was to enter the world stage.

The Siege of Londonderry 1688-9

Under Tyrconnell the Protestant civil and military establishment in Ireland was dismantled, and by 1688 the King's army in Ireland was overwhelmingly composed of Roman Catholics. Furthermore, the existing charters of cities and towns were superseded by new ones that gave Roman Catholics power in the corporations.

[34] Irish Society (*c.*1898), 412-3.
[35] *D.N.B.* (1917), **xix**, 333.

Londonderry's charter was changed on 3 August 1687, and a new corporation in which Roman Catholics predominated was established: it cannot have been very effective in a city where the majority of inhabitants was Protestant. As the winter of 1688 began, Londonderry's garrison was made up of forces containing the very few Protestants remaining in the Irish Army under the command of William Stewart, 1st Viscount Mountjoy (1653-92). Tyrconnell ordered Stewart's forces to Dublin to replace Irish troops sent to England to help King James, and instructed that Londonderry be garrisoned by Irish troops under the command of Alexander MacDonnell (1615-99), 3rd Earl of Antrim. On 7 December 1688 the apprentices of Londonderry shut the gates of the city against Lord Antrim's men (many of whom were bare-legged 'Redshanks', Scots Highlanders, with a fearsome reputation for savagery, whose very appearance put the fear of God into the inhabitants of the city), most Roman Catholics within the city left it, and the fearful citizens prepared to defend the walls. When Tyrconnell heard the news he burned his wig in a rage.

It was a difficult situation, for James was still perceived as the rightful King. The bishop of Derry, for example, was committed to unconditional submission to a divinely instituted monarch, and so was unable to agree to the shutting of the gates which he perceived as an act of rebellion against the legitimate King of Ireland. Hopkins, in short, firmly believed in upholding the existing political and religious powers. Consequently, the bishop prudently withdrew his presence from Londonderry.

Tyrconnell ordered Stewart and Lieutenant-Colonel Robert Lundy to proceed with forces to Londonderry, and Lundy was appointed Governor of the city which was now beginning to fill with Protestant refugees from the surrounding countryside. Lord Antrim's men withdrew, The Irish Society in London was informed of events, and agents were sent to Scotland to buy arms. In February 1689 William III and Mary II (1662-94) became joint monarchs of England and Ireland, but King James landed in County Cork with Jacobite and French officers. A representative of the citizens of Londonderry, David Cairn(e)s (1645-1722), reached London, and was able to acquaint The Irish Society and the new monarchs with conditions in the walled city. The ship *Deliverance* under the command of Captain James Hamilton, and escorted by a naval frigate, landed arms, ammunition, and cash at Londonderry, and brought a commission for Lundy, who was obliged to take an Oath of Allegiance to William and Mary. Lundy has not enjoyed a good reputation and he has been associated with defeatism and treachery by Protestants. His position, however, was very delicate as a commissioned officer in Tyrconnell's army, which was loyal to King James,[36] but his rôle in the siege was inglorious.

Cairns got back from London in April, bringing promises of assistance from William and Mary. Nevertheless, the atmosphere in Londonderry was uneasy, and steps had to be taken to stop able-bodied men from leaving the city. Opinions expressed by Lundy and others that Londonderry could not be defended against a well-armed Jacobite army had to be countered. Meanwhile, a Jacobite force under the command of Lieutenant-General Richard Hamilton was moving north to Ulster, and appeared near Londonderry on 13 April.

The Reverend George Walker (*c*.1645-90), rector of Donoughmore, Co. Tyrone, raised a regiment to defend Protestants against possible massacre, and he arrived in Londonderry to report that the main Jacobite army was marching towards Londonderry

[36] Simms (1966), *passim*; Simms (1969), *passim*; Macrory (1988), *passim*; Black (ed.) (1990), *passim*; Lacy (1998), *passim*.

under the command of the Lithuanian general, Conrad von Rosen, who had seen service in the French army. Lundy refused to acknowledge the seriousness of the threat, but was prevailed upon to oppose the Jacobites at Cladyford, Lifford, and Long Causey, engagements that ended in a rout, with Lundy leading the flight and locking his own troops outside the city so that many were subsequently killed by the Jacobites. Walker himself had to break into Londonderry with great difficulty and 'some violence upon the Centry'. Lundy and the council of war agreed to surrender the city, but the soldiers and citizens refused to countenance this, one of the most vociferous of the 'No Surrender' party being Colonel Adam Murray (d. 1700), whose father, Gideon, had settled on Skinners' Company lands in 1648. Murray raised a troop of horse, and, having been ill-served by Lundy, taxed the latter with cowardice, and was proposed as the new Governor by the people. However, when Lundy and the council were deposed, Murray refused the Governorship, and Major Henry Baker (d. 1689) and Walker were elected Governors of Londonderry (but not before Lundy had sent away two regiments provided by King William and intended to strengthen the garrison[37]). On 18 April King James himself arrived outside Londonderry, where negotiations between the Jacobites and the defenders were taking place. James and his party rode quite near the walls and were met by a hail of bullets which killed several members of the entourage. The citizens sent a message to James pointing out that King William was as capable of rewarding their loyalty, and that they would 'for ever' maintain the cause they had undertaken. Londonderry was not to be surrendered, and all attempts by James to change the minds of the defenders were rejected. The siege had begun.

41 Gun presented by the 'Marchant Taylers' on the walls of Londonderry. (*A/CC/UM*)

Earthworks were constructed outside the walls, guns were mounted on the city walls **[41]** and on the tower of the cathedral, and cannons were trained on the gates just in case the Jacobite forces should manage to break through **[42]**. Some 7,500 men were available to garrison the city, but figures for the besiegers are difficult to assess. What is clear, though, is that the Jacobites were ill-equipped to besiege anything, and had no siege-guns or machinery. Instead, they relied on mortar-bombs fired high,

[37] Simms (1966), *passim*; Simms (1969), *passim*; Macrory (1988), *passim*; Black (ed.) (1990), *passim*; Lacy (1998), *passim*.

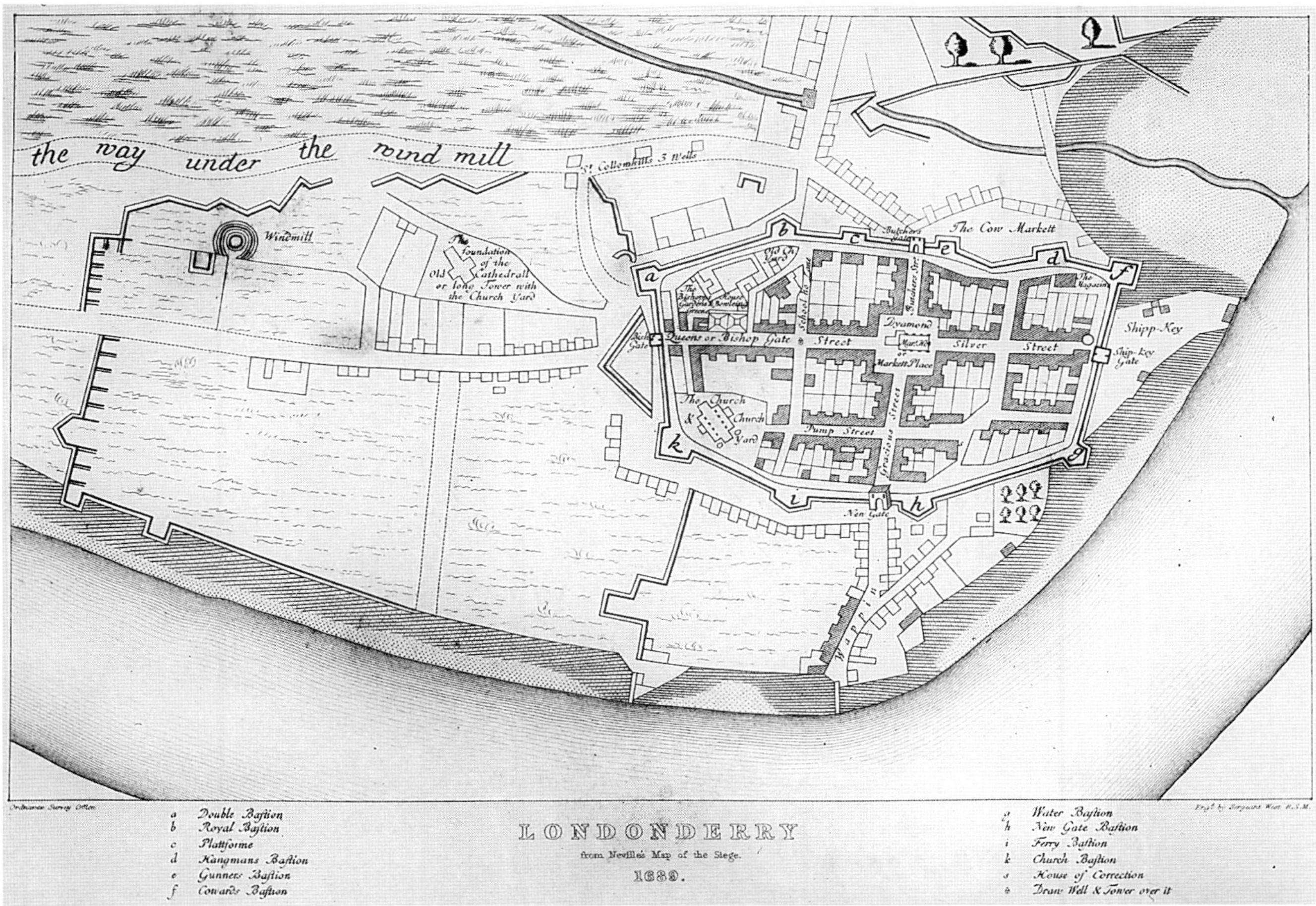

42 Plan of Londonderry during the siege of 1689. Note the arcaded market-house in the 'Diamond', the orientation of St Columb's cathedral, the bastions, and fortifications outside the city. (*Colby [1837]/ AC*)

which wrecked the upper floors of buildings but did no harm to Londonderry's walls or defences. Occasionally the defenders sallied forth to attack the Jacobites, as at the engagement of Pennyburn, when the besiegers were badly mauled by a force commanded by Murray, and the French commander, Jacques Fontanges, Marquis de Maumont, killed. A few days later Pennyburn was again attacked, and Major-General Pusignan, the French commander, perished.[38]

Rosen brought fresh troops to the aid of Hamilton in June, but it appears he had no great opinion of his Irish troops. A floating barricade or 'boom' was constructed across the River Foyle to prevent the naval contingent under Major-General Percy Kirke (*c.*1646-91) from sailing to the relief of Londonderry. Designed by a French military engineer, Jean-Bernard Desjeans, Sieur de Pointis (1643-1705), the 'boom' was covered by batteries of guns at both ends, and the Williamite ships did not attempt to break through. Meanwhile, conditions rapidly deteriorated inside Londonderry as to hunger the terrors of disease were added, and fever began to take its toll. Baker died in June, and was replaced by John Mitchelburn (1647-1721) as military Governor, who, with Walker, encouraged the determination and spirit of defiance among the defenders. Mitchelburn's wife and all seven of his children perished during the siege.[39]

[38] See note 37.
[39] *Ibid.*

Irritated by the stalemate, von Rosen rounded up all the Protestants in the area and assembled them before the city's walls. By this tactic he hoped they would be admitted and deplete the victuals held in Londonderry even more. The defenders then threatened to hang Jacobite prisoners in full view of the besiegers. Hamilton gave orders that the Protestants should be sent home, at which point the defenders cunningly allowed the fittest men in and sent the weakest members of the garrison out. There were a few skirmishes outside the walls, various attempts at negotiated surrender, and parleys, always followed by yet more bombardments. Added to the tribulations of both besieged and besiegers was the dreadful weather: true to form the Ulster summer was extremely wet, and the rain poured down with almost continuous ferocity. Morale among the Jacobites was very low, and they were very badly equipped.

A peremptory order to the cautious Kirke from Frederick Herman, Duke of Schomberg (1615-90), commander-in-chief of the Williamite forces in Ireland, eventually forced action. Kirke's fleet, consisting of the ships loaded with supplies (the *Jerusalem*, the *Mountjoy*, and the *Phoenix*), the frigate *Dartmouth*, and his own ship, the *Swallow*, returned to Lough Foyle. The *Dartmouth* (under the command of John Leake [1656-1720]) was to attack the Jacobites at Culmore, while the *Swallow*'s longboat and the *Mountjoy* were to attack the boom. A party from the longboat began to smash the boom with axes while the *Mountjoy* rammed it. On the evening of 28 July the *Phoenix* reached the beleaguered city, followed by the *Mountjoy*, whose gallant captain, Michael Browning, was killed by Jacobite gunfire from the shores. On 31 July the Jacobite forces lifted the siege, and the relieving forces under Kirke were received with jubilation by the depleted and starving garrison. The siege had lasted 105 days. Walker was sent to London with a loyal address to William and Mary, received a gift of £5,000 from the monarchs, and promised the bishopric of Derry when it fell vacant. Walker was entertained at a banquet given by The Irish Society, given honorary degrees by the universities of Oxford and Cambridge, and thanked by the House of Commons, which voted a sum of £10,000 for assistance of the ruined city of Londonderry, but this was never paid. It was an ominous foretaste of things to come.[40]

In September Walker's *A True Account of the Siege of London-Derry*[41] was published in London, and went through many subsequent editions. The book caused bad feeling among Londonderry's Presbyterians (who far outnumbered the Anglican defenders) as they felt their contributions were not given suitable prominence. John Mackenzie of Derryloran, the Presbyterian chaplain in Walker's regiment during the siege, felt obliged to publish *A Narrative of the Siege of London-Derry: Or, the late Memorable Transactions of that City. Faithfully Represented, To Rectifie the Mistakes, and supply the Omissions of Mr Walker's Account* (1690)[42] in which he suggested Walker had never been a real governor, but only a corrupt quartermaster given to cowardice and a fondness for the bottle. Mackenzie went as far as to state that Walker was 'guilty of shedding no other blood to stain his coat but that of the grape', and even accused him of having plotted to betray Londonderry, like another Lundy. Clearly the enforced collaboration between Anglicans and Presbyterians that had been evident during the siege had once more degenerated into venomous enmity. Walker himself published a *Vindication* (1689)[43] of his *Account* (which also appeared in translations, notably in a German version

[40] See note 37; Dwyer (ed.) (1893), *passim*.
[41] Walker (1689a).
[42] Mackenzie (1690).
[43] Walker (1689b).

published in Hamburg in 1689[44] and a French edition published in Amsterdam in 1690[45]).

In June 1690 Bishop Hopkins died, and the see thus became vacant for Walker. However, a Williamite force under Schomberg arrived at Carrickfergus on 13 August 1689, some 6,000 French officers and men landed in Kinsale, Co. Cork, under the command of Antonin Nompar de Caumont, Comte (later Duc) de Lauzun (1632-1723), on 12 March 1690, and on 14 June 1690 William himself, escorted by ships commanded by Sir Cloudisley Shovell (1650-1707), landed to lead his cosmopolitan armies of Danes, French, Huguenots, Germans, Poles, Courlanders, Dutch, Swedes, Scots, Irish Protestants, and English, part of which (the Danish corps) was under the command of Ferdinand Wilhelm, Duke of Württemberg-Neustadt (1659-1701), a German aristocrat. Soon afterwards William himself joined up with Schomberg, and on 1 July 1690[46] secured a victory over the Jacobites at the Battle of the Boyne, though both Schomberg and Walker perished in that engagement.[47] The victory was celebrated in the Holy Roman Empire, where the *Te Deum* was sung and the church-bells of Vienna resounded in joyous peals.

How was this, when modern commentators ignorantly refer to the 'Ulster Protestant victory' over the Roman Catholics? The point is that late 17th-century Europe was dominated by France, and it was the France of King Louis XIV (reigned 1643-1715) which had revoked the Edict of Nantes in 1685, causing many thousands of French Protestants (Huguenots) to leave and seek asylum in other countries. The revolution of 1688 in England also changed the European balance of power, for King William became a major figure in the Grand Alliance (1688-97) which opposed King Louis. France had become aggressive and expansionist, and in 1672 invaded the Dutch Republic: under the leadership of William of Orange the Dutch flooded their country and wrecked the French attempt at over-running the land. William became Louis's implacable enemy from that time. In 1673 Leopold I, Holy Roman Emperor from 1658 to 1705, supported William of Orange not only to prevent French aggression in The Netherlands, but because Louis had his eye on the Empire for further spoils. Eventually, an alliance was formed between Leopold, William, and the King of Spain, and peace was concluded by the Treaty of Nijmegen (1678). Soon afterwards, however, the French began to threaten the western frontiers of the Empire, and war broke out in 1682. The Ottoman Turks saw their chance, and a huge army invaded the Empire, laying siege to Vienna in 1683: only the intervention of a Polish army under King John III Sobieski (reigned 1674-96), allied with forces under other European princes, saved the imperial capital from capture. As the Turks were driven back, the exasperated Papacy intervened, alarmed by French intransigence. Apart from the serious threat to western Christendom posed by an aggressive Ottoman Empire under Mohammed IV

[44] Walker (1689c).

[45] Walker (1690).

[46] Not on 12 July as is popularly supposed. The anomaly lies in the use of the Old Style calendar introduced by Julius Caesar in 45 BC. The new Gregorian calendar, established by Pope Gregory XIII (1572-85) in a Bull of 12 February 1582 corrected the slightly inaccurate Julian calendar by prescribing that the day after 4 October 1582 should be 15 October and that the year should begin on 1 January instead of Lady Day (25 March). Protestant states did not follow the new calendar until the 18th century, Great Britain not until 1752 by an Act of Parliament (24 Geo. III, c.23) which prescribed that 2 September should be followed by 14 September. The Old Style Julian calendar was 10 days behind the New Style Gregorian calendar from 5 October 1582 to 28 February 1700 (Old Style), and 11 days behind from 29 February 1700 to 2 September 1752. Thus 1 July Old Style 1690 should really be 12 July New Style after 1752.

[47] Simms (1966, 1969); Black (ed.) (1990), Lacy (1998). See especially Dwyer (ed.) (1893), for Walker's *Account*, *Vindication*, and other matters concerning the siege.

(1648-87) and the ambitious Grand Vizier, Kara Mustafa (d. 1683), Pope Innocent XI (1676-89) was deeply troubled by the French Declaration of Gallican Liberties (1682) that, among other things, claimed that Church Councils in France had jurisdiction over the Papacy. Furthermore, papal infallibility (which did not become defined as a dogma until 1870 under Pio Nono [Pius IX (1846-78)]) was denied by the French, and King Louis insisted on making clerical appointments unacceptable to the Pope, seeing himself as the *de facto* head of the Church in France. The revocation of the Edict of Nantes caused widespread alarm, not least in the holy see, for Pope Innocent was not only outraged by the persecution of French Protestants, but regarded the revocation as folly. Matters came to a head in 1688, when further French aggression occurred. Louis sent French troops into the Rhineland Palatinate to back a French protégé to fill the vacant archiepiscopal-electorate of Cologne: Louis's favoured candidate was unacceptable to both the Emperor and the Pope, and the French moves alarmed German and north-European Protestant Princes. Perceiving Louis's pretensions as threats to order in a Europe so recently torn asunder in the Thirty Years' War, and determined to put a stop to French attempts to over-rule the Papacy in matters of Church appointments, the Pope became a key figure in cementing the Grand Alliance against France. Louis's invasion of the Palatinate was the last straw, but matters were further complicated by the removal of King James II and VII in the autumn of 1688, for the departure of William of Orange for England was interpreted in some quarters (incorrectly, as it turned out) as leaving the field clear for Louis. To the chagrin of the French, an expected civil war did not break out in England, and the transition of power to William of Orange was peaceful. In 1689, therefore, partly to create a diversion from events on the Continent, Louis assisted James to land in Co. Cork, but one supremely important support for the Jacobite cause was missing: the Pope was unsympathetic to James, regarding him merely as Louis's puppet. In May 1689 the Grand Alliance of England, Brandenburg, Denmark, Hanover, The Netherlands, Saxony, Bavaria, Savoy, Spain, the Empire, and sundry princes was formed, and, faced with strong Dutch, north-German, Bavarian, and imperial armies, Louis was obliged to withdraw from his advanced positions. Williamite forces suffered a reverse in Scotland at Killiecrankie, but the death of the Scots commander (John Graham of Claverhouse, 1st Viscount Dundee [*c.*1649-89]) led to the collapse of the Jacobite cause in that country, so Great Britain, by the time of the lifting of the siege of Londonderry, was firmly in the Williamite camp.

The need to pacify Ireland saved Louis from a triple invasion of France, for many allied troops were sent to Ireland to counter the Jacobite/French threat. This weakened the Alliance on the Continent, and indeed the French inflicted a series of disastrous defeats on their enemies in the course of 1690. William's arrival in Ireland and the victory at the Boyne was therefore a major morale-booster, but events in Europe forced William (who, in any case, regarded the Irish campaigns as a nuisance, and as a distraction from the main theatre of war) to return first to England and then to resume military operations against Louis on the Continent. James, meanwhile, had once more fled to France, leaving the Jacobites, French, and Allied forces to battle it out. Eventually, on 12 July 1691[48] the Jacobite army, commanded by the virulently anti-Protestant Frenchman, Charles Chalmont, Marquis de Saint-Ruth, and Patrick Sarsfield, Earl of Lucan (*c.*1650-93), was defeated by the Williamite forces under Godert de (or van) Ginkel (1630-1703) at the Battle of Aughrim, and by the Treaty of Limerick

[48] See note 46.

(October 1691) the war in Ireland was over. The Irish army was permitted to leave for France to continue fighting in the exiled King James's service.

Not until 1697 did hostilities on the Continent cease. It is clear that Louis had misjudged the determination of so many European princes to oppose him (the presence of Polish troops in the Williamite army is an astounding indication of this, despite John III Sobieski's marital ties with France), and he certainly seriously underestimated William of Orange. The foundations had been laid for both England and Austria to become major powers, though France's fortunes had by no means begun to wane. By the Treaty of Rijkswijk, however (1697), Louis was obliged to recognise William of Orange as King William III (Mary II had died in 1694), although he was to proclaim James's son, the Prince of Wales (the 'Old Pretender'), the rightful King of Great Britain and Ireland ('James III and VIII') on the death of James II and VII in 1702, prompting William to sign the Abjuration Bill that excluded the Prince of Wales from the succession.[49]

It is intriguing to speculate on what might have happened had King James managed to subdue Londonderry rather than waste time in a futile siege. If he had been able to get his forces over to Scotland to link up with those of the Scots Jacobites under Dundee, the history of the wars might well have led to a different outcome. Unfortunately for his cause, James seems to have been indecisive, lacked the capacity for broad strategic ideas, and was hamstrung for lack of funds.

The Aftermath of the Wars in County Londonderry

When the siege of Londonderry had ended, the relieving forces, themselves doubtless not in the best of shape after so long at sea, found the city to be in a dreadful state. The odour of decaying corpses lay heavy over the badly damaged settlement, and steps were taken to dispose of the bodies and clean up the place. Craters formed by bomb-shells had to be filled and houses needed to be repaired or, in some cases, completely rebuilt. However, the relieving troops had to be fed and housed, and constituted a serious drain on the resources of the weakened and impoverished populace. Very large sums of money were owed to the 'citizen-army' that had defended the city, but, in spite of many remonstrations sent to London, virtually nothing was ever paid out. Many distressed citizens travelled to London to attempt to claim financial help for themselves and for the city, but found themselves incarcerated in debtors' prison for their pains. For many years afterwards royal promises, official commissions, various recommendations, and endless reports were made, shuffled about, passed on, and never acted upon. Even Mitchelburn, the former military Governor of Londonderry, who had also fought at the Boyne and other engagements during the wars, and who failed to secure the governorship of Culmore Fort[50] from The Irish Society (which body felt, not unreasonably, that, as the said fort was then quite demolished, and not capable of any garrison, 'there could be no occasion for a Governor, and, therefore, no obligation to pay any stipend'), was jailed in the Fleet Prison in London (1709) during an attempt to claim compensation, although the *D.N.B.* states that 'some portion of what was due was at length paid to him'. Curiously, in 1691 a governor was indeed appointed to Culmore Fort, and The Society paid his salary. In the course of the following years The Society also paid out various sums to officers who had served in the siege.

[49] Black (ed.) (1990), *passim*.
[50] Colby (1837), 240.

Suggestions have been made that Mitchelburn was the author of *Ireland Preserv'; or, the Siege of London-Derry. A Tragi-Comedy*, and *Ireland Preserv'd; or, the Siege of London-Derry. Being the second part of the Battle of Aughrim* (both 1705), two popular plays that brought events in Ireland before a wide audience. Interestingly, Walker was referred to in the *Dramatis Personae* as the 'Commissary of the Stores', which would seem to support Mackenzie's contention. Some commentators have also connected the Londonderry-born George Farquhar (1678-1707) with the plays, proposing that he assisted Mitchelburn, but this is speculation.[51] More than a century after his death The Irish Society erected a monument over Mitchelburn's grave in Old Glendermot(t) churchyard: it was designed by William Tite (1798-1873), and was built in 1836-7 **[43]**. Nearby the Londoners also erected a monument over the grave of Colonel Adam Murray, and both tombs, protected by handsome Neoclassical cast-iron railings, are maintained in perpetuity by The Honourable The Irish Society.

43 Mitchelburn tomb (1836-7), Old Glendermot(t) churchyard, designed by William Tite. (*A/CC/UM*)

It should have been obvious to every settler, by the end of the 17th century, that he or she was on his or her own, and that any help from the State would always be too little and too late. In fact the City of London and the unfortunate settlers were being used by the Crown for purposes that might be described as Colonisation-on-the-Cheap. The bitterness that set in after the euphoria occasioned by the defeat of the Jacobites was very real, as a reading of William Hamill's pamphlet, *A View of the Danger and Folly of being Public Spirited and Sincerely Loving One's Country* (1721), will demonstrate. By the time Hamill brought out his polemical work estimates of expenses and wages owed to the citizen-garrison came to some £350,000, a vast sum then, and one that was never paid by a parsimonious Government. Not only were the settlers in County Londonderry treated appallingly by the State, which clearly felt their lives and wellbeing were dispensable, but their poverty and isolation was obvious to any reasonable observer. The fact is made overt by an examination of two 17th-century funerary monuments of wondrous crudity on the wall of the north aisle of St Columb's cathedral **[44a, 44b]**. The first (1678) commemorates Alexander Tomkins of Prehen

[51] Lacy (1998), 114.

44a Elvin/Tomkins funerary monument in the north aisle of St Columb's cathedral, Londonderry. (*A/CC/UM*)

44b Edwards monument in the north aisle of St Columb's cathedral, Londonderry. (*A/CC/UM*)

(d. 1642), his wife Margaret (d. 1674), and her second husband, John Elvin (d. 1676 *aet* 101), and was made by someone who had no idea of how Classical architecture worked at all: two clumsy attempts at representations of twisted or Solomonic columns (with ludicrously outsize bases and capitals embellished with leaves owing more to windswept kale than acanthus) flank the inscriptions and two sets of Arms. The second monument (1674), probably by the same bucolic hand, commemorates Hugh Edwards, and has its inscription flanked by three colonnettes (with spiral flutes and bands) on each side: above the entablature is a Coat of Arms flanked by what purport to be scrolls and garlands, but resemble twisted bed-linen, while under the aedicule is a panel ornamented with skulls, bones, and emblems of death. Originally covered with a coating of red, black, and white paste, these distressingly rustic monuments, so old-fashioned, so behind English and Continental contemporary taste, and so incompetently designed and executed, are pathetic testimonies as to how isolated and provincial Londonderry had become: here indeed was a cultural and impoverished backwater.

When the siege was over, County Londonderry was not only a backwater (though for a brief period one in the limelight), but a ruined one as well. Much had to be done. King William had sent a message to the Governor of Londonderry praising the 'eminent and extraordinary service' performed by the 'late resolute and unparalleled defence' of the city, and promising that everything would be done 'to recompense' services and sufferings.[52] William and Mary made various donations towards restoration of the city, the repair of the cathedral, and the rebuilding of the town-house, which had been badly damaged during the siege: they also presented a silver mace and other gifts to Londonderry, but were unable to sway Parliament in the rather important matter of paying the citizen-soldiers their wages owing to them.[53] Much was published concerning the siege, the heroism of the garrison, and their great victory over the Jacobites, but not much appears to have been done by the State in real terms to help the Londonderry Plantation which had suffered grievously twice in only 80 years.

George Walker 'attended The Society and represented that most of the houses in Derry were demolished by the military operations' of the enemy: he 'stated the necessity of some immediate assistance being sent to the inhabitants'.[54] As a result of Walker's eloquent appeal The Society applied to the Lord Mayor, Aldermen, and Common Council of London 'to induce the twelve chief Companies to advance £100 a-piece, to be paid to The Society's Treasurer, that thereby The Society might be enabled to send such immediate relief, as might encourage the City's tenants to continue in their habitations, until the season of the year should invite those, who had abandoned the place, to return and build their houses again'.[55]

A survey of the damage done to Londonderry during the siege was prepared by Captain Francis Nevill (*c.*1648-1727),[56] who presented his findings to The Irish Society. Nevill also produced *A New Map of the City of Londonderry with its Confines; As it was besieged by the Irish Army in the year 1689* and other material relating to the siege, subsequently published by Edward Sandys. Nevill was the architect of Londonderry's second town-house, really a court-house, council-chamber, and guard-house with its ground floor open and arcaded to accommodate the market. The building was in the Artisan Mannerist style[57] (that is, an architecture derived from pattern-books, not designed by trained architects, and showing an imperfect understanding of how Classical elements are put together to form a satisfactory whole), had a clock-tower with a bulbous cupola on top **[45]**, and replaced the earlier town-house of 1622 (probably represented on the Raven map of 1625[58]), so badly damaged in 1689.

The Mayor and Corporation of Londonderry obtained further assistance from The Irish Society, which was deeply concerned about the future of the settlements in Ulster, and increasingly aware that it would have to be the agency through which the ravages of war would be made good as no reliance was to be placed on fickle State aid. Considerable resources were required for building works, and in May 1691 some 60 tons of timber were made available from The Irish Society's depleted woods towards new structures and repairs, but by December it had become clear that double that amount at least would be needed as Londonderry was in a 'very sad and deplorable condition',[59] and Coleraine was in not much better shape, while in the country much

[52] Schultes (1822), 72-3.
[53] Lacy (1998), 147.
[54] Schultes (1822), 74.
[55] *Ibid.*, 75.
[56] *Ibid.*, but see also Milligan (1948), *passim*, and Milligan (1951), 50, 122, 171. For Nevill, see Loeber (1981), 79-80.
[57] Colby (1837) 115; Curl (1999), 36.
[58] Illustrated in Colby (1837), between 98 and 99.
[59] Schultes (1822), 76.

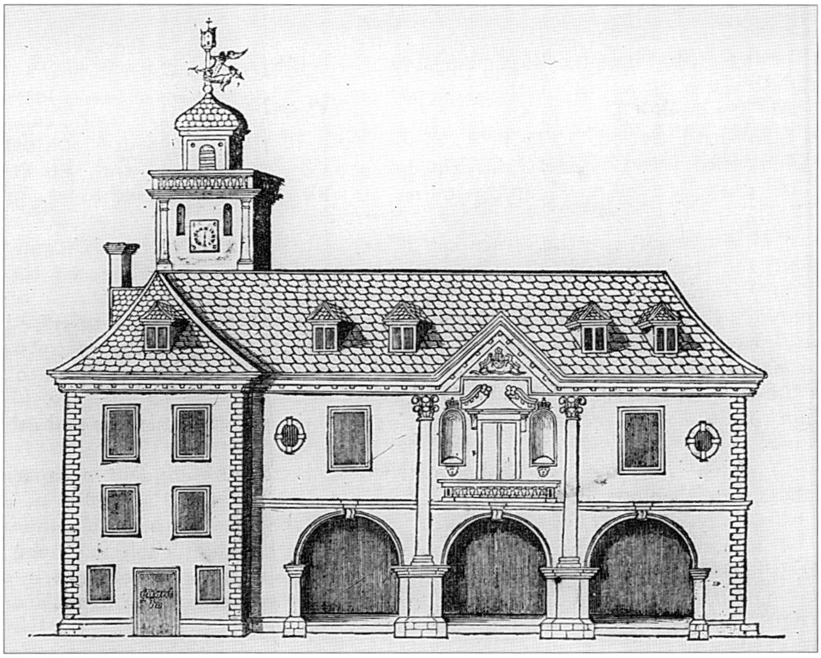

45 Nevill's design for the new town-house (1692), erected in the Diamond, Londonderry, to replace the first building destroyed during the siege of 1689. (*Colby [1837]/AC*)

had been laid waste. In order to establish the facts, commissioners were despatched 'to view the waste and ruins' left by 'the late Siege and Calamities made', to 'abate' rents 'newly or formerly in arrear, to make abatements to the tenants, according to the occasion or the Tenant's Disability and Circumstances, and to augment their Terms to 40 years from beginning of the Year [i.e. 25 March] 1692 ... The Commissioners from Londonderry went to Coleraine and discharged the like Trust there for the City of London, a people never wearied with charitable offices for necessitous cities or countries.'[60]

Two commissioners, Robert Rochfort and David Cairn(e)s, were appointed by The Society to establish the best means by which Londonderry would be re-edified, and to grant leases on favourable terms that would encourage tenants to rebuild their properties. John Mogridge (a lawyer who was Town-Clerk of Londonderry and later Agent for The Irish Society) was given the job of collecting rents in Londonderry, and Richard Lynam was appointed to the same capacity for Coleraine:[61] to discourage any embezzlement each collector had to enter into a bond for performance of his trust in a penalty of £1,000.

From surviving accounts, then, it is clear that the siege of 1689 caused considerable damage to the fabric of Londonderry within the walls. The cathedral, for example, suffered greatly from the bombardment: one bomb landed among the bells, another on the roof, one smashed through a window, and several cannon-balls ended up embedded in the walls. The defenders' guns, mounted on the tower and on the roof, cannot have done the fabric much good either. Very considerable repairs, therefore, had to be carried out. Nevill's design for the town-house **[45]** was realised, and the foundation-stone was laid in 1692 in a ceremony presided over by the Mayor and William King (1650-1729), Bishop of Derry from 1691-1703.

[60] Memorandum of John Mogridge (1700) in Moody and Simms (eds.) (1983), 328.
[61] Schultes (1822), 77.

Acrimonious Disputes between The Irish Society and the Bishops of Derry

Antrim-born, King was a formidable and determined Churchman, with a chequered history. He had been Dean of St Patrick's Cathedral, Dublin, from 1689, an unenviable position to hold at that time, for it led to his imprisonment by the Jacobites. While in gaol he wrote *The State of the Protestants in Ireland under the Late King James's Government*[62] in which he vindicated the transfer of loyalty from James to William by Irish Protestants. His appointment as Bishop of Derry was made in December 1690, and he was consecrated in January 1691. In March he arrived in Londonderry to take up his position, and, not surprisingly, found the see 'much disordered and neglected', the 'land almost desolate', country 'houses and dwellings burnt' and everything depressingly run down. In the diocese, 'before the troubles',[63] there were about a quarter of a million cattle, but after the siege was raised only 300 were left; out of 360,000 horses only two lame and wounded beasts remained; and there were virtually no sheep, pigs, or fowl. Only 10 clergymen were resident in the diocese, and of these nine were Pluralists (i.e. they held more than one benefice at the same time). When the new bishop attempted to force his clergy to resign their benefices or else provide for curates, 'no little odium' was 'excited' against him.[64] The bishop was also frustrated by private patronage of livings and by those in the Irish Parliament who had interests in maintaining the *status quo*.[65]

However, difficulties between The Irish Society and the Bishop of Derry over various matters started to boil up. Among these was the question of the division of the advowsons which could not be resolved, so it was referred to the Archbishop of Canterbury.[66] It seems that, after the confiscation of the City's Plantation the bishops usurped the advowsons, but The Irish Society re-asserted its rights in 1675. Discussions about allocation of advowsons between 1685 and 1692 never seem to have led to any resolution: by one means or another, by 1827 the Bishop of Derry held the patronage of the livings with the exception of the rectory of Coleraine which The Society managed to retain until 1869, when the Irish Church Act disestablished the Church of Ireland and put an end to the old system.[67] Another problem was the bishop's claim to certain lands, an irritant for The Irish Society that went back to Bishop Montgomery's time (1605-10), and, of course, the fishings were always to be a bone of contention. These matters will be discussed below.

In the early part of King's time as Bishop of Derry any difficulties seem to have been debated with gentlemanly restraint, and King began to effect improvements in his see. By 1693, 28 beneficed clergy were recorded in the diocese, and many ruined churches had been repaired with support from the Companies, The Irish Society, private individuals, and the Crown. King also secured adequate funds from The Society for the maintenance of the school in Londonderry, and, most surprisingly (and sensibly), he promoted the teaching of Irish at Trinity College, Dublin, to ensure that Irish-speaking clergymen were available to minister to non-English-speaking congregations in Donegal and other places under his care.[68]

[62] King, William (1692), *passim*.
[63] An Irish euphemism for war, mayhem, disorder, murder, etc.
[64] King, Sir Charles Simeon, Bt. (1908), 9.
[65] Orr (1997), 54.
[66] Schultes (1822), 77.
[67] 32 & 33 Vict., c. 42.
[68] Orr (1997), 54.

Apart from all these by no means minor matters, the bishop had to contend with the very large numbers of Nonconformists in the diocese of Derry, the presence of whom was a challenge, even a threat, to the Established Church (after all, in the 1640s the bishop had been forced to leave, and the cathedral had ceased to function as such). Having tried (unsuccessfully) persuasion during his Visitations, Bishop King soon attempted a more radical approach by publishing *A Discourse concerning the Inventions of Men in the Worship of God* (1693) in which he endeavoured to show that the Anglican mode of worship was conformable to Scripture, but that that of the Presbyterians was 'contrary thereto'.[69] This predictably stirred up a hornet's nest, and the disputatious Presbyterians responded with several public pamphlets.[70] King replied with *An Admonition to the Dissenting Inhabitants* (1694)[71] and a *Sound Admonition* (1696).[72] Much of the debate concerned the use of music in services, forms of prayer, the application of Scripture, the meaning and place of Communion, and the essence of worship. The bishop hoped that, by getting the Presbyterians to think about their faith, he would be able to undermine their confidence, but the Presbyterians felt the 'publick debates ... were manag'd ... to heighten rather than allay the animosities of the contending parties'.[73]

This war of words made Londonderry Corporation, by then dominated by Presbyterians, less well-disposed towards the bishop than might have been the case if the 'publick debates' had been less acrimonious. Thus, when disputes over ownership of land claimed by the bishop were again revived, the corporation tended to side with The Irish Society. This long-drawn-out and infinitely tedious business is exhaustively chronicled (with the arguments about fishing-rights) in the scholarly volumes edited by Moody and Simms.[74] Bishop King made a determined effort to claim rights over certain parcels of land in the neighbourhood of Londonderry known as the Quarterlands and to fishing-rights in the Foyle and Bann rivers. These claims involved The Irish Society in an immense amount of work and expense in order to defend itself and its property, as can be gleaned from the memorandum prepared by John Mogridge for The Society in 1700.[75] In essence, the main difficulties seem to have stemmed from uncertainties of distinction between temporal and Church lands, compounded by grants made by the Crown which conflicted with claims of The Irish Society, by the hiatus following the Star Chamber proceedings, and by the taking over of control of the Londonderry Plantation lands by the Irish Government. In Bishop Montgomery's time the Crown had assigned termon and erenagh lands to the Ulster bishops in demesne, and Bishop Bramhall (who had been involved in the sequestration [1635] of The Irish Society's rents) had managed to gain possession for the see of some of The Society's fishings and the Quarterlands of Mullenan, Ball(y)ougry, Termonbacca, Upper and Lower Creevagh, Killea, Ballymagowan, and Termonderry (the 'island' of Derry). Thus something like 1,500 acres of the lands 'laid' to Londonderry (part of the Liberties) within the parish of Templemore were said to have been Church lands improperly included in The Irish Society's grant.[76] Bramhall had argued that the Quarterlands should be 'restored' to the see of Derry subject to

69 King, Sir Charles Simeon Bt., (1908), 37.
70 See, for example, Boyse (1728), *passim*.
71 King, William (1694), *passim*.
72 King, William (1696), *passim*.
73 Quoted from Boyse (1694) in Orr (1997), 55.
74 Moody and Simms (eds.) (1968, 1983), *passim*.
75 *Ibid.* (1983), 279-421.
76 Moody (1939), 392.

a perpetual rent charge of £90 10*s*. reserved to the corporation, and then leased by the bishop to the corporation for £50 per annum. Thus the bishop would acquire the freehold and an annual income, and the corporation would have its income assured. At the time, this was accepted by the corporation and ratified by Wentworth, then Lord Deputy. The result was that the bishop received, in 1637, a grant of the Quarterlands, and the corporation a lease (1638) of the same lands for 60 years from 1634. However, Bramhall did not long enjoy his dubious acquisitions as he fell from grace in 1641 for his part in Wentworth's régime.[77]

Immediately after the Londoners had been relieved of all their lands the unfortunate settlers began to experience how little King Charles cared about the Plantation or for those British undertenants. The Irish Society and the Companies had repeatedly claimed to be fair and just landlords, yet those claims had been rejected at the time of the Star Chamber trial. Once the Londoners had been removed, rack-renting began in earnest, for the King was only interested in obtaining as much cash as possible for the English exchequer: as Moody noted, 'neither beneficence nor policy can be discerned in Charles's treatment of the planters in Londonderry'.[78] To be fair to Wentworth and Bramhall, they rapidly became deeply concerned about Crown policies, and did their best to argue for fair treatment of the settlers. Wentworth had striven to make the Irish revenue exceed Government expenses, but Charles's policies demanded that the lands be drained of money, and it was clear the settlers would soon be reduced to penury. Thus many of the inhabitants of County Londonderry began to long for the return of The Irish Society and the Companies, while at the same time turning against the Crown and the Established Church. However, when the fury of the 1641 rebellion was released, questions of rack-renting and collecting of rents became of little moment: the very survival of any part of the Plantation was at stake.

Having been restored to its property the City of London was in no position to repossess all its lands in Ulster, and, as has been mentioned above, The Irish Society was only re-established in 1657, thus there was an effective break in continuity for more than twenty years, so it was little wonder, given the disturbed state of Ireland, that a certain amount of confusion reigned. Even though the Londoners had been the victim of Charles's whimsical and arbitrary policies, they lost no time in sending provisions, clothing, arms, ammunition, and other aid to their settlements in Coleraine and Londonderry, so footholds were preserved, and machinery was set up by which the management of the Londonderry Plantation would be resumed as soon as possible.

Following the Restoration of the Monarchy in 1660 Bramhall, who had gone into exile for a period, was translated to the archbishopric of Armagh and succeeded as Bishop of Derry by Wild. In 1661 the Irish House of Lords ordered that the bishop should have lands held by his predecessor in 1640-1 restored, but The Irish Society resisted, and renewed disputes regarding the fisheries, including even the Cutts fisheries on the River Bann, dragged on until 1677 when it was agreed that the bishop should lease all fishing-rights in the Foyle and Bann for 21 years at a rent of £200 per annum. Bishop Hopkins, however, again adopted an aggressive stance, and in 1683 proceeded against The Irish Society in the Irish Courts, winning the case in 1687. The Irish Society then took matters to the English Court of King's Bench, but the Jacobite/Williamite Wars once more brought things to a standstill. On 27 January 1690 The Society optimistically advertised its fishings in *The London Gazette* for letting, but the

[77] Moody and Simms (eds.) (1968), 6-7.
[78] Moody (1939), 405.

arrival of Bishop King in the diocese heralded a difficult period for The Society. As was mentioned above, Bishop Bramhall had let the Quarterlands to Londonderry Corporation, and the lease was due to expire in 1694. In 1692, therefore, the Corporation began negotiations with Bishop King to renew the lease, and the bishop's refusal of the Corporation's offer had the effect of drawing The Irish Society's attention to the whole rather important question. Clearly The Society's built-in structure was again contributing to such oversights, exacerbated by the winding-up of The Society that had occurred after the Star Chamber débâcle, the great rebellion of 1641, the Civil War, and the more recent disturbances.

At one stage John Mogridge was acting for the bishop ('a man of strong and tenacious character'[79]), with whom he fell out, and was promptly hired by The Society, becoming that body's solicitor in 1700. It seems to have been Mogridge who was the catalyst in persuading the Presbyterian-dominated corporation to make common cause with The Irish Society against the bishop, not least because of memories of rack-renting, the proposed increases of rent demanded by the bishop, and the Anglican/Presbyterian animosities that were being inflamed by the pamphlet war. Mogridge was able to demonstrate that the 1,500 acres of the Quarterlands were part of the 4,000 acres granted to The Irish Society to provide the Liberties of Londonderry. The Society duly entered into possession of the lands on the expiry of the corporation's lease, but the bishop tried to recover his own possession, failed, and filed a bill in Chancery against The Society in October 1694.[80]

The affair then lurched into dangerous territory, almost provoking a major constitutional crisis. The bishop brought his case from the Irish Court of Chancery to the Irish House of Lords (a body not entirely well-disposed towards The Irish Society), and won his appeal in 1697. An order was obtained re-establishing the bishop in his possessions, which was opposed by the Sheriffs and other inhabitants of Londonderry. Things deteriorated further, when an attachment was obtained and the Sheriffs and others taken into custody and removed to Dublin. The Society then appealed to the English House of Lords which in May 1698 determined that the bishop's appeal to the Irish House of Lords was *coram non judice* (before one not a proper judge) and that all the proceedings thereon were null and void. The implications of this ruling for any consideration of Irish 'independence' are obvious.[81] The bishop airily ignored the judgement of the English House of Lords, so the Lords requested of the King that the bishop should be arrested and brought before the Bar of the House to answer for high contempt. The Lords determined that the disputed lands be restored to The Irish Society, the Lord Chancellor made an order to that effect in 1699, and the Sheriffs of Londonderry were instructed to reinstate the lands to The Society's possession.

Mogridge noted in a memorandum of 18 July 1699 that since it was 'evident that the present case and your [i.e. The Irish Society's] suit about the lands ... had never happened had your honours [i.e. The Irish Society] at first indented with the City of Londonderry for those lands and lodged their counterpart among your rolls to be produced as needful, so if the lands be once recovered it will be worth your time to take care for the future'.[82] He pointed out that the Quarterlands were 'never

[79] Moody and Simms (eds.) (1968), 8.
[80] *Ibid.*
[81] See, for example, Molyneaux (1698), *passim*. See also Schultes (1822), 80, and Reed (1865), 52-3.
[82] Moody and Simms (eds.) (1983), 252.

denominated' in the letters patent, but granted as part of the 4,000 acres, and that there were 'a great many' lands in the county to which The Society had 'good title founded in general words thus'. He warned The Society that many properties were 'invaded and held for several descents in fee' and that others were 'possessed by tenants of the various Companies without any profit or rent' to The Society or the Companies '*or title from either*'. Mogridge advocated that a general survey of the county should be made to find out who owned what, to distinguish 'such as are made by your grant from such as are native freeholds, being such as are pretended to be purchased from the natives *who had no right in themselves*' and '*consequently could not transfer one*'.[83] In other words, Mogridge was proposing a major inventory and greater care in book-keeping and paperwork in future, yet the lack of continuity among the membership of The Society was undoubtedly inimical to his sensible proposals, making their implementation even more imperative. A reading of Mogridge's voluminous contributions engages respect, and it clear he did much to re-establish The Society in a position of some strength at the beginning of the 18th century. The bishop's attempts to acquire the Quarterlands (especially Termonderry itself) 'caused a general disturbance', for the citizens of Londonderry concluded they could easily be 'pent up within their walls or at least within a little hill', unable to develop the lands within the Liberties as 'laid' to the city.[84] It began to be believed that the bishop's 'aim or at least his predecessor's was to grasp the whole Island of Derry, whereof before his predecessor had possessed himself of a good part, and the adjacent lands' disputed.[85] Suspicions of the bishop's motives were exacerbated by the growing ill-feeling between members of the Established Church of Ireland (often of English origins) and Presbyterians (often of Scots birth or descent) that followed the siege, the bitterness fuelled by Walker's *True Account*,[86] and the various controversies that mushroomed afterwards, not only as a result of Walker's claims, but because of King's publications.[87]

Thus The Irish Society defeated the bishop over the Quarterlands (which were, it should be emphasised, three-eighths of the area of Londonderry's Liberties, and included the city itself [Termonderry]) issue, and the King commanded the bishop to be brought to London to answer his contempt, but, pleading ill-health, the bishop's excuse was accepted by the English House of Lords. However, the Quarterlands were one thing, but the fishings were another. In 1697 Bishop King attempted to gain possession of several fishings which The Society resisted, so the bishop replied with a Bill in Chancery in 1698, and litigation proceeded at a snail's pace until King was translated to the archbishopric of Dublin in 1703. The bishop was able to inform his successor as Bishop of Derry, Charles Hickman (1648-1713), who held the see from 1703 until his death, that an agreement had been reached: The Society was to have all the bishop's fishings and tithes of fish, while the bishop was to receive the previously disputed Quarterlands, and £200 from The Society. This was subsequently altered so that The Society retained the Quarterlands and paid the bishop £250 per annum, a compromise that was enshrined in an English Act of Parliament in 1704.[88] The Society also paid the £90 10s. per annum to the Corporation of Londonderry, the rent-charge reserved to the corporation by the bishop in 1637.

[83] Moody and Simms (eds.) (1983), 252. The italics are mine.

[84] *Ibid.*, 329.

[85] *Ibid.* See also King, Sir Charles Simeon, Bt. (1908), *passim*.

[86] Walker (1689a) .

[87] For example Walker (1689a, 1689b, 1689c), Boyse (1694), King, William (1692, 1694. 1696), and other works. See Mant (1840), Phillips (1933), and Reid (1867).

[88] 3 and 4 Anne, c.1.

It was little wonder the fishings on the Foyle and Bann aroused such animosities for they were extremely profitable and important items in any overall picture of Irish trade. Salted salmon was exported in huge quantities to Spain and Italy, and in 1689 George Phillips, grandson of Sir Thomas, estimated the annual salmon catch of the Foyle and Bann at 500 tons: at the Cutts (Salmon Leap upstream from Coleraine) he described the 'innumerable company of fish riding on the backs of one another, even to the top of the water, and with great ease and pleasant divertisement taken up in loops'.[89] When it is remembered that in the 1680s a lessee paid the colossal sum of £1,600 per annum for the Foyle fishing and the part of the Bann below the Salmon Leap at Coleraine alone, some idea of the importance of the fish may be gauged.[90]

Hickman (an Englishman) does not appear to have troubled himself very much about his new diocese, and lived most of the time in England, even being buried in Westminster Abbey rather than in Londonderry. Archbishop King had him in mind when he wrote that 'we have, by great application, augmented our bishopricks; and now they are become valuable, we [i.e. Irishmen] are told we must not expect any of them ... As to those clergymen who are sent us from England, I believe it will not be pleaded that they are the brightest ... though I confess, to my observation they seem notably dexterous and industrious to make money for their wives and children. Thus the See of Derry was served by Dr. Hickman, my successor, who entirely rooted up and destroyed a large flourishing wood, which I, with care and cost, had planted whilst at Londonderry'.[91]

This was the not altogether satisfactory state of affairs that evolved as the 17th century drew to its close. Much had happened in some ninety years to the Londoners' Plantation, but more was to come, and although perhaps less overtly dramatic, just as difficult for The Irish Society and the Companies, and had its longeurs as well as moments of satisfaction.[92]

[89] Moody and Simms (eds.) (1968), 10.
[90] *Ibid.*, 9.
[91] Mant (1840), **ii**, 553.
[92] This chapter owes much to material listed in Aldous (ed.) (1993 – relating to various papers at the London Records Office, Guildhall, City of London), and to sources in the Public Record Office of Northern Ireland. Other sources are Beckett (1966), Black (ed.) (1990), Boyse (1694), Colby (1837), Curl (1986), Dwyer (ed.) (1893), Freshfield and Freshfield (1898), Graham (1829), King (1692, 1694, 1696), Lacy (1998), Mackenzie (1690), Macrory (1988), Milligan (1948, 1951), Moody, Martin, and Byrne (eds.) (1982), Moody and Simms (eds.) (1968, 1983), Mullin (1986), Parker (1851), Perceval-Maxwell (1990), Orr (1997), Phillips (1933), Reed (1865), Reid (1867), Schultes (1822), Simms (1966, 1969), Simpson (1847), Smith (1966), Walker (1689a, 1689b, 1689c), Ware (1739/45). John Mogridge's Memorandum of 1700, prepared for The Irish Society, is among the papers in the Corporation of London Record Office, and is reported in Moody and Simms (eds.) (1983), 279-421.

CHAPTER VII

The Londonderry Plantation from the Beginning of the Eighteenth Century to the Early Years of the Reign of King George III

> Between the accession to the Primacy of Narcissus Marsh [(1683-1713), Archbishop of Armagh (1703-13)] and the death of Primate Stone [George Stone (*c.*1708-64), Archbishop of Armagh (1747-64)] ... ecclesiastical statesmen were almost as prominent in the government of Ireland as they had been in that of France during the seventeenth century. The Lords Lieutenant were largely non-resident, and during their absence the country was governed by two or three Lords Justices, one of whom was almost invariably the Primate or an [A]rchbishop. Sometimes the clerical element even outnumbered the lay, as, for instance, in May 1715 when a single layman, the Earl of Kildare, was associated with two [A]rchbishops, King of Dublin and Vesey of Tuam, as Lords Justices. The Church, it might be said, could not be cognizant of every act of State, and every legislative proposal. She was in a most favourable position to attain her aims or amend her defects so far as this could be done by administrative action or by parliamentary statute
>
> WALTER ALISON PHILLIPS (ed.) (1864-1950): *History of the Church of Ireland from Earliest Times to the Present Day* (London: Oxford University Press, 1933), **iii**, 175

The Politico-Religious Settlement at the Beginning of the Eighteenth Century

Mindful of the numerous Presbyterians in Ulster, King William, in June 1690, had ordered that the *Regium Donum* be increased. Victory in 1691 led to the restoration of the Church of Ireland as the Established Church, supported by State endowments and by the tithes that everyone, Roman Catholics and Nonconformists included, had to pay to the Anglican clergy. The Presbyterians, who had supported the Williamite cause almost from the beginning, found themselves in a very weakened position, in spite of the *Act for the Encouragement of Protestant Strangers to settle in this Kingdom of Ireland* of 1692,[1] which permitted Protestants to worship in the form to which they had become accustomed. In 1695 Scotland suffered the first of a series of very cold, wet summers followed by bitter early frosts that encouraged massive emigration to Ulster, and greatly increased the Presbyterian population. By the end of the 17th century Presbyterianism was restored in Scotland by constitutional act, but in Ireland animosities between adherents of the Church of Ireland and their erstwhile allies, the Presbyterians, flared up, as the many pamphlets of the period demonstrate.

For Roman Catholics the Williamite victory was an unmitigated disaster. Although the Treaty of Limerick (October 1691) seemed to promise them religious privileges enjoyed in King Charles II's reign, the Penal Laws soon began to be enacted and to

[1] 4 Will. & Mary, c. 2.

bite. Under an Act of 1691[2] Roman Catholics were barred from membership of Parliament and other public positions in Ireland, and in 1695 other Acts[3] forbade Roman Catholics to send their children abroad for education, to keep arms, or to keep horses valued at £5 or more. In 1697 the Banishment Act[4] required Roman Catholic bishops, vicars-general, deans, and regular clergy to leave Ireland by 1 May 1698. Later enactments included one to 'prevent Papists being sollicitors' (1699)[5] and to 'prevent Popish Priests from coming into the Kingdom',[6] one to ensure the registration of 'Popish Clergy' (1704)[7] an 'Act to prevent the Further Growth of Popery' (1704)[8] and many others that restricted or penalised Roman Catholics. The last Act also imposed a sacramental test for public office, applicable equally to Protestant Dissenters, so Presbyterians were also debarred. As a result, 24 of the 38 members of Londonderry Corporation were obliged to resign, as they refused to take Communion according to the Anglican rite. Such discrimination rapidly exacerbated animosities between erstwhile allies, and would lead, in the course of the 18th century, to massive emigration of Presbyterians and to a short-lived and historically extraordinary alliance between Roman Catholics and Dissenters at the end of the century.

It should be realised that the Penal Laws were passed in reaction to the threat of a Jacobite invasion, which was a constant worry for Irish Protestants after the wars of 1689-91. After the death of Innocent XI the Roman Catholic authorities were committed to a Jacobite restoration, recognised James as the rightful King of Great Britain and Ireland, and accepted the exiled Stuarts' nomination of Roman Catholic Irish bishops until 1766, when the 'Old Pretender' (known as 'James III and VIII') died. By then even the Papacy could no longer support the drunken, failed, embarrassing Prince Charles Edward Louis Philip Casimir (1720-88), commonly called 'The Young Pretender', or 'Bonnie Prince Charlie': Charles had settled in Rome, expecting to be acknowledged by Pope Clement XIII (1758-69), but he was treated with coldness, and his pretensions to the thrones of England, Scotland, and Ireland were repudiated by all the great Roman Catholic powers. To incur the hostility of Great Britain was not regarded by the holy see as wise, and Pope Clement XIV (1769-74) hospitably received members of the British royal House (by that time the Hanoverians), at the same time diminishing traditional papal support for the exiled Stuarts.[9] Prince Charles's younger brother, Henry Benedict Maria Clement (1725-1807), became a Cardinal in the Roman Catholic Church, so was known as the Cardinal Duke of York, and, after the death of Prince Charles (known, improbably, as 'Charles III'), the Jacobites styled him 'King Henry IX'. By his death the male line of King James II and VII came to an end. While the Jacobite threat was real, however, no conscientious Roman Catholic could take any oath denying the legitimacy of Jacobite claims, and without such an oath (e.g. the Act of 1703 requiring office-holders, lawyers, and schoolmasters in Ireland to take the Oath of Abjuration declaring Queen Anne to be the rightful Sovereign and disclaiming the Pretender[10]) no Roman Catholic could be regarded as a loyal subject. The real purpose of the Penal Laws was not, in fact, to destroy Roman Catholicism,

[2] 3 Will. & Mary, c. 2.
[3] 7 Will. III, c. 4, and 7 Will. III c.5.
[4] 9 Will. III, c.1.
[5] 10 Will. III, c. 13.
[6] 2 Anne, c. 3.
[7] 2 Anne, c. 7.
[8] 2 Anne c. 6.
[9] Kelly (ed.) (1986).
[10] Anne, stat. 2, c. 17.

but to ensure that its adherents were kept in positions of economic, political, and social inferiority, debarred from power, and therefore rendered relatively harmless.[11]

Certainly the costs of the Franco-Jacobite attempts to win Ireland were very high, in terms both of life and money. In Ulster the Londonderry Plantation had once again been badly set back, as property had been ruined, livestock decimated, land left uncultivated, and many people had died. There was also a considerable exodus of those supporters of the Jacobite cause who chose to continue fighting in the Continental wars between France and the Allies. Sarsfield, for example, was to perish in the Battle of Landen (Neerwinden) in 1693, but there was one unique case of a most highly-placed personage changing allegiance later. James Butler, 2nd Duke of Ormonde (1665-1745), had been a close friend of the Prince of Orange, and supported the revolution which brought William III and Mary II to the throne. His estates were declared forfeit by the Irish Parliament in 1689, and he accompanied William to Ireland in 1690, seeing action at the Boyne. Gradually, though, he began to resent William's preferential treatment of Dutchmen, but nevertheless took part in various engagements in 1702. In 1703 he became Lord Lieutenant of Ireland, later serving with distinction in Flanders, replacing Marlborough as Captain-General of the army. Towards the end of Queen Anne's reign, however, his allegiance began to be transferred to the Jacobite cause and, after the accession of George Lewis, Elector of Hanover (1660-1727), as King of Great Britain and Ireland (1714-27), his wavering loyalty lost him all his positions, and, like many Tories (those who formed a party that sprang from the 17th-century Royalists or Cavaliers, and who leaned towards the dethroned House of Stuart and high-church principles), he was regarded by the new Establishment as a crypto-Jacobite. Impeached in 1715, he fled to France and his estates were declared forfeit. When John Erskine (1675-1732), 6th or 11th Earl of Mar, raised the Jacobite standard at Braemar, Aberdeenshire, on 6 September 1715, Ormonde landed at Plymouth to lead the Jacobite rising in the west. The Rising soon foundered, however, and although he commanded an abortive expedition to invade England in 1719 (the fleet foundered off Finisterre), thereafter his life was spent in exile in Spain and France.[12]

Such a history demonstrates that the post-Williamite settlements were not regarded by many (not by any means always Roman Catholics) as necessarily permanent, and there was a certain instability that became manifest at certain times during the 18th century, notably after the accession of King George I, in 1715, and again (more seriously) in 1745-6. In Ireland, however, with the Irish aristocratic and landowning classes either exiled or politically emasculated (unless individuals converted to Protestantism, as several did) and the Penal Laws firmly keeping the lid on any aspirations to support the Stuarts, nearly a century of peace ensued, and with it a growth in prosperity. It is to this period we now turn.

The Protestant Ascendancy

Eighteenth-century Ireland saw a remarkable change when compared with earlier times. The victories in the Protestant cause and the suppression of political opposition heralded something very like stability (though there were sporadic outbreaks of violence, often associated with objections to rack-renting and other grievances) that was not to end until the 1798 rebellion. Scotland experienced two major rebellions (1715 and

[11] Beckett (1966), 159.
[12] Black (ed.) (1990), 324-5.

1745-6), but nothing like these affected Ireland, which seems to have wearied of the Stuarts, and, in any case, many of those who might have supported the deposed dynasty had themselves become exiles.

Georgian Ireland was dominated by what we now call the Protestant Ascendancy, the Anglo-Irish ruling class that was almost entirely Anglican (Church of Ireland) in its religious persuasion, and provided the British Empire with soldiers, Churchmen, administrators, and governors in impressive numbers. George A. Birmingham (James Owen Hannay [1865-1950]), the scholar and novelist, referred to the Ascendancy as a 'doomed aristocracy', but its sons and daughters were, in the words of William Butler Yeats (1865-1939) 'no petty people', who created the great landed estates and gave architects scope to design some of the loveliest country-houses in the British Isles.[13]

Because of the rather peculiar circumstances surrounding the Londonderry Plantation there are no country-houses of the first rank in the county, although there are a few fairly modest architectural ensembles, including the very pretty Springhill, near Moneymore (*c.*1660-*c.*1820), the seat of the Conynghams (Planters from Ayrshire), and the fine Drenagh, near Limavady, a much later (1836) and rather splendid house by (Sir) Charles Lanyon (1812-89), built for the McCausland family. There are several decent houses built by the Companies for their agents (e.g. the Ironmongers' Lizard Manor [1860-1], by John Mullins [*c.*1795-1880], and the Mercers' Manor-House at Kilrea [1832], by William Barnes [1807-58]),[14] but by far the grandest houses were those erected for Frederick Augustus Hervey (1730-1803), Bishop of Derry from 1768 until his death, and 4th Earl of Bristol from 1779, who will be mentioned below.[15]

Given the Protestant Ascendancy's importance, it is not surprising that clerics played such significant rôles during the 18th century, not only at local and regional levels, but nationally as well. In 1714, for example, Thomas Lindsay (d. 1724), Archbishop of Armagh (1714-24), and John Vesey (1638-1716), Archbishop of Tuam (1678-1716), were sworn in as Lords Justices (the commissioners to whom, in the early 18th century, the vice-regal authority was entrusted), though Lindsay (who appeared to have Jacobite sympathies[16]), was replaced a few months later by Archbishop King of Dublin, formerly Bishop of Derry.

If the Jacobite defeat had raised hopes among all classes of Protestants (many of whom had settled on the Londonderry Plantation), the history of 18th-century Ireland was to dash those of certain groups. Precedents set by the English Act of Parliament of 1704[17] settling the dispute between the bishop of Derry and The Irish Society over fishings, lands, and other matters (outlined in the previous chapter), by which the supremacy of the English Parliament over Irish affairs was established, led to another clash in 1719 when the Irish House of Lords presented an address to the Lord Lieutenant for submission to the King protesting against the proceedings of the British House of Lords in *Annesley* v. *Sherlock*, the appellate case that led to the Declaratory Act of 1720 asserting the British Parliament's right to legislate for Ireland.[18] At the same time the Declaratory Act denied the appellate jurisdiction of the Irish House of Lords, so it was obvious that Ireland was to be treated very much as an inferior

[13] See Bence-Jones (1987, 1988).
[14] See Curl (1986), *passim.*
[15] See also Rankin (1972), *passim.*
[16] Phillips (ed.) (1933), iii, 193.
[17] 3 & 4 Anne, c. 1.
[18] 6 Geo I, c.5.

colony, though it supposedly was an equal Kingdom. This tendency is amply borne out by the draconian restrictions imposed on imports and exports into and out of Ireland that bedevilled the economy and made it excessively dependent upon one product, namely linen. In the event of a slump, Ireland would suffer untold miseries.[19]

The Penal Laws[20] (as the various enactments favouring Anglicans and restricting everyone else were known) impinged greatly on the sensibilities of Presbyterians who, as has been noted above, played no small part in the defence of Londonderry and in the history of the Plantation. As the 17th century progressed, the Londonderry Plantation became more densely populated by Scots, which is not surprising given the geographical closeness of the northern parts of Ireland to Scotland. Those Scots were essentially tough, no-nonsense Lowlanders from the Borders, Dumfries and Galloway, Ayrshire, Lanarkshire, Renfrewshire, the central belt between Edinburgh and Glasgow, the Lothians, and the lower pastoral lands in the vicinity of the Moray Firth, for the Government most certainly did not want Highlanders from Argyll and the Isles, natural allies of the Antrim MacDonnells, to settle in Ulster.[21]

Between 1660 and 1715, it appears, the number of Presbyterian congregations (predominantly Scots) in Ulster approximately doubled,[22] yet their strength led to discrimination against them in favour of the Established Church of Ireland. In the 1630s, for example, the administration of Wentworth and the high-church Laudian party became inimical to Presbyterians (as Nonconformists) but for a time during the Protectorate Presbyterianism was in the ascendant. The Restoration in 1660 had led Presbyterians to hope that their resolve in the face of the Irish attack on the Plantation from 1641 might gain them some favour and concessions, but they were driven from their churches and discrimination against them continued. During the wars of 1689-91 Presbyterians fought with determination for the success of the Williamite anti-French, anti-Jacobite cause, but hopes of being treated fairly were dashed by the Act of 1704 that not only imposed restrictions to 'prevent the growth of Popery', but insisted upon a sacramental test for potential holders of public office that applied equally to Protestant Dissenters.[23]

It is very odd that, after the fragility of Protestant supremacy and of English power in Ireland had been demonstrated again and again (e.g. during the Nine Years' War, the great rebellion and the wars after 1641, and the mayhem of 1689-91), the English and Irish Parliaments contrived to undermine Ireland's economic stability and alienate a large section of the Protestant population. As a stable and secure Ireland was absolutely essential for England's defence and even survival (as had been demonstrated on several occasions), the measures taken against Ireland's well-being were extraordinary. By 1715 Ireland was suffering from narrow-minded English commercial interests far more than were the American colonies.

Linen

Attempts were made to strengthen the economy by introducing a new industry. An Act of Parliament[24] had been passed in 1696 for 'encouraging linen manufacture in

19 Moody, Martin, and Byrne (*Eds.*) (1982) is a useful synopsis of Acts, events, etc.
20 Anonymous (1813), Atkyns (1689), Blackerby (1689), Wall (1967).
21 Ford (1915), Hill (1873), Perceval-Maxwell (1990).
22 Dickson (1966), 5.
23 2 Anne, c. 6. See Reid (1867), *passim*.
24 7 & 8 Will. III, c. 39.

Ireland' permitting the import of plain Irish linen into England free of duty (an important concession). However, there were counter-measures, and in 1697 the first of a series of Bills was introduced that effectively banned the export of Irish woollen goods. In the following year the King was presented with an address requesting him to discourage woollen manufacture in Ireland and to encourage the making of linen, and in 1699 duties were imposed on woollens exported from Ireland,[25] and a few months later an Act[26] was passed prohibiting the export of Irish woollens to lands other than England. Ostensibly to protect the English trade in wool (which had been in the doldrums) and to encourage the growth of a new Irish linen industry, these enactments seem to have been only part of a campaign to sacrifice Irish interests in favour of English merchants and landed proprietors. By 1715 the manufacture of woollen goods in Ireland (that had been introduced by Protestant Planters from Britain) was virtually non-existent.

To promote the manufacture of linen, a warrant was issued to the Lords Justices enabling them to pay a subsidy to Louis Crommelin (1652-1727),[27] a Huguenot exile from Picardy, who had been encouraged under the 1696 Act to settle in Ireland. Crommelin was appointed 'Overseer of the Royal Linen Manufacture in Ireland', imported looms from Flanders and The Netherlands, and encouraged Netherlanders and Huguenots to emigrate to Ulster in order to teach flax-growing to farmers and to supervise bleaching operations. Very soon the markets of Dublin and London were being supplied with linens and cambrics of a quality previously only found in goods imported from the Continent. In 1705 an Act of Parliament[28] permitted the export of Irish linen to the American colonies, but, in general, Ireland's trading and commercial possibilities were severely curtailed by enactments of Parliament in London.

The main manufacturing district established by Crommelin was the Lagan Valley, especially at Lisburn and in the surrounding area. He found the old Irish spinning-wheel to be a superior tool to anything on the Continent (or England), and at once set about improving it for the cottage industries that were to supply the yarn for the looms. Very soon, the growing of flax and the manufacture of linen yarn became features of the north of Ireland, where the fragile economy, ominously, began to depend very largely on the linen trade. Should anything go wrong, and demand for linen slump, the result would be poverty and economic ruin, for there was little to fall back on. In its 18th-century manifestations in Ulster the making of linen was largely a cottage industry, augmenting the unimpressive profits from precarious small farming tenancies. When it is remembered that linen exports accounted for about half the value of Ireland's total export trade, the seriousness of any calamity affecting the linen industry may be understood, and by 1728 the northern counties of Ireland were making in excess of 80 per cent of all linen marketed in the country.[29] Most linen-yarn and brown linen cloth was produced on small farms, sold in the markets to bleachers or supplied to the makers of the linen-cloth, and brought in a useful income. Nevertheless, there was not much left over as costs (notably rents) inevitably rose.

In 1709 the Corporation of Coleraine solicited The Irish Society for help to establish a 'linen manufacture in the town, as a means of increasing the trade and prosperity thereof', but The Society did not feel that such an 'undertaking was practicable and

[25] 10 Will. III, c. 5.
[26] 10 & 11 Will. III, c. 10.
[27] *D.N.B.* (1917), v, 145-6.
[28] 3 & 4 Anne, c. 8.
[29] Beckett (1966), *passim*; Dickson (1966), 8.

consistent with the constitution' of The Society.[30] A certain amount of optimism was in the air, for in May 1707 the union of the English and Scots Parliaments came into effect, prompting hopes that the Irish Parliament would also be united with that of Great Britain for the benefit of all institutions, commerce, manufacturing, and trade, but this was not to be until almost a century later. It became clear that the Government intended to ensure that conformity in matters of religion and political stability were established, for in 1709 registered Roman Catholic priests in Ireland were required by law to take the Oath of Abjuration recognising Queen Anne and renouncing all allegiance to the Old Pretender.[31] In the same year the first Irish Banking Act[32] became law (which facilitated trade and increased prosperity), and a Board of Trustees for linen manufacture was set up.[33]

The refusal of The Irish Society in the matter of establishing a linen manufacturing facility in Coleraine (September 1709) suggests intimations that all was not well with relations between the Coleraine Corporation and The Society. One of the difficulties facing The Society stemmed from the fact that, although it had agents on the spot, it was, in fact, an absentee landlord, and its views less audible than those of the local magnates whose power and influence had steadily grown. Coleraine (like Londonderry) had a Corporation that was largely self-electing, and by the second decade was virtually controlled by the Jackson family. As with the City of London, historically the Commonalties of Coleraine and Londonderry consisted of Freemen, and traders and artisans were penalised for not taking up the Freedom. In 1709 a bye-law approved by The Society exempted from such penalties all Protestant weavers engaged in the manufacture of goods from hemp or flax,[34] so clearly some attempt was made by The Society to encourage the nascent industry. One of the problems with the Corporations of Londonderry and Coleraine was the tendency to grant large numbers of Freedoms at the discretion of local dignitaries: in 1709, for example, 72 people were granted Freedoms by ticket, thereby possibly devaluing the old rights to Freedoms for those who had served Apprenticeships to Freemen, and enabling the Corporation to 'pack' meetings in one interest or another. The Society sought to control the powers of the Common Councils, to reduce the number of Freedoms granted, and to attempt to prohibit the election of any person to a Corporation without residential qualifications.

As the century progressed, however, The Irish Society could view with some satisfaction the growing prosperity of County Londonderry. Flax-seed was imported, and huge amounts of linen were exported; cottages hummed with industry; bleach-greens proliferated; and rural rents rose. At Upperlands (Ampurtaine *or* Ampertaine) in the 1740s Alexander Clark & Son founded the celebrated linen-mills, soon to be powered by water. Bounties were paid by the Trustees of the Linen and Hempen Manufacturers of Ireland to encourage the cultivation of flax in the county in the last decades of the century. By 1802 Sampson recorded that the 'staple of the country is the linen manufacture'.[35] While some encouragement was given at national and regional level, the Londoners played their part, and the linen trade and industry were established by private individuals, often having to contend with ever-increasing rents set by the 'farmers'. As will be outlined below, this was to bring about further serious problems later.

[30] Schultes (1822), 86.
[31] See 2 Anne, c. 6, 2 Anne, c. 7, 8 Anne, c. 3.
[32] 8 Anne, c. 11.
[33] 9 Anne, c. 3.
[34] Smith (1966), 65.
[35] Sampson (1802), 347. *See also* Johnston (1959), *passim.*

The Plantation and The Irish Society in the Early Eighteenth Century

Betts, in his *The Story of The Irish Society*,[36] claimed that after the Jacobite/Williamite Wars, 'The Society was at last to settle down in peace, and, as a consequence, the remainder of the record is tame and uneventful compared with the excitements under James and Charles. In fact, beyond the ordinary work – all the more useful perhaps because prosaic – there is little to tell'. Like the absurd tale of the prefabricated timber-framed houses being shipped over from a timber-starved London to an area where dense woodlands had survived intact at the very start of the Plantation (a fable Betts swallowed whole[37]), this is rather remote from the truth. Certainly the history of the Londonderry Plantation during almost a century of peace was not so fraught as was the case on numerous occasions during the 17th century, but that history was nonetheless momentous for other reasons. The attention of the City of London was often distracted from its Ulster interests, but The Irish Society and the Companies gradually accomplished an improvement of estates ravaged by warfare, and indeed had taken immediate emergency action to help Londonderry after the siege.

In 1693 The Society wrote to the Lord Lieutenant about helping the 'poor desolate City of Londonderry'[38] and ensuring the re-establishment of its Corporation: slowly the work of reconstruction proceeded, aided by grants of timber and cash. In 1698, at the time of the additional problems with the bishop over the Quarterlands and the fishings, The Society was called to attend a committee of the House of Commons to discuss petitions relative to the sufferings of the inhabitants of Londonderry, but it was generally left to the City of London and the Livery Companies to pick up the tab for making good damage done during the wars. Given the many problems The Irish Society had experienced in the course of the 17th century, the additional irritants of the bishops of Derry and their claims cannot have helped matters. Indeed, these 'caused great trouble and charge' and were 'the occasion of great heats and animosities'.[39] As has been noted above, The Society effectively bought off the bishop for a yearly sum following the settlement of 1704 for 'quieting all differences between' the see and The Society, 'and for remedying ... inconveniences, and for preventing the like for the future'.[40]

The Londoners' Plantation did not benefit from the grants of forfeited estates in Ireland,[41] and attention was once more diverted from the country by the War of the Spanish Succession which began in 1702, and was again concerned with containing the ambitions of King Louis XIV of France. However, that King's sworn enemy, King William III, died in that year and was succeeded by William's sister-in-law, Queen Anne (1702-14), the last of the Stuart monarchs, in whose reign the Allies inflicted several major defeats on the French. It was also a reign in which various enactments were passed that consolidated Anglican privilege: for example, as it had become impossible for Presbyterians,[42] as Dissenters, to hold public office,[43] Londonderry Corporation became exclusively Anglican as a result.

36 Betts (1913), 87.
37 *Ibid.*, 42.
38 Schultes (1822), 78.
39 *Ibid.*, 81.
40 *Ibid.*
41 Under 11 & 12 Will. III, c. 2.
42 Reid (1867), *passim.*
43 2 Anne, c. 6.

In 1705 The Irish Society determined to establish a free school in Coleraine, and this was duly accomplished: regular reports concerning the scholars, master, and condition of the school were required from the Corporation, but even so the schoolmaster had to be admonished for 'attending to the advice of other persons in the affairs of the school', and he was reminded that The Society was the founder, chief authority, and patron of the school. Once again, control from a distance had proved difficult, and voices nearer to hand (clearly local factions) were more audible.

By 1706 the population of Londonderry was just under 3,000, and reconstruction of the shattered fabric proceeded. Sir Thomas Molyneaux (1661-1733), the physician and scientist, who was the first writer to opine that the Giant's Causeway was a product of nature rather than an edifice created by humans, visited Londonderry in 1708 and was struck by the new and restored buildings, though he noted that prosperity had not returned. He was able to record with approbation the establishment of the diocesan library, founded by Bishop King.[44]

At Coleraine in 1713 disputes arose over the calling of a Court of Common Council when 13 members, desiring a Court, were over-ruled by the Mayor, and appealed to The Irish Society. The reason for the Mayor's refusal appears to have been that he (and his faction) desired the election of a non-resident Burgess which was opposed by the Coleraine members as such an event would be contrary to the Charter. 'Violent and tumultuous proceedings ensued at the Coleraine Common Council', during which 'the sword and mace were forcibly seized'.[45] The Society, not surprisingly, 'reprehended these proceedings'.

The upshot of the 'dissensions' was that The Society had to make representations to the Government in Dublin, and the matter was also referred to the Lord Lieutenant. Very soon afterwards the Mayor of Coleraine (who seems to have regarded the town as his personal fiefdom) was served with an order from the Privy Council of Ireland to appear and answer complaints, and in due course the Privy Council determined in favour of the Corporation (supported by The Irish Society), although disagreements continued for many years. The rot probably set in quite early on, even before the Proby/Springham commission, but the incident with the sword and mace was repeated in 1715, and the English Attorney-General was approached by The Society for an opinion. As originally established, control of the Common Councils in both Londonderry and Coleraine also carried with it control of Parliamentary franchise and representation of both settlements in Parliament (the source of influence and power). The Society therefore had a threefold interest: its authority over the Common Councils; its position as patron; and its pivotal rôle in carrying out the policies and supporting the interests of the Crown. Parliamentary representation secured Crown influence in the Irish House of Commons,[46] but Coleraine became increasingly under the control of the Beresfords and Jacksons who by the middle of the century had secured the patronage of Coleraine as the influence of The Irish Society declined. Even after the Act of Union[47] of 1800 Coleraine remained a closed Corporation under the control of the Beresfords.

[44] Lacy (1998), 149-50.
[45] Schultes (1822), 89.
[46] Smith (1966), 67.
[47] 39 & 40 Geo. III, c. 67, and 40 Geo. III, c. 38.

The Woods

When King was succeeded as Bishop of Derry in 1703 by the largely absentee Hickman, certain aspects of the Plantation and its economy deteriorated. Hickman seems to have been interested in the diocese primarily for his own financial gain, and proceeded to destroy King's carefully tended woodlands for precisely that reason. Of course there was a huge demand for timber for purposes of urgent reconstruction, and The Irish Society had been speedy and diligent in the provision of timber from its lands to help the work of rebuilding the shattered settlements, churches, public buildings, and private dwellings.

During the early part of the 18th century The Society endeavoured to protect the woodlands, many of which were on the Company Proportions. It had been the practice of The Society to distribute any profits it received as 'dividends' to the Companies, as the latter had put up all the capital for the Plantation in the first place. By 1707, however, The Society attempted to exert some pressure on the Companies by withholding dividends and hearing 'matters of controversy' by calling the clerks before it. Such pressures were attempted at various times in regard to the woods, but it all seems to have been an unproductive enterprise, for widespread destruction for profit continued unabated despite an Act imposing obligations on landowners and leaseholders to plant and preserve trees.[48] Timber and fish provided considerable profits for those who 'farmed' the Company (and other) estates and fishings, and The Society and the Companies depended largely on the rents, 'fines', and other income as agreed in the original papers concerning the Plantation.

Conservation of the woodlands on Company Proportions was again urged in 1712 by The Irish Society, which prepared a statement setting out its rights to the woods on the Plantation. On some Proportions wood-rangers were appointed at a total cost of £203 per annum to inspect and care for the woods, but it was a dangerous job, and wholesale theft continued. Some huge squared timbers, deliberately sunk in Lough Neagh, had to be recovered 'by means of an engine'[49] in 1713. Even though the woods were being looted, saplings destroyed, and mature timbers stolen (in 1714 £1,000-worth of timber was reported as 'having been embezzled away'[50]), The Irish Society was obliged to provide good timber for the repair and upkeep of buildings, bridges, and other fabric, and there was a constant and voracious demand for pipe-staves to make barrels, especially for the flourishing export trade in salted salmon. In 1718 and 1719, for example, The Society provided timber to repair the church at Magherafelt on the Salters' Proportion, and timber was given for the 'new steeple' at Coleraine. It was clear that the precious fishings would suffer 'great detriment' if the woods were not properly managed, and that tenants on the Company lands 'would suffer for want of timber for their necessary buildings and reparations'.[51] The Companies were 'earnestly recommended' to 'provide such timely and suitable remedies' to reverse the results of a century of profligate destruction of what had been ancient woodlands. Special committees were appointed with responsibility for the woods, and The Society also formed its own committee to deal with those Companies who responded (not all did so). However, the abuse of the woodlands continued (they were endemic from the start), notably on the Vintners', Salters', and Skinners' Proportions.

[48] 10 Will. III, c. 12.
[49] Schultes (1822), 89.
[50] *Ibid.*, 91.
[51] *Ibid.*

By 1736 The Irish Society had decided that 'no regulations' could 'prevent depredation and plunder of timber', and called for a commission of Justices to inquire into the 'wastes, transgressions, and mismanagement in The Society's woods'.[52] The wood-rangers were dismissed for 'misconduct' (they appear to have colluded in asset-stripping and poaching activities), and in 1741 The Society believing that 'the chief hindrance and discouragement to the planting of young trees' was the perception that The Society would claim the timber once the trees matured, declared that all young trees planted within the previous 15 years, or thereafter, on any Proportion, would not be demanded by The Society or by its successors. Even this ploy failed to bring results, however, and the woods were denuded at an even faster rate.

So, by 1741, the woods in County Londonderry were not only decayed, but almost totally consumed,[53] and there had been 'a very great and almost general neglect and disregard for many years past to the planting of young trees by ... Companys or their Tenants ... for the raising and providing a future Supply and Stock of Timber for the Uses and Occasions of the Plantation'.[54] Attempts were made to ensure that timber should be 'disposed of ... for and towards the Buildings and Reparations or other necessary use', but it was no good: the lands that, only a century and a quarter before, had been covered with mature forests, were almost completely stripped of timber. Sampson, writing in 1802,[55] recalled hearing old people tell that in parts of the county 'now entirely naked, their own fathers' had seen 'the martin jumping from bough to bough', and that the 'woods extended 30 or 40 miles in several parts of the County'. Sampson attributed these catastrophic losses to several factors: the policy of clearance to remove cover for the wood-kernes and to provide farmland; the use of timber for fuel; the demand for pipe-staves, both for the making of barrels in which to export salmon, and to supply the coopers of England and Europe; and the production of charcoal to smelt lead and iron, especially in England, by then itself critically short of timber. 'Many of those glens and banks, which once were shaded with natural oaks', he wrote, 'are now naked; and sorry I am to record their destruction, to which many more are inexorably doomed'.[56] Sampson referred to the destruction of the woods as 'barbarous havoc, perpetrated by those, who should rather adorn, than despoil'.[57] It would be difficult to dissent from his views. However, in the early 19th century, it was Sampson who would propose huge schemes of replanting, especially on the Fishmongers' Proportion.[58]

The Fishings

As has been described earlier, The Irish Society had been granted enormous rights over the salmon, eel, and other fishings. Problems arose with claims by the bishop of Derry, the sequestration, and the Quarterlands matter. Those were resolved in 1704, but later in the century even more troublesome claims were made that threatened The Society's rights in the Bann.

This is a long, involved, and tortuous tale, so it can only be outlined here. The Irish Society's original grants scheduled all the 'fishings and fowlings' within the city

[52] Schultes (1822), 109.
[53] Irish Society, (*c.*1898), 712.
[54] *Ibid.*
[55] Sampson (1802), 441.
[56] *Ibid.*
[57] *Ibid.*, 442.
[58] Curl (1986), *passim.*

of Londonderry, in 'all lands and tenements' granted to The Society, in the 'river or water' of Lough Foyle 'to the reflux of the sea', and in the river or water of Bann to Lough Neagh. Specifically, mention was made of the 'river of Lough Foyle so far as the river floweth, and in the Bann to Lough Neagh'. The King promised not to grant any new patents or privileges within The Society's lands. It is clear that the fishings were among the most attractive and desirable aspects of the territory, and were an essential lure to bring the City of London into the venture in the first place: without these remarkably fecund waters there can be little doubt that the Londoners (who were reluctant colonisers anyway) would have declined an involvement.

In the event, as has been indicated, the City had to buy out various private interests already granted on its lands. In 1606 Chichester had acquired rights to the fishings in the Bann from Lough Neagh to the Salmon Leap and from the Salmon Leap to the sea in two purchases from James Hamilton. In 1611 Chichester sold and surrendered all his interests in the fishings to the Crown, which also bought out from Hamilton his remaining interests, including certain fishing-rights in Lough Neagh.[59] After the trial and forfeiture, The Society recovered its fishings by letters patent of 1656, and in 1662, under the charter of King Charles II, was confirmed in its rights. Unfortunately a grant had been made to Chichester of Lough Neagh, the soil and fishings thereof, the eel-weirs at Toome, and the fishings of the Bann between Toome and the Salmon Leap in 1621, a clear example of contradictory grants being made by the Crown. David Babington, Law Agent to The Society, in his *Narrative of The Fishing Cause*,[60] opined that he doubted if The Society 'ever availed themselves of the grant of that part of the river which lies between the rock and the Lough',[61] but that stretch of the river was in constant use for transporting timber down-river to Coleraine, and it appears that the Bann was indeed fished. In 1622, Chichester granted Lough Neagh to The Society in fee-farm, in perpetuity, for £100 per annum, which makes it clear that The Society had interests upstream from the Salmon Leap.[62] Edward Chichester (*c.*1570-1648), 1st Viscount Chichester, Arthur Chichester's brother, and *his* son, Arthur (1606-75), 1st Earl of Donegall (from 1647), surrendered their premises granted in 1621 to the King in 1640, who then re-granted to them all the estates *except* the lough and the River Bann. However, in 1656, under the Protectorate, Sir John Clotworthy (d. 1665), created 1st Viscount Massereene (from 1660), managed to obtain a lease for 99 years of the lough, Toome, with fishings and soil thereof, and the Bann as far as the Salmon Leap. Clotworthy displayed great animosity towards episcopacy and anything connected with High Churchmanship, even sneering at Laud on the scaffold just before the latter's execution with questions about 'on what his assurance of salvation was founded' and what was 'the comfortablest saying for a dying man'.[63] He was also one of the most grasping of personalities: while representing the interests of Irish adventurers and the soldiers settled in Ireland, he succeeded in obtaining even better terms for himself. The King confirmed Clotworthy in his lease in 1660, but the very next year, by letters patent under the Great Seal of Ireland, granted to Chichester, by then Earl of Donegall, the fishings in Lough Neagh and the River Bann from the lough to the Salmon Leap. Then, in 1662, the same King re-granted rights under the Patent of 1613 to the Londoners, so that part of the Bann between Lough Neagh and

59 Schultes (1822), clxxiii.
60 Printed as an Appendix in Schultes (1822), clxxii-cc.
61 *Ibid.*, clxxiv.
62 Reed (1865), 37.
63 *D.N.B.* (1917), **iv**, 582.

the Salmon Leap had been granted at different times to different parties, a muddle that was sorted out later.[64]

Although The Irish Society began a determined attempt to recover its rights during its battles with the bishops of Derry, it seems to have lost its grip on the Bann fishings, for by 1739 it appears to have believed its fishing-rights on the Bann extended from the sea to the Salmon Leap, about a 'mile above Coleraine',[65] but still knew its Foyle fishings, from the 'main ocean up the river', extended about twenty-five miles in all. Mogridge had been right, and the regular changes of personnel in The Irish Society did not help continuity: by 1739 it is clear that The Society, for whatever reasons, was acquiescing in the usurpation of its fishing-rights by the Chichester family, now Earls of Donegall.

Then, in 1769 Donegall filed a Bill in the Exchequer against The Society alleging trespass by The Society's lessee (Sir Henry Hamilton) who had erected salmon-traps at the Salmon Leap. Donegall claimed *his* fisheries upstream were being injured by the traps at the Cutts. Clotworthy's lease expired in 1755, so Donegall's reversion became operative, giving him claims of title to the Bann by 1769. Claiming in a 1771 action against The Irish Society that the Londoners' charter had not been ratified under the Great Seal of Ireland, and challenging the rights of The Society to *any* fishings in the Bann, alarms began to sound in London. Donegall claimed that the grant of 1662 was invalid, and he, or those acting for him, began to disseminate pamphlets claiming he had defeated The Irish Society and its tenant (by then [1784] Lady Hamilton), but litigation dragged on leading to judgements in favour of Donegall in 1794 and 1795. However, an Act of the Irish Parliament was passed in 1795 whereby all grants of land in Ireland under the Great Seal of England were recognised to be as equally valid as those given under the Great Seal of Ireland.[66] In 1798 the Courts issued an injunction to force the removal and demolition of four of the 'cuts'. However, The Irish Society appealed to the Irish House of Lords, which again found for Donegall. David Babington, on behalf of The Society, prepared a closely argued petition to the Lord Chancellor, who gave his decision in The Society's favour, with costs (12 November 1801). On the death of Lady Hamilton the lease determined, and The Society recovered direct control over the fishings. Babington concluded his account with an opinion that 'nothing but the extreme of stupidity, or the grossest neglect in those that may have the honor of conducting the affairs of the Society hereafter' could lead to a defeat in any action brought against the Londoners.[67]

Healy, in his study of 1913,[68] refers to verdicts for Donegall being 'fraudulently obtained', and indeed many of the hearings took place in obscure courts in County Armagh. It is also difficult to avoid coming to the conclusion that Donegall's friends in high places were not always above showing bias in his favour and against the distant London-based Irish Society. In 1869 The Society grasped the nettle and bought out 'sundry rights of fishing claimed by certain parties' in the Bann above the Cutts, and so regained possession of the whole fishery in the Bann from Lough Neagh to the sea. However, The Society's title to the fishing from Coleraine to the sea was then challenged, but in 1873, at the Assize Court in Londonderry, the Judge stated that The Society had proved a clear and distinct title to the fisheries in the Bann from the

[64] For a detailed study of this murky business see Healy (1913), *passim*.
[65] Schultes (1822), 111.
[66] 35 Geo. III, c. 39.
[67] Schultes (1822), cxciii.
[68] Healy (1913), *passim*.

sea to Lough Neagh. He added that rarely had he seen a title more clearly proved and decidedly evidenced by written and printed documents.[69] Nevertheless, the aftermath of those events was not finally resolved until 1981, as will be described below.

Problems with the fishings were not only concerned with dodgy grants (sometimes giving the same rights to different people at almost the same time), but with the economics of catching and marketing the fish themselves. If Healy's story is shocking, then so is that of the The Society's other problems regarding the fishings. Although the fishings were extremely important during the 17th century, and a good source of revenue, things changed during the 18th century, and there were times when The Society had great difficulty finding tenants. There were also periods when expenses exceeded income, as in the Foyle fisheries in 1722. A glance at the evidence shows that there was a huge fall in the value of the fishings after the siege, reflecting the depressed state of the country after the wars. On occasion tenants were found and agreements reached, but when it was found no profits could be made at all, tenants gave up. In 1720, for example, a disastrous year for the economy in London, the fishings were advertised and Irish tenants were found, to pay £2,000 per annum for 41 years, half the rent to be paid in advance: however, the potential takers declined to complete the contract.[70] In 1721 salmon sold in London (120 tons) by The Society's Agent was valued at £2,160, and in 1723 profits were only £1,462 10s., but there were great expenses maintaining labour, equipment, the breeding-ponds in rivers, fishing-stations, stores, and so on, and there were always costs associated with providing barrels and transporting produce. So great were the charges and so difficult the management of the fishings from so great a distance that more attempts were made to lease them, but these again failed until in 1729 Alderman William Jackson contracted to take them at £1,200 a year. Even this arrangement had ended by 1735, so The Society, 'embarrassed in what manner to dispose of' its salmon, decided to export casks (marked with the dagger of the City or the name of The Society) containing salmon to Leghorn (Livorno) and Venice. The Society 'accordingly became merchants of their fish'[71] but profits were very small, and the venture ended in disaster when the cargo-ship was wrecked off Venice with the loss of all hands save the Captain. Although 335 'barrels' were 'recovered, ... the fish were in bad condition', but the cargo had been insured for £1,000.[72]

In 1749 the fishings were let to William Richardson (who had purchased the Merchant Taylors' Proportion in 1729, the year he became The Irish Society's General Agent for good measure) at only £620 per annum, determinable after seven years, and in 1756 better terms (£910 per annum) were obtained by leasing them to the General Agent, Sir Henry Hamilton, who renewed the arrangements in 1762 and 1769. Thereafter, the fishings were let for the rest of the century, but, apart from the exhausting, tiresome, and expensive litigation, expenses rose. 'Independent of clerks, fishermen, boats and boatmen, in the fishing season there must be a number of persons employed as guards and watchmen, in the neighbourhood of all the little rivers communicating with the Bann, and into which the mother-fish resort in the breeding season', observed Robert Slade, in his *Narrative*[73] of 1802. Furthermore, the advent of the linen industry also affected the fishings, though enhancing the value of

[69] Smith (1966), 172.
[70] Schultes (1822), 96.
[71] *Ibid.*, 108.
[72] *Ibid.*, 110-111.
[73] *Ibid.*, ccxiv-ccxv. See Slade (1802), *passim.*

The Society's land in some respects: 'the increased cultivation of flax, and the establishment of additional bleaching-grounds' contributed to 'injure the fishery, by poisoning the waters and producing additional stoppages in their course', while 'the workmen themselves, who, if not properly managed by douceurs and indulgencies' became 'poachers, capable of doing much mischief'.[74]

The South Sea Bubble Disaster

As if these enormous problems were not enough, a financial disaster of the greatest magnitude almost overwhelmed the City of London in 1720, and was all the more strange as it followed immediately from the French financial crisis of 1719 occasioned by the Mississippi Company mania and collapse. When the War of the Spanish Succession ended, it was hoped to establish a flourishing trade (mainly in slaves) with Spanish America, and a South Sea Company was formed with this end in view in 1711. Stock in the Company was offered with guaranteed interest of 6 per cent to holders of Navy and Ordnance Bonds in this Government-sponsored venture, and a monopoly of trade with South America and the Pacific was promised for the Company. Robert Harley (1661-1724), 1st Earl of Oxford (from 1711), Lord High Treasurer of England (thus, for all intents and purposes, the equivalent of Prime Minister), and Governor of the South Sea Company (a post from which he retired in 1714), introduced the scheme (intended to fund the National Debt, no less). The War of the Spanish Succession ended in 1713 with the Peace of Utrecht by which, *inter alia*, King Louis XIV recognised the British Protestant Succession and undertook to give no further help to the exiled Stuarts. France also ceded to Great Britain Newfoundland, Nova Scotia, the Hudson's Bay Territories, and the island of St Kitts. Spain, in return for the recognition of the Bourbon Philip V (reigned 1700-46) as King of Spain, and other benefits, ceded Gibraltar and Minorca to Great Britain, but granted only a limited trading concession restricted to a single ship per year that could not even enter the Pacific Ocean. Other expected benefits regarding commercial and mercantile matters were not forthcoming. The first voyage under the aegis of the South Sea Company (1717) brought only limited profits, but the appointment of the new King, George I (reigned 1714-27), as Governor of that Company created new confidence in the dodgy enterprise, and stock rose to dizzy heights. Hysterical demand for stock, which stood at 128.5 in January 1720, rose to 1,000 in July-August, but by December had dropped back to 124. This fall brought down Bank of England stock at the same time. The boom in South Sea Company shares was caused not only by a perception of spurious respectability, but by a scheme whereby the Company took over the whole of the National Debt except that owed to the Bank of England and the East India Company in 1720: investors were persuaded to exchange their State Annuities for South Sea stock, sold at a huge premium, and some, who prudently sold their holdings when they reached astronomical heights, made vast profits, but very many others were ruined.[75] After the South Sea Bubble burst, an inquiry was undertaken by a committee of the House of Commons, and its report (1721) concluded that at least three ministers of the Crown had accepted bribes and speculated (with inside knowledge) in the Company's stock. John Aislabie (1670-1742), for example, was found guilty of 'most

[74] Schultes (1822), ccxv. *See* Slade (1802), *passim.*
[75] *Encyclopaedia Britannica* (1959), **21**, 96.

notorious, dangerous, and infamous corruption',[76] and it was established that he had 'promoted the Dangerous and Destructive execution of the South Sea scheme with a view to his own Exhorbitant Profit'.[77] Aislabie was expelled from the House and committed to the Tower of London, but managed to hold on to his vast estates at Studley Royal, near Ripon, Yorkshire. The properties of most of the Company's Directors, however, were confiscated. It was a scandal beside which contemporary so-called 'Sleaze' pales to insignificance. Nevertheless, despite its history, the South Sea Company managed to continue its existence, making modest profits, but sold most of its rights in regard to Latin America and Spain to the Spanish Government in 1750. It survived until 1853, and in its later years was largely involved in the Greenland whaling fisheries. For a period (1789-92) Charles Lamb (1775-1834), the essayist and humourist, worked as a clerk in the London offices of the South Sea Company.

London suffered immeasurably from the collapse of the Bubble, and the slave trade in London was virtually destroyed, although Bristol profited, and Liverpool (on a far extended scale). Many Liverymen of the City of London were ruined, as the records of some Companies (which make sobering reading) make clear, and so resources were strained. The Irish Society had considerable difficulties letting its fishings from precisely that time, and it is clear there was a major problem with finance that only resolved itself considerably later (the price of salmon alone fell to very low levels, e.g. in 1721, when it stood at only £12 Irish per ton). Ripples of the disaster spread out over a very wide area, and affected a large number of people. Ulster did not escape, partly through the Londoners' involvement in the province. It seems to have been rather a grim period, one way or another.

The Bishops and the Diocese, 1718-68

As has been made clear, Presbyterians in the diocese of Derry had little about which to rejoice. The Anglican see, however, offered attractions to Anglican clergymen. After Hickman's death, a protégé of the Ormondes, John Hartstonge (1654-1717), was translated to Derry from the see of Ossory in 1714. Although Hartstonge only held the bishopric for a brief period, he again caused problems by presenting a clergyman to the living of Camus Macosquin in 1716. The Master and Wardens of the Merchant Taylors' Company (which had the right to the advowson) made representations to The Irish Society for help in sorting things out, so The Society was obliged to investigate 'all the former proceedings' in order to establish the facts[78] relating to all the advowsons in the Londonderry Plantation, some of which seem to have reverted to the bishop by default,[79] as Mogridge had warned would happen[80] unless careful stock was taken, noted, and referred to. Clearly The Society was so constituted that its rights were being lost sight of at regular intervals.

Hartstonge was succeeded by St George Ashe (1658-1718), who did not live long, and he, in turn, was followed by William Nicolson (1655-1727),[81] who became Bishop of Derry in 1718, an appointment that demonstrated the wish of the Whigs to have an episcopal bench of Whiggish persuasion in both the English and Irish House of

[76] *D.N.B.* (1917), **i**, 204.
[77] *Ibid.*
[78] Schultes (1822), 95.
[79] The studies of the late Mr. Hugh Alexander Boyd are illuminating in this respect.
[80] Moody and Simms (ed.) (1983), 279-421.
[81] James (1956), *passim.* See also *D.N.B.* (1917), **xiv**, 500-3.

Lords. The bishopric of Derry was then worth £2,000 per annum, a satisfactory sum at the time, and the new bishop did not long delay practising nepotism on an heroic scale, ensuring his younger son, son-in-law, and nephews were given benefices.[82] The lucrative deanery of Derry, however, went to George Berkeley (1685-1753) in 1724, who was to busy himself promoting Anglicanism in America before becoming Bishop of Cloyne in 1734. On his arrival in the diocese of Derry, Berkeley found Londonderry to be run by 'good Churchmen', and the city to be 'throughout English, being a colony from London'. He thought the location 'agreeable … , the town standing on a peninsula in the midst of a fair spreading lake, environed with green hills …' and the settlement 'the most compact, regular, well built town' … with … 'the town house (no mean structure)' standing 'in the midst of a square piazza from which there are four principal streets leading to as many gates. It is a walled town, and has walks all round on the walls planted with trees, as in Padua'.[83]

The bishop,[84] on the other hand (who had been translated from the see of Carlisle), was deeply shocked by the poverty he saw in his diocese. He had 'never beheld … such dismal marks of hunger as appeared in the countenances of most of the poor creatures' that he met 'with on the road. The wretches ly in reeky sod-hovels, and have generally no more than a rag of coarse blanket to cover a small part of their nakedness … These sorry slaves plow the ground to the very tops of their mountains, for the service of their lords: who spend the (truely rack-rent) at London. A ridge or two of potatoes is all the poor tenant has for the support of himself, a wife and (commonly) ten or twelve bare leg'd children. To complete their misery, these animals are bigoted papists: and we frequently meet them trudging to some ruin'd church or chapel, either to mass, a funeral, or a wedding, with a priest in the same habit with themselves'.[85] The bishop also noted in 1721 that one of his coach-horses was killed in an accident, but before the hide could be taken off the dead animal some 50 or 60 'cottagers' armed with axes and cleavers, immediately 'divided the carcase', every man 'carrying home his proper dividend for food' for his respective family.[86] Nicolson was also concerned about lawlessness, the difficulties of bringing criminals to justice, and the fact that many Irish murderers believed 'there was no more sin in killing an Heretick, than in knocking a Wolf on the head'.[87]

From early in the century poorer classes of people began to erect houses huddled near the walls of Londonderry although the Corporation did what it could to prevent this), many of them being Roman Catholic Irish. Some were car-men (those who drove cars or carts, i.e. carters) who had insufficient grazing for their horses, which then ruined private gardens and other property. Londonderry became 'overburdened' with poor, the children of which were often left as a charge on the parish. Several poor people moved into the city and suburbs as servants to Protestant citizens, and numerous Roman Catholics settled in the Long Tower district.[88] But, apart from the Roman Catholics, there were many Presbyterian families in the diocese of Derry, to which the bishop was reasonably sympathetic, supporting the limited Toleration Act[89] of 1719 that exempted Protestant Dissenters from obligations to attend services of

82 Mant (1840), ii, 445.
83 Quoted in Lacy (1998), 150-2. See Stock (1777), *passim*, and *D.N.B.* (1917), **ii**, 348-56.
84 James (1956), *passim.*, and Ware (1739/45), *passim.*
85 James (1956), 247.
86 James (1956), *passim.* See also *Ulster Journal of Archaeology* (1954), **xvii**, article on Bishop Nicolson's letters.
87 *Ibid. (U.J.A.)*, 180.
88 Lacy (1998), 152-3; Parker (1851), *passim.*
89 6. Geo. I, c. 5.

the Established Church and removed the penalties levied on Dissenting ministers from the time of the 1666 Act of Uniformity.[90] However, Nicolson was opposed to anything that might erode Anglican hegemony of public office.[91] Of Roman Catholics, his opinion was that they were essentially disloyal: ruefully, he noted that in spite of 'all our Acts of Parliament, unlicensed priests swarm amongst us'.[92] Among attempts to reduce the 'swarm' was an 'anti-popery' Bill of 1719 by which unregistered priests found in Ireland after 1 May 1720 were to be branded on the cheek, a penalty amended by the Irish Privy Council to castration, but the English Privy Council, horrified, rejected this. Included in this Bill was an attempt to invalidate reversionary leases by Roman Catholics, and it was on this account that the House of Lords rejected it.

Nicolson, who as Bishop of Carlisle (not exactly the most prosperous part of England) obviously found the squalor and poverty of his Irish diocese very distressing (and even horrifying), nevertheless put up with the shock to his system and resided in his diocese, where he affected considerable improvements, both spiritual and material. During his 1719 Visitation he noted with satisfaction the appearance of 'fifty of the best, and richest, clergy that are in any one diocese in this Kingdome'.[93] Gratifying increases in numbers taking Communion in the cathedral were recorded, and Nicolson was as zealous as Bishop King in visiting the more remote parts of his diocese. He supported the supremacy of the British House of Lords over the Irish House (of which he, of course, was a member): he thus ran contrary to the views of Archbishop King and others who favoured a greater degree of independence for the Irish Parliament, a controversy Nicolson called a 'little Ruffle'.[94] Industrious and intellectually curious, Nicolson was an effective prelate and an astute politician who did much for his diocese. Translated to the archbishopric of Cashel in 1727 he died a month later, so was unable to make anything of his exalted new position. During his time as Bishop of Derry there were various concerns connected with proposals to create a major port at Rathmullan on Lough Swilly (Co. Donegal) which The Irish Society and the Corporation of Londonderry opposed 'as likely to be prejudicial' to the city's 'rights and interests',[95] and in 1726 the first of a series of harvest failures obliged The Irish Society and other bodies to raise subscriptions to purchase corn for the poor, a state of affairs that continued for several seasons until 1730. Given all these concerns, charitable efforts and endemic problems, it is with something of a jolt, therefore, that we learn of the burning at the stake in 1725 outside the Bishop's gate of the city (within yards of the cathedral) of Cicily Jackson, 'servant to the bishop', for murdering her natural child.[96] We often think of Georgian times in a different light, but it is as well to recall that such barbarities were then perpetrated.

Under Henry Downes (1667-1735), Bishop of Derry from 1727 to 1735, there were 35 beneficed clergy and 22 curates in the diocese, and in the cathedral at 'great festivals' there were 500 communicants, a gratifying improvement when it is remembered that less than a century earlier the survival of Anglicanism under the Protectorate looked decidedly unlikely. Bishop Downes established the Clergymen's Widows Fund in the diocese, and when he died left money for the relief of the

90 17 & 18 Chas. II, c. 6.
91 Orr (1997), 63.
92 *Ulster Journal of Archaeology* (1954), **xvii**, 180.
93 *Ibid.*, 177.
94 *Ibid.*, 179.
95 Schultes (1822), 98.
96 Colby (1837), 48.

poor.[97] It seems to have been Dean Berkeley who was mostly in charge of the cathedral, by that time a 'substantial fabrick' ... with ... 'a good steeple, a ring of bells, a good organ, and every thing necessary for the decent performance of Divine Service'.[98]

Downes was succeeded by Thomas Rundle (*c*.1688-1743), bishop from 1735 to 1743, who in his earlier years had been tainted with Arianism,[99] a fact which caused him to be opposed when nominated for the see of Gloucester. He seems to have found Derry 'an easy Diocese', with clergymen 'all regular, decent, and neighbourly', although he deplored the tendency of some curates to marry with only about £40 per annum to support them and their families.[100] Carew Reynell (1698-1745) followed as bishop from 1743 to 1745, and had little time to make any impact. George Stone (*c*.1708-64) was bishop from 1745 to 1747 before being translated to the primacy of Armagh where it was said he saw himself as a second Wolsey,[101] carrying considerable political clout. He, in turn, was succeeded by William Barnard (1697-1768), bishop from 1747-1768, largely an absentee, like other 18th-century bishops of Derry (with the exception of Bishops King and Nicolson). His episcopate was followed by that of Frederick Augustus Hervey, a bishop of marked eccentricity, who nevertheless was to enrich County Londonderry in various respects. His career will be outlined below.

Emigration

Throughout the century, beginning seriously in 1718, many Ulster-Scots left the north of Ireland for North America, thereby undoing one of the main aims of the Plantation. Archbishop King, observing the phenomenon as it began in earnest, noted that 'no papists stir',[102] for only Protestants were leaving, and the Establishment began to worry about the emigration and the tenacity of Roman Catholic Irish in staying put and paying exorbitant rents which the canny Ulster-Scots refused to countenance. It should be remembered that many Presbyterian Planters from Scotland had only been in Ulster for a relatively short time, and the obviously inferior status of 18th-century Ireland, with all its attendant problems, did not encourage all of those Ulster-Scots to remain where they did not enjoy equal status with Anglicans.

On the face of it, linen had seemed to be Ulster's salvation, but the tenant farmers benefited but little, for the landlords increased rents, and the price of land 'kept pace with the linen manufacture'.[103] One of the results of the wars of 1689-91 was that lands were often leased for 21- or 31-year terms, but massive immigration from Scotland, the exploitation of improvements made during the short-term leases, and the tendency of landlords to charge more if linen was being manufactured on the lands drove rents up. On the Mercers' Company Proportion in County Londonderry, for example, much had been destroyed in the great rebellion from 1641, but in 1658 the Company leased its Proportion to Gervaise Rose for a fine of £500 and an annual

[97] Mant (1840), **ii**, 366-8 and *passim*. See also Orr (1997), 65-7.

[98] Quoted in Orr (1997), 67.

[99] A heresy promulgated by Arius (d. 336) that held the Three Persons of the Trinity were not coequal and coeternal, but that the Father preceded the Son, and the Holy Spirit was inferior to both.

[100] Rundle (1789), clix.

[101] Mant (1840), ii, 603.

[102] King, Sir Charles Simeon, Bt. (1908), 207-8. See Dickson (1966), Ford (1915), Mant (1840), Phillips (1933), Perceval-Maxwell (1990).

[103] Copies of papers of The Merchant Taylors' Company, Box 126, No. 33, Public Record Office of Northern Ireland.

rent of £300 for a term of 41 years. By 1663 the Jackson family of Coleraine was in possession for the same fine and rent, but in 1714 the Proportion could command a fine of £6,000 and an annual rent of over £400. Under the terms of the lease the 'farmer' was obliged to build a manor house, to plant trees, to enclose the waste lands and to encourage the linen industry.[104] Needless to say, these requirements, the hefty fine, and the rents pushed up costs all down the line and exacerbated the problems of the small tenant-farmers, causing them to live in a state of permanent insecurity and poverty. This system was endemic and led to a century of continuous bleeding of the resources of an impoverished land suffering from many years of warfare and political instability. In England, great estates were being properly managed, run on sound principles, and developed under the direction of educated agents versed in all aspects of advanced agriculture. In Ireland, notably on the Company Proportions, management was poor during the 18th century, and neither the chief landlord (the Company) nor the 'farmer' was much concerned with improvements or with ploughing back capital. All too often the 'farmer' was a glorified rent-collector who could take for himself what he could after the chief landlord had been satisfied. Matters were made worse after the South Sea Bubble burst, and the Londoners sought to recoup their huge losses, not least from their estates in Ulster.[105] About a third of the total rents in the whole of Ireland was siphoned off to Great Britain in 1729, and so the proportion of rent that did not get spent in Ireland was very high, causing resentment against absentee landlords who appeared to 'pillage' the country in order to spend the 'product of thousands of poor people' on 'vanity and luxury' in fleshpots such as Bath.[106]

It has to be said that, regrettable though the state of tenants was in County Londonderry during the 18th century, it was a lot better than the oppression endured under private individuals in south Antrim and the Belfast area that led to the 'Steelboy' disturbances[107] from 1769. Conditions that lead to emigration, however, are not only determined by problems at home, but by the attractions (real or imagined) offered by the place to which potential emigrants aspire. In 1636, during the Wentworth period, there was an abortive attempt by 140 persons to leave Belfast Lough for New England, but bad weather forced the ship back. Discontent among Ulster Scots in the 1680s encouraged small numbers to emigrate as a result of 'Episcopal Aggression',[108] but this had the effect of establishing footholds in America, and attracting potential settlers who were friends or relatives thereafter. It is perhaps significant that some of the emigrants from 1718 were encouraged and even led by Presbyterian ministers: William Boyd, minister in the Merchant Taylors' 'capital' of Macosquin, promoted emigration to Boston, Massachusetts, and James McGregor, Presbyterian minister at Aghadowey, seems to have seen himself as a latter-day anti-episcopal Moses leading his flock to the Promised Land.[109] Approximately 1,000 people from the north of Ireland landed in Boston in 1718, and some settled in New Hampshire, where Derry and Londonderry attest to their success in founding settlements.

Now the enthusiasm for emigration, some (at least) of which was whipped up by Presbyterian ministers, is rather curious, for the accession of King George I in 1714

104 Mercers' Company Acts of Court, 1714-31.
105 Curl (1986), 130-1.
106 Dickson (1966), 14.
107 *Ibid.*, 14-15.
108 Ford (1915), *passim*, Dickson (1966), 20.
109 Dickson (1966) 21, 26-30, 104, 127, 222n.

and the rise of the Whigs had removed some of the difficulties faced by Irish Presbyterians. The *Regium Donum* was increased, and in 1719 the Toleration Act[110] became law, easing, as explained earlier, the restrictions on Protestant Dissenters. In reality, toleration in County Londonderry and elsewhere had been practised for at least five years before it reached the statutes, so there must have been other reasons why Presbyterian ministers were so keen to leave.[111]

Reasons are not hard to find.[112] The Presbyterians in Ireland were riven by dissent among themselves, and it became very difficult for some ministers in Ulster to obtain even the bare necessities for life, being 'forc'd to lay down their charge … and transport themselves to America'.[113] In some instances, after the worst of discrimination against Presbyterians had been officially removed, we learn of ministers 'bellowing from their pulpits against ye Landlords and ye Clargey, calling them Rackers of Rents and Scruers of Tythes'.[114] Certainly tithes caused much resentment among poor Presbyterians who objected to being forced to pay to maintain a Church whose services they did not attend and whose clergy were often absentees. Tithes also ate into the small margin of profit (if any) made by subsistence farming while rents were high and increasing year by year. The observant Hugh Boulter (1672-1742),[115] Archbishop of Armagh from 1724, noted that very little remained to any small tenant-farmer after he had paid his rent. However, to the ordinary Presbyterian a landlord and a rector were much of the same, each collecting money that was scarce. Even worse was the system of 'canting' tithes to tithe 'farmers' who paid a sum for the privilege of collecting the tithes which were thereby increased. The tithe farmers were likened to wolves left behind by the shepherds to take care of the flocks in their absence (often in London, Bath, or elsewhere). Those 'wolves' also 'screwed' the tenants and used the poor people very severely.[116]

So tithes and high rents played their parts in encouraging emigration, but smouldering resentment also stemmed from the various restrictions imposed on Dissenters (e.g. being barred from official positions, having their places of education declared illegal, and having the validity of their marriages questioned), which branded them as inferior to Anglicans. When it is remembered that toleration of Presbyterian forms of worship was only granted in the teeth of bitter opposition from some Anglican bishops in Ireland, something of the hostility may be understood that still survives today in Ulster between members of the Church of Ireland and the Presbyterians. Jonathan Swift (1667-1745) observed that the 'screwing' of tenants had reduced the people to worse conditions than those suffered by the Poles, and that virtually everything was taken from them to pay their landlords, their tithes, and their taxes.[117]

Worse was to come, for abnormal weather conditions (e.g. the very hot and dry 1723) ruined the crops and reduced the tenants to penury. 1727 and the following two years also saw climatic inclemencies that severely reduced crop yields and produced near-famine conditions just as rents were jacked up. Matters were made worse by the purchase of corn to make up for losses in Great Britain. Failure of economic stability caused widespread misery and desolation and created a promising and lucrative field

110 6 Geo. I, c. 5.
111 Dickson (1966), *passim*; Ford (1915), *passim*.
112 Mant (1840), 333 *et seq.* .
113 Quoted in Dickson (1966), 28.
114 *Ibid.*, Note 1.
115 Boulter (1770), *passim*.
116 *Ibid.*, 40-41.
117 Swift (1720), 25 and *passim*.

in which emigration-agents could flourish. Rosy pictures of life across the Atlantic were painted, and it seems that these favourable accounts, together with economic deprivation and famine, led many to leave Ulster in the 1720s. In 1729 alone 1,155 emigrants from Ulster landed in Philadelphia.

The lure of America was very powerful, especially when promoted by agents and by captains of ships seeking passengers for what was a profitable trade. Tenants were supposed to become landlords quickly, and all sorts of benefits were said to await the unwary and gullible who flocked to the ports to take ship. Emigrants without means to pay for the passage often signed an indenture by which they undertook to serve the master of the ship or those to whom he assigned his interest for a specified period. Once the emigrant had landed in America the indenture was sold to the highest bidder. Some emigrants undertook to pay the fare within an agreed time by raising or earning money in America, but if they failed to redeem the pledge, then their services were sold by the ship's master as though the emigrant was an indentured servant. Even those capable of paying for their one-way journey often had to wait for so long before a ship sailed that their passage-money was gone by the time they embarked so that they, like those without means, had to mortgage their future labour by signing themselves into lowly positions. Whilst many of the emigrants came to grief and rued the day they ever decided to leave Ulster, others played no small part in the creation of the United States, and some families rose to positions of eminence. Andrew Jackson (1767-1845), for example, 7th President of the U.S.A., was the son of emigrants who left Carrickfergus, Co. Antrim, in 1765; William McKinley (1843-1901), 25th President, was descended from Scots-Ulster emigrants of the 1740s from Co. Antrim; Thomas Woodrow Wilson (1856-1924), 28th President, had ancestors from Ulster; and there were many other Americans who made names and fortunes for themselves whose forbears were of Ulster-Scots stock. Contrary to popular belief, Irish Roman Catholics did not constitute the majority of emigrants in the 18th century, but left in droves from the 'Hungry Forties' (the 1840s) when potato blight wrecked the agricultural economy. This does not mean that no Roman Catholics or Anglicans emigrated in the 1700s, because they did, but by far the largest numbers who sailed from Londonderry and other ports in Ulster for British North America were Ulster-Scots Presbyterians. Francis Makemie (1658-1708), a Presbyterian minister, emigrated in 1682, and, with other emigrants, organised the first Presbytery in America in Philadelphia in 1706, becoming Moderator. From that time he was in almost constant difficulties with the authorities in New York and Long Island who accused him of transgressing various enactments. Clearly, hopes that Anglican oppression of Presbyterians would not occur in America were merely wishful thinking.[118]

Emigration was not only encouraged by the agents (who took their cut from what was a very lucrative trade) and by the sea-captains, but by the many advertisements that appeared in the public prints, especially in Belfast and Londonderry. The main ports of embarkation for colonial America were Newry (Co. Down), Belfast, Larne and Portrush (both Co. Antrim), and Londonderry. Most people emigrating from the Bann Valley or the area round Coleraine left from Londonderry or Portrush, as the entrance to the Bann was extremely dangerous for sailing-ships. Word sometimes came back to Ulster recounting the horrors of the transatlantic voyage. Not only might a ship have to lie at anchor for many days or even weeks before a fair wind rose to bear it westwards, but storms, pirates, and other dangers threatened the often

[118] Dickson (1966), is full of information on these matters.

small vessels. Voyages could take seven to ten weeks or more,[119] while overcrowding, shortage of provisions and water, and appalling lack of attention to hygiene (that often converted ships to floating pest-houses) made the experience so horrible it hardly bears thinking about. Ships often brought bulky flax-seed to Ireland (one of the few commodities that could be imported without official interference) and took linen (which took up less room) back to America, so emigrants could be accommodated on the voyage west. Apart from interminable delays in sailing, passengers were often prevented from disembarking in America if fever had broken out on board, and had to stay on the stinking ships until, supposedly, danger of infection had passed.[120] Starvation and thirst were by no means unknown (often because ships were becalmed or blown off-course by westerly storms): in 1729, 175 people died on two ships on a journey from Ulster to Pennsylvania; in 1741 six of the 46 people who died on a hellish voyage from Belfast to Philadelphia were eaten by the 60 survivors;[121] and, of the 300 emigrants who sailed from Londonderry in 1772, 80 died and the remainder disembarked at Hampton Roads virtually skeletons, hardly able to walk.[122] The chances of survival for any child born *en route* to America were almost nil, and the mothers often died too. Few children under seven years of age were alive by the time passengers disembarked: on one voyage in 1774 only one of the 50 children under four years of age survived the journey.[123] Portholes were introduced only gradually to improve ventilation, so the stench, when the sole mode of ventilation was the hatchway, can only be imagined.[124] Famine during the 1740s caused by inclement weather encouraged massive emigration which led to even more grotesque overcrowding of the ships, so that in 1741 a hospital had to be provided for German and Irish immigrants by the Provincial Assembly of Pennsylvania. Diseases such as typhus or smallpox, once on board, did very well at the expense of the unfortunates confined to such a small space.

At first, emigrants from Ulster appear to have settled in Maryland and in the New York area, but after 1720 most emigrants went to Philadelphia or Newcastle in Delaware as land was becoming scarce in New England. In any case the Charter of Privileges (1701) that granted widespread toleration in religious matters in Pennsylvania attracted emigrants disenchanted by discrimination. By 1775 about a third of the population of Pennsylvania was comprised of immigrants from the north of Ireland or their descendants, but even then immigrants of Ulster-Scots origin were moving into Virginia and the Carolinas.[125] Charleston became an important destination for emigrants from Ulster in the 1760s: one of the townships established in North Carolina at the time was called Londonderry. Decline of the linen industry in the 1770s again increased emigration, and between 1772 and 1773 about 6,000 emigrants left for America. As desirable lands near the eastern seaboard of the American colonies were taken up and cultivated, so many Ulster-Scots became frontiersmen, facing new hardships and the terrors of attack by native Americans (known once as Red Indians).

[119] The shortest voyage (1772) was 27 days, and the longest (1773) 17 weeks.
[120] Dickson (1966), 206.
[121] Ford (1915), 207.
[122] Dickson (1966), 209.
[123] *Ibid.*, 217-8.
[124] *Ibid.*, 214.
[125] *Ibid.*, 226.

Afterword

One of the most important aspects of the Ulster-Scot emigration was the laying of a foundation of education in America. The tradition of sound education imported by the Scots to Ulster was carried across the Atlantic and continued (a surprisingly high proportion of Ulster Scots, even in humbler stations, was literate). The original building (1756) of the College of New Jersey was called Nassau Hall, erected 'to the immortal memory of the glorious King William the third who was a branch of the illustrious house of Nassau',[126] and owed much to the liberal contributions made by Presbyterians in Great Britain and Ulster. That institution, so closely connected with Ulster-Scots, is now the University of Princeton (founded 1746). Many other educational establishments were founded as a result of Ulster-Scot activities.[127]

It is perhaps symptomatic of Georgian Ireland that short-sightedness and torpor seem to have prevented any counter-measures that might have changed history and encouraged a thrifty people with a respect for hard work and learning to stay in Ireland. The Government, for example, only began to notice emigration when it realised it reduced the Protestant (and therefore theoretically loyal) population, but, the Establishment being largely Anglican, it was equivocal, as most would-be emigrants were Ulster-Scot Presbyterians, and therefore their departure was not altogether regretted by the powers-that-were. However, excessive emigration could have the effect of lowering rents by reducing the demand for land (and so hurt the landlords and their agents, who were, in effect, the Establishment). In the 1720s tentative proposals were made invoking the aid of Presbyterian ministers to dissuade their flocks from emigrating, but unease simmered among some Irish bishops as the Presbyterians would be granted access thereby to the ear of the London Government.

It was discovered that, under a law of Richard II,[128] only lords, other great men of the realm, and 'true and whole Merchants', and the 'King's Soldiers' were allowed to leave Ireland, but anyone else forfeited all his goods. Furthermore, the 'wardens and searchers' of ports were to forfeit their offices and suffer imprisonment if they did not stick to the letter of the law. Archbishop Boulter was very much opposed to such extreme measures[129] as he was deeply concerned about the welfare of those who could not find food or employment, and, in any case, he believed that any restrictions on emigration should entail obligations on the authorities to those forced to stay contrary to their wishes. Boulter was also unimpressed by those landlords who professed anxieties about the well-being of religion, but who, in reality, were more concerned with loss of income when those who had had enough of being 'screwed' voted with their feet and left the country. In any case, enforcement of laws made only a few years earlier was not carried out with much rigour in Ireland, so reliance on ancient enactments of the reign of Richard II was unlikely to be effective. Besides, the London Government did almost nothing to prohibit emigration, despite appeals from the authorities in Ireland to stop the granting of lands in America to Irish immigrants, although it did try to lean on the Dublin authorities to remove the causes that obliged so many Ulster-Scots to leave.

Matters worsened in the late 1760s when violent agrarian protest exploded against rack-renting and other practices of landlords (including evictions of those unable to

126 Ford (1915), 432.
127 *Ibid.*, 447-457.
128 Dickson (1966), 184.
129 *Ibid.* See also Boulter (1770), **i**, 209-11.

pay the huge increases of rent introduced just as the linen trade went into decline). The protestors, including, notably, the 'Steelboys' or 'Hearts of Steel', were harshly dealt with by the authorities, so that many ejected tenants and 'Steelboys' fled to America in the 1770s. In 1775 the War of Independence began in America, and Washington's forces contained a strong Ulster-Scots element (which some have computed as the dominant group in the American army). When it is realised that the Ulster-Scots population (either immigrants or descended from immigrants) was about a sixth of the entire population of the American colonies at the time of the Declaration of Independence,[130] such a claim is not excessive. Indeed, it is beyond the bounds of possibility that the Americans would have won their independence without the determined Ulster-Scots, still smarting from memories and handed-down tales of their treatment in the north of Ireland.[131]

[130] Ford (1915), 526.

[131] Sources for this Chapter are given in the footnotes. An immense amount of material exists on 18th-century Ireland, but by far the best account is Vol IV of *A New History of Ireland, 1691-1800*, published by Oxford University Press. Accounts of the Ulster-Scot emigration are admirably handled in Ford (1915), Dickson (1966), and Perceval-Maxwell (1990). See also Parker (1851) for valuable information on the early Ulster-Scot settlers in New England. For Presbyterianism generally in Ireland the most sober account is that of Reid (1867). For the history of the Anglican Church in Ireland, see Phillips (1933). For emigration from 1815 to the Famine *see* Adams (1935), *passim*.

CHAPTER VIII

The Londonderry Plantation in the Second Half of the Eighteenth Century to the Act of Union

As the century passed into its last quarter signs of greater religious toleration began to appear. In 1774 the oath of allegiance was modified in such a way as to be more acceptable to Roman Catholics, in that they were only required to renounce allegiance to the Stuarts; to repudiate the opinion that heretics might be lawfully murdered, that faith need not be kept with them, and that excommunicated sovereigns may be deposed or murdered; and to acknowledge that the Pope had not, and ought not to have, any temporal or civil jurisdiction within the realm. This was only the prelude to a long series of Acts sweeping away by degrees the whole fabric of the Penal Laws. In truth, whatever may have been the circumstances of the late seventeenth and early eighteenth centuries, it had long become impossible seriously to defend the existence of this code. The Roman Catholics could point to eighty years during which they had never, as a body, raised a weapon against the Government, although two rebellions in Great Britain had given them ample opportunity and perhaps strong temptation. Not only was this so, but among the Protestants the support for legislation of this kind was gradually crumbling away

WALTER ALISON PHILLIPS (1864-1950): *History of the Church of Ireland from the Earliest Times to the Present Day* (London: Oxford University Press 1933), **iii**, 248-9

Introduction

Once again the truth about relations between the London Government and Ireland was demonstrated during the 18th century. It was almost as though the wars of the 16th and early 17th centuries, the 1641 Rebellion and ensuing war, and the battles of the Jacobite/Williamite wars of 1689-91 had been forgotten. Although Parliament in London had shown that it would over-rule any legislation by the Irish Parliament or overturn rulings in the Irish Courts or House of Lords,[1] there was definitely a sense that an Establishment (Anglican and landowning) had been put in place and given powers to keep Irish affairs under control. Should Ireland's growing prosperity threaten Great Britain's economic well-being, though, the Government in London would ensure that this was stopped, and Ireland was treated very much like a colony, but preferably ignored unless notice had to be taken. It always seems to have been thus: England (i.e. the Government in London) only reacted to events in Ireland if forced to do so, otherwise it was not much interested in Ireland: as long as Ireland was quiet and gave no trouble, things were left alone. Immediately after the defence of Londonderry by what was largely a citizen-army of settlers in the City of London's Plantation in Ulster, there were public pronouncements, bombastic rhetoric, extravagant praise, and many

[1] As in 3 & 4 Anne., c. 1 (1704), and 6 Geo. I, c. 5.

empty commitments, but it was not long before those events, like earlier wars, slipped into oblivion. The London Government would show pronounced signs of amnesia, on more than one occasion. The fact that The Irish Society, the Companies, and individuals had to make good widespread damage caused by international events, with very little financial help from the Government (apart from paltry amounts from the King for the repair of, e.g., the cathedral in Londonderry [all of £200] and other structures), pointed to an unpalatable truth: the settlers were largely on their own, and had to make the best of it.

As far as The Irish Society was concerned, it is clear from the vast amounts of records, correspondence, litigation papers, and other material which have survived that it did its best to ensure that the Plantation was managed according to the agreements made with the Crown. Having lost its lands and interests in Ulster once, under King Charles's grasping rule, it was not keen to do so again, and the Companies (which were responsible for financing the Plantation and The Society) were anxious to recoup some of their enormous outlay. Damage caused by wood-kernes, by the Rebellion of 1641 and the widespread destruction that followed, and by the wars of 1689-91 should not be underestimated: a great amount of the fabric of towns, villages, settlements, and isolated dwellings had been completely destroyed and many lives had been lost. The bombardment of Londonderry had also done much damage. Very little help from the Government materialised, and the Londoners and their tenants reluctantly faced the fact that they would have to make things good themselves.

In the previous chapter The Irish Society's difficulties with the woods, the fishings, the Corporation, and the bishops have been outlined. By the 1740s it was clear nothing could be done about the woods, and The Society threw in the towel. Even armies of wood-rangers would have had no effect, for they would easily be intimidated or even killed, and it was always more agreeable to accept bribes and collude in theft and poaching than to be beaten up or murdered. It was the same with The Society's fishings: one man could do little to protect these from determined gangs of armed poachers. By 1803, when John Claudius Beresford, The Society's Agent, reported on the timber growing on the Companies' Proportions, he found the following:

Skinners' Proportion (Mr Ogilby, tenant): no wood whatever, except a few scattered trees … not worth £500;

Fishmongers' Proportion (Mr Beresford, tenant): wood of some magnitude, part mature, and part planted 30 years earlier;

Drapers' Proportion (Mr Rowley, tenant): no timber whatever;

Salters' Proportion (Lord Londonderry and Mr Bateson, tenants): some trees in hedgerows near Magherafelt, but very little besides, probably worth from £500 to £800;

Haberdashers' Proportion (Lord Waterford, tenant [i.e. descended from Tristram Beresford]): no timber, apart from 'an odd tree or two to shelter the houses of the peasants';

Ironmongers' Proportion (Mr Dupree, tenant): nothing except for a small wood of 10 to 12 acres on one of the native freeholds;

Merchant Taylors' Proportion (sold to William Richardson): not a tree 'except at Mr Richardson's demesne, which is just adjoining to the Coleraine Fishery, and which has been entirely planted by the tenant, the late Mr Richardson';

Clothworkers' Proportion (Mr Jackson, tenant): destitute of timber 'except immediately about the demesne of Mr Jackson, which is at the entrance to the town of Coleraine, where there are a good many old ash-trees of some value and some ornamental plantations';

Grocers' Proportion (Mr Conolly, tenant): a good wood of 30-40 acres, but the trees, being young and small, were of little value 'except for the bark, being oak, – that may be worth from £500 to £1,000';

Vintners' Proportion (sold to William Conolly and his heirs): about Bellaghy 'a good deal of scattered timber, but no regular wood or plantation', but the demesne of Castle Dawson had a 'considerable quantity of new plantation and some old trees';

Goldsmiths' Proportion (Mr Ponsonby, tenant): no timber except on the 'demesne of Mr Hamilton Ash', valued at £1,200 to £1,400;

Mercers' Proportion (Mr Stewart, brother of Lord Londonderry, tenant): very little timber of any kind.

Beresford ended his report by stating that 'the County of Londonderry is perhaps the worst wooded county in the King's dominions', which is a shocking indictment of the plundering that had reduced a densely wooded part of pre-Plantation Ireland to such a state.[2]

The fishings, though a problem from time to time, brought in a reasonable income, and remained a major concern of The Society. However, there were major disbursements connected with general repairs and improvements to the Londoners' property that had to be made, and these deserve some attention.

Buildings and Repairs on the Londonderry Plantation

As was chronicled earlier, the Companies paid £100 apiece to The Irish Society to provide 'immediate relief' after the siege and this was duly distributed 'among the sufferers'. Funds were also raised for the rebuilding of the town-house to Captain Nevill's designs **[45]**, and Nevill also prepared a detailed survey of damage done to Londonderry during the bombardment. Large quantities of timber were supplied by The Society for the new town-house, making repairs to the gates, and carrying out other works. Every effort was made by The Society to encourage repairs, rebuilding, and everything necessary to restore Londonderry and Coleraine, including the abatement of rents, supply of materials, and extension of leases. The Society also ensured it was fully informed of what was going on by sending special commissioners to Ulster to establish the facts and take necessary decisions on the spot.

Even though Culmore Fort had been very badly damaged (and was never rebuilt as a fort), The Society 'entered upon' its lands at Culmore, and, as the King appointed a governor there (Sir Charles Fielding rather than Mitchelburn), was obliged to pay his salary (£200 per annum). This was, in fact, a military sinecure, and from 1691 appears to have been united with the governorship of Londonderry.[3] Nevertheless, The Society had to continue paying out £200 per annum until 1861 when it managed to buy the fort and surrounding lands from the commissioners of Woods and Forests for £12,000.[4] Of course there was considerable annoyance caused and expense incurred

[2] Beresford's report is bound in with Schultes (1822), ccxxi-ccxxii.
[3] Smith (1966), 97.
[4] *Ibid.*, 97-8.

over the bishop of Derry's 'pretended right'[5] to the Quarterlands and other properties. There seems to have been a general tightening up of all matters relating to The Irish Society lands at that time, for it was ordered that, before any lease be granted, a survey should be made establishing exactly what 'perches and acres' belonged to each house, and that these should be 'numbered in every lease'. Freehold life interests were also created to give better continuity.

Apart from general repairs and new buildings, the cathedral required much work done to make good damage. The monarchs provided £200, but The Irish Society was obliged to donate various sums. There were also the several churches in the county (The Society claimed to have built or rebuilt 12 of these) which had to be supported and repaired after the wars. A free school was established in Coleraine in 1705 which had to be maintained and the salaries of staff paid, though 'from the mismanagement and incapacity of the master, and the gross negligence of the Corporation' the school was soon in trouble, and it fell into disuse in 1739, but was revived in 1740. Timber was supplied for building the market-house at Moneymore on the Drapers' Proportion, repairing Magherafelt church on the Salters' Proportion, and building a new steeple at Coleraine in 1718-19. More timber was allowed by The Society for building the charity-school in Londonderry, and for repairing Ballinascreen church in 1721 and Coleraine bridge in 1727. New fishing-houses had to be built on the Bann, and others kept in repair. Surveys of Irish Society land were ordered to be made, and Archibald Stewart (*fl.* 1727-38) was employed for this purpose, though the job was inaccurately done and the work had to be gone over again. Proposals for ports at Rathmullan and Ballycastle were opposed by The Society as such developments would have been detrimental to the ports of Londonderry and Coleraine. By 1730 it was decided to build a stone bridge over the Bann at Coleraine, and The Society allocated £500 for this purpose.

However, there were problems with the two main settlements, and The Irish Society had to engage in constant tussles with the two Corporations in order to assert its rights, even though it had wide powers, and virtually everything relating to the governance of Londonderry and Coleraine had to be submitted to The Society for approval, for The Society owned the soil on which the settlements stood. Thus The Irish Society was landlord, guardian, and trustee, with responsibilities towards the two Parliamentary boroughs, the aims of the Plantation, the Crown, the Livery Companies, the City of London, the settlers and their descendants, the Church and the fabric of churches, several advowsons, the woods, and a great deal besides, including the administration of law, common holdings, ferries, gaols and houses of correction, schools, the creation of freeholds, support for the mayoralties and corporations, confirmation of bye-laws, bridges, and much else. It was an awesome responsibility. On occasions, such as the events of 1736 when Londonderry Corporation, 'having manifested a reluctance to conform to the wishes of The Society, in regard to their bye-laws', had the annual grant of £90 10s. from The Society suspended until it 'conformed to the provisions of the bye-laws … ratified by' The Society,[6] the latter body, bound by its charter 'resolutely to maintain' its rights and 'jurisdiction by all possible means', had to take action by appealing to higher authority. The Privy Council of Ireland, in 1738, found for The Society, and in 1740 differences were resolved.

All that cost money, and the chronicler of events regarding The Irish Society cannot but help being amazed by the almost constant battles that had to be waged

5 Schultes (1822), 78.
6 *Ibid.*, 109.

just to retain what had been foisted on the reluctant City of London in the first place. Any estimate of the cost of the litigation is now very difficult, but it must have been astronomical. It is tantalising to speculate what could have been accomplished by The Society and the Companies had not so much capital been committed to defending interests and fighting off predators, including the King, various bishops, and countless others.

Bad weather brought hardship and shortages, prompting The Society to contribute money for the relief of the poor. A school was founded at Coleraine for teaching poor children to 'read, write, and comprehend accounts' in 1740, and a master appointed at a salary of £20 per annum (that appears to have been a resurrection of the 1705 free school), which contrasts painfully with the 100 guineas expended on a gift of a silver cup and cover to be presented to the Lord Chief Justice for services to The Society (which he refused to accept). Other activities at Coleraine included the closing in of the quay 'at the charge of' The Society 'for the benefit of the traders and inhabitants' and the removal of all duties or impositions for 'quayage or otherwise' on 'goods and merchandise imported'. A market-house for Coleraine was also to be built 'at the charge and contribution' of The Society, but afterwards the Corporation would be obliged to 'maintain and keep the same ... in good and sufficient repair'. Sheds and stalls were also to be provided which could be 'taken down and replaced on every market day'.[7] The Irish Society declared that by making such arrangements it would 'promote thereby the good and benefit' of the town and inhabitants. £700 and 35 tons of timber were provided by The Society for the Coleraine market-house. At this point the historian sits up for 'the plan was designed by Mr. Dance, the architect'.[8]

Now this is extremely interesting, for it is the first indication that architectural considerations were entering into the reckoning of The Society. Nevill's Londonderry town-house **[45]** was stylistically old-fashioned for its time (1690s), and St Columb's cathedral in Londonderry, though an interesting work of Gothic Survival, is insufficiently documented in its earlier stages to shed light on the whys and wherefores of its inception. The choice of Dance, however, is significant, for he was no mean architect. George Dance, Senior (1695-1768), was the son of Giles Dance, mason and a member of the Merchant Taylors' Company. Father and son had worked on South Sea House in London, headquarters of the infamous South Sea Company, and George became a Freeman of the Merchant Taylors' Company in 1725. In 1719 he married the daughter of James Gould (d. 1734), surveyor, the designer of South Sea House (built 1724-5 – demolished 1902). Gould and the Dances built the church of St Botolph, Bishopsgate, London (1725-8), and in 1735 George Dance became Clerk of the Works to the City of London (really the City Architect) which gave him virtually a monopoly of the City's architectural work, and in 1737 his designs for London's Mansion House were accepted (built 1739-42). He also designed the churches of St Leonard, Shoreditch (1736-40 – a very handsome ensemble), and St Botolph, Aldgate (1741-4).[9] His designs for the Coleraine market-house (*c.*1740) were realised in 1740-3, but the building was demolished in 1857. It consisted of an arcaded, partly open ground floor, with a court-house on the first floor, a common arrangement in Ireland,[10] and a tower at the west end.

7 Schultes (1822), 117.
8 *Ibid.*, 117.
9 Colvin (1995), 287-8.
10 Brett (1973), *passim.*

46 Coleraine town-house or town-hall, from The Irish Society's tercentenary window in Coleraine, showing what purports to be Dance's building, though it is wrongly shown as four bays plus one bay long instead of 3+1. As the tower is missing, the image must be based on how the structure looked after 1787 when the tower was removed. Note the filled-in 'piazzas' or pentices on the buildings on the right. (*A*)

Proposals for building a new market- and court-house (also called a town-house) at Coleraine were first mooted in 1735, and The Society allocated £200 for this purpose as well as ordering timber to be provided for its construction. The building was to be useful and ornamental, and was intended to galvanise the tenants of the town to build better houses by reference to its sophisticated architecture. Although some early plans seem to have been prepared in Ulster in 1735 (we do not know by whom), nothing further happened until The Society was approached with a memorial concerning the proposed building, and drawings were sent over to London by the Corporation of Coleraine. Dance was asked to inspect the designs and estimates, and was then asked to make a new set of plans which was duly sent to the Corporation of Coleraine and recommended by The Society as 'more agreeable and better approved by the Court' than the original submitted from Coleraine. The Society asked for assurances that the proposed building would be erected according to the approved plans, and in due course the Mayor of Coleraine sent to London an agreement made with Alexander Miller, master-builder and carpenter, to build the market-house. Dance approved the tenders, made copies of the drawings, and was paid for 'attendances and trouble'.[11] Dorothy Stroud, in her biography of George Dance Junior (1741-1825), stated that the tower and steeple of Coleraine's present town-hall were reminiscent of the elder Dance's London churches 'in spite of extensive alterations in 1859'.[12] The town-hall was not 'extensively altered': it was completely rebuilt.

[11] Irish Society Court and Committee Minute Books, Corporation of London Records Office, IS/CC/5, 24 January 1735, 2 May 1735, IS/CC/6, 87, 91, and *passim*.

[12] Stroud (1971), 41.

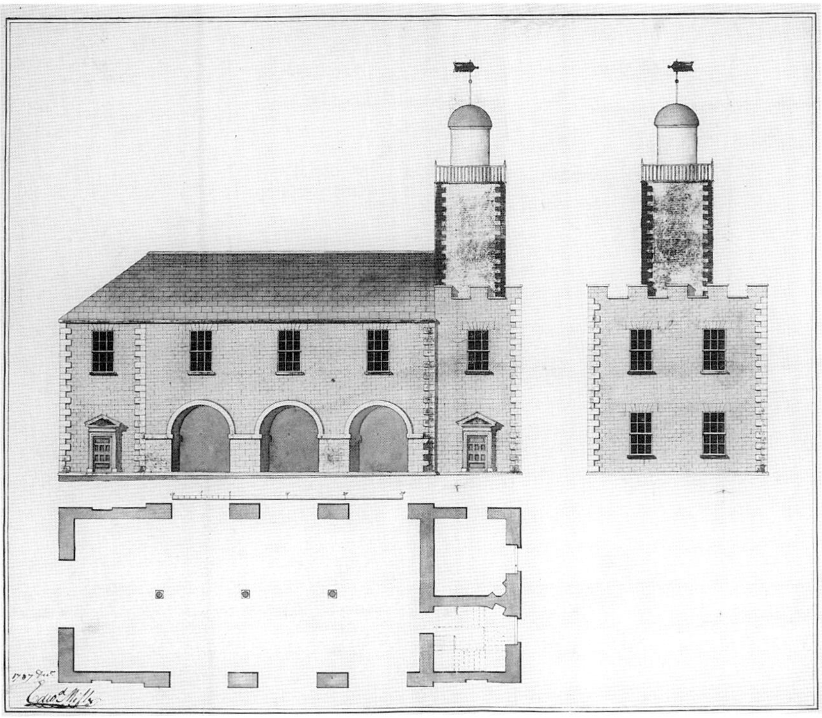

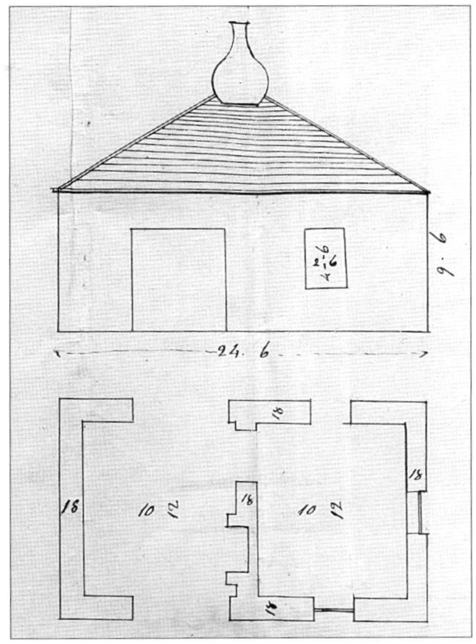

48 Mills's design for the Coleraine weigh-house and store (*c.*1788). (*IS/GLCL/2nd Series No.14 [3]*)

47 Edward Mills's proposals, *c.*1787, for the repairs and rebuilding of Dance's town- or market-house, Coleraine. (*IS/GLCL/2nd Series No. 14 [1]*)

Dance's town-hall was badly damaged by lightning in 1787 and the tower had to be taken down. Edward Mills prepared designs for the reconstruction of the building, and The Irish Society was approached again for money. Dance's original tower seems to have been very plain, and Mills's rebuilding did not add any frills **[46-47]**. The structure was again altered in 1830-5 to contain courts for the Quarter-Sessions, apartments for transacting the town business and the election of members, a news-room, library, ballast-office, and a savings-bank, so it looks as though the open arcaded ground floor was filled in to accommodate everything. Again, The Irish Society funded the works.[13] Mills also provided drawings for a weigh-house and store for Coleraine to cost the princely sum of £47 6s. 7d.: it was to have a curiously bulbous chimney on the roof **[48]**.

The Irish Society provided £2,050 more towards the building of Coleraine bridge in 1745. This project followed the failure of oat and potato crops in the autumn of 1744, resulting in more relief having to be given, and there is evidence of various works being attempted to try to improve the sagging economy. In 1752 directions were given to determine the true value of The Society's property, and moves were made to improve the Bann for the passage of ships. Legislation was passed in 1753 for making the River Lagan navigable and connecting Belfast with Lough Neagh by water:[14] in due course it was hoped that ships would be able to travel from Belfast to Coleraine via Lough Neagh thus bringing new prosperity to County Londonderry, but although Coalisland, Co. Tyrone, was linked by water to Belfast by 1 January 1794, major extensions to the north-west failed to materialise.

[13] Curl (1986), 419-20. See also Brett (1973), 84, 87 (which has an image of the Dance building).
[14] 27 Geo. II, c. 3.

Unrest and Disturbances

In 1765 inventories were made of The Society's records and moves in the direction of granting leases in perpetuity were made. This was a time of general improvements carried out to roads and bridges (the records show Irish Society grants for many bridges) largely because of the growth of the linen industry and the need to transport that product. However, most of the cash needed for roads, etc., was raised by *cess*, levied by Grand Juries on counties and baronies, and this, with the lesser tithes paid to Anglican clergy, led to the 'Oakboy', or 'Hearts of Oak', agrarian protest movement among all shades of religious persuasion, from 1763, mostly in Counties Tyrone, Armagh, and Monaghan, where there were several outbreaks of disturbances.

The Irish Society's grants of stone from its quarries at Termonbacca, and its largesse generally, helped to contain unrest for a while, and relieved the populace from the worst of cess demands. In 1768 the quays at Londonderry were repaired with stone, and every effort seems to have been made to improve communications, the accuracy of information about holdings, and the management of the Plantation. It was also in mid-century that The Society and the Companies began to standardise their method of granting leases. These were often for a fixed term and three lives, usually including a royal personage. With quite remarkable bad luck, some landlords nominated King George III as one of the three lives: as he did not die until 1820, the leases did not fall in until then. The Grocers' and Fishmongers' Companies fell into this trap, and the Ironmongers leased their Proportion in 1767, one of the nominated three lives being Nathaniel Alexander, later Bishop of Meath, who did not die until 1840.

However, from 1769 to 1772 the 'Hearts of Steel', or 'Steelboy', agrarian protesters were active in parts of County Londonderry. As indicated earlier, the 'Steelboy' disturbances were occasioned by rising rent levels, evictions, and objections to other forms of taxation, including cess and tithes, though the price of food played no small part in raising passions. 1770-2 'saw the climax of half a century of rack-renting and the years 1772 and 1773 saw a sudden and disastrous collapse in the linen trade'.[15] The 'lack of demand for linen hit most families in districts' such as the Lagan, Foyle, and Bann valleys and led to 'a shortage of money and to a decline in all branches of trade'.[16] The result was universal distress and widespread starvation, and rents started to fall, 'a striking comment on the immensity of the linen catastrophe which thus succeeded where insurrection had failed'.[17] 'Steelboy' violence flared up during the general re-letting of the Donegall (i.e. Chichester) estates in County Antrim from 1769, when the then Earl of Donegall tried to raise £100,000 in 'fines' for the privilege of granting leases at the old levels of rent to his tenants: this gigantic sum, about three-and-a-half times the annual rental of the estates, was beyond the means of the unfortunate tenants, who were already over-burdened by financial demands. Tenants who could not raise the funds were evicted or their leases taken over by unscrupulous local middlemen (notably Thomas Greg [1721-96] and Waddell Cunningham [1729-97][18]) who raised the rents of some under-tenants and converted the rest of the land to pasture. The result was an immediate outbreak of 'Steelboy' outrages against the landlords and their middlemen. When Cunningham, a magistrate, ordered the arrest

15 Dickson (1966), 77.
16 *Ibid.*, 78.
17 *Ibid.*
18 Clarke, R. S. J. (1988), 107-9, 121; Strain (1961), *passim*.

of one of the protesters (David Douglas) from the Templepatrick area (where Clotworthy Upton [d. 1785], 1st Baron Templetown [from 1776], advertised 96 farms to let [about 4,000 acres in all] in 1769), a group of angry farmers not only marched on Belfast to rescue Douglas, but looted and burned Cunningham's house as well. Five protesters were shot by troops, and feelings began to run high. Cattle and property were attacked, sometimes in broad daylight, and the disturbances spread to other parts of Counties Antrim, Down, Londonderry, Tyrone, and Armagh. Troops had to be sent north, but it is clear the Lord Lieutenant (from 1767), George Townshend (1724-1807), 4th Viscount Townshend from 1764, was sympathetic towards the Steelboys, believing that those disturbances were entirely due to the excessive rents, and that some leniency by landowners, rather than force, would restore peace. Nevertheless, it was a Parliamentary enactment sanctioning force[19] to suppress the 'Steelboy' outrages, and the ensuing trials, that brought peace. As soon as possible, however, this Act was repealed[20] in 1774 as the Government became alarmed by the possibility of further widespread emigration, but not before several 'Steelboys' had been tried and executed. It is worth noting that the 'Steelboys' phenomenon, as a movement of social protest, insisted on its exclusively Protestant origins and character, and has been perceived by some as a forerunner of both the United Irishmen and the Orange Order.

So, unlike the 'Oakboys', the 'Steelboys' had a considerable impact on County Londonderry, where the Salters' Proportion rents were increasing at a phenomenal rate under the Bateson/Stewart régimes. Indeed, early 18th-century leases on the Salters' Proportion show that there were under-tenants, even on farms of only 20 acres or so. It was little wonder that Townshend referred to the Irish as the 'most wretched people on earth … in a state of poverty not to be described'.[21] For this judgement to come from Dublin Castle from the Lord Lieutenant, no less, was a startling indictment. It was little wonder that the wretched settlers voted with their feet and fled in their thousands to the New World, where they became determined and implacable adversaries of British colonial rule in North America.

Attempts were made to reclaim land, such as the enactments of 1772 enabling Roman Catholics to take 61-year leases expressly to reclaim boglands.[22] The collapse of the linen-based economy also prompted conditions by which the Mendicity Act (1772) was passed to establish workhouses and identify beggars.[23] Events in North America obliged the Government to pass the Quebec Act[24] allowing Roman Catholics in Canada to practise their religion while also exempting them from the Oath of Supremacy. Then, not without warning, the storm broke. In 1775 the beginnings of the American War of Independence sent belated shivers down spines. The Government in London learned of the reconstitution of Irish regiments in French service in 1775, and an Act of Parliament[25] was passed to 'prevent tumultuous risings' in Ireland: the last was occasioned by the Whiteboy agrarian disturbances in southern Ireland, starting in 1761, which were similar to the Steelboy outrages in the north.

The American War of Independence is a huge subject, and cannot be dealt with here except to outline its immediate effects on Ireland. In 1777 Burgoyne's army

19 11 & 12 Geo. III, c. 5.
20 13 & 14 Geo. III, c. 4.
21 Dickson (1966), 79.
22 11 & 12 Geo. III, c. 21.
23 11 & 12 Geo. III, c. 30.
24 14 Geo. III, c. 83.
25 15 & 16 Geo. III, c. 21. See also 40 Geo. III, c. 96.

surrendered to the Americans at Saratoga, New York, and in 1778 John Paul Jones, American privateer, twice raided Belfast Lough. Mindful of potential trouble brewing in Ireland, the Catholic Relief Act[26] became law in 1778, enabling Roman Catholics to take leases for 999 years and inherit in the same way as Protestants. In 1780 The Protestant Dissenter Relief Act[27] was also passed repealing the sacramental test imposed by the Act[28] of Queen Anne's reign. In the same year Ireland was permitted to trade with British colonies in America, the West Indies, and Africa on equal terms with Great Britain.[29] There was nothing like an emergency, a major crisis, to force the British Government to sit up and take notice, and the message did not escape watchful eyes in Ulster. When Cornwallis surrendered at Yorktown in 1781, the virtual end of the American War of Independence, events moved quickly.

1782 saw the Catholic Relief Act[30] allowing Roman Catholics to acquire land; the Protestant Dissenter Relief Act[31] declaring the validity of marriages carried out by Presbyterian ministers, and various other measures were passed, including the British Act for the repeal of the Declaratory Act,[32] the Independence of Judges Act,[33] another Protestant Dissenter Relief Act[34] exempting seceders from kissing the Bible when taking oaths, and a further Catholic Relief Act[35] permitting Roman Catholics to teach in schools and act as guardians. Bills approved by both Houses in the Irish Parliament were transmitted unaltered to England by the important Act of 1782.[36] Then, in 1783, came the Renunciation Act,[37] acknowledging the exclusive right of the Irish Parliament to legislate for Ireland, and the 1784 Act for Regulating the Corn Trade,[38] providing for export subsidies when prices were low, and prohibiting exports when prices were high. This was the period when Henry Grattan (1746-1820) was a dominant figure in the Irish Parliament: legislative independence from 1782 was regarded as his personal triumph, but this was largely an illusion. A bigger, more violent storm was still to come.

The Earl-Bishop of Derry

The Irish Society's experiences with the bishops of Derry had not always been happy, as has been indicated above. This changed in 1768, when Frederick Augustus Hervey was translated from the bishopric of Cloyne to that of Derry. In 1779 he also became 4th Earl of Bristol, so he has been known ever since as 'The Earl-Bishop of Derry', sometimes irreverently shortened to 'Mitred Fred'. Urbane, cosmopolitan, cultured, sceptical, and with a mind refreshingly free from cant and hypocrisy, he carried out his episcopal duties with the minimum of conviction and the maximum of style. By 1770 he had made such an impression on his new diocese that he was presented with the Freedom of the city of Londonderry, a compliment never paid to any of his

26 17 & 18 Geo. III, c. 49.
27 19 & 20 Geo. III, c. 6.
28 2 Anne, c. 6.
29 20 Geo. III, c. 10.
30 21 & 22 Geo. III, c. 24.
31 21 & 22 Geo. III, c. 25.
32 22 Geo. III, c. 53, repealing 6 Geo. I, c. 5.
33 21 & 22 Geo. III, c. 50.
34 21 & 22 Geo. III, c. 57.
35 21 & 22 Geo. III, c. 62.
36 21 & 22 Geo. III, c. 47.
37 23 Geo. III, c. 28.
38 23 & 24 Geo. III, c. 19.

predecessors. 'At a time', the *Dictionary of National Biography* informs us, 'when sectarian jealousies ran high', he 'did much by his example to soften their asperities and to cultivate a spirit of toleration.' John Wesley (1703-91), no less, formed a high opinion of the bishop, finding him 'easy and unaffected in his whole behaviour, exemplary in all parts of worship, plenteous in good works'.[39] Although he never came anywhere near the grandeur of Clemens August, Prince-Bishop and Elector of Cologne (d. 1761 – who carried out his infrequent diocesan visitations seated like a mandarin of Cathay in a palanquin decorated in the Chinese Rococo style[40]), he attended the Grand Convention of the Volunteers (the part-time military force raised in 1778-9 to guard against possible invasion and to support law and order in Ireland after regular troops had been withdrawn to fight in America and the Government lacked the wherewithal to revive the Militia), in 1783, accompanied by a troop of dragoons, proceeding from his diocese to Dublin with all the pomp and ceremony of a royal progress. 'Dressed entirely in purple, with diamond knee- and shoe-buckles, with white gloves fringed with gold lace, and fastened with long gold tassels, he entered Dublin seated in an open landau, drawn by six horses, caparisoned with purple trappings, and passed slowly through the principal streets to the Royal Exchange ...'.[41] No Prince of the Roman Church could have asked for more.

Hervey supported Catholic Emancipation, and was on good terms with Dissenting groups in his diocese. Known as the 'edifying Bishop', he managed the finances of the see with great efficiency, and was able to indulge his tastes for building (hence 'edifying') on an unprecedented scale in Ulster. He conducted a diocesan Visitation to ensure all was well, established a superannuation fund, encouraged the erection of glebe-houses, and discouraged the appointment of clergy to benefices from outside the diocese or Ireland. He used some of his income to build roads, develop agriculture, explore geology, restore the fabric of churches, promote the construction of a new bridge across the Foyle, and embellish his cathedral in Londonderry. He built a great house at Downhill (with the exquisite circular Mussenden temple high on the cliffs above the sea), the palace and casino in Londonderry, the Pantheon-like Ballyscullion House (the portico of which now fronts St George's parish-church, Belfast), and a second great rotunda at Ickworth in Suffolk. Intended to house the works of art he collected during his frequent trips abroad (his absenteeism was legendary), his building activities nevertheless gave much-needed local employment, encouraged indigenous talent (such as the architects Francis Sandys (*fl.* 1788-1814], Michael Shanahan, and the McBlain dynasty), and gave County Londonderry some real architecture (e.g. the Mausoleum at Downhill, based on the Roman tomb of the Julii at Saint-Rémy in Provence). Some works at Downhill were erected under the direction of an Italian architect, Placido Columbani (b. *c.*1744), in 1783-5, but Shanahan seems to have been responsible for most of the designs, possibly with additional input from others.[42] Among the churches he re-edified or embellished (with the help of small grants from The Irish Society) were Ballyscullion (Bellaghy), Tamlaghtfinlagan (Ballykelly – with a particularly felicitous steeple), and Banagher. He also organised the building of the steeple as an eye-catcher on Church Island, Lough Beg.

[39] *D.N.B.* (1917), **ix**, 730-2. See also Childe-Pemberton (1924); Fothergill (1974); and King-Hall (1951). Wesley's comments are recorded in his *Journal* (1909-11), **xvi**, 170. See also T. G. F. Paterson (July-December 1966): The Edifying Bishop in *Irish Georgian Society Quarterly Bulletin*, **ix**, 3/4.

[40] Honour (1961), 112.

[41] *D.N.B.* (1917),**ix**, 732.

[42] Rankin (1972), *passim*. Mr. Rankin's study is indispensable, and has shed much light on the confused history of the origins of several of the bishop's projects.

49 View of Londonderry by Paul Sandby (1793), engraved by W. & J. Walker, and published by Harrison & Co. of London. It shows the spire of the cathedral, created by the Earl-Bishop of Derry to designs probably by Michael Shanahan. (AC)

In Londonderry the bishop did much to improve the cathedral of St Columb. It will be recalled that this building, completed in 1633, had been damaged in 1689, and repairs were slow in being carried out. The timber lead-clad spire had been taken down and the lead used to make bullets during the siege. Hervey, who was fond of spires, ordered that the top of the tower should be reconstructed and raised some seven metres, and that a tall slim spire should be placed on top. Unfortunately we have only contradictory illustrations of how the ensemble appeared, but in a painting of the Earl-Bishop by Pompeo Batoni (1708-87), done in Rome in 1778, the cathedral is shown with an elegant octagonal Georgian-Gothick spire resembling the almost contemporary spires of St Malachy's church, Hillsborough, Co. Down (1768-71), and of the cathedral at Lisburn, Co. Antrim, with which we know the McBlains were concerned. However, there is also some evidence that Michael Shanahan may have designed St Columb's steeple,[43] which had to be taken down in 1802 as it started to fail. The spire, with its quatrefoil openings, is depicted in a view of Londonderry drawn by Paul Sandby (1730/1-1809) and engraved by W. & J. Walker of 1793 **[49]**.

Other alterations were carried out at the cathedral in the 1770s. In the 1740s plans had been made for placing all the gallery at the west end, at which time the gallery over the north aisle already existed for some years. Indeed this north gallery, a simple timber structure of plain panel-fronted balustrades carried on Tuscan columns, tucked behind the stone nave-arcades, was matched by a similar gallery over the south aisle, and the whole ensemble appears in a lithograph preserved in the chapter-house of the cathedral **[50]**. Primate Stone, Bishop of Derry (1745-7), presented the organ in 1747,

[43] *Ibid.*

50 Interior of St Columb's cathedral, Londonderry, before the alterations of the 1860s, showing the nave-arcades, galleries, and plaster ceiling, with east window. Note the central pulpit, rudimentary chancel, and furnishings, including box-pews, Bishop's, dean's, and mayoral thrones. (Drawn by A. McFarland, lithographed by Westminster-Gainford, 1862.) (*sic*)

the fine case of which survives in the western gallery. So in Bishop Hervey's time, the cathedral had its 17th-century walls, nave arcades and clerestorey, a restored low ceiling constructed to look like late-Gothic vaulting, rib-vaulted aisles (probably of plaster resembling masonry), a short chancel, a pulpit placed centrally near the east end of the nave, galleries over the north and south aisles, a gallery at the west end, and Georgian box-pews in the nave and aisles. There is an intriguing possibility about the aisle galleries: Nevill's 1689 delineation of the south elevation of the cathedral shows that the aisle windows were always low down in the walls with a large expanse of masonry above, suggesting that there were galleries, or galleries intended, even then **[37]**. Regrettably, the documentary evidence regarding St Columb's is thin, so there is not much upon which to base descriptions before the draconian alterations carried out in the 19th century which will be outlined below.[44]

However, it is probable that some of the Classical mouldings, such as that on top of the external plinth, date from the 18th-century repairs, and there seems to be evidence that, on the north aisle wall, the three-light windows were set lower down than they are today, and that there were approximately elliptical windows punched through the walls above: this arrangement would have enabled light to enter below and above the north gallery. Hervey also presented the bishop's throne (or *cathedra*) to the cathedral: it is a fine piece of furniture in the Chippendale style of *Chinoiserie*.

The bishop seems to have been refreshingly free of any bigotry. Opposed to the Penal Laws, he sought religious toleration for all, including Presbyterians and Roman

[44] Exhaustive enquiries and examination of cathedral archives concerning the building's early history have proved unilluminating.

Catholics. As was mentioned above, many poor Roman Catholics began to settle outside Londonderry from the early years of the 18th century, and the Roman Catholic enclave outside the Bishop's gate, known as the Long Tower district, at the end of the Penal era was served by Father John Lynch (d. 1786), who, with his bishop, Dr. Philip McDevitt (d. 1797 – Bishop of Derry from 1766), took the Oath of Allegiance in 1782, a truly remarkable testament to the achievements of the Earl-Bishop in creating a climate of tolerance. In 1784 Lynch began to construct a church, to which Bishop Hervey gave £210 and the all-Protestant Corporation a further £50. What is more, Hervey, an enthusiastic collector of antiquities, presented four very fine Corinthian capitals he had acquired in Naples (some sources say he gave the column-shafts as well) to the new church, which was completed in 1786.[45] This was St Columb's, or the Long Tower Church, subsequently much enlarged, which many believed (erroneously) to stand on the site of the ancient Irish cathedral. In 1786, with characteristic forthrightness, Hervey gave money to the Roman Catholic rector of Desertmartin whom he described as an 'ingrained & thorough-paced sinner' for the 'Popish Chapel', and in 1784 in County Down, he noticed some unroofed walls intended as a 'Romish Chapel' which could not be roofed because of the poverty of the locals. His Lordship immediately repaired to the priest's place of abode and presented a sum to enable the work to proceed.[46] Hervey was equally generous to the Dissenters, distributing largesse to the Presbyterians at Macosquin and giving liberally to the building of the new Presbyterian church in Rosemary Street, Belfast (1783), designed by Roger Mulholland (1740-1818).

Yet Hervey deemed Presbyterians 'much more dangerous than the Papists' for their principles were 'truly republican'. He said that a 'reasonable indulgence to the Presbyterian and Papist may save the Kingdom'.[47] Here was a prelate of the Enlightenment indeed. Hervey was closely involved with the Volunteers, but that militia quickly became affected by events in American, and thus developed into a potentially menacing force, one of the most important pressure-groups in Ulster at the time. The Irish Society, prodded by the bishop, had made a donation to the Volunteers in 1781, and this organisation became a powerful advocate of Irish legislative and judicial independence, relaxation of the Penal Laws, and a general liberalisation. Hervey himself was Colonel of the Londonderry Corps of Volunteers, but his forthright opinions put him in bad odour with some elements within the Protestant Ascendancy. Having seen the 'bad effects of intolerance' in Italy and the 'excellent effect of a reciprocal toleration through all the great towns of Germany',[48] he argued that trouble in Ireland could be avoided if everyone were to be treated with enlightened benevolence. Feeling that the Crown 'should be the patron of all dissenters, seceders and schismatics whatever', and should 'either pay them or be the cause of their being paid', because then rebellion would be torn up 'by the roots' and preachers preach 'loyalty instead of disaffection': 'where the treasure is', he opined, 'there would be the heart likewise', a robustly sound and reasonable view.[49]

In the 1780s, too, The Society worked with the Corporation to embank part of the strand of Lough Foyle from the old wharf and quay, and to improve the road from Inishowen leading to the Butcher's gate. Major repairs were ordered to be carried

45 Lacy (1998), 153; Rankin (1972), 11.
46 Rankin (1972), 45.
47 Childe-Pemberton (1924), **i**, 238.
48 *Ibid.*, i, 219.
49 Walsh (1972), 31.

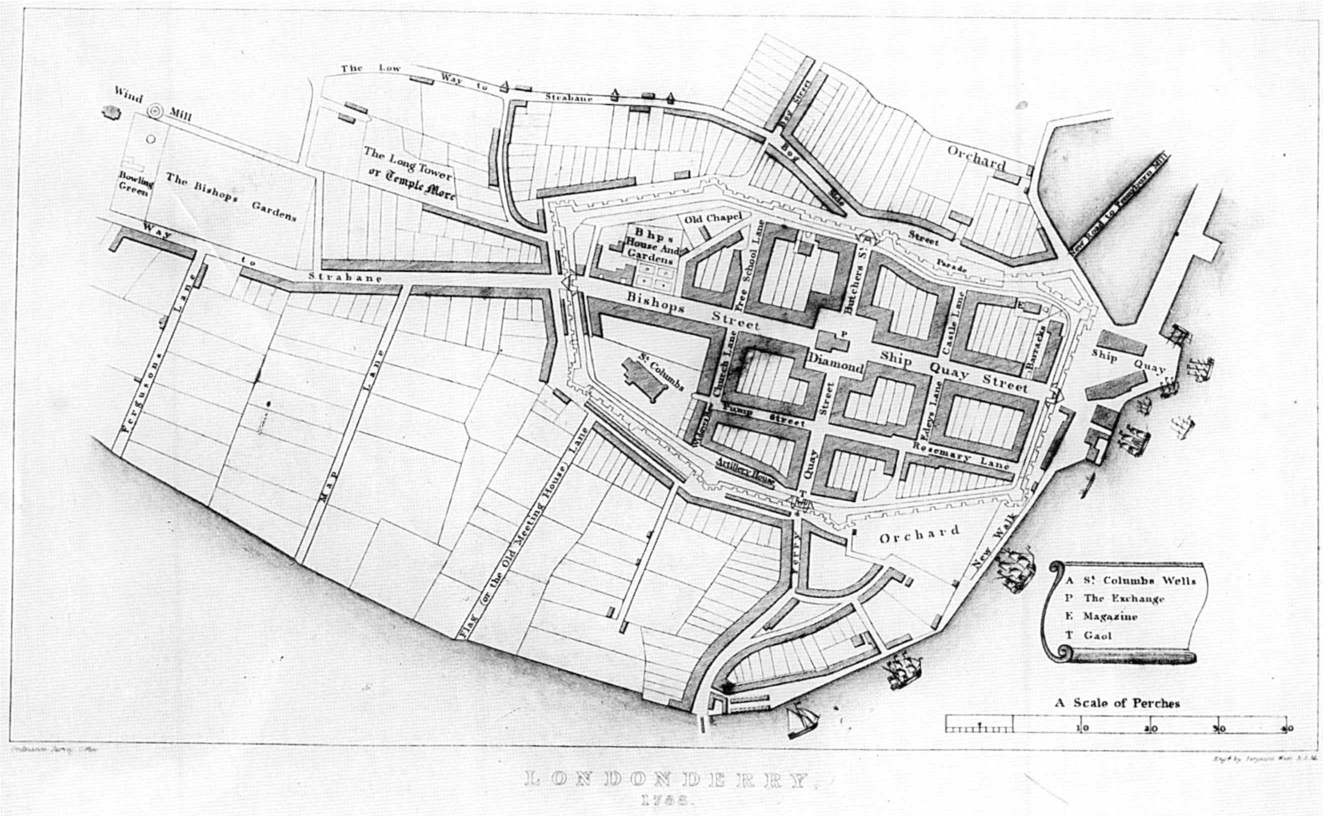

51 Plan of Londonderry in 1788. Access to the city from the east was either by sea, by ferry over the Foyle, or the long way round from the west, where the river was bridged upstream. (*Colby [1837]/AC*)

out at The Society's headquarters in London, The Irish Chamber in Guildhall, in 1785, as the rooms were insufficiently large by then. Before the work could be done, all the furnishings and records had to be moved to the offices of the City Chamberlain 'for their greater safety', which turned out to be illusory, for fire broke out and destroyed much valuable material in 1786. 'Books and papers rescued from the late fire' were ordered to 'be examined and arranged', and a list made, but 'this important work was very negligently performed' and no care 'was taken to investigate the burnt fragments'.[50] Some of this material survives 'in irretrievable confusion'[51] and Schultes attempted some record of these fragments in 1821-2.

So, in the 1780s, Londonderry had been re-edified, and building extended along the main roads out of the city. Within the walls the gardens behind the houses were still extensive, and the Londoners' settlement presented a neat and orderly face to the world **[51]**. However, travellers were inconvenienced by having to wait for the ferry to convey them over the River Foyle, and it was obvious that the relatively isolated position of Londonderry was affecting the city's economy. Things doubtless would have continued but for the intervention of the indefatigable Earl-Bishop, one of whose schemes (he called them, appropriately, 'luminous ideas') was to build a bridge over the Foyle, as travel by ferry was slow and unreliable. In 1786 The Society agreed to the proposition, spurred on no doubt by the £1,000 donation from the bishop, and estimates of £10,000 for a timber structure were obtained. In 1789 The Society granted

[50] Schultes (1822), 132.
[51] Moody (1939), 422.

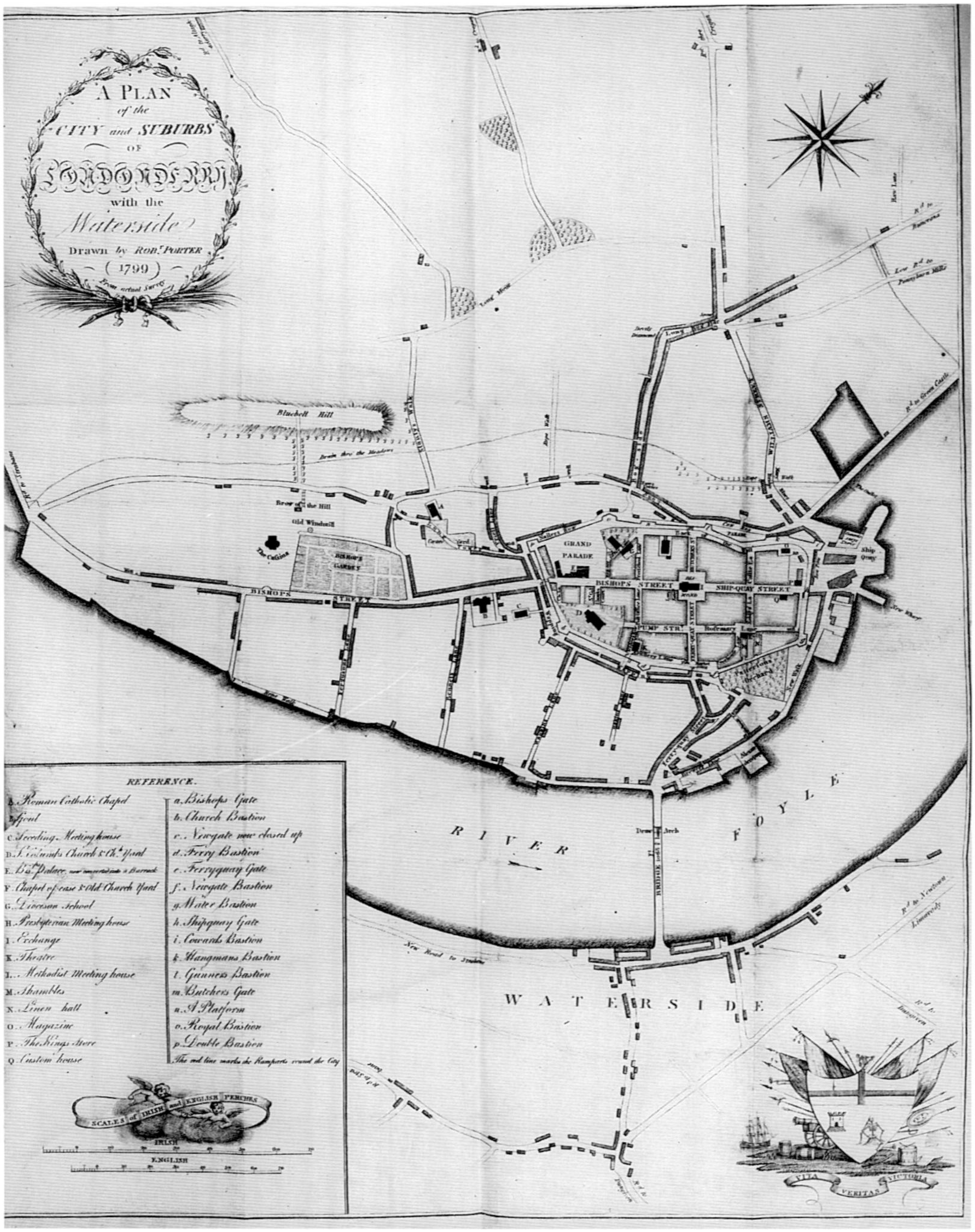

52 A Plan of the city and suburbs of Londonderry, with the Waterside (1799) drawn by Robert Porter. This shows Lemuel Cox's new bridge across the Foyle, linking Waterside with Ferryquay Street. (*AC*)

a lease of the tolls of the ferry to the Corporation to enable that body to borrow money on the security of the tolls. In due course the contract was awarded to Lemuel Cox (1736-1806) and Jonathan Thompson of Boston, Massachusetts, who had experience of erecting bridges in New England over rivers as large and fast-flowing as the Foyle (e.g. the Charles River bridge between Boston and Charlestown [1785-6], which was 1,503 feet long, and the Essex bridge between Salem and Beverly).[52] Cox

[52] *Dictionary of American Biography* (1946), **iii**, 479-80. See Johnson (ed.) (1946). I am indebted to Madame Françoise Roux and Mr. Gerald Beasley for these items.

53 View of Londonderry, *c.*1790s, by J. Ford, showing the Earl-Bishop's cathedral spire (demolished 1802) and the timber bridge built by Lemuel Cox. (*GVS/AC*)

also built (1793) the timber bridge over the River Suir at Waterford, some 832 feet long, of 'American oak'.[53] Construction of the Foyle bridge began in 1789 and the bridge was opened to horse-drawn traffic in 1791. It had a lifting section to enable boats to pass through, and water- and, later, gas-pipes were laid across it **[52-53]**. Arthur Young (1741-1820), the writer, visited Londonderry in 1776 and had to wait two miserable hours in the dark before the ferry-boat took him across the Foyle. Later, *The Post-Chaise Companion Through Ireland* commented upon the 'curious and handsome wooden bridge' opened in 1790, a 'plain and elegant structure [the first of its kind introduced into Ireland]' which, we are assured 'was framed in America and transported thence across the Atlantic. It was built in 13 months at the expense of the Corporation by Messrs. Lemuel Cox and Jonathan Thompson, natives of America'. The 'framed houses from London' story thus gained new potency, but this time there may indeed have been some truth in the matter, for America had plenty of wood, and the well-established trans-Atlantic shipping trade would have made the importation of American timber to Ireland more than feasible, though whether or not the bridge was prefabricated in the U.S.A. remains unclear. The prudent Colby, in his description of 1837, eschews mention of timber-frames being imported from America.

1789, of course, marked the centenary of the siege. In the previous year there had been elaborate junketings to celebrate the closing of Londonderry's gates 'against a bigoted tyrant', including a visit by a warship, *H.M.S. Porcupine*, which answered a 21-gun salute from the walls by returning an equal number. Lundy's effigy was burned, and the Volunteers paraded, re-enacting the ceremony of shutting the gates. A dinner was given in the town-hall attended by local dignitaries, including the Roman Catholic clergy. The 1789 celebrations commemorating the breaking of the boom and the relief

[53] Coyne (*c.*1850), **i**, 161. See also Watkins (1907), *passim.*

of the city included a great procession to the cathedral, led by the Earl-Bishop, and including the Roman Catholic Bishop, Dr. McDevitt, and his clergy, Presbyterian clergy and elders, the Mayor and civic dignitaries, and a corps of the Londonderry Independent Volunteers. A sermon was preached by George Vaughan Sampson (of whom more later), and the procession then moved out to the Bishop's gate, where the foundation-stone was laid for a fine new Neoclassical triumphal arch designed by Henry Aaron Baker (1753-1836), a pupil of James Gandon (1742-1823 – who had been consulted by the bishop about the tower and spire of the cathedral).[54] The sculptured panels and other embellishments of the new gate were carved by Edward Smyth (1749-1812), one of the most gifted sculptors working in Ireland at that time **[54]**.

Hervey left for an extended time (the many 'Hotel Bristols' in Europe named after him testify to his indefatigable energies as a traveller) after the 1789 celebrations, returning in triumph the following year, being met on the new bridge by the Corporation and a Company of Volunteers and greeted by an enthusiastic populace which would probably have had to go on using ferry-boats until the end of time if it had not been for His Lordship's 'luminous idea'. A procession was formed to accompany him back to his palace, and at the great welcoming banquet that evening the bishop's many contributions to the well-being of the city and its inhabitants were extravagantly praised. However, control of the national Volunteer movement, to which the bishop had aspired, passed to James Caulfeild (1728-99), 4th Viscount and (from 1763) 1st Earl of Charlemont, and gradually the Volunteers moved from being a politically radical force to one entirely in conservative hands. Many of the heady aims of the Enlightenment-inspired 1770s and 1780s, including the rapprochement with Roman Catholics, fell by the wayside. In 1791 Bishop Hervey left his diocese and Ireland, and never returned. In 1792 the Corporation which, influenced by the bishop's refreshingly open mind, had behaved with great benevolence, began to oppose any moves against the Protestant Ascendancy. The Earl-Bishop died in his beloved Italy in 1803 and his body was brought back to Ickworth and placed in the vault beneath the church there. Charlemont called him a 'bad father, a worse husband, a determined deist, very blasphemous in conversation, and greatly addicted to intrigue and gallantry'; to Horace Walpole (1717-97), 4th Earl of Orford from 1791, he was a 'mitred Proteus'; and Martin Sherlock (d. 1797), the bishop's chaplain, referred to Hervey as a 'gentle soul, a spirit great and just – the friend of mankind'. In the grounds at Ickworth stands a large obelisk erected by the inhabitants of the diocese of Derry to the Earl-Bishop's memory: the inscription reads that he 'endeared himself to all denominations of Christians resident in that extensive Diocese', that 'he was the friend and protector of them all', that his 'great Patronage was Uniformly administered upon the Purest and Most disinterested principles', that 'various important public works were undertaken at his instigation and completed by his munificence', and that 'hostile sects which had long entertained feelings of deep animosity towards each other were gradually softened and reconciled by his influence and example'. Both the Roman Catholic Bishop of Derry and the 'Dissenting Minister' resident in Londonderry contributed to the costs of creating this eloquent memorial. It is regrettable that the spirit of benevolent, enlightened, reasonableness conferred by the Earl-Bishop on his diocese, which the inhabitants could 'never forget', according to the inscription, appears to have been forgotten, and a brief period of hope gave way to recriminations and suspicion.

[54] Lacy (1998), 154-62.

54 Bishop's gate, Londonderry, by H. A. Baker, in *c.*1890. (*IRC/PH2619*)

The Final Decade of the Eighteenth Century

The key to this shift was the French Revolution. As relations between Great Britain and France once more deteriorated, Ireland once again became a potential threat to Great Britain and a political opportunity for France. In 1791 a group of Presbyterian radicals within the Belfast Volunteers formed a secret organisation that gave birth to the Society of United Irishmen which aimed to obtain Parliamentary Reform, Catholic Emancipation, and other concessions. With the outbreak of war between Great Britain and Revolutionary France the Irish Government was prodded by William Pitt's (1759-1806) administration into making numerous concessions to Roman Catholics: among these were the Catholic Relief Act of 1793, extending Parliamentary franchise to Roman Catholics, allowing them to hold civil and military offices, and removing the statutory bar to University Degrees;[55] and the Militia Act[56] under which each county and county borough was given a quota of recruits to provide the regiments needed to meet the potential menace of politicised Volunteer units and the ever more radical United Irishmen. The Militia Act was revolutionary because it ended a long prohibition against Irish Roman Catholics bearing arms. However, the system of recruitment by compulsory ballot provoked widespread and violent resistance, so voluntary recruitment for the Militia was substituted, realising 12,000 soldiers by 1795. The Londonderry Militia came into existence in 1793, in relatively painless circumstances.

[55] 33 Geo. III, c. 21.
[56] 33 Geo. III, c. 22.

Matters were further complicated by the growing threats to public order posed by secret oath-bound sectarian rural societies organised in lodges with quasi-Freemasonic signs, pass-words, and rituals: the Defenders, for example, was composed of poor rural Roman Catholics, wholly opposed to the existing State, and ruthless in its barbaric cruelties (in 1791 Defenders attacked a Protestant schoolmaster, his wife, and brother-in-law at Forkhill, Co. Armagh, and cut their tongues out); and the organisation known as the Peep O'Day Boys was the Protestant response. Defender violence became common in North Leinster and South Ulster in 1792-3, and the Dublin Society of United Irishmen called on the Volunteers as 'citizen-militia' to take up arms. Revolution was in the air, and an alliance of radical United Irishmen and Defenders to establish a French-style Irish Republic was formed under the leadership of Theobald Wolfe Tone (1763-98 – the Protestant founder of Irish Republican Nationalism) who managed to persuade middle-class urban Roman Catholics to make common cause with radical-minded Dissenters. By 1797 it was clear to the Government that the Militia had been penetrated by Defenders and United Irishmen, leading to a series of courts martial followed by executions, though in Londonderry things were almost trouble-free.

In 1795 there took place an affray between the Defenders and the Peep O'Day Boys at Loughgall, Co. Armagh. This, the so-called 'Battle of the Diamond', led to the founding of the Orange Order, an exclusively Protestant political society devoted to the memory of King William III and the politico-religious settlement following the defeat of the Jacobites. Drawing on ritual and organisational precedents established by the Defenders and derived from the Freemasons, the Order owed its birth to bitter sectarian violence and extreme rural poverty. The reaction to the hideous outrages of the Defenders led to the Armagh responses, concerted attacks on Roman Catholic households in Armagh and neighbouring counties in 1795-6, which caused numerous Roman Catholic families to flee the area, many settling in Connacht.[57] The Orange Order grew rapidly in strength in south and west Ulster in the 1790s, recruiting some landed gentry and penetrating both the Yeomanry (part-time local forces raised from 1796 to counter the threats posed by the Revolutionary Wars and the United Irishmen and Defenders) and the regular army.

The 1798 rebellion cannot be described in any detail here. It began in May in Leinster, and in Wexford the local Militia and Yeomanry were almost wiped out, after which the insurgents lost sight of all idealistic principles and indulged in a particularly nasty bout of sectarian violence, massacring Protestants at Scullabogue, near New Ross, Co. Wexford. When the rebellion broke out in Ulster it was led by the inexperienced Henry Joy McCracken (1767-98) and others, but was quickly put down. The Wexford insurgents were defeated at Vinegar Hill, near Enniscorthy, but although the French managed to land troops in Counties Mayo and Donegal, and a French invasion force was engaged by a British squadron outside Lough Swilly, the rebellion was crushed[58] under the military leadership of Charles Cornwallis (1738-1805 – created 1st Marquis Cornwallis in recognition of his services as Governor-General and Commander-in-Chief in India [1786-93]), Lord Lieutenant of Ireland and Commander-in-Chief (from 1798), to whom the French invaders under Jean-Joseph-Amable Humbert (1755-1823) surrendered on 8 September 1798 at Ballinamuck, Co. Longford. As 2nd Earl (from 1762), Cornwallis had been in command of the British Army which surrendered at Yorktown, Virginia, in 1781, to American and French forces,

57 Connolly (ed.) (1998), *passim*.

58 An attractive and informative source of information on 'The '98' is Maguire (ed.) (1998), *passim*.

thereby virtually ending the American War of Independence, so his victory over the French in Ireland must have been all the more sweet.

The immediate result of this was that the union of Great Britain and Ireland became inevitable. Only within a United Kingdom 'could the safety of Ireland from foreign invasion and internal subversion be guaranteed and emancipation be safely granted to Irish Catholics – a permanent minority in the United Parliament.'[59] Of course the Irish Parliament had to abolish itself, but, being open to persuasion, if the funds were available, did so,[60] and the British Act of Union was passed in 1800,[61] coming into effect on 1 January 1801. The key figure, as head of government administration in Dublin during the crucial period of the rebellion and its aftermath, including the realisation of the Act of Union, was Robert Stewart (1769-1822), Viscount Castlereagh (from 1796), later (from 1812) Foreign Secretary, and (from 1821), 2nd Marquis of Londonderry.[62] Even the Earl-Bishop voted (by proxy) for the Act of Union having been horrified by the excesses of the French Revolution and revolutionary armies, and disgusted by the possibilities of similar descents into barbarism in Ireland.

County Londonderry immediately after the Act of Union

During the rebellion there had been concern for Londonderry because of its strategic position, and the attempted French invasion through Lough Swilly bore this out. However, the Londonderry Yeoman Cavalry had been successfully formed, and it seems the authorities in County Londonderry as a whole were able to ensure that the rebellion did not spread to the north-west of Ulster. The Irish Society gave £100 towards suppressing the rebellion, and voted certain sums for the relief of the poor in Londonderry and Coleraine. By the end of the 18th century the population of Londonderry stood at around 11,000, and the city, a 'neat'[63] Georgian settlement, was still largely contained within its walls. **[51-52]**

From the time of the Act of Union a change of attitude towards the Ulster lands became apparent, and there was a definite movement by The Irish Society and the Companies towards becoming more involved in their properties. In some cases, where property had been let for 'three lives' direct control would not be regained for two more decades, but the Union seems to have galvanised a great deal of interest. In March 1802 hostilities with France temporarily ceased by the Peace of Amiens, and it was in that year that the Secretary to The Irish Society (from 1789-1831), Robert Slade **[55]**, visited Ulster and recorded his impressions in 1803. This valuable first-hand account of the estates of The Society and the Companies was published by The Society.[64]

Slade noticed the 'want of accommodation and the apparent poverty' of the Mercers' Proportion, and immediately appreciated that in a place which never saw the 'face of the owner of the soil, or even his under-tenant' the 'lower order of the people' toiled 'for a miserable subsistence' and saw 'the fruits of their labour carried off from time to time by an agent of their landlord, to be spent in a foreign country'.

[59] Maguire (ed.) (1998), 271.
[60] 40 Geo. III., c. 38.
[61] 39 & 40 Geo. III, c. 67.
[62] Hyde (1933), *passim.*
[63] 'Neat' was a favourite adjective of the period, meaning clean, elegant, decently made, well-proportioned, agreeable, simple with no fripperies, and well-built.
[64] Schultes (1822), cci-ccxvi.

55 Robert Slade (Secretary of The Irish Society 1789-1830) by John Opie (1761-1807), 1806. (*IS*)

The 'want of example, assistance and consolation from the resident land owners' deprived the 'inhabitants of all inducement' to better themselves.[65] Slade was concerned about the poor management of several Company estates, the extreme poverty, the squalor, the bare appearance of the country (denuded of timber), and much else.

On the Fishmongers' lands Slade saw the 'handsome house' built by the tenant, John Beresford, and the new plantations of 'oak, ash, and other timber trees', before proceeding to Londonderry over the 'wooden bridge over the lake [*sic*]'. There, he found the cathedral 'to be in a very ruinous state ... , the weight of the steeple ... having cracked the tower and walls which support it almost to the foundation'. The Irish Society had voted £200 towards repairs, and the Corporation gave directions to take down and rebuild the steeple, at an estimated cost of £2,600. Scaffolding for this work was erected during Slade's sojourn in Ulster.

'The linen-market of Londonderry', Slade wrote, formed 'an object of great curiosity': it was 'held twice in every week, and lasted 'for two hours only, within which short period of time ... linens were purchased ... to the amount of' £5,000 'and upwards in ready money'. The makers of the linen lived in 'cabins' in the vicinity of the city and had 'a few acres of land for the sake of keeping a cow and raising some potatoes and flax' for which, using the produce of their looms, they were able to pay a 'heavy rent'. It was this circumstance, Slade noted, that made the 'Society's land so valuable'.[66]

On the Quarterlands the 'bog-ground' was being destroyed by 'being improperly cut' with the result that turf would 'shortly become very scarce'. Slade suggested that The Society should arrange for careful apportionment of the bog among the tenants, and that a 'bog-keeper' should be appointed to ensure that the land was not misused. Throughout the century The Irish Society was anxious to protect the turbaries, and the Companies also became involved in their conservation. As several tenants indicated they would apply for new leases, Slade recommended that a new survey should be made and that encouragement should be given to tenants to build houses by granting leases for 'a sufficient number of years and three lives'.

Slade argued that accurate maps should be made of The Society's lands, and that many new roads should be constructed. Furthermore, he proposed the erection of a

[65] Schultes (1822), cciii. See also Johnston (1959), *passim*.
[66] Schultes (1822), ccvi.

fountain 'which might serve as a monument to perpetuate the Union', 'draw the people into a state of society, and ultimately lead to some plan for supplying Londonderry with water, which is much wanted'. It should be remembered that water was drawn from wells, which were often polluted, and, although the great River Foyle flowed round the city, its waters (being tidal) were not suitable for drinking. It was also necessary to erect fences, plant hedges, and enclose land which appeared 'like a barren waste, hardly accessible even in summer months'.

The policy of the Companies to let their lands for heavy 'fines' to individuals (who often never saw any part of the estates) brought no benefit to the Proportions, failed to inculcate any feelings of obligation in tenants towards landlords, and created instability and poverty. No improvement could be expected while such a system prevailed. However, the various properties that lay between Londonderry and Culmore had been enormously enhanced because tenants enjoyed security of tenure, landlords engaged the interest of tenants, and, by concerted effort, lands were greatly improved.

On the Clothworkers' Proportion, held by Richard Jackson, the rents had been raised so much in order to cover the 'fine' Jackson paid the Company that they 'produced an almost total emigration to America' and thus 'brought about the surrender of the British Army at Saratoga'. Coleraine, Slade thought, 'would ... be preferred by strangers to Londonderry', and had 'a handsome bridge' over the Bann, a 'sightly' parsonage-house and church, and a 'broad and spacious' main street. He saw the Cranagh 'or fish-house, where the fish are taken with nets ... about two miles below the town' and the 'rock or salmon-leap, where the traps are erected ... about a mile above the town'. There was 'no house of residence for the fishermen at the cuts ..., a matter of serious regret ...'. The 'cut next adjoining the shore' had 'a constant supply of water', and was of little use for taking fish, so could easily be used to drive machinery should The Society build a mill there. Slade was fully aware of the labour and expense necessary to operate and protect the salmon fishery as well as of the threats to it (from flax-growing, the linen industry, and poachers).

Like many before and after him, Slade saw for himself the danger posed to vessels by the bar at the mouth of the Bann, and favoured the cutting of a new canal linking Coleraine to the sea. Near Coleraine Slade saw the improvements carried out by Richardson (notably the planting); the 'little cultivated' Clothworkers' lands; the 'desirably situated' Ironmongers' Proportion; the Earl-Bishop's house at Ballyscullion 'ornamented in a style of eastern magnificence', but 'left unfinished ... the new-built offices ... falling to decay'; and 'Maraghfelt (i.e. Magherafelt) which he mistakenly thought was the 'chief place' of the Clothworkers' Proportion (it was on the Salters' Estate). Timber plantations were few and sparse throughout the county.[67]

The Reverend George Vaughan Sampson

It appears, therefore, that, by the time of the Union, the original intentions of the Plantation scheme had been obscured. In 1802 the Rev. George Sampson's *Statistical Survey of the County of Londonderry, with Observations on the Means of Improvement* was published,[68] a massive book which deals with geology, agriculture, industry, and social conditions of the inhabitants of the county, among other matters. Sampson made numerous recommendations, including the erection of soundly built model cottages

[67] Schultes (1822), *passim*.
[68] Sampson (1802).

by landlords; leases longer than 21 years and one life; the more realistic division of farms (those of four acres or less he said were too small and could not guarantee survival); the squaring of fields; the provision of adequate agricultural drainage; better breeding methods for farm animals; the supply of fertiliser and seeds at prime cost to tenants; the establishment of enormous nurseries for forest trees so that timber could once more be grown on land unsuitable for other crops; the planting of fruit-trees on arable land (on the French model) far enough apart so that cultivation could proceed without difficulty or damage to the trees; massive schemes of drainage and reclamation of the 'slob-lands' (i.e. the mud-flats by Lough Foyle that extended from the mouth of the River Faughan to the estuary of the River Roe); a rational system of storage and transportation of fuel to save time and energy (conservation of the turbaries became of considerable importance and concern to The Irish Society and the Companies, as was mentioned above); the standardisation of all weights and measures on the decimal system; the planting of hedgerows with thorn-quicks to enclose fields and protect soil; and a radical overhaul of the system of rack-renting (i.e. the imposition of very high, excessive, or extortionate rents, sometimes equal [or nearly equal] to the full value of the land, which stripped the poor tenants of any possibilities of improving themselves or their properties).

Sampson and others were agreed on the main problems of County Londonderry: the poor lived in dens of indescribable wretchedness without hope or incentive; absentee landlords were a curse, uninterested in their lands or their tenants other than to screw as much cash out of them as possible; the land, once so well wooded, had been stripped of its trees, and something needed to be done to remedy this; vast areas of bog- and slob-lands could be reclaimed for use, and in any case the bogs needed to be better managed or they would be ruined as a resource (rights to the turbaries were granted to The Irish Society at the very beginnings of the Plantation); holdings were far too small to support the families living on them, as, if any part of the system (making linen, growing potatoes for food, etc.) broke down, rents could not be paid, and eviction and starvation would follow; cash collected from tenants should be ploughed back into the estates to improve them, build houses and other structures, and transform the economy, rather than squandered on dissipations in London or Bath; and a huge transformation and much effort were needed to bring prosperity, civilisation, peace, and other benefits to a land ruined by a century of exploitation and neglect. It is greatly to the credit of The Irish Society and to some of the Companies that the recommendations of men like Sampson were eventually heeded, and an era of great reform commenced, though not until the French Wars were over.[69]

So who was this George Vaughan Sampson (1762-1827), whose two great publications[70] were so important in promoting the ideas that would greatly improve County Londonderry? He was rector of Aghanloo (1794-1807) before being translated to the rectory of Errigal, where he remained until he died, and was for a time Agent of the Fishmongers' Company (1820-4). The references to the metric system and to French farming methods mixing the growing of fruit-trees with other agricultural activities are interesting and significant, for Sampson was a keen observer of Continental (especially French) ideas.

In 1784, having taken holy orders, he became assistant chaplain to John Frederick Sackville (1745-99), 3rd Duke of Dorset (from 1769), when the latter was Ambassador-

[69] Curl (1986), 112.
[70] Sampson (1802, 1814).

Extraordinary and Plenipotentiary to the Court of France (from 1783 to 1789), and it was during that time he imbibed much that was to be of value to him later (not least the rational ideas and humane views of the *Encyclopédistes* Diderot, d'Alembert, and others). In 1789, as noted above, he preached an 'able sermon' in the cathedral in Londonderry during the centenary celebrations of the relief of the city, and in 1790 was appointed Master of the diocesan school in Londonderry before becoming rector of Aghanloo in 1794. Later, at Errigal, he found the parish-church ruinous and the glebe a 'barren and heathy waste': he left the former 'one of the best finished' in the diocese 'and the latter in a state of cultivation and improvement'.[71] As a result of the publication of his 1802 *Statistical Survey* he was elected a member of the Royal Irish Academy and an honorary member of the Geological Society of London. His radical Continental-inspired ideas may also have been influenced by his brother, William (1764-1836), United Irishman, writer, and lawyer, who was exiled from 1799 and eventually deported to America, where he became legal adviser to Joseph Bonaparte (1768-1844), King of Naples (1806-8) and King of Spain (1808-19), during the last's sojourn in the United States.[72] William Sampson had been a friend of Theobald Wolfe Tone, became a leading figure at the American Bar, and eventually took on as a legal trainee Wolfe Tone's son, William Theobald Tone (1791-1828 – who had seen distinguished service in the French army, and from 1820 to 1826 was an officer in the American forces). William Theobald Tone married William Sampson's daughter, Catherine Anne, in 1825, and it was she who painted the famous miniature portrait of the Irish patriot, later published by Charles Joseph Hullmandel (1789-1850), the important English lithographer. The Irish lawyer, orator, Member of Parliament, and defence counsel in almost all the trials of leading United Irishmen after the 1798 rebellion, John Philpot Curran (1750-1817), stood godfather to William Sampson's son (1795-1820), who received his sponsor's names and became head of the New Orleans Bar shortly before his early death. There was another American connection: Michael Sampson (1759-1813), George Vaughan Sampson's eldest brother, was a lawyer, and settled at Sampson Hall, near Wilmington, N.C., where he died.

George Vaughan Sampson, who does not appear to have been harmed professionally or socially by William's activities, was of English descent, though born in Londonderry, and derived his forenames from Colonel George Vaughan (Governor of County Donegal, third in descent from Sir John Vaughan, the distinguished Governor of Londonderry under whom the cathedral had been built) whose sister married a Sampson. The Irish Society became patron of G. V. Sampson's great *Chart and Survey of the County of Londonderry*, the prospectus of which was issued in 1810. This duly appeared in 1813, and was followed by the *Memoir* of 1814 to which The Irish Society and several Companies also subscribed. In this volume Sampson advocated the following:

1. reversion of all estates to their proprietors;
2. the ending of absenteeism, the establishment of a residential class of gentlemen (who would also function as magistrates), and direct improvement of estates by proprietors;

[71] Colby (1837), 97.

[72] *D.N.B.* (1917), **xvii**, 723-5, which states, erroneously, that William Sampson was the son of a Presbyterian minister of Londonderry. His father was the Rev. Arthur Sampson (*c.*1735-81), an Anglican clergyman. See Leslie (1937, 1993). I am indebted to Mr. Malley for these references.

3. a stop to the excessive subdivision of farms and to the process of rack-renting which was causing Protestants to emigrate and Roman Catholics to stay put on ever smaller farms to their ruin;
4. reduction of all rents to reasonable levels;
5. resumption of Proportions under the direct control of the Companies and abolition of excessive 'fines';
6. inculcation of a sense of responsibility towards tenants on the part of landlords;
7. in all new undertakings, where much expense and labour were involved in effecting improvements, leases should be extended to encourage, not punish tenants;
8. the establishment of nurseries for forest trees;
9. planting of boglands for forestation;
10. programmes of draining and enclosing land by means of walls and fences to improve and protect it;
11. a scheme of reclamation of 12,000 acres of slob-lands involving joint efforts by The Irish Society, proprietors, and freeholders;
12. drainage and conversion to arable land of all peat-mosses, any rocky knolls being planted with hardy trees;
13. planting of all thin soils with rape to provide spring food for sheep, and later oil, involving the erection of a mill for processing the rape;
14. amalgamation of small farms to form establishments of 20 to 200 acres;
15. the creation of small townships on each Proportion as trading-centres and residences for workers in new factories to be built;
16. reclamation of all waste lands;
17. a programme of building of farm-houses to suitable model standards;
18. encouragement given to the industrious to stay rather than emigrate;
19. the building of mills at the expense of the landlords;
20. improvement of all roads, bridges, and other infrastructure;
21. the establishment of model schools in decent buildings, with schoolteachers, books, and other equipment provided and paid for by the Companies.[73]

It says much for Sampson and the esteem in which he was held that during the first half of the 19th century many proprietors, including some of the Companies, began to implement his proposals with an evangelical zeal unknown even at the start of the Plantation venture. On the Fishmongers' Proportion, for example, a very beautiful model farm was erected (1823) under Sampson's aegis, and numerous other improvements were achieved. Sampson's funeral-procession from his rectory to his burial-place at Aghanloo was attended by large numbers of people, and it is obvious he was greatly loved and respected.[74] He is commemorated by a mural monument on the south wall of Tamlaghtfinlagan parish-church. It is inscribed:

To the Memory
of
The Rev'd George Vaughan Sampson,
Rector of Errigal, A.M., M.R.I.A., H.M.G.S.L.
This Tablet was Erected

[73] Sampson (1814), *passim.*
[74] Colby (1837), 98.

A.D. MDCCCXXVIII
By the Wardens and Commonalty
Of the Mistery of Fishmongers of London,
As a Tribute of Respect
For his Talents and Virtues
And as a Testimony of Their Sense
Of the Great Services Rendered by Him
To Their Estates in the County of Londonderry
Of which he became Their First Agent
A.D. MDCCCXX;
He died on the X Day of March
A.D. MDCCCXXVII,
And was buried at Aghanloo, of which Parish
He had formerly been Rector

The Evangelical Conscience

Sampson's promotion of concern for the underdog, improvements, reinstatement, philanthropic works, education, investment, and so on was a refreshing change after a century in which the main object seems to have been to get as much cash out of the lands as possible, without any thought given to those who had to provide that cash. This enormous change of hearts and minds did not suddenly occur, but was the result of an evangelical revival within the Anglican Church, the most influential movement of which became known as the Clapham Sect. The last evolved after Henry Venn (1725-97) became curate of Clapham in 1754, and developed a friendship with John Thornton (1720-90), a munificent supporter of the first generation of Evangelicals, whose son, Henry Thornton (1760-1815), was the best-connected member of the Clapham Sect and a close associate of William Wilberforce (1759-1833). Venn's son, John (1759-1813), became the central figure of the Sect after he became rector of Clapham in 1792: he was one of the founders of the Church Missionary Society (1797), an active participant in the suppression of the slave trade, and a tireless campaigner in numerous philanthropic movements. Venn owed his appointment to Clapham to the trustees of John Thornton who had bought up numerous advowsons so that he could present the livings to those of like mind to his own so that furtherance of his principles would be ensured.

Bound by faith, philanthropic zeal, and a network of well-heeled persons in positions of influence, the Clapham Sect sought education and betterment for the poor, extricating them from all future want; the elevation of minds to a state by which self-help would be encouraged; and a concerted campaign against drunkenness, vice, sloth, apathy, and immorality. Clapham was the first home of the Evangelical Conscience, and because so many members of the Sect were wealthy and prominent they were able to exert influence far greater than might be suggested by their numbers. Among the many achievements of those connected with the Sect were abolition of the slave trade, reform of the penal code, religious emancipation (especially of Roman Catholics), the suppression of press-gangs, and the prohibition of the employment of child chimney-sweeps. There can be no doubt that the Evangelical Conscience that evolved from the Clapham Sect was the formative influence on 19th-century England. Never in the history of the Anglican Church has any group within it exerted such a powerful effect on the ethos of the nation. Those steeped in the beliefs and principles of the Clapham Sect included Anthony Ashley Cooper (1801-85), 7th Earl of Shaftesbury from 1851; James Stephen (1758-1832), who married Wilberforce's sister in 1800, and whose son, Sir James Stephen (1789-1859), married Jane Catherine, daughter of John Venn, rector of Clapham, in 1814, and wrote an essay on the Clapham Sect; Zachary Macaulay (1768-1838), editor of *The Christian Observer*, the organ of the Clapham Sect, from 1802 to 1816; John Shore (1751-1834), 1st Baron Teignmouth (from 1798), President of the British and Foreign Bible Society from 1804 until his death; and Charles Grant (1746-1823) who was closely involved in the promotion of missionary work, the building of churches, and the foundation of the East India College at Haileybury, among other activities.[75]

It is clear that the Evangelical Conscience affected the management of the Plantation lands, for the 19th-century *Reports of Deputations* of The Irish Society and the Companies have a distinctly moral and improving tone, and it is clear there was a profound change of attitude from around the time of the Union. The facts that Slade's *Narrative of a Journey to the North of Ireland* was printed by order of The Society, and that so much support was given to and notice taken of Sampson's radical views indicate a massive shift of perception, a new sense of responsibility, and beginnings of determined efforts to transform a neglected county into prosperous and exemplary estates.

The Act of Union that came into effect on 1 January 1801 was concerned not only with the political union of the Kingdoms, but also with ecclesiastical order. Church and State were closely linked, and the Union had ecclesiastical as well as political consequences. The fifth clause of the Act[76] stated that the 'Churches of England and Ireland, as now by law established', were to be called 'The United Church of England and Ireland', and that the 'continuance and preservation of the said United Church, as the established Church of England and Ireland' was 'deemed and taken to be an essential and fundamental part of the Union'.[77] For a considerable part of the history of the Church of Ireland, however, an Evangelical tone was prominent, and the Tractarian high-church movement did not enjoy the success it had in England from the 1830s.[78]

[75] See Curl (1983), 72-3; Hennell (1958), *passim*; Sheppard (1971), 202-46. See also Stephen (1891), which includes the essay on the Clapham Sect.

[76] 39 & 40 Geo. III, c. 67, and 40 Geo. III, c. 38.

[77] For a useful examination of Irish Anglicanism see Hurley (ed.) (1970), *passim*. For quotation see *Ibid.*, 1.

[78] For the philosophies behind the new concern for the welfare of the Plantation lands, see Sampson (1802, 1814), Schultes (1822), and the sundry *Reports* of Deputations (see Irish Society [1815a, 1821, 1826, 1827, 1832, 1834, 1835, 1836, 1838, 1841, etc.], and the *Reports* of Deputations of the Companies listed in full in Curl ([1986], *passim*). For the Evangelical Conscience see Curl (1983), *passim*; and Sheppard (1971), *passim*, and for the Clapham Sect see Hennell (1958) and the essay on the Sect by Sir James Stephen (1789-1859) published in 1849 and 1867 (see Stephen [1867], *passim*.

CHAPTER IX

Consolidation and Development in the First Part of the Nineteenth Century

> Throughout the eighteenth and nineteenth centuries ... [The Irish Society] ... is seen managing its property, spending large sums upon public works, and dividing the balance between the London Companies. Sooner or later, however, the discharge of the last duty was bound to give cause for offence. The Society interpreted its functions as being first and foremost those of a trustee for public purposes. On the other hand ... [the Companies, which] ... had found the money ... urged that [The Society] held property in trust for them after the needs of the whole estates had been satisfied. Whatever balance remained was theirs ...
>
> JOHN BETTS (1880-1967): *The Story of The Irish Society. Being a Brief Historical Account of The Foundation and Work of the Honourable the Irish Society of London* (London: The Irish Society, 1913, reprinted 1921), 87-8

The Bishopric from the Death of Hervey

War again broke out between the United Kingdom and France in May 1803, and in July another rebellion, led by Robert Emmet (1778-1803) and Thomas Russell (1767-1803), occurred, but was swiftly crushed and the ringleaders executed. Thereafter, determined efforts were made to ensure some stability in Ireland as the wars were to continue with the rise of Napoléon Bonaparte (1769-1821), Emperor of the French (1804-14 and 1815).

William Knox (1762-1831) was translated to the see of Derry from Killaloe and Kilfenora (where he had promoted education and improvements in the condition of the poor) in 1803. Although he only spent about a third part of every year in his new diocese, and the other two thirds in London, he fostered high standards of conduct among the clergy, the building and repair of churches and glebe-houses, educational provision, and numerous charities, all of which attested to his evangelical credentials. He helped to found the Mendicity Association and the Charitable Loan which advanced small sums to Londonderry's poor to enable them to purchase fuel for the winter. He was to give £500 and many garments to help to clothe the poor, and advocated that linen should be collected to relieve the destitute of his diocese in the 1820s. The manufacture of clothing from linen would give work to weavers and sempstresses as well as keeping the poor warm and decently dressed. The bishop contributed £1,000 towards the building of Foyle College and another £100 per annum for its upkeep, as well as giving other generous grants to the school for the poor.

As bishop, Knox improved clerical behaviour, endeavoured to enforce legislation[1] of 1808, the main provision of which was that incumbents should reside where their livings were for nine months each year,[2] and increased the number of ecclesiastical

[1] 48 Geo. III, c. 66.
[2] Phillips (1933), **iii**, 291.

buildings in the diocese. From his own funds he contributed to the building of several Anglican and Roman Catholic churches. He also had to contend with the problems of a cathedral-church in very poor condition. Hervey's steeple, as noted above, had failed and had to be taken down in 1802, and the bishop donated £1,000 towards repairs and rebuilding. Although The Irish Society also contributed funds, the fabric of the building generally needed much done to it, but work was very slow, not least because, unlike many cathedrals, it had no endowments for maintenance, and cash had to be raised from parishioners and from voluntary donations within the diocese. Work on the building fabric, including the tower, enabled the building to be used for worship again from 1805. Seven bells were re-cast and the peal re-hung in 1813 at the expense of the Corporation.

Other works at St Columb's included the addition of the present elegant, yet reassuringly sturdy, stone spire, added in 1822-3, probably to designs by John Bowden, who was also the architect of at least five almost identical early Gothic Revival Anglican churches in County Londonderry (e.g. Aghanloo [1823], Bovevagh [1823], Faughanvale at Eglinton [1821], Fahan [1820], and Maghera [1819]). In 1822 it was found that the roof-timbers at St Columb's were 'incapable of repair' and, contrary to the advice of the bishop, a contract was signed with a local firm to carry out the repairs, which were badly done. The lead was stripped from the roof and replaced by slate, but this work was of poor quality, and the slates had to be taken off again. Meanwhile the contractor went bankrupt. Much disputation followed while the cathedral lay unused and roofless and questions were asked in Parliament: Knox was also unjustly criticised for allowing the building to fall into decay. The *Evening Post* of Dublin[3] published an attack entitled 'The Rich Church and the Ruined Cathedral' which, in turn, led to the publication of *A Statement and Refutation of the Charge against the Bishop of Derry* (*c.*1824). Eventually the roof was completed and made watertight, and the 'open rafter work' exposed and lime-washed.[4] However the building suffered considerable damage at that time.

Simpson, in *The Annals of Derry*,[5] states that the galleries were 'erected about 30 years ago by subscription', which would be about 1817, that is, under Bishop Knox. Now it is clear that there were galleries at earlier stages of the cathedral's history, but it is possible that the Georgian panelling and Tuscan columns shown in the lithograph by Westminster-Gainford of 1862, based on a drawing by A. McFarland, date from Bishop Knox's time **[50]**. This lithograph also shows a Gothic vaulted ceiling over the nave and aisles (clearly a plaster-on-timber construction that attempted to emulate the earlier 17th-century scheme); Georgian box-pews; and cast-iron stoves for heating the building. It appears that Bishop Knox, although not required by law to do so, had taken it upon himself to build the spire at a cost of £863, and he also paid £978 for the new ceiling to emulate stone vaulting.[6] The Irish Society also granted various sums towards the works at the cathedral, and the building was re-opened in January 1826. It would appear that during these extensive alterations and repairs, the two circular turrets at the south-east and north-east corners of the building that hitherto had been crenellated (i.e. with battlements at the tops) acquired their curious ogee-shaped caps. These towers appear to have been partly rebuilt from at least half their height, and the little corbelled turrets were added to the corners of the clerestorey,

[3] *Derry Journal*, 1 May 1824.

[4] *Derry Journal*, 13 May 1885. Presumably the plaster ceilings resembling stone vaults were reconstructed shortly afterwards.

[5] Simpson (1847).

[6] Orr (1997), 82.

56 Knox monument in St Columb's cathedral, Londonderry, by William Behnes. (*A/CC/UM*)

terminating the crenellations. It is not clear when the tops of the buttresses on the south front were built: some hold that they date from Parrott's time, but it is equally likely they are early 19th-century in date. At the east end, too, there were two three-light windows, one set above the other, set in the end-walls on either side of the taller chancel, indicating two-storey arrangements flanking the chancel.[7]

Knox is commemorated by a fine Neoclassical monument depicting a sarcophagus (on which a mitre rests) flanked by figures of Faith and Charity set in the wall of the south aisle: it is by William Behnes (1795-1864) of London, in the style of John Flaxman (1755-1826) and Sir Francis Legatt Chantrey (1781-1841), and was erected at a cost of £500 raised by the clergy and laity of all denominations **[56]**.

The Irish Society and the Plantation to 1825

In 1814 The Society sent a large Deputation (comprising the Deputy Governor [Nathaniel Saunders], John Thomas Thorp [Governor from 1817 to 1835], Charles Foster, Thomas Wiltshire, and the Secretary [Robert Slade]) to Ireland, where the property was seen and surveyed, and the precise rights of The Society and the Companies re-established. The Deputation was charged with several tasks:

- to ascertain the value of lands to let and to establish the value of any leases due to expire or which had expired;
- to view The Society's school in Coleraine;
- to find out what rights of manorial privilege and of presentation to Church livings existed;
- to liaise with The Society's Agent (J. C. Beresford) and his underlings in order to examine any documents;
- to consult with the Law Agent (David Babington);
- to call for and inspect any leases granted by the Court;
- to draw on the Treasurer and General Agent for any sums necessary;
- to obtain the opinion of professionals as might seem expedient;
- to report generally on the state of The Society's property in Ireland.[8]

[7] Rowan (1979), 379, believed the 'crocketed dome finial' was by the later architect Ferguson carried out in the 1880s, but photographs of the east end before Ferguson carried out his drastic alterations show these ogee-capped towers virtually as they are today.

[8] Irish Society (1815a), 3, 4.

57 Foyle Arts Centre, Londonderry, formerly Foyle College. (*A*)

There was also the question of the school in Londonderry itself. The Irish Endowed Schools Act[9] had been passed in 1813, providing for permanent commissioners to direct royal schools and supervise others, and The Society was mindful of its duties to ensure proper educational establishments were provided and maintained. The relationships of The Society to the Corporations of Coleraine and Londonderry were delicate, and needed careful nurturing; drainage and reclamation of the slob-lands on the shores of Lough Foyle (in The Society's ownership) were matters that had to be dealt with; the future and management of the bogs required urgent attention; and the ownership of lands was once more a problem.[10]

Once in County Londonderry the Deputation was joined by Charles Stewart, surveyor, of Kilrea, and a general inspection of buildings in Londonderry took place. The timber bridge, which had been very badly damaged by inclement weather and a severe battering by ice the previous winter, was being repaired, but this began to cause the Corporation financial problems, notwithstanding the hefty income from tolls. Given that the bridge had cost an average of £1,200 per annum to keep in reasonable repair under normal conditions, any major damage would seriously embarrass the Corporation.

Stewart was instructed to carry out surveys of the bogs, Liberties, and slob-lands. This was becoming more urgent because of the numerous unauthorised cabins and other buildings that were being erected on these lands without any formal agreement with The Society. Unregulated developments would inevitably cause problems in the future, and some nipping of buds was essential. The surveyor was also instructed to investigate where further land could be gained between the existing lands and the low-water marks on both sides of the Foyle.

The Deputation visited the charity-school 'recently built under the direction of the Bishop of Derry' where most of the children were Roman Catholics, living in the suburbs and neighbourhood of Londonderry. The 'great Classical School' (Foyle College) patronised by the Londoners (to which The Irish Society had donated £720) was starting its work:[11] in 1999 it was Foyle Arts Centre **[57]**. Much of the Deputation's time was taken up by addresses, welcomes (the members were each presented with the Freedom of the City), inspections of buildings, attendances of church services, and receiving memorials from tenants on various matters. Viewing of the fisheries, of course, took up a great deal of time, as the problem of usurpation of rights had again reared its head.

9 53 Geo. III, c. 107.
10 Irish Society (1815a), *passim*.
11 *Ibid.*, 8.

58 The Salmon Leap and mill at Coleraine, engraved by H. Adlard, *c.*1814. (*IS*)

Gratifying numbers of tree plantations had been created, and concerted attempts were being made to reverse the process of denuding the county of timber as a result of Sampson's publications and exemplary work on the Fishmongers' Proportion. At the Salmon Leap, near Coleraine, the Deputation visited the 'mill erected by Sir George Hill, agreeably to the covenants of his lease', which had 'two water wheels, eight pairs of stones, the whole machinery on a very extensive scale, and upwards of twenty persons employed'[12] The Deputation was able to pronounce this mill a 'work of great public utility'[13] **[58]**. At Coleraine itself, however, Lord Waterford (descendant of the early Beresfords) seems to have usurped many of The Society's rights and privileges, and the Deputation sought ways by which matters could be remedied.[14] By 1814 the ramparts and ditch had been partly removed and partly built over, again usurping property rights of The Society. Clearly the 18th century had seen considerable erosion of The Society's influence, not to mention properties, rights, and much else. Once again, action had to be taken concerning violation of The Society's fisheries by various parties.

At Coleraine the 'Rectorial House' was so dilapidated that the Deputation considered it should be rebuilt, and application made to the Board of First Fruits for funds.[15] First Fruits and Twentieth Parts were pre-Reformation papal dues, subsequently paid to the Crown, representing the first year's income of a Cure, and annual payment of a twentieth part of that income. Although abolished in England in 1704, negotiations, in which Dean Swift played a considerable part, led to the formation of a Board of First Fruits to fund the repair of Anglican churches and glebe-houses. Substantial Parliamentary grants to the Board in the 18th century, and the admirable management of William Stuart (1755-1822), Archbishop of Armagh from 1800 until his death, and of Charles Brodrick, Archbishop of Cashel from 1801 to 1822, enabled

[12] Irish Society (1815a), 47, 48.
[13] *Ibid.*, 48.
[14] *Ibid.*, 48, 49.
[15] *Ibid.*, 53.

the Board to fund an ambitious programme of building, the results of which may be seen all over Ireland even today. In 1833 the Board's functions were taken over by the Ecclesiastical Commissioners under part of the draconian measures of the Church Temporalities (Ireland) Act.[16]

The rectory was not the only building in a deplorable condition. The school-house at Coleraine was in such a parlous state that 'Mr Bogg, architect and surveyor', of Muff, was called in to provide designs and estimates for a new building 'sufficient for the education of 200 boys and 100 girls'... for 'children of all religious persuasions resident within the Liberties'.[17] This 'Bogg' must have been James Boggs, who lived at Muff (now Eglinton), and carried out various works in the 1810s and 1820s on the Grocers' estates.[18] His proposed school was costed at £774 1s. 8½d.

Other problems dealt with included the many memorials, petitions, applications, and begging-letters received by the Deputation during its stay of almost a month in County Londonderry. The very full *Report of the Deputation* published in 1815 gives details of matters it considered under various headings including 'The Cut-Out Bog', 'The Slob', 'The Erections under the Walls of Derry' (in which The Society's lands were being usurped by unauthorised buildings), 'The Weigh-House against the City Wall', 'The Houses of Mr Torrens, opposite the Weigh-House', 'The Sheriff's Mountain' (more Society property which seems to have been leased without agreement), 'The Corporation of Derry', 'House of Correction' (which had been converted into dwellings and a fish-market without any proper agreements), 'The Blue School' (where irregularities had again occurred), 'General Agent' (who was required to attend at Londonderry and Coleraine more frequently than had been his wont), 'Salmon Fishery', and 'Lands and Corporation of Coleraine' (regarding which 'affairs ... had been entirely diverted from their original channel, and so concentrated in the Marquis of Waterford ... that little remained to The Society, either in property or power'). The Society noted, with some pain, that 'very considerable property had also been fastened upon, without title, under a sort of usurped authority, by the Corporation, such as the rampart, the fosse, the bowling-green, the citadel, the waste adjoining thereto, ... the common, ... the court-house, ... various buildings erected upon the rampart and the fosse, entirely round the town', 'for all of which ... the Rev. Mr. Meara', who filled the 'double capacity of land agent to the Marquis of Waterford, and Chamberlain to the Corporation', charged the 'occupiers an annual rent'.[19]

It appears to have become a 'received opinion that by some means, now unknown', the patronage of the Borough of Coleraine which, by the Charter, belonged to The Society, 'had been transferred to the family of Lord Antrim, and that afterwards it had been wrested from them by the Beresford and Jackson families'. Until shortly before the Union the Jacksons assigned interests and 'pretensions to Beresford, Lord Waterford, in consideration of £7000'. The Irish Society viewed with horror the fact that the Marquis nominated all his placemen to positions of power: there were about 400 Freemen, 'none of which' were 'known as such in the town'. This 'mockery of national representation' obliged the Deputation to determine to 'rescue the town of Coleraine from ... a degrading and dependent state ... and reinstate' The Society in its 'chartered rights'.[20]

[16] 3 & 4 Will. IV, c. 37.
[17] Irish Society (1815a), 56.
[18] Curl (1986), 162-4.
[19] Irish Society (1815a), 68.
[20] *Ibid.*, 70-71.

Not to mince words, it would appear that The Honourable The Irish Society had rather lost control of Coleraine, as well as of very many other properties and rights. Mogridge's good advice of more than a century before had been forgotten. The shocking findings of the 1814 Deputation began to concentrate minds. A committee of The Society was formed to enquire into the charter, and this body reported to the Court in 1815.[21] First of all, it was found that no copy of the original charter had survived, and that The Society, acting under the charter of Charles II, was not bound to comply with the considerations and conditions expressed in the original charter of James I and VI. On the question of the advowsons, The Society clearly had given up trying to keep tabs on those, with the single exception of the rectory of Coleraine. However, all rents and profits collected by The Society were to be divided among the 12 Companies after the expenses of the 'undivided' lands of Londonderry, Coleraine, and their respective Liberties had been met (e.g. repairs to the cathedral, supporting schools, and other expenses essential to the objects of the charter). As 'early records' appear to 'have been destroyed by a fire … in the Irish Chamber … in … 1786', and The Society had considerable problems of retaining a collective memory thanks to the short service of members, so the general shambles of ownership and rights had to be sorted out. From 1814 The Society did what it could to regain control of that which it had lost, but certain rights had been usurped for so long they effectively passed from The Society for ever.

As the 1814 Deputation was carrying out its investigations, Londonderry itself was being embellished, and was acquiring its new court-house in Bishop Street. A new Act of Parliament was sought for this purpose in 1812, and the building was completed in 1817 to designs by John Bowden. It is a distinguished essay in the Greek Revival style **[59]**, with a tetrastyle (four-columned) portico based on the Ionic Order of the Erechtheion in Athens, and the wings derived from variations on the Choragic Monument of Thrasyllus, Athens, both Antique buildings having been published in the second volume of Stuart and Revett's *Antiquities of Athens*.[22] Sculpture, including the statues of Justice and Peace,[23] was said to be by Edward Smyth, but he died before the building was even started, so it would appear that the work was executed by Edward Smyth's son, John (*c*.1775-*c*.1834). The contract drawings for the court-house were dated 20 August 1813, signed by the Mayor of Londonderry, John Curry, two fellow-commissioners under the Act of Parliament,[24] and David Henry, builder, of Camden Street, Dublin (representing Henry, Mullins, and McMahon, the contractors). The foundation-stone was laid on 18 December 1813, but Colby notes that Bowden 'died before the work was finished'[25] at a total cost of £30,479 15s., including the purchase of ground and furniture.

Other improvements supported by The Irish Society were the rebuilding of Castle gate (1803), Shipquay gate, and Butcher gate (both 1805-8) in the city's walls as simple arcuated structures of sandstone. The New gate dates from 1787, and, as mentioned above, Bishop's gate, the finest of the city's gates, was erected in 1789 **[54]**. The Bishop's Palace on the opposite side of Bishop Street from the court-house was virtually rebuilt in 1803 after its use as a barracks from 1798: as Rowan[26] said, the

[21] Irish Society (1815b), *passim*.
[22] Stuart and Revett (1787/1789), **ii**, ch. 2, pl. 8, and ch. 4, pl. 3.
[23] Colby (1837), 116; Ferguson, Rowan, and Tracey (1970), 20.
[24] 52 Geo. III, c. 182. See also Schultes (1822), 139.
[25] Colby (1837), 116 .
[26] Rowan (1979), 393.

59 The court-house, Londonderry, in 1999. (*A*)

palace is 'distinctly Regency in character', and suggested that Bowden might have been the architect. If Bowden died before 1817, however, it may be that the various County Londonderry churches and other works were at least partly attributable to Joseph Welland, a pupil of Bowden, and the latter's successor as principal architect to the Board of First Fruits.

In 1815 The Irish Society granted 300 guineas to Sampson for his *Memoir* and *Chart*, a huge sum for those days, so it is clear that Sampson's work was held in the highest regard. An important Act of Parliament[27] was passed in 1816 to facilitate the recovery of possession of land by landlords in Ireland thanks to the persuasive arguments of Sampson and some influential lobbying by The Society and others. This legislation was necessary to reform the agricultural economy, and from the years immediately following the end of the French Wars (1815) several Companies did indeed recover direct proprietorship of their estates, and started managing them through agents rather than letting them to individuals for large 'fines' and a lease. Almost at once ambitious programmes for building towns, developing facilities, draining land, planting forests, constructing roads, conserving resources (especially woodlands and turbaries) and generally improving the estates were set in motion. Failure of the potato crop in 1816 and the resulting famine brought Sampson's advice home with a vengeance: rural over-population had to be halted, a one-crop economy had to be

[27] 56 Geo. III, c. 88.

transformed, and farms had to be economically viable and larger in order to feed the poor and increase prosperity. When a late season and excessive rain could do to potatoes what they did in 1816 it became clear that drastic measures were needed. The monetary grants recorded at the time by The Irish Society for clothing poor children, alleviating want, and so on make depressing reading.

Gradually, a system of assisted emigration to remove surplus population from the land (as Sampson had proposed) began to be accepted, and very slowly larger farms began to be created, but not without difficulties. Famine in September 1816 (the first such major blight since 1742) was followed by a ferocious typhus epidemic which became widespread and continued until the end of 1819. In June 1817 Parliament was obliged to pass the Poor Employment Act empowering the Lord Lieutenant to appoint commissioners to direct public works financed by mortgages of rates.[28] Another Act[29] in July regulated expenditure on public works, and legislation[30] to provide for lunatic asylums was passed in the same month. So terrible were the epidemics that swept Ireland at the time that a Fever Hospitals Act[31] was passed in 1818 for the establishment of four hospitals and dispensaries. A select committee was appointed in 1819 to inquire into the state of the poor in Ireland, and reports were issued in the same year.

In 1819 The Irish Society sent another Deputation consisting of John Thomas Thorp (Governor), Samuel Favell, James Williams, Robert Slade (Secretary), and Henry Schultes (Assistant Secretary) to Ulster.[32] It was instructed to inspect records and accounts of the corporations of Londonderry and Coleraine; to settle the boundaries of the holdings of Londonderry Corporation under The Irish Society; to resume its rights to various holdings; to establish what houses, lands, etc., were held by the corporations of Londonderry and Coleraine 'without lease from' The Society and the precise arrangements by which such properties were actually held; to insist upon the 'immediate resumption' of The Society's right of confirming (or not) the bye-laws for the two corporations; to 'view the various charitable and other institutions in the city and county of Londonderry' and 'town of Coleraine' to which The Irish Society subscribed 'in order to ascertain whether' the 'bounty' was being 'properly applied';[33] to promote the leasing of such parts of the different bogs that had 'been cut out'; to view all properties at Coleraine to 'ascertain the progress … made in resuming' The Society's right to 'various parts thereof' that had been from 'time to time wrested from' The Society; to inspect and report on the rectorial and school houses at Coleraine then being erected with The Society's aid; to lease all parts of the slob-lands, 'wastes, or other undemised property'; to plan the erection of boundary-stones 'at the extremities of the lands … to prevent future encroachments and disputes'; to survey and report on the state of all lands, tenements, and hereditaments belonging to The Society and make suggestions for improvements 'conducive to the interest and dignity' of The Society and the 'welfare and prosperity' of the Plantation; and to deal with any other matters regarding the properties.

The Deputation made several recommendations concerning Londonderry, including improvements to the dirty and dilapidated properties built 'on the space surrounding the walls', and suggested the 'erection of cottages in Coleraine … for the

[28] 57 Geo. III, c. 34.
[29] 57 Geo. III, c. 107.
[30] 57 Geo. III, c. 106.
[31] 58 Geo. III, c. 47.
[32] Irish Society (1821), *passim*.
[33] *Ibid.*, 4.

accommodation of the poorer classes'. It seems that relations with the Corporation of Londonderry were amicable, but that Coleraine did not co-operate as fully as it might. Indeed, The Society felt obliged not to renew certain leases to Coleraine Corporation in an attempt to bring that body to heel. It is worthy of note that The Society made even-handed grants to numerous causes, including donations for the repairs to the Roman Catholic churches in both Londonderry and Coleraine, as well as other grants 'for charitable uses'.[34]

Not least of the problems the 1819 Deputation had to resolve was the leasing of properties by Londonderry Corporation to members of that body and their family connections. Finding widespread malpractice, The Society refused to renew certain leases, and attempted to organise lettings so that benefits would go to corporate funds. It was found that The Society had let properties that were then sublet for many times as much and still brought in an income far in excess of the sublet rent.

Moves Towards General Improvements

All this took place against disturbances occasioned by the failure to emancipate Roman Catholics from the time of the Act of Union. Yet some Roman Catholic prelates, such as John Thomas Troy (1739-1823), Archbishop of Dublin (from 1784), who had been antagonistic to all violence, saw the 1798 rebellion as extremely dangerous. Troy, the most influential Roman Catholic voice in Ireland of the time, believed that emancipation was much more likely to come from a Union Parliament than from an Irish Parliament, and so supported the Union, but when emancipation failed to materialise, lost influence as less moderate counsels began to prevail.[35]

The widespread failure of the potato crop led to the passing in 1822 of the Poor Employment Act[36] providing for the building of roads using destitute poor as labourers to be paid from a special fund set up for the purpose. Irish window- and hearth-taxes were abolished,[37] and police-forces were established in each county.[38] Duties on all articles imported from England to Ireland and *vice versa* were abolished in 1824,[39] removing a heavy burden on the Irish economy. In that year Thomas Frederick Colby (1784-1852) was directed to make a cartographic survey of Ireland, and the first of the Ordnance Survey maps, that covering County Londonderry, was published in May 1833. The *Memoir of the City and North Western Liberties* followed in 1837, the only part of the Londonderry O. S. Memoirs to be published in the 19th century, and a fine publication it is.

The prospects for the economy were enhanced by the Currency Act[40] of 1825 which made Irish and British currencies one and the same, thus avoiding cumbersome conversions. Other improvements included the reform of Irish licence duties, thereby bringing them into line with those of Great Britain; the speeding up of communications between Ireland and Great Britain as steam power began to replace sail in ships from 1815 and the infrastructure (e.g. the building of the road-bridge over the Menai Strait by Thomas Telford [1757-1834], opened 1826) became better; restrictions[41] were placed

[34] Irish Society (1821), 32, 60, and *passim*.
[35] *D. N. B.* (1917), **xix**, 1188-9; Maguire (ed.) (1998), 276-7.
[36] 3 Geo. IV, c. 34.
[37] 3 Geo. IV, c. 54.
[38] 3 Geo. IV, c. 103.
[39] 5 Geo. IV, c. 22.
[40] 6 Geo IV, c. 79.
[41] 7 Geo IV, c. 29.

on the sub-letting of lands and tenements; and provisions[42] were made for uniform valuation of all lands and tenements in Ireland for purposes of local taxation. However, the textile industry collapsed during the general recession of 1825-6, bringing widespread distress followed by the inevitable epidemics.

In 1828 Daniel O'Connell (1775-1847), a Roman Catholic, announced his intention of standing for election to Parliament for County Clare, and was duly elected M.P. In April 1829, as a result, The Roman Catholic Relief Act[43] was passed, providing a new Oath of Allegiance, enabling Roman Catholics to enter Parliament, belong to any Corporation, and hold higher civil and military offices. This is known as 'Catholic Emancipation', which seemed to herald a new era, for the Roman Catholic bishops issued a statement expressing thanks for Emancipation, and requested that priests should avoid political activities in future. On the Londonderry Plantation lands the Companies responded, taking care to show as much impartiality as was compatible with their obligations by helping Roman Catholic tenants to enjoy more appropriate places of worship, although the articles and the charter had to be watched carefully to avoid any legal problems.

The Irish Society proposed to make demises on parts of its estates for long terms on condition that lessees would carry out building operations and other improvements: Sampson's recommendations had not gone unnoticed. The Society clarified its rights *vis-à-vis* the corporations of Coleraine and Londonderry; settled the boundaries of Londonderry; determined what properties were held by any parties without leases from The Society; finalised yearly values and types of lease; re-established its rights of confirming bye-laws in Londonderry and Coleraine; examined all charitable and other institutions in the county; leased bogs in accordance with agreed principles for their proper management in order to protect the turbaries; re-asserted rights to various parts of Coleraine that had fallen into abeyance; watched very closely the rectorial and school houses at Coleraine, under construction since 1819; began negotiations with persons desirous of taking leases of the slob-lands and other undemised properties; set up boundary-stones to avoid further encroachments and disputes about land (of which there had been a great many); reported on and surveyed all its lands, tenements, and hereditaments; and set about improving its estates in a businesslike manner. Significantly, The Irish Society reaffirmed that, notwithstanding the division of the estates among the Companies, such estates were to be considered as still under the paramount jurisdiction of The Society, and liable to contributions in common with the 'individable' estates in The Society's lands, towards the general expenses of maintaining public works and edifices, supporting the civic government, repairing Anglican churches, establishing and maintaining schools, and adopting measures to promote the civil and religious interests of the tenantry.[44]

From this time onwards, the rather detached manner in which the Plantation had been run during the previous century was definitely at an end. Specifications and elevations of all houses proposed to be built in Coleraine or Londonderry were to be submitted to The Society for approval, and every effort was made to ensure that the Londoners' lands were improved after years of neglect. The Society and the Companies therefore functioned as early types of local planning authorities, and certainly took aesthetic matters into consideration. The Ironmongers' Company even suggested that the Companies

[42] 7 Geo IV, c. 62.
[43] 10 Geo. IV, c. 7.
[44] Schultes (1822), 152-4, 189.

should form a type of federation called the Ulster Association in order to promote general welfare and to defend the interests of the Companies in Ireland. Furthermore, Henry Schultes, who was to share the post of Secretary of The Irish Society with Robert Slade from 1827 to 1831, and who was Assistant Secretary in 1819, was charged with the preparation of an 'abridgement of all the principal matters contained in the books and papers belonging to' The Society, which was duly printed in 1822 as *A Concise View of the Origin, Constitution, and Proceedings of The Honourable Society of the Governor and Assistants of London, of the New Plantation of Ulster, within the Realm of Ireland.*

It was an interesting moment at which Schultes was instructed. In 1816 a notice of motion had been given in the Court of Common Council of the City of London that The Irish Society should annually lay before the Court a brief state of its accounts, but this The Society refused, lest a precedent should be set. Various arguments were put forward, but it was decided that the Common Council had no foundation on which to base its claim as The Society was 'a trustee for the twelve companies', who were 'absolute owners of their estates', which were 'not clothed with any trust, either for individuals, for any other public body, or for a charity'. This sudden interest in the affairs of the Plantation was ominous, for the rest of the century would bring problem after problem for The Society, involving it in long procedures of litigation, and wasting enormous sums of money.

However, although the early decades of the 19th century were not without their concerns, The Society and the Companies began to take steps to improve their estates beyond all recognition, and in a new atmosphere of determination, established regular plans for Deputations to visit Ulster. Clearly, far greater involvement was anticipated, and that is what transpired.

Activities and Concerns of The Irish Society

In order to have worthy quarters from which to conduct its affairs, The Irish Society determined to build new premises in London, bearing in mind the necessity of preserving records and other papers. Accordingly, under a lease dated 31 January 1825 the Corporation leased a site in Guildhall Yard to The Society for 60 years as from Christmas 1822 at a ground rent of £50 per annum, plans having been prepared in 1821 by Joseph Walker (*fl.* 1815-*c.*1834), who practised from 21 Earl Street, Blackfriars. These designs were duly approved, and Joseph Griffith, of Coleman Street, tendered to build the Irish Chamber (as it became known) for £1,576. The foundation-stone was laid by the Governor, Alderman John Thomas Thorp, on 30 July 1824, and during 1825 the building was completed, decorated, and furnished, ready for the first meeting on 20 January 1826. The Society had decided the building should not exceed £2,000, but on 24 March 1825 the site was purchased outright, and the freehold was duly conveyed to The Society on 27 October 1825. In the event the total cost of the new headquarters of The Society was £4,226 or 'thereabouts'. Walker was paid £174 9s. 6d. for his pains.[45] His building was a chaste Classical two-storey structure of brick, the ground-floor elevation arcuated and faced with stone **[60]**. Above the crowning stone cornice was a mansard arrangement with dormer-windows set behind the plain parapet. In Londonderry itself, for about a century until the 1980s, The Society's house was at the corner of St Columb's Court and Bishop

[45] Court and Minute Books, Vols. 18-19, 1821-6, in the Corporation of London Records Office. See Aldous (ed.) (1993), *passim*. See also Schultes (1822), 187 and *passim*. The Society's Chamber was formerly within Guildhall itself.

60 The Irish Chamber, Guildhall Yard, London, in *c.*1920. (*GLCL/108*)

61 The former offices of The Honourable The Irish Society at the corner of Bishop Street and St Columb's Court, Londonderry, 1984. (*A/CC/UM*)

Street, a simple three-storey Georgian building with an elegant door-case dated 1768 on a quoin-stone **[61]**.

After the Act of Union various improvements were achieved. Among these were the new gates in the walls **[54]**, the splendid Greek Revival court-house (1813-17) **[59]**, the extension to the gaol (1791 – designed by Edward Miller) in Bishop Street (1819-24 – carried out by the same builders who worked on the court-house [Henry, Mullins, & McMahon of Dublin] – mostly demolished), Foyle College, Strand Road (1808-14 – originally designed by Richard Elsam [*fl.* 1790-1821][46] in the Gothic style, but subsequently completed by John Bowden in a simplified Classical manner **[57]**), and the Walker testimonial, on the Grand Parade on the west face of the city wall, a fluted Roman Doric column on a pedestal supporting a statue of 'Governor' Walker allegedly by John Smyth of Dublin, but probably by his son, John. This memorial column **[62]** was erected in 1826-8 of Portland stone, at a cost of £4,200, again by Henry, Mullins, & McMahon: it appears to have been designed by James Henry, whose knowledge of entasis[47] seems to have been shaky, but demonstration of this is no longer possible as the testimonial was destroyed by an explosion in 1973 (not, it transpires, on purely architectural grounds). In the 1820s it was also decided to provide gun-carriages for the ancient cannon on the walls, and this work was carried out in due course. Most of the money for the testimonial and the gun-carriages was raised by public subscription, but The Irish Society and the Corporation contributed small donations. (In the case of the Walker monument The Society gave 50 guineas.)

The Irish Society's Deputation (consisting of G. Gorst [Deputy Governor], J. Drinkald, Edward Hamblet Noy, and Henry Schultes [Assistant Secretary]) of 1825

[46] Elsam's design was published as a frontispiece to his *The Gentleman and Builders Assistant* (1808), and was also issued as a separate engraving by Martyn of Dublin as *Plan and Elevation of the Free School Proposed to be Erected at Londonderry*. See Colvin (1995), 344-5.

[47] The diminution of diameter with height in a column, resulting in a subtle convex curve of the shaft.

took great pains to examine all fines, arrears, income, and expenses in relation to its estates with the aid of its Law Agent, David Babington. Londonderry produced £2,890 2s. 0d. in rent in 1824-5, Coleraine £1,659 19s. 0d., and the Quarterlands £1,724 13s. 9d., all of which was reasonably gratifying. The Deputation saw the ruined mill **[63]** at the Salmon Leap near Coleraine (it had been destroyed by fire), where one and a half tons of fish were 'taken in the course of an evening',[48] and inspected various properties in Coleraine, including 'The Society's Institution', where the school and General Agent's offices were situated, and which was partly intended as a residence for the rector (who refused to live there). Finding the building 'much dilapidated', repairs were directed 'forthwith'.[49] The Deputation was critical of the poor quality of the workmanship and the 'inconvenient construction and bad arrangement of the building and offices generally',[50] which does not say much for Mr Boggs's expertise as an architect. There was much discussion concerning reinstatement of the mill and building other mills, especially in relation to possible injury to the fisheries, then bringing in £1,252 per annum in rent. It is of considerable interest to note that The Irish Society was well aware that salmon was 'frightened or driven away from many of the rivers in North Britain and elsewhere, by the numerous steam vessels navigating them', so that 'the Fishery in the Bann' was likely to 'become more valuable ... every day'.[51]

62 The Walker testimonial, Londonderry, drawn by G. Petrie, engraved by J. Duncan, in *c.*1835. (*Colby [1837]/AC*)

63 The ruined mill at the Salmon Leap, Coleraine, *c.*1825, from the tercentenary window in the town-hall, Coleraine. (*A*)

At the time (1825) The Society noted that the 'children of the peasantry and lower classes' were 'in no want of employment, being occupied in the cottages of their parents in the various branches of linen manufacture'.[52] The 'introduction of Cotton Spinning Mills' might enable 'children to earn more money, and ... give more lucrative employment to a number of other persons', but The Society was well aware that factories and mills were 'invariably accompanied by vice and immorality' and were 'often destructive of the health of the children employed'. The voice of the Clapham Sect was audible.

The Deputation inspected the slob-lands by Lough Foyle before proceeding to Londonderry. The timber bridge over the River Foyle was the subject of some discussion. By statute[53] the Corporation was required at all times to maintain and support this bridge from the proceeds of the tolls, and £1,000 at least therefrom was to be set aside each year for that purpose. Unfortunately the bridge had been badly damaged after ice and floods in 1814, and the Corporation had borrowed heavily to repair it. However, the bridge had brought new prosperity to Londonderry, and the city expanded by developing towards the water's edge, even reclaiming land so that the river was pushed further away from the walls. The pattern of present-day Londonderry began to emerge. Nevertheless, The Society was concerned about the Corporation's financial position.

In due course the Deputation viewed all the properties with which it was directly involved, including the schools in Londonderry and Coleraine. In the latter town there were 108 boys and 50 girls: the Deputation examined several children, who appeared healthy and clean, and found their educational attainments satisfactory. It was decided to establish a good library for the use of the pupils.

48 Irish Society (1826), 9.
49 *Ibid.*, 10.
50 *Ibid.*, 12.
51 *Ibid.*, 12.
52 *Ibid.*, 13.
53 54 Geo. III, c. 230.

The 1826 Deputation *Report*[54] was largely taken up with problems concerning encroachments made on the shore of the River Foyle, agreements for demising the slob-lands,[55] the general state of Coleraine and Londonderry, and the preservation of The Society's rights. When the Deputation saw a 'thatched dwelling-house, in Meeting-house Lane', the General Agents (John Claudius Beresford and his son [also John Claudius Beresford (1799-1866)]) were instructed 'to give notice to the proprietor to cover the house with slates',[56] clearly to lessen the danger of fire and to improve the appearance of the town. The Deputation visited the new hotel, *The Irish Society's Arms* 'near the bridge', which was 'fitted up with every convenience', and regarded the amenity as a great improvement 'affording comfortable accommodation to any guests'. In order to preserve the rights of The Society to their estates in Coleraine the Deputation recommended that 'perambulation should annually be made by the Master and Boys of The Society's School on Holy Thursday ... to ascertain and perpetuate the Boundaries of Property'.[57]

From Londonderry the Deputation viewed various farms in the vicinity, 'most of which' were 'in a slovenly and dilapidated state, and the major part of the occupants of the lower class of Irish Peasantry'.[58] Other rural districts, including Rossnagalliagh (adjacent to the Goldsmiths' Proportion) were seen: there, the Deputation 'found 28 Mud Cabins, inhabited by persons of low description'. The land 'appeared to be badly cultivated; very few Fences made or maintained, and not above two dozen trees discoverable on the Estate'. Furthermore, the sub-tenants appeared 'to be in a state bordering on pauperism'. An examination of the leases revealed that the tenants 'had engaged to improve their Farms', but The Society 'considered them totally unable to perform any such conditions', and so the Deputation conferred with The Society's lessee who was prevailed upon to 'put the Estate into better condition' and to plant 'the same with timber trees'.[59]

The *Reports* make reference to members of The Irish Society's Deputation being honoured with the Freedom of the City of Londonderry, and being given sumptuous public dinners and 'entertainments'. Clearly the ceremonial aspects reflected close connections between the Plantation and the City of London, and the Deputations were received almost like royalty. Donations to various causes were sought and given: The Society was even-handed in its distribution of largesse to the various religious denominations, including Dissenters and Roman Catholics. It seems to have been a widespread belief that The Irish Society never gave anything to Roman Catholic clergymen or causes, but this is simply untrue, as the records of disbursements make clear, although there were difficulties in making financial donations to Roman Catholics for the purposes of building churches, but that was no fault of The Society: it was a built-in restriction in the original grants. Education, however, became a prime concern of The Society, which established schools in the Liberties as well as the main urban settlements. The Deputation of 1826, for example, visited the 'New School erected at Ballywogry in the Upper Liberties of Derry', a 'substantially constructed' building 'well adapted for the purpose of educating the Children of the Neighbouring Tenantry'.[60] 'Ballywogry' is an error for Ballougry, and there the Deputation ordered

54 Irish Society (1827), *passim*.
55 *Ibid.*, 3.
56 *Ibid.*, 12.
57 *Ibid.*, 13.
58 *Ibid.*, 14.
59 *Ibid.*, 18.
60 *Ibid.*, 20-21.

that more desks 'and other requisites' should be supplied, together with funds for buying books for the children and an annual grant to pay the salary of the schoolmaster.

The 1826 Deputation gave money to the Londonderry Penny Society for the relief of sick and indigent room-keepers, and also supported the proposal to erect the testimonial to commemorate the 1689 defence of Londonderry. Some degree of frustration regarding ideas for improving the condition of sub-tenants on farms comes out in the *Report*.[61] Not one 'of the numerous applicants for taking Leases … appeared to attach the slightest value to that part' of the proposals 'that Stone Slated Cottages should be erected at the expense of' The Society, for 'however wretched the condition of the Tenantry of this description' might appear in the 'estimation of men accustomed to visit English Farms', it was evident that the 'Tenantry' would not be 'rendered happier by any immediate transition from Cabins surrounded by muck, and accessible to their Pigs, Poultry, and all kinds of Domestic animals' to the 'comparatively comfortable Cottage' which The Society proposed to erect. The members of the Deputation were convinced that 'any improvement in the habits of this description of persons' could only be 'effected by the residence of their landlords or other individuals accustomed to superior habits and acquirements' on the lands, thus reforming by means of education and example.

Gratifying improvements were found at the county gaol, where cleanliness and discipline were impressive: much effort was expended on the 'intellectual and moral improvement' of the 'unfortunate inmates', several of whom had been taught to read and write 'during the periods of incarceration'. However, the Deanery in Bishop Street immediately opposite the Bishop's Palace, had a 'very old and dilapidated appearance', so something had to be done about that too, but matters had to be put on hold as once again there were problems over Church property in the diocese.

Money was granted to numerous causes, including the Presbyterian and Roman Catholic schools, the Londonderry Library Association, the Londonderry Dispensary, the Poor Shop, and other organisations. The Deputation was able to consider 'that the objects for which' it had been sent to Ulster had been 'accomplished' apart from the building of houses for the poor rural tenantry for reasons given above. However, there were endemic problems concerning tenants who failed to pay rents, and difficulties with occupiers of the slob-lands who 'had not acceded' to The Society's terms. Instructions were issued to the Law Agent (Babington) to take immediate steps to recover rents due for the fishings, and proceedings were instigated against the lessee to oblige him to repair the mill at the Salmon Leap. Furthermore, the Corporation of Londonderry also had to be proceeded against for failure to provide £1,000 per annum towards building a substantial bridge to replace Lemuel Cox's timber structure that was costing a fortune to keep in repair. Londonderry Corporation also appears to have acquired the tolls and customs without authority, while the dean of Derry had managed to get hold of 12 acres of land 'by some means'.

In 1827 a Bill was introduced into the House of Commons to regulate the salmon fisheries but, as its provisions appeared to be detrimental to the interests of The Society, the latter body opposed it, and, after 'a long and arduous contest, the promoters of the Fishery Bill were obliged to abandon the measure',[62] but not before Jacob George Cope (Deputy Governor) and Schultes had been over to 'take a survey' of The Society's fisheries, to consider the horny old question of the advowsons, to

[61] Irish Society (1827), 28.
[62] Reed (1865), 86.

survey the bogs in the neighbourhood of Coleraine, and to deal with any other 'matters regarding' The Society's property. It is interesting to note that J. C. Beresford Senior 'had made considerable progress on his description book' of The Society's estates,[63] so *The Book of Coleraine* was still being compiled in 1827, and work on it may have continued well into the 1830s, which would explain the changes made to 'Tristram Beresford's House' from the time of the Ordnance Survey sketch **[13]** to the drawing in *The Book of Coleraine*, thought to be of the same building **[15]**.

The Irish Society in the early 1830s

Various attempts had been made to undermine the Waterford (Beresford) hold on Coleraine. In 1830 the Governor of The Irish Society, Alderman Thorp, was nominated (without his knowledge or agreement) by certain Freemen of Coleraine as Member of Parliament in opposition to Sir John Brydges, a relative of Lord Waterford. Subsequently, a petition was presented to the House of Commons by The Society against the return of Brydges, and matters grew so fraught that The Irish Society's Deputation of 1830 was actually barred from entering Coleraine town-hall which had been built by The Society. At the 1831 elections Coleraine Common Council again nominated Brydges, who was opposed by Alderman William Taylor Copeland (1797-1868) in the interests of the Liberals: Copeland was returned as M.P. on petition in 1831 and 1833. Under the Representation of the People (Ireland) Act, 1832,[64] the 'Rotten Boroughs' were dissolved, and some semblance of rationality began to be established. Nevertheless, The Irish Society's support for the Freemen of Coleraine against the Waterford interests incurred very heavy costs.[65]

The Deputation of 1832 consisted of John Locke (Deputy Governor), John Ebenezer Davies, Warren Stormes Hale, William Shearman, and Henry Schultes (by then Secretary). As usual, the Deputation was to view all lands and properties, but it was also to consider the possibilities of constructing embankments on the shores of Lough Foyle 'contiguous to the Fishmongers' and Grocers' Proportions' to enable the slob-lands to be reclaimed 'to the benefit of the tenantry at large'.[66]

The Deputation saw the new Presbyterian 'meeting-house' in Coleraine, which was regarded as 'a considerable ornament to the street', and a donation was made to carry out further embellishments.[67] Help was also given to the 'seceding Scotch congregation' in Coleraine to enable a new meeting-house to be built. Problems still continued in certain places, however: the mill at the Salmon Leap remained ruinous, and at Rossnagalliagh the occupiers were 'in a state of great poverty and destitution, residing in cabins of the most wretched description', so nothing had been done to improve matters. The Society determined to 'apply to Mr Babington to relinquish his holding': this was William Charles Babington, son of The Society's Law Agent, no less, and was proving to be an appalling chief tenant. Further improvements were suggested for Ballougry School, where a schoolmistress was to be hired to teach the girls separately, but problems at Londonderry were multiplying. The Corporation had got itself into great financial difficulties, and had gone bankrupt, largely because of the expenses on the bridge. Meetings were held to establish the best means of building a

[63] Irish Society (1829), 7.
[64] 2 & 3 Will. IV, c. 88.
[65] Smith (1966), 70.
[66] Irish Society (1832), 4.
[67] *Ibid.*, 5.

new structure, and the Deputy Governor stated that The Society would be prepared to set aside 'a considerable sum' per annum 'for the purpose of raising a fund to build a permanent bridge free of toll', but emphasised that the Corporation's debts had to be paid off, and that it would not be advisable for The Society to 'interfere' until the Corporation was 'relieved' from its 'existing encumberances [*sic*]'.

How had the Corporation got itself into such a mess? Very briefly, it had obtained an Act of Parliament in 1790 to build the bridge to replace the ferry, and The Society leased the site and the tolls in perpetuity for £20 per annum. From 1790 to 1813 the Corporation gained net revenue of £34,253 from the bridge, but the damage done by floods and ice in 1813-14 created major problems. An Act of Parliament[68] authorised the Government to advance £15,000 for the rebuilding, and enabled the Corporation to borrow money on the security of the tolls provided the Corporation repaid the money over 20 years *and* set aside £1,000 each year to provide a fund for the future repair and maintenance of the structure. However, no fund was established, and nothing was paid back at all. As mentioned above, The Society had been obliged to proceed against the Corporation to enforce the funding of an annual sum, but the latter body had been living beyond its means for years, and was in very serious trouble. The Irish Society refused to prop up the Corporation, an attitude which, though perfectly justifiable under the circumstances, called down the wrath of local opinion on the heads of The Society: the improvident local worthies spread the word that The Society had a duty to use its revenues to finance the Corporation (no such duty existed). The Society held that a new constitution was required, and Parliament passed an Act (1832) which established the right of the citizens of Londonderry to manage their own affairs and raise local taxes.[69]

The Skinners' Suit

Very soon The Society found itself in even further difficulties. A Bill was filed in Chancery by The Skinners' Company against The Society on 16 July 1832 challenging it to show just cause why it should not surrender its estates to be administered for the benefit of the Livery Companies of the City of London. The Skinners claimed that the Companies had contributed to the expenses of the Plantation, and so were 'beneficially entitled to the rents and profits of the ... ferries, fisheries, and town lands, subject only to the payment of ... yearly sums to the Bishop of Derry and the Governor of Culmore Castle'. They further argued that The Society was essentially a group of trustees of the rents and profits, and should be 'restrained by the injunction ... from collecting, getting in, and receiving the same rents and profits'.[70]

One of the chief complaints of the Companies was that The Society appeared to operate independently of the City and any other controlling bodies for the benefit of its members and had 'unlawfully or improperly applied large sums of money in law expenses ... without the consent ... of any' of the Companies. Furthermore large sums had gone on tavern expenses, 'gratuities', fees to members of The Society, portraits of members, plate for the use of The Society and as gifts for members, and defraying the costs of journeys to Ireland. The Skinners wanted to know if the money had been 'improperly applied'. Court Minutes and Deputation *Reports* do indeed record

68 54 Geo. III, c. 230.
69 2 & 3 Will. IV, c. 107.
70 Reed (1856), 250-1.

the commissioning of portraits and expenditure on gifts of plate, and there is no doubt that the Deputations did not concern themselves with economies. Some of the enormous expenditure on litigation was undoubtedly no fault of The Society, and can be laid firmly at the doors of greedy individuals (notably in the case of the fisheries), but some was ill-advised, and suggests, perhaps, that certain employees of The Society had acted in interests other than those of The Society they were supposed to serve.

Those who have read Charles Dickens's *Bleak House* (1852-3) will recall the case of *Jarndyce* v. *Jarndyce* in Chancery which only ended when the costs had absorbed the whole of the estate in dispute. If Dickens's satire on the abuses of the old Court of Chancery (which brought misery and ruin on its suitors) has its tedious moments, the Skinners' suit is definitely more so, and the catatonically dreary transcriptions[71] are considerably longer than several *Bleak Houses*. The saga of the Skinners' suit did not end until 8 August 1845, and had three distinct phases: the preliminaries and interlocutory hearings (1832-6); the Chancery case (1838); and the appeal to the House of Lords (1845).

The Irish Society admitted it was a trustee for the Companies in respect of any *surpluses* that might remain after its public duties and obligations had been discharged, but that it held discretionary powers to apply what income it thought fit to public purposes without having to be accountable to the Companies. The other 11 chief Companies, 29 minor Companies, the Corporation of London, and the Attorney-General were associated with The Society as respondents in the course of the suit, but the Skinners also appear to have had covert support from the Mercers, Grocers, Drapers, Fishmongers, Salters, and Clothworkers at various times.

During the Skinners' suit The Society had certain serious problems which did not help its case at all. One of the Deputation members in 1826 had claimed expenses and charges of £400 which the Deputy Governor considered 'too bad': such claims fuelled rumours about excessively high 'tavern expenses' and costly Deputations. Schultes seems to have spent much time in Ireland, leaving his accounts, correspondence, and papers 'very much in arrears, and consequently ... mystified', and Slade 'interfered not at all in the business or duties of the office and accounts'. In January 1831 Slade (who was getting on) resigned (though his departure was sweetened with '500 golden arguments'), and Schultes was appointed Secretary, with Richard Howell as his Assistant.[72] This arrangement did not last long. In 1832 The Society instigated an inquiry going back to 1826 in respect of expenses, personal charges, and costs of Deputations, salaries, and 'fees charged for renewal of leases' which should have gone to The Society. It seems that controls over the expenditure by employees of The Society were somewhat lax, and Schultes relinquished his post in April 1833 on grounds of 'incompetence' according to Sharp: nevertheless, the Court Minutes are at pains to avoid suggesting anything of the sort, though Schultes's resignation was somewhat unceremoniously, even brusquely, accepted by the Court. At the same time Schultes's young assistant, who appears to have been appointed in an irregular manner, was dismissed as 'unnecessary'. Presumably to save face and keep the affair under wraps, Schultes was exonerated from any whiff of wrongdoing, and given a pension of £175 per annum. However, a pointer to what the problem might have been is found in a letter to Schultes referring to his 'work and fatigue in the Dungeons of Armagh', and in another letter from Matthew Wood (1768-1843 – who was to become Governor of The Society in 1835) mention is made of Schultes's habit of taking 'more Physic than

[71] Irish Society (1836, 1838, 1839, 1845).
[72] Court Minute-Books IS/CM/52.

food', according to his accounts of his travelling expenses: in other words, the Demon Drink may have been at the bottom of it all.[73] In 1834, not before time, the accounts of the Law Agent, David Babington, were called for, with all his official documents and papers. The author of *Retrospect* wryly noted that Babington's 'connexion' with The Society had been for many years as 'flattering for his services as it had been costly to The Society',[74] but this may have been an overstatement, as Sharp's tone was generally critical of The Society. However, such internal problems at such a time were major, but things were stabilised with the appointment of John Ebenezer Davies as Secretary, a post he held until 1865. During his tenure The Society achieved a great deal, and its philanthropic character became overt.

In 1835 the Skinners gave notice of intent to apply to the Court of Chancery that The Society should pay into the Court the balance of funds held; to pray for the appointment of a receiver to handle all future rents and profits; and to restrain The Society from collecting anything in future. Eventually, the Lord Chancellor, Charles Christopher Pepys (1781-1851), Lord Cottenham (from 1836), delivered his judgement (27 February 1836), refusing the application, with costs.

The Society then proceeded to distribute £6,000 among the 12 Companies less rents due to The Irish Society. The Clothworkers withdrew their support for the Skinners at this stage, but the Skinners determined to proceed with their principal suit in the Rolls Court before Henry Bickersteth (1783-1851), Lord Langdale (from 1836), Master of the Rolls, in 1838. Judgement was delivered on 19 November 1838, and included the opinion that the powers granted to The Society and the trusts reposed in them were part of a general and public nature, independent of the private benefit of the Companies, and were intended by the Crown to benefit Ireland and the City of London and to promote the general purposes of the Plantation. Although the Companies might have an interest in any surplus that remained 'after general purposes', they had no right to control the exercise of the powers given to The Society for general and public purposes. The Bill was dismissed with costs.

At this juncture the Drapers, Merchant Taylors, and Salters (who alone had paid out £2,127 toward the suit) deserted the Skinners, who, however, decided to press on by taking the case to the House of Lords, whose judgement was delivered by John Singleton Copley (1772-1863), Lord Lyndhurst, the Lord Chancellor, who agreed with the opinions expressed by Lords Cottenham and Langdale that the suit could not be maintained. The Irish Society had public duties to perform and was given wide discretionary powers in order to carry out those duties: afterwards, any surpluses could be paid to the Companies at The Society's discretion, but The Society could not be trustees for the private benefit of the Companies, although it was answerable to the Crown and the Corporation of London. In a concurring judgement, John Campbell (1779-1861), Lord Campbell from 1841, stated that The Society had the function to act as trustees for public purposes, and would ever have this rôle.[75]

Progress in the 1830s: Tite's Reports

From the beginning The Irish Society had carried out its difficult task with a strong sense of public duty. From the time of the Act of Union The Society's devotion to

[73] Court Minute-Books IS/CM/20, 460-70.

[74] Smith (1966), 122-3. See also Sharp (1843), *passim*, but especially 19-32. The Court Minutes are discreet, even coy, about these matters, but things were quite clearly amiss.

[75] Smith (1966), 122-130.

its obligations became more zealous, prompted by the stirrings of the Evangelical Conscience noted earlier. The Skinners' suit strengthened The Society, confirmed it in its rôle, and corrected some mistaken views held of its situation and duties. In the *Report* of the 1835 Deputation,[76] for example, the obligations of the Companies regarding their Proportions were spelled out, and the well-managed estates of the Drapers', Fishmongers', and Grocers' Companies were contrasted with the 'deplorable appearance' of the Skinners' Proportion, let on a long lease, where the 'iron hand of an intermediate party was exacting from the poor tenants the uttermost farthing'.[77] The behaviour of Companies such as the Skinners was 'completely at variance with the object of the charter', and was 'introducing into the New Plantation ... the system to which is mainly to be ascribed the evils which afflict the southern and western parts of Ireland'.[78] The Drapers', Fishmongers' and Grocers' estates were under the direct control of the Companies, managed by resident agents, whereas the Skinners' Proportion was let, and The Company was an absentee landlord, completely uninterested in its lands except to collect its dues. The Society noted that the Mercers' Proportion had 'lately come into' the hands of the Company once more (actually in 1831), and 'great ameliorations had taken place'; ... enough had 'been done to make it apparent that the tenantry' had 'reason to rejoice in the change'.[79]

One of the most interesting documents of the time is the *Report of a Visit*[80] to The Irish Society's estates in 1834 by William Tite (1798-1873), who was a member of the Court in 1833-4, and sat on various committees of The Society. It was Tite who seems to have been instrumental in sorting out several problems at the time, especially in relation to mismanagement and even dishonesty on the part of some employees. Tite spent a great part of his professional life in the valuation, purchase, and sale of land for railways, designing many of the early railway-stations, and was architect of the South Metropolitan cemetery, Norwood (1838), the Royal Exchange, City of London (1842-4), the London Necropolis cemetery, Brookwood, Surrey (1853-4), and St James's church, Gerrards Cross, Buckinghamshire (1858-9). Elected a Fellow of the Royal Society (1835) and of the Society of Antiquaries of London (1839), he was President of the Royal Institute of British Architects (1861-3 and 1867-70), Liberal M.P. for Bath (from 1855 until his death), a member of the Metropolitan Board of Works, a director of the London and Westminster Bank, Master of The Spectacle-Makers' Company of the City of London (1861), was knighted in 1869, and was appointed a Companion of the Bath (1870).[81] His report is mercifully succinct and avoids the prolixity of many Deputation *Reports*. Tite's *Report* makes overt what was hinted at in earlier Deputation *Reports*: David Babington was at the very least tardy in producing papers The Society required, and there was more trouble over the letting of The Society's fisheries. Tite inspected the farm leased to W. C. Babington at Rossnagalliagh and found it presented 'the same deplorable picture of dilapidation and wretchedness as that described' by the 1832 Deputation.[82] He advised that The Society should repossess it so that it might become 'an ornament rather than ... a disgrace to the neighbourhood of Londonderry'.

[76] Irish Society (1835).
[77] *Ibid.*, 44. For conditions in 1834 *see* Johnston (1959), *passim.*
[78] *Ibid.*
[79] *Ibid. See* Johnston (1959), *passim.*
[80] Tite (1834), *passim.*
[81] Colvin (1995), 980-2. See also *D.N.B.* (1917), **xix**, 198-9, and Papworth (1892), **viii**, 58-9.
[82] Tite (1834), 8.

Tite was impressed by J. C. Beresford's knowledge of the area and by his efforts on behalf of The Society. The architect had been given powers to issue orders to put anything right that was necessary, and one of the first instructions was to order the repair of part of the city wall near the Butcher Gate. Tite approved of the new Wesleyan chapel for which The Society had contributed a grant, but was concerned that the subdivision of lands for letting along the river bank had occurred, because the slob-lands were a 'very great nuisance' and should have been embanked, which was only possible by concerted effort. In fact this is what Tite recommended – a 'joint embankment on a fair principle' erected through the cooperation of the various lessees.[83]

It appears that several parcels of land had been let for development, but that various improvements intended by The Society had 'not been attended to'. The architect's eye was offended by general squalor and untidiness, and Tite urged a far greater tightening up of permissions, conditions, leases, and what we now would call 'planning control'. Tite noted that there was nothing in many agreements that compelled developers to 'arrange' buildings 'so as to give a uniform' appearance. Three houses built by a Mr. McCrea were stated to be 'first class houses', but Tite said categorically that they were nothing of the sort, and had not been erected according to approved plans: frontages 24 feet wide on the drawings were built 18 feet wide, floor-to-ceiling heights were reduced from those indicated on the drawings, and just about everything else was skimped. Tite recommended that McCrea should be 'called upon to take down and re-build these houses consistent with his agreement with' The Society.[84] This sort of thing appears to have been endemic, with The Society granting permission and the lessees cheating, cutting corners, and messing up every good intention. To The Society's agents on the spot much blame for the state of affairs should be laid. The Society was treated like a benevolent, distant, absentee landlord, to be milked for funds at every opportunity. Tite saw this at once.

Several fields west of Londonderry had been occupied by the Recorder, 'the Right Hon. Sir George Fitzgerald Hill', in 1819 'for as long a time as he should continue Recorder'. Tite noted that Hill had never taken out a lease, nor paid any rent, and had 'for some time ceased to be the acting Recorder'.[85] Tite recommended that The Society should resume possession. This kind of chicanery was more usual than not, and it is clear that, contrary to popular belief in the latter part of the century, The Irish Society was not a grasping landlord, but, on the contrary, was being defrauded right, left, and centre, and losing a fortune every year in rents that were either far too low or were never paid, while properties, intended to be improved or repaired, were allowed to deteriorate to the point that they could not be saved without great expense. Mogridge had warned of such problems as long ago as 1700, but The Society had lapsed into languid torpor, and its grip on things was loose, to be charitable. During the 18th century The Society had evolved into a kind of substitute for a gentleman's Club, with predictable consequences that Tite was quick to spot.

To his surprise Tite found that the 12 acres of the 'Dean's Park', referred to by the 1826 Deputation, were still in the possession of the dean, and that ownership had not been resolved. Richard Ponsonby (1772-1853), Bishop of Derry from 1831 to 1853, desired to erect a school and a public room for meetings on ground 'at the gate

83 Tite (1834), 11.
84 *Ibid.*, 13.
85 *Ibid.*, 14.

of the Cathedral yard', and Tite recommended that the land should be leased for such purposes reserving powers of re-entry in case of any attempt to change its use.

Tite also inspected various encroachments made upon the fishery of the Foyle, and was in no doubt as to the blatant illegality of those who usurped The Society's rights. At Cloughglass and Springtown there were several farms, the leases on which were due to expire in 1841. Tite advised that no separate renewal should be entertained because the opportunity should be grasped of re-organising the field-boundaries and the sizes of various holdings, as well as encouraging rebuilding where possible. Tite deplored the fact that in Ireland the landlord did not normally erect any of the farm-buildings, in consequence of which 'more hovels' were thrown up. He proposed, therefore, that The Irish Society should set an example by establishing farms of no less than 60 or 70 English acres on which moderate farm-houses, barns, and sheds should be erected to reasonable standards. Tite pointed out that one farm, Buchanan's at Springtown, was well run and had a 'neat, comfortable' farm-house 'in good repair', although the farm-buildings were 'only mud hovels, thatched, and greatly dilapidated', which meant that crops were 'ill saved' and corn 'sent to market in a damaged and dirty condition'.[86] Tite estimated that a barn, a stable for three horses, a shed for two cars, a cow-house for four cows, calf-pens, pigsties, and a house of four rooms and a kitchen could be erected for £280 to appropriate standards.

At Pennyburn Tite supported proposals by Sir Robert Ferguson to develop the land with 'substantial and respectable' houses 'erected upon a uniform and well-considered plan, both as to site and elevation'.[87] Repairs to the decayed parts of the wooden bridge over the Foyle were being carried out under the direction of Captain Stewart, the harbour-master, but Tite considered that the tolls were a 'dead weight' on the prosperity of Londonderry.[88] Stating that Londonderry had more 'natural advantages' than Belfast, Tite could not help contrasting the rapid development and prosperity of the latter town, and was convinced that the tolls were at least partly to blame for retarding Londonderry's evolution. He urged The Irish Society to create a special fund to build a new toll-free bridge at the Gallows Strand, some 1,300 yards upstream from the wooden bridge **[64]**. Sir John Rennie (1794-1874), who had completed London Bridge in 1831, had proposed a suspension-bridge about 600 feet upstream from the timber bridge, but Tite felt that the site did not fully address the problem of the 'extremely precipitous' hill of Derry, and argued that his own proposals solved several problems.

Tite found that the settlements of Muff and Ballykelly on the Grocers' and Fishmongers' Proportions respectively were 'highly creditable', resulting in a 'happy, contented, and decent peasantry', largely, of course, as a result of reforms promoted by Sampson earlier. At Coleraine, however, he had much to say about the general standard of development, and proposed sundry improvements to the planning of roads and bridges. The mill at the Salmon Leap was still ruinous, but the fishery 'had greatly fallen off' because of widespread and blatant poaching.

The schools in Coleraine were 'creditable', apart from the boys' school, where the master, one Hinde, was 'much embarrassed by his debts'. Tite recommended that Hinde 'should be allowed to retire' and suggested that The Society 'should afford … the means' by which Hinde and his numerous brood should emigrate to America or

[86] Tite (1834), 16, 17.
[87] *Ibid.*, 17.
[88] *Ibid.*, 18.

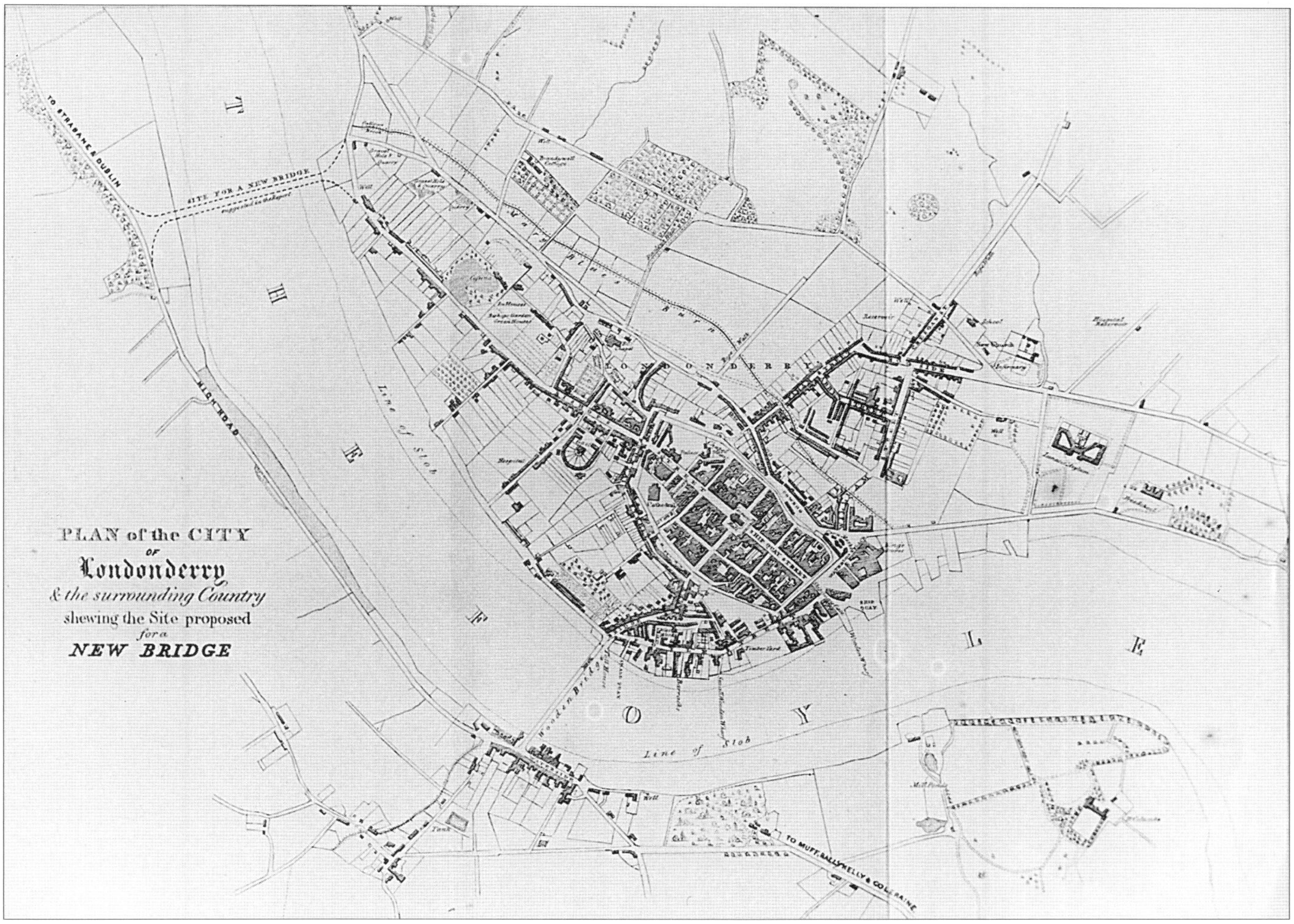

64 'Plan of the City of Londonderry & the surrounding Country shewing the Site proposed for a New Bridge' of 1834. William Tite showed the old bridge and his ideas for a new structure upstream. (*IS*)

Australia. It appears that Hinde owed about £150 locally (a huge sum then), and Tite made it clear that The Society would not 'undertake the liquidation of any part of this debt', having bailed him out eight years before and 'adjusted the claims of his creditors'. The contrast with Miss Rippingham's well-run girls' school was painful.

Tite urged the establishment of an 'Infirmary, or Hospital' as Asiatic cholera had made its first terrible appearance in Ireland in 1832, and, although the people of Coleraine had heroically helped poorer townspeople in their distress, the absence of proper facilities had contributed to the horrors of the epidemic. In conclusion Tite urged The Society to send 'frequent Deputations' to Ulster to keep a tighter rein on the affairs of the Plantation, for The Society was 'placed, to a certain extent', in the class of those who had caused and do still cause much of the misery and wretchedness prevailing in Ireland:- viz. absentee landlords, … and therefore … it was [The Society's] obvious duty to obtain by all means … an intimate acquaintance with [its] Tenantry, and … to afford … support, assistance, and encouragement which … contributes as much to the interest of the Landlord as to the well-being and comfort of the Tenantry'.[89] The arguments of Sampson, the Evangelical Conscience, and exemplary

[89] Tite (1834), 34-5. *See also* Johnston (1959), 151-4 and *passim*.

work by the Drapers', Fishmongers', and Grocers' Companies were creating a new climate, and Tite hoped The Irish Society would inaugurate a new era on its properties as well.

Further Deputations and their Reports

The Deputation of 1835 (consisting of W. A. Peacock [Deputy Governor], John Evans, Edward Tickner, and John Ebenezer Davies [Secretary from 1833 to 1865]) found that some of the improvements agreed by Tite at Coleraine had not been complied with, so various extensions were granted to enable them to be carried out. The new schoolmaster had given the boys' school a fresh lease of life, and the pupils were 'all dressed in their new round frocks ordered by The Society'. However, many of the boys had no shoes or stockings, so the Deputation ordered these to be obtained and distributed at once. The girls, too, were given 'shoes and stockings, and cloaks', so some idea of the appalling poverty may be gained. The school buildings had 'very imperfect' ventilation, and the air was 'close and suffocating', which was probably a euphemism for an overpowering stench of unwashed bodies. Orders were given to introduce 'two or three ventilators'. Books in the lending library in each school were 'much worn', so annual sums were allocated for a 'constant supply' of books.[90] Miss Rippingham's school, in a 'beautiful cottage on the banks of the Bann, very near The Society's School', was much admired, and the Deputation increased The Society's allowance to the school from £10 to £15 per annum.

Other matters discussed were road improvements, the slob-lands running up-river from the bridge opposite Hanover Place (which the Deputation recommended should be reclaimed and developed), the derelict mill (to be advertised in the Manchester and Glasgow papers as there were no local takers), the building of a 'Roman Catholic chapel' to plans approved by The Society, grants towards the building of a vestry and school-room behind the Presbyterian meeting-house, and various other affairs relating to Coleraine and its inhabitants (who do not seem to have been very enthusiastic about Tite's proposals for an infirmary).

In Londonderry, needless to say, nothing had been done about the slob-lands because the various lessees would not agree to accept the new leases, and would not co-operate in the improvements so necessary and desirable. The Society immediately directed the General Agent to write to all the lessees saying that if they did not execute the leases at once, they would never be granted any thereafter, and that all the rent owing would be levied on the one who impeded settlement of the question. Patience had been tried once too often. This produced immediate results, and all the lessees complied, so that 'desirable improvement' would be 'carried into effect'.[91]

Much of the *Report* is taken up with trying to sort out problems caused by procrastinating, obstructive, bloody-minded individuals, who seem to have had no concept of ideas about the public good, civic improvements, or even tidiness. Another problem was that of the slob-lands: the bishop and *his* tenants, for example, believed that they had a right to the slob adjoining their lands, but The Society disputed this. The General Agent was instructed to confer with the Law Agents concerning these matters. Further difficulties had arisen over the slob-lands above the bridge on the city side which The Society had leased to the Corporation at £1 per annum to enable

90 Irish Society (1835), 4-5.
91 *Ibid.*, 21.

a quay to be built, but this had not happened because of the 'embarrassments' of the Londonderry Corporation. Instead, the Corporation had sold the site on, yet another example of a benevolent action being abused. The Society called in Stewart Gordon, the county surveyor, to investigate. Clearly, accurate plans of holdings were becoming more and more necessary.

The Deputation was approached by the usual large number of people asking for grants and other hand-outs: donations were dispensed with customary liberality, including £200 towards the building of the school-house at the cathedral yard gates, the site for which was granted by The Society at £1 per annum. Not every request for money was met, though: the parish-priest of Killowen, near Coleraine, had prayed for aid to build a school, but 'previous to any grant being made' The Society asked where the £25 'formerly granted for that purpose … had been appropriated'.[92] A certain amount of caution became detectable in the 1830s.

Inspection of the fishings revealed to the members of the Deputation that it was 'a matter of surprise' that these 'should have been overlooked for so long', and that they 'had no idea of the extent of The Society's rights'.[93] The Deputation found that The Society's fishings comprised 'upwards of two hundred miles of fishing ground', much of which had been neglected, usurped, and robbed. When the Deputation reflected that the fisheries of the River Spey in Scotland, 'though not one twentieth of the extent of The Society's fishings', were leased for £8,725 per annum, clearly something was very wrong. In fact, at the Donegal Summer Assizes, 1835, the Lough Foyle Fishery Cause had been heard before the Hon. Baron Richard Pennefather (1773-1859) and a special jury. The case involved an action for trespass by Sir George Duckett against the Rev. John Molesworth Staples, rector of Upper Moville. Duckett claimed the sole and exclusive right of fishing in and over the whole waters of Lough Foyle as he had his lease from The Irish Society, while Staples based his case on the Chichester usurpations and grants going back before The Society's charter. In due course the jury found a general verdict for Duckett, with six pence damages and costs, but the 'Cause' once more established the exclusive rights to the fishings of the Rivers Bann and Lough Foyle and River Foyle held by The Honourable The Irish Society.[94] The Deputation recommended that Captain Stewart, harbourmaster, should be appointed Deputy Vice-Admiral to watch over all The Society's rights and privileges regarding the fishings, and to supervise the eight 'conservators or waterkeepers' appointed for Lough Foyle.

If the Deputation might seem to have been unduly concerned with the slob-lands (a recurring subject in 19th-century Deputation *Reports*), one example, consisting of 450 acres between Londonderry and Lifford Bridge, had been reclaimed from slob-land at a cost of £15,000, sold for £18,000, and was let for between £5 and £7 per acre, so brought in between £2,250 and £3,150 *per annum*, so reclamation paid well. What was worse, the land 'would have belonged to The Society, had it been properly noticed at the time', but that, and other property, had 'to a great extent … been lost' to The Society, 'from the want of sufficient information', while 'encroachments' had 'been permitted for so long a time' that the period was past 'in which they could be legally recovered'. The implications are obvious: failure to send annual Deputations, the ever-changing members of The Society, lackadaisical (and possibly less than alert)

92 Irish Society (1835), 19.
93 *Ibid.*, 40-41.
94 Davies (1835), *passim.*

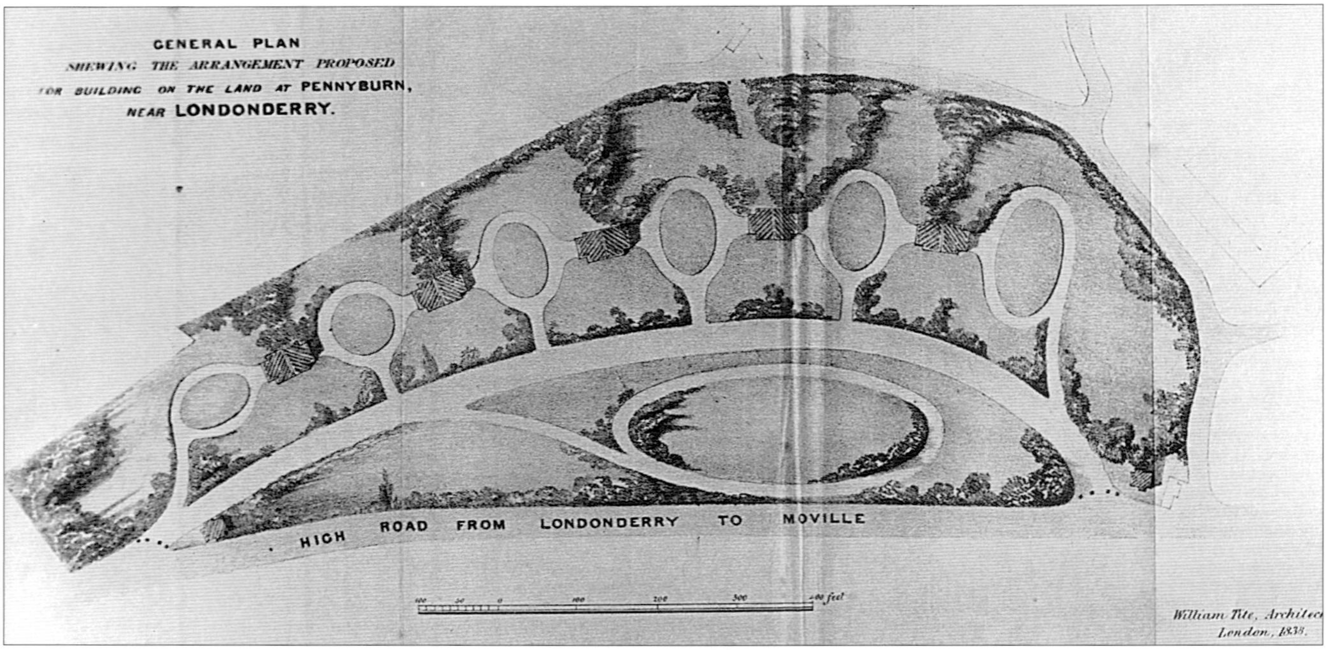

65 'General Plan shewing the arrangement proposed for building on the land at Pennyburn, near Londonderry.' Tite's layout of 1838 (based on his *Report* of 1834) for 'substantial and respectable' houses. (*IS*)

agents, and rapacious locals all contributed to a system that must have cost The Irish Society millions of pounds over the years, not to mention the enormous expenses incurred in fighting endless litigation.

The Deputation called on the Lord Lieutenant at Dublin Castle, not only to pay its respects, but to acquaint the Secretary, Lieutenant Thomas Drummond (1797-1840), an enlightened and liberal administrator, with the necessity of giving orders to the inspectors of police stationed along the shores of the Bann and Lough Foyle to assist the men engaged in the fisheries and to protect them against the brutal attacks, and to 'warn the magistracy not to employ the police in protecting the persons employed in ... illegal fishings'. Drummond assured the Deputation that the police would be cautioned, and that he would be happy to deal with any complaints from The Society at any time. Tite, in his *Report*,[95] had reported that the police refused to execute warrants against offenders in fishery cases, and it is likely there was at least widespread corruption, and probably intimidation as well, not for the first time in Irish history.[96]

The following year the Deputation (consisting of Edward Tickner [Deputy Governor], James Harmer, John Kinnersley Hooper, and Secretary Davies) produced a fuller *Report* [97] than usual. The horny old problem of the advowsons had resurfaced, and was to involve The Society in further disputes. However, the bulk of the 1836 *Report* contains details of the various Company Proportions, contrasting those under the direct control of Companies through their agents with the estates that had either been sold or let to others whose only purpose was to increase their fortunes by making the most of their bargains.

William Tite's design for a new monument over the grave of Colonel Mitchelburn in Glendermott (Clondermott) churchyard[98] was ordered to be realised **[43]**, and the

95 Tite (1834), 30.
96 For Drummond's reaction see Irish Society (1835), 45.
97 Irish Society (1836), *passim*.
98 It and the similar monument over the grave of Colonel Adam Murray have been maintained ever since by The Honourable The Irish Society.

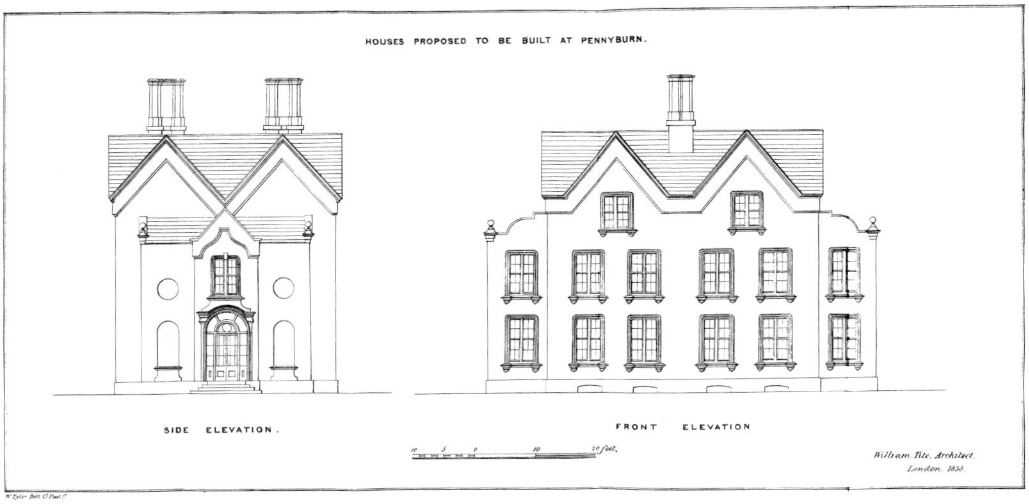

66 Houses proposed to be built at Pennyburn. Elevations of 'substantial and respectable' houses proposed by William Tite, 1834-8. (*IS*)

same architect's proposals for 'good and substantial houses' were accepted **[65-6]** to be erected by Sir Robert Ferguson on land at Pennyburn provided that Sir Robert paid The Society an increased rent of £150 per annum after the existing term of 45 years at a rent of £49 6s. 5d. had expired.

Plans were projected to build a railway between Londonderry and Enniskillen, to which The Society contributed £100. The Deputation also inspected all the coasts and rivers by steamship (provided *gratis* by the North-West of Ireland Steam Packet Company), accompanied by the Deputy Vice-Admiral, the General Agent, and others. During the voyage, the Deputation observed 'the vast tracts of reclaimable slob' by the shores of Lough Foyle, and regretted 'no effort had been made to reclaim the same, inasmuch as the employment it would give to vast numbers of the labouring poor, now destitute of work'.[99] In particular, the slobs from 'Culmore down to the sea' offered great attractions.

Improvements were proposed to the meat, fish, and vegetable markets in Londonderry, but nothing had transpired to improve anything at Rossnagalliagh, although W. C. Babington had died, and efforts were made to see if the lease could be surrendered to The Society. The General Agent, based in Coleraine, complained that he often had to carry important papers and records to Londonderry, which was both inconvenient and dangerous. It was therefore agreed to establish an office 'with a strong closet' in Londonderry for The Society's Agent. At Coleraine itself Stewart Gordon was supervising works for The Society, including reclamation of slob-lands, the new road from Coleraine to Portrush (which the Grand Jury had agreed to on condition The Society built the required bridges), and the improvements to Dance's court-house and town-hall.[100]

Apart from the usual memorials, applications for grants, and concern for the slob-lands, the Deputation applied itself to the problem of improving the 'wretched state' of dwellings. Accordingly, it was decided to erect model cottages and small farm-houses on various parts of The Society's estates. Tite provided the plans **[67]**. There were also strong recommendations to plant trees on The Society's estates not only to

[99] Irish Society (1836), 21.
[100] *Ibid.*, 30-31.

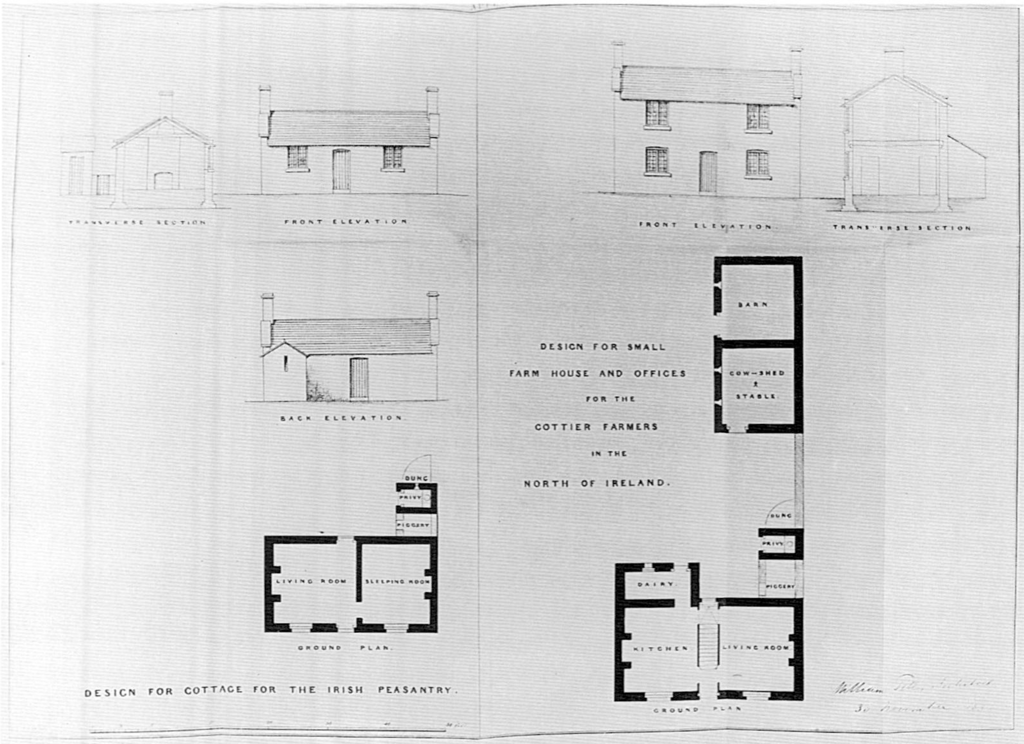

67 'Designs for Cottage for the Irish Peasantry' and 'Design for small Farm House and Offices for the Cottier Farmers in the North of Ireland' of 1836 by William Tite. (*IS*)

beautify the landscape and provide employment, but to secure future supplies of timber and fuel for the rural poor.

Further Deputations visited Ulster in 1838 and 1840. Once more the benefits of afforestation were stressed, but long-standing problems remained. The burnt-out mill at Coleraine was still unlet; encroachments were being made on the slob-lands; and the fisheries were constantly being threatened by poachers 'encouraged by' the Marquess of Donegall. Offices for the General Agent had been obtained in a house in Foyle Street, Londonderry, but the 1840 Deputation considered that The Society 'should erect a large and commodious house, to be called Government House, where the General Agent might reside, and have his office for the transaction of the business of The Society and the security of the papers, &c.' This house 'ought to be sufficiently large to accommodate the Governor, Deputy Governor, and Members of the Deputation with commodious apartments' during their visits.[101]

The Society at one time had contributed 50 guineas per annum for a race-plate to be presented at the recently re-established races. However, this had to be discontinued when The Society received a petition signed by nearly 1,000 persons (including, naturally, all the clergy) stating that the race-meetings were 'extremely prejudicial, subversive of decency and propriety, and destructive to the morals of the working classes and the peace of the community in general'.[102] The Society could only regret in the circumstances that the races 'should have recommenced'. This was not the only difficulty facing The Society at the time.

[101] Irish Society (1841), 17. See also Court Minutes IS/CM/25-26 at the Corporation of London Records Office. See Aldous (ed.) (1993), *passim*.
[102] *Ibid.*, 18.

CHAPTER X

Events relating to The Irish Society until the Aftermath of the Royal Commission of 1853-4

> Through the long course of eventful years since the citizens of London became the undertakers of the settlement of (the) escheated estates – through all the strife by which the hardy colonists held their own against native marauders and foreign foes – through those long and wasting sieges which tried the endurance and evoked the stern virtues of heroic courage and unexampled bravery in her faithful and devoted people – the City of London through her Irish Society, has been the firm and unflinching ally of the Maiden City and her sister town Coleraine
>
> CHARLES REED (1819-81): *An Historical Narrative of the Origin and Constitution of ... The Honourable The Irish Society* (London: The Irish Society, 1865), ix

The Church and The Irish Society

Under Bishop Richard Ponsonby, who had been translated to the see of Derry from Killaloe and Kilfenora in 1831, the diocese faced growing challenges. Following the famous enactment of 1829[1] the Roman Catholic population of Ireland began to demand more and more political clout under the leadership of Daniel O'Connell. Not least of the demands related to the position of the Established Church, for in 1831 there were major disturbances relating to non-payment of tithes. An Act to facilitate the recovery of tithes in certain cases in Ireland and for relief of the clergy of the Established Church[2] was passed in June 1832, but the process of commutation of tithes began shortly afterwards with the Irish Tithe Composition Act.[3] What is more, in the general election of 1832 under the new Representation of the People (Ireland) Act,[4] out of 105 Irish seats at Westminster 42 went to those opposed to the Act of Union (known as Repealers), 33 to the Liberals, and 30 to Conservatives. Opposition to the Established Church was found not only among Roman Catholic Irish, but among those utilitarians who had been most vociferous during the Great Reform debates. In 1833 was passed the draconian Church Temporalities (Ireland) Act[5] which abolished no fewer than 10 bishoprics, provided for appointments of ecclesiastical commissioners with powers to divide livings, suspend appointments, and use the revenues of suppressed bishoprics and the produce of a graduated income tax on livings worth over £200 to build and repair churches as well as to augment poor livings. Not only were the archbishoprics of Cashel and Tuam abolished, but the revenues of the remaining 12 sees were to be reduced and taxed. The diocese of Derry was united with that of Raphoe.[6]

1 10 Geo. IV, c. 7.
2 2 & 3 Will IV, c. 41.
3 2 Will. IV, c. 119.
4 2 & 3 Will. IV, c. 88.
5 3 & 4 Will IV, c. 37.
6 Phillips (1933), **iii**, 304-312.

The Church Temporalities (Ireland) Act of 1833 created uproar, not least in England. It prompted John Keble (1792-1866) to preach his famous sermon on 'National Apostasy' and led, indirectly perhaps, but nevertheless steadily to the Tractarian or high-church movement within the Anglican Church. Certainly rights to the advowsons were of singular importance, and The Irish Society sought to recover the patronage of all livings usurped by the bishops of Derry. When it is remembered that the *annual* value of these livings in the 1820s was around £6,000 we are not considering something insubstantial. The Irish Society attempted to re-assert its rights to the advowsons in the 1830s in a *Quare Impedit* suit (a form of writ issued in cases of disputed presentation to a benefice, requiring the defendant to state why he should hinder the plaintiff from making the presentation) in the Court of Common Pleas in Dublin before a judge and jury. This tried the right of The Society to the patronage of the living of Killowen against the bishop of Derry and involved extensive research and heavy expenses, largely because during the 18th century (in spite of its 17th-century experiences chronicled by Mogridge) The Society had failed to keep adequate tabs on its rights and properties.[7] The judge left it to the jury to decide if the Crown had been legally entitled to the living at the time of the original grant to The Society, but the jury (of the county of Londonderry) returned a verdict in favour of the bishop. Yet there can be no doubt of the Crown's rights at the time the advowsons were granted to The Society, and it would appear that the judge failed to instruct the jury with the facts. The judge in question was William Conyngham Plunket (1764-1854), 1st Baron Plunket (from 1827), Lord Chancellor of Ireland from 1830 to 1841, whose decisions frequently had been reversed on appeal, who had the reputation of being 'hasty and imprudent', and who was given to nepotism to a scandalous degree.[8] Fearing that the outcome of the suit would deprive The Society of the 'extensive patronage' to which it was entitled, that body determined to prosecute a new trial with the bishop of Derry and to present 'Clerks ... forthwith ... to several Livings in question' in order to preserve rights 'either in the event of a Parliamentary measure being introduced upon the subject, or the following up those presentations by suits at law against the Bishop'.[9]

In 1837 the incumbent of Camus-juxta-Bann on the Merchant Taylors' Proportion died, and the bishop installed his nominee to the living. The Society, claiming the advowson was its property under the charter, instituted a suit against the bishop and the incumbent in 1838, claiming damages of £5,000: it dragged on for almost five years, and involved investigations into the history of titles going back to the reign of King Henry VIII. In 1840, the Lord Chief Justice of Ireland (from 1830), John Doherty (1783-1850), delivered a very clear summing-up at the Court of Common Pleas[10] which was favourable to The Society, and legal opinion, based on historical investigations, was clear about The Society's rights. However, juries tended to find against The Society (reflecting a growing animosity in Ireland against anything English), and eventually the suit went to the House of Lords in 1842. In 1843 it was decided to stop defending the advowsons under the governorship (1843-63) of John Humphery, who admitted in 1854 that The Irish Society 'would have got into an expense from £8,000 to £10,000 more ... in the ... suits' had he not set his face 'resolutely against

[7] Irish Society (1836), *Appendix* to the *Report of the Deputation* of 1836.
[8] *D.N.B.* (1917), **xv**, 1332-5.
[9] Irish Society (1836), *Appendix* to the *Report of the Deputation* of 1836, 123.
[10] Given in Appendix III in Irish Society (1841): *Report of the Deputation ... in the Year 1840*, 80-102.

68 The Deanery, Bishop Street, Londonderry of 1833. (*A/CC/UM*)

it, and ... put a stop to litigation'.[11] His evidence for the 1854 commissioners also referred to difficulties The Society experienced in its dealings with Irishmen, including the unfortunate tendency of Dublin lawyers to overcharge for services.[12] Humphery expressed an opinion that The Society would be more efficient if its members served for at least four years or longer.[13] As it was, the advowsons litigation cost The Society about £6,000, and left it only with the rights to the presentation to the rectory of Coleraine, but even that was lost by The Irish Church Act[14] of 1869 which disestablished and partly disendowed the Protestant episcopal Church, and became effective in 1871. The Society applied to the Irish Church commissioners for compensation, which was duly granted.

This momentous Act, which was a severe blow to the Church of Ireland, also deprived many parishes of their glebe-houses, but these could be repurchased at a fixed rate, and The Irish Society was approached for assistance towards the costs of buying them. Among the properties bought with financial help from The Society were the handsome Deanery **[68]** in Bishop Street, Londonderry (as the glebe-house of the parish of Templemore), and the glebe-house (of 1828, later called Chapelfield House, Laurel Hill) and land for Killowen parish.[15]

William Higgin and the Diocese of Derry

William Higgin (1793-1867), Bishop of Derry and Raphoe (1853-67), a Lancastrian (he is commemorated in a handsome stained-glass window in the north chapel of the priory church of St Mary, Lancaster [reset in 1908]), instigated an energetic period in the history of the diocese. During the 1863 Visitation he found that many churches had no fonts, that Communion was administered rarely, and that things were generally unimpressive throughout the lands under his pastoral care. Under Higgin no fewer

[11] Commissioners Appointed to Inquiry into the Existing State of the Corporation of the City of London (1854), Questions 8399-8401. Humphery's evidence is given in Questions 8338-8439.
[12] *Ibid.*, Question 8399.
[13] *Ibid.*, Questions 8436-7.
[14] 32 & 33 Vict., c. 42.
[15] Reed (1917), 72. See also Smith (1966).

than 17 new churches were erected in the diocese, and a further 27 were altered and enlarged during his episcopate. His zealous restoration and re-ordering of the cathedral was of considerable importance, and it is worth considering this in some detail.

In 1858 the bishop (clearly influenced in part by fashionable ecclesiology) began to campaign for major works to be carried out at St Columb's. These were carried out in 1861-2, but during excavations necessary for construction purposes opinion was excited by the 'unceremonious manner' in which human bones, the 'memorials of the defenders of Derry' were treated by the 'parties in temporary charge of the Cathedral'.[16] In this remark can be detected something of the extreme sensitivity to anything relating to disturbing certain aspects of history, and in particular a whiff of animosity towards the English bishop who was behind major changes to the built fabric: those alterations included removal of the galleries in the north and south aisles; destruction of the 'clumsy' Georgian box-pews and their replacement with 'handsome' Gothic Revival Riga-oak open benches and stalls; tidying-up of the western gallery (holding seats for about 120 persons) including the erection of the Gothic screens; the addition of the canopy over the *cathedra* (bishop's throne); provision of gas-lighting and a new heating system; construction of a new stair and floor in the tower; and the addition of some stained-glass memorial windows. The plastered ceilings in imitation of stone vaulting survived these alterations, which cost £4,000 towards which The Irish Society made a hefty grant of £750 **[38]**. Champneys, however, noted that the 'old low aisle windows' had been made 'architecturally absurd by the removal of the galleries',[17] which remark suggests that the fenestration was not as it is now.

The Dublin Builder reported on the re-opening of the cathedral in 1862.[18] The improvements, it was said, 'had their origin in a correct and cultivated taste'. The 'ricketty, whitewashed wooden staircase and broken flags' of the old building, together with the 'useless and ungainly stoves' in the 'central aisle' had spoiled the look of the building: there were no stalls, except for the bishop and dean, and these were 'incongruous in style', while the 'high-backed pews' were 'inconvenient'. The old galleries were 'dark and cumbrous', overhanging the 'side aisles' and destroying the 'fair proportions' of the building, while the 'dusty windows' were filled with 'common glass'. Improvements included the timbers of the bell-ringers' loft left exposed, the erection of 'graceful stairs', and the panelled ceiling to the 'effective' vestibule with its tracery panels and doors filled with plate glass. The 'groined ceilings' of the church proper had their bosses 'illuminated', and the episcopal throne, with its 'canopied and traceried gablets, decorated finials, and handsome spirelet', was much admired. Also approved of were the carved bench-ends with their Gothic poppy-heads, and the new stained-glass window in the east end.

For these works the designer was Joseph Welland, architect to the ecclesiastical commissioners, and the contract was supervised by Welland and Gillespie.[19] The general contractor was James Henry of Belfast; the hot-water provisions for heating and the gas-light were by J. W. Smith of London; stained-glass was by Wailes of Newcastle upon Tyne; and floors to the porch, vestibule, nave, and chancel were laid with Minton's encaustic tiles. Stalls for the dean and prebendaries were placed at the

[16] *The Dublin Builder* 3 (1861), 548.

[17] Champneys (1910), 202-3.

[18] 4 (1862), 112-3, 123-4.

[19] There were two Wellands, Joseph and William. The latter retired in 1875. William Gillespie died in 1896. Joseph Welland succeeded Bowden, and was probably responsible for realising Bowden's designs for several Anglican churches in Londonderry: he would have been getting on when he carried out the works in Londonderry cathedral in the 1860s.

69 Monument to Captain Boyd in the north aisle, St Columb's cathedral, Londonderry. (*A/CC/UM*)

west end, in front of the timber traceried screen separating the body of the church from the vestibule. The octagonal pulpit, reading-desk, lectern, and Communion-rails were 'richly decorated' with 'specimens of mediaeval art'. In addition, the north aisle was ornamented by two 'splendid' windows. It was at that time that the monument was erected to Captain John McNeil Boyd, R. N. (d. 1861), who was lost when H.M.S. *Ajax* was hit by a hurricane: by (Sir) Thomas Farrell (1827-1900), it is in the north aisle, and features Hope with her Anchor above a relief of the Captain and crew battling against the storm **[69]**.

Mindful of the vociferous attacks being made on the Church before disestablishment, Higgin insisted on high standards of clerical conduct within his diocese in order to deflect criticisms, and also promoted the idea that Church property should be kept in good repair. At considerable personal cost he managed to get one dubious rector deprived of his living, but he ran foul of some opinion when he refused permission for the crimson flag associated with the siege and relief of Londonderry to be flown above the east window. Interpreted as an 'outrage upon the Protestant community',[20] the bishop's action was a response to the Party Processions (Ireland) Act of 1860[21] which became law on 28 August in an attempt to strengthen powers against 'provocative' behaviour during marches, processions, and public displays. In 1850 Parliament had passed the Party Processions (Ireland) Act[22] which provided for the confiscation of emblems and arms, but the 1860 Act was intended to give extra powers to the authorities. As a member of the House of Lords, Higgin had supported the Bill on its first reading, so he found himself in an invidious position. In the event, the Apprentice Boys of Derry Club (founded 1814) raised the flag and occupied the belfry for a couple of days.

[20] *Londonderry Sentinel* (17 August 1860).
[21] 23 & 24 Vict., c. 141.
[22] 13 Vict., c. 2.

Sectarian Difficulties

However, it was not just an Act of Parliament, a bishop endeavouring to be consistent, and local organisations that were on collision courses. Sectarian tensions had been steadily rising in Londonderry as working-class Roman Catholic districts grew up with the influx of rural poor. The Ordnance Survey *Memoir* painted a ghastly picture of the poverty, squalor, and disease prevailing,[23] partly as a result of the arrival of very large numbers of destitute persons from County Donegal. Among the reasons for this migration was the failure of the potato crop in 1821, but the rural economy was even more severely hit when the widespread and flourishing manufacture of illegal whiskey (*potheen*) was virtually ended by the zealous activities of Excise officers operating under new laws to tighten up the collection of revenue and encourage *legal* stills.[24] Relations between Roman Catholics and Protestants had been fairly amicable in the 18th century until the 1798 rebellion quickly degenerated into sectarian outrages, but frictions became more overt as the numbers of Roman Catholics increased. Agitation for 'Catholic Emancipation' and the beginnings of annual parades to celebrate the siege and the relief exacerbated sectarian trouble. The Roman Catholic bishop, Charles O'Donnell (1747-1823), who succeeded the conciliatory Bishop McDevitt (who was probably his uncle) in 1798, attempted to steer a course of moderation, but soon fell foul of those in favour of more radical activities, and earned himself the unfortunate nickname of 'Orange Charlie'. O'Donnell was actually threatened in 1813 by a priest, Cornelius O'Mullan (d. 1821), who was associated with Ribbonism, the secret oath-bound agrarian sectarian society, partly descended from the Defender society, which regularly clashed with Protestant organisations. The bishop, who had arranged a meeting in the Long Tower church, had to seek protection in the court-house when O'Mullan and a mob arrived at the church. Subsequently, O'Mullan was excommunicated, tried, and imprisoned for a short time.[25]

The annual Protestant parades were attacked in 1822, but O'Donnell's successor as bishop (from 1824), Peter MacLaughlin (1760-1840 – who had witnessed the storming of the Bastille in Paris in 1789), attempted to calm things down, or, as Colby put it, interfered 'in political matters only so far as to endeavour to prevent the people of his own persuasion from indulging in party violence',[26] and was 'distinguished for his piety, and very generally esteemed ... for his zealous and unremitting exertions to promote concord and good feeling among all sects'.[27] MacLaughlin's efforts were not assisted by the arrival in Londonderry of fiery itinerant Protestant proselytising preachers, events which were excuses for riots. Other 'Missions' of the 1820s had a similar effect on the populace, but controversy resulted in a very surprising series of public debates in 1828 between six Protestant clergymen and six Roman Catholic priests covering topics such as the Papacy, Transubstantiation, Purgatory, Luther, and the Bible, transcripts of which were published in a vast tome in Dublin later that year. A cursory look through the volume is sufficient to make the reader thankful not to have been at the debates.

[23] Colby (1837), 194.

[24] 4 Geo. IV, c. 23, and 4 Geo. IV, c. 94. Such draconian measures against illegal distilling, like the success of Customs officers in the 1960s in preventing cross-border smuggling of sausage-skins and other commodities, were referred to locally as 'ruining the economy'.

[25] Colby (1837), 70; Lacy (1998), 169-7. See also Daly and Devlin (1997), 12-13, 146.

[26] Colby (1837), 70.

[27] *Ibid.*

Removal of all remaining restrictions on Roman Catholics by the Act of 1829[28] (apart from those relating to royal marriages[29]) created its own problems, for many Protestants in Ireland felt threatened, and indeed disestablishment was only 40 years away. In all these controversies, however, The Irish Society managed to avoid becoming too embroiled, although, like every other landlord in Ireland, it attracted the opprobrium of Nationalists simply because it was a landlord.

The Society and Londonderry from the 1840s

By far the greatest transformation to County Londonderry to occur, apart from the enormous schemes of tree- and hedgerow-planting encouraged after Sampson's important publications of 1802 and 1814, was that brought about by the coming of the railways. Two were promoted in 1844: one was a line from Londonderry to Enniskillen, and the other linking Londonderry, Ballykelly, and Coleraine. The Irish Society was closely involved in both projects (especially in regard to the provision of land for railway purposes), but the Londonderry-Coleraine line was far more important, and not only as a transport link, for its construction involved the reclamation of a very large area of slob-land which, it was held, would pay for the construction costs. However, the terrain involved the making of tunnels through the solid rock at Downhill below Bishop Hervey's great house, and English labourers had to be brought over to carry out the works. The line took eight years to build, and was soon in financial trouble, but the Belfast & Northern Counties Railway (as it became in 1860) took over the small Ballymena & Portrush Railway in 1861, and the construction of a railway-bridge downstream from Coleraine over the Bann by a nominal company, The Belfast & Londonderry Junction Railway, linked Belfast and Londonderry by 1860, thus improving economic prospects.[30]

The bridge was constructed on timber piles with an iron lattice-structure spanning them: in the centre was a masonry pier supporting a span that revolved when ships needed to pass beneath. Although the Londonderry & Coleraine line co-operated with the Belfast & Northern Counties Company, it did not amalgamate with the B. & N. C. R. until 1871. As the old L. & C. fabric, including the stations, was in a deplorable condition, the new company was obliged to replace just about every structure, and simple designs for red-brick buildings with different brick dressings were provided by John Lanyon (1840-1900), son of one of the original surveyors of the line, Charles Lanyon (the other surveyor had been Robert Stephenson [1803-59]). John Lanyon was also responsible for the handsome Italianate railway-station at Londonderry-Waterside (1875), but it was his father, Charles, who designed the fine arcaded station at Coleraine (1855).

The railway was responsible for the development of the holiday-resort of Castlerock by the Clothworkers' Company, and clearly the amalgamation of companies and the bridging of the Bann did much to stimulate the economy. The Londonderry and Enniskillen Railway did not reach Enniskillen until 1854 (its Londonderry terminus was sited at Letterkenny Road), but it did not long remain independent either: it was absorbed first by the Irish North Western Railway and then by the Great Northern Railway (Ireland). A third company, The Londonderry & Lough Swilly Railway,

[28] 10 Geo. IV, c. 7. For Ireland in the 1840s *see Parliamentary Gazetteer* (1846), *passim.*

[29] Royal Marriage Act, 1772.

[30] Currie (1973), *passim.*

connected Londonderry to Letterkenny, and also, via other lines, Inishowen and Burtonport. When the Carlisle Bridge **[89]** was eventually erected over the Foyle at Londonderry in 1861-3 at a point upstream from its expensive and troublesome timber predecessor, it had two decks: the upper one was a carriageway, and the lower supported railway-tracks. The Port & Harbour Commissioners constructed a line in 1868 linking the Waterside terminus, the Graving Dock terminus of the Londonderry & Lough Swilly Railway, the Foyle Road station of the line to Strabane and Enniskillen, and the City Goods Station. Later, when the County Donegal Railway opened its terminus at Victoria Road (near the south-east end of the bridge) in 1900, it was connected with the other systems.[31]

With all these developments The Irish Society, as a benevolent landlord and owner of much of the soil on which construction took place, was closely concerned. Grants were distributed throughout the years, not only for charitable purposes, but for building work, including a pier at Moville Bay. However, the 1840s saw considerable restlessness in Ireland as O'Connell's agitation for repeal of the Union, and the close connection between Nationalism, religion, and politics once again began to create ominous rumblings. Even the Papacy became concerned, and the Prefect of Propaganda, Cardinal Fransoni, wrote in 1844 to William Crolly (1780-1849), Roman Catholic Archbishop of Armagh from 1835, prescribing that bishops and priests should eschew politics and urging the archbishop to take action against those who refused to obey. This letter followed an earlier one of 1839 *exhorting* bishops and priests to avoid politics, but does not seem to have had much effect because in 1848, in a communication published in the *Dublin Evening Post* (5 February 1848), the Papacy urged Irish bishops to forbid political activity by the clergy. The Popes at the time were Gregory XVI (1831-1846 – who was hostile to modern trends, notably Italian Nationalism, outbreaks of which he had had to crush with the help of military aid from Austria, and who had written to Polish bishops in 1832 condemning the Polish uprising against Russia [1830-1]) and Pius IX (1846-78 – who is identified with Ultramontanism, who opposed the view that the Pope should reconcile himself to, or agree with, liberalism, progress, and modernity, and who forbade Roman Catholics to take part in political life in the 'usurping' Kingdom of Italy).

In September 1845, potato blight made its first appearance in Ireland, heralding disaster for the rural economies of many counties. G. V. Sampson had warned of the dangers of a single-crop agriculture, and the problems should have been anticipated, for collapse of demand for linen in the past, bad harvests, and other problems had quickly reduced small tenant-farmers to destitution. Myth has it that the Government did nothing to alleviate problems caused by potato blight, but in 1845 Sir Robert Peel (1788-1850), the Prime Minister, ordered the purchase of cheap corn from the U.S.A. for shipment to Ireland, and a relief commission was established. It should be remembered that Peel had established the Devon commission in 1843 to enquire into the state of the law and practice in respect of the occupation of land in Ireland, which reported in February 1845. Peel was also a leading figure in getting legislation through Parliament to give financial support to St Patrick's College, Maynooth, the educational establishment of the Irish priesthood,[32] and to create the new Queen's colleges for higher education on a non-sectarian basis.[33] The Roman Catholic bishops objected to

[31] Currie (1973), 115-6. See also Boyd (n.d.), *passim.*
[32] 8 & 9 Vict., c. 25.
[33] 8 & 9 Vict., c. 66.

the proposed new non-denominational colleges as dangerous to faith and morals, but the establishments flourished, and developed to become important centres of university education (e.g. The Queen's University of Belfast).

Various enactments to relieve distress caused by the Potato Blight were passed, including the Public Works (Ireland) Act of 1846[34] and others,[35] which saw an enormous amount of construction work (e.g. piers, harbours, walls round estates, roads, bridges, etc.). Nevertheless, smallholders who could not pay rent were evicted in large numbers, so food had to be distributed by relief committees, and public health enactments were rushed through to create a Central Board of Health with powers to direct the Poor Law Guardians to provide fever hospitals, dispensaries, medicines, and food. In June 1846 Peel's famous repeal of the Corn Laws[36] became law by which duties on imported corn, meal, and flour were abolished in order to enable the starving Irish peasantry to be fed, but what is always forgotten is that the protection the Corn Laws had given British agriculture was removed, thereby permanently and drastically changing the nature of society.

Nevertheless, in spite of these measures, the potato crop again failed disastrously, and the Government passed further legislation empowering the Board of Works to execute schemes backed by Treasury loans for the employment of the destitute poor on various public construction proposals. Amazingly, corn was *exported* from Ireland, and there were riots in Youghal, Co. Cork, when a ship laden with oats set sail. Matters were made worse by an unusually hard winter in 1846-7, and the British Association for the Relief of the Extreme Distress in the Remote Parishes of Ireland and Scotland was formed in 1847 (it should be remembered that the Highlands and Islands of Scotland also suffered from famine at the same time and for the same reason). Soup-kitchens[37] were established as well as public works, and the Boards of Guardians were empowered to grant outdoor relief.[38] Crimes and outrages multiplied, and a series of murders of landlords and their agents took place, prompting the Crime and Outrage (Ireland) Act of 1847,[39] by which extra police were appointed and powers given to control the possession of arms.

The general failure of the potato crop in 1848 led to a further deterioration of conditions, law, and order. Where famine and destitution are found, disease and death follow closely behind: typhus, typhoid, and cholera claimed their victims, including Archbishop Crolly himself, who died of cholera in 1849, the year in which the potato blight reappeared, causing widespread distress and more evictions. The Great Famine began to affect Londonderry and its environs towards the end of 1846, by which time many destitute poor from rural areas were endeavouring to obtain relief in and around the city. Towards the end of 1845 the Corporation of Londonderry, realising a disaster was occurring, expressed to the Government its unanimous opinion that immediate steps should be taken to 'guard against the melancholy consequences ... of the scarcity of food', including the issue of an Order in Council 'admitting the immediate importation of Corn at a minimal duty'[40] and '*prohibiting the exportation of provisions to foreign parts*'.[41] This was an extraordinarily far-sighted position to take for the time,

[34] 9 Vict., c. 1.
[35] 9 Vict., c. 2.
[36] 9 & 10 Vict., c. 22.
[37] 10 Vict., c. 7.
[38] 10 Vict., c. 31.
[39] 11 Vict., c. 2.
[40] Lacy (1988), 184-5.
[41] My italics. See also Murphy (1981), *passim*.

given the *laissez-faire* climate that then prevailed, and The Irish Society was a prime mover in this approach to the Government.

A special committee was established to deal with the crisis, but it was no time to be having a famine, as Londonderry was experiencing severe economic decline which left it unable to respond with unlimited resources. It should be remembered that such difficulties were not confined to Ireland, for throughout the British Isles there was a considerable slump in economic well-being. With the best will in the world, the city of Londonderry was not in a strong position to give support to large numbers of poverty-stricken refugees from rural areas (mostly in Donegal), and this was made clear, deterring all but the most desperate from seeking relief.[42]

All this, set against an uneasy political climate, led to campaigns being mounted against Protestant parades. In those agitations Dr. Edward Maginn (1802-49 – who had been nominated to the see of Orthodosia, in the archbishopric of Tyre, *in Partibus Infidelium*, in 1845, and consecrated Roman Catholic Bishop of Derry in 1846), was prominent: he became active in public arguments about responsibility for the famine, supported O'Connell's campaigns for the repeal of the Union, and was vociferous in his condemnations of Protestant parades. Thus he was consciously going against the official line promoted by the Papacy. The bishop attempted to stop the 1848 Protestant parades, and the ensuing 1849 Roman Catholic St Patrick's Day parade led to serious riots. Bishop Maginn founded St Columb's College as a seminary, and worked tirelessly for the victims of the Great Famine, channelling aid from abroad to help them. He himself died of typhus, one of the attendant diseases of hunger.

From the 1830s, as is clear from the Deputation reports of The Irish Society and local newspapers, the tone of Londonderry was changing. Scrupulous observance of 'The Sabbath', the conversion of the theatre into a wash-house, the discontinuance of concerts, and the growing aversion to horse-racing were all symptomatic of a move towards increasing puritanism, even joylessness. Persons who had once patronised social occasions and trade began to move out of the city, with the result that inhabitants tended to be those who had 'yet their fortunes to gain':[43] philistinism, fundamentalism, Sabbatarianism, economic decline, sectarian animosities (whipped up by both persuasions), and a perceptive shift in class structure did not do much to improve the Londoners' city, and the coming of the railways was just too late to halt this transformation.

Londonderry had long been associated with shipbuilding (on a small scale) and emigration (on a large one). The construction of ships was inhibited by the lack of ship-ways and dry-docks until the 1830s, when some improvements enabled the building of sailing vessels for transatlantic routes and steam-powered ships for cross-channel journeys. In 1843 the *Great Northern*,[44] then the largest steam-propelled ship in the world, was launched, but it was badly timed in the middle of the economic slump, and the shipbuilding industry failed to develop, though it flourished during the 1914-18 war. As one of the most westerly ports in Europe, Londonderry was well-placed for emigration to America. As was mentioned above, most of those who left for the New World in the 18th century were of Ulster-Scots stock, fleeing from rack-renting and middle-men, but from the 1840s the flow of Roman Catholic emigrants began in earnest, prompted by the disaster of the Famine. The Roman Catholic bishop noted

[42] Murphy (1981), *passim*. For the Great Famine see Kennedy, Ell, Crawford, and Clarkson (1999), *passim*.
[43] Colby (1837), 194.
[44] *Illustrated London News* (14 January 1843).

that within the diocese there were nearly a quarter of a million of the faithful, of which about 50,000 people were starving. As was mentioned earlier, American ships carrying flax-seed for the linen industry arrived in Londonderry and took emigrants back on the return journey. As demand for ships increased and emigration from the overcrowded countryside began to be supported by the Companies, local entrepreneurs acquired ships to carry emigrants (mostly to Canada at first), returning with loads of North American timber, and used in the winter months to bring cotton back from southern American ports (e.g. New Orleans) to Liverpool. By the 1840s the ships were larger, and the main American port of disembarkation for emigrants from Londonderry became Philadelphia: in the spring of 1847 alone nearly 2,000 emigrants left Londonderry for Philadelphia on eight local sailing vessels.[45] Emigration continued, largely in the hands of local firms, and in the 1860s was augmented by demand from America for war supplies and emigrants to replace Americans fighting in the Civil War (1861-5), at the end of which the Londonderry shipping and emigration trade was at its height. Very soon the trade was taken over by steamships calling at Londonderry: it is very strange that local firms persisted with sailing vessels which simply could not compete with the speed of steam-powered vessels. Given that sailing-ships could be delayed for weeks while they waited for favourable winds to take them westwards across the Atlantic (with all the associated ghastliness on board ships teeming with emigrants unversed in basic hygiene), it is hard to fathom the mentality that refused to move with the times.

By 1849 The Irish Society had done much to promote the railways, facilitate the improvement of the quays, and alleviate the worst effects of the Famine by means of donations to various benevolent bodies. However, endemic unrest led to its own difficulties, and employees of The Society had a hard time of it, sometimes finding themselves in great danger. Leah Johnston, the widow of 'a servant of The Society murdered in County Donegal' was just one of many who prayed to The Society for aid and got it.

During the construction of the Londonderry & Enniskillen Railway material was excavated from the bed of the River Foyle in order to build the quays, and this caused problems for the fisheries and the banks generally. Difficulties were also experienced at Culmore Fort, where a cabin The Society had permitted a destitute family affected by the Famine to occupy was demolished and a two-storey house erected, blocking up the loop-holes of the fort. The family also levelled the historic earthworks and effectively became squatters. It appears that the instigator of this episode was a nephew of the family, also a priest, who was clearly out to embarrass The Society, probably as part of the general anti-Union, pro-Repeal, anti-landlord, sectarian uproar prevalent at that time.[46] The Society was obliged to take proceedings to recover its lands, but it was one of many instances where a benevolent gesture at a time of emergency and crisis was taken advantage of and abused for political ends, not unconnected with greed.

The Irish Society and Building Activities

Mindful of the need to give employment to local people, and particularly to provide exemplars as there were 'but few good houses' in the neighbourhood during the

[45] Cooke (*c.*1950), *passim*; Lacy (1998), 190-1. For emigration from 1815 to the Famine *see* Adams (1935).

[46] Court Minutes for 1849, 15/CM/25-26, at the Corporation of London Guildhall Records Office. See Aldous (ed.) (1993), *passim*.

1840s, The Society decided to build a house as its headquarters, the cost not to exceed £2,100.[47] This had been mooted earlier and 'Government House', as a residence for the General Agent and base for visiting Deputations, was referred to in the *Report* of the 1840 Deputation.[48] In 1846 land was purchased for £300 to buy out the interests of one Captain James Taylor at Termonbacca.[49] It appears that designs were prepared by Stewart Gordon, the surveyor, but these were comprehensively worked over by William Tite, and the Court Minutes for 1846 record that Tite's plans were a 'great improvement'. Once Parliamentary approval had been sought and obtained (the reason being that The Society, though the owner of the soil, was also subservient to the Crown), tenders were sought, but these exceeded the agreed figure.

Here we come up against a recurring theme in the history of the Londoners' Plantation. There always seem to have been difficulties with Irish labourers, Irish contractors, Irish lawyers, and Irish employees generally: overcharging, shoddy work, and dishonesty were problems with which The Society and the Companies had to contend, time and again. The Governor of The Society referred to grotesque attempts by Dublin lawyers to screw money out of The Society in his evidence to the commissioners enquiring into the state of the Corporation of the City of London in 1854,[50] and the Drapers' Company, exasperated by their problems, found it less trouble and expense to bring clerks of works and even contractors over from London (and keep them) than to attempt to employ locals.[51]

However, in the case of Government House at Termonbacca the contract was awarded to a local man, John McCarter, who tendered £2,950, and building began in 1846. The first instalment of payment to McCarter was certified by Tite in January 1847, and the building was roofed by November 1847. During the winter of 1846 a garden-wall was built at Termonbacca to give McCarter and some 50-60 men work during inclement weather at a cost of £390. Government House was completed early in 1848 and Tite reported on McCarter's final bill, which was £385 more than the contract: Tite opined that the building was 'remarkably well executed, ... certainly for Ireland', but noted that McCarter (who claimed to have lost money having carried out the contract) was in severe financial difficulties. Tite contrasted the 'skilful and punctual' tradesmen of London with the 'somewhat uneducated' workers of Londonderry operating under a contractor of 'limited means'.[52] Chronic lack of capital seems to have been a universal problem among Irish builders at the time, and the unfortunate McCarter was no exception. Stables and other offices were erected at Termonbacca in 1848, and an examination of the records at Guildhall reveals other interesting information: stone for the building of Government House was imported from Scotland, and the chimney-pieces (that in the main reception-room being exceptionally fine work in a Neoclassical style) and kitchen range from England. As usual with contracts of the time, the house required a long time to dry out (because of the use of lime-mortar and slow-drying plaster), so was not painted and papered until 1850. The total cost of Government House, including roads, walls, outbuildings, the formation of the garden, and planting was £5,814 3s. 11d.[53] Tite was paid £183 18s. 11d. as architect,

[47] Court Minutes for 1849, 15/CM/25-26, at the Corporation of London Guildhall Records Office. See Aldous (ed.) (1993), *passim.*

[48] Irish Society (1841), *Report of the Deputation ... in ... 1840*, 17.

[49] Called 'Termonbacco', No. 325, in the Court Minutes.

[50] See note 11.

[51] Curl (1986), 193 and *passim.*

[52] 1S/CM/25-26.

[53] *Ibid.*

70 Government House, Termonbacca, in 1984. The ugly dormer-windows are not original, and have since been removed. The chimneys with arch between them were demolished in the 1990s. Over the porch is a keystone with the emblem of The Irish Society on it. The architect was William Tite. (*A/CC/UM*)

but the clerk of works was Garrett Payne, who designed the outbuildings. A vignette of the house adorns James O'Hagan's map of 1847: with its fittings, and superb site with stunning views over the River Foyle, it was a worthy residence for The Society's Agent **[70]**. Over the doorway The Society's Arms were set.

The Society retained Government House until 1906, when it was sold to the Cooke family, together with a 'strip of land to the other side of the main road', for £5,500: in the 1980s it was in the hands of the Christian Brothers, who eventually sold it, and it passed again to private hands. The handsome chimneys with an arch between them on the entrance front were demolished in *c*.1997. Government House was intended as a catalyst to encourage the erection of salubrious villas along the banks of the Foyle. The Society sought to improve its estates, and Stewart Gordon was instructed to prepare plans for 'Cottiers' houses' and various other buildings **[71, 72]** in the 1850s. Gordon was the architect of an elegant (if conservative for its date) design for a house at Killea to cost £400 **[73]**.[54]

Stewart Gordon (d. 1860) was a competent surveyor (he not only served The Society but was county surveyor as well) and could be a reasonable designer of buildings at times. Among his best works are the Great James Street Presbyterian church (1835-7 – with its handsome Ionic portico and steps flanked by huge scrolls); the court-house at Coleraine with its Doric portico **[74]** modelled (rather unusually, and very loosely, minus the triglyphs and other refinements) on the Roman temple at Cori (first century B.C.), and built in 1852;[55] and the bridge over the Bann at Coleraine, linking the Clothworkers' Proportion on the Killowen side of the river to Bridge Street in Coleraine itself. This bridge, which The Irish Society played a major part in promoting, was built by the contractor John Lynn of Coleraine and completed in 1844, and it is one of the most handsome of such stone structures in Ireland **[75]**. This major development also involved reclamation of slob-lands, embanking of the Bann (under Gordon's

[54] Curl (1986), 414. See IS/V/31, MS. Report of 1859 Deputation.
[55] Curl (1992), 36-7.

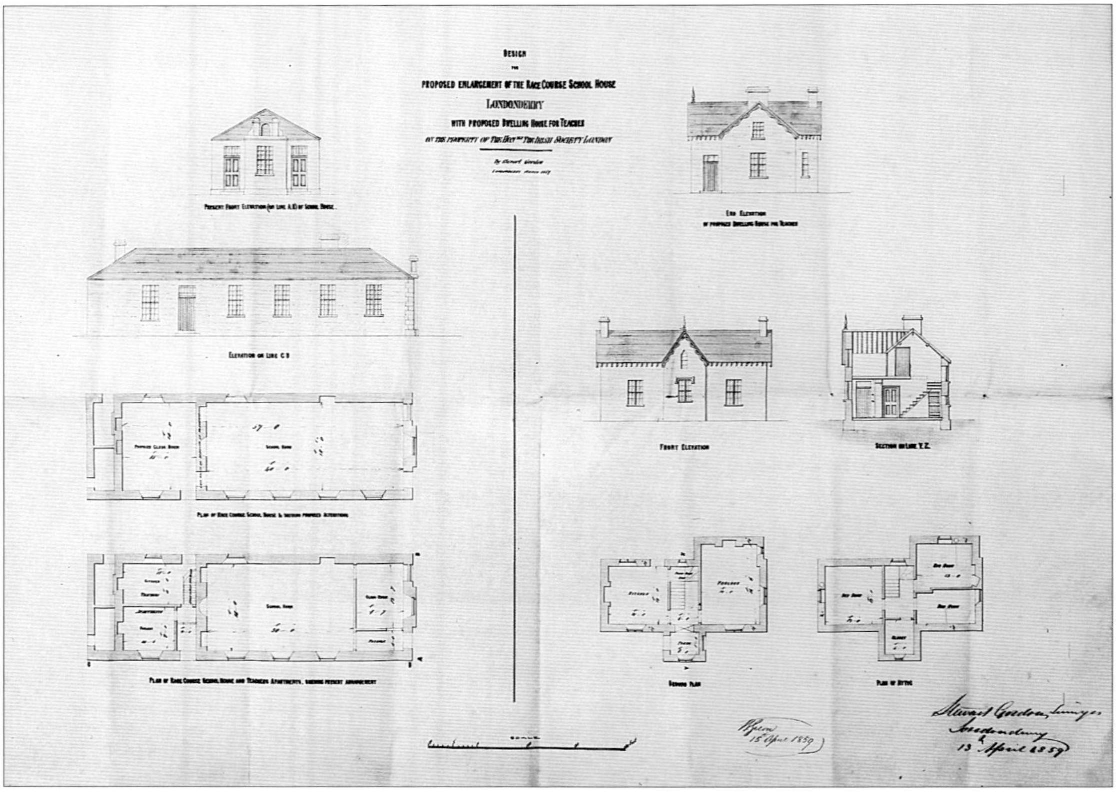

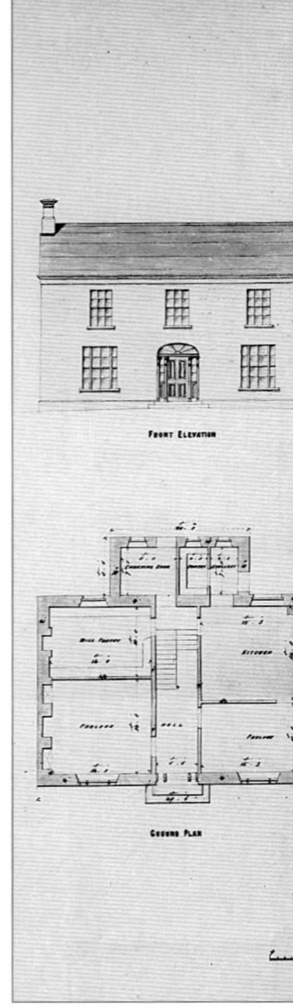

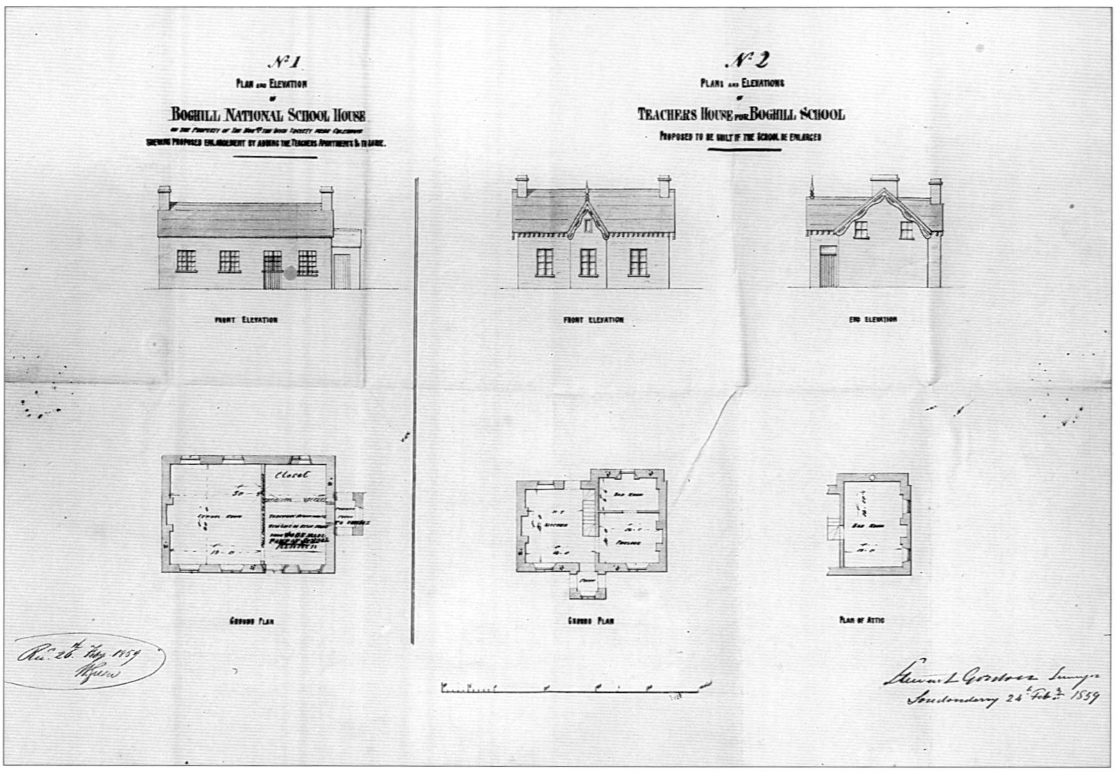

71 Stewart Gordon's designs of 1859 for the enlargement of the Race Course School House, Londonderry, with Proposed Dwelling House for Teacher. *(CLRO/GLCL/IS/2nd Series No. 36)*

72 Stewart Gordon's plans of 1859 for the Boghill National School-House and Teacher's House, near Coleraine. *(CLRO/GLCL/IS/2nd Series No. 44)*

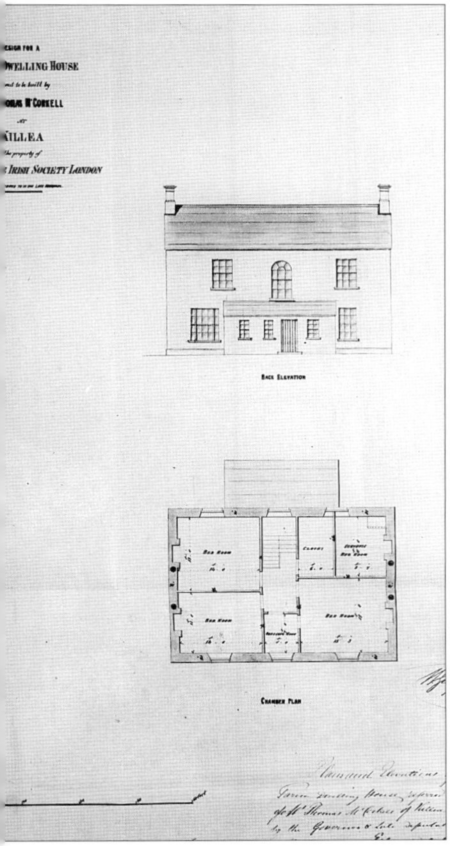

73 Stewart Gordon's design for a house at Killea for The Honourable The Irish Society, 1859. The design is almost identical to that of Cutts House at the Salmon Leap, Coleraine, The Irish Society's offices in County Londonderry from the 1990s. (*IS*)

74 Court-house, Coleraine, completed in 1852 to designs by Stewart Gordon, in 1983. (*A/CC/UM*)

75 Stewart Gordon's bridge over the River Bann of 1844, in 1987. The former *Clothworkers' Arms* hotel can be seen on the left behind the tree, and County Hall stands above the first arch on the left. (*A*)

76a Prospect of Coleraine from Killowen, *c.*1848. On the left is the *Clothworkers' Arms* hotel by Samuel Angell, with the Waterside cottages shortly to be replaced by more salubrious houses. The bridge over the Bann is in the centre, and the town-hall tower is visible above the roof-tops. From a sepia water-colour. *(AT and DMacL)*

supervision), the raising and widening of the road on the Killowen side, and considerable building works. On the Clothworkers' side of the river the dignified houses and hotel at Waterside were designed by Samuel Angell (1800-66), surveyor to the Clothworkers' Company, and he, with Gordon, greatly improved the approaches to Coleraine.[56]

Two panoramic views of Coleraine, rendered with sepia water-colour, show what The Irish Society's town looked like in *c.*1848. *The Clothworkers' Arms* hotel and stable-block were built in 1844-6, and these are shown on the drawings which, though somewhat amateurish, are nevertheless important as a record of the town's development. Visible are St Patrick's church, the new bridge over the Bann, St John's Roman Catholic church, Killowen, and the tower of the old town-hall **[76a-b]**. Coleraine then was very compact and neat, and it did not sprawl untidily over the countryside: indeed it nestled pleasingly by the banks of the majestic river, and was a considerable credit to The Society and its management. In 1849-50 the burnt-out mill at the Salmon Leap above Coleraine (which had not been let for many years) was demolished and the site cleared for the buildings that stand on the site today.[57]

During the 1850s The Irish Society approved the establishment of the Coleraine Academical Institution, the site for which was provided by the Clothworkers' Company in 1853, and the building, designed by Isaac Farrell of Dublin (*fl.* 1849-63 – the architect of the handsome Methodist church in Coleraine [1851-2]**[77]**), was opened in 1860. The Society also gave substantial sums towards the building of Magee Presbyterian

[56] Curl (1986), 374-97.

[57] IS/V/31 MS. Report of Deputations. I am indebted to Mr Daniel MacLaughlin for showing me the panoramic views.

76b Prospect of Coleraine looking upstream. On the left is old St Patrick's church. The town-hall tower can be seen above the roofs of the houses. On the right is the *Clothworkers' Arms* hotel and stable-block, and on the hillside above the bridge is St John's Roman Catholic church, Killowen. From a sepia water-colour. *(AT and DMacL)*

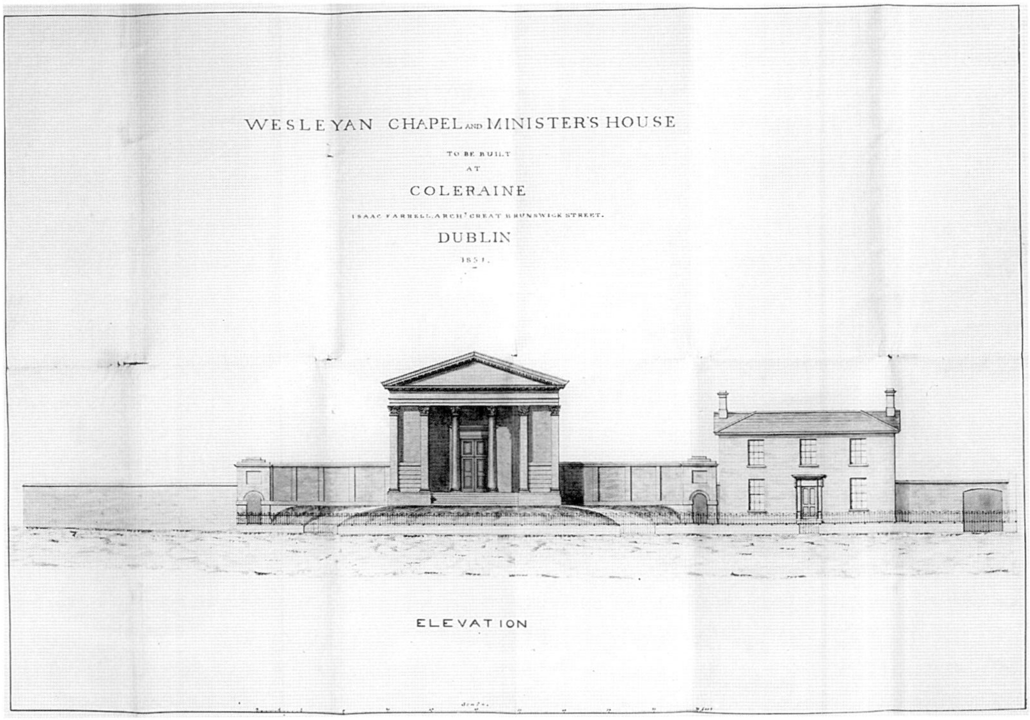

77 The 'Wesleyan Chapel and Minister's House' at Coleraine. Drawing by Isaac Farrell, architect, of Great Brunswick Street, Dublin, 1851. (*GLRC/GLCL/IS/2nd Series No. 89*)

College, Londonderry in 1853, designed by E. P. Gribbon of Dublin (d. 1899) in 1856 in the Gothic Revival style, completed in 1865, partly under the direction of Stewart Gordon who died before the work was finished. 'Magee' became a college of the Royal University of Ireland in 1879, was affiliated to Trinity College, Dublin, in 1909, and is now part of the University of Ulster.[58]

Much effort and cash were expended on improvements to the banks of the Rivers Foyle and Bann, reclamation of slob-lands, quays, navigation, and roads throughout this period. Large sums were expended at Londonderry to improve the docks, and The Society agreed to build a cemetery-chapel and chaplain's residence. Grants totalling £2,100 were made towards the construction of water-works for Londonderry.[59] At Coleraine schools for infants were built by The Society, designed by Stewart Gordon and built by Coyle, a local contractor.[60] During the 1850s it was decided to replace the old Dance-Mills market-house in Coleraine with a new town-hall, and construction began in 1857, supervised by Gordon, but he did not design the building. The architect was Thomas Turner (*c.*1820-91), probably a brother of Richard Turner (1798-1881), the Dublin iron-founder who worked with Charles Lanyon on the design and manufacture of the Palm House, Botanic Gardens, Belfast (1839), and then with Decimus Burton (1800-81) on the Palm House at the Royal Botanic Gardens, Kew (1845-8). Richard Turner's firm made the fine cast-iron grilles in the Coleraine town-hall tower's belfry-stage, and the general contractors were McLaughlin & Harvey, who completed the building in 1859 at a cost of £4,146 19s. 10½d. A fine building of masonry, the town-hall combines Italianate and Baroque features **[78a-b]**, and proudly displays in its carved roundels **[79a-b]** the connections between Coleraine and London: the *Sigillum Villae Coleraine* roundel has a shield on which is a St George's cross and in *Dexter* chief a sword erect, and in *Sinister* chief a salmon; and the other roundel, inscribed *Soc. Gubernat. Et. Assist. Lond. Novae. Plantat. in Ultonia. Ine. Regn. Hiberniae* (the shortened and incorrect Latin form of The Society of the Governors and Assistants, London, of the New Plantation in Ulster within the Realm of Ireland – it should read *Inf. Regn. Hiberniae*, the '*ine*' being wrongly given instead of '*inf*', short for *infra*), contains the escutcheon of The Irish Society in which the field is divided into two (*party per pale*) by a vertical line on the *Dexter* part the Cross and Sword (in the first quarter) of London and on the *Sinister* the hand of Ulster (though it is the

78a Coleraine town-hall from the west, in 1983, designed by Thomas Turner, completed in 1859. (*A*)

78b Coleraine town-hall from the south-east, in 1997. (*A*)

79a Roundel on Coleraine town-hall featuring the escutcheon of the town. (*A*)

79b Roundel on Coleraine town-hall featuring the escutcheon of The Society of the Governor and Assistants, London, of the New Plantation in Ulster within the Realm of Ireland. The Latin INE is incorrect: it should be INF, short for 'infra'. (*A*)

[58] Ferguson, Rowan, and Tracey (1970), *passim*. See also Reed (1865), 93-95.
[59] Reed (1865), 94.
[60] IS/CM/27. See Curl (1986), 420, 482.

SIGILLUM VILLAE COLERAINE

SOC. GUBERNAT. ET ASSIST. LOND. NOVAE PLANTAT. IN ULTONIA INF. REGN. HIBERNIAE

Sinister rather than the *Dexter* hand that is couped at the wrist) [see **Frontispiece**]. The London connection is also underscored in The Irish Society window, created by Campbell Brothers of Belfast to celebrate the tercentenary of The Irish Society in 1913: this depicts the Arms of Sir Alfred James Newton, Governor, from 1906 to 1921, the Arms of The Irish Society, and the old Seal of Coleraine Corporation, together with four vignettes showing The Society's schools, the ruined mill at the Salmon Leap, the Diamond in *c.*1815 with the old market-house, and the parish-church as restored in 1775 **[80]**. It is a splendid object, this window, but it perpetuates the drivel about 'the framed houses sent from London', whose myth has been exploded above. The town-hall was sensitively extended to the east in 1902 by the local architect W. J. Given. Turner's building has certain affinities in terms of style and detail with his Northern Bank, Shipquay Place, Londonderry, completed in 1866, and built on land reclaimed from the river.

80 The tercentenary window of The Irish Society (1913) in Coleraine town-hall. (*A*)

Turner entered into a professional partnership in 1861 with Richard Williamson (d. 1874), architect and civil engineer, who succeeded Stewart Gordon as county surveyor in 1860 and as surveyor to The Irish Society at a salary of £100 a year. As Turner and Williamson the firm produced many works throughout the county, and Williamson's association with The Irish Society began almost as soon as he settled in Londonderry. In 1860, on the death of Sir John Byng (1772-1860), Earl of Strafford from 1847, Governor of Londonderry and Culmore Fort from 1832, The Irish Society opened negotiations with the Government to obtain possession of the lands of Culmore, and eventually managed to secure the property by purchasing the fee simple from the commissioners of Woods and Forests.[61] By 1862 The Society was considering building cottages as model dwellings and £1,000 per annum was set aside for this purpose, the idea being to persuade other landowners to erect decent dwellings by example. Plans were drawn up by Williamson for semi-detached pairs of cottages to face seaward: these were under construction by 1864, and the contractor was Robert Ferguson **[81]**. However, they were not original designs, but based on plans by Henry Roberts (1803-76), architect, of London, entitled *Pair of Labourers' Cottages Adapted to Agricultural Districts With Two Bed Rooms on the Upper and one on the Ground Floor*, published by the Society for Improving the Condition of the Labouring Classes, and dating from *c.*1851 **[82]**.[62]

This was a period of major building activity. The Irish Society's schools at Culmore were found to be in a dangerous condition and The Society gave instructions that they were to be rebuilt. Williamson produced the designs, and by 1866 the building

[61] Reed (1865), 95.

[62] Curl (1983), *passim*, and Plate 77b. See also *Report* of the Deputation of 1861 and IS Court Minutes at Guildhall.

81 Model dwellings at Culmore, designed by Richard Williamson, drawing heavily on plans by Henry Roberts. (*A*)

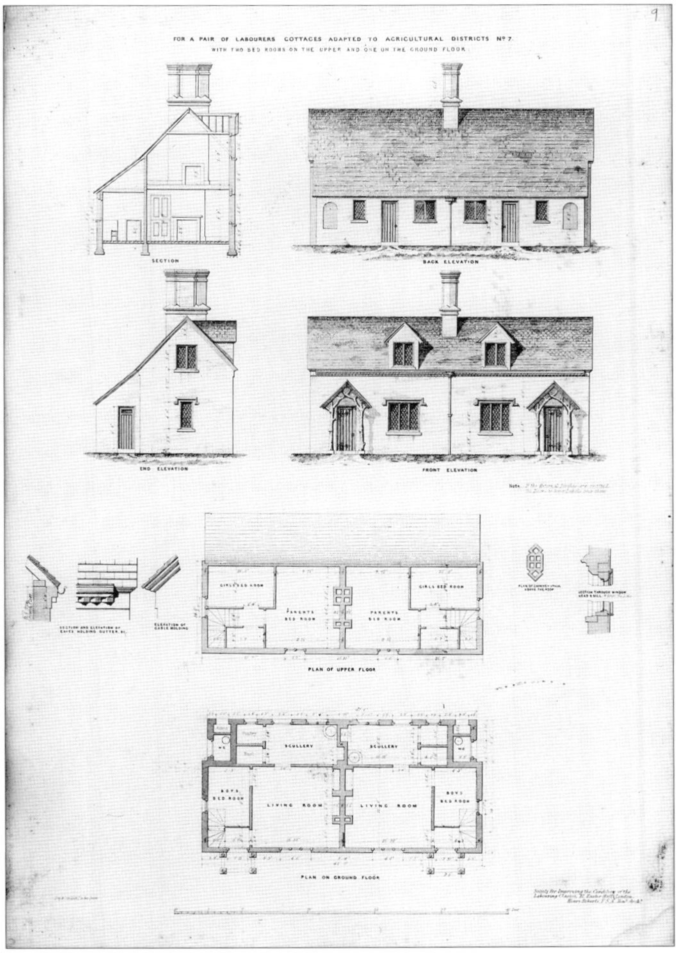

82 Henry Roberts's design for 'A Pair of Labourers Cottages Adapted to Agricultural Districts … with two Bed Rooms on the Upper and One on the Ground Floor'. (*AC*)

83 The Irish Society's schools at Culmore, in 1998. (*A*)

84 The Irish Society's schools at Ballougry, in 1997. (*A*)

was completed **[83]**, to the considerable satisfaction of all. On one of the gables is a roundel containing the Arms of The Society. At almost the same time Williamson also designed the pretty Irish Society schools at Ballougry, a charming building with gabled pavilions at each end **[84]**, and the Gothic lodge and belfry at Killea burial-ground of 1864 (in 1999 derelict and vandalised).

At Culmore, too, The Society ordered and paid for the construction of a new road along the shore, with a wall to protect it, the whole costing £530. It also decided to support the rebuilding of the parish-church to replace the old Plantation church erected for the use of the garrison of Culmore Fort. Williamson was appalled that the ecclesiastical commissioners had 'sanctioned' the 'act of vandalism' involving the demolition of almost all of the old building.[63] The new parish-church of Holy Trinity, Culmore **[85]**, was designed by John Guy Ferguson (1829-1901), the son of the builder, Robert Ferguson, who had spent some time in Philadelphia, Pennsylvania, in his early 20s, but returned to Londonderry where he began his practice in *c*.1856. In 1861 he

[63] Deputation *Report* of 1866.

85 Holy Trinity parish-church, Culmore, in 1999, by J. G. Ferguson. (*A*)

was appointed diocesan architect to the Church of Ireland diocese of Derry and Raphoe, but did not eschew working for other denominations: among his churches are those at Buncrana, Moville, and Raphoe, all in County Donegal, for the Presbyterians. Later in his career he designed Christ Church, Burt (County Donegal), of 1868, St Augustine's, Londonderry, of 1872, and St John's, Killowen, near Coleraine, of 1875, all for the Church of Ireland. His work at St Columb's cathedral, Londonderry, will be described below.

The Irish Society expressed regret that the 'interesting ruins of the old church had been completely destroyed', which is not quite true as part of a 17th-century gable-wall survived Ferguson's drastic attentions. It is clear Williamson did not approve of Ferguson's attitudes, and it has to be said that the destruction of so much of the old Planters' church (wrecked by the Jacobites in 1689) was inexcusable. In spite of the devastation of part of The Irish Society's heritage, Holy Trinity was liberally endowed by the Londoners, who gave a window for the east end made by Ward & Hughes.[64] Constructed of rubble with sandstone dressings, the church (built 1865-7) is small, cruciform, and subdued First and Second Pointed in style **[85]**.

[64] Deputation *Report* of 1867.

Also at Culmore The Irish Society recommended in 1867 that a parsonage and more model cottages should be built, but no progress was made on the cottage question until 1875, when William Harte (who succeeded Williamson as surveyor on the latter's death in 1874) designed several robust but rather pretty buildings with decorative

86 Model cottages at Culmore, in 1998. (*A*)

87 The Irish Society's schools at Coleraine: contract-drawing by Richard Williamson, signed by the contractor, Robert Ferguson & Son. (*CLRO/GLCL/IS/R.P. No. 2*)

88 The Irish Society's schools at Coleraine, from the tercentenary window in Coleraine town-hall. (*A*)

rustick barge-boards on the dormers and gables as concessions to frivolity **[86]**: floor-plans were typical two-up, two-down, with back-yards and external privies, hardly advanced for their date. In 1877 the contractor, one Craig, was found to be cheating The Society, and another builder had to be found. There were problems with Harte too, for he and the local agent did not get on, and The Society had to ask both men to give an undertaking that they would endeavour to work together on an amicable basis. Harte designed the school at Rossnagalliagh in 1880, and also carried out alterations to Williamson's schools at Ballougry (The Society called it Molenan) **[84]** and to Tite's Government House **[70]**.

Williamson was the architect for The Society's most impressive and dignified schools, those at Coleraine, built by Robert Ferguson & Son, contractors, in 1867-9, at a cost of £5,500. Throughout the 1850s and '60s there had been much debate about rebuilding the schools, and in 1866 plans were drawn up by Williamson in a freely treated asymmetrical Gothic style **[87]**. The buildings were of red brick with stone dressings, and the entire composition was handled with great verve **[88]**. Many sources state that this building was by Turner, but the documentary evidence shows it was designed by Williamson.[65] The schools were extended in 1935 to designs by Malcolm McQuigg, but the future of the buildings was in doubt by the 1960s, and the school moved out in 1978 as it had outgrown the premises. The buildings were then leased to a youth-training organisation, but by 1999 they were in a parlous state.

[65] Curl (1986), *passim*.

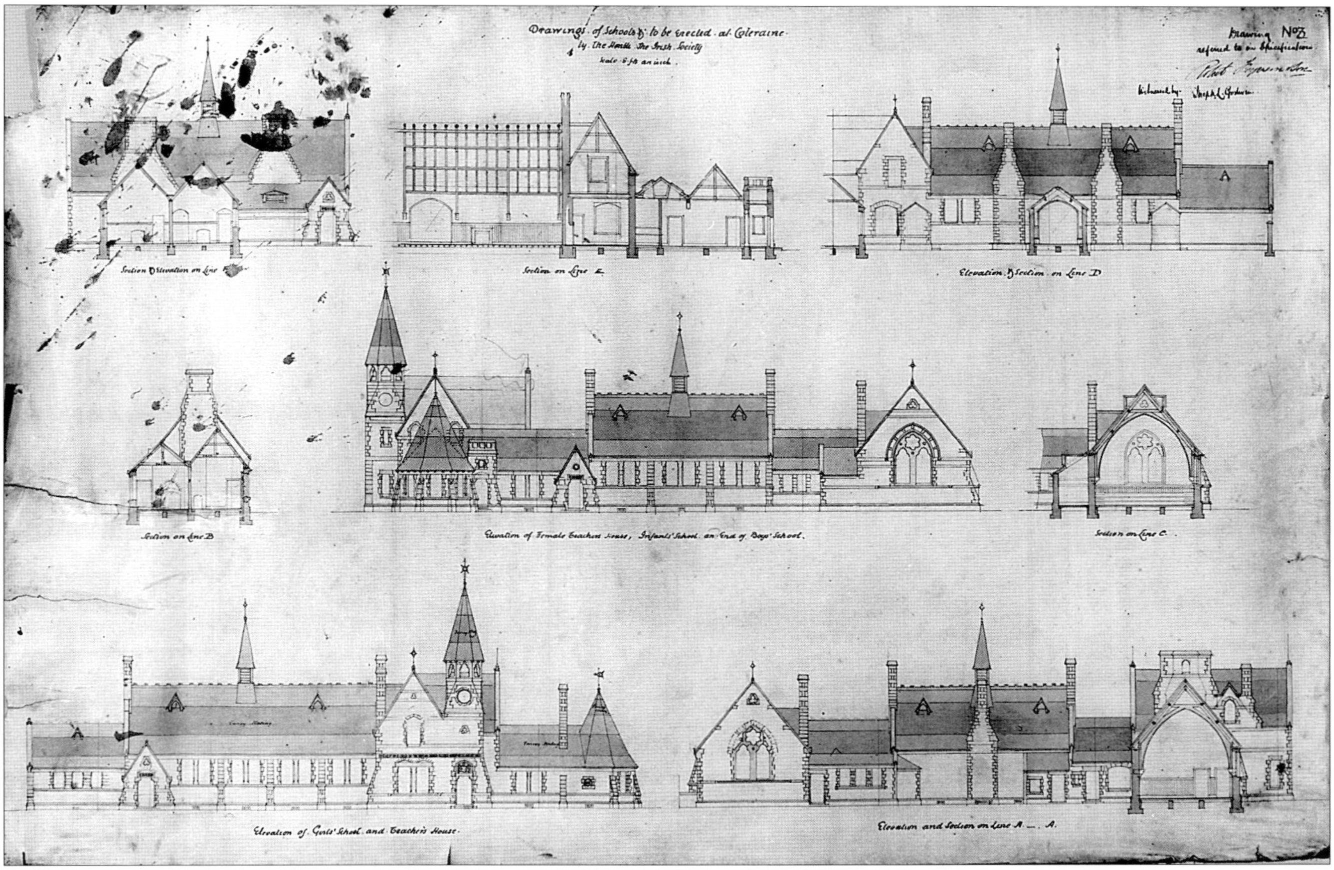
Drawings of Schools &c to be Erected at Coleraine
by The Honble The Irish Society
Scale 8 ft an inch
Drawing No 3
referred to in Specification
Section & Elevation on Line
Section on Line E
Elevation & Section on Line D
Section on Line B
Elevation of Female Teachers House, Infants' School an End of Boys' School.
Section on Line C
Elevation of Girls' School and Teacher's House
Elevation and Section on Line A — A

89 Carlisle Bridge, Londonderry, opened in 1863. The upper deck was a carriageway and the lower supported railway-tracks. Photograph of *c.*1880 by Alex Ayton. (*IRC/U/LON-LON/PH2625*)

The Irish Society's relationship with Londonderry and Coleraine changed during the period discussed above. Under the Act for the Regulation of Municipal Corporations in Ireland of 1840[66] municipal privileges were granted to Londonderry, but Coleraine Corporation was suppressed, and the town was administered by commissioners appointed under an Act of Parliament of 1828,[67] but the rights and duties of The Society were reaffirmed. Any bye-laws had to be approved by The Society before submission to the Viceroy. In 1854 under the Towns Improvement (Ireland) Act[68] town commissioners could be elected, and it was not until the Local Government (Ireland) Act of 1898[69] that the creation of County and Urban District Councils came into being, and Coleraine became an Urban District Council. The Society made an annual grant towards the support of the Mayor, Recorder, and Officers of Londonderry, and, as has been made clear above, gave liberal financial help to schools, charities, churches, and other bodies.

One of the works supported munificently by The Society was the new Carlisle Bridge at Londonderry, mentioned above, which was opened in 1863 **[89]**. The Honourable The Irish Society contributed £10,000 towards its construction, as well as facilitating the parliamentary, legal, and land-acquisition aspects associated with the project. It was called the Carlisle Bridge because it was opened by the Lord Lieutenant, George William Frederick Howard (1802-64), 7th Earl of Carlisle (from 1848), who

[66] 3 & 4 Vict., c. 108.
[67] 9 Geo. IV, c. 82.
[68] 17 & 18 Vict., c. 103.
[69] 61 & 62 Vict., c. 37.

was the appointee of Palmerston as Viceroy in 1855-8 and again in 1859-64. Carlisle devoted much energy to improving manufactures and agriculture in Ireland, and he was tactful and successful in office.[70]

£10,000 was also granted in 1864 to improve the mouth of the River Bann, where the 'bar' or ridge of sand posed a great danger to shipping, even steam-powered vessels. This bar, created by the very strong currents in the area, had been a problem, and was certainly a menace in the days of sail. In 1997 the present writer voyaged in a small motor-powered boat down the Bann into the sea and experienced for himself the powerful forces and fearsome currents there. A dredger was at work on the bar to keep the entrance to the river navigable **[90a-c, 91a-c]**.

Space does not permit the inclusion of every donation, grant, act of benevolence, or building activity by The Irish Society, but some idea may be gained by reference to a few more examples. In 1864 money was given to the Presbyterians for their new 'meeting-house' at Londonderry-Waterside; in 1865 a donation was made to the Londonderry Female Penitentiary in addition to the annual grant for the 'reclamation of fallen women'; money was given to assist the erection of a new Anglican church at Londonderry-Waterside; Boghill school near Coleraine and St Patrick's church, Coleraine, were enlarged with financial help from The Society in 1866; and various church-bells, railings, walls, endowments, etc., were paid for by The Society.

The philanthropic flavour of The Irish Society at the time was strengthened by the presence of Charles Reed (1819-81) as a member of the Court. Reed was the second son of Andrew Reed (1787-1862), philanthropist and Nonconformist clergyman, and was involved in the printing-trade in London. In 1844 Charles Reed joined the Sunday School Union, and published various pamphlets dealing with the education of the poor. In 1855 he became a member of the City of London's Common Council for the Ward of Farringdon Within, and was active in promoting Guildhall Library and the City of London School. He was a leading light in the campaign to preserve Bunhill Fields burial-ground[71] and took a profound interest in The Irish Society's estates in Ulster, taking part in official Visitations, and arguing persuasively for improvements of every kind, notably in education and housing (in 1869 he was an executor of the will of George Peabody [1795-1869], the philanthropist who gave the then huge sum of around half a million pounds to the City of London for the benefit of the poor, and whose generosity enabled the series of Peabody Model Dwellings to be erected, starting with the block in Spitalfields designed by Henry Astley Darbishire [1825-99] in 1864).[72]

In 1868 Reed was elected Liberal Member of Parliament for Hackney, and made his maiden speech on introducing a bill for exempting Sunday and Ragged Schools from poor-rates. An advocate of elementary education for all, he was a passionate supporter of Bible instruction free from any sectarian bias. In 1874 he was unseated as M.P. for Hackney on a technicality, but was returned for St Ives in 1880. Throughout the 1870s he devoted much time to the affairs of the London School Board.

His interest in Bunhill Fields was indicative of his antiquarian predilections, and in 1849 he was elected a Fellow of the Society of Antiquaries of London (F.S.A.). In 1865 The Irish Society published his *An Historical Narrative of the Origin and Constitution of ... The Honourable The Irish Society*,[73] later updated in 1878, 1899, and 1917: it was,

[70] *D.N.B.* (1917), **x**, 19-21.
[71] See Reed *et al.* (1867), *passim.*
[72] *D.N.B.* (1917), **xv**, 575-6, and **xvi**, 832-4; Pevsner (1968), **ii**, 18-37.
[73] Reed (1865), *passim.*

and remains, a useful synopsis, and is clearly written. He was involved in the translations of the *Liber Albus*, published in the Rolls Series of the City of London, contributed for many years to *Notes and Queries*, and was active in the direction of the Religious Tract, British and Foreign Bible and London Missionary Societies.

Knighted in 1874, he also had the degree of Doctor of Laws conferred on him by Yale University after a visit to the U.S.A. in 1873. He was buried in Abney Park cemetery, Stoke Newington, the Nonconformist Valhalla of London. His third son was Talbot Baines Reed (1852-93), the historian of English typography and one of the founders of the Bibliographical Society, who was better-known as a contributor to the *Boys' Own Paper* and author of such yarns as *The Adventures of a Three-Guinea Watch* (1880) and *The Fifth Form at St Dominic's* (1881). T. B. Reed married (1876) Elizabeth Jane, daughter of Samuel MacCurdy Greer (1810-80), the Irish politician and lawyer from County Londonderry (where his father, the Rev. Thomas Greer, had been the Presbyterian minister of Dunboe), who demanded the Three Fs for agricultural tenants (Fixity of Tenure, Fair Rents, and Free Sale), and was Recorder of Londonderry from 1870 until 1878.[74] Time and again the historian finds many such quirky details concerning the relationships between the philanthropically inclined in the City of London and those of benevolent turn of mind in Ulster: the Reed-Greer connection is only one such example, but it is clear that The Irish Society was permeated with ideals of philanthropy, and that the Evangelical Conscience, derived from the work of the Clapham Sect, was a powerful influence in its deliberations.

The Royal Commission of 1853-4

In the face of political and journalistic agitation a royal commission was established in 1853 to enquire into the Corporation of the City of London. Earlier, in 1837, commissioners appointed to enquire into municipal government in England and Wales reported on London and the Companies, and interpreted The Irish Society as a committee of the Common Court superintending the undivided estates of the London Companies in Ulster.[75] While finding the Londoners were benevolent landlords who managed their estates with great liberality to the benefit of their tenants, the commissioners felt that The Society exercised 'municipal supremacy' over Londonderry and Coleraine which they found 'anomalous' and saw no reason why it should be permitted to go on. Unfortunately the report contained a passage referring to 'control of this kind, maintained ... by the municipality of one town in England, over another in Ireland' appearing to be 'indefensible in principle', but made no reference to the historical background. Any evidence The Society offered was rejected, and its voice was not heard. This wholly unhistorical and irresponsible *Report* was eagerly embraced by enemies of The Society and used to attack virtually every aspect of its interests, chartered duties and responsibilities, and its very existence.

The 1853 commission was chaired by Henry Labouchère (1798-1869), Baron Taunton from 1859. It found the The Society was, in substance, a committee of the Corporation appointed under special regulations, and piously noted that Ulster in 1853 was prosperous, peaceful, and stable, quite unlike conditions in the reign of King James I and VI. According to the commissioners The Society had evolved into

90a Dredger at work on the bar and the mouth of the Bann in 1997. (*A*)

90b Coastline near the mouth of the River Bann, with the ruins of Downhill and the Mussenden temple on top of the high ground. (*A*)

90c Approach to the mouth of the River Bann, showing the moles completed in 1882. A dredger is at work on the bar in the centre. (*A*)

[74] *D.N.B.* (1917), **viii**, 529.

[75] See *Parliamentary Papers* xxvi: *Second Report of the Commissioners on Municipal Corporations in England and Wales: London and the London Companies* (1837), 16, and 191-3 (paragraph 349).

a charitable trust, distributing annual endowments, but, given that the trustees were in London and the trust property was in Ireland, administration was cumbersome, difficult, and expensive.[76] Questions were raised regarding relations between The Society and its tenants, and the commissioners found that neither The Society nor the Companies were beneficially interested in the revenues of the estates. The commission recommended the abolition of The Society and the vesting of its properties in trustees appointed by the Lord Chancellor of Ireland.[77]

The commissioners questioned 15 witnesses about The Society: eight were Londoners and seven were from County Londonderry. The Skinners' suit clearly influenced the Irish witnesses, who believed that The Society's main duties lay in helping Londonderry and Coleraine, but that its expenses were far too large, with the result that money which should have been distributed was wasted on entertainment, travel, management, dinners, and fripperies. As 12 members of The Society retired each year, there was a recurring problem in that promises were made and hopes raised, then the members retired from The Society and were never seen again. That there was a certain amount of truth in this, and that continuity had always been a problem, is beyond dispute.

However, reading the transcripts[78] it is clear that there was a certain amount of resentment against the Londoners, not only because they were absentees, but were perceived as having no understanding of land tenure or of anything else in Ireland, and as aliens telling locals what to do (a perennial problem of perception). Short leases, however, did not encourage tenants to establish businesses or carry out improvements, and The Society was criticised for not listening to arguments for renewal of leases until they had almost expired.

Some of the Ulster witnesses do not appear to have understood that the only income The Society had came from rents, and that it was out of that income that grants for benevolent or corporate purposes came, and it is clear from the many anti-Irish Society polemics of the period that many people in County Londonderry saw that body as possessing untold riches and a bottomless pit full of gold for potential largesse which was squandered on 'tavern expenses' and other frivolities. There is more than a touch of thin-lipped puritanism here. The explanation lies in the fact that in English collegiate and other establishments conviviality was a part of life, and bibulous dinners were normal events in the City of London, the Inns of Court, and Oxbridge colleges. In Ulster, however, a much grimmer mode of existence, the result of privation, relative poverty, and an essential need to eschew all luxuries and show (partly because there was insufficient money, and partly because of abstentionist principles), ensured that any 'wasteful' expenses would be looked upon as almost sinful, and certainly as rubbing the noses of the deprived in their own less than prosperous state. Some of the witnesses,[79] however, did understand that The Society could not distribute largesse to its tenants *and* execute its various duties and trusts under the charter. There was also the problem that The Society had been in the habit of giving any surplus revenues to the Companies after performing its obligations, so the duties of a landlord (as in England) could not be exercised in Ireland.[80]

[76] Commissioners Appointed to Inquire into the Existing State of the Corporation of the City of London (1854), xxxi-xxxiv.
[77] *Ibid.*, xxxiv.
[78] *Ibid.*, from Question 8009.
[79] *Ibid.*, Question 8257.
[80] *Ibid.*, Question 8148-54 and 8338-8439.

91a The River Bann near its mouth, in 1997, with Inishowen in the distance. (*A*)

91b The River Bann with the sea beyond. (*A*)

91c The River Bann from the west bank near its mouth. (*A*)

It became 'quite plain that whatever The Society did or did not do, either as landlord or trustee, it was liable to attack. It is also plain that The Society took the only course open to it, namely to carry out its public duties responsibly and honestly, and as reasonably as it could having regard to its constitution under the Charter'.[81] On behalf of The Society, the Governor explained that nearly the whole of Coleraine and a very large part of Londonderry had been leased in perpetuity, but the lessees did not adhere to their covenants, and enforcing those covenants was almost impossible. Furthermore, as a result, the properties were deteriorating and The Society had no powers to improve them having leased them (under pressure) in perpetuity. Long leases, he argued, should not be granted unless very tight and enforceable clauses were included to compel lessees to demolish poor-quality property and rebuild in a substantial and 'uniform' manner. By 'uniform' he meant some degree of conformity to appearance, height, width, style, etc. (i.e. aesthetic control), but that, in Ireland, was often beyond the comprehension of the average tenant. The Governor reminded the commissioners that The Society had been forced to intervene to demolish some 'shocking places … with … an accumulation of filth and wretchedness beyond all idea', and was endeavouring, by erecting model cottages to decent standards of design and layout, to create exemplars. He said that if the Irish critics of The Society were correct in their diagnoses, then the body of which he was Governor had no right to make improvements and would be forced to leave the poor people to rot in their present state. While it was true The Society could not build on agricultural land, make repairs to buildings, or construct drainage (because it had insufficient financial resources to do this), tenants holding farms for long leases on moderate terms should invest money in improvements according to the covenants of their leases, but far too often failed to make any improvements at all.[82]

On the thorny question of expenses and income, representatives of The Society pointed out that the very heavy outgoings on litigation had been forced upon it, as a public trustee, in order to defend its legitimate rights, otherwise it would have lost everything. For example, a fortune had been spent protecting the fisheries and the advowsons from usurpers, and, although the fisheries had been eroded and pillaged, they were still partly intact, but the advowsons (apart from Coleraine) had been lost. Defence against the Skinners' suit had cost The Society £8,000 and there had also been long-running disputes with the Donegall family over the fisheries, and with the bishops of Derry over advowsons and the Quarterlands. One former Assistant of The Irish Society stated that The Society could either defend itself or give everything up, including any chance of doing anything useful in Ulster.[83] Representatives of The Society suggested, perfectly reasonably, that, if that body had not been financially crippled by having to defend its rights in various suits, it would have had many thousands more to expend on the Plantation lands. Gross legal expenses from 1832 to 1849 totalled the gigantic sum of £32,000 and forced The Society to borrow £18,000 from its bank.

Some Ulster witnesses claimed that The Society's expenses were grotesquely excessive, and were some 60 per cent of revenue. This is nonsense. From 1833 to 1853 the picture looked something like this:

[81] Smith (1966), 136.
[82] Note 76, *passim*, but especially Questions 8338-8439.
[83] *Ibid.*, Questions 7737-94.

Average Annual Revenue	
(not counting loans and repayments)	£10,650
Average Annual Expenditure	£ 9,125

Out of the £9,125, £3,340 was spent on Londonderry and Coleraine to support the magistracy, churches, schools, charities, improvements, and employment; £990 went to the Crown and on rents and local rates; £1,020 accounted for salaries and incidental expenses in Ulster; £1,470 went on salaries in England, incidental expenses, expenses of members, and Deputation costs; £1,450 was expended on law costs and interest on loans raised to fund legal costs; £240 was laid out on equipment for and protection of the fisheries; £285 was paid out as dividends to the Companies; £210 went on pensions to officers of The Society, and £50 was expended on various surveys. Thus average expenses on management (salaries, incidental expenses, Deputation costs, expenses of members, etc.) came to about 27 per cent of total expenditure, or 23 per cent of revenue. In 1853-4, the year of the commissioners' inquiry, revenue was £12,571; expenditure £10,953; balance carried forward £1,618; and expenses of management etc., £2,637. The last represents about 21 per cent of revenue or 24 per cent of the total expenditure, which is nothing like the 60 per cent claimed by Irish witnesses, and dramatically emphasises the kind of misrepresentation with which The Irish Society had to contend. It is clear that The Society's enemies added the costs of litigation and defence to its 'management expenses'.[84] When the short period of service of the Assistants of The Society was discussed, former Assistants themselves agreed that the two-year stint was far too short and ought to be increased, but pointed out that the Corporation could do nothing about this without a special Act of Parliament which, in the climate of the times, might be difficult to obtain, and in any case, could well stir up a hornet's nest of adversaries. In other words London was lumbered with an arrangement it itself could not change.[85]

Although the 1853-4 *Report* was less antipathetic towards The Society than that of the 1837 commission, it too was used by enemies of the Londoners. At least it was comprehensive, at 875 pages of close print, but its recommendations[86] showed little understanding of conditions in Ireland or of the predicaments of The Society itself. Had those recommendations been implemented, the inhabitants of County Londonderry would have found the new bureaucratic machinery proposed much less benevolent than the organisation of the Londoners, and certainly more likely to be controlled by local factions, leading to corruption and bad management. In the event, the recommendations of the commissioners regarding The Irish Society were not carried out. However, the main *raison d'être* of the *Report* was not just The Irish Society, but the running of London. It should be remembered that the growing metropolis was beset by problems in the 1840s and '50s, not least those connected with disease, absence of hygiene, bad housing, traffic congestion, disposal of the dead, and the state of the River Thames. One of the results of the *Report* was the establishment of the Metropolitan Board of Works under the Metropolis Local Management Act of 1855.[87]

[84] Smith (1966), 145; Commissioners Appointed ... (1854), xxxiii.
[85] Commissioners Appointed ... (1854), Questions 7438, 7477, 8443.
[86] *Ibid.*, xxxiv.
[87] 18 & 19 Vict., c. 120.

Aftermath

Every now and then the sport of bashing the City of London has been pursued, usually by those with an agenda of their own. In the mid-19th century attacks on The Irish Society seem to have evolved as part of the broad strategy of an increasingly vociferous Irish Nationalism. In 1866, in the House of Commons, the 1853-4 recommendations were raked up, but the only result was a plethora of pamphlets and abuse in Ireland and a resolution demanding returns from The Society for all receipts and expenditure from 1845 to 1865 and copies of standing orders for the same period relating to leases. Those who have had dealings with parliament, government at central or local level, or the 'management-structure' of large organisations (even universities) will be familiar with the demands for endless papers and the massive amount of work this entails. The Society complied: the 'returns were duly prepared by the Secretary, and laid upon the table of the House'.[88] Three years later, the Nationalist M.P. for Cork, John Francis Maguire (1815-72), who 'took a very prominent part'[89] in all debates concerning the Irish land question, having first proposed the appointment of a royal commission to enquire into the administration of The Society's estates and those of the Companies with a view to the annulling of the charters and the sale of the estates, moved for an enquiry to consider if it would not be advisable to carry out the recommendations of the royal commission of 1853-4, but, after a six-hour debate, the matter was withdrawn.[90] It was a foretaste of things to come.[91]

[88] Reed (1865), *Continuation of The Historical Narrative* (*c.*1880), 4. See House of Commons *Paper* 514 (1866) which shows a nil return regarding standing orders relating to leases.

[89] *D.N.B.*(1917), **xii**, 774-5.

[90] Reed (1865), *Continuation of the Historical Narrative* (*c.*1880), 10-11.

[91] This chapter owes much to the papers in the Corporation of London Records Office (see Aldous [ed.] [1993]); Adams (1935); Curl (1986); Johnston (1959); *Parliamentary Gazetteer* (1846); Reed (1865), and Smith (1966). It also draws extensively on the Royal Commission *Report* (1854) and the various Deputation *Reports*. Mr. Daniel MacLaughlin very kindly gave access to valuable material, as did The Honourable The Irish Society.

CHAPTER XI

Ireland, The Irish Society, and the Political Climate from the 1860s

> Still carrying on its efforts to assist in the material prosperity of Londonderry, Coleraine, and Culmore, by supporting Educational and Charitable Institutions, by stimulating local energy whenever devoted to a good object, the Society has, during the last few years, especially given its aid to large and important works of public improvement, such as the Freeing of the Derry Bridge from Toll; the improvement of the Navigation of the River Bann; and other works in connexion with Coleraine ... The record will shew that The Irish Society has still faithfully carried out its trust in connexion with the Plantation in Ulster ...
>
> JOSEPH BECK, DEPUTY GOVERNOR (1829-91): *Preface* to *A Continuation of the Historical Narrative of The Honourable The Irish Society, being a Memoranda* [sic] *of Principal Occurrences from 1864 to 1878* (London: The Irish Society, 1878), v-vi

Introduction: the Historical Background, 1860s to the Partition of Ireland

Disestablishment of the Church of Ireland[1] in 1869 was only one of numerous enactments that severely weakened the privileges of the Protestant Ascendancy. The Anglican Church in Ireland was thereby put on the same footing as the Roman Catholic and Presbyterian Churches, and thenceforth all religious denominations were to achieve equal status, though the overwhelming number of Roman Catholics ensured that Church would achieve a pre-eminent position in Ireland which would be expressed by a certain triumphalism in architectural terms. Capital sums were paid to the Presbyterians in lieu of the *Regium Donum*[2] and to the Roman Catholics instead of the Maynooth College grant.

By that time, however, the Fenian Brotherhood, an Irish-American revolutionary secret society, had been formed with the intention of establishing an Irish Republic. The end of the American Civil War in 1865 was significant, for Irishmen who had fought in that conflict returned to Ireland, and there were various outrages, arrests, and disturbances. In 1867 a police-sergeant was killed in Manchester while conveying two Fenian prisoners, and 12 persons died and about 120 were maimed in an unsuccessful attempt to rescue Fenians held in Clerkenwell gaol, London. The Fenians were among the movements that contributed to the rise of modern Irish Republicanism.

Of course the political aspects cannot be ignored, and the unremitting attempts of Irish Nationalists to unravel the Union and undermine the Establishment were really

[1] 32 & 33 Vict., c.42.

[2] The annual grant of public money to Nonconformist ministers in England, Scotland, and, especially, Ireland. The first grant to Presbyterian ministers in Ireland was in October 1672 in the reign of King Charles II; under William & Mary it increased to £1,200 per annum in 1690 as a reward for support during the Jacobite wars; King George I increased it again to £2,500 per annum; and by 1868 the total grant to Presbyterian ministers in Ireland alone stood at £45,000. The first payment in England was in 1721.

effective partly as a result of the Union, for by the 1870s the 'Home Rulers' as a faction held a powerful position in Parliament: in the 1874 general election, for example, 60 Home-Rulers were returned; in 1880, 63 (including 27 supporters of Charles Stewart Parnell [1846-91]); in 1885 the Nationalists were returned for 85 seats in Ireland and one in Great Britain, which gave the Nationalists strength equal to the Liberal majority in the House of Commons; and in 1910 the 82 Nationalists held the balance of power. Under Parnell's leadership, Irish Members of Parliament systematically obstructed the business of the House, and it became clear that they would effectively paralyse the workings of Parliament until they got what they wanted. Disestablishment had been achieved. Next on the agenda was land tenure, and it was a combination of political clout in the House of Commons and the activities of the Irish National Land League (founded 1879) that proved to be powerful forces in the evolution of things to come.

This study cannot attempt a history of Irish Nationalism, a subject already well served by innumerable publications, but it must perforce describe Nationalism and the political background against which The Irish Society had to operate, otherwise the story makes little sense. One cannot separate the personality of William Ewart Gladstone (1809-98) from the Irish Question: in 1868, for example, he spoke in a debate advocating the disestablishment and disendowment of the Church of Ireland, and it was under Gladstone's first Liberal administration as Prime Minister that the Irish Church Act of 1869 became law: it was 'emphatically Gladstone's work'.[3] In 1870 Gladstone introduced the first Irish Land Bill giving tenants compensation for disturbance if they were evicted for any other reason than not paying rents and for making improvements (reversing the old presumption concerning the property of the landlord). The Act[4] also made it easier for tenants to buy their holdings. Then, in 1881, came the Land Law (Ireland) Act[5] which established special Courts for the fixing of rents, allowed for the appointment of land commissioners (one of whom would have the status of a judge) with powers to advance three-quarters of the purchase-money as loans to tenants who wished to buy their holdings, and provided for other machinery relating to the ownership and rights over land. This enactment took place against the disturbed state of Ireland, the increasingly violent activities of the Land League, outrages against landlords, their agents, and their property, and the passing of the Protection of Person and Property Act (1881)[6] and Peace Preservation (Ireland) Act[7] of the same year. The second Gladstone Land Act was not enough for the League or Parnell, and more concessions were demanded. Various Land Leaguers were arrested, serious disorder broke out as a result of what became known as the 'Land War', and Parnell himself was arrested in October. From Kilmainham gaol, in Dublin, Parnell and his colleagues issued the 'No-Rent Manifesto' urging tenants to pay no rents until the Irish leaders were released from gaol and all arrears of rent were wiped off the slate.

Early in 1882 Gladstone indicated in an elliptical way that he was not opposed to 'Home Rule', but expressed concern as to how it might be achieved under the British Constitution while acknowledging the supremacy of the imperial Parliament. The Opposition quite reasonably pointed out that this stance was at least a partial surrender

[3] *D.N.B.* (1917), **xxii**, 722.
[4] 33 & 34 Vict., c. 46.
[5] 44 & 45 Vict., c. 49.
[6] 44 & 45 Vict., c. 4.
[7] 44 & 45 Vict., c. 5 .

to the Nationalists and that Gladstone could no longer oppose Irish demands for a Parliamentary inquiry. Parnell and his associates were released from custody in May, when Gladstone promised an inquiry into reasons for all persons detained, settlement of arrears of rent, and other concessions in what had become known as the 'Kilmainham Treaty'. Much disquiet was occasioned by Gladstone's wobbly position, and William Edward Forster (1818-86), the Irish Secretary, and the Lord Lieutenant, Francis Thomas de Grey (1834-1905), 7th Earl Cowper, resigned, taking the view that political terrorism and agrarian crime were being encouraged by the Parnellites and Land Leaguers, and that it was asking for trouble to appease them. John Poyntz Spencer, 5th Earl Spencer (1835-1910), was appointed Viceroy with Lord Frederick Charles Cavendish (1836-82) as Chief Secretary in April 1882, but on the very day of Spencer's swearing-in (6 May) Cavendish (who had only just arrived in Ireland) and the Under-Secretary, Thomas Henry Burke (1829-82), were murdered in Phoenix Park, Dublin, where they were taking a late-afternoon stroll. Cavendish was Gladstone's nephew by marriage, but even the murders did not deflect the Prime Minister from his declared purpose of settling 'the Irish Question'. Indeed, he even went as far as to introduce an Arrears Bill into the House of Commons intended to wipe out arrears of rent in Ireland, confined to tenancies below the annual value of £30, using the surplus of the Irish Church (the Church of Ireland) to raise most of the gigantic sum of two million pounds required. The Opposition, outraged, suggested that Parnell and his associates had been released as a result of a secret bargain by which the Parnellites would support the Liberals in Parliament and control outrages in Ireland (which they [the Parnellites] had been partly responsible for encouraging). Further concessions made by Gladstone to Parnell led to revolt, but the Government did not resign, even though it found itself in a minority by 13 votes. Resignation, however, did follow in June over an amendment to the Budget proposed by the Opposition, which was carried, six Liberals and 39 Irish members voting with the Conservatives, while many Liberals abstained.

The Queen then sent for Robert Arthur Talbot Cecil (1830-1903), 3rd Marquis of Salisbury, who was persuaded to head a 'Caretaker' Government. Salisbury appointed Edward Gibson (1837-1913), 1st Baron Ashbourne, Lord Chancellor of Ireland, and it was Ashbourne who, in August, introduced the Purchase of Land (Ireland) Bill to the House of Lords. This Bill became law,[8] providing for the advance of the entire purchase money and for annuity payments lower than rents.

It was the result of the general election in December 1885, mentioned above, which seems to have made Gladstone's mind up: 335 Liberals were returned, against 249 Conservatives and 86 Irish Nationalists exactly balancing the Liberal majority in numerical strength. Gladstone became converted to Home Rule, an event disclosed prematurely in the newspapers in December: he favoured an Irish legislature sitting in Dublin and an Irish executive responsible for Irish affairs. Although he claimed that, unless the Irish Question were speedily resolved, the parties of violence and assassination would get the upper hand in Ireland, it now seems obvious that the obstructive policies of Irish Members of Parliament and the fact that they held the balance of power in the House of Commons contributed much to Gladstone's change of position.

In 1886 opposition to Home Rule mushroomed with demonstrations and meetings in Ulster, and at the Liberal Party Convention in Belfast a split developed on the

[8] 48 & 49 Vict., c. 77.

Home Rule question, part becoming the Ulster Liberal Unionists. Gladstone's Home Rule Bill was defeated in the Commons, some 93 Liberals voting against the Government. In the General Election in July the Liberals lost 144 seats, but 77 Liberal Unionists were returned. Serious rioting broke out in Belfast, leading to the withdrawal of the Royal Irish Constabulary from certain districts including the Shankill Road. There was open talk of forcible resistance to Home Rule.

Under Salisbury's second administration various inquiries were set up to investigate disorder, the operation of the Land Acts, Irish Public Works, and other matters, and in 1887 Parnell and other Home Rulers were accused of complicity in outrage and murder in articles published by *The Times*. In August the Land Law (Ireland) Act[9] became law, giving the Land Courts powers to fix rents of leaseholders and to revise certain rents determined judicially between 1881 and 1885. At an open-air meeting of Nationalists and Radicals in London's Trafalgar Square to support agrarian agitation in Ireland, police and troops clashed with demonstrators, and there were over 100 casualties, an event referred to as 'Bloody Sunday'.

In 1889 William Henry O'Shea (1840-1905) filed a petition for divorce on the grounds of his wife Katharine's adultery with Parnell, and a decree nisi was awarded in 1890. This undermined support for Parnell, and the Catholic Episcopal Standing Committee publicly denounced him in December, leading to a split into 'Parnellite' and 'anti-Parnellite' political factions. The anti-Parnellites became the Irish National Federation, and began to defeat Parnell's supporters in by-elections. Meanwhile, in August 1891 the Purchase of Land (Ireland) Act[10] had become law, extending facilities for land-purchase and establishing the Congested Districts Board,[11] but Parnell was a broken man, and died in October.

During 1893 Gladstone, Prime Minister for the fourth time, introduced the second Home Rule Bill which was duly defeated in the House of Lords. In 1903 George Wyndham (1863-1913), Chief Secretary for Ireland in the Conservative administration of Arthur James Balfour (1848-1930), introduced the Land Purchase Bill which became law as the Irish Land Act:[12] it made the sale of land much more attractive to landlords without requiring the immediate payment by the tenant-purchasers, so sales, not surprisingly, were immensely increased, having almost ceased under the earlier acts which did not favour landlords at all, and really gave them ludicrously low prices. Wyndham's Act made bold use of imperial credit. Wyndham, however, resigned as a result of a scheme of 'Devolution' brought in by his Permanent Under-Secretary, Sir Anthony Patrick MacDonnell (1844-1925), with the approval of the Lord Lieutenant, William Humble Ward (1867-1932), 2nd Earl of Dudley.

The Liberal Government passed the Irish Land Act[13] in 1909, which increased facilities for the purchase of lands by tenants and gave powers of compulsory purchase to the Congested Districts Board.[14] Then, in 1910, Sir Edward Henry Carson (1854-1935)[15] was elected leader of the Irish Unionists in the House of Commons, and

[9] 50 & 51 Vict., c. 33.

[10] 54 & 55 Vict., c. 48.

[11] A body invested with considerable powers to encourage agriculture and industry in parts of the country suffering from acute poverty (roughly one third of Ireland). It sponsored schemes ranging from the employment of agricultural instructors and the promotion of cottage industries to the purchase of land for resale to tenants. By 1909 it had a quarter of a million pounds to dispose of annually, but the management of its finances was eccentric, and it was abolished in 1923 under the Land Law (Commission) Act of the Irish Free State (1923/27).

[12] 3 Edw. VII, c. 37.

[13] 9 Edw. VII, c. 42.

[14] See footnote 11.

[15] Hyde (1953), *passim*. For the Ulster Crisis of 1912-14 see Stewart (1997), *passim*.

opposition to Home Rule hardened. In 1912 the Home Rule Bill was introduced into the House of Commons by Herbert Henry Asquith (1852-1928), and a proposed amendment to exclude Counties Antrim, Armagh, Down, and Londonderry from the provisions of the Bill was defeated. Soon Unionists in Ulster began to drill and arm with a view to resisting the Bill if it became law, and in September the Solemn League and Covenant to resist Home Rule was signed by Unionists throughout Ulster. Although the House of Lords threw out the Home Rule Bill after its third reading in January 1913 and again in July after its fourth, the Government made it clear it would not tolerate continued obstruction by the Lords, and the Unionists knew it was only a matter of time before Home Rule became law. In January 1913 the Ulster Volunteer Force was created expressly to oppose Home Rule, and in September Carson announced that a Provisional Ulster Government would be set up in the event of Home Rule coming into effect. In November Nationalists established their own volunteer force to counteract the Ulster army.

However, in March 1914 the Government became seriously alarmed when General Hubert de la Poer Gough (1870-1963) and 57 out of 70 of his officers stationed at the Curragh Camp, County Kildare, announced they would prefer dismissal from the Army rather than march north to enforce Home Rule. In June the Government of Ireland (Amendment) Bill, introduced in the House of Lords, provided for the 'temporary exclusion' of parts of Ulster from the Home Rule scheme, and in July a further amendment in the Lords allowed for the permanent exclusion of all Ulster. Two days later the provisional government of Ulster met in Belfast. Gun-running continued and anxiety increased, for on 23 July Austria-Hungary presented its ultimatum to Serbia following the assassination of the heir to the throne, the Archduke Franz Ferdinand (1863-1914) and his wife, Sophie Chotek, Duchess of Hohenberg (1868-1914), at Sarajevo on 28 June.

The 1914-18 War swiftly followed Austria-Hungary's declaration of hostilities on Serbia on 28 July, and very soon Europe was engulfed. Home Rule became a fact in September by the Government of Ireland Act,[16] but was put on ice by means of another Act.[17] The Ulster Volunteer Force provided men to form the 36th (Ulster) Division of the British Army, and the leader of the constitutional Nationalists, John Edward Redmond (1856-1918), pledged Irish support for Great Britain for the duration of hostilities. Opposition to conscription ensured that never happened in Ireland, and many Nationalists opposed Irish involvement in the war, Redmond's leadership, and any partition of Ireland. Sir Roger David Casement (1864-1916) attempted negotiations with the Germans for help in the Nationalist cause.

Early in 1916 the Irish Republican Brotherhood decided to launch an insurrection, and in April Casement was landed by a German U-boat. On 24 April various buildings in Dublin were seized by the Irish Volunteers and Citizen Army, and the proclamation of the provisional government of the Irish Republic was posted. The 'Easter Rising' or 'Sinn Féin Rebellion' had begun. Martial law was declared, and on 29 April the insurgents surrendered. 450 people had been killed, 3,000 wounded, and many buildings in Dublin badly damaged. Early in May the execution of the rebels began, and Redmond (who had not foreseen the rising) warned the Government that opinion unsympathetic to the insurrection was being alienated by the killings.

16 4 & 5 Geo. V, c. 90.
17 4 & 5 Geo. V, c. 88.

These events have often been told, and can only be outlined here. Nevertheless, it is difficult to know what else the Government and military authorities could have done, for there was a major European war going on (and going badly for the Allies at the time, as the Central Powers seemed to have the upper hand). Any hint of rebellion in their territories was certainly not tolerated by Germany and her allies: had Ireland been under German rule, for example, history shows that the reprisals would probably have been considerably greater. By May 1916 David Lloyd George (1863-1945) had been entrusted with negotiations of a settlement of the Irish Question: this was to result in a scheme to implement Home Rule but to exclude six of Ulster's nine counties from its application for the duration of the war, and the 'six-county' proposal was accepted by the Ulster Unionist Council and ratified by a convention in Belfast.

In July the Somme offensive saw the 36th (Ulster) Division and other units of the British Army suffering grotesquely severe casualties. Casement was hanged for high treason in August, and various enquiries and commissions were set up to find out the facts about the rising. In a public meeting in Londonderry opposing the partition of Ireland, the foundations were laid of the Anti-Partition League (afterwards the Irish Nation League): early in 1917 at the North Roscommon by-election the candidate endorsed by the League and Sinn Féin won but refused to take his seat in the House of Commons. It was a taste of things to come.

Meanwhile, in December 1916, Lloyd George had become Prime Minister of a Coalition Government, and in March 1917 told the House of Commons that the north-east of Ireland was as hostile to Irish rule as the rest of Ireland was to British rule, and that part of Ulster was 'as alien in blood ..., religious faith ..., traditions ..., and outlook' to the rest of Ireland as were the inhabitants of Fife or Aberdeen. Redmond and the Nationalists withdrew from the House in protest. In May 16 Roman Catholic and three Church of Ireland bishops signed a declaration against Partition, and in the same month at the South Longford by-election a Sinn Féin candidate, languishing in gaol, was elected, defeating the Nationalist. In June, some 120 Irish prisoners, serving sentences for their parts in the Rebellion, were released from gaol. In the East Clare by-election in July one of those released, Eamon de Valera (1882-1975), was elected for Sinn Féin, severely defeating the Nationalist. The pattern was repeated thereafter: it was obvious that the 'Constitutional Nationalists' were on the way to extinction.

Under the Representation of the People Act and the Redistribution of Seats (Ireland) Act, both of 1918,[18] all men over 21 and most women over 30 were enfranchised, while constituencies were made approximately equal in size according to the numerical strength of the electorate. Lloyd George attempted to introduce conscription for Ireland which was vehemently opposed by Republican-Nationalist opinion, and a one-day General Strike was called. In May 1918 the Viceroy, Field Marshal Sir John Denton Pinkstone, Viscount French of Ypres (1852-1925), later (1922) 1st Earl of Ypres, in a proclamation, stated that Irish rebels were collaborators with Germany, and various leaders of Sinn Féin were arrested. Thereafter, matters went from bad to worse, and attempts were made to govern the country by means of military authority supported by the police and special auxiliaries, but restrictions of every kind led to degeneration into campaigns of outrages and reprisals, aggression and punishment.

[18] 7 & 8 Geo. V, cc. 64, 65.

In the general election of December 1918 (the war having ended in November) Sinn Féin won 73 seats, the Nationalists six, Unionists 25, and Independent Unionists one. Among those elected was Constance Gore-Booth (1868-1927), Countess Markievicz, who had served with the Irish Citizen Army during the rising of 1916, been sentenced to death (commuted to life imprisonment), released in the general amnesty (1917), re-arrested in May 1918, and, from Holloway gaol in London, elected as Sinn Féin Member of Parliament for St Patrick's Ward, Dublin. Although Countess Markievicz was the first woman to be elected to the House of Commons, in accordance with Sinn Féin policy she did not take her seat, but, at the first meeting of the Dáil Éireann (the Irish Parliament), was appointed Minister for Labour. Independence was declared, addresses were prepared to the free nations of the world, and a programme was proposed. De Valera escaped from Lincoln gaol in February, and all remaining Sinn Féin detainees were released in March.

The Dáil Éireann was declared illegal in September 1919, there was an unsuccessful attempt to assassinate the Lord Lieutenant in December, and in January 1920 the Royal Irish Constabulary enrolled the first of several thousand special constables recruited from ex-officers of the British Army, later known as the 'Black and Tans' from their composite uniforms. In Londonderry at the mayoral elections a Nationalist was elected, and in June the city experienced severe outbreaks of disorder, resulting in 18 deaths and many injuries. Thereafter, murder, arson, and mayhem continued. In August there were 30 deaths in Belfast alone, and a curfew had to be imposed. Special constables were recruited in Ulster, and martial law was decreed in Counties Cork, Kerry, Limerick, and Tipperary. Then, in December 1920, came the Government of Ireland Act[19] providing for two subordinate Irish Parliaments and administrations, with a Council of Ireland for consultation on matters of common interest.

In February 1921 Carson resigned as leader of the Ulster Unionists, and was succeeded by Sir James Craig, Bt. (1871-1940), later (1927) 1st Viscount Craigavon. In May 124 Sinn Féin candidates and four Independents were returned to the southern Parliament, and in the north 40 Unionists, six Sinn Féiners, and six Nationalists were elected. The Custom house in Dublin was destroyed in an attack by the Irish Republican Army (I.R.A.) in May 1921, involving the loss of local government and other records. In June, King George V (reigned 1910-35) opened the Northern Ireland Parliament in Belfast's Baroque city-hall,[20] but the southern Parliament was attended by only 15 of a possible 64 senators and four of a possible 128 members. Following a truce between the British Army in Ireland and the I.R.A., the second Dáil Éireann met, attended by Sinn Féin members elected to the southern Parliament, and in December an Anglo-Irish treaty was signed in London.

This conclusion contained in essence the relationship of Ireland with the British Empire, bearing in mind that Irish National aspirations had to be satisfied after such a bloody war. However, any such relationship was incompatible with Irish Republican goals. The Irish delegation agreed to accept continued association with Crown and Empire (then starting to be called the 'Commonwealth') in exchange for something called 'essential unity'. Craig rejected any truck with an all-Ireland Parliament, and Lloyd George offered a boundary commission to delineate the extent of Northern Ireland. When fiscal autonomy was offered to the new southern Irish State, the Irish delegates, faced with the threat of renewed war, accepted a settlement 'within the

[19] 10 & 11 Geo. V, c. 67.
[20] Designed by Sir Alfred Brumwell Thomas (1868-1948), and built 1898-1906.

Empire', knowing it was only a matter of time before the Empire (fatally weakened by events in Ireland and the Government's responses to those events) could be ignored. The Irish Free State had come into being as a self-governing Dominion within the Empire.

The treaty, however, was rejected by de Valera and other leaders of Sinn Féin because it continued subordination to the British Crown represented by the Oath of Allegiance to the King and the office of Governor-General (which replaced that of the Lord Lieutenant from 1922). After much vitriolic debate the treaty was ratified in the Dáil by a very small majority, and in March the Irish Free State (Agreement) Act, 1922,[21] became law in the U.K., providing for the transfer of powers to the provisional government.

Predictably, the immediate result was the outbreak of civil war between factions opposed to the treaty and those supporting the provisional government. Anti-treaty forces seized the Four Courts in Dublin, and attacks on property became endemic. In the north the I.R.A., the Irish Volunteers, the Irish Republican Brotherhood, and other organisations were declared illegal, and the Royal Ulster Constabulary was established as the police force.[22] Field Marshal Sir Henry Hughes Wilson, Bt. (1864-1922), Chief of the Imperial General Staff (1918-22) and Conservative M.P. for North Down, was assassinated on the doorstep of his home in Eaton Place, London, on 22 June. Irish provisional government forces attacked the anti-treaty occupants of the Four Courts, resulting in the destruction of the Public Record Office (making life for historians of Ireland even more difficult). Lloyd George's coalition fell in October, and a new administration in Westminster under Andrew Bonar Law (1858-1923) was formed.

The Dáil approved the constitution of the Irish Free State, and this was ratified, together with the treaty Articles, by the Irish Free State Constitution Act of 1922.[23] Meanwhile, given the appalling difficulties occasioned by the civil war, the Dáil established military courts with draconian powers, and in November the first of a series of 77 executions of anti-treaty combatants (known as 'Irregulars') took place. In the Northern Ireland Parliament both Houses agreed to opt out of the Irish Free State. In December the office of Lord Lieutenant in Northern Ireland was replaced by that of Governor, and James Albert Edward Hamilton, 3rd Duke of Abercorn (1869-1953), became first Governor, a position he held until 1945. Fighting in the civil war ended in May 1923 when the I.R.A. gave orders for its arms to be dumped to await another day, but there was no negotiated peace, so the war never really ended in any official sense.

The Irish Society and the Churches from 1868

The Irish Society (which had opened [1868] new offices in an 18th-century house in Bishop Street, Londonderry **[61]**, for the transaction of its business) and the London Companies were obliged to function in the climate described in the *Introduction* to this chapter. They had not had an easy time of it since the very beginning of the Plantation venture, but by the last decades of the 19th century the position of landlords in Ireland had become virtually untenable. Given that the Londoners were supposed to

21 12 Geo. V, c. 4.
22 12 & 13 Geo. V, c.8.
23 13 Geo. V, c. 1.

have removed the native Irish (except those who conformed to the Established Church and took various Oaths of Allegiance, etc.) from their lands, which, as we have seen, did not happen to anything approximating to the extent intended, and given that the Londoners were also expected to promote the interests of the Established Church, they found themselves in an anomalous position by 1871 when Gladstone's Irish Church Act of 1869 came into effect.

During the 1853-4 inquiry the Governor of The Society was subjected to close examination on various matters, including religion. He stated that no preference was given to one religion in the choice of tenants, and that The Society had 'not restrained' itself in giving grants to Roman Catholic 'chapels' and schools.[24] The Governor told the commissioners that the 'original object [of the trust imposed upon The Society] was to create and improve' the two main settlements 'and to encourage the Protestant religion in those two places, so as to establish the Protestant faith throughout the country'. He went on to remark that in the 'first instance, the Scotch and English settlers were exceedingly rigid in the profession of their faith, and the Roman Catholic was almost prohibited from possessing any church or chapel in the country; but as religion [became] more tolerant [Roman Catholics erected] churches and chapels indiscriminately with the members of the Presbyterian Church and the Church of England'.[25]

Nobody in Parliament seems to have understood the predicament in which The Irish Society found itself, as the entire State structure in Ireland set up from the time of King James I and VI was dismantled (in some areas with almost indecent haste, indicative, perhaps, of something like panic), yet the Londoners' charter and obligations remained unchanged. It is remarkable that The Society managed to adapt to circumstances, continuing a process that had begun from the time of the Act of Union when, as has been described above, a benevolent involvement in Ulster replaced the absenteeism partly forced on the Londoners after the South Sea Bubble disaster. Changes in the political and religious climate are demonstrated most dramatically and obviously by the built fabric, especially churches.

During the 18th century the Roman Catholic 'Long Tower Church' had been erected outside Londonderry's walls (1784), subsequently extended in 1810 and 1820-9, and greatly remodelled in 1908. As has been described above, the handsome Corinthian capitals of the high altar were the gift of the Anglican Bishop of Derry and Earl of Bristol. Under Bishop Peter McLaughlin St Columb's Roman Catholic Church, Chapel Road, was commenced (1838) to designs by James Joseph McCarthy (1817-82), the style being a desiccated Perpendicular Gothic. In 1838 Bishop McLaughlin began to promote the idea of building a new cathedral, but matters did not progress far until the episcopate (1849-89) of Dr Francis Kelly (1812-89), who was more concerned with ecclesiastical matters than politics (in this he took the then prevailing line of the Papacy, unlike his bellicose predecessor, Dr Edward Maginn [1846-9]). Bishop Kelly (who was coadjutor Bishop of Derry and titular Bishop of Titopoli [1849-64]), succeeded as Bishop of Derry in 1864. He introduced the Irish Christian Brothers, the Sisters of Mercy, and the Society of St Vincent de Paul to the city in order to develop educational and charitable services.[26] He also energetically pursued the cathedral-building project,

[24] Commissioners Appointed to Inquire into the Existing State of the Corporation of the City of London (1854), Questions 8406-8.

[25] *Ibid.*, Question 8405.

[26] Lacy (1998), 186. For information concerning the Roman Catholic diocese see Daly and Devlin (1997), *passim.*

and in 1851 the foundation-stone of Londonderry's Roman Catholic cathedral of St Eugene was laid.

The dedication is unusual. There was another church, at Ardstraw, County Tyrone, also named after St Eugene: Ardstraw was the seat of the first bishopric that evolved into that of Derry, but the patron of the diocese was neither St Eugenius of Carthage (d. 505 at Albi in France, where his relics are venerated) nor St Eugene (Pope 654-7), but Eogan, Eogain, or Eóghan (of a Leinster family on his father's side and an Ulster one on his mother's), who died around 580,[27] founded the monastery of Ardstraw, and was consecrated bishop (*c.*550). According to other sources, he died in *c.*618. His name was Latinised as Eugenius and Anglicised to Eugene.

St Eugene's cathedral was designed by J. J. McCarthy, cost £40,000 and was consecrated in 1873 by Dr Kelly. However, McCarthy seems to have inherited the plan, but had to strengthen the foundations before his design (in the Second Pointed style of Gothic) was realised.[28] Supervision of the construction work was by Charles Whelan, and the builder was Robert Maxwell. The church is very large, but the detail is bare, giving it a stripped, severe appearance, and it has to be admitted the building is more impressive from a distance than from near by. This hard, spare Gothic is reminiscent of the work of Augustus Welby Northmore Pugin (1812-52), the English architect and polemicist, who was one of the key personalities of the Gothic Revival, and whose churches often had a mean, pinched look owing to shortage of funds. Indeed, McCarthy has been called 'the Irish Pugin'. Curiously, the nave arcades, although taller, are not unlike those of the Anglican cathedral in general conception. At the west end is a tall tower capped by a spire: the ensemble was designed by Edward J. Toye (1857-1932), with George Coppinger Ashlin (1837-1921 – a pupil of Pugin's son, Edward Welby Pugin [1834-75], with whom he was in partnership [1860-9]) and Thomas A. Coleman (d. 1950) as consultants, and was built 1900-3 during the episcopate (1890-1907) of John Keys O'Doherty (1833-1907). It owes something, perhaps, to the elder Pugin's church of St Giles, Cheadle, Staffordshire (1840-6), and to elements from Continental Gothic architecture, but again the steeple is better seen from afar: closer to its detail is rather ungainly, even coarse. Much of the stone used is granite, which does not lend itself to elaborate carving or invention. The final consecration of the completed parts of the cathedral did not take place until after all debts were paid: this was in 1936, and Bernard O'Kane (1867-1939), Bishop of Derry from 1926 until his death, officiated.

The triumphalism of 19th-century Roman Catholicism is well expressed by St Eugene's, for the steeple is much higher than that of St Columb's cathedral, and the building dwarfs the Church of Ireland Christ Church near by (built under the aegis of Bishop Knox in 1803-31 by John and Robert Ferguson. This church was worked over by Welland and Gillespie in 1862 and enlarged in 1881-2 to designs by J. G. Ferguson). Following an arson attack, Christ Church was rebuilt 1997-8, and The Irish Society (which had presented the original organ in the 1860s) again contributed to funds in 1998. Similar architectural domination is clear at Letterkenny, County Donegal, and in Armagh the two cathedrals compete for attention.

Although The Irish Society gave sums of money to Roman Catholic causes (presumably in contravention of its original charter), the problem of supporting such

[27] Baring-Gould (1914), **ix**, 251; Bonner (1982), O'Hanlon (n.d.), 333-48.

[28] Ferguson, Rowan, and Tracey (1970), 28 (No. 55); Rowan (1979), 383-4; Sheehy (1977), 42-3; *Building News* (19 March 1858), 304; *Dublin Builder* (15 April 1862), 89; *Irish Builder* (1 and 15 February 1873), 36-37, 47.

a vast undertaking as a cathedral for the Roman Catholic Church was considerable: as the Governor had said during the 1853-4 inquiry, some grants were given to Roman Catholic establishments. In the case of St Eugene's, the site was purchased from William Hazlett (or Haslett) but The Society found itself in considerable difficulties in respect of funding buildings for Roman Catholic worship, not only because of the specific wording of the original grants. Diehard Protestants were always on the alert for any deviation from the principles of upholding Protestantism, and sworn enemies of The Society of all sorts (including Members of Parliament) created problems at every turn. Paths had to be trodden with care and much sensitivity. It should be remembered that the Anglican Bishop Higgin had come into conflict with much Protestant opinion in the 1860s, and The Irish Society had to be very careful when disestablishment, political uncertainty, and militant Nationalism were very much evident everywhere. On at least two subsequent occasions, therefore, The Society sought legal opinions about what it could and could not do.

Higgin was succeeded as Anglican Bishop of Derry and Raphoe by William Alexander (1824-1911), bishop from 1867 to 1896, who took disestablishment hard. Influenced by the Oxford High Church Movement and Tractarianism, he almost followed John Henry Newman (1801-90) by converting to Roman Catholicism while at Oxford, but remained an Anglican and became curate of Templemore during the Great Famine. Horrified by that calamity and by the insanitary conditions within the diocese, he resolved to do all he could to improve the conditions of the poor, and to beautify and strengthen the Church of Ireland in its coming times of tribulation. Alexander was a formidable scholar and churchman, and was greatly assisted in his life's work by Cecil Frances Humphreys (1818-95), whom he married in 1850. Cecil Frances Alexander (as she became) also fell under the influence of the Tractarians, and wrote numerous hymns, including *All Things Bright and Beautiful*, *Once in Royal David's City*, and *There is a Green Hill Far Away*, the last said to have been inspired by the hills around Londonderry, probably the Creggan, but the hymn dates from 1848 (two years before her marriage, and 19 years before the Alexanders moved to Londonderry), and so was probably suggested by the hills around her home near Strabane, County Tyrone. There is also a Green Hill Road at Aghadowey, County Londonderry, which is a link with Bishop Alexander's father, sometime rector of Aghadowey. After his wife's death Bishop Alexander was elected Archbishop of Armagh and Primate of All Ireland in 1896, but resigned in 1911 when he became infirm.

It should be remembered that disestablishment meant confiscation of Church property (except churches and graveyards), although compensation was paid. Nevertheless, when the Church had to rely almost entirely on donations from parishioners, and the landed gentry (its main support) were being badly hit by the various land enactments, it was an anxious time, and there is no doubt the Church of Ireland suffered most grievously.

Not surprisingly, the Church sought to assert itself in an aggressive programme of building, not only because compensation money suddenly flooded into the coffers, but because the Roman Catholics were building vast, expensive piles in the atmosphere of Nationalist triumphalism of the times. It was inevitable, therefore, that discussion should commence concerning the enlargement of St Columb's cathedral in Londonderry, not only as a riposte to St Eugene's cathedral, but because the building had become too small for major services. However, some opinion felt that it would be desecration to tamper with the 'Cathedral of the Siege' and to disturb the remains and monuments of those who had been associated with the heroic period of Londonderry's history. Furthermore, greatly enlarged chancels savoured of 'Ritualism', ecclesiology, and even 'crypto-Popery', none of which went down well in the climate of the time. A glance through contemporary local newspapers is sufficient to understand how high feelings were running.

However, in 1885 a faculty was granted to enable the cathedral to be enlarged, and in 1885-7 the cathedral-church of St Columb was altered and extended to designs by John Guy Ferguson, who had been the architect for the little church of St Augustine (1871-2) on the site of the ancient monastery used as the cathedral before St Columb's was completed in 1633. St Augustine's (to which The Society contributed a grant) is a decent essay in the First Pointed style of the 13th century.[29] The new chancel Ferguson added to the cathedral is also partly First Pointed, but there are touches of Perpendicular too, notably in the east windows. This chancel is said to be partly erected on the foundations of the original 17th-century chancel, but it is difficult to see how this could be so, as the surviving pictorial evidence indicates that the east wall was always between the two circular eastern towers until the extension of the 1880s. The contractor was M. McClelland, of Strand Road, Londonderry, and the contracted sum was for £5,600 to which The Irish Society contributed £1,000.[30] It has to be said that Ferguson had not grown more sensitive since Williamson's strictures over his treatment of Culmore church 20 years earlier, and those who were concerned about the conservation of earlier fabric associated with the siege must have despaired. Ferguson's interventions were nothing short of drastic: he renewed all the windows of the clerestorey (destroying the panels of the reveals); put new mullions in the aisle windows; removed the old ceilings and erected new timber trusses and roofs, with new corbels (bishops' heads, of singularly lumpish design) in the nave [compare **38** with **96-97**]; and added an extra bay to the nave by extending the arcades where the old north and south chancel walls stood. Ferguson's two arches, new piers, and responds are not quite the same as the 17th-century arcades, so he patched these up to smarten them and make them conform to his new work (as can be seen when photographs of the pre-1884 fabric are compared with the structure

92 St Columb's cathedral, Londonderry: the photograph from the east before Ferguson's drastic alterations in 1885-7. The post-1802 steeple is shown, together with the two circular turrets and the fenestration of the east end. The many monuments in the churchyard should be noted. (*DB*)

[29] *Irish Builder* **13** (1871), 265, and **14** (1872), 184.
[30] Vestry Minutes in St Columb's cathedral, 1884-5.

93 East end of St Columb's cathedral, Londonderry, showing it in *c.*1875 before the alterations of 1885 and after. (*AC*)

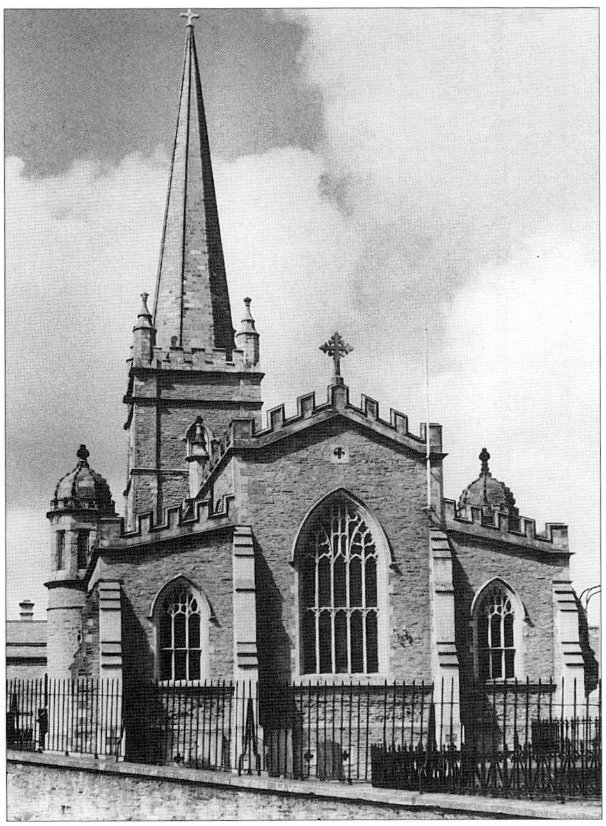

94 East end of St Columb's cathedral, Londonderry, in 1984 showing the two new Perpendicular Gothic windows and the ends of the chancel-aisles and what appears to be the re-set east window. (*A/CC/UM*)

photographed later, and which survives today). He filled joints with composition and introduced hard lines to suggest very thin masonry joints, and he rubbed down the mouldings, destroying much of their character. He also made new windows in the north and south aisle walls (which can be seen as the openings are formed of brick rather than stone). Ferguson's work is hard and mechanical, with insensitively handled detail, and his intervention can only be regretted, even though he bought in stone from Monk's Park, Bath, for the internal dressings rather than stone from Dungiven. In the new east wall of the chancel he appears to have reinstated the large window (with tracery in the Perpendicular style of Gothic) that appears to be the window in a photograph taken after the Welland alterations 25 years earlier, and which may even be earlier than that. Ferguson added new Perpendicular-style windows at the east ends of the north and south chancel-aisles **[92-94]**. The organ was restored by Peter Conacher of Huddersfield for £875.[31] Repairs to the organ following vandalism in the 1990s were costed at £400,000, which is an eloquent testimony to declining values in more senses than one.

In 1909 the cathedral acquired its chapter-house, designed by Sir Thomas Drew (1838-1910), and paid for by Mrs Corscaden **[95]**. Drew also designed the 1887 pulpit, made by E. P. Sharpe of Dublin,[32] and it was Drew who took over from Ferguson in 1889, designing the mosaic, marble, and elaborate reredos and other details. According to the vestry minutes held in the cathedral, consideration was given to the employment of Drew, William Henry Lynn (1829-1915), and one or two other architects before the local man, Ferguson, was decided upon. Lynn was an architect who often rose to distinction, even genius, and Drew was sound, though not quite in the same league as Lynn. It is perhaps Londonderry's loss that Ferguson got the job of adding the chancel and otherwise altering the building: his handling of the fabric lacked subtlety, to be charitable. Moreover, the damage done to the nave arcades since the 1860s was considerable **[96-97]**.

31 Vestry Minutes in St Columb's cathedral, 1884-5.
32 *Ibid.*

95 St Columb's cathedral, Londonderry, in 1999, from the adjacent bastion, showing the 'post-1802' steeple and Drew's chapter-house below it. (*A*)

Drew was also responsible for the designs of St Patrick's church, Coleraine. It will be recalled that The Irish Society had built the early 17th-century church, and added a tower and spire in 1714. A south transept, funded by the corporation, was built in 1784, and an illustration of that church with its additions appears in the 'Book of Coleraine' **[20]**. Joseph Welland, architect to the ecclesiastical commissioners, designed a new chancel and south aisle with porch, and re-fenestrated the tower in 1851: The Irish Society gave a grant towards those works. A north transept was added in 1862.

96 Interior (looking east) of St Columb's cathedral, Londonderry, in 1983, showing Ferguson's chancel and roof, with the earlier east window re-set. Note the poppy-heads on the pew-ends. (*A/CC/UM*)

97 Interior (looking west) of St Columb's cathedral, Londonderry, in 1997, showing the organ-case, screen, and nave-arcades (the arches nearest the camera are much harder and less subtle in detail, and are Ferguson's work). The rest of the arcades was patched and renewed in the 20th century. (*A/CC/UM*)

The Society held the advowson of Coleraine until disestablishment in 1869-71, but nevertheless clearly felt a close connection with the parish, and facilitated Drew's major rebuilding in 1883-4, which included a new tower to the south of the extended nave, a north aisle, the clerestoreyed nave on its arcades, and a new chancel. Materials were roughly coursed basalt with Dungiven and Draperstown sandstone dressings, with interior stone of a warm red colour. The contractors were Dixon & Co., of Belfast, and the work cost £6,400 **[98, 99]**.[33]

Welland's large south transept window is in the manner of the 14th-century Second Pointed style, and really set the stylistic agenda for the rest of the church, although Drew's handsome five-stage tower **[98]** is almost pure English Perpendicular (based on 15th-century exemplars), and the west and east windows are also of that style. Although slightly attenuated and somewhat hard and mechanical in its detail, the tower owes something to medieval church-towers of the west of England. It is very unlikely that Drew himself had any part in supervising the works, as the 17th-century

[33] *Irish Builder* **26** (1884), 169, 367, 371, and **27** (1885), 262. See also *The Coleraine Chronicle* (25 April 1885 and 11 August 1894).

98 St Patrick's parish-church, Coleraine, in 1999, showing Drew's work, from the south. (*A*)

99 Interior of St Patrick's church, Coleraine, in 1999, looking east. The re-set monuments can be seen in the north and south transepts. (*A*)

monuments to Rowley **[39]** and Beresford were not re-assembled correctly, the Rowley monument in particular having elements in the wrong place, upside-down, and pieces missing. The Beresford monument **[100]** may be partly a copy, and also appears to have been put together in a curious order. Both the Munro (*c*.1647) **[40]** and Dodington (*c*.1610) memorials are of some interest (though damaged), and the latter contains an inscription in dog-Latin to the effect that Sir Edward Dod(d)ington was the first to build in the English manner in the area.

The rebuilding of the church was supported with a large grant (£2,000) from The Irish Society,[34] and a memorial stone was laid with full Freemasonic honours by the then Governor, Sir John Whittaker Ellis, Bt., M.P. (1829-1912). Connections with London were also made overt in the window in the north transept which is embellished with the Arms of the Clothworkers' Company (the Proportion of which adjoined Coleraine at Killowen on the west bank of the river) and The Irish Society. In addition to its benevolent grants towards the rebuilding and beautifying of St Patrick's, The Society had the communion plate repaired and also provided a new chalice to the same pattern as that of 1613. Contributions were also made towards other stained-glass windows, a peal of bells, and various furnishings.

Apart from St Columb's cathedral-church at Londonderry and St Patrick's parish-church, Coleraine, The Irish Society also supported Glendermott parish-church **[101]** at Clondermott (in the churchyard of which some of the memorials to heroes of the

[34] Reed (1865, in the 1899 edition, 104).

100 Beresford monument in the north transept of St Patrick's church, Coleraine. (*A*)

siege of Londonderry were also erected and maintained by The Society **[43]**) and Culmore parish-church (where a stained-glass window at the east end was put in in 1867). Houses for clergy were purchased or funded at Culmore, Killowen, Clooney (Londonderry), Faughanvale, Christ Church (Londonderry), St Augustine's (Londonderry), and Bishop Street (Londonderry) – the Deanery. Help was also given towards the erection of school buildings and to support the running of schools associated with churches: examples included Coleraine parish-church school; the fourth Presbyterian congregation school, Londonderry; Terrace Row and the second Presbyterian church-schools, Coleraine; the national school-house associated with Killowen parish-church; the national schools at Waterside, Londonderry, associated with the Roman Catholic church there; the Roman Catholic college of St Columb, Londonderry (original buildings designed by O'Neill & Byrne [1877-9] and Croom & Toye [1892-8]); Magee College, Londonderry; Clooney parish-school, Waterside, Londonderry; St Augustine's, Londonderry; the Hawkins Street Methodist schools, Londonderry; new national schools associated with the Roman Catholic church in Coleraine (which The Irish Society had supported for many years); the Deanery schools, Londonderry; new national schools associated with the first Presbyterian church, Londonderry; a new national school for the Roman Catholics of Culmore; the Long Tower national schools; St Eugene's cathedral national schools; national schools associated with Christ Church, Londonderry; Strand Road Presbyterian Church national schools; additional help for St Eugene's cathedral's new national schools; and the Presbyterian Church at Waterside, Londonderry, national schools.

Furthermore, The Society built and supported its own schools (e.g. at Ballougry, Coleraine, Culmore, and Rossnagalliagh); provided scholarships to enable girls educated

101 Glendermot(t) parish-church, in 1983, with tower of 1789 in rudimentary Georgian Gothic. The plate-tracery of the windows is Victorian, as is the chancel. (*A/CC/UM*)

in Londonderry or Coleraine to study for three years at Girton College, Cambridge (1881); established funds so that boys educated at The Society's schools at Coleraine could go on to the Coleraine Academical Institution (1895); set up a scholarship for girls tenable at Trinity College, Dublin (1906); and otherwise encouraged or funded educational projects.[35]

On the election of Bishop Alexander to the primacy in 1896, George Chadwick (1840-1923) was translated to Derry and Raphoe, and remained bishop until 1916. The diocese experienced a decline in the numbers of clergy: in 1870 the united diocese had 34 curates, but by 1904 only 18 curates. Isolated cures with tiny congregations were unattractive, but the bishop found that alterations to church buildings were being carried out without faculties and without his consent, and urged clergy to become familiar with the Church's laws. As animosities between Roman Catholics and Protestants became more pronounced, not only because of the growing aggressiveness of Irish Nationalists, but because of doctrinal problems such as papal infallibility (1870) under Pius IX and the Decree *Ne Temere* (1907) under Pius X (1903-14 – which required the non-Roman Catholic partner in a 'mixed marriage' to consent that any children should be brought up as Roman Catholics), Chadwick worked to bring some degree of unity to the various Protestant sects to counteract what he saw as desperate surrenders to expediency by unscrupulous politicians.[36] He believed that political unity among Protestants was of paramount importance in the face of the Home Rule Bill, and that the constitutional crisis of 1912-14 proved the mutually exclusive positions of Ulster Unionism and Irish Nationalism. The 1914-18 war suspended Home Rule for the time being, but the events of 1916 polarised opinion even more, with Irish Republicans being identified as allies of the Germans by one side and as martyrs dying for Ireland by the other.

[35] All this information from Reed (1865) in the 1917 *Continuation* of the *Historical Narrative*, and from The Irish Society papers at Guildhall, City of London. See Aldous (ed.) (1993).

[36] Orr (1997), 95-8.

Joseph Irvine Peacocke (1866-1962), Bishop of Derry and Raphoe from 1916 until 1945, was consecrated at the same time as the Easter rising, a prelude to an episcopate marked by political instability, violence, and lawlessness in Ireland during its first decade. Despising what he perceived as a timid Government, paralysed with fright, he hoped that Irish Protestants and Roman Catholics could still be reconciled, but his faith was dashed. Partition brought grim battles and riots to Londonderry, where 40 lives were lost in the early summer of 1920. With a diocese straddling the new border, the bishop found it difficult to get around, and indeed travel in those times was fraught with dangers.

The Parliamentary Inquiries 1889-91

Following the inquiry of 1853-4 and Maguire's attempts to get a royal commission established to enquire into the administration of The Society, a further attack was launched in 1875 by the Conservative Member of Parliament for the city of Londonderry, a Presbyterian Londoner, Charles E. Lewis. Upon his motion a return was required to be made to the House of Commons of The Society's receipts and expenditure from 1865 to 1875, together with copies of all orders and resolutions relating to the granting of leases since 1820.[37] The report of the commission of 1853-4 was resurrected, and political pressure was brought urging its recommendations be passed in the House of Commons.[38] Much emboldened by his popular success, Lewis pressed for the appointment of a select committee to report on the best means of realising the recommendations of the commissioners of 1853-4, but was opposed by various petitions from various Livery Companies and by individuals in Londonderry and Coleraine. In 1877 Lewis brought forward in the House of Commons a motion calling attention to the constitution of The Irish Society and the management of its income and property; moving that a select committee be appointed to inquire into the workings of The Society; to report as to what changes, if any, might be made to The Society; and to investigate if The Society's property might be better placed in the hands of public trustees resident in Ireland.[39] The Governor of The Society, Sir Sydney Hedley Waterlow, Bt., M.P. (1822-1906), replied on behalf of The Society, and the motion was defeated.

However, trouble never went away, and in 1884 the Government introduced a Bill concerning the government of the City of London in which lurked clauses providing for abolition of The Irish Society. The City petitioned against this Bill, which was subsequently withdrawn.[40] Then, in 1889, a select committee was appointed by the House of Commons to inquire into and report on the terms of the charter or other instruments by which the estates were granted to The Irish Society and to the London Companies, including trusts and obligations attaching to the ownership of the estates. In particular the committee was to look into the mode in which the sale of the estates had been effected or would be effected in the light of trusts and obligations.[41]

37 Reed (1865), 1899 edition, 80.

38 Anonymous (1875), *passim*. It is interesting that many of the pamphlets antipathetic to The Irish Society and the City of London do not carry the name of the author or authors. See, for example, J.C.W. (1890) – which is relatively mild compared with some of the semi-literate and ignorant publications that stirred up great animosity. J.C.W. (1890) clearly referred to the 'Oppression' of County Londonderry by the Londoners, which is nonsense.

39 Reed (1865), 1917 edition, 86.

40 *Ibid.*, 104-5.

41 *Ibid.*, 111.

The amounts of work generated, expenses incurred, and time spent on the interminable reports, inquiries, and resisting attacks are incredible, and must have exasperated the Court of The Society. The published papers relating to the Skinners' suit and the 1853-4 commission, augmented with volumes such as the *Concise View* and the *Deputation Reports*, contain more than anyone could ever want to know about The Society and its workings. These apparently never-ending attacks appear to have been intended to wear The Society down, for there was really nothing more that could be added to the mass of material already available in published form. So why yet another select committee in 1889?

The answer appears to lie in the change caused by the various land enactments intended to improve the lot of the small tenant-farmers, to break up the big estates, appease the Nationalists, and so on. Many Livery Companies which, only a few decades earlier, had regained direct control over their estates and set about improving them with evangelical zeal, gave up and sold their holdings. Now, with the benevolent landlords no longer there, generous handouts for educational, charitable, and other purposes ceased to exist, so that was wrong too, and the squeals were loud and shrill.

For example, the Grocers' Company sold its estates in 1877 and at once all allowances and grants towards buildings ceased. The Drapers had a great deal of trouble during the worst of the agitation in the 1880s, and income virtually dried up: this did not encourage the Company to hand out large sums to its belligerent tenants for charitable purposes. The Fishmongers, who had been benevolent landowners, also found themselves in a quandary when tenants refused to pay rents, settle arrears, or buy out the Company. The Fishmongers' Agent observed that the tenants were 'an awful lot of ungrateful blackguards'.[42] The Clothworkers and the Merchant Taylors were more fortunate, and managed to sell lock, stock, and barrel in 1871.

Parliamentary interference and commissions (which invariably raised red herrings about whether or not the Companies actually owned their lands or merely held them in trust, though the position was quite clear), badly drafted Acts, corrupt and tardy bureaucrats, an 'unsettled', easily led, and greedy tenantry, and politicians and press inimical to the Londoners did not help. In nearly every case where the Companies were still owners of estates by the end of the 1880s, hatred was whipped up by agitators, rents were permanently in arrears, and a general lack of confidence made its presence felt in squalor, failure, and decay. The tactics of the tenantry (which had been treated with open-handed generosity in most cases) and its political manipulators alienated the Londoners, so contributions to dispensaries, charities, individuals, and churches, not surprisingly, ceased. Some Companies did not manage to extricate themselves finally until just before the 1914-18 war, and when connections with Proportions were finally severed the papers of the Companies indicate degrees of bemused regret, exasperated relief, and more than a touch of righteous indignation. For the Companies the Plantation of Ulster had been three centuries of trouble, expense, bother, and impossible demands, pleasing nobody. To give some idea of how deeply the sense of betrayal, exasperation, and hostility had penetrated, the Clothworkers' Company (which had dispensed largesse with liberality from 1840 to 1870) refused to send representatives to attend the centenary celebrations of Castlerock parish-church on its former Proportion in 1970.[43]

42 Fishmongers' Papers at Guildhall Library, City of London, M.S. 7273, loose letter.

43 For details of Company reactions see Curl (1986), *passim*.

The 1889 committee presented its report in July of that year.[44] No doubt to the irritation of its enemies, The Irish Society came out blameless, with no complaints against the way in which that body performed its duties. Furthermore, the committee concluded that the loss of the London Livery Companies' benevolent and charitable support for local causes in County Londonderry was and would be a disaster, but it was rather too late to conclude that, as the Companies had had enough: those Companies which had managed to sell out wanted nothing more to do with Ulster, and those (like the Mercers, Fishmongers, and Drapers) that were still embroiled in the incredibly unpleasant and messy business of trying to extricate themselves wanted to be shot of everything as soon as possible, and were in no mood to continue giving largesse as before. However, the committee, despite having mountains of *published* papers readily available, felt it could not report on the legal aspects of the trusts and obligations attaching to ownership of the estates by The Society and the Companies. So, almost inevitably (the weary historian quickly learns to see such things coming) yet another inquiry was suggested.

Thus, in May 1890 a committee was appointed, and presented its findings in 1891.[45] The committee had three Irish Nationalists sitting on it, and consisted of the 1889 committee less one member but with three new ones, and had 13 members in all, giving it a suitably solemn, almost biblical air. Its terms of reference were to hear full statements from all the parties concerned of the various positions maintained by them, to collect all the arguments by which those conditions were supported and defended, and to report to the House of Commons if any case had been established by those who insisted that the Crown's grant of the estates was associated with public purposes and trusts in Ulster that were wholly independent of any benefit to the Companies. Having heard evidence (mostly from Ireland) the committee, chaired by John Morley (1838-1923), reported that a *prima facie* case existed for the view that permanent public objects still adhered to the estates of The Irish Society, the Companies, *and the proceeds of the sale* of the estates.[46] From the point of view of the Londoners, this was an appalling result, but it was not really surprising. Morley had become Chief Secretary for Ireland in Gladstone's 1886 administration, and was partly responsible for drafting the first Home Rule Bill of that year. Morley, an agnostic, was associated with what might be called 'humanitarian rationalism', had been a champion of disestablishment since the 1860s, and, with Joseph Chamberlain (1836-1914) and Sir Charles Wentworth Dilke, Bt. (1843-1911), had advanced disestablishment, secular education, land reform, progressive taxation, and pressure to changes of old-established Corporations (e.g. the City of London). Attached to this triumvirate too was more than a whiff of Republicanism, and Dilke was on friendly terms with numerous Continental Radicals and Republicans. To say that Morley was sympathetic to Irish Nationalism would be an understatement: he received the Freedom of the city of Dublin in 1888, and once more became Chief Secretary for Ireland in 1892, a post he held until the Government fell in 1895. He was raised to the peerage in 1908 as Viscount Morley of Blackburn.

The 1890 committee's findings were curious, to say the least, for several horses had bolted. The Haberdashers had shed their load in the 17th century; the Merchant Taylors had sold their estate in the 18th century (except for interests they had held in

44 House of Commons *Paper* 290 (1889).

45 House of Commons *Papers* 322 (1890), 222 (1891).

46 House of Commons *Paper* 222 (1891), iii, xi.

the Clothworkers' Proportion, and those, too, had been sold by 1890); the Goldsmiths and Vintners had got rid of their estates in the 1730s; the Clothworkers (and their Merchant Taylor associates) had sold out in 1871; the Grocers were thankful to have disposed of their property in 1877; the Fishmongers, Drapers, Skinners, Salters, and Ironmongers were in the process of selling their estates under the various Irish Land Acts of the 1880s; and the Mercers kept their estates virtually intact until after 1903.[47]

The 1891 *Report* of the committee held that Irish tenants of the Companies should benefit from the various land purchase enactments, not only by being able to buy property on advantageous terms, but from the proceeds of the sales, as it would be indefensible to allow the vendors to divest themselves of the responsibilities attached to their Ulster estates. In short, the committee argued that a fund should be established into which the proceeds of the sales should be paid, and that this fund should be used entirely for Irish purposes and objects.[48] Furthermore, Morley and his committee concurred with the findings of the 1853-4 commission and recommended that The Irish Society should be abolished and its charter repealed by Act of Parliament.[49] Once more the committee made adverse comments about the excessive costs of management and the enormous expenditure on law charges and administration in London and Ireland. Given the almost continuous attacks on The Society, the immense amounts of work needed to prepare evidence and brief lawyers to defend interests, it is ludicrous that the committee should have come to these fatuous conclusions: Members of Parliament and bureaucracies do not seem to understand that they can generate vast amounts of paperwork at no personal costs, but when individuals or others have to prepare cases and answer charges they have to pay people to do the work, and that does not come free.

It had long been established that The Society held its lands as a trustee for public purposes (especially the improvement of Londonderry, Coleraine, and their Liberties), but the Companies had obtained their titles from The Society, and so investigations as to how far the Companies were bound by the same obligations of public trusts delved into the affairs of the Plantation. Ever since the 1850s attempts had been made to abolish The Irish Society, and one has to come to the unfortunate conclusion that the 1890-1 committee was not unbiased at all, but had political motives. This conclusion is reinforced by an examination of Morley's leading questions and constant harking back to the 1853-4 commissioners' *Report*. Attempts to have draft reports by other than the chairman adopted were foiled by the three Irish Nationalists and three Liberal supporters of Home Rule voting together, and when there was any chance of a tie the chairman added his casting-vote, so it was Morley's draft that was adopted.[50] One of the rejected drafts (by Sir William Thackeray Marriott, M.P. [1834-1903]) pointed out that The Irish Society's practice of devoting to public purposes the net revenues of the estates held by The Society ought 'not to be disturbed'. It also stated that there was 'no excessive fund', and nor was there any likelihood of such a fund ever accumulating: given that The Society was always having to spend money defending itself and briefing lawyers this was absolutely certain. Marriott's draft stated that no case had been 'made out for any alteration in the constitution of' The Society,[51] and

[47] The Mercers largely sold out under the Irish Land Act of 1903 (the 'Wyndham Act', 3 Edw. VII, c.37). See Curl (1986), *passim*.

[48] House of Commons *Paper* 222 (1891), xi.

[49] Commissioners Appointed to Inquire into the Existing State of the Corporation of the City of London (1854), xxxvii, 26.

[50] House of Commons *Paper* 222 (1891), viii, xxvi-xxx.

[51] *Ibid.*, xix-xx.

cautioned against any consideration of the Company estates being held subject to trusts as no court of law would enforce this, the evidence simply not being there. It is not insignificant that Marriott's draft was not even discussed.

Witnesses questioned by the committee were reported to have been 'pretty unanimous' in denouncing The Society's management costs as excessive; in objecting to The Society's expenditure on legal costs in London; and in finding the requirement to submit bye-laws and other matters to The Society for approval as inconvenient and subject to delay. A careful reading of these intolerably tedious and bigoted documents shows that the 'witnesses' all wanted bigger slices of The Society's cake from personal or partisan motives: an educationalist stated The Society was neglecting education (it quite obviously was doing nothing of the sort); Roman Catholics complained they were not getting anything (they were); Presbyterians were dissatisfied with the size of grants to Presbyterians, and moaned about grants to other sects (they had done very well); a speculative builder found The Society was not spending enough on property (its outlay was enormous); and two witnesses made it clear they regarded grants as degrading, even suggesting they were 'bribery'. It is perfectly clear that the Archangel Gabriel himself, if he had had London connections, would have been unable to satisfy those witnesses. Relations between the Corporation of Londonderry and The Irish Society were 'indefensible in principle', but nobody could agree what system would be better. The 'immense delays' in getting sanction for new bye-laws do not stand up to serious examination either: the last bye-law submitted to The Irish Society by Londonderry Corporation was considered in 1878, had been received on 2 February, and returned on 12 February involving ten days between receipt and despatch, and had occurred 12 years prior to the Morley committee's first meeting in 1890.[52]

In 1891 the committee was 'irresistably forced' to opine that The Society and the Companies were bound by identical trusts and obligations, and early in 1892 a writ was issued summoning The Honourable The Irish Society, the Twelve Great Companies and other Companies, and the Corporation of the City of London to appear in an action at the suit of the Attorney-General for Ireland in the Court of Chancery, Dublin, at the relation of an otherwise somewhat obscure Presbyterian minister, John Johnston, who was clearly a figurehead for the venture. The object of the exercise was to have The Society and the Companies declared to be trustees as regards their Ulster estates, and, *inter alia*, settling on the future management of The Society.

When it is considered that preliminary pleadings in the suit were spread over seven years and generated mountains of paper, any whisper that The Society spent too much money on legal matters has to be treated with the contempt it deserves: The Society had no option, and did not start the business. Eventually, in 1898, the trial began before the Master of the Rolls in the Chancery Court, Dublin, and judgement was delivered on 2 December.[53] He said that everything bearing on the case had been considered, and referred to the 'immense mass of documents' and 'enormous amount of the property involved'. He wondered why the case had been permitted to drag on for 'nigh on seven years in Court, unheard', and wryly remarked that 'never in the history of litigation was there a case in which the burthen of proof lay so heavily upon a plaintiff'. The Judge outlined the history of the Plantation before turning with wholly admirable clarity to the main issue. The Irish Society had not paid any money for its

[52] For these dreary matters see House of Commons *Paper* 322 (1890), Questions 2355-63, 3104-11, 3257, 3682, 3992-3, 7025-8, and *passim*.

[53] It is given in full in an Appendix in Reed (1865), 1917 edition, 200-231.

estates, but the Companies did, so they were 'purchasers', and their rights to any profits were specifically acknowledged in virtually every document relating to their title. Unequivocally, he said that the Companies were never trustees, and that the relator had 'wholly failed to prove his case', the evidence having completely failed. The Judge 'presumed' that the Attorney-General of the day 'was satisfied that' the Reverend Johnston 'was a competent relator'. In fact, Johnston was a shadowy figure who only appeared through Counsel: the Judge was obviously unimpressed by the fact that Johnston was not heard in person. In his conclusion, the Judge said he was clearly 'of opinion that no Court' had 'any right' to say the Companies were 'mere trustees for the plantation which was undertaken and completed more than 250 years' before. As to The Irish Society, no case had been made that would entitle the relator to a decree against it. The City of London, which represented interests of the Brownbakers (Clothworkers' Company associates who had ceased to exist) and the Coopers (associates of the Ironmongers), was only a nominal party in the long-winded affair. The Judge dismissed the information with costs.

However, the strange saga demonstrates that hearsay, mythology, and false beliefs have powerful influences in Irish matters, for the positions of the Companies and of The Irish Society were perfectly clear, not only from the original grants, but as a result of the Skinners' case in the 1830s. Documentation is unusually full, for Dr Edwin Freshfield, the solicitor representing all the defendants except the Corporation of the City of London and The Irish Society, prepared three hefty volumes dealing with the documents, pleadings, and proceedings which were printed by Spottiswoode & Company. Freshfield also produced a useful *Statement of Facts* to help counsel during the 1898 trial.[54] Also of interest is the report of Sir John Whittaker Ellis Bt., Governor of The Society during the troubled years 1883 to 1893, prepared in 1891[55] for the House of Commons committee sitting under Morley's chairmanship. Sir John's report was not voted on by the committee (of which he was a member), but it was a clear and factual statement of policies and activities of The Society. It began with a brief historical introduction. It dealt with leases, pointing out that perpetuity leases were granted by The Society with strict conditions concerning building improvements and certain precautions taken to prevent properties falling into the hands of unscrupulous middle-men. One by one his report dealt with specific complaints raised by witnesses:

	Complaint	*Response*
1.	The Society retarded the evolution of Londonderry and Coleraine by refusing to grant leases in perpetuity.	Not true. The Society not only granted such leases (with appropriate conditions) but permitted lessees to purchase fee-farm rents to convert their holdings into fee-simples.
2.	The Society gave its funds away as small grants instead of applying them for a great public undertaking.	True that The Society gave many small grants to many causes, but if it ceased spreading its largesse it would then be accused of favouring one group instead of another. Primary schools, for example, had to be numerous as very young children could not travel far, and so resources had to be distributed with an even hand. This did not mean The Society neglected intermediate schools, for it supported (among others) Foyle College (essentially an Anglican foundation), The Londonderry Academical Institution (mainly Presbyterian), its own schools in Coleraine, Coleraine Academical Institution, and other educational establishments.

[54] Freshfield and Freshfield (1898), *passim*.
[55] House of Commons *Paper* 222 (1891), xx-xxvi.

The Society also gave funds for numerous public undertakings: Londonderry cathedral was a case in point; the water-works; the freeing of Londonderry bridge from tolls; providing a Guildhall for Londonderry and converting the old town-hall for educational purposes; a town-hall for Coleraine; restoring and rebuilding the parish-church at Coleraine; improvements to navigation of the River Bann; providing cemeteries; and ensuring decent water supplies. The exercise of a wide discretion had enabled The Society to fund enormous improvements. To restrict this discretion would create more discontent and adversely affect many public interests.

3. Favour was shown to the Anglican Church and the Roman Catholics failed to benefit from handouts.	One of the main objects for which The Society was founded was to support and encourage the Protestant Established Church, so The Society could hardly be blamed for that. In any case, The Society used its discretionary powers to support St Columb's Roman Catholic College, and monies given to Londonderry Corporation, to support public works, and to maintain primary-schools conducted on the Irish national school system (open to children of *all* religious denominations) were bound to benefit Roman Catholics as well as Protestants. Claims that nothing went to Roman Catholics were untrue.
4. Expenditure by The Society for its establishment, Deputations, etc., was too high.	The Society's estates were subdivided into numerous smallholdings, most of which were held in fee-farm, so management was costly. Most rents had been fixed many years before, and were far too low for 1890. Dinners given annually to tenants and others in Londonderry and Coleraine were expensive, but were popular occasions: their abolition would be counter-productive. As for the annual Deputations or Visitations, they were necessary for many reasons, not least to maintain the close links between the Plantation lands and London.
5. 'Jobbery' (i.e. unfair means to secure a private end) had been used in relation to the granting of leases.	This red herring was raised by one witness, a building-contractor, who was unable to substantiate his allegations.
6. Members of The Society held office for only two years.	Administration was continuous, for Governors held office 'during good behaviour' and permanent officers (e.g. the Secretary) ensured continuity.
7. Funds devoted to Irish purposes should not be administered by a 'body of gentlemen residing in London'. The Society should be dissolved and property vested in a body of local or Irish trustees.	The Plantation of the area had been effected by the City of London. Both Londonderry and Coleraine owed their existence to London, and it was not unreasonable the association should be retained. Opinion was so divided as to the purposes to which the funds of The Society should be devoted that it was worthless. The builder wanted money spent on buildings; the Secretary of the Londonderry Port and Harbour Commissioners wanted the harbour debt paid off; and the parish-priest of Dungiven wanted the Londoners 'cleared out body and bone' leaving the property behind, of course (Sir John felt that such a comment was wholly predictable). When local opinion was sought as to whether The Society's property would be better managed by Irish trustees, total confusion reigned, one faction expressing its suspicion of the others, and so on. The consensus was that it was far better to leave well alone, and retain The Society.

Sir John ended his report with observations that modern communications had to a very large extent removed the previous inconveniences of referring matters to London, and that no unanswerable case had been made for the abolition of The Society. In short, it would not be sensible, either economically or rationally, to destroy an existing organisation that worked well, nor would it be wise to sever connections with London just to transfer administration to a new bureaucracy that would be subject to all sorts of interests and factions.[56]

The Irish Society became very concerned about this turn of events. Having taken legal advice in the 1870s, it did so again in 1893: by the 1890s there was an 'earnest drive on behalf of Roman Catholics' to obtain a 'substantial share' of The Society's donations, so it was decided to establish if Society funds 'should be devoted to objects connected with the propagation of the Roman Catholic religion'.[57] In its evidence to the select committee of 1891 The Society reiterated that it was restricted by its charter to making grants to 'the Irish Church'.[58] Only occasionally did it make grants to Nonconformists.[59]

However, in the volatile political climate of the 1890s, following disestablishment by the Irish Church Act of 1869, it began to be felt by The Society that it should *either* make no distinction between denominations and should distribute funds evenly, *or* should abstain from making any grants to *any* religious bodies, devoting its funds to public purposes unconnected with religion. The Honourable The Irish Society and the Companies met and decided to seek an independent legal opinion on the proper course they should adopt as by 1875 there was no religious denomination in Ireland that was Established and that, strictly speaking, operated according to Her Majesty's laws.

Counsel opined that the granting of sites for the building of churches, schools, and colleges was a special case, and that there could be no legal objections to this. Concerning Roman Catholic churches or schools, 'special cases' would have to be made when applying for grants, but generally, in order to avoid controversy, The Society should abstain from giving grants to bodies for *religious* purposes.[60] Nevertheless, counsel felt that a certain amount of discretion remained, and that there was some leeway in the post-1869 climate.

Sir John Whittaker Ellis, Bt., was another personality in The Irish Society in whom the Evangelical Conscience brightly burned. There is a revealing private letter, dated 31 July 1893,[61] from him to his successor, George Faudel-Phillips (1840-1922), who later became a baronet. In this document, Sir John gave his opinion of the various personalities with whom he had had to deal, and particularly mentioned the 'late Roman Catholic Bishop' of Derry as a 'friend' (this would have been Francis Kelly, bishop from 1864 to 1889). Sir John also praised 'Mr Leverington' as a sound and trustworthy servant of The Society: this was James Robert Leverington, Secretary of The Honourable The Irish Society from 1917 to 1925 in succession to Durie Miller, who served from 1865 to 1917 during a period of great transition. As will be seen below, however, Leverington, who started life as the butler, and then messenger and housekeeper to The Society, was not an entire success, and his rise to the responsible position of Secretary is rather strange.

This was a curious chapter in The Society's history, indicative, perhaps, of the rather bumbling and amateurish way in which things were done. It is rather sad, too, for the gentlemanly ways of the 1890s were not to survive long in the century that was to come: Ireland, The Irish Society, Great Britain, Europe, and the world were to go through massive trials. Nothing would ever be the same again.

[56] Smith (1966), 157-164. This chapter draws largely on Court Minute-Books and Letter-Books in the Corporation of London Record Office (see Aldous [ed.] [1993], and on other sources cited in the footnotes.

[57] Corporation of London Records, IS/Box 4.7 Loc. 422B.

[58] i.e. The Church of Ireland (Anglican).

[59] xxiv of House of Commons *Paper 222* (1891).

[60] This principle was upheld by the Local Advisory Committee in the 1970s, '80s, and '90s.

[61] Corporation of London Record Office IS. Box 10. 18.

CHAPTER XII

County Londonderry, Ireland, The Irish Society, and Events from the 1880s to 1984

> Some perchance there yet be who would prefer local administration, but, however that may be, it is idle to deny that Londonderry and Coleraine are fortunate in the twentieth century in the possession of The Irish Society. The benefit is theirs, wholly and altogether. The London Corporation, forced though it was to undertake the responsibility and incur great trouble and expense at the dictation of an arbitrary government in troublous times, has never reaped the slightest pecuniary advantage from the association
>
> JOHN BETTS (1880-1967): *The Story of The Irish Society. Being a Brief Historical Account of the Foundation and Work of The Honourable The Irish Society of London* (London: The Irish Society, 1913), 89-90

The Society's other Achievements in County Londonderry

Given the enormous hassle with which The Society had to contend in the second half of the 19th century, it is amazing that it managed to achieve anything at all, so much of its energy and resources being absorbed by having to defend itself. Sir John Ellis could have listed many more benefactions than he did. Many of these are given in *A Brief Historical Narrative of the Origin and Constitution of ... The Honourable The Irish Society* in its various manifestations, but intelligence of other grants lurks among the papers of The Society held in London.[1]

Apart from the schools built by The Society, the major public works it supported (e.g. the bridge over the Foyle at Londonderry, the water-supplies, the quays, the cathedral, Coleraine parish-church, Coleraine town-hall, and other projects listed above), the greatest building was the Guildhall in Londonderry. It should be remembered that The Society gave small grants (for which it was adversely criticised, but would have also been abused if it had given nothing at all) to numerous building projects, including many churches, church-halls, church-schools, and the like. In 1873, for example, it gave £200 to the Londonderry Academical Institution in addition to the previous grant of £1,000 made in 1869 (the building was erected to designs by Richard Williamson in 1870, but no longer survives). Money was also given in 1874 to the Young Men's Christian Association to help to enlarge and repair its hall in Londonderry, and £200 was given to help build the memorial-hall for the Apprentice Boys (a Protestant political society founded in 1814, named after the 13 apprentices who on 7 December 1688 shut Londonderry's gates against Lord Antrim's troops[2]). The latter

[1] Aldous (ed.) (1993), *passim.*

[2] The Apprentice Boys celebrate the shutting of the gates on 18 December and the lifting of the siege of Londonderry on 12 August, dates which are incorrect: the difference between Old Style and New Style Calendars from 5 October 1582 to 28 February 1700 (Old Style) was ten days, and from 29 February 1700 to 2 September 1752 it was eleven days. Thus the true anniversaries should be 17 December and either 10 or 11 August, depending on the date accepted for the Jacobites' departure.

might be considered a contentious grant today, but in 1874 the connection between apprentices in 1688 and London would have been clear, given the numbers of young men sent over from the capital to serve their time in Londonderry and Coleraine, and so the grant towards the building would not have been seen as partisan, but rather as part of even-handed benevolence. In the event, J. G. Ferguson designed the building, which was not only a memorial to the apprentices and a reminder of 'civil and religious liberties', but a working-men's club. As a work of architecture it is a curious and rather ungainly hybrid of styles including Tudor Gothic, Scottish Baronial, and Irish medieval (e.g. the crenellations): it was completed in 1877 at a cost of £3,250.

The Society in 1882 granted a site for the Roman Catholic Temperance hall at a nominal rent, but the Temperance Society did not proceed further as the proposed lease contained a condition that the proposed building should be used solely for the promotion of temperance principles. In due course (1888), however, St Columb's Temperance hall was erected in Newmarket Street to designs by Croom & Toye in a coarse Renaissance-Italianate style, the façade of which was crowned by figures of Erin, Temperance, and Vulcan carved by Charles W. Harrison (1835-1903) of Dublin. Just as Protestants used the siege as a focus for their traditions, Roman Catholics exploited the mystic legends of early saints associated with the city, notably Saint Columba, Columb, Colmcille, or Columcille (*c.*521-97), and by 1900 the two communities were polarised socially, religiously, and politically, with their own institutions, buildings, and meeting-places. The Apprentice Boys' memorial-hall and St Columb's hall are only two examples of the architectural expression given to such polarisation. Though The Irish Society, by the 1890s, was doing its utmost to give support to a very large range of causes, and the published documents record some of the donations in a laconic way, some of the letter-books occasionally reveal despair and exasperation. It is not surprising that this was so, but what is amazing is the even-tempered way in which The Society behaved.

Money was given for many new buildings, repairs to buildings, and general improvements. Every application was given due consideration, and a steady flow of grants went out of The Society's coffers. Hospitals were supported, and a very considerable amount went on annual grants, not for buildings, but for other purposes. For example, The Society gave £250 each year to the Roman Catholic College of St Columb towards the support of the 'Classical English Assistant Masters',[3] and grants were made to Nazareth House, Londonderry, for the relief of aged and 'destitute infirm and respectable poor of both sexes, irrespective of religion, together with orphan, abandoned, or invariably infirm children'.[4] There were also grants made for and assistance given to the promotion of railways in order to improve the economy, but very large sums were expended on improving the River Bann for shipping and on freeing Londonderry Bridge from tolls (the last involved the raising of £40,000 by the issue of debentures of £100 each, at 4 per cent, at a minimum price of £95, and the Bann improvements attracted a grant of £30,000 from The Society, both enormous sums for 1877-8). These grants did not discriminate against who used the bridge or the River Bann. The works at the Bann included the construction of the two moles **[90c]**, completed in 1882.

[3] Reed (1865), 1899 edition, 116, and Court Minutes for 1892. A list of colleges, schools, and other institutions receiving annual grants from The Society is given in an *Appendix* to Reed (1865), in the 1878 edition, 53-6. This list was greatly extended by 1900 .

[4] *Ibid.*, 117.

102 The Governor of The Irish Society laying the foundation-stone of Londonderry's Guildhall in 1887. (*PRONI/T2416/2/28*)

A very odd aspect of The Irish Society's affairs surfaced during investigations of the papers held in the Corporation of London Records Room in 1999. It will be recalled that Sir John Whittaker Ellis, Bt., in 1893, wrote to his successor as Governor, George Faudel-Phillips, about various people, including J. R. Leverington, whose probity he commended. As noted above, Leverington was The Society's butler, then messenger and housekeeper, yet in 1883 he and his wife accompanied the Visitation, or Deputation, to Ireland, which is curious, to say the least, though they may have helped with catering and other matters at Government House, Termonbacca. Thereafter, though, Leverington's rise was even odder, because he was admitted to the Freedom of the City of London in 1887, and seems to have established himself very firmly at The Irish Chamber, with the full *Imprimatur* of the Governor and other powerful personalities within The Society.[5] The workings of The Society were sometimes mysterious, but, as will be described below, the case of Leverington defies probing. It was a bizarre affair.

However, as Leverington was building his base, The Society continued to support major works. In 1885 help was given to tenants on the Ballykelly and Myroe reclaimed slob-lands, flooded when the sea-wall was damaged during a severe storm. During the same year The Society agreed to grant Londonderry Corporation £16,000 and a site reclaimed from the slob-land of the River Foyle at Shipquay Place for a new town-hall, and in 1887 the foundation-stone was laid by the Governor of The Irish Society **[102]**,

[5] Corporation of London Records Office, IS Box 10.18; IS/CM/38, 48, 49; IS/CM/38, 440. The author is indebted to Mrs. Aldous for these items.

Sir John Whittaker Ellis, Bt., M.P. The Guildhall (as the building became known, to emphasise the London connection) was officially opened in 1890 by the Lord Lieutenant (1889-92), Lawrence Dundas (1844-1929), 3rd Earl of Zetland (1st Marquess from 1892).[6] It was quite an occasion, for the Viceroy passed through the 'principal streets' of Londonderry in the State Carriage (specially forwarded from Dublin), accompanied by the Governor of The Irish Society, the Mayor of Londonderry, and Colonel Garrett, A.D.C., followed by the High Sheriff, the Deputy Governor, and members of The Society's Visitation.

103 The town-hall in the Diamond, Londonderry, re-edified in 1823-6, from Bishop Street, as shown on James O'Hagan's map of Londonderry of 1847. (*CLRO/GLCL/IS/ Plans R.P. No.16*)

This was really the fourth town-hall: the first had stood in The Diamond, but was destroyed during the siege **[26]**; the second was erected in 1692 **[45]** to designs by Captain Nevill (Phillips's fantastic 'citadel' of 1622 **[28, 30]** was never realised); and the third was a major re-working of Nevill's building in 1823-6. The last **[103, 104]** was donated to the school of art by the corporation when the Guildhall opened, and The Irish Society gave £150 towards the cost of adapting the old town-hall for the purpose. This building was demolished in 1909-10 and the site laid out as an ornamental garden, now occupied by the robust and vigorous war-memorial, a splendidly heroic centrepiece for the city **[105]**. The new Guildhall cost £20,000 and was designed by the ubiquitous J. G. Ferguson, the builders being Colhoun Brothers, a local firm. However, the building demonstrated all Ferguson's weaknesses as an architect: uncertain stylistically (it was vaguely First Pointed [Gothic] based loosely on 13th-century precedents), it had tourelles plonked uneasily at the bases of the gables, but the dominant clock-tower was altogether more successful as a work of architecture.

In 1900 Coleraine Urban District Council (as it had become in 1898) decided to enlarge the town-hall of 1857-9, and The Society made a grant of £70 per annum for 30 years for the purpose. Work was completed in 1902 to tactful designs by the local architect, W. J. Given, and alterations included an extra piece added to the east end, a new pedimented entrance, and the blocking-up of the original way in. Thus The Irish Society's two urban settlements were suitably embellished with fine municipal buildings.

However, on 19 April 1908 (Easter Sunday) Londonderry's Guildhall was destroyed by fire, and the Court of The Irish Society responded to an appeal from Londonderry Corporation for assistance to rebuild it. A grant of £5,000 was voted, conditional upon the total expenditure on the new building not exceeding (with the insurance money) £16,300. Plans were subsequently submitted to The Society for approval, and a memorial- or foundation-stone **[106]** was laid by the Governor (from 1906 to 1921), Sir Alfred James Newton, Bt. (1845-1921), during The Society's Visitation of 1909. However, the designs turned out to be unsatisfactory as they 'would not afford all the accommodation required', and a larger building was evolved **[107]** to cost £24,000. In

[6] *Irish Builder* **32** (1890), 185.

104 The former town-hall in the Diamond, Londonderry (then the school of art), from Shipquay Street, showing Sir Robert Ferguson's monument, *c.*1890. (*IRC/U/LON-LON PH2621*)

1910 The Society resolved to increase the grant to £13,000, the balance to be raised by borrowing a sum to be secured on the rates of the City of Londonderry. Principal and interest were to be paid off over 50 years at an estimated rate of about £600 per annum, this amount being provided by The Society each year until the loan was extinguished. A further condition of this generous arrangement was that the Corporation would not apply to The Society for further assistance for 15 years from 1910.[7]

[7] Reed (1865), 1899 edition, 137-8.

105 The war-memorial in the Diamond, Londonderry, in 1999. (*A*)

Ferguson's clock-tower, entrance vestibule, and parts of the building nearest the river were retained **[108a]**, but otherwise the red sandstone Guildhall was a new design, and much more successful it is too. The architect was a former pupil of Messrs Robert Magill Young (1851-1925) & John Mackenzie (1844-1917) of Belfast and former assistant to John Lanyon, Matthew Alexander Robinson (1872-1929), city surveyor, engineer, and architect from 1909, whose free treatment of late-Gothic Revival is wholly admirable. The Tudoresque turrets rise up logically in a series of stages, and the elevation to Shipquay Place is charming, elegant, and very beautifully composed. Particularly felicitous is the combination of oriel window set beneath a large Perpendicular window, with elements rising up above the gable **[108b]**. Tracery is delicate and well handled, and roundels on the gable contain heraldic devices connecting Londonderry, London, and The Irish Society.

This connection was made even clearer in the stained-glass windows by Campbell Brothers of Belfast. Many aspects of Londonderry's history were alluded to, and events such as the arrival of the apprentices, the four-man Deputation at the very beginning of the Plantation, and the siege were celebrated together with mythologies (e.g. the timber-framed houses from London). Arms of the City Companies, The Irish Society, and the former Irish Chieftains were also vigorously presented in the windows. It was at the suggestion of the Governor that the Livery Companies were 'invited to provide suitable stained-glass windows for the building'.[8]

This proposal was connected with the tercentenary of The Society in 1913, but was also related to commemorating Edward VII (1841-1910), King of Great Britain and Ireland (1901-10), who, with Queen Alexandra (1844-1925), had visited Londonderry on 28 July 1903. The Irish Society was also concerned to demonstrate the 'valuable services rendered by the City of London and the Livery Companies in the establishment of the Plantation of Ulster, and satisfactory replies [to the invitation to contribute to the costs of the stained-glass windows] were received' from the Mercers', Grocers', Drapers', Fishmongers', Skinners', Salters', Ironmongers', Vintners',

[8] Betts (1913), xxvii.

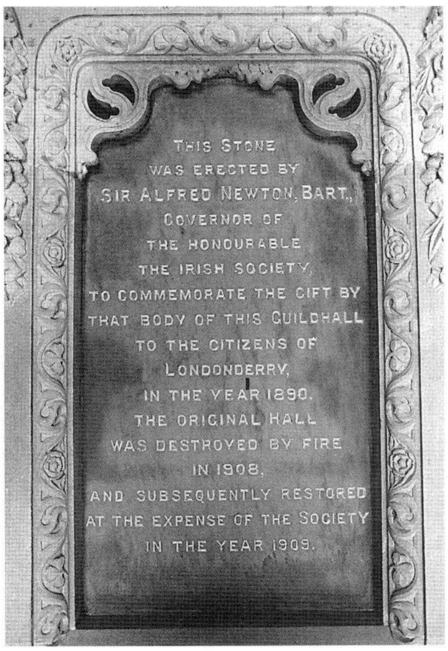

106 Memorial-stone in the Guildhall, Londonderry laid by the Governor of The Irish Society in 1909. (*A*)

107 Work proceeding on the Guildhall, *c.*1909. (*PRONI/T2416/2/31*)

Pewterers', Cutlers', Girdlers', Carpenters', Painter-Stainers', Scriveners', Musicians', Turners', and Glaziers' Companies. Of the Twelve Great Companies, therefore, the Goldsmiths, Merchant Taylors, Haberdashers, and Clothworkers did not return 'satisfactory replies', but it is interesting that several 'Associated Companies' obliged: the Musicians and Glaziers, it will be recalled, were associated with the Fishmongers; the Painter-Stainers with the Goldsmiths; the Girdlers with the Skinners; the Turners with the Haberdashers; the Cutlers with the Salters; and the Pewterers, Carpenters, and Scriveners with the Ironmongers. Thus the Painter-Stainers and Turners seem to have 'broken ranks' and acted independently of the Goldsmiths and Haberdashers, and it is interesting that the Merchant Taylors and Clothworkers (who were associates) both failed to support the proposal.[9] The handsome windows were paid for by the Governor, Sir Alfred Newton, Bt., Lady Margaret Waterlow, widow of Sir Sydney Hedley Waterlow, Bt. (Governor 1873-83), Sir John Whittaker Ellis, Bt. (Governor

[9] Reed (1865) in the 1917 edition, 142-3.

1883-93), Sir George Faudel-Phillips, Bt. (Governor 1893-1906), Sir Henry Miller, Alderman Ballantine, and Sir John McFarland, Bt. (former Mayors of Londonderry), W. C. Simmons, Sir Robert Hargreaves Rogers, Millar Wilkinson, George Briggs, Mann Cross, Alexander Tillie, W. J. Berriman Tippetts, Harry Bird, Thomas Goldney and J. Stuart Pollock (past Deputy Governors), The Irish Society itself, and several Companies. The tercentenary was also marked by a Ball given for the inhabitants of Londonderry and Coleraine held in the newly edified and embellished Guildhall during the 1913 Visitation. It was on this last Visitation before the 1914-18 war that The Society determined to commission a stained-glass window for Coleraine's town-hall, and the work was carried out (including more allusions to the spurious timber-framed houses from London) for £100 **[80]**.

Something of the formality of Irish Society occasions may be gleaned from reading extracts from the copious papers that survive at the Corporation of London Records Office, but photographs are even more eloquent testimonies. A fine photograph of 9 August 1898 survives showing a party at Boom Hall hosted by the Mayor and Mayoress of Londonderry, with the Governor of The Irish Society, Lady Faudel-Phillips, and other members of the Visitation **[109]**.

So three hundred years had passed since The Society had come into existence. The outbreak of war in 1914 put a

108a The Guildhall, Londonderry, from the east, in 1999, showing part of the 1887-8 building (nearest the camera). (*A*)

108b The Guildhall, Londonderry, from the walls, in 1999, showing the elevation to Shipquay Place and the clock-tower. In the gable are the Arms of The Irish Society and the city of Londonderry. (*A*)

109 Garden-party at Boom Hall (built *c.*1770) on 9 August 1898 hosted by the Mayor and Mayoress of Londonderry, Mr and Mrs John B. Johnston. On the second seated row (left to right) are the Mayoress, the Mayor, Lady Faudel-Phillips, and Sir George Faudel-Phillips, Bt. (Governor of The Irish Society [1893-1906] — in top hat). Some of the men standing in the centre were members of The Society's Visitation of 1898. (*DB*)

temporary end to the customary Visitations, and in that year no Visitation took place, but in 1915 the Visitations were resumed. In 1916-18 new maps of The Society's estates were made by R. Eccles Buchanan, civil engineer, to replace those of 1858. These survive, and show that The Society then still owned an enormous amount of urban property. However, although the municipal buildings in both Coleraine and Londonderry were in good shape, changing circumstances had led to the sale of Government House, Termonbacca, in 1905, but the offices at the corner of St Columb's Court and Bishop Street were retained **[61]**, as was The Irish Chamber in Guildhall Yard, City of London **[60]**.

When The Society sold Government House, it did so at a time when it was, like the Companies, shedding much of its property. Enactments of 1870, 1881, and 1887 gradually gave tenants possibilities to buy out their landlords, and money was made available on easy terms for this purpose. The 1891 Purchase of Land (Ireland) Act greatly extended the facilities for transferring land from landlords to tenants, and a further Act of 1896 helped to meet the claims of landlords by means of Land Stock guaranteed by the Treasury. In the early years of the 20th century, therefore, The Society's agricultural tenants mostly held their lands under judicial agreements at low rents fixed either by the land commissioners or by mutual agreements settled out of Court. Wyndham's Act of 1903 made things even easier for tenants to buy out landlords on very favourable terms with payments spread over 68 years, and landlords who agreed to sell were offered bonuses. The Honourable The Irish Society disposed of 198 holdings by 1903, and commissioners determined the total sum to be received by The Society as £99,207, but there were other burdens, for the commissioners required that all interests secured or chargeable on the lands should be discharged. Included were the Londonderry Bridge bonds, Coleraine Bann bonds, and a loan from the commissioners of public works. Once these obligations had been paid off, The Society was left with £17,638.[10]

The Society began to sell off properties in Londonderry and Coleraine by granting leases in perpetuity on condition that suitable buildings were erected by the tenants to designs approved by The Society.[11] Such leases involved charging 'fair ground rents', and the 'liberal terms' offered resulted in marked improvements of several thoroughfares. Leases in perpetuity had been granted in the 18th century, but The Society found that if strict, enforceable conditions were not attached, properties would decay, and there was little could be done to remedy matters, so the practice was discontinued in 1832. By the 1860s, 80- or 99-year leases were being granted to encourage an adequate outlay on buildings, but various criticisms of The Society led to a policy of selling freeholds or granting leases in perpetuity backed by conditions to ensure improvement to properties would ensue. Even so, the post-1916 maps show many urban properties still in The Society's hands, reflecting the general decay of prosperity in the area at the time, for there were not all that many takers, even at the advantageous terms on offer. These maps are interesting documents, showing ownership, rents, and other information, all based on the Ordnance Survey.[12]

More Difficulties and Litigation

As if things had not been difficult enough for The Irish Society, matters concerning the fisheries had again become troublesome. An outline of earlier problems has been given above, but, at the same time as Nationalist and Land agitation had flared, further difficulties arose regarding the use of drift-nets to take salmon at the mouths of the Rivers Foyle and Bann. A drift-net is one that is allowed to drift with the tide, extended by weights at the bottom and floats at the top, and is often of considerable length.

In the 1860s no such nets were in use, but by 1890 there were between 80 and 90, varying in length from 500 to 800 yards (1,500 [457.2 metres] or 2,400 feet [731.52 metres]), and this excessive use began to affect the fishings in the two rivers. Not only was there ample evidence of salmon being injured by drift-nets,[13] but the numbers of fish showed a steady decline. In 1908, therefore, The Irish Society decided to find out if remedies were to be had through the courts. Matters were not helped by sewage effluent discharged directly into the River Foyle, and The Society drew the attention of 'Derry Borough Council' to the growing necessity of rendering effluent innocuous. After much discussion The Society, supported by the Fishmongers' Company and the fishery lessees, resolved to take proceedings to test the legality of such nets.

In April 1909 writs were duly served on Edward Harold and other defendants. The documentation was again enormous, and costs high, but some of the information gathered is of considerable interest. For example, between 17 June and 29 July 1908 Edward Harold had consigned considerable quantities of salmon to Bradford, Manchester, Liverpool, Birmingham, Sheffield, and Leeds from Clonmany, Moville, and Londonderry using the Midland Railway Company, the books of which provided the evidence.[14] The fish was packed in 168 boxes and the net total weight was almost 13 tons, representing a lot of salmon.

[10] Betts (1913), xxv.
[11] Reed (1865), 1917 edition, 48, 59, 72, 96, 99, 113.
[12] They are held (1999) at Cutts House, Coleraine.
[13] Irish Society (1911), Appendix 28.
[14] *Ibid.*, Appendix 24, 220-3.

On 14 May 1910 the Master of the Rolls (Ireland) gave his Judgement against The Society and the other plaintiffs. The Society appealed against the decision, but the Lord Chancellor, with other Judges sitting in the Court of Appeal in Ireland, upheld the Judgement of the Master of the Rolls. Much of the argument appears to have centred on definitions of drift-nets, and it was decided these could not be regarded as 'fixed':[15] such a myopic view wholly failed to take into account the damage being done to the river and coastal fishings. In the appeal documentation prepared meticulously by B. H. Lane and Leonard Maton (the appellants' agent and solicitor respectively) there are several maps drawn by R. Eccles Buchanan, civil engineer, of Londonderry. These maps show 11 drift-nets in the North Channel north of Magilligan Point to the east of Greencastle on 24 June 1908; 29 in the same channel on 30 June; 21 on 2 July; and 14 on 8 July. Off the north coast of Inishowen there were 17 drift-nets west of Glengad Head on 24 June 1908; and 11 east of Culdaff Port on 1 July. So alarmed had the Londonderry Board of Conservators become by the great increase of the use of drift-nets off the north-west coast of Ireland, and more particularly off the coast of Donegal and at the mouth of the Foyle (with increased impediments to the passage of salmon into the rivers) that it passed a resolution restricting the use of drift-nets (21 March 1906). Similar concerns and resolutions were expressed and passed by the Ballyshannon (24 March 1906), the Letterkenny (1 April), and Coleraine (5 April) Boards of Conservators. The result was that the Department of Agriculture and Technical Instruction for Ireland proposed a bye-law to regulate the use of drift-nets on 2 January 1907.[16] Twelve fishermen from Inishowen (four of whom could sign their names) appealed to the Lord Lieutenant in Council against this bye-law.

The Irish Society and others took their case to the House of Lords in 1911, but this appeal was also dismissed in 1912. Things looked very black for The Society and for the future of one of its most precious assets, the fisheries. It is hard not to come to the conclusion that the various decisions were coloured by the prevailing political climate and by a misplaced sympathy for the drift-net fishermen who were clearly doing a lot of damage. Some London-bashing could have been involved. However, the Department of Agriculture in Ireland, alarmed, as the evidence piled up, by the deteriorating state of the fishings, held an inquiry into the whole question of the use and restriction of drift-nets. The results of the deliberations were that it became illegal to use drift nets longer than 1,500 yards (which was not a great deal of use as most nets by then were between 600 and 1,000 yards long), and drift-nets were prohibited within a mile of the mouth of the River Bann.[17]

Matters were not helped by the outbreak of war (when the population of Londonderry stood at 45,000) and by the ensuing political uncertainty, although in 1914 there had been a decrease in the tension between Roman Catholic and Protestants as men flocked to the colours. The Roman Catholic Bishop of Derry from 1907 to 1926, Dr. Charles McHugh (1856-1926), initially gave his support to the war effort, but subsequently figured prominently in the campaign against conscription of Irishmen into the British Army: in 1917 he signed the manifesto against the partition of Ireland. During the war, however, there was a temporary upsurge of the economy: the shipyards re-opened, employment improved, and wages rose. However, after the Easter rising

15 13 & 14 Vict., c.88.
16 Under 62 & 63 Vict., c.50 and 32 & 33 Vict., c.92.
17 Betts (1913), xxvi; Reed (1865), 1917 edition, 139.

of 1916 and the growing call for Home Rule, excluding six Ulster counties, tensions grew, and pressure mounted against such exclusion as sympathy for Britain waned.

During the 1914-18 war The Society maintained its close connections with County Londonderry, and the annual Deputations (or Visitations, as they became known), as noted above, were resumed in 1915. Money was donated to various funds for war wounded and to relieve distress experienced by families bereaved by the war. Annual grants were made to the various schools in the county, including those not under the direct control of The Society (e.g. the Coleraine Academical Institution). During the 1917 Visitation, the Deputation was regaled by choruses of boys at The Society's Schools at Coleraine: among these musical renditions were *Sons of the Sea* and *The Deathless Army*, works which no doubt entertained The Society in more ways than one.

In 1918, Londonderry returned Eoin MacNeill (1867-1945) as Sinn Féin Member of Parliament: however MacNeill took his seat, not in the House of Commons, but in the Dáil Éireann in Dublin. In local elections in 1920 the Roman Catholics (now about 5,000 more numerous than Protestants) elected 21 municipal councillors to 20 Unionists, and Hugh C. O'Doherty became the first Roman Catholic Mayor of Londonderry (although Cormack O'Neill, mayor for a brief period in 1688-9, was probably 'a Papist' [his wife certainly was]). Predictably, the Nationalist Press waxed ecstatic, referring to the 'Citadel' being 'Conquered After Centuries of Oppression' and to the 'Overthrow of the Ascendancy'. For a time the Union Flag ceased to be flown, but the Corporation did not throw its lot in with the Dáil, continuing to have links with the British authorities in Dublin.

Ugly sectarian riots and disorder blew up from April, and there were many deaths, properties burned, and tit-for-tat outrages. In June the British Army was ordered into action and a curfew was imposed. The police, reinforced by the auxiliary 'B' Specials, established an uneasy peace. The Government of Ireland Act of 1920 legalised the partition of Ireland into Northern Ireland (which remained part of the United Kingdom, now called the United Kingdom of Great Britain and Northern Ireland) and the Irish Free State. As a result of partition the boundary between the two States followed the Foyle, separating Counties Londonderry and Tyrone (in Northern Ireland) from County Donegal (in the Free State). However, Londonderry and its Liberties on the west bank of the river were within the County of Londonderry, so the boundary moved westwards around the Liberties and returned to the bank of the Foyle just south of Muff. Londonderry was now in Northern Ireland, which was a problem for the Nationalist majority.

One of the main difficulties was that Londonderry and its Liberties, once a bastion of Protestantism, had gradually changed in politico/religious colour during the course of the 19th century. In 1886 the Roman Catholics had demonstrated their numerical strength by returning a Roman Catholic, Justin McCarthy (1830-1912), as Member of Parliament for Londonderry in the Irish Parliamentary Party (Nationalist) cause,[18] and the election of O'Doherty as Mayor was an eloquent testimony of change. Dr McHugh was in the vanguard of opposition to elections for the new Parliament of Northern Ireland in 1921, yet, mindful of legal niceties, he cautioned against a proposed motion of allegiance to the Dáil Éireann by the city council.

In 1922 the Government of Northern Ireland abolished the proportional representation voting system in local elections and required declarations of allegiance

[18] *D.N.B. 1912-1921* (1927), 351-2.

from anyone elected to or employed by local authorities.[19] This, obviously, was an attempt to restore power to Protestants, and, when the electoral areas were rearranged, Unionist/Protestant advantage was re-affirmed. In 1923 the Unionists recovered control of the Corporation and Nationalists withdrew in protest, not to return for a decade. However, the Nationalists decided (for the most part) to await the findings of the Boundary Commission, which took evidence relating to Londonderry and its hinterland in 1925. Among the proposals was one that the centre of the Foyle should be the boundary, putting Londonderry and its Liberties into the Irish Free State and Londonderry/Waterside (on the east bank of the river) into Northern Ireland. This suggestion was not implemented and arguments that Londonderry was connected to Northern Ireland and Great Britain by trade (many of its factories being allied to British undertakings) won the day. Londonderry stayed in Northern Ireland and the U.K.

The end of the 1914-18 war (which had brought some prosperity to Londonderry) saw post-war depression on a dreadful scale. Soldiers returning from the war could find no work; the shipyard closed again; and even the local distillery (in common with other Irish distilleries) failed.[20] The new boundary cut the city off from its hinterland in County Donegal, and many old-established firms closed, so that by the mid-1920s the *official* unemployment figure stood at nearly 30 per cent. It is impossible to estimate what the impact of partition actually was, for there was widespread economic decline in Europe as a whole, but the Roman Catholics in Londonderry were certainly severely affected more than the Protestants (though life was not rosy for them either). Once more emigration proved to be the only course open to many.

Partition also brought yet more headaches for The Irish Society, for before the boundary became a fact The Society could protect its rights and privileges through the Courts of the Kingdom of Ireland, with recourse to Parliament and the House of Lords in London if necessary. Problems concerning the fisheries multiplied, for offences involving illegal nets, poaching, pollution, etc., could not be dealt with through legal process in the Free State, as The Society swiftly found courts there would not convict, and questions were again raised on grounds of title which were not within the jurisdiction of the courts: in Donegal one judge went so far as to rule that The Society had no fishing rights in the area under dispute, despite the fact that those rights and titles were very clearly stated in the 17th-century grants and subsequently tested in law.

The Irish Society found itself in a difficult position. If it appealed to a higher court this action could well imply recognition of legal authority in Dublin (at that time not fully resolved), and, in any case, political and other considerations might well have led to a hostile judgement in any higher court. Alternatively, if The Society did not appeal, the Donegal judge's ruling could well be regarded as sound, and weaken the Londoners' position. During the 1920s poaching increased, and considerable losses were experienced by The Society, mostly in Lough Foyle, where poachers from Inishowen pillaged the fisheries, and in the River Foyle upstream from Londonderry.

Somehow, matters had to be resolved, and the Court of The Irish Society, sitting in London, determined to take its case to the highest authorities.[21]

[19] 12 & 13 Geo. V, c.15.

[20] Not unconnected with a boycott of Irish products in Great Britain as a response to events from 1916 on: the boycott damaged Ulster industries as well as those of the Free State.

[21] Smith (1966), 173-7.

The Fishery Cause

As indicated above, The Irish Society found itself awkwardly placed at the end of the 1914-18 war and when the border partitioned the two States in Ireland. That border cut part of the area with which it was concerned into two, and problems of poaching mushroomed. In 1918 the Court of The Irish Society recorded its concerns after the legislation relating to Ireland became law, and the unsettled state of the country also caused major worries as there were attacks on Society properties, and employees of The Society were intimidated. So severe were these attacks and difficulties that The Society sent a delegation to meet Winston Churchill (1874-1965), then Colonial Secretary, to discuss the matter, but Churchill referred the business to the Prime Minister of Northern Ireland, Sir James Craig, Bt. (1871-1940).[22]

The Society raised these difficulties with the Governments in Westminster and Belfast, and in 1927 attempts were made by the two Irish Governments to introduce reciprocal Bills to establish some sort of control over the Lough Foyle fisheries. These moves came to nothing, and an exasperated Irish Society approached the British Government for help in the form of a fishery patrol vessel, but, having only recently managed to extricate its forces from Ireland, the Government was in no mood to help. The Society and the lessees of the fisheries determined to acquire, equip, and operate a well-protected but unarmed motor patrol-boat crewed by employees of the fishery lessees. As some of the poachers and their accomplices did not have any qualms about using violence or weapons, the patrol-boat's crew was often placed in great danger. It was not a simple matter of poaching, but of hatred fuelled by Nationalism, anti-landlordism, and even religious prejudice. It should also be remembered that there was a very long history of friction over the fisheries going back to the beginning of the Plantation, and The Irish Society had often employed men to protect the woods and the fisheries in the past, not always with success. This patrol-vessel continued to operate until the outbreak of the 1939-45 war.

If 1914-18 had brought changes to Londonderry, 1939-45 brought even more. The Foyle became an important naval base, and the presence of many naval vessels associated with the protection of the north-western approaches so close to the Donegal coastline made poaching in the lough difficult. Poachers turned their attention upstream, stealing salmon which was exported from the Free State. It should be remembered that food supplies in the United Kingdom were almost immediately affected by the outbreak of war, and that, as in all such times, a black market evolved to supply goods not readily available. Salmon became a great luxury, but a price was paid: the Foyle fisheries were raided and exploited so comprehensively that they were almost destroyed. Over-fishing has caused major difficulties in the world's oceans in recent years, so the damage done to the far more compact Foyle can be imagined: in only a short time the fish stocks were so depleted that the river was almost fished out. Repeated appeals to the Governments in Belfast and London brought no satisfaction.

Faced with complete destruction of the fisheries, in 1944 The Irish Society, in collaboration with its lessees, decided to grasp the nettle by attempting once more to assert and establish the legal validity of its long title to the fisheries, this time in the

[22] Churchill's relations with Ireland are very curious, and deserve more attention than they have been given hitherto. His views and position seem often to have been at least coloured by his personal relations with those with whom he dealt, and it may (or may not) be significant that he got on exceptionally well with Michael Collins (1890-1922), the Irish Revolutionary leader and chairman of the provisional government of the Irish Free State in 1922. Collins himself said Churchill's help was fundamental to the signing of the treaty (1921).

Irish Free State courts. The Society instituted a suit relating to a fishing at Clonleigh, near Lifford, County Donegal, and a vast assemblage of documents was prepared. In this suit the plaintiffs were The Irish Society and their lessees, the Foyle and Bann Fisheries Ltd., and the defendants were the Attorney-General (representing the public) and a large number of fishermen. Proceedings started in the High Court in Dublin, on 2 June 1945, the hearing went on for 48 court-days (from December 1947 to March 1948), and Judgement was delivered by the President of the Court (Gavan Duffy, J.) on 13 October 1948.[23]

Several expert witnesses were employed to investigate and present the historical evidence, including Professor T. W. Moody for The Irish Society and Professor Robert Dudley Edwards (1909-88) for the Attorney-General. Drawing on the early records of The Irish Society and on the collection of manuscripts deposited by W. K. Ellis of Clonleigh in the Public Record Office of Northern Ireland, the Fishery Cause enabled 'voluminous transcripts' to be 'made and assembled', and from those transcripts (by William O'Sullivan) Moody and John Gerald Simms (1904-79) prepared the material published in 1968 and 1983 by the Stationery Office, Dublin, for the Irish Manuscripts Commission.[24] Thus we have in print an unusually full record of The Irish Society's history and problems, especially those relating to the bishops of Derry and the fisheries.

As the Judgement was 35,000 words long and took four hours to deliver, only the briefest of outlines can be attempted here. In essence, the plaintiffs claimed a declaration of title to an exclusive fishery in the waters of a link of the River Foyle in the parish of Clonleigh, County Donegal. As was described above, this fishery had been one of the many subjects of dispute between the bishops of Derry and The Irish Society: the bishops claimed rights included in patents granted to them, and The Society claimed its charter granted the whole fishery of the Foyle as far as the town of Lifford and to the highest point of the ebb and flow. This dispute was settled in 1704[25] by an Act of Parliament that required The Irish Society to pay an annual sum to the bishop, and the settlement included fishing-rights in the River Bann and on lands near Londonderry. So, from 1704 until 1948 The Society remained in continuous possession of the Clonleigh fishery by virtue of the charter and the compromise agreement with the bishop. The defendants, on the other hand, denied that the Clonleigh branch formed part of the River Foyle at all, or that there ever were exclusive fishing-rights, or that The Society or its lessees had been in exclusive possession, or that the bishops or deans of Derry had ever claimed any rights to the fishery, or that, if they had, they were exclusive rights, or that title had ever been granted by letters patent, leases, or the 1704 Act. Finally, the defendants argued that no exclusive fishery had ever existed in 1189 or before that date, and that, because the waters were tidal, under *Magna Carta* the Crown could never have given any such grant.

In his Judgement, the President of the High Court expressed doubts about the validity of the Stuart title as derived from previous ownership, but did not come to any definite conclusion. When he considered the charter of 1613 and The Society's claims under the 1662 charter, he could not find evidence that in the 17th century The Society had enjoyed exclusive possession of the branch-stream other than as lessees of the bishops of Derry. The 1704 Act mentioned fishings belonging to the

[23] *Irish Law Times* (1949), lxxxiii, 29-42; Moody and Simms (eds.) (1968), 1-10. See also Davies (1835), *passim*, for earlier problems.

[24] Moody and Simms (eds.) (1968, 1983), *passim*.

[25] 3 & 4 Anne, c.1.

bishop in the Rivers Bann and Foyle within the county of Londonderry, and also fishings in other waters within the county and in the counties of Antrim, Donegal, and Tyrone. The defendants claimed that this ruled out any part of the 'River of Loughfoyle' that lay within County Donegal, and the President concurred with this view. He also held that the 1704 Act was passed to facilitate a private agreement, and did not affect any of the rights of the public (who were certainly not part of any agreement or compact). The President ruled that The Society and its lessees had no exclusive rights to the fishing in the branch stream at Clonleigh, and dismissed the application.[26]

To say that this was unfortunate for The Society would be an understatement, and it was decided to appeal against the Judgement. The reason the President's findings were so significant was that, although it seemed only the fishing-rights in one small area were in question, in fact greater issues were at stake: these included The Society's property; its income from the fisheries; its trusteeship; the future of all the fisheries in the Foyle; the powers of the two Governments; and much else. The Society made strong and urgent representations to the Government of Northern Ireland, emphasising the effects of the Judgement then and in the future, and the business was raised at high level in London as well.

On 21 December 1948, only a couple of months after the President's Judgement, the Republic of Ireland Act, 1948, was passed, repealing the Executive Authority (External Relations) Act of 1936 by which the British Crown had been recognised in the Free State for the purpose of diplomatic representation and international agreements. De Valera, as *Taoiseach*, had asserted in the Dáil Éireann in July 1945 that the Free State was in effect a Republic, but in 1949 Éire formally became a Republic and left the Commonwealth. This meant that three Governments had to be involved, and under the aegis of the British Government various matters relating to The Society were thrashed out. Negotiations were set in motion between the Attorney-General of Northern Ireland, his counterpart in the Republic, The Irish Society's General Agent in Northern Ireland, and Counsel. In June 1950 The Honourable The Irish Society was informed that the Governments of Northern Ireland and the Republic would acquire *by purchase* The Society's fishing-rights in Lough Foyle and the River Foyle and would establish a fishery commission with full powers of control, run by both Governments. The Society was offered £100,000 plus various sums to be agreed relating to other interests, the total costs to be met equally by the two Governments. This offer was made subject to the condition that The Society would not proceed with its appeal against the 1948 Judgement.[27]

The Irish Society gave the matter mature consideration, and it is clear that the Court of The Irish Society felt that there was no real alternative to accepting this solution to the contentious, expensive, and tedious difficulties in which it had been placed. Among the most important benefits that The Society perceived might ensue were that the two Irish Governments would collaborate, and certain unpleasant bones of contention would be removed. Immediately, the decision to accept the offer was conveyed to the two Governments, and for almost two years representatives of the *three* Governments thrashed out details of the legislation essential for the establishment of the commission. Naturally, precise details of the extent of the properties and interests involved had to be determined, and in due course an Act of Parliament enabling the

[26] Moody and Simms (eds.) (1968), 1-3. See also Barratt (1957), 132-6.
[27] *Ibid.*, and Smith (1966), 177.

Government of Northern Ireland to legislate (in conjunction with the Government of the Republic) was passed in Westminster. On 8 April 1952 the Foyle Fisheries Purchase Agreement was signed in Dublin by the Minister of Agriculture (Republic of Ireland), the Minister of Commerce (Northern Ireland), and four members of The Honourable The Irish Society. Thus the Foyle fisheries were transferred from The Society to the two Governments. The commission was one of the first 'Cross-Border' bodies to be established.

Clearly the outcome, even though The Society had incurred very heavy legal expenses, justified The Society's concerns for the well-being of the fisheries, and, equally clearly, the two Governments recognised these concerns, even though President Duffy's Judgement appeared to ignore them. Had not the three Governments intervened there can be no doubt that wholesale looting of a natural resource would have destroyed the fisheries.[28] As things transpired, The Society was greatly helped by the Act of Parliament of 1704,[29] which specified it had rights to 'all the fishings and rights of fishings, and also all and all manner of tithes of fishing belonging' to the bishop or see of Derry, 'of what nature or kind soever, in the rivers of Ban and Loughfoile, within the county of Londonderry, or of or in any other rivers, waters, of counties of Antrim, Tyrone, or Donegall, and which at any time heretofore been claimed or enjoyed by the bishops of the said see of Derry'. The Foyle is a tidal river, as far upstream as Strabane, and the 1952 settlement related only to the *tidal* waters of the Lough and the River Foyle: tributaries of the Foyle (Lough or River), *not being tidal*, were exempted. Gradually The Society came to realise it had major assets in the many non-tidal rivers, nearly all of which had potential as fishings, and over the following decades gradually consolidated its position.

The overall outcome appears, on the whole, to have been beneficial. The fisheries were protected (in part by the Republic's Government), The Irish Society's powers in relation to its trusts and its non-tidal fishings were unaffected, and the settlement fostered co-operation between the two Governments in Ireland that all too often had been at loggerheads.

Other Activities of The Society from 1918

In 1917 James Robert Leverington, butler, messenger, housekeeper, and later assistant secretary to the ageing Durie Miller (who had been in the saddle, so to speak, since John Ebenezer Davies's time from 1865), was appointed Secretary to The Irish Society, having been acting secretary for a brief period.[30]

His son, Robert, was appointed assistant secretary in 1919, and in 1922 James Robert Leverington completed writing the Appendix to *The Story of The Irish Society*[31] and was paid for so doing.[32] However, by that time J. R. Leverington was in financial difficulties,[33] possibly because his son was running up debts, and the father was desperately trying to bail him out. By 1924 the situation was becoming untenable, and the son resigned as assistant secretary in that year,[34] but soon after attempted to

[28] Smith (1966), 177-8, and Irish Society Papers in the Corporation of London Records Office. See Aldous (ed.) (1993), Misc MSS 69.8, and Barratt (1957).

[29] 3 & 4 Anne, c.1. See Moody and Simms (eds.) (1983), 497-500.

[30] Corporation of London Records Office IS/CM./47, 151-3, 408-10.

[31] Betts (1913).

[32] IS/CM/48, 249. It is not an impressive piece of work.

[33] IS/CM/48, 398-9.

[34] IS/CM/49, 265-6.

withdraw his resignation, but this was refused by the Court. J. R. Leverington resigned as Secretary in 1926,[35] and died in 1928 in straitened circumstances. His daughter was obliged to petition The Society for financial help in the year her father died,[36] but the prime cause of the trouble would appear to have been Robert. In 1930 the manager of the *City Hotel*, Londonderry, tried to recover debts run up by Robert Leverington, who, it seems, had used his position as a servant of The Society to obtain credit. It was an unpleasant business, and a sad end to the career of J. R. Leverington, who had once enjoyed the favour of Governors such as Whittaker Ellis and Faudel-Phillips.[37] The Society came to a settlement, and the matter faded from view.

The period during which Leverington was Secretary was difficult enough for The Irish Society without further problems of an internal nature. The 1914-18 war was not going well, the economy was suffering, and the future of Ireland (Home Rule having been put on ice for the duration of the war) was unclear: the Easter rising of 1916 and its aftermath were instrumental in swinging Irish Nationalist opinion into a more extreme anti-British direction, and if London and Londoners had had a difficult time of it before the war, the indications were that once Home Rule became a fact things would become more fraught than ever. It is therefore strange that The Society should have appointed an ex-butler as its Secretary, especially then, but this may reflect the decent, well-meaning amateurishness of the organisation at that time, as well as the shortage of able candidates due to the war.

The post-1914-18 war period saw The Society investing in major repairs to the schools at Ballougry, Culmore, and Coleraine. Major contributions were also made to the funds for the war-memorials in Coleraine, Limavady, and Londonderry, and a scroll of honour was placed in The Society's schools in memory of the Old Boys who had lost their lives in the war. Of the three memorials, that in the Diamond, Londonderry, is the most impressive and vigorous, with splendid figures of servicemen in powerful attitudes: these bronze figures were by Vernon March, the Kentish sculptor, and the Portland-stone memorial stands over the basement of the old town-hall. The vigour and expression of the figures almost rise to the impressive impact achieved by Charles Sergeant Jagger (1885-1934) **[105]**.[38]

However, The Society's income was much reduced, and consequently it could not dispense grants as it once had done. In 1925, for example, the Court of The Society had to take stock of the last of the measures transferring agricultural land from landlords to the occupying tenants by compulsory sale. All unpurchased tenanted land was to be vested in a land purchase commission under the Northern Ireland Land Act, which followed a similar Act of 1923 passed by the Irish Free State.[39] Prices were fixed in Northern Ireland as 18½ years' purchase. So, by the end of the 1920s, and even well into the 1930s, agricultural land was still being transferred in ownership, and the once vast holdings of the Londoners (The Society and The Companies) were no longer controlled by them, though The Society retained certain rights relating to the fisheries, shooting, and other matters specifically noted in the original grants (the Drapers' Company, for example, still has interests in stone in the Draperstown area).

[35] IS/CM/50, 2.

[36] IS/CM/50, 401-2.

[37] Mrs. Aldous was most generous in pointing out these interesting, if distressing, facts, and has the author's gratitude.

[38] Compton (ed.) (1985), *passim*. See also Borg (1991), *passim*.

[39] 15 & 16 Geo. V, c.34, and 1923/42, I.F.S.

In 1929 questions were raised in London concerning the provision of the charter relating to the appointment of members to The Society: in particular it was queried if the Corporation of the City of London had acted contrary to the charter or to the standing orders of The Society by the appointment of an existing Assistant to the position of Deputy Governor, and whether the custom by which the Recorder was never included among those members obliged to retire was in accordance with the charter.[40] The Court of Common Council appointed the Governor, Deputy Governor, and 12 Assistants (consisting of three Aldermen and nine Commoners) which, with the Recorder, two Aldermen, and nine Commoners, comprised The Society in any one year. During the following year the Common Council appointed the Governor, Deputy Governor, and 12 Assistants (two Aldermen and 10 Commoners) which, with the Recorder, three Aldermen, and eight Commoners (all of whom by then had served for one year), comprised The Society for that year. As the Recorder did not retire, the Deputy Governor was elected from the second-year Assistants (i.e. who had already served for a year). However, close examination of the charter showed that The Society was doing its best to comply with that unwieldy document, which stipulated that half the number of Assistants should retire in any one year.[41] However, in 1943 the problems that had long been noted concerning the two-year period of service were once more scrutinised, largely as a result of the investigations and arguments of A. H. Thomas, Deputy Keeper of Records of the Corporation of London.

Dr. Thomas emphasised that the charter was quite clear in stating The Society should consist of 26 citizens of London (the Governor, Deputy Governor, and 24 Assistants). Of these, the Governor and five Assistants had to be Aldermen, and one of the Assistants the Recorder. Each year the Deputy Governor and 12 Assistants had to retire (13 persons), so in one year the Deputy Governor, three Aldermen, and nine Common Councilmen should retire, and in the following year the Deputy Governor, two Aldermen, the Recorder, and the other nine Common Councilmen should retire, but the Recorder's retirement would be a token retirement only, since he had to be an *ex officio* Assistant, and would be re-appointed. Dr. Thomas pointed out that because it was desirable to have a Deputy Governor with some experience, that office was filled by a second-year Assistant, who was therefore replaced by another Assistant so that the numbers would be correct. Nevertheless, Thomas opined that this was not actually the intention of the charter at all, for the charter of 1662 clearly stated that the Court of the year had a Deputy Governor who was not an Assistant, and was not included among the 18 Commoners. Therefore, The Society should be re-constituted by re-appointing one of the retiring Assistants as Deputy Governor, thus ensuring the office was held by someone with two years' experience, and the matter could be formalised if the Common Council simply adopted a report from The Society or passed a resolution to that effect. However, the City Solicitor, mindful of the ambiguities of the 1662 charter that had been the cause of endless disputes and much litigation, took a more cautious view, and he and the Recorder recommended that an amending charter should be obtained.

The Court of The Honourable The Irish Society did not care for this proposal, anticipating all sorts of trouble from just about every possible source, and felt that opportunities would be grasped to raise all the old hares about abolition, reconstitution, and so on. So matters were left as they were, and no change was made to the established

[40] Minutes of the Court of Common Council (1929), 60, 212.

[41] Smith (1966), 181-2.

practice of electing the Deputy Governor.[42] In 1962 the matter of continuity was resurrected by one of the Court of Assistants who proposed that one of the Assistants should, having retired after two years, be re-elected after one year for a further two-year term. If this were to be adopted every Commoner would serve four years of any five-year period, and this time the legal people saw no difficulties looming, and the scheme was adopted in 1963.[43] Furthermore, Alderman Assistants were to stand down for two years and then return for a further two years. Thus the thorny problem of collective amnesia was finally grasped.[44]

A certain degree of dignity and occasion continued when the annual Visitations occurred, even during the 1920s and 1930s. Not only were there grand civic occasions, performances by the children in the various schools, and church services, but special trains were laid on by the directors of the railway companies to convey the Deputation. Station-masters were met and greeted by members of The Society, and formal wear was very much *de rigueur*. By the inter-war period, however, some of the trappings, such as the salute by cannon-fire from the Vice-Admiral's boat, had been abandoned. (Under the charters, it will be recalled, The Society was granted the Vice-Admiralty on all coasts or shores of Tirconnell, Coleraine, and the county of Londonderry, together with grants of all wrecks of ships, goods, and merchandises belonging to The Society or the Mayor, Aldermen, or citizens of Londonderry, in Ballyshannon and Olderfleet, and on the shores, coasts, ports, and creeks between those two places, with all royalties and profits. In other words The Society had very considerable rights over the coastline from the mouth of the River Erne at Ballyshannon, past Donegal town, Killybegs, Malin Bay, Ardara, Aran Island, the Bloody Foreland, Dunfanaghy, Fanad Head, Lough Swilly, Malin Head, the rest of the Inishowen peninsula, Lough Foyle, Magilligan, the north coast past the mouth of the Bann, Portstewart, Portrush, the Giant's Causeway, Ballycastle, and the Antrim coast as far as Olderfleet at the entrance to Larne Lough).[45]

The Deputations had attracted critical comment during the 19th century, being perceived by some as pleasant junketings paid for out of The Society's rents and other income. Certainly it was the custom of The Society to entertain gentlemen of the county, local notables, the principal tenants, and (of course) a good smattering of clergymen of all denominations (Roman Catholics and Protestants).[46] It should be remembered that Deputations in the 1830s involved long and arduous journeys before transport improved; visits to many properties; tedious sessions listening to innumerable problems, complaints, and demands for hand-outs; and much else besides, including what were sometimes painful renditions of choruses by schoolchildren. These detailed inspections based on first-hand observations were invaluable to the Court: The Society was a caring and benevolent landlord, and did not wish to be classed as an 'absentee', so it took a personal interest in the welfare of and problems affecting its tenants. Individual contacts, business meetings, visits to sites, and so on not only helped The Society to understand what was going on, but helped it to run its estates. As for the special trains, cannon salutes, and lavish dinners, all those helped The Society's public

[42] Smith (1966), 184. *See also* Minutes of the Common Council (1943), 110, 194, and (1944), 50.

[43] See Research Papers, Corporation of London Records Office, 1.26: Report of special committee 12 April 1962 (Aldous [ed.] [1993], 7, 9).

[44] Smith (1966), 179-185, discussed these matters in great detail.

[45] Irish Society (*c.*1898), 248-5. *See also* Irish Society (1836), map showing the Vice-Admiralty district, and Schultes (1822), 24-5, 68-9.

[46] It is quite clear that this was so, though it has been held by some that entertainments (such as dinners) were not extended to Roman Catholics. This assertion is simply untrue: if some persons chose to stay away that does not mean they were not invited.

image and set the general tone. Quite apart from those matters, the members (who in the early part of the 19th century were away from home for about a month at a time) deserved some respite from their duties and some pleasures.

The Irish Society and Londonderry, 1921-39

The arrival of a new rector, Richard G. S. King, in 1921 heralded a new interest in the documents and books belonging to the cathedral and diocese, and when he became dean in the same year, considerable alterations were carried out to the fabric of St Columb's. In 1924-5, for example, the organ was renovated and the console moved to the south aisle: all the crenellations were taken down and rebuilt, with new flashings; the tower and other parts of the exterior were repointed; the plaster was removed from the interior walls of the aisles, porch, and west end; marble was substituted for sandstone on the chancel floor; the screens and choir-stalls were moved back on each side of the chancel; additional oak doors were placed in the porch as draught-excluders; electric lighting was installed; and *all decayed stone throughout the building was renewed.* At a total cost of £6,000 those renovations were pretty radical, and appear to have been carried out by Buchanan & Reid of Londonderry, with Frederick Batchelor (d. 1931) and Frederick George Hicks (1870-1965) of Dublin as consultant architects. It is clear from documentary evidence[47] that drastic renewals of the nave arcades were carried out during Ferguson's alterations of the 1880s, but the changes of the 1920s were also crass in the extreme. In 1922 Richard Francis Caulfeild Orpen (1863-1938), architect, who had been articled to Sir Thomas Drew, no less, and later worked with Drew as his managing assistant, was asked to inspect the cathedral. Buchanan & Reid (the latter was an architect) were asked to prepare plans and specifications on which contractors could estimate (December 1923), and various works were agreed in 1924, including repairs to the 'cutstone shafts of the nave arcade' using 'crushed stone and shellac'. Some of the discoloured patching that disfigures the piers today is therefore due to Buchanan & Reid's interventions. 'All interior plaster' was 'cut off', and 'new pointing in cement' in an 'approved manner' was to be carried out.

Now the removal of the plaster not only revealed the stone, but Ferguson's brick dressings around the easternmost windows of the north and south aisles as well. The 'new pointing in cement', unbelievably, was a dark-grey Portland cement ribbon-pointing, wholly inappropriate, and of singular ugliness. A photograph of 1933, published in an illustrated booklet on the cathedral dated 1935, shows that the ribbon-pointing was in existence then, and its hideous amateurishness has disfigured the cathedral ever since it was perpetrated. The stone was never intended to be exposed anyway, but the introduction of unhistorical ribbon-pointing was a major error of judgement. Also in the 1924 alterations, defective Bath stone was replaced in the chancel, and many repairs to masonry were carried out with 'composition of crushed stone and cement'. Some of this fearsome patching is still visible today, making the 'stone' look like discoloured blancmange.

It is clear that the ways in which these works were proposed aroused the antagonism of The Irish Society, which had promised £2,000 towards *necessary* repairs to the fabric of the *structure*. The vestry minutes[48] record that one of the members travelled to

[47] In the select vestry minutes held in the chapter-house of St Columb's cathedral. The author is indebted to Mr. Gallick for steering him through these papers.

[48] *Ibid.*

110 Clergy processing through the new gates presented by The Irish Society at St Columb's cathedral, Londonderry, 18 July 1933. (*DB*)

London to see the Governor (Sir Thomas Vansittart Bowater, Bt. [1862-1938]), who was extremely 'nettled'[49] to be asked for more money, and sent the member of the vestry away with a large flea in his ear. The Society made it very clear it was not going to increase the grant for interior works (the proposals do not seem to have impressed Orpen). It is amazing that, many decades after William Morris (1834-96)[50] had led attacks against 'Scrapers' of old buildings and the enthusiastic 'renovators' who would 'restore' buildings within an inch of their lives, such enormous (but doubtless well-meant) damage was done to the fabric of a very important building, one that is, arguably, the most important in north-west Ulster. The experienced and practised eye, inspecting the building at the end of the 20th century, can only regret that there is very little of any antiquity left in the cathedral: the greatest loss is the integrity of the fine 17th-century nave-arcades (as is demonstrated by comparing the photographs of the post-1860 restoration with the structure today **[38, 96, 97]**). In 1928-9 the bells were re-cast and re-hung, and five new bells were added: at this time new floors and stairs were made for the ringing-chamber in the tower at a total cost of £2,400. Then, in 1931, the oak screen at the west end of the south aisles was extended upwards, and new doors were provided to improve the access to the gallery.

The tercentenary of St Columb's cathedral in Londonderry, the great church erected by The Society and completed in 1633, deserved to be marked in some way, and The Society, under the Governorship (1928-32) of Sir Louis Arthur Newton, Bt. (1867-1945), resolved in 1932 to erect entrance-gates at the eastern end of the cathedral

[49] *Sic.*

[50] Curl (1999), 436; Pevsner (1968), **ii**, 108-17; Thompson (1993), *passim.*

111a The Irish Society's gates at St Columb's cathedral, Londonderry, from the north-east, in 1999. (*A*)

111b The Irish Society's gates at St Columb's cathedral, Londonderry, from the north-west, in 1999. (*A*)

precincts at a cost not exceeding £750. William Henry Randoll Blacking, architect (1889-1958), was commissioned to design the gates, and eventually his proposals (costed at £990) were approved. In 1933 the elegant wrought-iron gates were erected, and at the tercentenary service the new gates were dedicated by the Bishop of Derry and Raphoe (Joseph Irvine Peacock) **[110]**. The then Governor of The Society (from

1933 to 1938),[51] Sir Charles Albert Batho, Bt. (1872-1938), and the Lord Mayor of London, Sir Percy Walter Greenaway (1874-1956 – created 1st Baronet, October 1933), read the lessons and participated in the ceremony. Blacking's design was eminently successful, as would be expected of an ecclesiastical architect of long experience, and certainly rose to the occasion. It is one of the most beautiful objects in Londonderry, and features on either side the Arms of The Society and of Londonderry, while above, on the overthrow, is set the escutcheon of the see of Derry featuring *Gules* two Swords in saltire proper pommeled and hilted gold, on a chief *Azure* an Irish harp gold stringed *Argent* **[111a, b]**. It should be noted that the Church of Ireland bishops do not wear mitres, presumably because of the low-church character that generally prevailed in the Church since the fall of Wentworth. It is worth observing that Blacking's son, John Anthony Randoll Blacking (1928-1990), was a distinguished anthropologist and ethnomusicologist, an outspoken opponent of apartheid when living in South Africa in the 1960s, and the first holder of the Chair of Social Anthropology at The Queen's University of Belfast (1970-90).[52]

As part of the improvements to the cathedral graveyard, much of the ground was levelled, decayed and ruined walls of table-tombs were removed, many iron grave-surrounds were also taken away, and retaining-walls were built for the walks. Nineteenth-century photographs show that the graveyard was indeed untidy and cluttered, but then death is not a tidy thing. It is perhaps unfortunate that adequate records do not appear to have been made before the 1933 work on the grounds was carried out, and much of historical and genealogical interest may have been lost.

1933 also saw the completion and opening of the new Craigavon Bridge over the Foyle. Named after the first Prime Minister of Northern Ireland, Sir James Craig, Bt., created Viscount Craigavon in 1927, the steel structure, like its predecessor, the Carlisle Bridge **[89]**, has two decks: the lower, now used for road traffic, was originally intended for railway purposes. The ceremony of opening the bridge was carried out by the Lord Mayor of London, and The Irish Society, which had supported the project to replace the older work, was represented. Speeches at Londonderry's Guildhall were broadcast in Ulster, but it appears that the B.B.C. refused to permit historical accounts of the history of the Plantation and of the long association between London and Londonderry to be broadcast throughout the United Kingdom.[53]

This is a very curious business, and obviously puzzled The Society, though the written minutes and other papers are very discreet about it. The term 'flatly refused' is used in connection with the B.B.C.'s action. It is as though the extraordinary and widespread ignorance about the Plantation as a whole (which is unquestionably and regrettably a fact) has been deliberately fostered, but by whom it is not clear. Obviously the national Broadcasting Corporation took a decision at high level, but it is at the least very odd that part of the history of these islands and of the story of London seems to be (or has been) subject to suppression.

During the 1933 tercentenary celebrations The Society's normal visits to the various parts of its surviving estates and to the schools with which it was associated continued, and photographs survive showing the Governor and Horace Bowles (Deputy Governor) inspecting The Society's schools at Culmore **[112]**. Thereafter, business

112 Group at Culmore School during the Visitation of July 1933. The Governor of The Irish Society, Sir Charles Batho, Bt. (with boy on his knee), the Deputy Governor, Horace Bowles, and Mrs T. C. Wylie, wife of the school manager (with glasses), with pupils. Members of the Visitation are in the background. (*DB*)

113 Group at war-memorial, the Diamond, Londonderry, in *c.*1933. The Governor of The Irish Society, Sir Charles Batho, Bt., is in the front row, holding his top-hat in his right hand and his gloves in his left. On the extreme right is Sir Dudley McCorkell, Mayor of Londonderry (1929-34), and on his right is the High Sheriff, Sir Basil A. T. McFarland, Bt. (*DB*)

51 Select Vestry Minutes of St Columb's cathedral.

52 *D.N.B. 1986-1990* (1996), 36-7.

53 All the above from the Court and minute-books at the Corporation of London Records Office. See Aldous (ed.) (1993), IS/CM/52, and sundry other papers at Guildhall. Other information from papers in the chapter-house at St Columb's cathedral, Londonderry.

AUCTIONEER

114 The Governor of The Irish Society, Sir William Phené Neal, Bt., inspecting a guard of honour of past pupils of The Society's schools at Culmore, 17 July 1939. (*DB*)

continued without much disturbance **[113]**. The Society maintained its connections with Londonderry and Coleraine, helping when possible, and continued trying to protect the fisheries which it clearly recognised as among the area's most important assets, requiring protection and active measures of conservation in the teeth of widespread depredations.

In 1938 Batho was succeeded as Governor by Sir William Phené Neal, Bt. (1860-1942), who had been Lord Mayor of London (1930-1), and is also recorded photographically during an inspection of Culmore schools on 17 July 1939 **[114]**. Three days later, on 20 July 1939, The Irish Society's dinner at Londonderry's Guildhall was also captured by the camera lens **[115]**. Neal, in a speech, was sanguine about the future, and was convinced there was no danger of a European war breaking out. Meanwhile, the I.R.A. issued an ultimatum to the British Foreign Secretary, Edward Frederick Lindley Wood (1881-1959), 3rd Viscount Halifax (from 1934), demanding the removal of all British troops from Irish soil, and the first of a series of bomb-attacks occurred on 16 January 1939: on 25 August an I.R.A. bomb in Coventry killed five people and wounded 70 more.

The Second World War

On 1 September 1939 Germany invaded Poland and annexed Danzig, de Valera confirmed on 2 September his statement of 19 February that the Government of the Free State (by then known as Éire) intended to remain neutral in the event of war, and on 3 September the United Kingdom and France declared war on Germany. At

115 The Irish Society's annual luncheon in the Guildhall, Londonderry, 20 July 1939. Sir William Phené Neal, Bt. (with The Society's badge), stands at high table. On his right is the Bishop of Derry (the Rt. Rev. Dr. Peacocke), then the Mayor (Sir Basil McFarland, Bt.), Sir Dawson Bates, F. S. Alexander, R. H. Smith, Colonel Gottwaltz, M.C. (the officer commanding the South Wales Borderers), J. H. Welch, S. Hanna, G. Scott Robertson, Alderman J. M. Mark, and John Archer (Town-Clerk, Belfast). On the Governor's left (i.e. right on the picture) is John F. Gordon (Minister of Labour), J. J. Buchanan (President of the Chamber of Commerce), Sir Horace Bayer (High Sheriff of Londonderry), and Lieutenant-Colonel G. L. S. Smith (officer commanding the 9th Londonderry, Anti-Aircraft Regiment). (*DB*)

once the Government of Northern Ireland declared its commitment to the British cause, and in Londonderry, as in 1914, local political enemies declared a truce. The shipyard re-opened, and a huge amount of construction-work brought employment on a gratifying scale. Factories that made shirts began turning out clothing for troops, and a secret agreement with the United States of America (1941) provided for the establishment of a naval base in Londonderry and the Foyle (before the U.S.A. entered the war). Several hundred 'civilian technicians' arrived in Londonderry in June 1941, and by 8 December of that year (when the U.S.A. and Britain declared war on Japan) the Americans had a huge new quay constructed, and had created camps for personnel, officers, storage depôts and ammunition dumps, a radio station, facilities to repair ships, and much infrastructure ready for emergencies. The first U.S. troops to arrive in Europe landed in Northern Ireland, and by 5 February 1942 the U.S. naval base at Londonderry was operational. Londonderry became the terminal for U.S. convoys bound for Britain.

In April 1941 Northern Ireland experienced the first attacks from the *Luftwaffe*, and in the air-raids of April-May over 1,000 people were killed in Belfast, and some 56,000 houses (50 per cent of the city's housing stock) damaged or destroyed: as the fires raged the fire-brigades of Dublin and other towns in Éire were sent to render assistance. Next month the Germans inflicted severe damage on the shipyards and aircraft factories in Belfast, and the North Strand, Dublin, was bombed by the *Luftwaffe*, destroying 300 houses, killing 34, and injuring 90, for which the German Government 'expressed regret' and 'promised compensation'. Considering that the *Luftwaffe* had already bombed Campile, County Wexford (26 August 1940), and various other places in Counties Carlow, Dublin, Kildare, Louth, Meath, Wexford, and Wicklow (1-3 January 1941), the Irish Government's determined neutrality was sorely tested, and the *Luftwaffe*'s actions looked, at best, like carelessness.[54]

It has been recognised that Londonderry once more assumed enormous strategic significance in the 1939-45 war, just as it had done in 1688-90. It held the key to victory in the Atlantic Ocean, and was the most westerly naval base on the eastern side of the ocean for the repair and refuelling of the smaller warships. By 1943 it was the most important escort-base for convoys in the north-western approaches (149 such escorts were based in the Foyle, twice the number at Liverpool and Greenock combined[55]). What is more, the huge programme of slob-land reclamation, carried out under the aegis of The Irish Society and the Fishmongers' Company adjacent to the eastern shore of Lough Foyle during the 19th century, which added thousands of acres to the size of County Londonderry, provided valuable bases for four large military airfields. Thus the lands of the Londonderry Plantation and of the London Companies played a pivotal rôle in the preparation for the invasion of Europe and the defeat of Naziism. The natural harbour of Lough Foyle became the first safe haven for merchant- and war-ships arriving from the west, and it is not any exaggeration to claim that without the Plantation a major port and major facilities would have been denied the Allies. It should also be remembered that certain ports in Éire (involving harbour, aviation and storage facilities reserved to the United Kingdom at Berehaven, Queenstown [now Cobh], Lough Swilly, Haulbowline, and Rathmullen (or Rathmullan) under the Anglo-Irish Treaty [1921]) had been handed back to Irish control in 1938 in spite of Admiralty objections, as the British chiefs of staff, citing costs and the difficulties of defending installations in wartime against a hostile host country, felt they were not worth the candle, and the last British troops had left the Cork harbour defences in November 1938. The refusal of de Valera to sign a defence agreement because of the existence of Partition was also a contributory factor in the unconditional return of the ports to Éire. However, the loss of the 'Treaty Ports' left the north-western approaches somewhat vulnerable to enemy attack, so the facilities of Belfast and Londonderry were invaluable to Allied naval and air forces, especially after de Valera informed the Dáil of the Irish Government's 'unwillingness' to lease the 'Treaty Ports' to Britain (7 November 1940).

[54] For a synopsis of key events see Moody, Martin, and Byrne (eds.) (1982), *passim*.
[55] Blake (1956), *passim*; Lacy (1998), 240.

The 1939-45 war brought employment and prosperity to Northern Ireland (unemployment, 20 per cent in the 1930s, fell to under 5 per cent by the end of the war), and agriculture, industry, and commerce developed enormously to meet wartime needs. Between 1942 and 1945 some 300,000 American soldiers were stationed in the province of Ulster, in addition to the British, Empire (or Commonwealth – mostly Canadian) , Free French, Belgian, and Dutch forces, and many of them were based in County Londonderry. The impact on the atmosphere of sleepy, provincial, poor Londonderry was colossal, and a huge 'black economy' of wartime smuggling between Northern Ireland and Éire flourished.

The area did not escape without some damage inflicted by the enemy: the *Luftwaffe* bombed an ex-servicemen's housing-estate at Messines Park, and a mine fell on Pennyburn (which The Irish Society and Tite had tried to develop as a salubrious residential area in the 1830s and '40s) in 1941, but the rapid build-up of formidable defences soon proved to be an admirable deterrent. Not many Germans were to see Londonderry and its hinterland again until very large numbers of German U-boats were instructed to proceed to Lisahally (Lissahawley) in the Foyle, the naval base just opposite Culmore Fort. The surrender of the first group of submarines was taken by Admiral Sir Max Kennedy Horton (1883-1951), commander-in-chief of the western approaches, watched by the Prime Minister (since 1943) of Northern Ireland, Sir Basil Stanlake Brooke, Bt. (1888-1973: created 1st Viscount Brookeborough in 1952).

All through the 1939-45 war The Irish Society (whose Society House in Londonderry became a library for visiting servicemen) maintained its close relationship with County Londonderry, and members of the Court continued to keep themselves informed about the lands in Ulster **[116]**. If anything, links between London and Londonderry were greatly strengthened by the experience of the war.

County Londonderry from 1945

With the end of the war and the departure of the troops the endemic problems of Londonderry and its surrounding area re-surfaced: unemployment, poverty, and bad housing had not gone away, although serious violence did not break out for some time. Nationalists managed to fix the green-white-orange tricolour[56] of the Irish Republic (as the Free State/Éire had become) to the top of the Walker testimonial in 1951: that the most imposing memorial of the siege, precious to the Protestants of Londonderry, should be 'defiled' in this way caused no little stir at the time.

Renewed I.R.A. activity in the 1950s included a driverless goods-train sent hurtling at top speed into the Foyle Road station, which was very badly damaged, and there were numerous other incidents. Bad housing in the Bogside and other parts of Londonderry, unemployment, and other problems gave the place an air of unredeemable depression, and wits observed that the skeleton on the City's Arms was a Londonderry Roman Catholic waiting to be re-housed. Government attempts to attract industry to the area led to the establishment of some 68 firms from Britain and elsewhere establishing factories there, including Du Pont, which located itself on the disused 1939-45 war airfield at Maydown. As a result of such policies unemployment

[56] Supposedly symbolising peace between Roman Catholics and Protestants, the tricolour was first adopted, it seems, in the 1830s. However, the orange is often replaced by yellow, and this has been interpreted either as indicative of the symbolism being lost, or that the tricolour is actually the white-and-gold or white-and-yellow flag of the Papacy with the green of Irish Nationalism. However, orange is notoriously unstable as a colour, and, if exposed to the elements, soon turns yellow, which might explain much.

116 Members of The Irish Society processing into the Diamond from Bishop Street to lay a wreath on the war-memorial. The Deputy Governor, Captain George James Cullum Welch (1895-1980), who was Lord Mayor of London 1956-7, Governor of The Society 1967-70, and created a baronet in 1957 (with moustache and badge of office), walks with Councillor F. J. Simmons, Mayor of Londonderry 1940-45. Photograph *c.*1940. (*DB*)

was reduced (by 2,000 between February 1967 and October 1968), and the then Minister of Commerce (1963-9), Arthur Brian Deane Faulkner (1921-77 – Baron Faulkner of Downpatrick from 1977),[57] declared in 1966 that the Government intended to have full employment established in Londonderry very soon 'through industries already established or in the pipeline'. Other developments included the building of Altnagelvin hospital, designed by Yorke, Rosenberg, and Mardall of London, built by Robert Colhoun Ltd and Stewart & Partners, opened in 1960, the first general hospital completed in the U.K. after 1945; the new psychiatric hospital at Gransha; and some progress was made with the provision of new housing. However, only one railway-line survived (that connecting Londonderry Waterside with Coleraine and Belfast).[58]

In March 1960 a campaign was mounted to make Londonderry the location for a second university in Northern Ireland, supported by all shades of opinion, but in

[57] *D.N.B. 1971-1980* (1986), 304-6.
[58] Lacy (1998), *passim.*

1965 the committee established in 1963 to review facilities for higher education under the chairmanship of Sir John Francis Lockwood (1903-65) reported,[59] and recommended that Coleraine should be the site for the new university. It was also proposed that Magee College should be discontinued as a university institution. Despite widespread opposition the Government ratified the Lockwood report, the New University of Ulster was established at Coleraine, and the limited undergraduate programmes in Londonderry ceased: Magee became a centre for 'second-chance' learning for adults. In 1984 the University of Ulster was formed by an amalgamation of the N.U.U. at Coleraine with the Ulster Polytechnic at Jordanstown and the Art and Design Centre in Belfast, and with Magee (where a limited range of undergraduate courses was re-established).

Some of the factories that had raised hopes for Londonderry closed, so by 1967 the unemployment figures for Londonderry were ten times greater than those for Great Britain, and there was widespread discontent. Electoral 'gerrymandering', to ensure that Unionist control was maintained, began to be noticed by London journalists and politicians, as was discriminatory employment. Subsequent events have been exhaustively covered in many publications, so any full description here would be superfluous. In 1968 the B.B.C. broadcast a television documentary about Londonderry's electoral system and gave Nationalists the chance to air their complaints: during the summer of that year the civil rights movement began its demonstrations against discrimination in matters of housing. This movement was not unconnected with other protests in Europe and America, and on 5 October 1968 a civil rights march (banned by the then Minister of Home Affairs on grounds that it would be provocative and would clash with an Apprentice Boys' march at the same time and over the same route) led to widespread rioting and pitched battles with the Royal Ulster Constabulary. Later, youths from the Bogside rioted, and film taken of the events was shown world-wide. From then on Londonderry, previously barely noticed by the media, was on the world stage.

On 22 November 1968 the Prime Minister, Terence Marne O'Neill (1914-1990 – later [from 1970] Baron O'Neill of the Maine),[60] announced a programme of reform, including the abolition of the business vote in local government elections and the overhaul of the local government system; fair allocation of local authority housing; the appointment of an ombudsman to investigate grievances arising out of Government administration; the Civil Authorities (Special Powers) Act (N.I.)[61] to be reviewed and certain clauses conflicting with the U.K.'s international obligations to be removed; and the Londonderry city council to be superseded by a development commission.

However, early in 1969, a march from Belfast to Londonderry organised by People's Democracy, a left-wing organisation, was harassed and then attacked by a hostile crowd, and during the next day, as rioting spread, the police were involved in battles in the Bogside (and severely criticised by the commission set up under the chairmanship of Lord Cameron). Tension rose in the days leading up to the Apprentice Boys' March on 12 August, and the 'Battle of the Bogside' began, which lasted for three days. There was talk of the army of the Irish Republic occupying the city; the barricades went up; and theoretical revolutionaries from Europe arrived to study the riots and ask earnest questions about how the Bogside unemployed had learned to fight.[62]

[59] Cmd. 475 (N.I.). See also local newspaper reports of the time.

[60] *D.N.B. 1986-1990* (1996), 336-7.

[61] 12 & 13 Geo. V, c.5; 23 & 24 Geo. V, c.12.

[62] Described in Devlin (1969), *passim*.

After three days of mayhem the exhausted police could no longer cope, and the Government, headed by James Chichester-Clark (O'Neill had resigned as Prime Minister on 28 April), requested help from the U.K. Government: the Home Secretary, James Callaghan, agreed, and on 14 August a company of the British Army took over the control of security in Londonderry from the police. Sectarian riots broke out in other parts of Ulster, notably in Belfast. The die was cast. The 'Troubles' had begun.

In August 1971 internment without trial was re-introduced, leading to violent reactions. By this time Faulkner was Prime Minister, Chichester-Clark having resigned in March, and the British Army had killed two Roman Catholics in Londonderry. The I.R.A. targeted numerous buildings, and the architectural losses began to mount: as the damage to 'economic targets' increased, some graffiti exhorted citizens to SHOP NOW WHILE SHOPS LAST. Then, on Sunday 30 January 1972, British troops killed 13 men following a banned anti-internment march (an event called, predictably, after earlier precedent, 'Bloody Sunday'). A film taken of events shows a local priest waving a white handkerchief as he helped to convey casualties from the line of fire: two years later (1974) that priest, Edward Daly (b. 1933), became Roman Catholic Bishop of Derry (until 1993).

Repercussions included the burning of the British Embassy in Dublin, killings, explosions, and woundings. Then, when Faulkner refused to accept the transfer of security to Whitehall, the British Government under Edward Heath announced the suspension of the Northern Ireland Parliament and Government, and the introduction of direct rule from Westminster. William Whitelaw (1918-99) was appointed Secretary of State for Northern Ireland. In July 1973 the Northern Ireland Parliament was abolished.[63]

But the immediate result of 'Bloody Sunday' was the intensification of the Provisional I.R.A. bombing campaign. In June 1972 Londonderry's Guildhall was very badly damaged; 22 explosions in Belfast killed 11 people and injured 120; and on 31 July three car-bombs exploded in Claudy, County Londonderry, killing six and injuring 32 people. The Claudy outrage was perpetrated only a few hours after 'Operation Motorman', in which the British Army moved into the Bogside and Creggan areas of Londonderry with heavy machinery to tear down the barricades and end the status of 'No-Go Areas' (where the police and security forces were 'unwelcome', to use a euphemism).

Londonderry City Council was established in 1973, restoring some degree of limited municipal government. The moderate Nationalists were returned as the largest party (Social Democratic and Labour Party), but the council set up an enlightened power-sharing arrangement for the posts of Mayor, Deputy Mayor, and committee chairmanships. However, violence also continued, leading to the destruction of thousands of houses, hundreds of business premises, and damage to many important landmarks, including the Walker testimonial (blown up in 1973). One of the saddest losses was Gwyn's Institute, Brooke Park, a chaste classical composition of 1840 designed by Thomas Jackson (1806-90), whose handsome Ulster Bank, Waterloo Place, was also bombed, and subsequently demolished.

One of the greatest changes brought about to some extent by the many years of violence in Londonderry has been the huge demographic shift. Protestants have deserted the west bank of the Foyle and moved to Waterside or further away. It has been suggested that about 14,000 Protestants have left the historic city and its immediate

[63] 1973, c.36.

117 The Guildhall, Londonderry, in 1983. (*A*)

surroundings, abandoning the walled settlement created by The Irish Society. Yet, although in 1984, in accordance with general usage, Londonderry City Council voted to change its name to 'Derry City Council', the tercentenary of the siege was widely celebrated, and support given by that city council. The fact that Londonderry's Guildhall has been superbly restored, and its connections with London commemorated in the fine stained-glass windows, may be indicative of a spirit of tolerance and of an acceptance of historical reality at last **[117]**.[64]

[64] This Chapter draws on Court minute-books and letter-books in the Corporation of London Records Office (see Aldous [ed.] [1993]), and on sources cited in the footnotes. Some material is taken from the masses of material examined in 1982-5 in preparation for Curl (1986), *passim.*

CHAPTER XIII

Conclusion
The Irish Society from the 1950s to the End of the Century

> The Irish Society has always taken its own perpetuity, and the responsibilities and duties that go with that, very seriously. It cannot – and would not – simply will itself out of existence and walk away from a task that it believes so important and relevant. [It] has always been willing and able to adapt to the shifting circumstances of history, constantly revising its rôle to suit the requirements of the times whilst remaining mindful and proud of its ancient heritage
>
> IRISH SOCIETY (1994): *The Honourable The Irish Society* (London: The Irish Society), 13

The Society and the Cathedral

The Foyle fishery matter was described above, and led to The Society giving careful consideration to its position. The connections with the cathedral, Londonderry, and Coleraine, were, of course, very strong, and links with St Columb's were maintained during the periods when Robert McNeil Boyd (1890-1958) and Charles John Tyndall (1900-71) were bishops of Derry and Raphoe (1945-58 and 1958-69 respectively). Tyndall in particular had a difficult episcopacy, for, by trying to work with his Roman Catholic colleague, Dr. Neil Farren (1893-1980 – bishop from 1939 to 1973 – who prudently guided his diocese through the 1939-45 war and after), he incurred the wrath of Protestant extremists, and for a time was obliged to leave the city. Cuthbert Irvine Peacocke (1903-94) succeeded Bishop Tyndall, and was bishop of Derry and Raphoe from 1970 to 1975; thus his episcopacy coincided with the worst of Londonderry's 'Troubles'. He, in turn, was succeeded by Dr. Robert Eames (b. 1937), bishop from 1975 to 1980 before being translated to Down and Dromore and then (1986) becoming Archbishop of Armagh and Primate of All Ireland. When bishop of Derry and Raphoe, Dr Eames spoke of the need for Protestants to take part in public affairs in the city of Londonderry. Eames was succeeded by Dr James Mehaffey (b. 1931), who worked with his Roman Catholic colleague, Bishop Daly, to promote inter-community relations, thus earning him considerable opprobrium from some quarters, and praise from others.

In 1950-1 new frontals, falls, markers, chancel-carpet, and altar-rails were given to the cathedral, designed by (Sir) Albert Edward Richardson (1880-1964) and his son-in-law Eric Alfred Scholefield Houfe (1911-93),[1] but major transformations to the fabric of the building were carried out under the direction of Alexander Theodore Marshall (1914-75), a Scot who was also architect to The Irish Society and city

[1] Personal communication from Mr. Simon Houfe.

architect.[2] In 1952 Marshall prepared a major report on the building in which he recommended an expenditure of over £23,000 over several years. Marshall's approach to the cathedral was ruthless: he had no compunction in replacing materials with modern construction (e.g. removing roof-timbers and substituting concrete), and he renewed much of the stonework of the fenestration. The success of a world-wide appeal for funds ensured there was money available for wholesale renewal, which is why the stone dressings, mullions, and mouldings have such a harsh appearance: they are entirely based on Marshall's drawings and specifications. In the 1950s the whole of the north and south sides of the cathedral and the upper part of the tower were 'completely restored', and by 1964 £24,000 had been spent. In 1966 the stonework of the east window was largely renewed, with new mullions, and 1967 'marked the conclusion of a massive work' of restoration going back many years and costing £50,000, a huge sum of money then.

Much of the stone was renewed, therefore, under Marshall's direction in the 1950s and 1960s, and he certified monies for 'cleaning down and pointing stonework' *inside* the building in 1964. It looks very much as though some further damage was done to the nave arcades in the 1960s, but the external works were drastic in the extreme. In spite of Marshall's specifications requiring stone to be cleaned with bristle-brushes and water, mechanical means were sometimes used, and hard cement-pointing was liberally applied, giving a 'rendered' effect[3] in many places. Ribbon-pointing,[4] too, is much in evidence. Such hard cement-rendering has further damaged the stonework, and the ribbon-pointing, causing water to run back into the masonry, could be regarded as an aesthetic and practical disaster. It is difficult to avoid coming to the conclusion, perhaps, that the work was inadequately supervised, and that it would appear that much damage has been done to an unusually fine 17th-century building. It has to be said that the building works have not contributed to the maintenance of the authenticity of the cathedral-church, and indeed that much of the 20th-century intervention has not helped to maintain the fabric but rather to erode it. Undoing what has been done will not come cheap, nor will all the damage be capable of repair.

In 1962 The Honourable The Irish Society presented a handsome silver-gilt Decanal Insignium to the cathedral to commemorate the 350th anniversary of its foundation by royal charter of 1613: it features the Arms of The Society **[Frontispiece]** and those of Coleraine, Londonderry, and Northern Ireland (as it was). The following year The Society was given the Freedom of the City of Londonderry in celebration, and links between London and County Londonderry were again emphasised. Shortly afterwards there were major celebrations to mark the completion of the long programme of 'restoration': special services were held, speeches were made, and fulsome articles published. Deterioration of the exterior, however, began almost at once (especially on the south side), as was noted in 1971.

Since Marshall's time and the very considerable works carried out then, the cathedral has had to be maintained and repaired on several occasions, not least after bomb-blasts. In 1971-2 the interior of the building was cleaned by H. L. Stuart-Cox & Co Ltd.: in Stuart-Cox's report, the managing director of the firm specifically deplored

[2] Personal communication from Miss Margaret Brown, Mr. Marshall's secretary from 1949 to 1972. Other information relating to works at the cathedral from papers held in the chapter-house, and from Londonderry (1987), *passim*.

[3] i.e. a finish (e.g. plaster or harling) applied to a surface, thus concealing it.

[4] *Ribbon-pointing* is a hard, projecting band of mortar (usually stiffened with Portland cement) which should not be confused with the subtle *tuck-pointing* used in fine brickwork, and which should not be used at all.

the 'tuck-pointing' of the interior (it is, of course, nothing of the sort, but is ribbon-pointing), and drew attention to the exterior stonework that had been 'slurred over with sand/cement render' so that it would be unable to 'breathe'. The report also noted that the 'new stones of the East window' were 'efflorescing', and that certain stones should not have been selected for use at all. Furthermore, when new stones had been fixed, old stones nearby had been ground down with carborundum, and stones so treated had been 'ruined'. It would be difficult to quarrel with such a devastating assessment: the damage done has been widespread and serious.

Following bomb-blast damage, The Society assisted with modest grants, and after the severe blasts of the 1980s the Corporation of London itself made a substantial gift of £10,000 to enable restoration to proceed. Since 1975 Miss Caroline Dickson (daughter of The Society's former General Agent, Peter Dickson) has had charge of the fabric, and before her appointment The Irish Society's local architect, Malcolm McQuigg (1902-74), of W & M Given, architects, Coleraine, was involved, but only for a short time: neither was responsible in any way for the problems alluded to above. Considerable works will be required to repair the cathedral and undo the damage of the 1920s, 1950s, and 1960s, but the 'very good work' noted by Champneys cannot be recovered, and much has been irretrievably lost. It would not be an exaggeration to call it an architectural and historical tragedy, but the problem has been long-standing, going back to the 19th century (and probably the previous one as well).

Other Historic Fabric

Londonderry's walls, with the cathedral, remain among The Irish Society's greatest and most impressive achievements. Although the 17th-century fabric has undergone various changes, not least the replacement of the old gateways with handsome Classical structures from 1789 to 1865, the walls are of considerable architectural and historic interest. Responsibility for the upkeep of the walls was assumed by the Department of Finance in 1954, and The Irish Society gave £500 per annum to this end. However, when it transpired that this sum was merely absorbed in the general exchequer and was not used for the maintenance of the fabric, The Irish Society managed to terminate the agreement.

A curious situation arose as the 'Troubles' escalated and the Walker testimonial was blown up in 1973. This handsome monument had been erected by public subscription to which The Society had contributed, and it was The Society which actually owned the bastion on which the testimonial stood. Eventually, out-of-court compensation of £800,000 was paid to the Apprentice Boys (which organisation had been prominent in the original raising of the subscription) for the damage, on condition that the modest pedestal should be restored by the Apprentice Boys, and this was duly carried out **[118]**. The Society, however, did not benefit at all from the compensation, even though it had paid for repairs to the testimonial at various times in the past.

The Society and a Change of Direction

A climate of violence, destruction, hatred, and political change once more led in 1973 to calls from Nationalists to the Secretary of State for The Irish Society to be wound up. Once it was realised that if this happened certain assets and funds raised from the

118 Restored pedestal, all that remains of the Walker testimonial, in 1998. In the background is St Eugene's Roman Catholic cathedral. (*A*)

sale of property would have to be returned to London, calls for abolition grew less vociferous. However, it was decided by The Society to establish a Local Advisory Committee in order to bring the two main settlements into a closer relationship with the Londoners. This committee is not chosen by The Society: it consists of four elected representatives from Londonderry and three from Coleraine, each group including the two mayors *ex officio*, and the others elected by the Londonderry and Coleraine authorities. The town-clerks are eligible to attend in a non-voting capacity, so there are five representatives from Londonderry and four from Coleraine. In addition, The Mercers' Company (which had only decided to sever its connections with its Proportion in 1963, on the grounds that the very small income was insufficient to generate any funds for real help to be given to the former estate) formally transferred its interests to The Irish Society as trustees in 1965, and so the Kilrea Trust Fund (as it became) is represented on the Local Advisory Committee by one of the Coleraine Council members, usually from a Ward in the Kilrea area. This committee (which meets under the chairmanship of The Society's Representative in Ireland) *recommends* certain actions, grants, etc. to The Irish Society's Court, which then *ratifies* the committee's recommendations. Furthermore, the Local Advisory Committee has powers of co-option when necessary, should specialist advice be required.

The first meeting of The Society's Local Advisory Committee was held at Society House, St Columb's Court, Bishop Street, Londonderry, on 28 March 1974, with The Society's Representative in Ireland, Commander P. C. D. Campbell-Grove,[5] in the chair. It is interesting to reflect that the chairman could boast a very long connection with the Plantation, for his ancestors included members of the Gage family and Peter Benson, the London tiler and bricklayer, who built Londonderry's walls and who could also lay claim to be an architect. Very soon afterwards, in June, the Local Advisory Committee met members of The Irish Society's Annual Visitation. **[119]**

During 1974 the Local Advisory Committee, with limited funds at its disposal, advised the granting of a lease at Culmore Fort **[120]** to the Lough Foyle Sailing Club. It also recommended grants to St Joseph's House, Termonbacca (the former

[5] Now (1999) Commander Peter Colin Drummond Campbell, LVO, OBE, DL, to whom the author is indebted for help and information. When Commander Campbell-Grove was invited to take over as Agent he agreed to do so in an honorary capacity provided that: the title was changed to Representative; there should be a Local Advisory Committee; and accounts should be published. It was the last which showed that the capital was quite small, and this removed pressures for abolition of The Society. Nevertheless, politicians were still able to get grants for their Wards, thus ensuring a waiting list of would-be members of the Local Advisory Committee. It is a measure of the success of policies since then that the Nationalist council now running Londonderry participates fully, for in the past animosities would have precluded this.

119 Members of The Irish Society and some members of The Society's first Local Advisory Committee meeting at St Columb's Court, Londonderry, on 28 June 1974 during The Society's Annual Visitation to north-west Ulster (25 June to 1 July). *Back row* (left to right): C. Geary (Town-Clerk, Londonderry), E.H. Shackcloth (Secretary, The Irish Society), J. M. Keith (immediate past Deputy Governor, The Irish Society); *middle row* (left to right): Councillor Ivan Wilson (Coleraine), Councillor Marlene Jefferson (Londonderry), B. E. Manning (Assistant Secretary, The Irish Society), Commander P. C. D. Campbell-Grove (The Society's Representative in Ireland), Alderman Lindsay R. Ring (Member of The Irish Society's Visitation [who was to become Governor in 1981]); and *front row* (left to right) A.N. Clarke (Mayor of Coleraine), C. H. Murkin (Deputy Governor, The Irish Society), Alderman J. Allen (Mayor of Londonderry), and Councillor F. McAteer (Londonderry). Councillor John White and E. Andrews, Town-Clerk of Coleraine, were not present. (*Derry Journal [5 July 1974], 7*)

Government House of The Society, then an institution of the Christian Brothers); the Society of St Vincent de Paul; and to organisations helping deprived children. At its meetings the committee took on board The Irish Society's declared aim of helping to develop north-west Ulster. Because of the loss of so many venues in Londonderry, it was decided to hold any Society dinners in London (these were not annual affairs, but were occasions to further specific projects such as European Union funding for studies to link Londonderry with Donegal and Strabane). Given the appalling state of Londonderry and Ulster at the time it might be felt in some quarters that dinners were rather frivolous matters about which to be concerned, but they were far more important than mere gastronomic and bibulous junketings: dinners were means by which contacts could be made, the London connections strengthened for the benefit of Londonderry and Coleraine, and bridges built.

In 1975 the committee only had £8,500 for distribution. Decisions were made not to make any grants for religious purposes (parish funds, etc.) in order to avoid controversy, although listed buildings could be supported. For example, grants were made to St Columb's cathedral for the structure and for the development of youth work, and a grant was made towards the repair of St Patrick's church, Coleraine. It is interesting that this matter once again surfaced, opinions from counsel having been sought in the 1870s and 1890s, as indicated above.[6] Two years later a small grant was

[6] See, for example, Corporation of London Records Office, IS Box 4.7 Loc. 422B.

120 Culmore Fort in 1998. (*A*)

made to Magee College to help excavation work in Londonderry, and funds were also given to help to conserve two cannon from the wrecks of the Armada pending their transfer to the Ulster Museum. As properties had been destroyed by bombs, fires, and so on, opportunities were sometimes grasped to carry out archaeological investigations as detailed understanding of the early building history of the Plantation was not great. However, the shortages of archaeologists and of funds were such that not nearly enough investigations have been made, and an enormous amount could be done to improve matters in this respect.

During the mid-1970s help from Europe was sought, negotiations with the Department of Agriculture began to dispose of The Society's remaining timber rights in County Londonderry (these were on the former lands of the Haberdashers' Company which had been sold before The Society relinquished its rights), and tentative feelers went out to Williamsburg, Virginia, in the U.S.A., in an attempt to forge links with Londonderry (the American settlement was named after King William III, and its College of William and Mary ranks second to Harvard in seniority among U.S. colleges). By 1977 restoration of Londonderry's Guildhall was well under way, including the very fine stained glass, and in that year the Local Advisory Committee had £15,000 to distribute. During the 1970s grants were given to numerous causes including the Coleraine Music Festival Association, the Londonderry Children's holiday fund, and the Bogside festival.

In the 1980s grants were made to St Joseph's High School, Coleraine; for the refurbishment of the mayor's parlour in Guildhall, Londonderry; and larger grants for buildings (e.g. £1,000 towards restoration-work at St Patrick's church, Kilrea [1841-3], originally designed by George Smith [1783-1869] and William Barnes [1807-68] in a

Romanesque style). In 1986 the question of Brooke Park came up once more. In 1903 The Irish Society had given £6,000 towards the purchase of the property for the benefit of the inhabitants of Londonderry (six-thirteenths of the purchase-price). On consideration of the Corporation managing the park and museum at its expense, the property was conveyed to Londonderry City Council. When Jackson's very pretty building was destroyed by bombs in 1973, compensation of £440,327 was paid to the Council, and The Society felt that, as it had an interest in how the money should be spent consistent with the 1899 Act of Parliament passed to enable the lands to be acquired, it should be in a position to ensure the money was used for the benefit of the inhabitants. Matters were resolved in a satisfactory fashion.[7]

The 1933 gates at the cathedral were restored in 1957 (supported by a grant from The Society), and again in 1987, the drawings and specifications being given by The Society. This was within the remit of the Local Advisory Committee, but larger funds for schools and other purposes were outside its scope. Further refurbishment took place in 1994 (helped by donations from various Livery Companies), and in June of that year the restored gates were opened by the Governor of The Society and the Lord Mayor of London.

It was during the 1980s that The Society took a long hard look at itself. The granting of perpetual leases had, as expected, reduced income in real terms, so if The Society were to achieve anything its remaining assets would have to be developed. It soon became apparent that the key to the problem lay in the fecund waters over which The Society had enormous powers. It was decided to expand and improve The Society's fishings and shooting leases, make more effective use of The Society's influence in the City of London (and therefore in Europe, America, and Japan), and use the annual entertainments to publicise north-west Ulster and The Society's rôle.

This new confidence was, to a very large extent, thanks to the work of the Local Advisory Committee and to the tact of The Society's Representative in Ireland. Only 10 years after Nationalists were lobbying the then Secretary of State (Whitelaw) to terminate the existence of The Society, the advantage of having an influential and benevolent organisation independent both of the Government and local factions was once more appreciated. Furthermore, The Society not only was, *but was seen to be* non-sectarian, distributing limited funds in an even-handed manner. Thus the Roman Catholic community began to appreciate The Society's work. The importance of steering a careful course in troubled waters was demonstrated again and again, and, in every case, The Society's Court in London ratified the Local Advisory Committee's recommendations without demur.[8]

For many years The Irish Society had maintained schools, some of which (as we have seen) it had built. Under the Education Act (Northern Ireland) of 1947[9] The Society's school at Coleraine was transferred to the Local Education Authority having previously been wholly maintained by The Society. However, The Society was to have a majority on the school's management committee, the annual Visitation to the school and right to present prizes were to be preserved, and the buildings were to revert to The Society in the event of their ceasing to be used as a school, which happened in 1977. Other schools with which The Society had long been connected were also transferred to the L.E.A., including Ballougry school and teacher's residence and

[7] All from relevant papers held at Cutts House.

[8] Minutes and other papers of the Local Advisory Committee, held at Cutts House.

[9] c.3.

121 Coleraine Academical Institution, in 1983, designed by Isaac Farrell, completed in 1860. (*A/CC/UM*)

Culmore School and residence. As a result of the agreement in 1963-5, Swatragh and Movanagher Schools on the former Mercers' Proportion were conveyed to The Society, and duly reverted to The Society when the schools closed. Rossnagalliagh School, transferred to the L.E.A. under the Education Act (Northern Ireland) of 1923,[10] closed in 1977 and reverted to The Society. Despite the transfers of responsibility, The Society's Court in London still took an interest in, and gave support to, the schools at Ballougry, Culmore, Millburn Primary (Coleraine), the D. H. Christie Memorial School, Coleraine Primary School, and, in later years, Coleraine High School, as well as Foyle and Londonderry College (the descendant of Alderman Springham's School in the early years of the Plantation) and St Columb's College. Both Millburn Primary and the D. H. Christie Memorial were offshoots derived from the liberal principles established by The Society's school in Coleraine, and were run on similar lines. Other educational establishments were also helped at various times, and for many years Coleraine Academical Institution **[121]** had enjoyed the support of The Society. An annual grant had been made, and The Irish Society was represented on the Board of Governors, in an *ex officio* capacity, in the 1980s by The Society's Representative in Ireland.[11] Magee College, too, was encouraged to pursue courses that would eventually contribute to the industrial and commercial development of Londonderry and its hinterland.

So the 1980s saw many changes, not least to The Society's income and operational bases. In order to re-establish economic soundness, a careful examination of all The Society's properties, rights, and privileges was made. It will be recalled that regular changes to the Court of Assistants and failure to maintain adequate records had caused difficulties in the past.[12] In 1836 Charles Stewart, Deputy Vice-Admiral, had produced a series of maps showing the *Vice-Admiralty District* of The Society stretching from Ballyshannon all round the coasts to Olderfleet, *The Fisheries* owned by The Society,

[10] 13 & 14 Geo. V, c.21.
[11] Copies of voluminous correspondence at Cutts House.
[12] See especially Mogridge's Memorandum in Moody and Simms (eds.) (1983), **ii**, 279-421.

including the *Lake or River of Lough Foyle* (which indicates The Society's property formerly disputed by the bishops of Derry), and *The Fisheries and River of the Bann … Granted by the Charter & Purchased from the Bishop of Derry* as far as Lough Neagh, published as Appendices to the *Report of the Deputation* of 1836. Subsequently, these maps were updated and the rights (despite many usurpations and attacks) were largely preserved, apart from the tidal waters of the Foyle dispute which was resolved by buying The Society out in the 1950s. In 1931 The Society bought up certain fishing-rights in the River Bann and Lough Neagh, which permitted limited recreational angling in the lough, and it also made sure its title to various rivers such as the Roe, the Faughan, and the Agivey were protected. By 1980, concern was expressed about various activities (e.g. canoeing) causing damage to the spawning of salmon in various rivers (the problem was particularly bad in the Faughan), and it was decided to tighten up controls and the conditions in leases granted which would affect the waters.

On 17 November 1981 a deed of exchange between the Shaftesbury Estate of Lough Neagh Ltd (successors to the Chichester-Donegall interests that had been such a problem from the very beginning) and The Honourable The Irish Society was drawn up and signed. By this indenture the Shaftesbury Estate conveyed to The Society such rights as it owned over the bed and soil of the River Bann from Lough Neagh to the Salmon Leap at Coleraine (including the navigable channel through which the River passes across Lough Beg) and also the scale fishing-rights (if any) it had over the waters of the River Bann and Lough Beg in the counties of Antrim and Londonderry. In exchange, The Society conveyed to the Shaftesbury Estate such shooting-rights as it owned over the bed and soil of reclaimed land in County Londonderry bordering Loughs Beg and Neagh, as well as shooting-rights over the waters of Lough Beg in fee-simple. Thus a long-running issue of contention concerning doubts about the nature and extent of interests of the parties was finally settled, amicably, and without money changing hands.[13]

However, it became apparent that the terms of the leases granted in the Bann to a descendant of the persons formerly associated with the Fisheries bought out in the 1952 settlement were not being properly adhered to, and in 1984 it was decided to regain direct control of the River Bann and all goodwill associated with the fisheries at the earliest opportunity, once the Shaftesbury Estate difficulties had been resolved. By 1985, therefore, The Society had regained control of the Bann north of Lough Neagh with all fisheries and fishing-rights, and set up a new company, Bann System Ltd., wholly a subsidiary of The Society, but with half its board of directors from Northern Ireland. The costs of buying out other interests and setting up the new structure were considerable, so there was only a small profit in the first year of operation (1985-6), but there were other plans in the pipeline, for The Society was keen to encourage recreation, tourism, and educational facilities associated with the great river, so various sub-committees were established to deal with these matters, and also to study scientifically the flora, fauna, breeding of fish, and other subjects. Thus Bann System Ltd. is wholly owned by The Society and is The Irish Society's tenant as well, having a 49-year lease.[14]

There were still enormous problems to resolve, for poaching had once more become a major thorn in The Society's flesh. This was hardly an unfamiliar story, as

[13] Registered in the Registry of Deeds, Belfast, on 2 December 1981, Book 139, No. 59.
[14] Papers of Bann System Ltd. at Cutts House, and information from Commander Campbell.

it recurs from the very beginning of the Plantation,[15] but studies of the waters had demonstrated beyond doubt that strict controls were essential to prevent great natural assets being wasted. The sad story of Lough Neagh, once teeming with perch, is sobering, for, thanks to the selfishness and greed of those with access to the lough, the perch stocks were destroyed. Conservation, therefore, was essential, and conservation needed careful and firm management with clout. Leases were granted to the fishings of tributaries such as the Agivey and certain waters in Tyrone. Very soon the new policy of direct control, properly managed, showed that The Society could re-establish itself on a healthy financial footing. In five years, for example, the revival of its fortunes in the Bann alone raised its income from £8,000 to £25,000 per annum. By 1989 Bann System Ltd. had repaid The Irish Society the monies laid out to establish the Company, and a healthy profit was announced. It was not before time, for various problems arose during the 1980s that required immediate and large expenditure, and The Society sold off more properties it could not see much point in retaining.[16]

The first difficulty was caused by terrorist bomb-damage in Londonderry. Attacks made on the court-house in Bishop Street in 1988 and 1989 damaged St Columb's cathedral, the offices of The Irish Society (Society House) leased from the diocese, and other buildings. The court-house survived, but required considerable refurbishment. Having only just renovated its offices following an earlier bomb, The Society gave up its lease which was nearing expiry and moved to temporary accommodation in the Diamond, Coleraine, but that still left it with the question of where to establish its Irish headquarters. For some time the lands at the Salmon Leap, upstream from Coleraine, had been considered. The derelict mill that had been such a problem to let in the previous century[17] had long been demolished (in 1849-50), but there were available a double-fronted house in a late-Georgian style and the former manager's house beside it at the Cutts. It was decided to renovate both buildings, and on 31 October 1990 the fully refurbished Cutts House was opened, the work having been carried out to the designs of Alan Thompson **[122-124]**. This major work was achieved on the proceeds of reversions of various lands, including the old gas-works site in Coleraine. Situated in a spacious garden beside an impressively beautiful stretch of the River Bann, just before the waters tumble down over the Cutts and flow through the lock **[124]**, Cutts House (which bears a strong resemblance to the house at Killea designed by Stewart Gordon of 1859 **[73]**, and is probably also by him) functions as offices, meeting-rooms, and a base for visiting members of The Society (there are bedrooms, bathrooms, and sitting-rooms). There is also a large kitchen, so the meeting-room can also function as a dining-room.

Hardly had The Society's Irish headquarters been resolved before difficulties arose with The Irish Chamber in Guildhall Yard, City of London. Moves to vacate the Chamber were mooted in 1987, but damage was done to the Chamber during building-works on an adjoining site in 1990, and The Society moved out in 1992. Meetings

[15] John Macky, inspector of the waterkeepers on the River Bann in the province of Ulster, 1791-1804, in the diary he kept, recorded a fearful story of 'watchers' who were really poachers, together with much else of interest. In 1799 for example, he recorded 13,677 salmon being caught (officially), weighing 56 tons 5 cwt., and fetching £1,650 3s. 7½d., and in 1803 10,146 fish weighing 34 tons 14 cwt., selling at £1,797 10s. 9d. (the increase in costs reflecting economic conditions at the time). This diary, edited by Richard Moore-Colyer, survives in manuscript held by The Irish Society, and is entitled 'Rogue Watch; Rogue Catch; the Diary of John Macky'. The author is indebted to Commander Campbell and Mr. Montgomery for drawing attention to this interesting document.

[16] Papers at Cutts House. Nevertheless, The Society still owns many properties in County Londonderry.

[17] IS/V/31 MS. Report of 1859 Deputation.

122 The Salmon Leap, Coleraine, with Cutts House, 1997. (*A*)

123 Cutts House at the Salmon Leap, Coleraine, in 1998, the offices of The Irish Society in Ireland from 1990. This handsome double-fronted house was originally built to designs by Stewart Gordon (compare 73). (*A*)

124 View of the Salmon Leap, Coleraine, from the garden of Cutts House, 1997. (*A*)

125 The doorway to The Irish Society's former offices in St Columb's Court, Londonderry. The brass plate is now (2000) in The Irish Chamber in Watling Street, London. (*A/CC/UM*)

were held in several venues thereafter (including Guildhall) until London offices were acquired at 74-75 Watling Street, where The Society now (2000) meets. On the door of the rented 'Chamber' is the brass plate that adorned the front door of Society House in Londonderry until the late 1980s **[125]**. Meanwhile, The Irish Chamber building has been repaired and renovated, but, when the lease on the Watling Street premises runs out, The Society will not return to the Chamber which was sold to the Corporation of London in 1992. It is not yet known where its future home will be.

Epilogue

Commander Campbell **[126]** retired as The Society's Representative in Ireland in September 1996 and was succeeded by Mr H. E. J. Montgomery who, like Commander Campbell, has family connections going back to the beginnings of the Plantation (the Montgomerys originally came from Scotland). Under these able administrators, supported by the Court in London, the work of The Society continues as the century draws to a close and the four-hundredth anniversary approaches of the establishment of The Society of the Governor and Assistants, London, of the New Plantation in Ulster, within the Realm of Ireland.

In 1999 the Local Advisory Committee had around £50,000 to distribute, which is an eloquent testament to how the fortunes of The Society have been consolidated. The great rivers of the Foyle and Bann, with their tributaries, are not only superb amenities but contribute enormously to the local economy. The Irish Society has been in the vanguard of protecting these assets and ploughing back profits they generate into the lands that comprised the Londonderry Plantation. Furthermore, The Society indefatigably carries out many acts consistent with its obligations and duties: it encourages tourism; supports education by many means (including grants to scholars); fosters good relations between communities; promotes north-west Ulster in London, nationally, and internationally; makes donations to many causes; calls upon the offices of influential people to support the economy of County Londonderry; intervenes to secure benefits for Londonderry and Coleraine; provides unique educational and career opportunities for talented individuals who would otherwise lack such possibilities; and, among many other activities, nurtures the special relationship between the wealthy and powerful City of London and its 'offspring', the main settlements of the 17th-century Londonderry Plantation. Private visits, group excursions, personal exchanges, warm welcomes extended and returned, friendships formed, co-operation developed, practical help given, material interests carefully inter-related, and much else sustain that special relationship and assist it to evolve. As The Society itself has claimed, it 'has always sought to promote the healthy co-existence of the two communities whose situation it had a hand in creating. Its ways and means may have altered but the

126 Meeting of The Irish Society's Local Advisory Committee, at Cutts House, Coleraine, 20 March 1996. *Left to right*: E. Andrews (Town-Clerk, Coleraine Borough Council), Alderman J. White (Coleraine Borough Council), Councillor M. Bradley (Derry City Council), Alderman Pauline Armitage (Mayor, Coleraine Borough Council), Commander P. C. D. Campbell (Irish Society's Representative), Mrs J. Young (Secretary, The Irish Society's office at Coleraine), Councillor J. Guy (Derry City Council), Councillor Olive Church (Coleraine Borough Council), and Councillor S. Gallagher (Derry City Council). Councillor John Kerr, Mayor of Londonderry, was absent. (*Alan Leighton A10/CC/18, 20.3.96*)

peaceful prosperity of the people of County Londonderry, their welfare and security, is still, and will be for generations to come, its prime concern'.[18]

In recent years the Lord Mayor of London presented funds to an Irish-speaking school, an event which would have been unthinkable in the climate of the 17th or 18th centuries. Indeed, it was once the aim of much opinion in Ireland to discourage the retention of the Irish language for various reasons, some connected with the economy, and others with conformity, security, and the evolution of loyalties unconnected with a Gaelic past. One of the results of the 'Troubles' and the emergence of a very different economy within the European context has been a huge upsurge of Irish national pride, often involving study of Irish history, the Irish language and literature, and Gaelic antiquity. When the 26 counties of the Irish Free State determined that at least one hour of Irish should be taught in schools in 1922, some hoped that Irish would be restored, but the experiment only had limited success. In the 1990s, however, a new spirit seems to be abroad, and something very like enthusiasm for the language has blossomed. How permanent this will be is difficult to judge, for only time can tell, but, rather than being imposed, Irish is being eagerly and voluntarily sought.

It is extraordinary that, in Northern Ireland, Irish history, until recently, was given short shrift, and the Plantation was ignored. Today, attempts are being made to address this omission and some knowledge of the past encouraged rather than the half-baked mythologies that contributed to hatred and misunderstanding. When the history of Ulster is considered from an objective, cool approach, and the towns and settlements

[18] Irish Society (1994), 16.

studied, it is abundantly clear that the Plantation *cannot* and *should not* be ignored, for nothing makes sense unless it is taken into consideration. Even the names in a telephone-book or a directory can be informative, for English, Irish, and Scots names can be found, often concentrated in certain areas (though this is changing as the population becomes more mobile). There are even smatterings of French names, sometimes corrupted, which point to the Huguenots, but searches for Central European names associated with groups such as the Moravians are disappointing, for long ago those immigrants Anglicised their names so that they could merge more easily with their new surroundings.

When the Londonderry Plantation is considered, the efforts of the Livery Companies and The Irish Society deserve respect, and their remarkable achievements against considerable odds are certainly worthy of study, whether one approves of the principle of colonisation or not. The point is, it happened, and is an historical fact: it cannot be wished out of existence. The City of London was pushed into the venture by the Crown against its will, and only took part when it realised it had no real option in the matter: its very survival was at stake, for the Stuart monarchy, if thwarted, could be vindictive. Once things got going, however, the speed with which Londonderry, Coleraine, and the various Company settlements were established was remarkable, given the difficulties of communication. The reasons for this speed are many, and include the contractual obligations to meet certain targets set by the Crown, but there is another important factor, and that is precedent. The Munster Plantation was directed from London after the second Desmond Rebellion (1579-83), and by 1592 had a population of 3,030: rents paid to the Crown were about £1,900 by 1594, but during the Nine Years' War the colony was over-run. Re-established in 1601, the Plantation's population was about 14,000 in 1611 and 22,000 in 1641,[19] so there was expertise, methodology, and experience on which the Londoners could draw and from which they could learn: they were not blundering into wholly untested areas, and this may help to explain the awe-inspiring rapidity of construction work and colonisation. There was also the important Plantation of Virginia, the first colonists of which sailed from the Thames only shortly before the Flight of the Earls in 1607: among the incorporators named in the second Virginia Charter of 1609 were 56 City Companies (the 55 Companies involved in the Ulster Plantation plus the Worshipful Company of Gardeners), but the amounts subscribed were much smaller than those levied on the Companies for the Londonderry venture. It is probable that if the Ulster Plantation had not made such heavy demands on resources the Companies would have played a greater part in the Virginia Plantation than was the case. By 1613 the *total* amount raised for the Virginia Plantation by the Companies *and* several hundred individual adventurers was £30,000, but the Companies *alone* had contributed £40,000 towards the Londonderry Plantation by the same date. Nevertheless, those two precedents, Munster and Virginia, were important.[20]

Today, The Honourable The Irish Society, reluctantly born of necessity in the reign of King James I and VI, and obliged to serve a sectional interest, has evolved into a body which aims to promote the welfare of the whole populace of the lands of the Londonderry Plantation, and especially of the two settlements of Londonderry and Coleraine. Drawing on income from the residue of its once-extensive estates, its considerable investments, its magnificent fisheries **[127-129]**, and its sporting-rights,

[19] Connolly (ed.) (1998), 372-3.
[20] Moody (1939), 31, 83, 96-8, 133, 156.

127 The Cranagh on the Bann near the mouth of the river, associated with The Irish Society's fishings, in 1997. (*A*)

128 Structure over the Cutts, in 1997. (*A*)

it disburses charitable grants, maintains properties, runs its affairs, and funds the very important annual Visitations. Any person or group in County Londonderry may apply to The Society for financial assistance for any purpose that is consistent with The Irish Society's declared policy of promoting the well-being of the county, and, in particular, the city of Londonderry and the town of Coleraine. The Society also takes its pastoral rôle very seriously, and supports numerous other educational and religious bodies in various ways, although it avoids giving money for 'parish' purposes and it remains aloof from showing bias towards any particular creed. Any assistance, financial or otherwise, which The Society gives is based on an ideal of even-handedness across a wide social and religious spectrum. In the volatile and sectarian climate of Northern Ireland such an unbiased stance is essential, and in the last 25 years or so has earned The Society new respect. The establishment of the Local Advisory Committee has undoubtedly helped to mellow antipathetic perceptions and to undo some of the damage perpetrated by a host of mischievous, malicious, and wholly inaccurate pamphlets published during the last 175 years or so.

In the turbulent and bloody history of Ireland there were many 'good' landlords, benevolent towards their tenants, who ploughed profits back to improve their estates; there were also many 'bad' landlords, who were absentees, who asset-stripped their lands, and rack-rented their unfortunate tenants to such an extent they had no option but to emigrate. The historian, privileged to explore the huge amount of documentation concerning The Irish Society that survives, must arrive at one conclusion: on the whole The Society comes out of the story with honour. Not all the Companies do, though: while the 19th-century philanthropic achievements of the Mercers, Grocers, Drapers, Fishmongers, Salters, and Clothworkers (in association with the Merchant Taylors) were very considerable, some other Companies were less benevolent: careful inspection of documents and surviving built fabric (which is documentary evidence of another sort) shows very clearly who the benevolent landlords were and who were not. In all the documentation, however, The Irish Society was on the side of the angels, although there were times when its agents (e.g. Rowley) were less than angelic, and more interested in feathering their own nests than in furthering the aims of The Society. However, life in County Londonderry in the 17th century cannot have been

129 Carnroe weir and locks near Kilrea from the air. The prime salmon angling beat on the River Bann is known locally as the 'holy water'. (*IS*)

very agreeable, and one suspects that lining of personal pockets would have been regarded as legitimate perks by those unfortunate enough to have had to organise the infrastructure of the early Plantation in such hostile territory. Just how dangerous and vile conditions were may be gauged from a perusal of Canning's communications with The Ironmongers' Company.[21] Just as the Planters of Virginia were attacked by native Americans in 1622 and 1644, resulting in the deaths of several hundred settlers, the native Irish made life difficult for the Planters of Londonderry, especially in 1641. The connection between Williamsburg (the capital of Virginia from 1699) and County Londonderry is obvious, and explains why The Irish Society has attempted to foster links between Londonderry and Williamsburg, not, sadly, with instant success, possibly because the version of Irish history peddled in America tends to lean heavily towards romanticised mythology having little resemblance to fact.

It is very curious, when events of recent decades in Ulster are considered, that the historical perspective has been virtually ignored. There has been much glib talk (at one time even including the obscene term 'acceptable levels of violence'[22]) and uninformed comment betraying an appalling ignorance of *why* passions tend to run high in Northern Ireland. The legacy of history is a heavy burden, but it should not be brushed aside as irrelevant. Some pundits may deplore that Ulster still wallows in

[21] See British Museum Add. MS. 4790 and the collection of documents compiled by Richard Hunter, Clerk to the Company (1608-18), and papers of The Ironmongers' Company at Guildhall Library, City of London (M.S. 17276).

[22] Reginald Maudling (1917-79), Home Secretary 1970-2.

problems of earlier centuries that are no longer considered relevant in London's suburbia, but they never seem to ask themselves how those problems arrived in Ulster: the attitudes and problems did not suddenly become manifest. They were put there and they were fostered. Given that Ulster always was provincial, relatively isolated, and remote until comparatively recently (the time-lag in architectural fashions is a striking testament to this fact), it is not really all that strange that the sort of passions that led to the Gordon Riots in London (1780) and the anti-Ritualist attacks on Father Arthur Wagner (1824-1902), the Anglican parson, in Brighton in the 1870s, '80s, and '90s (his curates were denounced as crypto-Papists and his churches liberally decorated with obscene *graffiti*), survive in parts of Ulster. The Irish Society knows this, and treads carefully with immense tact and sensitivity.

The appearance of the county of Londonderry today owes much to the Plantation, and the many historic buildings, roads, arrangement of fields, hedgerows and mature trees exist because of the policies and management established by the Londoners (prompted by the eloquent and rational arguments of George Vaughan Sampson[23]). It is clear from documentary evidence and from surviving buildings themselves that the Companies and The Irish Society endeavoured to encourage building on sound principles taking into account aesthetic matters as well: today, it is very unfortunate that the appearance of buildings in the countryside or the towns does not seem to be given much consideration, for there is very little evidence that the subtle colours and delectable landscapes of one of the loveliest counties in these islands have brought out any response whatsoever in contemporary builders. Far too many old buildings have been altered unsympathetically (especially where fenestration is concerned), and visual chaos has replaced order and harmony in the towns and villages. The rash of bungaloid developments in the alien *hacienda* style of the Costa del Sol is not the most appropriate or tactful addition to landscapes rapidly being wrecked.

The Londonderry Plantation was a momentous event in the history of our islands, and had ramifications of many kinds. Not only was it the reason behind the creation of the last fortified city to be built in western Europe, but it was a catalyst in the events that led to the end of capricious absolute monarchy and its replacement by the supremacy of Parliament. It played a key rôle as the centre of communications for the north Atlantic campaigns and as a major factor in the build-up for the invasion of Europe during the 1939-45 war; it was of enormous importance in the defeat of the Jacobites and French in the 1689-91 war (and therefore most significant in the creation of the political settlement of the 18th century); and more recently the lands colonised by the Londoners saw the outbreak of renewed violence leading to direct rule and the abolition of the Stormont parliament. Images of the rioting in Londonderry have made the place known on the world stage once more. Local politicians have also raised the profile of the city of Londonderry: John Hume, the S.D.L.P. Member of Parliament for Foyle Constituency, Member of the European Parliament, and joint winner of the Nobel Peace Prize (1998), has done much to focus international attention on the area he has represented politically for many years.

Nevertheless, the visitor to north-west Ulster cannot fail to be impressed by the great variety of breathtaking scenery and gentle landscapes, by the two majestic rivers and their charming tributaries, by the huge expanse of Lough Foyle, protected by the Inishowen peninsula, and by the many historic buildings of County Londonderry that survive in spite of everything. The massive walls of the city of Londonderry, the 17th-

[23] Sampson (1802, 1814), *passim*.

century Gothic cathedral, the remains of fortified manor-houses (e.g. Salterstown castle or Ballykelly bawn), the clear layouts of Londonderry and Coleraine, and many other fine buildings (including Londonderry's Guildhall, Coleraine's town-hall, Ballykelly Presbyterian church [designed by Richard Suter (1797-1883) for the Fishmongers' Company in 1827], and Tite's Government House, Termonbacca) survive as eloquent testimonies of the Londoners' efforts.

It should be remembered that Ulster, once the most intractably Gaelic part of Ireland, was colonised in such a way that it contained a large number of Protestants, so was, from the State's point of view, a partial success, yet in Ireland as a whole Protestantism never became the main religion of the mass of the people, and the process of colonisation never succeeded in making the Irish loyal to the British Crown. So, what was only a *partial* success created problems because it left several counties of Ulster secured in Plantation terms but unwilling to be submerged into what was, in essence, a Roman Catholic Irish State. This has placed ordinary people in a very curious position given the wider aspects of historical events, for they are the victims of history and of policies that have long been abandoned because they no longer matter and have been forgotten. The fact of the matter is that the Protestants of Ulster are descended from people who were either put there or persuaded to settle as part of Crown policy: they were granted lands on condition they upheld British law, were loyal to the British Crown, and conformed to the Protestant religion, the objective being to outnumber a Gaelic-Irish, disaffected, Roman Catholic population with a strong and determined British, English-speaking, loyal, Protestant people. The attitudes such colonists were obliged to adopt as part of State policy remained, and cannot be eradicated overnight. They are explainable, but should not be dismissed because they appear to be absurd in other contexts. When Britain signalled the end of its Empire by giving Ireland up (having demonstrated it could not keep order in a country separated from Scotland by a mere 12 miles, the message for India was obvious[24]), it became clear that many of those who had served the Crown would be abandoned. Siege mentalities do not just happen: they develop because conditions make them. The settlers were left to their own devices on more than one occasion. The siege of Londonderry, after all, involved a defence by a *citizen* army, and relief came almost too late. Few commentators these days seem to be able to grasp the historical predicament of the descendants of the Plantation settlers and of those who resisted them. But predicaments they are, and it will take more than wishful thinking to alter the fact.

To the enormous credit of The Irish Society, the various positions adopted by Nationalist and Unionist opinion are fully understood by that body, which avoids any action liable to cause friction. On the contrary, it attempts to bridge divides, smooths rough ways, and works for the common good. As the century draws to a close it is clear that The Society has evolved into a major force for reconciling what many might once have seen as irreconcilable. The Londoners and their servants have given Ireland a remarkable legacy that is now as much part of the country's heritage as the relics of Gaelic Antiquity. The built fabric erected under the aegis of The Honourable The Irish Society and the Livery Companies, for example, is of very considerable architectural and historic importance. It should be recognised as such.

To some, of course, *any* reminders of the Plantation are unloved, and there are those who would wish to destroy *all* fabric associated with the Londoners. The contrast

[24] Carson made this very point in a speech in the House of Lords on 14 December 1921. See Hyde (1953), 462-8.

with the recent history of Germany and Poland is salutary: both those countries have been enemies for centuries, yet after the 1939-45 war, during which Poland suffered catastrophic losses of its heritage and people, the great fortress of the Teutonic Knights at Marienburg (now Malbork) has been superbly and lovingly restored by the Polish State, and the former Hanseatic City of Danzig (now Gdańsk) has been reconstructed having been left a pile of rubble. Furthermore, Polish craftsmen and architects were involved in major works of reconstruction, restoration, and conservation in the former German Democratic Republic, notably the old royal palaces at Potsdam and the medieval town of Quedlinburg. Even the post-office building in Gdańsk, scene of fierce fighting in 1939, has been restored, and the new Germany was associated with the re-opening of the building. Such co-operation and careful restoration of monuments of architectural and historical importance by peoples long enemies speak eloquently of reconciliation and the fact that history is important: without noble buildings and ancient monuments national and spiritual impoverishment ensue. If Poland and Germany recognise this fact, the inhabitants of a very small area of the British Isles should be able to do so too.[25]

This book has been written partly as a record of an extraordinary and little-known aspect of history, and is based on documentary evidence: it is also intended to contribute to understanding, to dispel ignorance, and to shed light in dark corners. If it succeeds in doing this to any degree, then it has achieved something positive. That it is a strange story is beyond dispute, for it is most certainly that: it is a tale of the cash-starved Crown forcing ancient Livery Companies to implement a State policy of what was in reality colonisation, and of its convoluted, messy, and rather terrible aftermath. The transformation of The Irish Society from a major force in the implementation of that colonisation to a benevolent agency for reconciliation and charitable purposes is itself of great importance, and augurs well for the future. As The Society nears its quadricentennial, having survived vicious attacks from virtually every quarter (including the Crown it was attempting to serve), fair-minded persons might be permitted an expression of good-will for its further evolution and achievement. The motto of The Society, like that of the City of London, is *Domine, Dirige Nos* (Lord, direct us): it is not inappropriate, given the constraints within which the Londoners have had to work for so many centuries.[26]

25 The author met several Poles working in Potsdam and Quedlinburg when a guest (under the aegis of The British Council) of the East German Ministry of Culture in 1986 and 1987. He visited the huge restoration works at Malbork in 1994, and these are now (1999) almost completed.

26 This chapter draws heavily on the Court Minutes and Local Advisory Committee Minutes at Cutts House, and on information kindly provided by Commander Campbell, Mr. Montgomery, and Mrs. Joy Young (Secretary to The Society's Representative in Ireland from 1987). It uses material taken from sources indicated in the footnotes as well as other matter listed in the present author's 1986 publication on the Londonderry Plantation. Other documents consulted are among The Irish Society's papers at the Corporation of London Records Office.

APPENDIX I

Governors of the Honourable The Irish Society from 30 January 1610

Each Governor was an Alderman of the City of London, and was elected each year at the first Common Council held after 2 February

1610	William Cokayne (*c.*1550-1626)	[6]
1614	George Smithes (d. 1615)	
1615	Thomas Bennett (d. 1627)	
1616	Peter Proby (*c.*1565-1625)	
1622	Robert Johnson (d. 1626)	
1625	Humphrey Handford (1565-1625)	
1625	Robert Parkhurst (d. 1636)	
1636	Edward Bromfield	
1657-60	Thomas Foot (d. 1687)	
1662	Sir Thomas Adams, Bt. (1586-1668)	
1668	John Lawrence (d. 1692)	
1676	William Turner (1615-1693)	
1687	Peter Daniel (d.1700)	
1688	William Prichard (*c.*1632-1705)	
1690	John Lawrence (again)	
1691	William Turner (again)	
1692	Robert Clayton (1629-1707)	
1706	William Withers (1625-1721)	
1721	Francis Forbes (d. 1727)	
1727	Robert Alsop (d. 1737)	
1735	John Barber (1675-1741)	[130]
1741	Daniel Lambert (d. 1750)	
1744	Robert Westley (d. 1745)	
1745	Robert Alsop (resigned 1785) (d. 1785)	
1785	Brass Crosby (1725-93)	
1793	Thomas Harley (1730-1804)	[131]
1798	Paul Le Mesurier (1755-1805)	[132]
1806	Harvey Christian Combe (d. 1818)	
1817	John Thomas Thorp (d. 1835)	[133]
1835	Sir Matthew Wood, Bt. (1768-1843)	[134]
1843	John Humphery (d. 1863)	[135]
1863	(Sir) William Anderson Rose (1820-81)	
1873	Sir Sydney Hedley Waterlow, Bt. (1822-1906)	
1883	Sir John Whittaker Ellis, Bt. (1829-1912)	
1893	Sir George Faudel-Phillips, Bt. (1840-1922)	

130 Portrait in oils on canvas (1737) by Bartholomew Dandridge (1691-*c.*1754) of John Barber (1675-1741), Lord Mayor of London (1732-3) and Governor of The Irish Society (1735-40). A friend of Jonathan Swift and other illustrious contemporaries, he was the lover of Mary de la Rivière Manley (1663-1724), the author of numerous works, after whose death he lived with her former servant, Sarah Dovekin (or Dufkin), as his common-law wife. As a High Tory, he was probably involved in transmitting financial aid to the exiled Stuart Court in 1722. He was a vigorous defender of the City's political liberties and trading interests. (*IS*)

APPENDIX II

Deputy Governors of The Honourable The Irish Society

1611 William Towreson
1613 Martin Bond
1614/25 William Stone
1626/30/32 Samuel Armitage
1631 John Cordell
1633 John Wollaston
1634/5 Samuel Armitage
1636 John Wollaston
1637 Roger Drake
1658 John Sanders
1659 Edward Storey
1660 John Sanders
1662 John Sanders (Charter)
1662 Sir Theophilus Biddulph
1663 Sir Charles Floyd
1664 Thomas Cullen
1665 Thomas Nevill
1666 Thomas Cullen
1667 Thomas Nevill
1668 Nicholas Delves
1669 Thomas Nevill
1670 Robert Jeffreys
1671 Thomas Pilkington
1672 John Short
1673 John Lane
1674 Ralph Box
1675 Thomas Pilkington
1676 Sir Richard Piggot
1677 Thomas Pilkington
1678 Thomas Vernon
1679 Michael Godfrey
1680 Arthur Baron
1681 John Morris
1682 Ralph Box
1683 Thomas Vernon
1688 Thomas Vernon
1689/90 Arthur Baron
1691 Ralph Box
1692 John Morris
1693 Arthur Baron
1694 John Flavell
1694 Robert Knight
1695 Daniel Dorvile
1696 Sir William Coles
1697 Sir Edward Wills
1698 Samuel Powell
1699 Sir B. Gracedieu
1700 Thomas Collett
1701 William Fazackerley
1702 William Walker
1703 John West
1704 John Eggleton
1705 William Walker
1706 John West
1707 Thomas Salter
1708 Sir Benjamin Ayloffe
1709 John Taylor
1710 John West
1711 Samuel Clarke
1712 John Taylor
1713 Braham Smith
1714 Samuel Clarke
1715 Nathaniel Turner
1716 Thomas Preston
1717 William Parrott
1718 Lancelot Skinner
1719 Thomas Breston
1720 Robert Alsop
1721 William Parrott
1722 Wiliam Jenkins
1723 John Cartlick
1724 Robert Alsop
1725 John Colt
1726 Thomas Breston
1727 Thomas Ravenscroft
1728 John Bateman
1729 William Sheldon
1730 John Child
1731 John Thomas
1732 Edward Chowne
1733 Samuel Smith
1734 Thomas Nash
1735 James Heywood
1736 Thomas Sandford
1737 Anthony Lucas
1738 John Webb
1739 Gyles Vincent
1740 John Forty
1741 Giles Mills
1742 Walter Bernard

1743 George Nelson
1744 Robert Alsop
1745 William Arnold
1746 Thomas Pestell
1747 Timothy Helmsley
1748 Thomas Long
1749 Samuel Southouse
1750 Robert Waite
1751 Thomas Harrison
1752 Nathaniel Nash
1753 Robert Wilson
1754 James Walton
1755 Francis Ellis
1756 Jonathan Granger
1757 Samuel Bridgman
1758 John Fashion
1759 Samuel Bates
1760 George Maynard
1761 John Moorey
1762 Samuel Beard
1763 Henry Kent
1764 Samuel Gordon
1765 Edward Ingram
1766 Phillip Milloway
1767 George Hayter
1768 John Pittway
1769 Philip Bell
1770 Thomas Burfoot
1771 Richard Townsend
1772 John Smith
1773 Lawrence Holker
1774 Ingham Forster
1775 Richard Windsor
1776 Stephen Unwin
1777 John Sealy
1778 Charles Sommers
1779 Thomas Holdsworth
1780 Richard Alsager
1781 John Hopkins
1782 Joseph Partridg(e)
1783 Peter Pope
1784 Clement Corderoy
1785 Henry Major
1786 Robert Wyatt
1787 John Adcock
1788 Stephen Langston
1789 Gabriel Leekey
1790 James Andrews
1791 Jacob Wrench
1792 Henry White
1793 Richard Causton
1794 George Bedley
1795 William Deane
1796 William Anderson
1797 James Taddy
1798 William Angell
1799 Benjamin Bovill
1800 Robert Albion Cox
1801 William Row
1802 Edward Kemble
1803 Timothy Baxter
1804 Charles Aldridge
1805 William Mathie
1806 William Hardy
1807 Edward Colebatch
1808 John Fitzwilliam Vandercom
1809 Richard Knight
1810 Edward Wigan
1811 Zachary Langton
1812 James Ebenezer Saunders
1813 Thomas Reeve
1814 Nathaniel Saunders
1815 John Paterson
1816 Thomas Ayres
1817 Edward Hughes
1818 Daniel Britten
1819 William Wadham Cope
1820 James Crook
1821 Mathias Prime Lucas
1822 John Platt
1823 Samuel Weddell
1824 Samuel Favell
1825 Gilpin Gorst
1826 John Drinkald
1827 Jacob George Cope
1828 Henry Prichard
1829 Thomas Whitby
1830 William Day
1831 Robert Westwood
1832 John Locke
1833 Richard Lambert Jones
1834 Thomas Whitby
1835 Walter Anderson Peacock
1836 Edward Tickner
1837 William Richardson
1838 David Allan
1839 John Blacket
1840 William Green
1841 James Toplis
1842 William Hunter
1843 Thomas Quested Finnis
1844 William Jones
1845 Thomas Henry Hall
1846 James Anderton
1847 William Knott
1848 Beniamin Hardwick
1849 Thomas Bridge Simpson
1850 Thomas Dakin
1851 Frederick Farrar
1852 Thomas Watkins
1853 James Low
1854 George Harker

1855	William Rathbone	1911	Sir Harry Bird
1856	Joseph Turnley	1912	Thomas Goldney
1857	Herbert Lloyd	1913	John Stuart Pollock
1858	William Gresham	1914	William Hurst Brown
1859	Thomas Henry Fry	1915	Sir John Pakeman
1860	Henry Wellington Vallance	1916	Sir Frances H. Green, Bt.
1861	George Bone	1917	Harold Elliott Sparks
1862	Frederick Maynard	1918	Charles Perry Whiteley
1863	William Cox	1919	Sir William Robert Dudley Pryke, Bt.
1864	Charles Rose	1920	Vickers Dunfee
1865	Blomfield Burnell	1921	Maurice Jenks
1866	Edward Burkitt	1922	Albert Egerton Legh Slazenger.
1867	Francis Wyatt Truscott	1923	Percy William Berriman Tippetts
1868	John Anderson Cotton	1924	Victor Brown
1869	William Brass	1925	Joseph James Redding
1870	Archibald McDougall	1926	Bertrand Johnson
1871	John Sewell	1927	Cecil Dudley King Farlow
1872	Robert Taylor	1928	Frederick Whittingham
1873	John Thomas Bedford	1929	Humphrey Morris
1874	Mark Sheppard	1930	Athro Charles Knight
1875	James Wyld	1931	George Josiah Berridge
1876	Charles Sawbridge	1932	Sir Charles James Hugh McCrea
1877	William Sutton Gover	1933	Horace Edgar Bowles
1878	Joseph Beck	1934	Robert James Blackham
1879	William Braham	1935	George Edward Withers
1880	William Clapton	1936	John Lockhart Gow
1881	Robert Parker Taylor	1937	George Sampson Elliston
1882	Thomas Loveridge	1938	William Edwyn Shipton
1883	William Charles Simmons	1939	George James Cullum Welch
1884	Richard Clarence Halse	1940	Frank Walter Brundle
1885	Benjamin Biggs	1941	Arthur Stanley Bell
1886	Frank Green	1942	Claud William Dennis
1887	Frederick Prat Alliston	1943	William Frederick Bonser
1888	Alfred Thomas Layton	1944	Charles Gordon Dickson
1889	Alfred Brookman	1945	William Edmund Sykes
1890	John Charles Bell	1946	Alfred Samuel Henderson
1891	Graham King	1947	Reginald Jack Hayward
1892	Pearse Morrison	1948	Thomas Ernest Chester Barratt
1893	George Taylor	1949	Cyprian Charles Oswald Whiteley
1894	Robert Hargreaves Rogers	1950	John Kenneth Newson-Smith
1895	Matthew Wallace	1951	Sidney Joseph Fox
1896	William Henry Pannell	1952	William Watkins Dove
1897	Benjamin Turner	1953	Edward Stuart Hunt
1898	George Berridge	1954	Walter Rose
1899	Thomas Hastings Miller	1955	Dudley Stewart Game
1900	Millar Wilkinson	1956	Donald Eustace Erlebach
1901	Thomas Briggs	1957	Oliver Gordon Sunderland
1902	Charles Valentine Hunter	1958	Frederick William Ingle Lowe
1903	George Briggs	1959	Benjamin George Arthur
1904	William Mann Cross	1960	Sir Gilbert Davis, Bt.
1905	Edward Lee	1961	Dennis Gordon Fisher
1906	Alfred William Read	1962	Norman Cleverton Tremellen
1907	William Cooper	1963	Thomas Cuthbert Harrowing
1908	Edward Ansted	1964	Cyril Frederick Lewis
1909	Alexander Tillie	1965	Norman Lancelot Hall
1910	William James Berriman Tippetts	1966	George Kimberley Perkins

1906 Sir Alfred James Newton, Bt. (1845-1921)
1921 Sir Thomas Vansittart Bowater, Bt. (1862-1938)
1928 Sir Louis Arthur Newton, Bt. (1867-1945)
1933 Sir Charles Albert Batho, Bt. (1872-1938)
1939 Sir William Phené Neal, Bt. (1860-1942)
1943 Sir Maurice Jenks, Bt. (1872-1946)
1945 Sir Percy Walter Greenaway, Bt. (1874-1956)
1950 Sir George Henry Williamson, Bt. (1885-1967)
1955 Sir Frank Samuel Alexander, Bt. (1881-1959)
1958 Sir Denys Colquhoun Flowerdew Lowson, Bt. (1906-75)
1961 Sir Noël Vansittart Bowater Bt. (1892-1984)
1964 Sir Cuthbert Lowell Ackroyd, Bt. (1892-1973)
1967 Sir George James Cullum Welch, Bt. (1895-1980)
1970 Sir Denis Henry Truscott (1908-1989)
1973 Sir Bernard Nathaniel Waley-Cohen, Bt. (1914-1991)
1976 Sir (Hamilton) Edward (de Coucey) Howard, Bt. (1915-)
1976 Alan Raymond, The Lord Mais (1911-93)
1981 Sir Lindsay Roberts Ring (1914-97)
1984 Sir Peter Drury Haggerston Gadsden (1929-)
1987 Sir William Alan Davis (1921-94)
1991 Sir David Kenneth Rowe-Ham (1935-)
1993 Sir Alan Traill (1935-)
1997 Sir Christopher Rupert Walford (1935-)
2000 Sir Richard Everard Nichols (1938-)

131 Portrait in oils on canvas (1794) by T. Hardy of Thomas Harley (1730-1804), Lord Mayor of London (1767-8) and Governor of The Irish Society (1793-7). (*IS*)

132 Portrait in oils on canvas (1798) by T. Hardy of Paul Le Mesurier, Lord Mayor of London (1794-5) and Governor of The Irish Society (1798-1805). His right hand rests on a copy of The Society's Charter of Charles II. (*IS*)

133 Portrait in oils on canvas (1818) by Sir William Beechey (1753-1839) of John Thomas Thorp (d.1835), Governor of The Irish Society (1817-35). (*IS*)

134 Portrait in oils on canvas (*c.*1840), unsigned, of Sir Matthew Wood, Bt. (1768-1843), Lord Mayor of London (1815-17) and Governor of The Irish Society (1835-43). (*IS*)

135 Portrait in oils on canvas (1851) by Henry William Pickersgill (1782-1875) of John Humphery (d.1863), Governor of The Irish Society (1843-63). (*IS*)

1967 Frederick Walter Utting
1968 Robert Guy Shillingford
1969 Thomas Hugh Clifford Amies
1970 Owen Campbell Jones
1971 Richard Theodore Beck
1972 Arthur Brian Wilson
1973 James Mansfield Keith
1974 Cyril Henry Murkin
1975 Sir Thomas Kingsley Collett
1976 John Trevor Yates
1977 Hugh Gansel Brewer
1978 Alfred Burnett Shindler
1979 John Louis Stevenson
1980 Henry Duckworth
1981 Edwin Stephen Wilson
1982 Reginald Thomas Dorrien Wilmot
1983 George Hubert Challis
1984 Laurence St John Thomas Jackson
1985 Duncan William Oxley Lawrence
1986 Cecil Douglas Woodward
1987 Robert Leith Turner
1988 John Holland
1989 Norman Harry Harding
1990 Douglas James Leslie Mobsby
1991 Frederick Michael Bramwell
1992 Ivy Margaret Sharp
1993 Gordon Robert Alexander Wixley
1994 Kevin Malcolm Everett
1995 Philip John Willoughby
1996 Peter Philip Rigby
1997 Gerald Albert George Pulman
1998 Christopher Barry Davies
1999 Keith Allen Sargant
2000 Joyce Carruthers Nash

APPENDIX III

List of Secretaries/Clerks of The Honourable The Irish Society

1615 Samuel Calvert
1621 Clement Moss
1662 John Sprackling (called The Clerk)
1683 William Porter
1685 Michael Ballowe
1697 Augustin Ballowe
1702 James Brace
1743 William Bedell
1747 Francis Sparrow
1760 John Paterson
1789 Robert Slade **[55]**
1827 Robert Slade and Henry Schultes
1831 Henry Schultes
1833 John Ebenezer Davies
1865 Durie Miller **[136]**
1917 James Robert Leverington
1925 Leslie Cyril Landragin
1959 Edmund (Edward) Henry Shackcloth
1968 Barrett Ernest Manning
1993 Simon Francis Norman Waley

136 Portrait in oils on canvas (1907) by Ernest E. Carlos of Durie Miller, Secretary to The Irish Society (1865-1917). (*IS*)

APPENDIX IV

General Agents of The Honourable The Irish Society in Ireland

1611 John Rowley
1613 Tristram Beresford
1664 Col. John Gorges
1675 John Davis
1692 David Cairn(e)s
1707 John Duckett
1729 William Richardson
1755 Henry Hamilton
1789 John Claudius Beresford
1823 John Claudius Beresford Junior
1837 Edward Fletcher
1844 William Green
1863 Walter Green
1874 Arthur Cecil Crampton Plunket
1884 Thomas Bedford Montgomery
1906 Benjamin Hugh Lane
1915 Benjamin Hugh Lane and Edward Maurice Fitz-Gerald Boyle
1916 Edward Maurice Fitz-Gerald Boyle
1925 William Aubrey Lane
1942 Peter William Dickson

From the 1970s the General Agents were called The Society's Representatives in Ireland
1974 Peter Colin Drummond Campbell-Grove
(Later P. C. D. Campbell)
1996 Hugh Edward John Montgomery

Select Glossary

These words were written by some glossator

THOMAS TAYLOR (1768-1835): *Apuleius*, **vii**, 164 n. (1822)

acre. Definite area of land, originally calculated as the amount a yoke of oxen could plough in one day, but settled under various statutes of Kings Edward I, Edward II, and Henry VIII as 4,840 *square yards*, a *yard* being the equivalent of 3 *feet* (36 *inches* or 91.44 *centimetres* [0.9144 *metres*]). An acre is equivalent to 0.405 *hectares*. An *Irish acre* was equivalent to 7,840 square yards English, so 1 *Irish acre* = 1.6155 *English acres* (but see **Plantation acre** below).

Admiralty rights. With the office or jurisdiction of an admiral, i.e. with the hearing and determining of civil and criminal causes associated with the sea; command of ships for defence purposes; policing of shores and inlets; command of fishing and merchant ships; and control of harbours, quays, etc.

advowson. Patronage of an ecclesiastical office, especially the right of presentation to a **benefice** or **living**. Originally the City of London was to enjoy the patronage (see **patron**) of all the churches in the lands to be planted, but subsequently the advowsons were divided between the City and the **bishops** in a ratio of 9 to 6. **The Irish Society's** rights as patron were gradually usurped, and eventually it only retained the rights to the presentation of the **rectory** of Coleraine: that, too, was taken away by the Irish Church Act (32 & 33 Vict., c. 42) of 1869. Advowsons were often held by the persons who built or endowed a church, and so became annexed to the **manor** in which a church stood. A *presentative advowson* was one in which the patron presented a clergyman to the bishop with a request that he be instituted into the vacant living, and the bishop, if satisfied about the presentee's credentials, would then admit and institute him. In a *collative advowson* the bishop himself held the patronage, either in his own right or in the right of the proper patron which had lapsed to him through not being exercised within a certain period after the vacancy occurred. Tardiness or lack of attention seems to have been among the reasons why The Irish Society lost to the bishop all its rights to present clergy to livings, with the one exception of the rectory of Coleraine.

agent. One authorised or with delegated powers to transact business, manage, etc., on behalf of an employer: a deputy, factor, steward, representative, substitute, or emissary. **The Irish Society's** Agent in Ulster became known as its *Representative* in the 20th century.

Alderman. **1**. Chief officer of a **Ward** (administrative division of the City of London). At its inception the **Court** of **Assistants** of **The Irish Society** included five aldermen, and the Governor of The Society was also an alderman. **2**. Magistrate next in dignity to a mayor.

Anglican. Of the Reformed Church of England and other Churches in Communion therewith (e.g. the **Church of Ireland**). The Anglican Church claims to be part of the Holy Catholic Church, approves of catholic dogma and ritual, but repudiates certain tenets of the **Roman Catholic** Church as corruptions and claims national independence of the Roman Papacy. The **Established Church** in England (and in Ireland until 1871), it acknowledges the Sovereign as its Supreme Governor, with the **Archbishop** of Canterbury as its senior churchman. Anglicanism falls into three main groups: *High-Church* (which gives a high place to the authority and claims of the episcopate (*see* **Episcopal**) and the priesthood, to the saving grace of the Holy Sacraments, and to those points of doctrine, discipline, and ritual by which Anglicanism is distinguished from Protestant Nonconformity (*see* **Dissenters**) and Continental *Calvinism*. In its most ritualistic catholic observances, it is sometimes known as *Anglo-Catholic*, *Ritualist*, or even *Smells and Bells*); *Broad-Church* or *Middle-of-the Road* (which avoids incense, many ritualistic trappings, and eschews images, Stations of the Cross, and the like); and *Low-Church* (which has a more **Protestant** character, shies away from anything suggesting Catholicism [even the Cross, and certainly vestments, images, and candles], and is sometimes called *Evangelical*, because it often tends to emphasise Salvation by the Atoning Death of Christ according to the Gospels, denying that either Good Works or the Sacraments have any saving efficacy). The **Church of Ireland** tends in the main to be of the low-church persuasion, especially in **Ulster**.

Anglo-Irish War. Guerrilla campaign by the Irish Volunteers (later known as the Irish Republican Army [I.R.A.]) against Government forces from January 1919 to July 1921. It was concluded by the **Anglo-Irish Treaty**.

Anglo-Irish Treaty. Agreement between the British Government and representatives of the provisional Irish Government on 6 December 1921 ending the **Anglo-Irish War**. By it the Irish Free State became a self-governing Dominion within the British Empire (later Commonwealth). It was ratified by both Governments in 1922.

Apprentice Boys. Protestant political society, founded 1814, so named after the 13 apprentices who shut the gates of Londonderry (7 December 1688) against the Earl of Antrim's Roman Catholic **Jacobite** troops, many of whom were **Redshanks**. This event is celebrated on 18 December, and the lifting of the siege (1689) is also remembered by the Apprentice Boys on 12 August (both dates assume a gap of 11 days between the Old and New Style calendars, rather than 10).

archbishop. **1**. Highest dignitary in an **episcopal** Church, with authority over the **bishops** in his **province**. **2**. A **metropolitan**.

Assistant. Senior person who manages the affairs of a London **Livery Company**, i.e. is a member of the **Court** of Assistants. At its inception **The Irish Society** consisted of a Governor, Deputy Governor, and 24 Assistants, five of whom were to be City of London **Aldermen**, and one of whom was the **Recorder**.

Assizes. Sessions held periodically in each **county** for the administration of civil and criminal justice.

Associated Companies. 43 Lesser **Livery Companies** associated with the 12 Great Companies in the **Plantation** of **Ulster** venture in 12 groups to develop the **Proportions** allocated.

attainted. Subject to an *attainder*, the legal consequence of *outlawry* or a *capital sentence* in respect of *treason* or *felony*, viz. forfeiture of estate real and personal, and corruption of blood, so that one *attainted* could neither inherit nor transmit by descent, and suffered the extinction of all civil rights and capacities. Following the **Flight of the Earls** the **Ulster** Lords suffered *attainder*, and lost their titles, estates, and rights.

auxiliaries. **1**. Recruited from demobilised officers of the British Army from July 1920 in response to the escalation of the **Anglo-Irish War**, they formed a division of the Royal Irish Constabulary (police force). Heavily-armed and highly mobile, they were used to support the R. I. C. Disbanded in 1922, they should not be confused with the **Black and Tans**.

ballibetagh, ballybetagh. Medieval Irish territorial unit consisting of from 12 to 20 **balliboes** or about 16 **townlands**. It was computed at about 960 **acres** assuming a townland contained about 50 or 60 acres.

balliboe, ballyboe. A parcel of land that varied greatly in area depending on the quality of the soil: in barren mountainous districts it might be enormous, but in rich lowland pastures it would be much smaller. It was essentially an *economic* unit, conceived as the residence of a food provider. Assumed by English **Jacobean Plantation** surveyors to be around 60 English **acres**, **The Irish Society's** grants (which included all classes of land) were calculated at a rate of 57 **acres** to the balliboe. The **Livery Company Proportions** tended to be much larger than they appeared on paper: in the Goldsmiths' Proportion, for example, the 44 balliboes contained actual acreages of between 97 to 609, so the average size of a Goldsmiths' balliboe was 143 Irish or 231 English acres. On the Haberdashers' Proportion (56 balliboes) the average size of balliboe was 252 Irish or 408 English acres. Using the balliboe as a measure of area its average size in County **Londonderry** was about 400 English acres rather than the 60 acres estimated by the surveyors and official grants. A balliboe was the approximate equivalent of a **townland**.

barony. Territorial subdivision of a **county** composed of several **townlands** formerly serving as bases for local administration, taxation, and law enforcement. County **Londonderry** was divided into 4 baronies, and there were 273 baronies in Ireland as a whole. Sometimes a barony was derived from the **cantred**. During the **Plantation** of **Ulster** baronies were sometimes called **precincts**.

bawn. Fortified enclosure, usually with projecting corner towers (**flankers**), usually associated with a **manor-house**. **Undertakers** in the **Plantation** of **Ulster** were required to build bawns, and some of those erected by the London **Livery Companies** survive in part.

benefice. **1**. An ecclesiastical **living**. **2**. To endow or invest with a church living.

bishop. Clergyman consecrated for the spiritual government and direction of a **diocese**, ranking beneath an **archbishop** and above the priests or presbyters.

Black and Tans. **1**. Former British soldiers and sailors recruited into the Royal Irish Constabulary (Police Force) from January 1920, who wore khaki military trousers and dark-green R.I.C. tunics, hence their nick-name. They were distinct from the **auxiliaries**, and were disbanded in 1922.

Bull. Papal or **episcopal** edict or mandate (from *bulla*, the seal attached to an official document).

cantred. Territorial unit established by the Anglo-Normans that provided the basis for the subdivision of counties (*see* **county**), not unlike the English **hundred**. Some **baronies** were derived from cantreds which often covered the same area as rural deaneries (*see* **dean**).

capite, in. *Tenere in capite* means to hold (of the King) in chief, so tenure *in capite* meant land held immediately of the King, or of the Crown. *Knight-service* was military service a knight was bound to render as a condition of holding his lands, so *knight-service in capite* meant service to the Crown as such a condition.

Caroline. Of or pertaining to the reign of King Charles I (1625-49).

Carolean. Of or pertaining to the reign of King Charles II (1660-85).

cess. **1**. Government tax 'assessed' to pay for garrisons during the **Tudor Conquest**. **2**. Tax levied by **Grand Juries** on **counties** and **baronies** for the upkeep of roads and bridges from 1634. **3**. Money levied by **Anglican** churchwardens for the upkeep of ecclesiastical buildings (abolished 1833).

Church of Ireland. **1**.The **Protestant Established Church** in Ireland from 1537 to 1871, with the English monarch as its Supreme Governor. Since **disestablishment** under the Irish Church Act (32 & 33 Vict., c. 42) of 1869 (effective from 1 January 1871) it has been independent and self-governing, though a member of the **Anglican** Communion.

Church lands. Land allocated under the **Plantation** scheme for the support of the **Established Church**. In **County Londonderry** Church lands belonged to the **bishop** and **dean** of Derry and to the **archbishop** of Armagh, and parcels were leased to individuals. Church lands comprised some 102,100 acres, plus 14,300 acres of **glebe** land for the support of incumbents.

Church Temporalities (Ireland) Act, 1833. By 3 & 4 Will. IV, c. 37, 10 of the 20 **Anglican** bishoprics in Ireland were united to adjacent **sees** (Derry, for example, was amalgamated with Raphoe); two of the four archbishoprics (Cashel and Tuam) were demoted to bishoprics; the rights of churchwardens to levy Church **cess** for the maintenance of ecclesiastical buildings were revoked; tenants on episcopal lands were permitted to purchase their holdings at a fixed annual rent; and provisions were made for the appointment of ecclesiastical commissioners with powers to divide **livings**, suspend appointments, and use the revenues of the suppressed bishoprics (plus a graduated income tax on livings worth over £200) to build and repair churches and augment poor livings. It significantly reduced the status of the **Church of Ireland** as a self-governing corporation and State Church. The Act caused uproar in England, and prompted John Keble (1792-1866), Anglican divine, Oxford don, and poet, to preach his celebrated sermon in Oxford on 'National Apostasy' (1833), generally reckoned to have triggered the Oxford Movement: this led to the evolution of the Anglo-Catholic, Ritualist, or high-church branch of the Anglican Church, which, in turn, prompted the flowering of **ecclesiology** and the Gothic Revival.

Civil Survey. With the **Gross** and **Down** Surveys, the Civil Survey (1654-6) was an investigation by inquisition of land and land-ownership in every Irish **county** except Clare, Galway, Mayo, Roscommon, and Sligo. It was concerned with **Church lands**, lands owned by the State, and properties owned by persons liable to forfeit: it was thus a preliminary leading to the **Cromwellian** confiscation and resettlement. It contains invaluable information on County **Londonderry** (*See* Simington [ed.][1937] 142-246).

clan. Descent group (*clann* means children, descendants, or race) often with common interests in land ownership. Political clout exercised by a clan chief was territorially based. The term identifies groups claiming a common ancestry and with a well-defined hierarchy controlling a larger area than would be dominated by a **sept**. Followers, tenants, and others living on a clan's territories were not necessarily related by blood to the clan proper. Powerful Ulster family-groups included O'Donnell (Ó Domhnaill) of Tír Conaill (Tirconnell), O'Neill (Ó Néill) of Tír Eóghain (Tyrone), O'Cahan (Ó Catháin) of Fir Lí (later the baronies (*see* **barony**) of Coleraine and Keena[u]ght), O'Doherty (Ó Dochartaigh) of Inis Eóghain (Inishowen), and Maguire (Mág Uidhir) of Feara Manach (Fermanagh).

common socage. *See* **socage**.

conacre. Subletting of land in small parcels for a season for one crop, commonly potatoes, by which agricultural labourers, investing all their earnings, sought to feed their families. The system broke down when potato blight appeared, and led to widespread famine (*see* **Famine**), ruin, and agrarian violence in Ireland.

Confederate War. Known as the *Eleven Years' War* (1641-53), it was associated with the War of the Three Kingdoms, and saw a general uprising of **Roman Catholics** in Ireland leading to general devastation, confiscation of land, and the **Cromwellian settlement**. It was named after the Confederation of Roman Catholic Irish, **Old English**, and some **New English** formed after the outbreak of the Great Rebellion of 1641.

Conformity. Compliance with the form of religion legally established, i.e. with the rites, discipline, and doctrines of the **Anglican** Church in Ireland (*see* **Established Church**) as prescribed by the various Acts of Uniformity. **Roman Catholics** who conformed, recanted their former religious persuasion, took Anglican Communion, and registered with the Court of Chancery were released from restrictions on property, public life, marriage, and entry to the legal profession. It follows, therefore, that anybody who did not conform as defined above was a *Nonconformist* or a **Dissenter**.

county. Territorial division, or **shire**, created from the time of the Anglo-Norman colonisation of the 12th century. **Ulster** west of the Bann was effectively shired from 1604, and to each county a **Sheriff** (in whom administrative, legal, and military powers were vested) was appointed by the Crown. Each county contained smaller administrative districts called **baronies**.

Court. **1**. Assembly or meeting of members of a Company, Corporation, or Guild, such as the Court of **The Irish Society**. **Livery** Company Courts were often referred to as the *Court of Assistants*. **2**. Assembly of judges or other persons legally appointed and acting as a tribunal to hear and determine any cause.

court-baron. Assembly of **freehold** tenants of a **manor** under the presidency of the lord of the manor or his steward.

court leet. **Court** of record held in a **manor** or **barony**.

Court of Wards and Liveries. An instrument of taxation, established in 1622 as an attempt to reduce the continual demands made upon the Royal Treasury by Ireland. In a nutshell, an heir to property was obliged to apply to the **Court** for legal delivery of his estates, by suing for his **Livery** (i.e. paying a sum of money, or a 'fine', into the Court for obtaining rights to his lands). It tended to discriminate against **Gaelic Irish** and **Old English**, who were, for the most part, **Roman Catholics**, and caused much resentment, as it did not apply to **Planters**. It was abolished in 1662 (14 & 15 Chas. II, c. 19).

Cromwellian land settlement. Following the **Confederate** (or *Eleven Years')* **War**, large tracts of Irish territory in the hands of **Roman Catholics** were seized and redistributed among those who had financed or served in the reconquest of Ireland by Oliver Cromwell (1600-58). A three-part survey was ordered in 1653 to facilitate the identification of land (the **Civil Survey** [by jury inquisition] the **Gross Survey** [by estimates] and the **Down Survey** [by mapping]), as a result of which over 1,000 adventurers acquired over a million **acres**, and several thousand soldiers obtained interests in estates. The system of estates thus created survived until late in the 19th century.

Customs and Excise. *Customs* are duties payable on imported or exported goods. *Excise* duties are taxes levied on goods produced within a country, or associated with certain trades or manufactures (e.g. alcoholic drink).

dean. **1**. Head of the *Chapter* of a cathedral-church. **2**. *Presbyter* invested with jurisdiction or precedence (under the **bishop** or archdeacon) over a division of a **diocese**. A **deanery** is **1**. a group of parishes, forming a division of a diocese, over which a rural dean presides, or **2**. the official residence of a dean.

Declaratory Act. An Act of Parliament (6 Geo I, c. 5) by which the dependancy of the Kingdom of Ireland upon the Crown of Great Britain was secured. It asserted the British Parliament's rights to pass legislation binding on Ireland, and denied that the Irish House of Lords had any appellate jurisdiction. It caused much resentment.

Defenders. **Roman Catholic** secret society which entered into a formal alliance with the **United Irishmen** in 1796. Intent on political and social transformation of Ireland, it was partly imbued with selective ideas promoted by the French Revolution, but by 1798 there were elements within the movement determined to settle scores with 'heretics' (i.e. **Protestants**), which led to the sectarian killings in the south-east that would be termed 'ethnic cleansing' today.

demesne. Possession as one's own, i.e. in one's hands as possessor by *free tenure*, or immediately from the Crown.

Derry. From *Doire*, meaning 'place of the oaks', an 'oak grove', or a 'thick wood', was situated on high ground commanding the west bank of the River Foyle. It does not appear to have been used by the Irish without an additional epithet, such as Derry-Calgach (oak-wood of Calgach). The site of an ancient monastery, modern Derry was founded by Sir Henry Dowcra (*c.*1560-1631) in 1600, but was completely replanned and newly edified by **The Irish Society** after 1613, and was called **Londonderry** thereafter.

diocese. Sphere of jurisdiction of a **bishop**; a **see**.

disestablishment. Removal of the privileged position of the **Church of Ireland**, intended by Gladstone as part of his policy of pacifying Ireland. The **Anglican Established Church** in Ireland was, in fact, a minority Church, and it was disestablished (effective from 1871) by the Irish Church Act of 1869 (32 & 33 Vict., c. 42).

Dissenters. All who refused to conform (*see* **Conformity**) to the requirements of the **Established Church**. In early use *Dissenters* included **Roman Catholics**, but from *c.*1660 the term came to mean **Protestant** *Nonconformists* who remained separated from the **episcopal Church of Ireland** (**Anglican**), and included Presbyterians, Baptists, Quakers, Independents, Unitarians, and Congregationalists. Immigrant groups, including Huguenots and Moravians, were also classed as Dissenters, although the former seem to have become Anglicans quite quickly. Later, Methodists and various small Protestant sects were also described as Dissenters. A *Dissenter* is sometimes distinguished from a *Nonconformist* in that the term is restricted to those who not only dissent from the National Established Church as constituted, but who reject any National or State Church. Some 18th-century Anglican opinion was less well-disposed towards Dissenters than to Roman Catholics, but the sectarian outrages of the 1798 rebellion changed such views.

Down Survey. At the end of the **Confederate War** much land was confiscated, and all forfeited lands previously identified in the **Civil Survey** were carefully mapped under the direction of Dr (later Sir) William Petty (1623-87). This vast exercise was so called because the information was set *down* on maps, and the results were drawn by parishes in a more accurate form than anything attempted earlier. It was intended as a record of land to be set apart and distributed to soldiers in 22 counties.

dressings. Cut or moulded stones, carved accurately and properly finished, as, e.g. round window- or door-openings, or quoins, etc.

ecclesiology. Study of church forms and traditions, especially relating to the design, furnishing, and decoration of churches. It blossomed from the 1830s, and led to the powerful movements of 19th-century religious revival in the **Anglican** Church and (most significantly) to the Gothic Revival in architecture and design.

Eleven Years' War. *See* **Confederate War**.

episcopal. Pertaining to a **bishop** or bishops. An episcopal Church is one with bishops, e.g. the **Anglican** Church.

erenach, erenagh. **1**. Lay guardian of a parish church, or administrator of ecclesiastical **temporalities** (i.e. material possessions of the Church or clergy), usually under dynastic control. The existence of such a system was frowned upon by the Papal authorities, and tended to undermine the authority of **archbishops**, **bishops**, and priests. **2**. By extension, therefore, an hereditary tenant of ecclesiastical lands, known, therefore, as *erenagh lands*.

escheat. An incident in feudal law whereby a fief reverted to the lord. Thus the lapsing of land to the Crown or to the lord of the **manor** on the death of the owner intestate without heirs. As any **attainted** person (one outlawed in respect of treason or felony, and thus having all civil rights and capacities extinguished) could have no legal heir, his property suffered escheat. One attainted suffered a 'stain or corruption of blood of a criminal capitally condemned, the immediate inseparable consequence of the Common Law'. The **Flight of the Earls** of Tyrone and Tyrconnell and the Lord of Fermanagh (Cúchonnacht Maguire) in 1607 was judged to be treason, and so their lands were escheated and forfeited to the Crown as attainted persons.

Established Church. The Church as by law established as the public or State-recognised form of religion. In England it was the English branch of the western Church, which, at the Reformation, repudiated the supremacy of the Pope, and asserted that of the Sovereign over all persons and in all causes, ecclesiastical as well as temporal, in his Dominions. In Ireland King Henry VIII was recognised as Supreme Head of the **Church of Ireland** by 28 Hen. VIII, c. 5 in 1536, and the **Anglican** Church remained the Established Church in Ireland until 1871 when Gladstone's Irish Church Act of 1869 (32 & 33 Vict., c. 42) disestablished (*see* **disestablishment**) and partly disendowed the **Protestant episcopal** Church.

Famine. Failure of food supplies has occurred since the beginning of time, and the causes have been many, including inclement weather, war, disease, and so on. Ireland suffered from severe famines from the end of the 12th to the beginning of the 20th centuries. Heavy rains and bad summers accounted for some disasters, but the **Confederate War** from 1641 wrecked the agricultural economy and brought about famine. The introduction of the potato to Ireland (possibly in the late 16th-century, but certainly by 1606) was a mixed blessing: easy to grow on small patches of ground, the potato was rich in food value, and could keep whole families well-nourished, but dependency on one crop was a potential source of trouble. The first potato crisis occurred in 1740-1, and probably killed as many people as the so-called *Great Famine* of 1845-9. The catastrophe of the Great Famine was caused by the failure of the potato-crop through a fungal disease ('potato blight', or *phytophthora infestans*), exacerbated by reliance on the potato as the staple diet by small farmers (about a third of the population). Although relief was provided by private individuals, the gentry, organisations, the Churches, and the Government, the problem was compounded by the prevailing belief that to disrupt *laissez-faire* by intervening on a large scale would wreck the economy. Furthermore, response in Great Britain began to become less sympathetic to Ireland's plight because an economic recession bit deeply in the 1840s, and 36 Irish anti-Union M.P.s were returned in the general election of that year. In 1848 the Chartist agitation in England, led by Feargus O'Connor (1794-1855), M.P. for County Cork, the revolutions in France and elsewhere in Europe, and the abortive Young Ireland rebellion in Ireland further alienated opinion in Great Britain. It should also be remembered that bad harvests and potato blight were not confined to Ireland: Great Britain suffered abominably too.

Yet in 1845-6 Sir Robert Peel (1788-1850) and the Tory Government purchased cheap corn from America for distribution in Ireland and began a programme of public works to be administered by the **Grand Juries** and the Board of Works. As a response to the failure of the potato crop in Ireland the Corn Laws were repealed in 1846 (9 & 10 Vict., c.22), enabling cheap corn to be imported, but driving huge numbers of agricultural labourers off the land in Great Britain and into the towns, and shifting the balance of power from the old landowning classes to the rising industrialists and entrepreneurs of the manufacturing districts. Very soon the majority of the population of Great Britain lived in towns, and protection of agriculture was withdrawn. The myth that England did nothing while Ireland starved is untrue: England destroyed the structure of its rural economy so that Ireland might be fed, and very soon became itself dependent on food imports rather than home-grown produce to survive.

Further attempts to feed the destitute in Ireland by means of soup-kitchens led to the distribution of three million meals per day in 1847 under the Destitute Poor (Ireland) Act (10 Vict., c.7), and the Poor Relief (Ireland) Act (10 Vict., c. 31) empowered the Boards of Guardians to grant outdoor relief to the poor, but here local Irish organisation proved inadequate to the task. Vitamin deficiencies led to disease and blindness among children in the workhouses, and throughout Ireland most deaths were not the results of actual starvation, but of disease caused not only by a lack of vitamins, but by widespread ignorance of basic hygiene (and lack of such provision) exacerbated by large numbers congregating in confined spaces. Typhus became widespread, and Asiatic cholera added to the horrors in 1848.

Some commentators believed that the disaster presented an opportunity to reform Irish agriculture by amalgamating very small farms and encouraging the surplus population to emigrate or move to the growing towns. The Government, ever mindful of economies, was keen to get as much money as possible out of Irish landlords to pay for the crisis and the provision of relief (several Boards of Guardians complained of the intolerable burdens of relieving the destitute from the local rates). Drastic falls in rent receipts and more taxation led to wholesale evictions (in 1849 the constabulary recorded some 90,000 evictions, and in 1850 over 100,000), and reduced the population still further through disease and emigration (between 1845 and 1851 Ireland's population declined by 20 per cent, and never rose again to its pre-Famine level). Thus the social structure of Irish society was drastically altered, leaving legacies of hatred to this day. Yet, but for the Great Famine, it is at least debatable if Ireland would be seen as more susceptible to famine than other European countries before then. Disputes still rage concerning questions about how much or how little the Government did or could have done to alleviate conditions. In such debates the unenviable fate of the English agricultural labourer, driven in tens of thousands from the land as a result of the repeal of the Corn Laws, is usually ignored. History is never as straightforward as some would like to believe. It has to be said, though, that 19th-century Ireland was very unlucky.

County **Londonderry** escaped the worst effects of the famine, as **The Irish Society** and some of the **Livery Companies** had reformed agriculture, amalgamated farms, and given financial assistance to potential emigrants, so the rural economy was better balanced and not entirely dependent on one crop. For these reforms George Vaughan Sampson was responsible. The main problem was the influx of destitute poor flooding into the **county** from County Donegal (where the rural economy had collapsed) and elsewhere which placed an intolerable burden on organisations and individuals, notably in Londonderry itself. Minutes of The Irish Society contain references to the problem, and record numerous grants and other attempts to alleviate matters. *See* Kennedy, Ell, Crawford, and Clarkson (1999) for the famine thoughout Ireland, and Johnston (1959) for County Londonderry in 1834.

farmer. **1**. One who collects revenues, taxes, etc. (e.g. rents or **tithes**), paying a fixed sum to the landlord for the privilege and retaining the balance as profit. Most London **Livery Companies** initially leased their **Proportions** to 'farmers', often for a 'fine' (i.e. a lump sum) and an annual rent, for a fixed term. **2**. One who has a lease of anything. **3**. One who rents land for the purpose of cultivation, i.e. a *tenant-farmer*. **4**. One who cultivates and develops land for the owner, i.e. a *bailiff* or *steward*. **5**. One who cultivates a farm, whether as tenant or owner, or who makes agriculture his occupation.

fee. Estate in land held on condition of homage and service to a superior lord by whom it is granted and in whose ownership it remains.

fee-farm. Tenure at a fixed rent without services. This was the common arrangement in Ireland, and the **native freeholds** were held of **The Irish Society** by Irish gentlemen in fee-farm. During the 19th century The Irish Society made grants of property on a large scale to tenants in Coleraine and Londonderry, very much in line with major changes as a result of the various enactments of the time.

fee-simple. Estate belonging to an owner and his heirs in perpetuity, without limitation: in absolute possession.

fee-tail. Estate of inheritance entailed, or limited, to some particular class of heirs of the person to whom it is granted.

fishings. The fishings or fisheries were among the most important assets that induced the City of London to become involved in the **Plantation** of **Ulster**. The Rivers Bann (from the sea to Lough Neagh, including the river-bed and the banks up to high-water level) and Foyle (upstream as far as Lifford) with their tributaries were included in the grant. Various disputes with persons who had also been granted or had usurped fishing-rights led to long and expensive litigation, notably with the bishops of Derry and the Chichester (Donegall) family. Following an Act of Parliament which resolved the dispute with the bishop, The Irish Society in 1705 also acquired fishings including those at Camus-juxta-Mourne (upstream from Strabane), on the Finn, and on the Derg (Ardstraw). It should be noted that these included fishings in the counties of Donegal and Tyrone. Details of the fishings are given throughout the chapters of this book.

flanker. Part of a fortification projecting to flank or defend another part, e.g. the projecting structures at the corners of **bawn** walls from which fire could be directed at any attacker.

Flight of the Earls. The sudden departure from Lough Swilly of Hugh (Aodh) O'Neill (*c.*1550-1616), 2nd Earl of Tyrone, Rory (Ruaidhrí) O'Donnell (1575-1608), Earl of Tyrconnell, and Cúchonnacht Óg Maguire (d. 1608), Lord of Fermanagh, with their followers, on 4 September 1607. It left huge tracts of land **escheat** to the Crown, and paved the way for the **Plantation** of **Ulster**.

free burgage. **1**. Tenure whereby lands or tenements in towns were held by the King or other lord for a certain yearly rent. **2**. Freehold property in a borough (in Ireland subject to an annual rent).

freehold. Property free of any duty save to the monarch. In Ireland a freehold was not quite what it was in England, and involved payment of a rent, so a native freeholder (*see* **native freehold**) was really the recipient of a grant of land from the major grantee, and was obliged to pay a rent. In County **Londonderry** Irish gentlemen held their freeholds of **The Irish Society** in **fee-farm**.

Freeman. One possessing the Freedom of a city, company, guild, etc., with certain rights and privileges.

Gaelic Ireland. Those parts of Ireland and its people adhering to the Irish language and customs, and where the **clan** system held sway. Its predominant religious persuasion was **Roman Catholic**.

Gallicanism. Reduction of papal power by the State or other means. It was particularly the case in France under King Louis XIV (reigned 1643-1715) that led to the intervention of the Papacy in cementing the Grand Alliance in which William of Orange (1650-1702) was a leading light against France. In Ireland the **Old English** attempted to reconcile their allegiance to the Crown with loyalty to the Papacy, which might be described as a variation on Gallicanism, and during the 19th century divided loyalties once more surfaced, the Irish **Roman Catholic** hierarchy accusing the teachers at Maynooth College of Gallican tendencies because that institution enjoyed the support of a State grant, had independent governing arrangements, and had strong connections with French ecclesiological scholarship.

gavelkind. System of tribal succession by which land, on the death of its occupant, passed into the common stock, and the whole area was redistributed among male members of the **sept**. Gavelkind encouraged fragmentation of landholdings and was probably a major factor in preventing the erection of permanent dwellings in Ireland. In certain districts redistribution of lands took place every year, even when no death had occurred.

glebe. Portion of land assigned to a clergyman as part of his **benefice**.

Graces. Concessions promised but not delivered to Irish **Roman Catholics** by King Charles I (reigned 1625-49) in return for subsidies and/or support.

Grand Jury. Nominated by the High **Sheriffs**, it was drawn from property owners in each **county**, and ruled on the validity of indictments at the **Assizes** before a case could be heard. It also levied the **cess** to pay for the roads and bridges in the county, and its powers were later extended to order the building of court-houses, gaols, infirmaries, lunatic asylums, fever-hospitals, etc. Matters concerning Grand Juries were consolidated under 6 & 7 Will. IV, c. 116, but the Juries were abolished in Northern Ireland during the 1970s.

Gross Survey. Part of the Great Survey of lands in Ireland from 1653, essentially a 'measurement of the surround of whole Baronies', carried out under the direction of Benjamin Worsley (*c.*1617-77), Surveyor-General of Forfeited Estates. However, the returns of the Gross Survey were so unsatisfactory that it was stopped in 1654, and work concentrated on the **Civil** and **Down** Surveys, under the direction of Dr (later Sir) William Petty (1623-87), who incurred the jealousy and hatred of Worsley.

High King. Term used to describe the most powerful Irish Kings of the period before the Anglo-Norman Conquest. Its precise meaning is disputed, but it implies some kind of overlordship.

Holy Roman Empire. There was a tradition of the old Roman Empire, preserved by the **Roman Catholic** Church as an idea, and by that Church as a fact in its imperial organisation. The Coronation of Charlemagne as Emperor of the West in 800 created an important precedent for the Holy Roman Empire of the German nation, a union of German-speaking lands, northern Italy, and (after 1032) Burgundy under single rule. The Empire is generally reckoned to have begun on Candlemas Day 962 with the Coronation by Pope John XII (955-64) of Otto I (born 912, German King from 936, and Roman Emperor 962-73), expanded with the acquisition of northern Sicily under the Hohenstaufen emperors (1152-1250), and became a federation of Princes under Rudolph of Habsburg (German King 1273-91), after which most of Italy was lost and the Empire became more Germanic in character. From about 1077 the principle of elected kingship became established (with the *Imprimatur* of the Papacy), and from the 13th century a body of German Princes was formed as Electors (*Kurfürsten*): after 1356 the Electors were the three Rhineland Archbishops of Cologne, Mainz, and Trier, and four lay magnates (the Count Palatine of the Rhine, the Duke of Saxony, the Margrave of Brandenburg, and the King of Bohemia). Later, as a result of upheavals during the Thirty Years' War (1618-48), the vote of the Count Palatine was transferred to the Duke of Bavaria, a new vote was created for the Count Palatine, and in 1708 a ninth vote was established for Hanover. The House of Habsburg, however, had established a *de facto* right to the imperial Crown, and this rendered the importance of the electoral college (with perquisites) of only symbolic value. With secularisation of the ecclesiastical principalities (1803) and abolition of the Empire (1806 — when the *Austrian Empire* came into being), the offices of Elector became extinct.

The Empire was an important ally of William of Orange in the wars of the late 17th century, and was of fundamental significance in stopping the Turkish advance into Europe, containing the expansionist aims of France, and eventually (as Austria) helping to defeat Napoleon in the early 19th century.

Home Rule. The aim of 'Constitutional Nationalism', it was nevertheless vague and ambiguous, meaning many things. Gladstone (influenced by the ideas of Isaac Butt [1813-79] and the colonial precedents of, e.g., Canada) envisaged an Irish 'Assembly' of two chambers to run internal affairs, with Parliament in Westminster retaining control of foreign policy, the armed forces, currency, security, and (of course) taxation. More extreme Republican Nationalists saw Home Rule as a stepping-stone to full independence and the establishment of an Irish Republic, but virtually all arguments for Home Rule ignored the interests of a (then) largely Protestant north-east **Ulster**, the demographic character of which was directly attributable to the **Plantation**. It is one of history's curiosities that the only part of Ireland granted Home Rule was two-thirds of Ulster, which was utterly opposed to the whole idea: in the south the concept foundered and a provisional Government, the Dáil Éireann, was established quite independently of any Home Rule arrangements. The whole matter of Home Rule split and virtually destroyed the old Liberal party, part of which joined the Conservatives (re-named the Conservative and Unionist party).

hundred. Subdivision of a **county** or **shire**, having its own **court**.

impropriation. Annexation of a **benefice** or its revenues to a corporation, office, or individual (especially to a lay corporation or lay proprietor). *Impropriate* is to place **tithes** or ecclesiastical property in lay hands. After the Reformation most impropriations passed to lay interests.

Irish Society, The. The Society of the Governor and Assistants, London, of the New Plantation in Ulster, within the Realm of Ireland, also known as The London Society, The Honourable The Irish Society, or The Irish Society, was established in 1610 as a body within the City of London to consist of a Governor, Deputy Governor, and 24 Assistants, the Governor and five Assistants to be Aldermen of the City, and the other Assistants to be Commoners. The **Recorder** of the City was always to be one of the Assistants. The Society was authorised to hold **Courts**, to treat of and determine all matters and causes concerning the **Plantation** of **County Londonderry**, to direct operations in Ireland by letter and by other means, to administer all cash raised (mostly by the **Livery Companies**) for the Plantation venture, and to exercise control on behalf of the City of London over the entire undertaking. Any decision of The Irish Society's Court would have the same authority as that of the Common Council of the City itself. The Court had full powers to appoint its own officers, and to collect and disburse money raised by the City for the Plantation.

The Irish Society resembled the governing bodies of other contemporary 17th-century **joint-stock companies** established for purposes of trade and colonisation (e.g. the East India Company, the Virginia Company, the Newfoundland Company, and the Bermuda Company). The East India Company (1600), for example, had a Governor and 24 'committees' to manage all of its activities. The Virginia Company's second charter (1609) established a 52-person council with sweeping powers to govern and establish the Plantation in America, and indeed there are many parallels between the Virginia and **Ulster** Plantations. Cokayne, first Governor of The Irish Society, was a leading light in financing the expedition of William Baffin (d. 1622) to explore Greenland (1612), and had 'Cockin's Sound' named after him. It should also be remembered that there were precedents for Plantations in Ireland itself, notably those in Munster (from 1583 and 1601). The Common Council of the City of London had a similar relationship with The Irish Society as the joint-stock companies associated with other schemes of Plantation had enjoyed with their committees of management. The Irish Society had been called a 'Standing Committee of the Common Council, entrusted with the general management' of the City of London's Plantation, 'and essentially subordinate' to the Common Council, but in practice it was (and is) virtually autonomous, and had enormous powers over the city and **Liberties** of Londonderry, the town and Liberties of Coleraine, the **Customs**, the **fisheries** of the Rivers Foyle and Bann and their tributaries, the waters of Lough Foyle and the rivers that flowed into it, **Admiralty rights**, **advowsons**, and much else, including a certain amount of control over the Company **Proportions**.

At the end of the 20th century it still has considerable assets, income from which is used for maintenance, administration, charitable and benevolent purposes.

Jacobean. Of or pertaining to the reign of King James I and VI of Great Britain and Ireland (1603-25).

Jacobite. Adherent of King James II and VII (reigned 1685-8) and his immediate descendants, the 'Old Pretender' (James Francis Edward Stuart — known to his followers as King James III and VIII [1688-1766]), the 'Young Pretender' (Charles Edward Louis Philip Casimir [1720-88]— called by some King Charles III), and Henry Benedict Maria Clement (1725-1807 — Cardinal Duke of York, styled King Henry IX by his followers).

joint-stock company. Company consisting of seven or more members having a permanent paid-up or nominal stock or capital of fixed amount, divided into shares, also of fixed amount, and formed on the principle of having for its members the holders of shares in such capital, and no other persons.

kern(e). Band of Irish foot-soldiers of guerrillas, from *ceithearn*, meaning a 'war-band'. An individual soldier was a *ceithearnach*. In the early days of the **Ulster Plantation** they were known as the wood-kern(e)s because they took to the forests and intimidated local inhabitants into feeding, sheltering, and protecting them.

knight-service. *See* ***capite, in***

Lady Day. 25 March (the Feast of the Annunciation), the start of a New Year according to the Old Style (pre-Gregorian) calendar.

Land Acts. A series of Acts of Parliament that transformed land-ownership in Ireland by breaking up the big estates and establishing small farms run by owner-occupiers. The Acts destroyed the power-bases of the largely **Protestant** Anglo-Irish landed gentry and aristocracy, and the first were introduced by W. E. Gladstone (1809-98), who, some claim, became convinced of the necessity to make concessions to Irish Nationalists in order to safeguard the United Kingdom, but others have seen his efforts partly as ill-advised appeasement and partly as a cynical attempt to buy the support of Irish M.P.s who often held such power that Government business could not proceed without their abstention or votes. In the event, Ireland was lost to the kingdom, and heralded the disintegration of the British Empire in the 20th century. The main enactments were the Landlord and Tenant (Ireland) Act, 1870 (33 & 34 Vict., c. 46), the Land Law (Ireland) Act, 1881 (44 & 45 Vict., c. 49), the Purchase of Land (Ireland) Act, 1885 (48 & 49 Vict., c. 73), the Purchase of Land (Ireland) Act, 1891 (54 & 55 Vict., c. 48), the Irish Land Act, 1903 (3 Edw. VII, c. 37), the Irish Land Act, 1909 (9 Edw. VII, c. 42), and subsequent legislation of the Irish Free State (1923) and Northern Ireland (1925).

The London **Livery Companies**, like other landlords, suffered during the so-called 'Land War' (a campaign of agrarian protest beginning in the 1870s, which encouraged the withholding of rents, and agitation [often violent] against property and persons). This 'Land War' was, like **disestablishment** and much else, part of the 19th-century campaign of Irish Nationalism leading to **Home Rule** and, eventually, the separation of 26 counties in Ireland from the United Kingdom.

Liberties. 1. Districts over which a corporation's privileges extend, such as those parts of **County Londonderry** formerly in Counties Antrim and Donegal forming the Liberties of, or lands laid to, Coleraine and Londonderry respectively, held by **The Irish Society**. **2.** Property of a church, or of an ecclesiastical foundation, exempt from certain secular powers.

linen. Flax was grown in Ireland from the earliest times, and linen garments were commonly worn throughout the medieval period. Rapid expansion of linen manufacture occurred during the 18th century, and the labour-intensive cultivation of flax rose dramatically from the Napoleonic wars to around 150,000 **acres** by 1850. Flax-seed was imported, mostly from America, Russia, and The Netherlands, and by 1800 about 80 per cent of all flax in Ireland was grown in **Ulster**, much on very small holdings rented out to weaver-farmers. The **Plantation** encouraged linen-workers and merchants from Great Britain and Europe to settle in Ulster, and Government policies from 1696 helped the industry to develop so that by 1796 exports included 47 million yards of linen. Growing flax, spinning yarn, and weaving cloth were activities suited to very small farms, but by 1830 linen was being produced in factories, most of which were in east Ulster. Belfast became the world's most important linen-manufacturing centre by 1860, earning the town the nickname 'Linenopolis'. The industry declined after the 1914-18 war, and virtually disappeared after 1945 as demand for linen sheets, table-cloths, napkins, shirts, and underwear suffered terminal collapse.

Livery. 1. Legal delivery of a property into a person's possession. To *sue for one's Livery* means to institute a suit as heir to obtain possession of lands e.g. in the hands of the **Court of Wards** (1622-62). This cost money, and led to considerable resentment. **2.** Special robes or clothes worn by members of a **Livery Company**.

Livery Company. Derived from the medieval guilds that were widespread throughout Europe, the Companies (such as those of London) were secular organisations associated with a trade or a craft, but were also very much concerned with the spiritual welfare of the brethren and sisters. It was expensive to keep an altar and maintain a priest expressly to offer Masses and prayers for the repose of the souls of those who had died: such an endowment was called a *chantry*, and only very rich individuals could afford this, so one of the functions of a Company or Guild was to endow a chantry ensuring that the dead would be given succour in perpetuity. Companies also regulated entry to a trade or craft by means of an apprenticeship system: once the process of training had been completed (normally lasting seven years) an apprentice could claim his Freedom, which granted privileges including immunity from tolls at markets and fairs, freedom from impressment into the armed forces, and rights to vote at **Ward** and Parliamentary elections. Those without the Freedom had no voice in the government of the City of London, the municipal structure of which was created on the principle of the Freedom.

Each Company, regulated by a governing body, acquired a **Court** composed of a **Master** (normally elected for one or two years at a time), one to four **Wardens** (from whom the Master would be elected), and a number of **Assistants**, with a clerk to keep the books, and a beadle to assist the clerk, lead processions, and so on. Members of a Company were Apprentices, Journeymen (or Yeomen who had served their apprenticeships but still had to obtain their Freedom), Freemen, and Liverymen (those who had set up in business on their own, were Freemen, had been admitted as full members of the Company, could eventually become members of the **Court**, and were entitled to wear a special **Livery** or set of robes). Many Companies obtained permanent meeting-places called *Halls*, where deliberations, feasts, and ceremonies took place, and to this day the Companies play an important part in the government of the City of London as well as supporting commerce, trade, and charities.

Fifty-five Livery Companies of the City of London participated in the **Londonderry Plantation**, and supplied the bulk of the finance for **The Irish Society** and the huge programme of construction works in **Ulster**. Each of the Great Companies (Mercers, Grocers, Drapers, Fishmongers, Goldsmiths, Merchant Taylors, Skinners, Haberdashers, Salters, Ironmongers, Vintners, and Clothworkers) was granted an estate (or **Proportion**) by lot in County Londonderry. The Grocers and Merchant Taylors were unusual in that they held their estates alone: the other Companies had Associates in the form of Lesser Companies (the Vintners, for example, had eight

Associated Companies as well as some connections with the Grocers, who had oversubscribed, so the balance went into the Vintners' Proportion).

living. An ecclesiastical **benefice**.

Londonderry. **1**. Name of the **county** created for the City of London to colonise as a key part of the **Plantation** of **Ulster**. **2**. Name of the new city erected on the site of **Derry** by **The Irish Society** on behalf of the City of London in the 17th century.

Londonderry, siege of. During the international conflicts at the end of the 17th century Londonderry was besieged by a **Jacobite** force (18 April - 31 July 1689) under French command. The heroism of the defenders (mostly a citizen army) was much lauded at the time and entered into folklore.

Lord Deputy. The chief governor of Ireland, essentially the Sovereign of England's representative (the monarch was Lord of Ireland from the 12th until the 16th centuries, when the lordship became a kingdom).

Lord Lieutenant. Title of the Viceroy of Ireland from the Restoration of the Monarchy in 1660. The office had considerable powers of patronage, and from 1772 Lords Lieutenant were expected to be permanently resident in Ireland.

Lords Justices. Temporary governors of Ireland in the absence of a **Lord Deputy** or **Lord Lieutenant**.

manor. Land held in **demesne** (by the lord of the manor) to which was attached a **seignory** over **freehold** tenants sufficient in number to constitute a **court-baron** which the lord was obliged to hold and the tenants to attend. It was a unit of territorial organisation, essentially an instrument of lordship for defence and to exploit agriculture and trade. Historically, the lord of the manor had considerable powers: under him knights held their lands by giving military service; tenants paid rent; burgesses (burgage tenants of a medieval borough) were entitled to plots fronting the high street of a town, and enjoyed certain privileges, including protection from external competitors, the right to have their own **courts** for the hearing of pleas within the borough, and ability to buy and sell burgage lands; and serfs had tenures by which they paid with labour, although they enjoyed some protection from the manorial courts (or **courts leet**). By the time of the **Plantation** manors and their organisation were much simpler, and the relationship was one of lord and tenants.

Master. **1**. Tradesman qualified by training and experience to teach apprentices and carry on a business on his own acccount. **2**. Presiding officer of a **Livery Company**.

mendicity. Appalling poverty in Ireland obliged citizens of several Irish towns (including Coleraine and **Londonderry**) to establish organisations to relieve destitution and reduce the very considerable nuisance of beggars on the streets. Help was given by means of money, food, and even accommodation, and no restrictions on grounds of religion, age, or trade were applied. The buildings erected as *Mendicity Institutes* were called asylums, and in Londonderry the asylum had 82 inmates, while 137 persons were given daily rations of food. Support was given by **The Irish Society** to the institutes in County Londonderry.

mere. Pure or unmixed (of a people or language). The term 'mere Irish' is not pejorative: it simply means Irish previously untouched by English influences or rule, speaking Irish, and observing Irish customs (e.g. in dress).

metropolitan. **Bishop** having charge over the bishops of a **province**. The term is synonymous with an **archbishop** in the west.

middle-men. Tenants holding extensive properties from landlords on long leases who sublet for short periods and were able to increase rents as market conditions changed, thus often making considerable fortunes. Apart from the disastrous period during the 18th century after the South

Sea Bubble burst, some of the London Companies were able to regain their lands and manage them under their direct control, thus cutting out the middle-man or **farmer** (**1**).

Militia. Part-time military force. The first Irish Militia was raised in 1666, and was exclusively **Protestant**. Disarmed in the reign of James II and VII (1685-8), it was replaced by a **Roman Catholic** Militia raised by Richard Talbot (1630-91), Earl (from 1685) and titular Duke (from 1689) of Tyrconnell. A Protestant Militia was organised during the 1689-91 Wars, and by 1716 Protestant males aged between 16 and 60 were required to muster and train for four days per annum. Mobilised in 1739-40 and 1745, it acquired its own uniform. An Irish Militia (full-time, and intended for service anywhere in the British Isles) was raised in 1793, and by 1800 had 25,000 soldiers. Commanded mostly by Protestants, the rank and file were largely Roman Catholics, but the reliability of this force was called into question by its penetration by **Defenders** and **United Irishmen** which led to several courts martial. During the 1798 Rebellion, however, the Militia was a decisive element in the defeat of the insurgents.

native. Original or usual inhabitant of a country or place, as distinguished from strangers or foreigners: someone born in a country, or one of a nation by birth. Not pejorative when used in this sense (e.g. a native of Bristol).

native freehold. Estate granted to Irish gentlemen. In County **Londonderry** Irishmen were granted **freeholds** in **fee-farm** of **The Irish Society** (i.e. they had tenure for a fixed rent without services).

Netherlands. The accession of Charles V as Holy Roman Emperor in 1515 brought The Netherlands into the enormous collection of States acquired by the Habsburgs through war and marriage. Protestantism gained ground very rapidly there, and conflicts were inflamed under Philip II (1555/6-98), who succeeded his father in his Spanish Dominions in 1555. Attempts to crush Protestantism exacerbated matters and led to powerful nationalist forces being unleashed under the leadership of provincial lieutenants (*Stadholders*). Pre-eminent was William the Silent, Prince of Orange, a House which rose to assume leadership of the **Protestants**. Spanish installations and ships were constantly harried both by the Dutch and by the English, and by 1648 Dutch independence was recognised. When William of Orange (1650-1702) was called to power, first as *Stadholder* of Zeeland, *Stadholder* of Holland, and Captain-General of the United Provinces of the Netherlands (1672), France acquired a formidable adversary, especially when William concluded formal alliances with the Holy Roman Emperor and Brandenburg against France. Military and diplomatic involvements were signalled by William's marriage (1677) to Mary, elder daughter of the heir-presumptive to the throne of Great Britain and Ireland (James, Duke of York). When King James II and VII was obliged to remove himself in 1688, William and Mary became King and Queen of Great Britain, but claims to the throne of Ireland were disputed by **Jacobites** who, supported by the French, determined to resist the new order. The war of 1689-91, with the celebrated **siege of Londonderry**, led to the establishment of William and Mary as monarchs of Ireland as well, and the eclipse of the Jacobites. It also led to a century of peace in Ireland.

New English. Officials, soldiers, and settlers from England who came to Ireland during the **Tudor Conquest** and thereafter. Increasingly **Protestant**, they began to supplant the **Old English**, and rose to pre-eminence from the time of the **Plantation** of **Ulster**.

Nine Years' War. Lasting from April 1593 until March 1603, it was an attempt by the Gaelic lords of Ireland under the leadership of Hugh (Aodh) O'Neill (*c.*1550-1616), 2nd Earl of Tyrone and last inaugurated O'Neill chief (called 'The Great O'Neill'), to destroy English **Protestant** supremacy with the aid of Spanish arms. Its failure, and the submission of O'Neill at Mellifont, led to the completion of the **Tudor Conquest** and effective control of all Ireland.

Northern Ireland. **Province** created by the Government of Ireland Act of 1920 (10 & 11 Geo. V, c. 67) consisting of the six counties (*see* **county**) of Antrim, Armagh, Down, Fermanagh, Londonderry, and Tyrone, retained within the United Kingdom after the 26 counties of the rest of Ireland became a Dominion by the **Anglo-Irish Treaty** of 1921. Sometimes loosely called **Ulster**, this usage should be avoided, as historically Ulster consisted of nine counties.

oireacht. **1**. Territorial council under a chief. **2**. Body of vassals. **3**. Territory of a chieftain.

Old English. Descendants of the Anglo-Norman conquerors of Ireland, mostly **Roman Catholics** loyal to the English Crown, they did not ally themselves with the Gaelic Irish until 1641 during the **Confederate War**.

Orange Order. **Protestant** political society founded in 1795 following a skirmish between a branch of the Protestant Peep O'Day Boys and the **Roman Catholic Defenders** near Loughgall, County Armagh. Devoted to the memory of William of Orange and his victories over the **Jacobites**, it drew upon the rituals and organisations of both the Defenders and Freemasonry (although much transformed), and its influence spread very rapidly in the increasingly embittered climate of the 1790s, gaining recruits in the army and the **Yeomanry**. British Governments were wary of Orangeism, even suppressing it for a time from 1825, but it survived, largely among rural workers and the urban proletariat. This changed with the Irish land agitation of the 1870s and 1880s when the Order gained support from beleaguered Protestant landlords, and very soon it became a vehicle by which a widely-based popular Unionist movement gained ground. During the 1880s, Orangeism made enormous advances, and provided a ready-made organisation for Ulster Unionism during the **Home Rule** crises. The Order remains closely associated with Ulster Unionism, a fact that has not escaped political commentators across the Irish Sea.

Ordnance Survey. Established in 1791, the survey was intended to map a Britain faced with a French invasion. When the survey began work in Ireland it was intended to be used as a means by which property should be re-rated. Under the sole direction of Thomas Frederick Colby (1784-1852) a county-by-county survey of unprecedented accuracy proceeded, involving the employment of over 2,000 staff, between 1825 and 1841. Work began in County **Londonderry**, and additional information was collected on place-names, antiquities, history, geology, and industry, only one volume on which (*Memoir of the City and North Western Liberties of Londonderry: Parish of Templemore*) was published, in 1837. It was a tremendous achievement, and remained the basis of most maps thereafter until well into the 20th century.

Pale. The fortified region around Dublin in which English rule was established, later including the 'four obedient Counties' of Dublin, Meath, Louth, and Kildare. The Pale retained its distinctive character until the medieval frontier began to move outwards with the **Tudor Conquest** of the rest of Ireland.

Pallium (*pl.* **Pallia**). Woollen vestment conferred upon **archbishops** by the Papacy in the **Roman Catholic** Church. Historically, the lambs from which the wool for this purpose were taken were blessed (on 21 January each year) in the Church of Sant'Agnese fuori le Mura, Rome.

Partibus Infidelium, in. Literally 'in the lands of infidels', in the **Roman Catholic** Church it describes a **titular bishop** in an uncivilised or heretical country. For example, until the Roman Catholic hierarchy was restored in England in the 1860s (denounced as 'Papal Aggression' at the time), Roman Catholic bishops were nominated to **sees** *in Partibus Infidelium* (called 'Pretended Provinces' by some who disapproved).

Patron. One who holds the right of presentation to an ecclesiastical **benefice**; i.e. the holder of the **advowson**. **The Irish Society** held the *patronage* of several **livings** in County **Londonderry**.

Penal Laws. Following the upheavals of the 1641-53 **Confederate War** and the wars at the end of the century, various discriminatory laws were enacted against **Roman Catholics**. Some of the most powerful legislation concerned land purchase and inheritance, the practising of law, the holding of office, membership of **Grand Juries** and municipal corporations, membership of Parliament, and service in the armed forces. As a result, many Roman Catholic aristocrats and gentry found it expedient to conform (*see* **Conformity**) to the **Church of Ireland**. Laws banishing Roman Catholic clergy, if enforced, might well have transformed the religious persuasion of Ireland in a couple of generations, but they were not enforced, and attempts to convert the population to Protestantism were spasmodic, generally feeble, and unsustained. Roman clergy could be found in most parts of Ireland from the 1720s, all through the century. It should be remembered that the

1704 Act to Prevent the Further Growth of Popery (2 Anne, c. 6), generally regarded as the most effective of the legal restrictions on Roman Catholics, imposed a sacramental test for public office, which applied equally to **Protestant Dissenters**, so the Penal Laws also made life difficult for all who did not conform to the requirements of the **Anglican** Church of Ireland.

Plantation. Settlement of persons in a locality, especially the planting of a colony. A term meaning colonisation (e.g. of **Ulster**, Virginia, etc.).

Plantation acre. Unit of estimated land areas in early 17th-century **Ulster** based on the assumption that a **balliboe** consisted of 60 **acres** of profitable agricultural land. As a balliboe, being an *economic* unit rather than any fixed size, could vary enormously in acreage, and in fact averaged 400 acres in **County Londonderry**, the 'Plantation acre' was not much help when trying to establish the extent of landholdings. Surveyors did not *measure* land areas until later in the century as it was far too dangerous to attempt to do so: therefore, they ascertained from the Irish **natives** how many balliboes were estimated in any given district, and multiplied the resulting figure by 60. Figures were further distorted by the fact that locals, 'not wishing their Countries to be discovered', would be economical with the facts. This would explain why the county of Coleraine, estimated to contain 34,187 English acres, actually had 307,278 acres. G. V. Sampson's map or 'Chart' of County Londonderry, published in 1814, came up with a figure of 470,835 acres for the county, and in his *Statistical Survey* (1802) estimated an area of 511,688 acres. The true area of the county is about 521,230 acres, but it should be remembered that considerable areas have been reclaimed from the **slob-lands**. Between the **Ordnance Survey** of 1830-2 and 1939 some 5,000 acres were added to the area of the county, and the coastline has altered very considerably.

Planter. Person who 'plants' or founds a colony; a settler, colonist, or pioneer. Especially an English or Scots **Protestant** settler in 17th-century **Ulster**.

poll. Unit of land in County Cavan, slightly smaller than a 60-Plantation-acre **balliboe**, estimated by English surveyors at around 50 **Plantation acres**.

Precept. Authoritative command, order, or mandate, e.g. that used by the Lord Mayor of the City of London demanding payments towards a common fund (e.g. for the **Plantation** of **Ulster**).

precinct. Subdivision of a **county**, approximating to a **barony**, for the purposes of the **Plantation**.

President. Provincial administrator to establish English law and order, first in the 1560s and '70s in Connacht and Munster, backed by two judges, a council of local lords and **bishops**, and a military force.

Privy Council. **1**. Body of advisers selected by the Sovereign, with certain persons who were members by usage (e.g. Princes of the Blood, **archbishops**, and chief officers of present and past Ministries of State). Its original function of advising the Crown in matters of state and administration is now discharged by the Cabinet. **2**. The *Irish Privy Council* was a body formed to assist the Viceroy in Ireland (*see* **Lord Deputy**, **Lord Lieutenant**). There are, of course, Privy Councillors who are eminent in science or letters, but most come from the ranks of dignitaries who have held high political, judicial, or ecclesiastical office.

Proportion. A portion or part of a whole, or a share usually applied in the present study to an estate of an **Undertaker**, **Servitor**, or London **Livery Company** in **Ulster**.

Protestant. Originally one of those who *protested*, i.e. made a declaration of dissent from the decision of the Diet of Speier (1529) which re-affirmed the Edict of the Diet of Worms against the Reformation, so a general designation of an adherent of the Reformed doctrines or Churches which repudiated papal authority: a member of a Christian Church outside the **Roman Catholic** Communion in the west. Settlers from Great Britain who took part in the **Plantation** of **Ulster** were required to be Protestants.

Protestant Ascendancy. The **Protestant** (usually **Anglican**) landed gentry who were dominant figures in Ireland after the enactments known as the **Penal Laws**.

province. **1**. One of four subdivisions of Ireland (Connacht [Counties Galway, Leitrim, Mayo, Roscommon, and Sligo], Leinster [Counties Carlow, Dublin, Kildare, Kilkenny, Laois, Longford, Louth, Meath, Offaly, Westmeath, Wexford, and Wicklow], Munster [Counties Clare, Cork, Kerry, Limerick, Tipperary, and Waterford], and Ulster [Counties Antrim, Armagh, Cavan, Donegal, Down, Fermanagh, Londonderry, Monaghan, and Tyrone]). **2**. Administrative division of a country or state, or any principal division of a kingdom (usually under a governor): the term was given to the six-**county** State of **Northern Ireland** from 1920. **3**. District within the jurisdiction of an **archbishop** or a **metropolitan**: in Ireland there were four historical ecclesiastical provinces, those of Armagh, Cashel, Dublin, and Tuam.

quarter. Irish land division, approximately 25 per cent of a **ballibetagh**. In County Donegal **townlands** seem to have evolved from quarters rather than from the smaller subdivision of a **balliboe**. The term derives from the Irish *ceathramhadh*, anglicised as *carrow* (corrupted to *quarter*).

quarterage. Charge paid each quarter-year, e.g. by members of London **Livery Companies**.

quit-rent. **1**. Small rent paid by a freeholder (*see* **freehold**) in lieu of services that might otherwise be required of him. **2**. Charge made upon an estate for some special purpose.

Recorder. Magistrate, a person with legal knowledge appointed by a mayor and aldermen (*see* **Alderman**) to record the proceedings of courts and the customs of the Corporation. The Recorder of London was appointed by the **Court** of Aldermen, and was often called upon to make oral statements concerning custom and usage that were regarded as having considerable weight. From its inception, **The Irish Society** included the Recorder as one of the Assistants (*See* **Assistant**).

rectory. A **benefice** held by a *rector*, i.e. a parson or incumbent of a parish whose **tithes** are not impropriate (i.e. placed in the hands of laymen). *See* **impropriation**.

recusant. One who refused to attend services of the **Established Church** or conform (*see* **Conformity**) to its beliefs and practices. The term became synonymous with **Roman Catholics** even though it could theoretically be applied to **Dissenters**.

Redshanks. Highland and Western Islands **Scots** mercenary infantrymen, so-called from their bare legs and feet, who were auxiliary troops employed by Gaelic chiefs (e.g. the O'Donnells, O'Neills, and Antrim MacDonnells). Often accompanied by their women and children, they looked strange and fearsome to English eyes.

Regium Donum. State grant towards the salaries of Presbyterian ministers, started in the 17th century and abolished during **disestablishment** (1869-71).

Remembrancer. Official of the Corporation of the City of London with responsibilities to represent that body at the royal court, before the **Privy Council**, before Parliament and parliamentary committees, and at council and treasury boards. He was also responsible for compiling records and memoranda to ensure continuity.

Roman Catholic. Adherent of the *Roman Catholic Church* recognising the spiritual supremacy of the Pope (or **Bishop** of Rome) and accepting the doctrines and teachings of that Church. The Irish and **Old English** were almost all Roman Catholics, so the English break with Rome (1533-4) under King Henry VIII (1509-47) led to immense problems: attempts to impose Protestantism (*see* **Protestant**) in Ireland generally failed, and caused severe stresses.

sacramental test. Requirement from 1704 that persons holding office under the Crown should take Communion according to the rites of the **Established Church** (**Church of Ireland**), so applied to **Roman Catholics** and Protestant **Dissenters**.

Scots. Lowland **Protestant** Scots were encouraged to settle in **Ulster** as part of the **Plantation** scheme. These should not be confused with the 'Antrim Scots' associated with the MacDonnells, who were Gaelic-speaking Roman Catholics from the Highlands and Western Islands, sometimes acting as auxiliary troops (**Redshanks**) during the 17th century in, e.g., Lord Antrim's army. Highland Scots were often regarded as Irish in pre-Plantation **Ulster**.

see. **1**. Seat of dignity or authority, so the throne or *cathedra* of a **bishop**. **2**. Territory under the jurisdiction of a bishop; a **diocese**.

seignory. Mastery or overlordship.

sept. Division of a **clan**, tribe, or nation. In pre-**Plantation** Ireland a sept (*sliocht*) was a distinct group associated with a particular territory and under a local chieftain (often a vassal of one of the powerful clan chieftains).

Servitors. Class of persons to whom lands were assigned in **Ulster** during the **Plantation**. They were normally those who had served in military or administrative capacities in Ireland, and so were mostly resident Crown officials who knew the people and territory well.

Sheriff. The Crown's chief administrative and judicial officer in each **county** with responsibilities to collect revenues, preside over the county court, summon juries, execute writs, levy fines, and organise defence in times of crisis.

shire. Administrative district consisting of smaller districts. It is synonymous with a **county**.

slob-lands. Muddy, low-lying lands by the sea-shore, partly covered at high tide; ooze or swampy land adjoining the sea. Under the aegis of **The Irish Society** and some of the **Livery Companies** several thousand **acres** of slob-lands were reclaimed during the 19th century, adding to the area of **County Londonderry**.

socage. Tenure of land by services other than **knight-service**, fixed and determinate in quality. **Free** or **common socage** is the ordinary form of such tenure, usually involving payment of rent instead of through services.

Star Chamber. **1**. Apartment in the Royal Palace at Westminster in which, during the 14th and 15th centuries, members of the monarch's council sat to exercise jurisdiction. **2**. A **court**, chiefly of criminal jurisdiction, developed in the 15th century from the judicial sittings of the King's council in the Star Chamber: the judges were the Lord Chancellor (or Lord Keeper), the Lord Treasurer, the Lord Privy Seal, and any peers who chose to attend. It became a powerful instrument in the hands of the Sovereign, and the abuses of it under Kings James I and VI (1603-25) and Charles I (1625-49) rendered it the proverbial type of an arbitrary tribunal. It was abolished in 1641, but not before it had done untold damage to the City of London, **The Irish Society**, the **Plantation** of **Ulster**, and the **county** of **Londonderry**.

Surrender and Regrant. Usually regarded as a Tudor mechanism to regularise order in Ireland by which an Irish lord would recognise the King as Sovereign, surrender his lands to the Crown, renounce his Gaelic titles and rights, promise to help to establish English laws and customs, give military service to the Crown, and pay rents to the Crown, all in return for a charter for his lands, the grant of a noble title, and the right to arbitrate with his kinsmen and vassals over privileges, rights, and duties. The intention was to stabilise existing tenures and social structures by feudalising them and making them conform to English practice. It was not to grasp communally held land and to offer it as a carrot to the Gaelic lords (as is often erroneously claimed). In the case of O'Neill, he became Earl of Tyrone, and other chieftains were ennobled. However, a system of Surrender and Regrant existed long before, as when King Reginald of Mona (1187-1226) bestowed his kingdom upon the apostolic see during the Pontificate of Honorius III (1216-27) to hold it thereafter of the Papacy. This had the advantage of ensuring the backing of the Papacy for legitimate dynasties, though part of the arrangement was payment of an annual sum to Rome, which became less attractive in time.

Tánaiste. Designated successor of a king or chief, nominated during his lifetime. *Tanistry* was the Gaelic system of political succession.

tate, tath. Division of land in Counties Fermanagh and Monaghan, equivalent to a **balliboe**, and the forerunner of a **townland**.

temporality. Temporal (i.e. worldly, material, or secular) power, jurisdiction, affairs, possessions, property, and so on, belonging to the Church or clergy.

termon. Land belonging to, or forming the precinct or **Liberties** of a religious house, free from all secular charges. It enjoyed special privileges of sanctuary and protection.

tithe. Tax levied on agricultural produce for the support of the **Established Church**, much resented by **Roman Catholics** and **Protestant Dissenters**.

titular. That which exists only in title or name. A *titular bishop* in the **Roman Catholic** Church is one deriving his title from an ancient **see** lost to the control of the Roman pontificate. In 1885 the title **titular bishop** was substituted for **bishop *in Partibus Infidelium***.

townland. Division of land varying greatly in area, not necessarily possessing any urban settlement. Ireland had over 60,000 townlands which were the smallest administrative parcels of land used in levying **tithes** and in valuations.

Tudor Conquest. The extension of English sovereignty through the whole of Ireland. Before 1534 English lordship was only really effective in the **Pale**, but the transformation of Ireland from a lordship to a kingdom under the English Crown in 1541 introduced centralised and effective Government that was gradually extended throughout the land. The Conquest was finally achieved with the end of the **Nine Years' War** in 1603.

turbary. **1**. The right to cut and take peat from another's land. **2**. Place where peat is dug, i.e. a peat-bog or turf-moss. **3**. Substance obtained from or forming a turbary; peat or turf. *Common of turbary* is the right to cut peat or turf for fuel on a common or on another person's land.

uirrí. A sub-king. *aireachta* or *urraghts* were terms used to describe Irish nobles of an area under a chieftain. *Uirríthe* controlled territories (called 'Countries') which, in turn, became **Plantation baronies** or **precincts**. O'Cahan was the principal *uirrí* of O'Neill, and his 'Country' was the **county** of Coleraine which became part of the county of **Londonderry** during the **Plantation** of **Ulster**.

Ulster. **1**. One of the four provinces (*see* **province**) of Ireland consisting of the nine counties (*see* **county**) of Antrim, Armagh, Cavan, Donegal, Down, Fermanagh, Londonderry, Monaghan, and Tyrone. Until the end of the 16th century the province of Ulster included County Louth but not County Cavan (which was part of Connacht). **2**. Loosely (and inaccurately) applied to the six counties of **Northern Ireland**. **3**. Before the Norman Conquest, an area approximately covering the northern counties of Antrim and Down. **4**. An earldom, by *c.*1350 consisting of the northern counties of Antrim and Down, with territories around Lough Foyle in what are now the counties of Donegal and Londonderry, and power extending into the O'Neill, O'Cahan, and O'Donnell Gaelic lands.

Ultramontanism. An *Ultramontane* was a representative of the **Roman Catholic** Church north of the Alps as opposed to an ecclesiastic in Italy (literally *beyond the mountain*). *Ultramontanism*, therefore, was the principle and practice of the Ultramontane party in the Church advocating absolute papal supremacy outside Italy (especially in France, Germany, Northern Europe generally, and the British Isles).

Undertakers. English or Scots grantees (**Planters**) of **Plantation** lands in **Ulster** charged with their development and settlement.

United Irishmen, Society of. Established in Belfast in 1791, it was largely a middle-class movement inspired by the American and French revolutions, leavened with strong dashes of Irish patriotism. It hoped to remove English control from Irish affairs, introduce universal male suffrage, and unite Irishmen of all religious persuasions. By the mid-1790s, however, a strong oath-based organisation within the Society, centred in **Ulster**, began to prepare for armed revolution. Although help arrived from France, the rebellion, when it occurred in 1798, rapidly degenerated into sectarian outrages. It was put down firmly by the Government and many of the ringleaders put to death.

urraghts (*aireachta*). Leading nobles of a district under a major chief (*See* ***oireacht***)

Volunteers. Part-time military force raised in Ireland 1778-9 to guard against invasion and to enforce law and order at a time when the regular army was fighting in America. Numbering over 60,000 by 1782, the Volunteers became significant politically in attempts to obtain legislative independence for Ireland. Largely middle-class, with officers from the landed gentry and aristocracy, the Volunteers became once more a force to be reckoned with after 1789, but growing political instability and prohibitions placed on the import of arms caused the decline of Volunteering, and its *raison d'être* as a defensive force was removed by the raising of the new **Militia** in 1793 and the formation of the **Yeomanry** in 1796.

Ward. Administrative division of the City of London represented by an **Alderman**. *But see* **Court of Wards and Liveries**.

Warden. Member of the governing body of a **Livery Company** under the authority of the **Master** or the *Prime Warden*.

Wild Geese. Irishmen who left Ireland to serve in foreign European armies from the late 17th and during the 18th centuries.

Yeomanry. Part-time force raised in 1796 to combat threats posed by the French, the **United Irishmen**, and the **Defenders**. It gradually became predominantly **Protestant**. It largely superseded the **Volunteers**.

Select Bibliography

You will find it a very good practice … to verify your references …

MARTIN JOSEPH ROUTH (1755-1854) in John William Burgon (1813-88): *Lives of Twelve Good Men* (1888), **i**, 73

ADAMS, WILLIAM FORBES (1935): *Ireland and the Irish Emigration to the New World from 1815 to the Famine* (New Haven: Yale University Press, and London: Humphrey Milford, Oxford University Press)

ALCOCK, N.W., BARLEY, M.W., DIXON, P.W. & MEESON, R.A. (1996): *Recording Timber-Framed Buildings: An Illustrated Glossary* (York: Council for British Archaeology)

ALDOUS, VIVIENNE E. (ed.) (1993): *An Interim List of The Irish Society's Archives held by the Corporation of London Records Office.* Typescript held by the City of London Records Office, Guildhall, London (London: Corporation of London Records Office)

ALEXANDER, ELEANOR (1913): *Primate Alexander, Archbishop of Armagh* (London: Edward Arnold)

ANALECTA HIBERNICA including the REPORTS OF THE IRISH MANUSCRIPTS COMMISSION (COIMISIÚN LÁIMHSCRÍBHINNÍ NA hÉIREANN) (various dates from 1930): See especially No 3 (*Survey of the Escheated Counties in Ulster, 1608* [1931]), No 8 (*Ulster Plantation Papers* and *Schedules of the Lands of Ulster allotted to the London Livery Companies* [1938]), and No 12 (*The Perrot Papers* and *The O'Kane Papers* [1943]) (Dublin: Stationery Office)

ANONYMOUS (1813): *A Sketch of the History and Proceedings of the Deputies Appointed to Protect the Civil Rights of the Protestant Dissenters* (London: Burton)

——— (1875): *The Irish Society of London. Its Management and Expenditure* (Londonderry: Journal Steam Printing Works)

ATKINSON, ERNEST GEORGE (ed.) (1893): *Calendar of The State Papers relating to Ireland of the Reign of Elizabeth, 1596-1597* (London: H.M.S.O.)

——— (1895): *Calendar of The State Papers relating to Ireland of the Reign of Elizabeth, 1598-1599* (London: H.M.S.O.)

ATKYNS, SIR ROBERT (1689): *An Enquiry into the Power of Dispensing with Penal Statutes* (London: Goodwin)

BAEDEKER, KARL (1930): *Rome and Central Italy* (Leipzig: Baedeker)

BAGWELL, RICHARD (1885-90): *Ireland under the Tudors* (London: Longmans)

——— (1909): *Ireland under the Stuarts and During the Interregnum* (London: Longmans)

BARING-GOULD, SABINE (1914): *The Lives of the Saints* (Edinburgh: John Grant)

BARRATT, T. E. CHESTER (1957): The Foyle Fishery Case in *Transactions of The Guildhall Historical Association*, **ii**, 132-6

BARTLETT, W.H. *See* COYNE, J. STIRLING (*c.*1850)

BECK, JOSEPH (1878): *A Continuation of the Historical Narrative of the Origin and Constitution of … The Honourable The Irish Society* (London: The Irish Society)

BECKETT, J. C. (1966): *The Making of Modern Ireland, 1603-1923* (London: Faber)

BENCE-JONES, MARK (1987): *Twilight of the Ascendancy* (London: Constable)

——— (1988): *A Guide to Irish Country Houses* (London: Constable)

BETTS, JOHN (1913): *The Story of the Irish Society. Being a Brief Historical Account of the Foundation and Work of The Honourable The Irish Society of London* (London: The Irish Society, Irish Chamber). A second edition was published in 1921 with a Preface by SIR ALFRED NEWTON, Bt., Governor from 1906 to 1921, and an Appendix entitled *Memoranda of Principal Events … 1609-1920*

BIGGER, DAVID and MCDONALD, TERENCE (1990): *In Sunshine or In Shadow. Photographs from the* Derry Standard, *1928-39* (Belfast: Friar's Bush Press)

BLACK, EILEEN (ed.) (1990): *Kings in Conflict: Ireland in the 1690s* (Belfast: The Ulster Museum)

BLACKERBY, SAMUEL (1689): *Account of Making the Penal Laws by the Papists against the Protestants and by the Protestants against the Papists*, etc., etc. (London: William Churchill)

BLAKE, JOHN W. (1956): *Northern Ireland in the Second World War* (Belfast: H.M.S.O.)

BODLEY, SIR JOSIAS (1910): Consideracons concerning such forts and garrisons in the north as I have viewed, in *Ulster Journal of Archaeology*, new series, xii (5 September), 61-4

BONNER, BRIAN (1975): *That Audacious Traitor* (Dublin: Foilseacháin Náisiúnta Teoranta)

——————— (1982): *Derry: An Outline History of the Diocese* (Dublin: Foilseacháin Náisiúnta Teoranta)

BORG, ALAN (1991): *War Memorials from Antiquity to the Present* (London: Leo Cooper)

BOULTER, HUGH (1770): *Letters written by His Excellency Hugh Boulter DD, Lord Primate of All Ireland … with an account … of transactions … from 1724 to 1738* (Dublin: Faulkner)

BOYD, HUGH ALEXANDER (1933): *A History of Coleraine from the Londoners' Plantation to the Restoration 1609-1660* (Unpublished MSS. in the possession of The Irish Society)

BOYD, J. I. C. (n.d.): *The Londonderry and Lough Swilly Railway* (Truro: D. Bradford Barton)

BOYSE, JOSEPH (1694): *Remarks on a Late Discourse of William Lord Bishop of Derry: Concerning the Inventions of Men in the Worship of God* (London: J. Lawrence & J. Dunton)

——————— (1728): *The Works of the Rev. and Learned Mr. Joseph Boyce of Dublin, being a Complete Collection of his Discourses, Sermons, and Other Tracts* (London: John Gray)

BRADLEY, SIMON and PEVSNER, NIKOLAUS (1997): *London I: The City of London. The Buildings of England Series* (London: Penguin)

BRAMHALL, JOHN (1842): *Works of the Most Reverend Father in God, John Bramhall: with a Life of the Author and a Collection of his Letters* (Oxford: John Henry Parker)

BRETT, C.E.B. (1973): *Court Houses and Market Houses of the Province of Ulster* (Belfast: Ulster Architectural Heritage Society)

BREWER, J.S. and BULLEN, WILLIAM (eds.) (1867-73): *Calendar of the Carew Manuscripts preserved in the Archiepiscopal Library at Lambeth,* usually referred to as *Calendar of Carew MSS,* or *Cal. Carew MSS* (London: Longmans, etc.) The relevant volumes are *1515-1574* (1867), *1575-1588* (1868), *1589-1600* (1869), *1601-1603* (1870), *1603-1624* (1873), and *Miscellaneous Papers* (1871)

BRUNSKILL, R.W. (1978): *Illustrated Handbook of Vernacular Architecture* (London: Faber & Faber)

BURKE, ASHWORTH, P. (1897): *Family Records* (London: Harrison & Sons)

BURKE, SIR BERNARD (1884): *The General Armory of England, Scotland, Ireland, and Wales* (London: Harrison & Sons)

BURKE'S PEERAGE See MOSLEY, *and see* TOWNEND

BUTLER, W.F.T. (1918): *Confiscation in Irish History* (Dublin: Talbot)

BYRNE, MATTHEW, J. (1903): *Ireland under Elizabeth. Chapters towards a History of Ireland in the Reign of Elizabeth. Being a Portion of the History of Catholic Ireland by Don Philip O'Sullivan Bear* (Dublin: Sealy, Bryers, & Walker)

CAMBLIN, GILBERT (1951): *The Town in Ulster* (Belfast: William Mullan & Son [Publishers] Ltd)

CARSON, W.R.H. (1968): *A Bibliography of Printed Material Relating to the County and County Borough of Londonderry* (Unpublished Thesis submitted for Fellowship of the Library Association, in The Irish Reference Library, County Hall, Coleraine)

CARTE, THOMAS (1736): *A History of the Life of James Duke of Ormonde from 1610 to 1688 … with an account … of the affairs of his time …* (London: Bettenham)

——————— (1739): *A Collection of Original Letters and Papers Concerning the Affairs of England from the year 1641 to 1660* (London: Bettenham)

CHAMPNEYS, ARTHUR C. (1910): *Irish Ecclesiastical Architecture* (London: George Bell & Sons)

CHART, D.A. (ed.) (1928): *Londonderry and the London Companies 1609-1629. Being a Survey and Other Documents Submitted to King Charles I by Sir Thomas Phillips.* Sometimes referred to as *Phillips MSS.* (Belfast: H.M.S.O.)

CHILDE-PEMBERTON, WILLIAM S. (1924): *The Earl Bishop. The Life of Frederick Hervey, Bishop of Derry, Earl of Bristol* (London: Hurst & Blackett)

CLARKE, R. S. J. (1988): *Gravestone Inscriptions, County Down*, ii, (Belfast: Ulster Historical Foundation)

COLBY, THOMAS FREDERICK (1837): *Ordnance Survey of the County of Londonderry: Memoir of the City and North Western Liberties of Londonderry. Parish of Templemore* (Dublin: Published for Her Majestys Government, Ordnance Survey Office, by Hodges & Smith)

COLVIN, HOWARD MONTAGU (1995): *A Biographical Dictionary of British Architects 1660-1840* (New Haven & London: Yale University Press)

——————— (1999): *Essays in English Architectural History* (New Haven & London: Yale University Press)

COMMISSIONERS APPOINTED TO INQUIRE INTO THE EXISTING STATE OF THE CORPORATION OF THE CITY OF LONDON (1854): *Report of the Commissioners ... together with the Minutes of Evidence and Appendix* (London: Printed by Eyre & Spottiswoode for Her Majesty's Stationery Office)

COMPTON, ANN (ed.) (1985): *Charles Sergeant Jagger: War and Peace Sculpture* (London: Imperial War Museum)

CONNOLLY, S.J. (ed.) (1998): *The Oxford Companion to Irish History* (Oxford: Oxford University Press)

COOKE, SHOLTO (*c.*1950): *The Maiden City and the Western Ocean. A History of the Shipping Trade between Londonderry and North America in the Nineteenth Century* (Dublin: Morris)

COYNE, J. STIRLING (*c.*1850): *The Scenery and Antiquities of Ireland*, illustrated by W. H. BARTLETT (London: George Virtue)

CURL, JAMES STEVENS (1983): *The Life and Work of Henry Roberts (1803-76), Architect* (Chichester: Phillimore)

——————— (1986): *The Londonderry Plantation 1609-1914. The History, Architecture, and Planning of the Estates of the City of London and its Livery Companies in Ulster* (Chichester: Phillimore)

——————— (1992): *Classical Architecture. An Introduction to its Vocabulary and Essentials, with a Select Glossary of Terms* (London: Batsford)

——————— (1999 and 2000): *The Oxford Dictionary of Architecture* (Oxford: Oxford University Press)

CURNOCK, NEHEMIAH (ed.) (1909-16): *The Journal of the Reverend John Wesley* (London: Epworth Press)

CURRIE, J.R.L. (1973): *The Northern Counties Railway. Beginnings and Development, 1845-1903* (Newton Abbot: David & Charles)

——————— (1974): *The Northern Counties Railway. Heyday and Decline, 1903 - 1972* (Newton Abbot: David & Charles)

DALY, EDWARD and DEVLIN, KIERAN (1997): *The Clergy of the Diocese of Derry: An Index* (Dublin: Four Courts Press)

DAVIES, JOHN EBENEZER (1935): *Report upon the Fishery Cause* (London: Printed by Arthur Taylor for The Irish Society)

DAVIES, SIR JOHN (1787): *Historical Tracts* (Dublin: William Porter for White, Gilbert, Byrne, Whitestone, W. Porter, & Moore)

DAVYS, JOHN (1856): Original Documents illustrative of Irish History, No 6. The Plantation of Ulster, in *Ulster Journal of Archaeology*, First Series, **4**, 192-7

DAY, ANGÉLIQUE, MCWILLIAMS, PATRICK and ENGLISH, LISA (eds.) (1995): *Ordnance Survey Memoirs of Ireland. Parishes of County Londonderry* (Belfast: The Institute of Irish Studies, The Queens University of Belfast, in association with the Royal Irish Academy, Dublin)

DAY, J. and PATTON, H.E. (1932): *The Cathedrals of the Church of Ireland* (London: S.P.C.K.)

DEVLIN, BERNADETTE (1969): *The Price of my Soul* (London: Pan)

DICKSON, R. J. (1988): *Ulster Emigration to Colonial America 1718-1775* (London: Routledge & Kegan Paul). Contains a very useful bibliography

DICTIONARY OF NATIONAL BIOGRAPHY (D.N.B.) (1917-96): Various Editors (London and Oxford: Oxford University Press)

DOOLITTLE, I.G. (1982): *The City of London and its Livery Companies* (Dorchester: Gavin)

DOWNHAM, GEORGE (1895-8) *See* REYNELL, W. A. (ed.)

DUBLIN BUILDER (various years)

DUGDALE, WILLIAM (1658): *The History of St Paul's Cathedral in London* (London: Thomas Warren)

DUNLOP, ROBERT (1913): *Ireland under the Commonwealth* (Manchester: Manchester University Press)

DWYER, PHILIP (ed.) (1893): *The Siege of Londonderry in 1689, as set forth in the Literary Remains of Colonel the Rev. George Walker, D.D.* (London: Elliot Stock)

ERCK, JOHN CAILLARD (ed.) (1846, 1852): *Repertory of the Inrolments on the Patent Rolls of Chancery in Ireland. Reign of James I* (Dublin: J. McGlashan)

EVANS, P. HEATHER (1970): *An Historical Account of the Bann Fisheries* (Dissertation in the Irish Reference Library, County Hall, Coleraine, U. 639. 21, c. 317713)

FALLON, T.M. (1894): *The Cathedral Churches of Ireland* (London: Bemrose & Sons Ltd)

FALLS, CYRIL (1950): *Elizabeth's Irish Wars* (London: Methuen)

FERGUSON, N. S., ROWAN A.J. and TRACEY, J. J. (1970): *Historic Buildings, Groups of Buildings, Areas of Architectural Importance in and near the City of Derry* (Belfast: Ulster Architectural Heritage Society)

FORD, HENRY JONES (1915): *The Scotch-Irish in America* (Princeton, N.J.: Princeton University Press)

FOSTER, R.F. (1988): *Modern Ireland 1600-1972* (London: Allen Lane)

——————— (ed.) (1989):

The Oxford Illustrated History of Ireland (London: Guild Publishing by arrangement with Oxford University Press)

FOTHERGILL, BRIAN (1974): *The Mitred Earl* (London: Faber & Faber)

FRESHFIELD, EDWIN and FRESHFIELD, EDWIN (Jr.) (1898): *A Statement of Facts Deduced from Ancient Records and Other Sources Relating to The Irish Estates of the City of London Companies in Ulster* (London: Spottiswoode). This was prepared for Counsel in the Trial in Dublin of 1898

GILLESPIE, RAYMOND (1987): *Conspiracy* (Belfast: Ulster Society for Irish Historical Studies)

GIRVAN, W. D. (1972): *Historic Buildings, Groups of Buildings, Areas of Architectural Importance in Coleraine and Portstewart* (Belfast: Ulster Architectural Heritage Society)

GRAHAM, JOHN (1829): *A History of the Siege of Londonderry* (Dublin: William Curry Junior & Co.)

GROSE, FRANCIS (1791): *The Antiquities of Ireland* (London: S. Hooper)

HAMILTON, HANS CLAUDE (ed.) (1860): *Calendar of the State Papers relating to Ireland of the Reigns of Henry VIII, Edward VI, Mary, and Elizabeth, 1509-1573* (London: Longmans, etc.)

——————— (1867): *Calendar of the State Papers relating to Ireland of the Reign of Elizabeth, 1574-1585* (London: Longmans, etc.)

——————— (1885): *Calendar of the State Papers relating to Ireland of the Reign of Elizabeth, 1588-1592* (London: Longmans, etc.)

——————— (1890): *Calendar of the State Papers relating to Ireland of the Reign of Elizabeth, 1592-1596* (London: H.M.S.O.)

HARDY, EVELYN (1966): *Survivors of the Armada* (London: Constable)

HARDY, WILLIAM LE (ed.) (1937): *County of Middlesex. Calendar to the Sessions Records*, New Series, **iii** (London: C. W. Radcliffe)

HARE, AUGUSTUS J. C. (1897): *Walks in Rome* (London: George Allen)

HARRIS, WALTER (1770): *Hibernica, or Some Ancient Pieces Relating to Ireland* (Dublin: Milliken)

HAYES, R. (1916): *A Guide to the Cathedral Church of St Columb, Derry* (Londonderry: The *Sentinel* Office)

HAZLITT, W. CAREW (1892): *The Livery Companies of the City of London* (London: Swan Sonnenschein)

HEALY, T.M. (1913): *Stolen Waters ... a page in the conquest of Ulster* (London: Longmans, Green). The book was re-issued in 1917 under the title *The Great Fraud of Ulster*

HEATH, BARON (1869): *Some Account of the Worshipful Company of Grocers of the City of London* (London: Grocers Company)

HENNELL, MICHAEL M. (1958): *John Venn and the Clapham Sect* (London: Lutterworth Press)

HERBERT, WILLIAM (1834-7): *The History of the Twelve Great Livery Companies of London* (London: The Author)

HILL, GEORGE (1873): *An Historical Account of the MacDonnells of Antrim* (Belfast: Archer)

——— (1877): *An Historical Account of the Plantation in Ulster at the Commencement of the Seventeenth Century, 1608-1620* (Belfast: McCaw, Stevenson, & Orr)

——— (1878): *The Flight of the Earls* (Belfast: *Northern Whig*)

——— (1889): *Plantation Papers … of the Great Ulster Plantation in the year 1610* (Belfast: *Northern Whig*)

HONOUR, HUGH (1961): *Chinoiserie: The Vision of Cathay* (London: John Murray)

HURLEY, MICHAEL (ed.) (1970): *Irish Anglicanism 1869-1969. Essays on the rôle of Anglicanism in Irish life presented to the Church of Ireland on the centenary of its Disestablishment by a group of Methodist, Presbyterian, Quaker, and Roman Catholic scholars* (Dublin: Allen Figgis Ltd.)

HYDE, HARFORD MONTGOMERY (1933): *The Rise of Castlereagh* (London: Macmillan & Co. Ltd.)

——— (1953): *Carson. The Life of Sir Edward Carson, Lord Carson of Duncairn* (London: William Heinemann)

IRISH BUILDER (various years)

IRISH HISTORICAL STUDIES. From 1938

IRISH SOCIETY, THE (1815a, 1821, 1826, 1827, 1829, 1832, 1834, 1835, 1836, 1838, 1841, etc): *Reports of the Deputations of The Irish Society to visit the City of Londons Plantation in Ireland* (London: Printed by Charles Skipper *et al.* for the Society)

——— (1815b): *A Report of the Committee of The Irish Society, respecting their Charter* (London: Charles Skipper for The Society)

——— (1825): *A Narrative of an Excursion to Ireland by the Deputy Governor, Two Members of the Court, and the Assistant Secretary, of The Honorable Irish Society, of London.* (London: Charles Skipper for The Society). A lively and entertaining account by the Deputy Governor, Gilpin Gorst.

——— (1830): *Transactions relative to the Corporation and Borough of Coleraine in Ireland* (London: Printed by Arthur Taylor for The Irish Society)

——— (1836): *The Skinners Company versus The Honourable The Irish Society and Others. Proceedings upon a Motion for a Receiver, at the Suit of The Skinners Company … in His Majestys High Court of Chancery* (London: Printed by Richard Clay)

——— (1838): *The Judgment of The Right Hon. Lord Langdale, Master of the Rolls, in the Case of The Skinners Company* versus *The Honourable The Irish Society, and Others* (London: Printed for The Irish Society by W. Tyler)

——— (1839): *The Skinners Company against The Honourable The Irish Society, The Corporation of London, and Others. Proceedings in Her Majestys High Court of Chancery upon the Hearing of the Cause in the Rolls Court before The Right Honourable Lord Langdale, Master of the Rolls* (London: Printed by William Tyler)

——— (1845): *The Skinners Company* versus *The Irish Society and Others. The Judgments of The Right Honourable The Lord Chancellor Cottenham* (London: Printed for The Irish Society by Arthur Taylor)

——— (1854): *Royal Commission of Enquiry into the State of the Corporation of London: The City and Liberties of Londonderry, and the Honourable The Irish Society* (Londonderry: n.p.)

——— (1889): *Report from the Select Committee on The Irish Society and The City Companies (Irish Estates)* (London: Eyre & Spottiswoode). See also other reports of 1890 and 1891

——— (*c.*1898): *In the Court of Appeal in Ireland. Attorney-General (for Ireland)* versus *The Irish Society and Others. Documents* (London: Printed by Spottiswoode & Co.)

——— (1911): *In the House of Lords. On an Appeal from His Majestys Court of Appeal in Ireland. Between The Irish Society and Others and Edward Harold and Others* (Londonderry: Printed by William Colhoun at the *Sentinel* Office)

——— (1994): *The Honourable The Irish Society* (London: The Irish Society)

JAMES, F. GODWIN (1956): *North Country Bishop: The Biography of William Nicolson* (New Haven, Conn.: Yale University Press)

J.C.W. (1890): *London and Londonderry. Transactions of Three Centuries Considered from a Historical and Legal Standpoint* (London and Belfast: Marcus Ward & Co. Ltd.)

JOHNSON, A. H. (1914-22): *The History of the Worshipful Company of Drapers of London* (Oxford: Clarendon Press)

JOHNSON, ALLEN (ed.) (1946): *Dictionary of American Biography* (New York: Charles Scribner's Sons)

JOHNSTON, JAMES H. (1959): 'Population Movements in County Derry [*sic*] during a Pre-Famine Year', in *Proceedings of the Royal Irish Academy*, **60**, Sect. C/3 (Dublin: Hodges, Figgis & Co.), 141-62.

KEARNEY, H.F. (1955): The Court of Wards and Liveries in Ireland, 1622-1641, in *Proceedings of The Royal Irish Academy*, **57**, Sect. C/2 (Dublin: Hodges, Figgis & Co.), 29-68. I am indebted to Mr John Gamble for this item.

KELLY, J.N.D. (1986): *The Oxford Dictionary of Popes* (Oxford: Oxford University Press)

KENNEDY, LÍAM, ELL, PAUL S., CRAWFORD, E.M., and CLARKSON, L.A. (1999): *Mapping the Great Irish Famine: A Survey of the Famine Decades* (Dublin: Four Courts Press Ltd.)

KILROY, P. (1994): *Protestant Dissent and Controversy in Ireland, 1660-1714* (Cork: Cork University Press)

KING, SIR CHARLES SIMEON, BT. (1908): *A Great Archbishop of Dublin: William King. D.D., 1650-1729* (London: Longmans, Green)

KING, R.G.S. (ed.) (1936): *A Particular of the Howses and Famylyes in London Derry, May 15, 1628* (Londonderry: The *Sentinel* Office)

——————— (1952): *Historical Guide to St Columbs Cathedral, Londonderry.* (Londonderry: David Irvine)

KING, WILLIAM (1692): *The State of the Protestants of Ireland under the late King Jamess Government* (London: Robert Clavell)

——————— (1694): *An Admonition to the Dissenting Inhabitants Of the Diocess of Derry* (London: R. Clavel)

——————— (1696): *A Second Admonition to the Dissenting Inhabitants Of the Diocess of Derry* (London: R. Clavel)

KING-HALL, MAGDALEN (1951): *The Edifying Bishop. The Story of Frederick Hervey, Earl of Bristol and Bishop of Derry* (London: Peter Davies)

LACY, BRIAN (1998): *Siege City. The Story of Derry and Londonderry* (Belfast: Blackstaff Press Ltd., for Eason & Son [NI] Ltd.)

LEIGH, SARAH and TAYLOR, SIMON (eds.) (1997): *The Livery Companies of the City of London* (London: Corporation of London)

LESLIE, JAMES B. (1937): *Derry Clergy and Parishes* (Enniskillen: R.H. Ritchie for the Author)

——————— (1993): *Clergy of Connor from Patrician times to the present day* (Belfast: Ulster Historical Foundation and Library Committee of the Dioceses of Down, Connor, and Dromore)

LEWIS, SAMUEL (1837): *A Topographical Dictionary of Ireland, Comprising the Several Counties, Cities, Boroughs, Corporate, Market, and Post Towns, with Historical and Statistical Descriptions, etc.* (London: Lewis)

L.L.D. (1883): *The Irish Society and the London Companies of Ireland: Should they be abolished ?* A Series of Papers republished from *The Morning News* (Belfast: *The Morning News* Printing Works)

LOEBER, ROLF (1981): *A Biographical Dictionary of Architects in Ireland 1600-1720* (London: John Murray)

LONDONDERRY (1929): *St Columbs Cathedral. A Book of the Bells 1614-1929* (Londonderry: David Irvine)

——————— (1955): *St Columbs Cathedral 1633-1955* (Glasgow: Ecclesiastical Press Ltd)

——————— (1987): *St Columbs Cathedral Londonderry: Historical Guide* (Belfast: BCD Printers)

MACADAM, ROBERT (ed.) (1853-62): *The Ulster Journal of Archaeology* First Series (London and Belfast: J Russell Smith and Archer & Sons)

MACKAIL, J.W. (Tr.) (1908): *The Aeneid of Virgil* (London: Macmillan)

MACKENZIE, JOHN (1690): *A Narrative of the Siege of London-Derry: Or, the late Memorable Transactions of that City. Faithfully Represented, To Rectifie the Mistakes, and supply the Omissions of Mr* Walkers *Account* (London: Printed for The Author by Richard Baldwin)

——————— (1861): *Memorials of the Siege of Derry, including his Narrative and its Vindication,* with notes by W. D. KILLEN (Belfast: Aitchison)

MACNEVIN, T. (1846): *The Confiscation of Ulster in the Reign of James the First, commonly called The Ulster Plantation* (Dublin: James Duffy)

MACRORY, PATRICK (1988): *The Siege of Derry* (London: Hodder)

MAGUIRE, W.A. (ed.) (1998): *Up in Arms! The 1798 Rebellion in Ireland. A Bicentenary Exhibition* (Belfast: Ulster Museum)

MAHAFFY, ROBERT PENTLAND (ed.) (1900): *Calendar of the State Papers relating to Ireland, of the Reign of Charles I, 1625-1632* (London: Eyre & Spottiswoode for H.M.S.O.)

——————— (1901): *Calendar of the State Papers relating to Ireland, of the Reign of Charles I, 1633-1647* (London: *Norwich Chronicle* for H.M.S.O.)

——————— (1903): *Calendar of the State Papers relating to Ireland, of the Reign of Charles I, 1647-1660* (London: Mackie & Co Ltd. for H.M.S.O.)

MANT, RICHARD (1840): *History of the Church of Ireland, from the Revolution to the Union of the Churches of England and Ireland, January 1 1801;, with a Catalogue of the Archbishops and Bishops, continued to November 1840; and a Notice of the Alterations made in the Hierarchy by the Act of 3 and 4 William IV., Chap. 37* (London: John W. Parker)

——————— (1841): *History of the Church of Ireland, from the Reformation to the Revolution; with a Preliminary Survey, from the Papal Usurpation in the Twelfth Century, to its Legal Abolition in the Sixteenth* (London: John W. Parker)

MANT, WALTER-BISHOP (1857): *Memoirs of the Right Reverend Richard Mant, D.D., M.R.I.A., Lord Bishop of Down and Connor, and of Dromore* (Dublin: McGlashan & Gill, and London: Bell & Daldy)

MAXWELL, CONSTANTIA (1923): *Irish History from Contemporary Sources. 1509-1610* (London: Unwin)

——————— (1954): *The Stranger in Ireland, from the Reign of Elizabeth to the Great Famine* (London: Jonathan Cape)

MILLIGAN, CECIL DAVIS (1948): *The Walls of Derry* (Londonderry: *Londonderry Sentinel*)

——————— (1951): *History of the Siege of Londonderry 1689* (Belfast: H.R. Carter Publications Ltd for The Corporation of the City of Londonderry)

MOLYNEAUX, WILLIAM (1698): *The Case of Irelands being Bound by Acts of Parliament in England Stated* (Dublin: The Author, with subsequent editions [e.g. 1719, 1725])

MOODY, T.W. (1939): *The Londonderry Plantation 1609-41. The City of London and the Plantation in Ulster* (Belfast: William Mullan & Son)

MOODY, T.W., MARTIN, F.X. and BYRNE, F.J. (eds.) (1978): *A New History of Ireland,* Vol. III, *Early Modern Ireland, 1534-1691* (Oxford: Oxford University Press)

——————— (1982): A *New History of Ireland*, Vol. VIII, *A Chronology of Irish History to 1976* (Oxford: Oxford University Press)

MOODY, T.W. and SIMMS, J.G. (eds.) (1968): *The Bishopric of Derry and The Irish Society of London, 1602-1705*. Vol. I: 1602-70 (Dublin: Stationery Office for the Irish Manuscripts Commission)

——————— (1983): *The Bishopric of Derry and The Irish Society of London, 1602-1705*. Vol. II: 1670-1705 (Dublin: Stationery Office for the Irish Manuscripts Commission)

MORGAN, HIRAM (1999): *Tyrone's Rebellion* (Woodbridge: Boydell & Brewer)

MORLEY, HENRY (ed.) (1890): *Ireland under Elizabeth and James the First* (London: George Routledge & Sons, Ltd.)

MORTON, GRENFELL (1971): *Elizabethan Ireland.* Seminar Studies in History series, PATRICK RICHARDSON (ed.) (London: Longman Group Ltd.)

MOSLEY, CHARLES (ed.) (1999): *Burke's Peerage & Baronetage* (Crans: Burke's Peerage [Geneaological Books] Ltd.)

MULLIN, T.H. (1986): *Historic City: Derry, Londonderry* (Coleraine: Coleraine Bookshop)

MUNN, ALFRED MOORE (various dates): Collection of papers, books, and pamphlets, held in the Chapter-House of the Cathedral-Church of St Columb, Londonderry

——————— (1925): *Notes on the Place Names of the Parishes and Townlands of the County of Londonderry* (Cookstown: Mid-Ulster Printing Co. Ltd)

MURPHY, DESMOND (1981): *Derry, Donegal, and Modern Ulster 1790-1921* (Londonderry: Aileach Press)

NEWMANN, KATE (1994): *Dictionary of Ulster Biography* (Belfast: Institute of Irish Studies, The Queen's University of Belfast)

O'BRIEN, GERARD (ed.) (1999): *Derry and Londonderry: History and Society. Interdisciplinary Essays on the History of an Irish County* (Dublin: Geography Publications)

O'DONOVAN, JOHN (ed.) (1856): *Annals of the Kingdom of Ireland by the Four Masters from the Earliest Period to 1616* (Dublin: Hodges, Smith, & Co)

O'HANLON, JOHN (n.d.): *Lives of the Irish Saints* (Dublin: James Duffy & Sons)

ORR, J.C.D. (1997): *Servants of Christ. A Short History of the Bishops of Derry since the Reformation 1605-1995* (Dublin: A.P.C.K.)

PAPWORTH, WYATT ANGELICUS VAN SANDAU (1852-92): *The Dictionary of Architecture issued by The Architectural Publication Society* (London: Thomas Richards [vols. i-vi] and Whiting & Co. [vols. vii-viii])

PARISH REGISTER SOCIETY OF DUBLIN (1910): *The Register of Derry Cathedral 1642-1703* (Dublin: Parish Register Society)

PARKER, EDWARD L. (1851): *History of Londonderry* (Boston, Mass.: Perkins & Whipple)

PARLIAMENTARY GAZETTEER OF IRELAND, THE, Adapted to the New Poor-Law, Franchise, Municipal and Ecclesiastical Arrangements, and compiled with a Special Reference to the Lines of Railroad and Canal Communication, as existing in 1844-5, etc. (1846): (Dublin, London, and Edinburgh: A. Fullarton & Co.)

PERCEVAL-MAXWELL, M. (1990): *The Scottish Migration to Ulster in the Reign of James I* (London: Routledge & Kegan Paul)

PETRIE, GEORGE (1845): *The Ecclesiastical Architecture of Ireland, Anterior to the Anglo-Norman Invasion; comprising an essay on the Origin and Uses of the Round Towers of Ireland* (Dublin: Hodges & Smith)

PEVSNER, NIKOLAUS (1968): *Studies in Art, Architecture, and Design* (New York: Walker & Co.)

PHILLIPS, WALTER ALISON (1933): *History of the Church of Ireland from the Earliest Times to the Present Day* (London: Oxford University Press)

PORTER, CLASSON (1884): *Frederick Augustus Hervey, Fourth Earl of Bristol and Bishop of Derry* (Belfast: *The Northern Whig*)

PORTLOCK, J. E. (1843): *Report on the Geology of the County of Londonderry and parts of Tyrone and Fermanagh* (Dublin: Milliken)

POTTERTON, HOMAN (1975): *Irish Church Monuments 1570-1880* (Belfast: Ulster Architectural Heritage Society)

PUBLIC RECORD OFFICE (1903): *Calendar of the Charter Rolls Preserved in the Public Record Office. Henry III* (London: H.M.S.O.)

RANKIN, PETER (1972): *Irish Building Ventures of the Earl Bishop of Derry* (Belfast: Ulster Architectural Heritage Society)

RANTOUL, ROBERT S. (1894): *The Building of the Essex Bridge* (Salem, Mass: Salem Press — reprint from the *Historical Collections of the Essex Institute* (1893), xxx)

REED, CHARLES (1865): *An Historical Narrative of the Origin and Constitution of ... The Honourable The Irish Society* (London: The Irish Society). The *Historical Narrative* was re-issued in updated form in 1878, 1899, and 1917. The last edition had the title augmented as *Together with Memoranda of Principal Occurrences from 1611 to 1898*, and was printed by Waterlow & Sons Ltd., for The Irish Society in 1917

——————— *et al.* (1867): *Proceedings in Reference to the Preservation of the Bunhill Fields Burial Ground* (London: Benjamin Pardon for The Corporation of London)

REEVES, WILLIAM (1850): *Acts of Archbishop Colton in his Metropolitan Visitation of The Diocese of Derry, A.D. MCCCXVII* (Dublin: Irish Archaeological Society)

REID, JAMES SEATON (1867): *The History of the Presbyterian Church in Ireland, Comprising the Civil History of the Province of Ulster from the Accession of James I*, etc., with notes by W. D. KILLEN (Belfast: William Mullan)

REPS, JOHN (1965): *The Making of Urban America: a History of City Planning in the United States* (Princeton, N.J.: Princeton University Press)

——————— (1972): *Tidewater Towns: City Planning in Colonial Virginia and Maryland* (Williamsburg, Va.: Colonial Williamsburg Foundation)

——————— (1980): *Town Planning in Frontier America* (Columbia, Mo.: University of Missouri Press)

REYNELL, W. A. (ed.) (1895-8): The Estate of the Diocese of Derry compiled by Dr George Downham, in *Ulster Journal of Archaeology*, New Series, **i-iv**

ROBINSON, P. S. & BRANNON, N. (1981-2): A 17th Century House in New Row, Coleraine, in *Ulster Journal of Archaeology,* 44-5, 173-8

ROBINSON, PHILIP S. (1984): *The Plantation of Ulster. British Settlement in an Irish Landscape, 1600-1670* (Dublin: Gill & Macmillan, and New York: St. Martins Press). See also the 1994 edition published by The Ulster Historical Foundation

ROWAN, ALISTAIR (1979): *North West Ulster: The Counties of Londonderry, Donegal, Fermanagh, and Tyrone* in *The Buildings of Ireland* series (Harmondsworth: Penguin)

RUNDLE, THOMAS (1789): *Letters ... to Mrs Sandys,* with an Introductory Memoir by J. DALLAWAY (Gloucester: R. Raikes, also published in Dublin in the same year)

RUSSELL, C.W. and PRENDERGAST, JOHN P. (eds.) (1872): *Calendar of the State Papers relating to Ireland, of the Reign of James I, 1603-1606* (London: Longmans, etc.)

——————— (1874a): *Calendar of the State Papers relating to Ireland of the Reign of James I, 1606-1608* (London: Longmans, etc.)

——————— (1874b): *Calendar of the State Papers relating to Ireland of the Reign of James I, 1608-1610* (London: Longmans, etc.)

——————— (1877): *Calendar of the State Papers relating to Ireland of the Reign of James I, 1610-1614* (London: Longmans, etc.)

——————— (1880): *Calendar of the State Papers relating to Ireland of the Reign of James I, 1615-1625* (London: Longmans, etc.)

SAMPSON, GEORGE VAUGHAN (1802): *Statistical Survey of the County of Londonderry, with Observations on the Means of Improvement; Drawn Up for the Consideration, and under the Direction of The Dublin Society* (Dublin: Graisberry & Campbell)

——————— (1814): *A Memoir, Explanatory of the Chart and Survey of the County of London-Derry, Ireland* (London: Printed by W. Bulmer for G. & W. Nicol). See also the important *Chart* (14 June 1814) itself, drawn by J. O'Kane and engraved upon the direction of Mr Arrowsmith (London: G. & W. Nicol)

SAYERS, JANE E. (1984): *Papal Government and England during the Pontificate of Honorius III (1216-1227)* (Cambridge: Cambridge University Press)

SCHULTES, HENRY (1822, with subsequent revised editions of 1832 and 1842): *A Concise View of the Origin, Constitution, and Proceedings of The Honorable Society of the Governor and Assistants of London, of The New Plantation in Ulster, within the Realm of Ireland, commonly called The Irish Society. Compiled, Principally, from their Records* (London: printed by order of the Court of The Irish Society by Gye and Balne)

SHARP, W. H. (1843): *Retrospect of the Affairs of The Honourable The Irish Society of London, of the New Plantation in Ulster, within the Realm of Ireland from 1824 to 1842* (London: J. H. Wilson)

SHEEHY, JEANNE (1977): *J. J. McCarthy and the Gothic Revival in Ireland* (Belfast: Ulster Architectural Heritage Society)

SHEPPARD, FRANCIS HENRY WOLLASTON (1971): *London, 1808-1870: The Infernal Wen* (London: Secker & Warburg)

SIMINGTON, ROBERT C. (ed.) (1937): *The Civil Survey A.D. 1654-6,* Vol. III, *Counties of Donegal, Londonderry, and Tyrone* (Dublin: Stationery Office for the Irish Manuscripts Commission)

SIMMS, J.G. (1966): *The Siege of Derry* (Dublin: A.P.C.K.)

——————— (1969): *Jacobite Ireland 1685-91)* (London: Routledge & Kegan Paul)

SIMPSON, ROBERT (1847): *The Annals of Derry* (Londonderry: Hempton)

SLADE, ROBERT (1803): *Narrative of a Journey to the North of Ireland in the Year 1802* (London: The Irish Society)

SMITH, RAYMOND (1966): *The Irish Society 1613-1963* (London: The Irish Society)

SPEDDING, JAMES (ed.) (1868-90): *The Letters and the Life of Francis Bacon*, iv (London: Longmans, Green)

STEPHEN, SIR JAMES (1891): *Essays in Ecclesiastical Biography* (London: Longmans, Green, & Co.)

STEWART, A.T.Q. (1997): *The Ulster Crisis. Resistance to Home Rule 1912-1914* (Belfast: Blackstaff

Press Ltd.)
STOCK, JOSEPH (1777): *An Account of the Life of George Berkeley DD, Late Bishop of Cloyne in Ireland* (Dublin: Hallhead)
STOKES, MARGARET (1878): *Early Christian Architecture in Ireland* (London: George Bell & Sons)
STRAIN, R. W. M. (1961): *Belfast and its Charitable Society. A Story of Urban Social Development* (London: Oxford University Press)
STUART, JAMES and REVETT, NICHOLAS (1787, but actually 1789): *The Antiquities of Athens*, **ii** (London: Haberkorn, etc.)
STURDY, DAVID J. (1997): *St Patrick's, Coleraine* (Coleraine: St Patrick's Church)
SWIFT, JONATHAN (1720): *A Proposal for the Universal Use of Irish Manufactures, in Cloaths and Furniture, etc., utterly rejecting and renouncing every thing wearable that comes from England*, in SCOTT, TEMPLE (ed.) (1897-1908): *The Prose Works of Jonathan Swift*, **vii** (London: George Bell & Sons)
TITE, WILLIAM (1834): *Report of a Visit to the Estates of the Honorable The Irish Society* (London: Printed by Charles Skipper and East, for The Society)
TOWNEND, PETER (ed.) (1963): *Burke's Geneaological and Heraldic History of the Peerage, Baronetage, and Knightage* (London: Burke's Peerage Ltd.)
TOWNSHEND, DOROTHEA (1904): *The Life and Letters of the Great Earl of Cork* (London: Duckworth)
ULSTER JOURNAL OF ARCHAEOLOGY (from 1894)
WALKER, GEORGE (1689a): *A True Account of the Siege of London-Derry* (London: Robert Clavel and Ralph Simpson)
——————— (1689b): *A Vindication of the True Account of the Siege of Derry in Ireland* (London: Robert Clavel)
——————— (1689c): *Kurtze Beschreibung der hart belagerten Stadt London-Derry in Irrland* (Hamburg: Thomas von Wiering)
——————— (1690): *Relation Véritable... du Siège de la Ville de Londonderry en Irelande* (Amsterdam: Paul Marret)
WALL, MAUREEN (1967): *The Penal Laws, 1691-1760* (Dundalk: n.p.)
WALSH, JOHN R. (1972): *Frederick Augustus Hervey 1730-1803* (Maynooth: Department of Modern History, St Patrick's College)
WARE, SIR JAMES (1739/45): *The Works of Sir James Ware Concerning Ireland … Containing The History of The Bishops of Ireland …* etc. (Dublin: Printed for The Author)
WATKINS, WALTER KENDALL (1907): *Lemuel Cox, Bridge-Builder and Inventor, 1736-1806* (n.p.: W. K. Watkins)
WILLIAMS, JEREMY (1994): *A companion guide to Architecture in Ireland, 1837-1921* (Blackrock: Irish Academic Press, Ltd.)
WYLIE, J.C.W. (1997): *Irish Land Law* (Dublin: Butterworth [Ireland])
YOUNG, ROBERT M. and BIGGER, FRANCIS JOSEPH (eds.) (1895-1909): *The Ulster Journal of Archaeology* Second Series (Belfast: Marcus Ward, McCaw, Stevenson, & Orr, and Davidson & McCormack)

Index

compiled by Mary Norris

The following abbreviations have been used: Abp = archbishop; arch.= architect; Bp = bishop; c.=century; Gov.= Governor; I.S.= Irish Society; N.I.= Northern Ireland; Plant. = Plantation; R.C/s= Roman Catholic/s; Sec. = Secretary; surv.= surveyor.
Page references in **bold** refer to plates. An asterisk (*) refers to material in the glossary. 'Mac' and 'Mc' names are treated as if all were spelt 'Mac'.